SRA ART Connections

Arts Education for the 21st Century

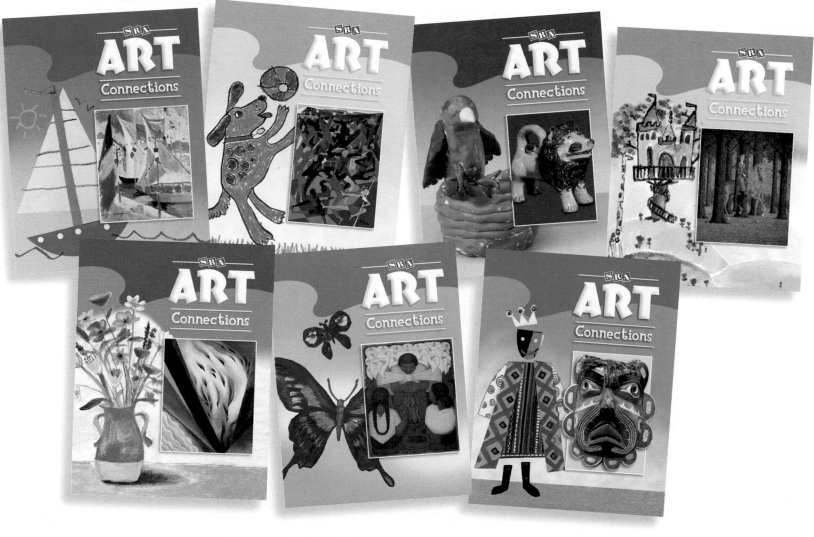

Culture   Personal Expression   Creativity

History   Beauty   Critical Thinking

Art encourages different ways of learning, knowing, and communicating.

i

SRA ART Connections

All the Resources you Need for Great Art Teaching!

Art Connections provides everything teachers need to offer meaningful art education.

Student Edition K-6

Comprehensive student materials in two formats:

Student Edition

LEVEL 6

Big Book

LEVEL 6

Teacher Edition

Everything classroom and art teachers need to teach art effectively

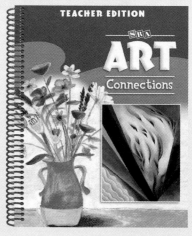

LEVEL 4

- Complete lesson plans to teach
  - elements and principles of art
  - art history and culture
  - art criticism
  - art production
- Art background
- Cross-curricular connections
- Program resources guide

Technology Components

e-Presentation for students and teachers

LEVEL K

e-Presentation offers the complete Student Edition as a presentation tool for teachers, complete with multimedia experiences, assessments, teacher materials, and a gallery of all artworks in the entire program.

This electronic gallery allows immediate access to all the artwork in the ***Art Connections*** program.

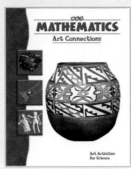

Cross-Curricular Art Connections include practical art projects for the classroom to help meet subject-area guidelines in

- Social Studies
- Mathematics
- Language Arts and Reading
- Science

LEVEL 3

Reading and Writing Test Preparation that reinforces art content

LEVEL 1

Home and After-School Connections for every unit, in English and Spanish

Professional Development Guide for both classroom teachers and art specialists

LEVEL 5

Assessment with tests in English and Spanish for every lesson

Art Around the World CD-ROM includes 150 works of art from the *Art Around the World Collection*, representing a variety of thought-provoking perspectives and activities.

The National Museum of Women in the Arts Collection CD-ROM dynamically explores the 200-print collection to introduce students to key women artists.

ART Connections

Enrich students' lives with exposure to the great masters and cultures of the world.

Fine-Art Resources

Transparencies Overhead transparency study prints for all lesson artwork allow for up-close examination.

LEVEL 5

Large Prints for each unit provide exemplary artwork to develop unit concepts.

LEVEL 2

LEVEL 1

Artist Profiles Pictures, background information, and profiles for every artist in the program provide valuable historical and cultural information at your fingertips.

The Polar Express

Literature and Art Videos and DVD develop art connections to literature.

Art Around the World 150-print resource explores the art of the world's cultures.

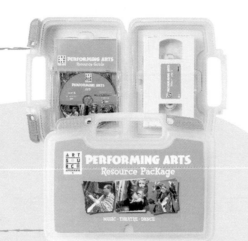

Elements and Principles of Art Teaching Resources

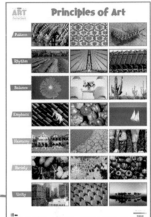

Artsource® Performing Arts Resource Package (Video and DVD) integrates the performing arts of dance, music, and theatre.

LEVEL 3

The National Museum of Women in the Arts Collection This 200-print resource provides famous artwork from famous women artists.

Elements of Art poster reinforces line, shape, color, value, form, space, and texture.

Principles of Art poster develops concepts of rhythm, balance, movement, harmony, variety, emphasis, and unity.

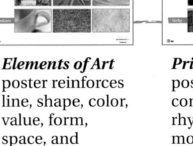

Use the *Color Wheel* to explore color concepts.

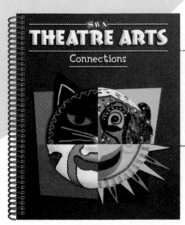

Theatre Arts Connections is a complete dramatic arts program that ties to *Art Connections*.

LEVEL 4

Flash Cards provide a quick review of the elements and principles of art.

v

Build a foundation in the elements and principles of art.

36 Lessons at every grade level develop the elements and principles of art in six-lesson units.

◄ Rembrandt van Rijn. *Portrait of Rembrandt.*

◄ Frida Kahlo. *Frida y Diego Rivera.*

8   9   **LEVEL 6**

Unit Openers introduce students to unit concepts and master artists.

Unit 5

Space, Proportion, and Distortion

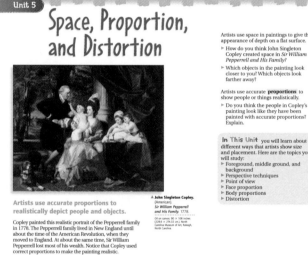

Artists use accurate proportions to realistically depict people and objects.

Copley painted this realistic portrait of the Pepperrell family in 1778. The Pepperrell family lived in New England until about the time of the American Revolution, when they moved to England. At about the same time, Sir William Pepperrell lost most of his wealth. Notice that Copley used correct proportions to make the painting realistic.

▲ **John Singleton Copley.** (American). *Sir William Pepperrell and His Family.* 1778

Oil on canvas, 90 × 108 inches (228.6 × 274.32 cm.) North Carolina Museum of Art, Raleigh, North Carolina.

Artists use space in paintings to give the appearance of depth on a flat surface.
► How do you think John Singleton Copley created space in *Sir William Pepperrell and His Family?*
► Which objects in the painting look closer to you? Which objects look farther away?

Artists use accurate **proportions** to show people or things realistically.
► Do you think the people in Copley's painting look like they have been painted with accurate proportions? Explain.

In This Unit you will learn about different ways that artists show size and placement. Here are the topics you will study:
► Foreground, middle ground, and background
► Perspective techniques
► Point of view
► Face proportion
► Body proportions
► Distortion

Master Artist Profile

John Singleton Copley

(1738–1815)
John Singleton Copley was a popular portrait painter during the eighteenth century. When he was seventeen years old he created a portrait of George Washington. In his attempt to capture details and to make his subjects appear natural, Copley sometimes required fifteen or sixteen sittings for a single portrait. Copley moved to England during the American Revolution and did not return to America.

154   Unit 5   Unit 5   155   **LEVEL 4**

Unit Wrap-Ups review concepts, explore Art Museums or Art Careers and allow students to experience Artsource® connections to dance, theatre, and music.

Wrapping Up Unit 5
Space, Proportion, and Distortion

▲ **Jacob Lawrence.** (American). *Study for the Munich Olympic Games Poster.* 1971.

Gouache on paper, 35½ × 27 inches (90.17 × 68.58 cm.) Seattle Art Museum, Seattle, Washington.

180   Unit 5

Wrapping Up Unit 5
Space, Proportion, and Distortion, *continued*

Show What You Know

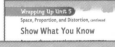

VISIT A MUSEUM
The Smithsonian

Art Criticism Critical Thinking

Describe What do you see?
During this step you will collect information about the subject of the work.
► How many people do you see? What kinds of facial expressions do they have?
► What are the people doing? What are they wearing?
► What is the setting?

Analyze How is this work organized?
Think about how the artist used the elements and principles of art.
► Which people or objects look closest to you? Which look farthest away?
► What is in the foreground, the middle ground, and the background?
► Where do you see a part of someone's body that overlaps and covers part of another person or object?
► What is the point of view of this painting?
► Where do you see distortion?

Interpret What is the artist trying to say?
Use the clues you discovered during your analysis to find the message the artist is trying to show.
► Which runner do you think will win the race? Why?
► What is the mood of this painting?
► What sounds would you hear if you could go into the painting?

Decide What do you think about the work?
Use all the information you have gathered to decide whether this is a successful work of art.
► Is the work successful because it is realistic, because it is well-organized, or because it has a strong message?

Space and Proportion in Music

...orn in Cuba. ...ld he moved to ...eard harp music. ...from his friend ...master harpist. ...but eventually ...fe to the harp.

...make a simple

...nd. Vibration is ...nsation caused in ...of air. You can hear ...a string tightly ...ack the string.

...tch rubber bands ...are that rubber ...knesses.

...e if you get ...s. The thickness, ...e strings will

...thicknesses of ...higher or lower

▲ Ortiz. *"Joropo Azul."*

Art Criticism

Describe Describe how you made your instrument.
Analyze What did you do to get a higher or lower tone or pitch?
Interpret What did you feel as you created an instrument and heard the sounds it made?
Decide Were you able to get a satisfying musical sound from your simple instrument?

Unit 5   181   Unit 5   183   **LEVEL 4**

vi

Integrate the four disciplines of art into every lesson for well-rounded exposure to all the dimensions of art.

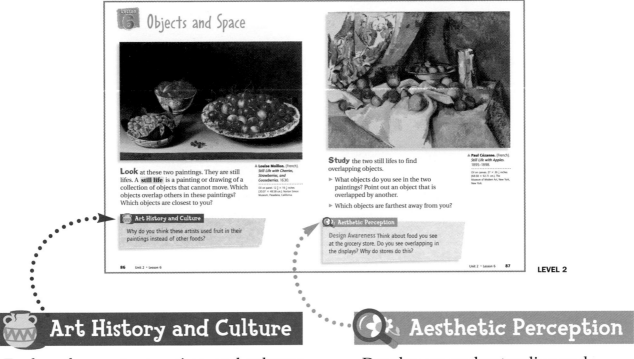

LEVEL 2

Art History and Culture

Explore the great art, artists, and cultures of the world.

Aesthetic Perception

Develop an understanding and appreciation for art.

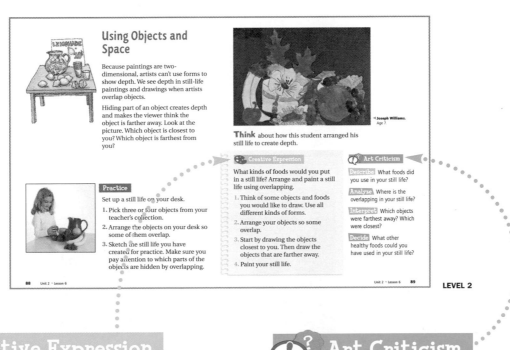

LEVEL 2

Creative Expression

Encounter a broad range of art media in a variety of hands-on art activities that give students an avenue for self-expression and self-esteem.

Art Criticism

Enrich critical-thinking skills as students learn about the elements and principles of art by examining their own and others' artwork.

Add dimension to all subjects with meaningful art connections.

Connect Art to Mathematics, Social Studies, Science, Language Arts and Reading.

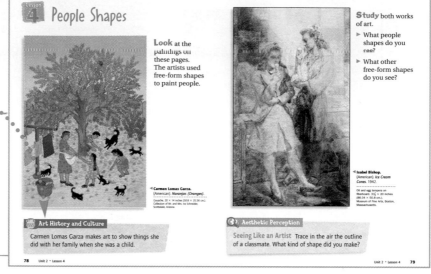

LEVEL 1

History
Develop historical understanding as students explore art history and culture in every lesson.

LEVEL 2

Reading and Writing Test Preparation
Use art content, information about artists, art concepts, and art history to practice reading and writing skills in every unit.

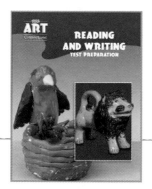

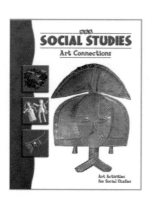

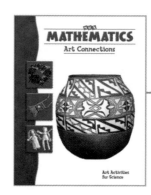

Cross-Curricular Art Connections
These books provide a wealth of exciting art activities designed specifically to support subject-area studies in Science, Mathematics, Social Studies, Language Arts and Reading as they reinforce art concepts.

Integrate the four disciplines of art into every lesson for well-rounded exposure to all the dimensions of art.

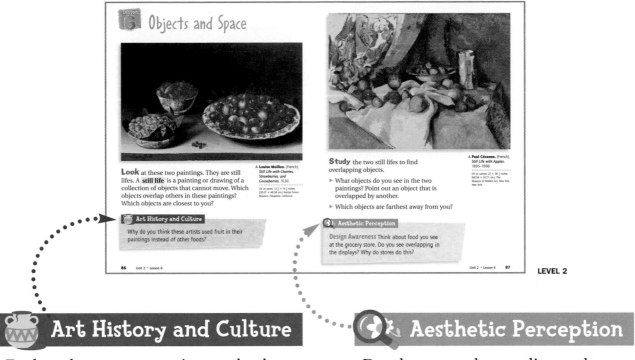

LEVEL 2

Art History and Culture

Explore the great art, artists, and cultures of the world.

Aesthetic Perception

Develop an understanding and appreciation for art.

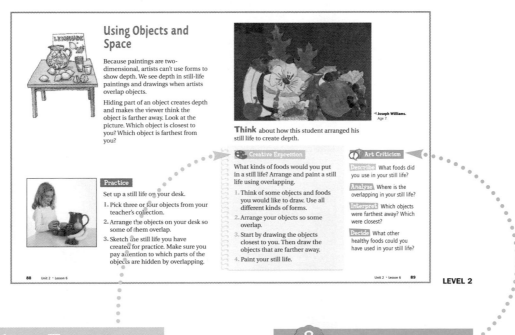

LEVEL 2

Creative Expression

Encounter a broad range of art media in a variety of hands-on art activities that give students an avenue for self-expression and self-esteem.

Art Criticism

Enrich critical-thinking skills as students learn about the elements and principles of art by examining their own and others' artwork.

ART Connections

Add dimension to all subjects with meaningful art connections.

Connect Art to Mathematics, Social Studies, Science, Language Arts and Reading.

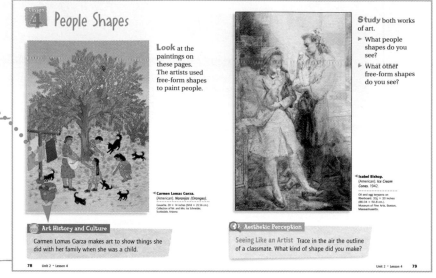

Lesson 4 People Shapes

Look at the paintings on these pages. The artists used free-form shapes to paint people.

◄ **Carmen Lomas Garza.** (American). *Naranjas (Oranges).* Gouache, 20 × 14 inches (50.8 × 35.56 cm.) Collection of Mr. and Mrs. Ira Schneider, Scottsdale, Arizona

Art History and Culture

Carmen Lomas Garza makes art to show things she did with her family when she was a child.

Study both works of art.
- What people shapes do you see?
- What other free-form shapes do you see?

◄ **Isabel Bishop.** (American). *Ice Cream Cones.* 1942. Oil and egg tempera on fiberboard. 33½ × 20 inches (86.04 × 50.8 cm.). Museum of Fine Arts, Boston, Massachusetts.

Aesthetic Perception

Seeing Like an Artist Trace in the air the outline of a classmate. What kind of shape did you make?

78   Unit 2 • Lesson 4   Unit 2 • Lesson 4   79

LEVEL 1

History
Develop historical understanding as students explore art history and culture in every lesson.

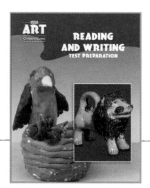

LEVEL 2

Reading and Writing Test Preparation
Use art content, information about artists, art concepts, and art history to practice reading and writing skills in every unit.

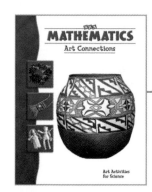

Cross-Curricular Art Connections
These books provide a wealth of exciting art activities designed specifically to support subject-area studies in Science, Mathematics, Social Studies, Language Arts and Reading as they reinforce art concepts.

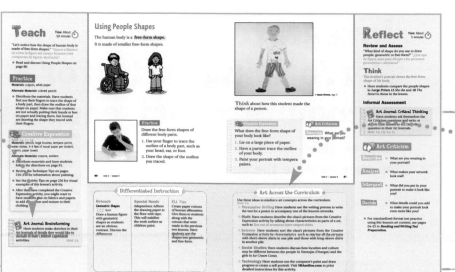

Writing Develop writing skills with Art Journal activities throughout each lesson.

Cross-Curricular Ideas Show students how artwork and concepts relate to science, mathematics, social studies, reading/language arts, and technology in every lesson.

LEVEL 1

LEVEL 2

Cross-Curricular Integration Integrate language arts and reading, math, science, and social studies concepts naturally as students work through each art lesson.

LEVEL 4

Vocabulary Development Key vocabulary terms are highlighted, defined, and reviewed to develop the language of art.

LEVEL 3

Literature Integration Integrate literature with Illustrator Profiles and Literature and Art video experiences at the beginning of every unit.

Research has shown that incorporating the arts into core curriculum areas in a way that actively involves students in the learning process produces "significant positive effects on student achievement, motivation, and engagement in learning, and notable changes in classroom practices" ("Different Ways of Knowing: 1991-94 National Longitudinal Study Final Report" in Schools, Communities, and the Arts: A Research Compendium).

Integrate all the Performing Arts for a complete Art education.

Expose children to music, dance, and theatre as they explore the visual arts.

LEVEL 2

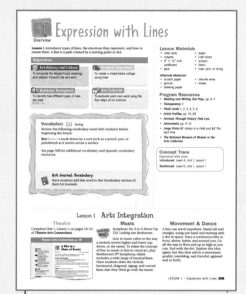

LEVEL 5

Music Connections
in every Unit Opener translate the visual arts elements and principles into music.

Music Experiences
in every lesson from Macmillan/McGraw-Hill's *Spotlight on Music* expand creativity and develop music appreciation.

Artsource®
music performances on video and DVD explore the elements and principles of art through the performing arts.

LEVEL 4

x

LEVEL 3

Artsource® dance performances on video and DVD explore the elements and principles of art through the performing arts.

LEVEL 5

Artsource® theatre performances on video and DVD explore the elements and principles of art through the performing arts.

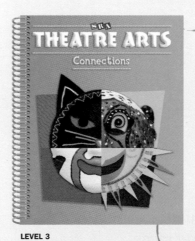

LEVEL 3

Theatre Arts Connections for grades K–6 lessons explore the elements and principles of theatre arts as students develop the elements and principles of visual arts.

Case studies have indicated that students perceive "that the arts facilitate their personal and social development." It also appears that to gain the full benefit of arts education, students should be exposed to all of the arts, including fine arts, dance, theatre, and music ("Arts Education in Secondary School: Effects and Effectiveness" in <u>Critical Links</u>, p. 76).

Meet Today's Standards for Art Education.

Art Connections exceeds the national standards for art education.

National Standards for Arts Education

Content Standard #1:

Understanding and applying media, techniques, and processes

The Creative Expression activity in every lesson of *Art Connections* develops understanding and experience with a wide variety of media, techniques, and processes. Practice activities in every lesson focus specifically on techniques.

Content Standard #2:

Using knowledge of structures and functions

Art Connections develops the elements and principles of art in every grade level, K–6. Units and lessons are organized to explore the elements and principles in exemplary art and then to practice techniques and create works of art that employ specific structures and functions of art.

Content Standard #3:

Choosing and evaluating a range of subject matter, symbols, and ideas

Art Connections introduces students to subject matter and symbols at the beginning of every grade level and then uses that knowledge throughout every lesson in the Aesthetic Perception questions and Creative Expression activities as students explore content to develop meaning in artwork.

Ali M. Forbes. Age 7.

Jasmine Krasel. Age 9.

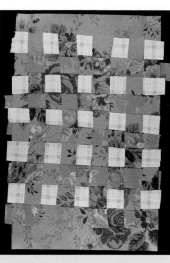

Briana Kittle. Age 6.

Content Standard #4:

Understanding the visual arts in relation to history and cultures

Every lesson in *Art Connections* has a specific objective related to the understanding of art history and culture. These objectives are met as students analyze and interpret exemplary artwork and develop their own artwork.

Content Standard #5:

Reflecting upon and assessing the characteristics and merits of one's own work and the work of others

The four steps of art criticism are explored in every lesson throughout the program as students analyze their own artwork and the work of others.

Content Standard #6:

Making connections between visual arts and other disciplines

Theatre, Dance, and Music are integrated into every unit of *Art Connections*. The elements and principles of visual art are translated into Dance, Theater, and Music through the Artsource® lessons and experiences. In addition, *Theatre Arts Connections* lessons and Music connections throughout the program develop a comprehensive understanding of the connections between visual arts and the performing arts.

Cross-curricular connections are built into every lesson through teaching strategies and ideas that integrate language arts and reading, math, science, and social studies concepts. Art Projects for each of the different subject areas are also included in the program.

Let the experts bring the best practices to your classroom.

Rosalind Ragans, Ph.D., Senior Author

Artist, Associate Professor Emerita

Georgia Southern University

Authors

Willis "Bing" Davis

Artist, Art Consultant

Associate Professor Emeritus,

Central State University, Ohio

Tina Farrell

Assisstant Superintendant, Curriculum and Instruction

Clear Creek Independent School District, Texas

Jane Rhoades Hudak, Ph.D.

Professor of Art

Georgia Southern University

Gloria McCoy

Former President, Texas Art Education Association

K–12 Art Director

Spring Branch Independent School District, Texas

Bunyan Morris

Art Teacher

Effingham County School System

Springfield, Georgia

Nan Yoshida

Art Education Consultant

Los Angeles, California

Contributors

Jackie Ellet

Elementary Art Teacher

Duncan Creek Elementary School

Georgia

Artsource® Music, Dance, and Theatre Lessons

Education Division

The Music Center of Los Angeles County

National Museum of Women in the Arts Collection

National Museum of Women in the Arts

Washington, D.C.

Your Fine-Arts Partner for K–12 Art, Theatre, Dance and Music

McGraw-Hill offers textbook programs to build, support, and extend an enriching fine-arts curriculum from kindergarten through high school.

**Senior Author
Rosalind Ragans**

Start with Art 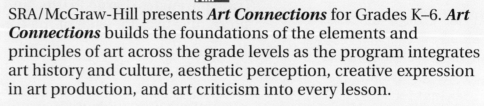 SRA

SRA/McGraw-Hill presents *Art Connections* for Grades K–6. *Art Connections* builds the foundations of the elements and principles of art across the grade levels as the program integrates art history and culture, aesthetic perception, creative expression in art production, and art criticism into every lesson.

Art Connections also develops strong cross-curricular connections and integrates the arts with literature, *Theatre Arts Connections* lessons, *Artsource®* experiences, and integrated music selections from Macmillan/McGraw-Hill's *Spotlight on Music*.

**Author
Rosalind Ragans
and Gene Mittler**

Integrate with Art Glencoe

Glencoe/McGraw-Hill offers comprehensive middle and high school art programs that encourage students to make art a part of their lifelong learning. All Glencoe art programs interweave the elements and principles of art to help students build perceptual skills, promote creative expression, explore historical and cultural heritage, and evaluate artwork.

- Introduce students to the many themes artists express.
- Explore the media, techniques, and processes of art.
- Understand the historical and cultural contexts of art.

ArtTalk offers high school students opportunities to perceive, create, appreciate, and evaluate art as it develops the elements and principles of art.

**Author
Rosalind Ragans**

Motivate with Music Macmillan McGraw-Hill

Macmillan/McGraw-Hill's *Spotlight on Music* offers an exiting and comprehensive exposure to music foundations and appreciation.

Sing with Style  Glencoe

Glencoe/McGraw-Hill introduces *Experiencing Choral Music* for Grades 6–12. This multilevel choral music program includes instruction in the basic skills of vocal production and music literacy, and provides expertly recorded music selections in many different styles and from various periods of history.

SRA
ART
Connections

Getting Started
The very basics...

Here are some tips for Getting Started with Art Connections.

Before School Begins

1 Explore the components you have (student materials, **Overhead Transparencies**, **Large Prints**, and so on). Consider uses and alternative uses for each of the components.

2 Plan your year.
- Consider how often you meet with students.
- Decide how many lessons you can present.
- Examine your curriculum requirements.
- Select the lessons that best meet your curriculum requirements.

3 Organize art materials.
- Identify the *Creative Expression* activities you will have students develop.
- Determine how you will budget materials to last the entire year.
- Compile a list of materials and order them.
- Arrange classroom space to store materials.

4 Arrange classroom space to create and store student artwork.

The First Day of School

1 Give an overview of your expectations, objectives, and what you want students to accomplish.

2 Introduce the artroom to students. Show them where things are kept.

3 Establish and communicate:
- rules for behavior.
- rules for handling art materials.
- rules for cleaning up.

4 Begin the **Art Connections** introductory lessons, including *What Is Art?*, *About Art Criticism*, *About Aesthetic Perception*, and *About Art History and Culture*.

Planning a Lesson

1 Review the lesson in the *Teacher's Edition*, including lesson objectives, in-text questions, *Practice*, and *Creative Expression* activities.

2 Assemble program components, such as **Transparencies, Large Prints,** and the **Big Book**.

3 Make any copies of activities or assessments that will be needed for the lesson.

4 Assemble art materials.

5 Determine how you will assess the lesson.

TEACHER'S EDITION

SRA ART
Connections

Level 5

Authors

Rosalind Ragans, Ph.D., Senior Author

Willis "Bing" Davis   Jane Rhoades Hudak, Ph.D.   Bunyan Morris
Tina Farrell   Gloria McCoy   Nan Yoshida

Contributing Author

Jackie Ellett

Education Division
The Music Center of Los Angeles County

Columbus, OH

The **McGraw·Hill** Companies

Authors

Senior Author
Dr. Rosalind Ragans, Ph.D.
Associate Professor Emerita
Georgia Southern University

Willis "Bing" Davis
Associate Professor Emeritus
Central State University - Ohio
President & Founder of SHANGO:
The Center for the Study of
African American
Art & Culture

Tina Farrell
Assistant Superintendent,
Curriculum and Instruction
Clear Creek Independent School
District,
League City, Texas

Jane Rhoades Hudak, Ph.D.
Professor of Art
Georgia Southern University

Gloria McCoy
Former President,
Texas Art Education Association
Spring Branch Independent
School District, Texas

Bunyan Morris
Art Teacher
Effingham County School System,
Springfield, Georgia

Nan Yoshida
Art Education Consultant
Retired Art Supervisor,
Los Angeles Unified School
District
Los Angeles, California

Photo Credit **Cover,** Diego Rivera, *Flower Day.* Los Angeles
County Museum of Art, Los Angeles County Fund. Photo
©1999 Museum Associates, LACMA. ©Banco de Mexico
Diego Rivera & Frida Kahlo Museum Trust. Av. Cinco de Mayo
No. 2, Col. Centro, Del. Cuauhtemoc 06059, Mexico, D.F.

SRAonline.com

Send all inquiries to:
SRA/McGraw-Hill
8787 Orion Place
Columbus, OH 43240-4027

Printed in the United States of America.

ISBN 0-07-600395-7

3 4 5 6 7 8 9 BCM 10 09 08 07 06

The McGraw·Hill Companies

Contributors

Contributing Author
Jackie Ellett, Ed.S
Elementary Art Teacher
Duncan Creek Elementary School
Hoschton, Georgia

Contributing Writer
Lynda Kerr, NBCT
Ed. D. Candidate, Art Teacher
Henry County, Georgia

 Artsource® Music, Dance, Theatre Lessons
Mark Slavkin, Vice President
    for Education
The Music Center of Los Angeles County
Michael Solomon, Managing Director
Music Center Education Division
Melinda Williams, Concept Originator and
Project Director
Susan Cambigue-Tracey, Project Coordinator
and Writer
Madeleine Dahm, Movement and Dance
Connection Writer
Keith Wyffels, Staff Assistance
Maureen Erbe, Logo Design

Music Connections
Kathy Mitchell
Music Teacher
Eagan, Minnesota

More about Aesthetics
Richard W. Burrows, Executive Director
Institute for Arts Education
San Diego, California

Art History
Gene A. Mittler, Ph.D.
Professor Emeritus
Texas Tech University

Resources for Students with Disabilities
Mandy Yeager
Ph.D. Candidate
The University of North Texas
Denton, Texas

Brain-Based Learning in the Arts
Jamye Ivey
K-12 Art Supervisor
Dougherty County School System, Georgia

Safe Use of Art Materials
Mary Ann Boykin

Director, The Art School for Children and
Young Adults
University of Houston–Clear Lake
Houston, Texas

Integrating the Four Art Forms
Susan Cambigue-Tracey
The Music Center of Los Angeles County

Using Writing to Enhance Your Art Curriculum
Mary Lazzari, EdS
Elementary Art Teacher
Clarke County School District
Athens, Georgia

Museum Education
Marilyn J. S. Goodman
Director of Education
Solomon R. Guggenheim Museum
New York, New York

Displaying Student Artwork
Jackie Ellett
Duncan Creek Elementary School
Hoschton, Georgia

Student Activities

Cassie Appleby
Glen Oaks Elementary School
McKinney, Texas

Maureen Banks
Kester Magnet School
Van Nuys, California

Christina Barnes
Webb Bridge Middle School
Alpharetta, Georgia

Beth Benning
Willis Jepson Middle School
Vacaville, California

Chad Buice
Craig Elementary School
Snellville, Georgia

Beverly Broughton
Gwinn Oaks Elementary School
Snellville, Georgia

Missy Burgess
Jefferson Elementary School
Jefferson, Georgia

Marcy Cincotta-Smith
Benefield Elementary School
Lawrenceville, Georgia

Joanne Cox
Kittredge Magnet School
Atlanta, Georgia

Carolyn Y. Craine
McCracken County Schools
Paducah, Kentucky

Jackie Ellett
Duncan Creek Elementary School
Hoschton, Georgia

Tracie Flynn
Home School
Rushville, Indiana

Phyllis Glenn
Malcom Bridge Elementary
Bogart, Georgia

Dallas Gillespie
Dacula Middle School
Dacula, Georgia

Dr. Donald Gruber
Clinton Junior High School
Clinton, Illinois

Karen Heid
Rock Springs Elementary School
Lawrenceville, Georgia

Alisa Hyde
Southwest Elementary
Savannah, Georgia

Kie Johnson
Oconee Primary School
Watkinsville, Georgia

Sallie Keith, NBCT
West Side Magnet School
LaGrange, Georgia

Letha Kelly
Grayson Elementary School
Grayson, Georgia

Diana Kimura
Amestoy Elementary School
Gardena, California

Desiree LaOrange
Barkley Elementary School
Fort Campbell, Kentucky

Deborah Lackey-Wilson
Roswell North Elementary
Roswell, Georgia

Dawn Laird
Goforth Elementary School
Clear Creek, Texas

Mary Lazzari
Timothy Road Elementary School
Athens, Georgia

Michelle Leonard
Webb Bridge Middle School
Alpharetta, Georgia

Lynn Ludlam
Spring Branch ISD
Houston, Texas

Mark Mitchell
Fort Daniel Elementary School
Dacula, Georgia

Martha Moore
Freeman's Mill Elementary School
Dacula, Georgia

Connie Niedenthal
Rushville Elementary
Rushville, Indiana

Barbara Patisaul
Oconee County Elementary School
Watkinsville, Georgia

Elizabeth Paulos-Krasle
Social Circle Elementary
Social Circle, Georgia

Jane Pinneau
Rocky Branch Elementary School
Watkinsville, Georgia

Marilyn Polin
Cutler Ridge Middle School
Miami, Florida

Michael Ramsey
Graves County Schools
Mayfield, Kentucky

Rosemarie Sells
Social Circle Elementary
Social Circle, Georgia

Jean Neelen-Siegel
Baldwin School
Alhambra, California

Debra Smith
McIntosh County School System
Darien, Georgia

Patricia Spencer
Harmony Elementary School
Buford, Georgia

Melanie Stokes
Smiley Elementary School
Ludowici, Georgia

Rosanne Stutts
Davidson Fine Arts School
Augusta, Georgia

Fran Sullivan
South Jackson Elementary School
Athens, Georgia

Kathy Valentine
Home School
Burkburnett, Texas

Debi West
Rock Springs Elementary School
Lawrenceville, Georgia

Sherry White
Bauerschlag Elementary School
League City, Texas

Patricia Wiesen
Cutler Ridge Middle School
Miami, Florida

Deayna Woodruff
Loveland Middle School
Loveland, Ohio

Gil Young
El Rodeo School
Beverly Hills, California

Larry A. Young
Dacula Elementary School
Dacula, Georgia

Table of Contents

▲ **Jaune Quick-to-See Smith.**
Spam.

Unit 1 Line, Shape, and Value

➡ **indicates Core Lessons**   **5**

Reading Comprehension Skills and Strategies

❶ Vocabulary, Using Literature, Comparing and Contrasting
❷ Vocabulary, Using Literature, Visualizing

❸ Vocabulary, Using Literature, Comparing and Contrasting
❹ Vocabulary, Using Literature, Comparing and Contrasting

❺ Vocabulary, Using Literature, Visualizing
❻ Vocabulary, Using Literature, Cause and Effect

◀ **Jan Vermeer.**
The Concert.

Unit 2 Space, Shape, and Form

6

●◆ indicates Core Lessons

Reading Comprehension Skills and Strategies

➊ Vocabulary, Using Literature, Comparing and Contrasting
➋ Vocabulary, Using Literature, Sequence

➌ Vocabulary, Using Literature, Point of View
➍ Vocabulary, Using Literature, Cause and Effect

➎ Vocabulary, Using Literature, Fact and Opinion
➏ Vocabulary, Using Literature, Point of View

Unit 3 Color and Pattern

➻ indicates Core Lessons

7

Reading Comprehension Skills and Strategies

➊ Vocabulary, Using Literature, Making Inferences
➋ Vocabulary, Using Literature

➌ Vocabulary, Using Literature, Artist's Purpose
➍ Vocabulary Using Literature, Comparing and Contrasting

➎ Vocabulary, Using Literature, Sequence
➏ Vocabulary, Using Literature, Visualizing

◄ **Viola Frey.**
Grandmother Series:
July Cone Hat.

Unit 4 Proportion and Distortion

8   ●◆ indicates Core Lessons

Reading Comprehension Skills and Strategies

❶ Vocabulary, Using Literature, Main Idea and Details
❷ Vocabulary, Using Literature, Predicting

❸ Vocabulary, Using Literature, Artist's Purpose
❹ Vocabulary, Using Literature, Cause and Effect

❺ Vocabulary, Using Literature, Drawing Conclusions
❻ Vocabulary, Using Literature, Sequence

◀ **Vincent van Gogh.**
House at Auvers.

Unit 5 Texture, Rhythm, Movement, and Balance

➥ indicates Core Lessons

9

Reading Comprehension Skills and Strategies

❶ Vocabulary, Using Literature, Drawing Conclusions
❷ Vocabulary, Using Literature, Classify and Categorize
❸ Vocabulary, Using Literature, Visualizing
❹ Vocabulary, Using Literature, Comparing and Contrasting
❺ Vocabulary, Using Literature, Point of View
❻ Vocabulary, Using Literature, Drawing Conclusions

▲ **Berthe Morisot.**
The Sisters.

Unit 6 Harmony, Variety, Emphasis, and Unity

10

➥ indicates Core Lessons

Reading Comprehension Skills and Strategies

➊ Vocabulary, Using Literature, Fact and Opinion
➋ Vocabulary, Using Literature, Main Idea and Details

➌ Vocabulary, Using Literature, Making Inferences
➍ Vocabulary, Using Literature, Comparing and Contrasting

➎ Vocabulary, Using Literature, Thematic Connection: Sharing Stories
➏ Vocabulary, Using Literature, Sequencing

Technique Tips

Activity Tips

Overview

The purpose of these pages is to open students' minds to the idea that visual arts include many components and take many forms. The arts satisfy the human need for display, celebration, personal expression, and communication. We use the visual arts to enhance our innermost feelings and to communicate ideas. Art is made by people. Even people who are not professional artists can enjoy the creative process.

Activating Prior Knowledge

- Ask students what they think art is. Encourage creative, divergent thinking. In visual art, there are many answers to a question.

Questions to Discuss

- Have students look at the images on pages 12 and 13 and name the things that are visual art. Then ask the following questions.

  ▶ Which of these things could you hold in your hands?

  ▶ Which one could you walk inside?

  ▶ Which ones would you hang on a wall?

  ▶ Which ones could you wear?

- Encourage students to think about things they have at home that fit the categories on these pages. The building they live in is architecture. They have dishes and other containers. Many of them have things hanging on the walls to enhance their visual environments. A few may have sculpture in the home. Many will have seen sculptures in and around public buildings.

What Is Art?

Art is . . .

Painting is color applied to a flat surface.

▲ **Vincent Van Gogh.** (French). *Houses at Auvers.* 1890.

Oil on canvas. 29¾ × 24⅜ inches (75.56 × 61.93 cm.). Museum of Fine Arts, Boston, Massachusetts.

Drawing is the process of making art with lines.

▲ **Pablo Picasso.** (Spanish). *Portrait of Dora Maar.* 1938.

Pencil on paper mounted on fiberboard. 30 9/16 × 22 7/16 inches (77.62 × 57 cm.). Hirshhorn Museum and Sculpture Garden, Smithsonian Institution, Washington, D.C.

Sculpture is art that fills up space.

▲ **David Bates.** (American). *Seated Man #4.* 1995.

Painted wood. 88 × 37½ × 45½ inches (223.52 × 95.25 × 115.57 cm.). Dallas Museum of Art, Dallas, Texas.

Architecture is the art of designing and constructing buildings.

▲ **Jørn Oberg Utzon.** (Danish). *Opera House.* 1957–1973.

Sydney, Australia.

Printmaking is the process of transferring an original image from one prepared surface to another.

▲ **Katsushika Hokusai.** (Japanese.) *Winter Loneliness,* from *One Hundred Poems Explained by the Nurse.* 1839.

Woodcut. 10⅛ × 14½ inches (25.5 × 36.8 cm.). Honolulu Academy of Art, Honolulu, Hawaii

Photography is the act of capturing an image on film.

◀ **Eliot Elisofon.** (American). *Asante Paramount Chief Nana Akyanfuo Akowuah Dateh II, Akwamuhene of Kumase.* 1970.

Photograph. National Museum of African Art, Smithsonian Institution, Washington, D.C.

Ceramics is the art of making objects with clay.

▲ **Artist Unknown.** (Kongo peoples, Congo and Democratic Republic of Congo.) **Bowl.** Late-nineteenth to early-twentieth century.

Ceramic and resin. 5⅞ × 4⅛ × 5⅞ inches (14.9 × 10.49 × 14.94 cm.). National Museum of African Art, Smithsonian Institution, Washington, D.C.

A mask is a covering for the face to be used in ceremonies and other events.

▲ **Charlie James.** (Southern Kwakiutl.) *Sun Tranformation Mask.* Early nineteenth century.

Royal British Columbia Museum, British Columbia, Canada.

Art is created by people

▶ to communicate ideas.

▶ to express feelings.

▶ to give us well-designed objects.

Using the Credit Line

The credit line is a list of important facts about the work of art that appears below or next to the work. For example, you can help students understand the size of an artwork and how it relates to their own size. Most credit lines contain the following information.

- Name of the artist.

- Title of the work. This always appears in italics. If the word *detail* follows the title, it means that the image is part of a larger work of art.

- Year the work was created. A *c* before the date indicates that the piece was made around the year given.

- Medium used by the artist.

- Size of the work. The first number is the height, the second is the width, and a third number indicates depth for three-dimensional works.

- Location of the work. This tells the museum, gallery, or collection in which the work is housed.

Art Studios, Galleries, and Museums

Works of art are created in ***studios.*** A studio is an artist's workplace, much like a classroom is a studio for students. Almost everything an artist needs to create an artwork will be found in his or her studio. It is possible for people to visit artist studios, but an invitation from the artist is usually required.

Art galleries are private businesses where art dealers display and sell works of art. Art galleries are typically open to the public, and the works of art may be viewed even if the patrons do not intend to buy anything.

A ***museum*** is a public or private building where valuable and important artwork is cared for and displayed for the public to view. *Curators* are people who supervise the museum and organize exhibitions. *Docents* are special tour directors who help explain the art to visitors.

Overview

These pages introduce students to the three components that define a work of art: the subject, the composition, and the content.

Subject

The subject is the image that the viewer can easily identify in a work of art. The subject may be one person or many people. It may be a thing. It can be an event, such as a party. In recent years, some artists have chosen to create nonobjective art. This is art that has no recognizable subject matter. In this type of art, the elements of art become the subject.

Composition

The composition is the way the principles of art are used to organize the elements of art. Notice how Benny Andrews uses color and shape to portray the image of a family dinner.

Content

The content is the message the work communicates to the viewer. The message may be an idea, such as family unity, or an emotion or feeling, such as joy or loneliness. If the work of art is functional, such as *Habitat*, then the function is the meaning. Does the work of art look like it could perform the function it is supposed to?

What Is Art?

Every work of art has three parts.

Subject

The objects you can recognize are the subject matter of a work of art. When a work has no recognizable objects, the elements of art such as lines, shapes, colors, and so on become the subject of the work.

Composition

The composition of the work is the way the artist has used the principles to organize the elements of art.

Content

The content is the message the artwork communicates. Content is the meaning of the work. If the work is functional, such as a chair or clothing, then the content is the function of the object.

▶ In which work of art do you think the subject matter is very important?

▶ In which artwork do you think composition is most important?

▶ Which work seems to have the strongest message? Explain.

▶ Which artwork's meaning relates to its function?

▲ **Benny Andrews.** (American).
Grandmother's Dinner. 1992.
Oil on canvas. 72 × 52 inches (182.88 × 132.08 cm.).
Ogden Museum of Southern Art, New Orleans, Louisiana.

▲ **William Sharp.** (English/American). *Great
Water Lily of America.* 1854.
Chromolithograph on woven white paper. 21¼ × 27 inches
(53.98 × 68.58 cm.). Amon Carter Museum, Fort Worth, Texas.

▲ **Artist Unknown.** (Maya/Huipil). *Huipil Weaving.*
c. 1950.
Backstrap woven plain weave with supplementary-weft pattern, silk on
cotton. 50 × 14½ inches (127 × 36.83 cm.). Museum of International
Folk Art, Santa Fe, New Mexico.

▲ **Mosche Safdie.** (Israeli). *Habitat.* 1967.
Concrete. Montreal, Canada.

Activating Prior Knowledge

▪ Ask students to say the first thing they
look for when they look at a work of art.
Students may say they look at color, size,
or what the work is about. Some may say
they look for the feeling or message they
get from the artwork. Give students time
to explore this question. It will provide a
good context for the discussion on these
pages.

Questions to Discuss

▪ Read with students the text on page 14
and look at the images on page 15. Share
with them some of the information above.
Encourage students to think about their
responses during the Activating Prior
Knowledge discussion as they look at
these images and think about the
information you have shared with them.

▶ Read the questions on page 14 and discuss
the answers. The subject matter is
important in *Grandmother's Dinner* and
Great Water Lily of America. Composition
is important in *Huipil Weaving*. *Huipil
Weaving* and *Habitat* are works in which
the meaning relates to function. Most
students will think that *Grandmother's
Dinner* has the strongest message.
However, it is important to point out that
the function of a work is an important
message *(Huipil Weaving* and *Habitat)*.

Overview

In art, subject means something an artist has depicted or represented in an artwork. For example, the subject matter of Paul Cézanne's painting of fruit is called a still life. Some subject matter, like the objects in Cézanne's still life, is easy to identify. Others are more difficult because the artwork may be symbolic or nonobjective. Artists create works of art on a variety of subjects: the natural world, literature, religion, the constructed world, history, and so on. These pages deal with several of the most common subject-matter topics—people, objects, everyday life, stories, things outside, colors and shapes, and things that have a deeper meaning.

Talk with students about each subject-matter topic description below. Encourage them to look for examples of different subject matter in the lessons. By helping them to look at each subject in greater detail and by asking thoughtful questions, your students will begin to develop an understanding for differences among subject matter in art.

Still Life

Artists create works of art that show a variety of objects. Traditional still lifes are bowls, vases, bottles, pitchers, fruit, flowers, food on a table, and/or musical instruments (among other things) that are artfully arranged.

▶ **Question:** What are the objects in this still life?

Subject Matter

Artists make art about many subjects. *Subject matter* is the content of an artist's work. For example, the subject of a painting can be a vase of flowers or a self-portrait. This subject matter is easy to see. The subject matter is harder to understand when the artwork stands for something beyond itself. Look at the artwork on these pages. Notice the different kinds of subject matter.

Still Life

▲ **Paul Cézanne.** (French). *Still Life with Basket of Apples.* 1895.

Oil on canvas. $23\frac{3}{5} \times 31\frac{1}{2}$ inches (60 × 80 cm.). The Art Institute of Chicago, Chicago, Illinois.

Landscape

▲ **Z. Vanessa Helder.** (American). *Rocks and Concrete.* c. 1940.

Watercolor on paper. 19 × 15⅞ inches (48.26 × 40.34 cm.). Cheney Cowles Museum, Spokane, Washington.

What Is Art?　**17**

Landscape

This area includes the natural world—plants, animals, or other things outside. The suffix *-scape* means "a view of." For example, a *cityscape* is buildings and city life seen in an artwork. A *seascape* is a scene of the sea.

▶ **Question:** What objects do you see in this landscape?

Genre

In art, the term *genre* is used to indicate subjects that have to do with ordinary people engaged in everyday activities.

▶ **Question:** What everyday activities is this boy doing?

▲ **Winslow Homer.** (American.) *Nooning.* c. 1872.

Oil on canvas. 13$\frac{5}{16}$ × 19$\frac{5}{8}$ inches (33.02 × 48.26 cm.). Wadsworth Atheneum, Hartford, Connecticut.

Nonobjective

◄ **Natalya Goncharova.** (Russian). *Maquillage.* 1913.
Gouache on paper. $4\frac{3}{8} \times 6\frac{3}{8}$ inches (11.13 × 16.21 cm.). Dallas Museum of Art, Dallas, Texas.

Portrait

◄ **Elizabeth Catlett.** (American). *Sharecropper.* 1970.
Color linocut. 26 × 22 inches (66.04 × 55.88 cm.). Smithsonian American Art Museum, Washington, D.C.

Nonobjective

Sometimes artwork is nonobjective. It does not have an identifiable subject matter—no familiar subjects are shown. People respond to the way the artwork has been organized and designed. Nonobjective art focuses specifically on the elements and principles of art: line, shape, color, and so on.

▶ **Question:** The artwork does not use a subject we can identify. What are some of the lines, shapes, and colors you see in this picture?

Portrait

This category includes portraits, self-portraits, and group portraits. Portraits are one of the oldest subjects in art history. Artists try to present both an accurate depiction and also other aspects of a person's character in a portrait.

▶ **Question:** What do you think the artist is telling us about this person?

Stories

A story is an account of some incident from a real person's life, a historic event, or from a myth, legend, or other piece of symbolic literature.

▶ **Question:** What story do you think is being told in this artwork?

What Is Art?

Allegory

▲ **Jan van Eyck.** (Flemish.) *Portrait of Giovanni Arnolfini and His wife Giovanna Cenami.* 1434.
Oil on wood panel. 32 x 23 inches. The National Gallery, London, England.

Symbolism

▲ **Artist Unknown.** (Huichol People/Mexico). *Mother of the Eagles.* 1991.
Braided yarn embedded in vegetable wax on wood. 15¾ × 19½ inches (40 × 49.53 cm.). Private collection.

Symbols

Sometimes works of art contain symbols—visual signs of something invisible. For example, a dove can be a symbol of peace, or an hourglass may represent the passing of time. Symbols represent a broader idea or sometimes have a secret meaning.

▶ **Question:** What symbols do you see in this work? What do you think they mean?

Overview

Each language has its own system of words and rules of grammar. To learn a new language, you need to learn new words and a new set of rules for putting the words together. The language of visual art also has its own system. The words of the language are the **elements** of art. They are the basic visual symbols in the language of art. Just as there are basic kinds of words such as nouns, verbs, adjectives, and adverbs, there are basic kinds of art elements. These are line, shape, color, value, space, form, and texture. These elements are the visual building blocks that the artist puts together to create a work of art. No matter what materials are used, the artwork will contain all of the visual elements. Sometimes one element will be more important than the others.

Visual images are organized according to rules. In language, these are the rules of grammar. In visual art, the rules for organizing the elements of art are called the **principles** of art. These principles include pattern, rhythm, balance, emphasis, harmony, variety, and unity.

Activating Prior Knowledge

- Ask students what they think of when they hear each of the following words: *line, shape, color.* Encourage them to look around the classroom for examples.

Questions to Discuss

- Have students examine the images on pages 22 and 23. Ask them what they can tell about each photo. What stands out in each image? How does each image help explain the element or principle?

Elements of Art

Art is a language. The words of the language are the elements of art.

Line

Shape

Form

Space

Color

Value

Texture

Principles of Art

Artists organize their artwork using the principles of art.

Pattern

Rhythm

Balance

Emphasis

Harmony

Variety

Unity

The Language of Art

The elements and principles of art are the concepts or ideas that artists use to organize their artwork. Artists use a variety of media and materials to make art. *Media* are types of art such as photography, watercolor, and so on. *Materials* are the things used to make the art, such as markers, paint, paper, clay, fabric, wood, metal, or glass.

There are specific techniques and processes that artists use to manipulate the materials. For example, the proper way to hold a brush to create a thin line with watercolor paint is a specific technique unique to watercolor painting. The process of creating a finished watercolor painting consists of many interwoven steps, such as thinking about what to paint, sketching several ideas, deciding which elements and principles will enhance the work, choosing the best sketch, deciding which watercolor techniques to use, and finally, producing the finished work.

Special techniques and procedures are used with each material. You will need to learn different techniques and follow different procedures for modeling clay than you will for creating paper sculpture. Drawing with crayons requires different techniques and procedures from drawing with oil pastels or chalk. Using the computer to make original art requires that you learn how to use specific computer hardware and software.

Overview

Art History and Culture

Art history is the record of art from the past to the present. By looking at art from the past, we learn what the people who lived before us were like—their feelings and beliefs, clothes, food, houses, and how they viewed the world around them.

Questions to Discuss:

Knowledge

▶ Who created the artwork?

▶ When was the artwork created?

▶ What is the artwork's title?

▶ Have you ever seen an artwork like this? Where?

Comprehension

▶ Is this artwork useful? How is it used?

▶ Compare this artwork with another work from a similar time period. How are the works alike and different?

▶ What interests you most about this artwork?

▶ What is the major theme of this artwork?

Application

▶ What types of materials were used to create this artwork?

▶ Demonstrate how the artwork was created.

▶ Explain how this artwork could have a different use today.

Analysis

▶ What are the main elements in this artwork?

▶ Compare this painting with another painting in this book. How are they alike? How are they different?

▶ What does this artwork mean?

▲ **Frida Kahlo.** (Mexican). *Frida y Diego Rivera.* 1931.
Oil on canvas. 39⅜ × 31 inches (100.01 × 78.74 cm.). San Francisco Museum of Modern Art, San Francisco, California.

Look at the artwork.

▶ What people or objects do you see?

▶ Do they look like people and objects you see around you today? Explain.

Look at the caption.

▶ When was the artwork created?

▶ What can you learn about the artist?

Learn more.

▶ Do some research to find out more about the artist, the artwork, and the time period.

Synthesis

▶ How many titles can you create for this artwork? Name them.

▶ Name a person you would like to give this artwork to as a gift. Why?

▶ Imagine that two people in this room are having a conversation. What would they say to each other? Why?

Evaluation

▶ Do you think this artwork is interesting? Why?

▶ Summarize this artwork's unique qualities.

What to Do

■ Have students research to find out information about the life and times of Frida Kahlo. Students may write a biography of the artist or dress up as the artist and tell the artist's story to classmates.

■ Have students research Kahlo and another artist who lived at the same time. Students should research information about the media, styles, techniques, and procedures the artists used. Have pairs of students role-play a discussion between the two artists about media, style, and personal beliefs about art.

■ Have students work in groups to act out this painting. They should write a script for what happened before, during, and after the moment shown in the painting.

About Art **25**

Overview

Aesthetic Perception

Aesthetic perception encourages students to make choices rather than give "correct answers." By understanding the process of aesthetic perception, students can see something from a new perspective and ultimately realize that art is all around them.

Journal writing is an integral part of aesthetic perception. It is an ongoing record of what a student does, notices, and thinks. Journals track the evolution of thoughts and experiences over time. Through this recorded journey, the student has the ability to reflect on where one has been and where one is going. Writing thoughts, reactions, perceptions, new information, and questions intensifies each student's life experiences.

Guidelines for Aesthetic Perception

Students like to know what is important about a work of art and what was important to the artist. They are fascinated with information, questions, and descriptions. There are some guiding principles in the development of aesthetic perception at this level that can profoundly influence teaching practice.

1. All aesthetic perception actively involves the learner.

2. All aesthetic perception involves reflection.

3. The works of art have substance. Their tools and a working vocabulary are vital to empower the learner.

4. Aesthetic perception is a process based upon examination of the artist's choices and the choices in response made by the viewer.

5. All responses are valid. Right and wrong are irrelevant issues when viewing works of art.

6. All works of art relate to each other, and each relates to all other areas of life.

About Art

▲ **Frida Kahlo.** (Mexican). *Frida y Diego Rivera.* 1931.
Oil on canvas. 39⅜ × 31 inches (100.01 × 78.74 cm.). San Francisco Museum of Modern Art, San Francisco, California.

Look

► Look at the work of art. What sounds, smells, or feelings are in this work of art?

► What happened just before and just after in this work of art?

► What kind of music would be playing in this work of art?

Look Inside

► Imagine you are one of these people. Who are you? What are you thinking? How do you feel?

► If you could add yourself to the painting, what would you look like? What would you be doing?

► Act out or tell the story in this work of art with a beginning, a middle, and an end.

► Draw what you can't see in this work of art. Are there hidden images that should be revealed?

Look Outside

► How is this like or different from your own world?

► What does the artist want you to know or think about in this work of art?

► Describe your journey in viewing this work of art. Include your thoughts, ideas, and changes in thinking.

► What will you remember about this work?

Questions to Discuss

► What is happening in this work of art?

► What is this work of art about?

► What is your favorite part of this work of art?

► What is most important in this artwork?

► What happened just before and just after in this work of art?

► If you were in this work of art, what would you be doing?

► What have you learned about the work of art?

► What does the artist want you to know or think about in this work of art?

► How do you feel about the work of art? What does it make you feel?

► What will you remember about this work of art?

► Has this work of art changed your thinking?

Things to Do

■ Draw yourself into the work of art.

■ Draw what you can't see in the work of art.

■ Act out or show the story in the work of art.

■ Collect objects that are similar to the objects in the work of art and make aesthetic judgments about them.

■ Role-play an interview with the artist about how the work of art was made.

Overview

Art Criticism

Art criticism is an organized system for looking at and talking about art. The purpose of art criticism is to get the viewer involved in a perception process that delays judgment until all aspects of the image have been studied. Learning art criticism also gives each viewer the confidence to discuss a work of art without worrying what other people might think.

Describe **What do I see?**

During this step, the viewer lists all the obvious things in the artwork. Objectivity is important.

Questions to Discuss

▶ List and describe everything you see in the artwork. Answers may include: We see the full figures of a man and a woman standing on a plain, brown floor. Above Frida's head flies a tan dove with blue-tipped wings. Frida looks tiny. She is wearing a floor-length, ruffled, dark blue-green skirt and a red scarf that is trimmed with diamond shapes and fringe. Diego is wearing a plain, dark blue suit (and so on).

Analyze **How is the work organized?**

During this step the viewer examines how the elements and principles of art are used in the artwork.

Questions to Discuss

▶ Describe the elements of art that you see. Answers may include: **Line**—There are horizontal lines where the floor meets the wall, on the wall, and in the rug. **Shape**—The tabletops, bookcase, lamp, doilies, and picture frames are geometric. The chairs, vase, flowers, leaves, and pitchers are free-form shapes (and so on).

▶ How has the artist used the principles of design? Answers may include: **Balance**—Informal balance; the large, plain shape of Diego is balanced by the small, busy shape and bright color of Frida. **Emphasis**—The bright red scarf leads our eyes to the clasped hands (and so on).

About Art

▲ **Frida Kahlo.** (Mexican). *Frida y Diego Rivera.* 1931.
Oil on canvas. 39⅜ × 31 inches (100.01 × 78.74 cm.). San Francisco Museum of Modern Art, San Francisco, California.

 **Art Criticism**

Describe

▶ List everything you see in this painting. Be sure to describe the people and their clothing.

Analyze

▶ How has the artist used line, shape, color, value, space, and texture?

▶ What kind of balance has the artist used?

▶ Has the artist used emphasis to make us notice one thing more than others?

Interpret

▶ What is happening?

▶ What is the artist telling us about these two people?

Decide

▶ Have you ever seen another artwork like this?

▶ Is it successful because it is realistic?

▶ Is it successful because it is well-organized?

▶ Is it successful because you have strong feelings when you study it?

More About Aesthetic Judging

You can use art criticism to make aesthetic judgments about functional objects such as cars or shoes. Follow the first two steps (**Describe** and **Analyze**) as described. During **Interpret,** consider the purpose of the object as its meaning. (Does a pitcher look like it will pour liquid without spilling?) As you **Decide,** consider whether the object works when it is used. (If a chair is not comfortable to sit in, it is not functioning properly and is not successful as a chair.)

Interpret — What is the artist saying to me?

During interpretation, viewers will make inferences about the message in the work of art. Each interpretation can be different because each is based upon the feelings and life experiences of the viewer.

Questions to Discuss

▶ What do I think about this work?

▶ What is the artist trying to tell us about these people and their lives? The clasped hands of these two people represent the link between them. They are married, and this is their wedding portrait. She leans toward him, but he turns away from her to the outside world. She shows her need for him; he shows his independence.

Decide

This is when the viewer decides whether or not the work is successful. There are two levels of judgment to be made. The first is personal: do you like the work?

The second level is also subjective, but it uses aesthetic theories to help the viewer decide whether the work is successful. More than one theory may be used to judge a work.

■ Some critics think that the most important thing about a work of art is the realistic presentation of the subject matter. This aesthetic theory is called **imitationalism** or **realism.**

■ Other critics think that composition is the most important factor in a work of art. This aesthetic theory, called **formalism** or **composition,** emphasizes the design qualities and the arrangement of the elements of art using the principles of art.

■ Some critics claim that no object should be considered art if it fails to arouse an emotional response in the viewer. **Emotionalism** or **expressionism** is a theory concerned with the content or the meaning of the work of art.

Questions to Discuss

▶ Have you seen any works in this book that look similar to the style of this artist?

▶ Which aesthetic theories would you use to judge the success of this work? The two people and the objects are realistic. The artist has used informal balance to organize the work, and has used the red scarf as a point of emphasis. The artist has shown the feelings of these two people.

Overview

Creative Expression

The creative process, like the writing process or the scientific method, is an organized approach to creative problem solving that can be used by professional artists and students alike. Throughout *Art Connections,* the Creative Expression activities are presented as problems to be solved. Remind students of the steps in the creative process as they work on the activities.

Get an idea.

- Inspiration can come from many places. In the *Art Connections* Creative Expression activities, the idea comes from the activity instructions. Professional artists may get ideas from a client who has commissioned a piece of art from nature, from a historical event, from everyday life, or from the available media and materials.

- Try the following to help students when they have trouble getting an idea.

  1. As a class, brainstorm about where to get ideas for artwork: works by other artists, personal experiences, stories students have read, and so on.

  2. Encourage students to write ideas in the Ideas section of their Art Journals. Remind students that they can make notes for ideas anytime, not just in art class.

  3. Pair students who are having trouble thinking of ideas with students who have many ideas. One student can model getting ideas for the other student.

Plan your work.

- Once students have an idea, they must decide the best way to execute that idea. Would a two-dimensional or three-dimensional artwork best convey the idea that students are trying to show? Should students use watercolor or pencil?

Make a sketch.

- Just like professional writers, professional artists do not make a perfect work on the first try. They may make several sketches, evaluate those sketches, and revise them before deciding on a final vision for the artwork.

- Encourage students to make sketches in the Ideas section of their Art Journals.

About Art

▲ **Frida Kahlo.** (Mexican). *Frida y Diego Rivera.* 1931.

Oil on canvas. 39⅜ × 31 inches (100.01 × 78.74 cm.). San Francisco Museum of Modern Art, San Francisco, California.

How does an artist create a work of art?

Art is a process. You can follow the same steps to create your own work of art.

1. Get an idea.
- ▶ Artists get inspiration from many places. Look around you. People, objects, and scenes may provide inspiration for a work of art.

2. Plan your work.
- ▶ Do you want your artwork to be two-dimensional or three-dimensional?
- ▶ Decide what media you want to use.
- ▶ What materials will you need?

3. Make a sketch.
- ▶ Think about how you want your artwork to look. Sketch several ideas.
- ▶ If your artwork will be three-dimensional, sketch it from different points of view.
- ▶ Then choose the best idea.

4. Use the media.
- ▶ Make an artwork based on your best idea. You may want to practice using the materials first.
- ▶ When making your composition, remember the elements and principles of art. How can you use them to make your artwork say what you want it to say?

5. Share your final work.
- ▶ Evaluate your work using the four steps of art criticism. What do you like best about your work? What would you do differently next time?

Use the media.

- ■ In this stage of the creative process, students make their artwork based on their plans. Encourage students to practice using unfamiliar media, and to try new techniques on a small practice piece before using those techniques on their artwork.

- ■ Even during this stage of the process, students may get new ideas. Encourage them to be flexible.

Share your final work.

- ■ Art is meant to be shared with and viewed by others. Encourage students to share their artwork with family or friends, display it in the classroom, or display it in the school display area. This is also a good time for students to self-evaluate their work using the four steps of art criticism.

More About Art Journals

- ■ Art Journals are a wonderful way to work through ideas. At the beginning of the school year, help students set up an Art Journal. This can be a spiral notebook or a three-ring binder with pages for writing and sketching. The Art Journal will be divided into sections for Concepts, Ideas, Critical Thinking (Art Criticism), Vocabulary.

1. Encourage students to use the Concepts section of their journals for summarizing unit and lesson concepts, writing questions they have, and listing other things they want to learn.

2. Students can use the Ideas section of their Art Journals for brainstorming, organizing, planning, and sketching. Remind students that they can write ideas in their journals any time; they do not need to wait until a designated time in art class.

3. Students can use the Critical Thinking section of their journals to self-evaluate their work using the four steps of Art Criticism. In *Art Connections,* students are asked to self-evaluate after each Creative Expression activity. This can be a valuable tool to help students review art concepts and get ideas for their next work.

4. Encourage students to use the Vocabulary section of their Art Journals to record unfamiliar words, summarize or explain definitions, and so on. Developing vocabulary is an important step in being able to think about and communicate about art.

Overview

Elementary teachers are responsible for the safety of their students. Specific guidelines have been established by the Center for Safety in the Arts, and these guidelines should be followed to ensure that both students and teachers use art materials safely. Following are some general tips for using art materials safely. For more detailed information, see "Safe Use of Art Materials" on page T12 of this book.

Safe Art Materials

- Use only water-soluble AP- or CP-designated markers. Never use permanent or scented markers.

- Use only dustless chalk.

- Make sure that crayons have the AP or CP label to ensure that they do not contain lead.

- When using tempera paint, use only liquid tempera, not powdered tempera. Do not use any spray paints or fixatives.

- Use only water-soluble printers' inks.

- Use pencils to carve into soft surfaces for printing blocks. Do not use mat knives or other sharp instruments.

- Do not allow young children to use sharp scissors; blunt points are safe.

- Do not use rubber cement unless it bears the AP or CP label. Do not use solvent-based glues.

Safety

▶ Use art materials only on your artwork.

▶ Keep art materials out of your mouth, eyes and ears.

▶ Use scissors and other sharp tools carefully. Keep your fingers away from the cutting blades.

▶ Wash your hands after using the art materials.

▶ Wear an art shirt or smock to protect your clothes.

▶ Use only art materials with a "nontoxic" label.

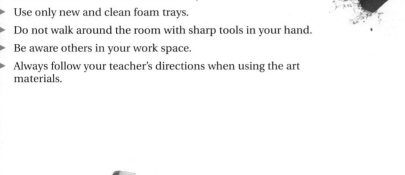

- Return art materials to their proper storage place.
- Be careful not to breathe chalk or clay dust.
- Use only new and clean foam trays.
- Do not walk around the room with sharp tools in your hand.
- Be aware others in your work space.
- Always follow your teacher's directions when using the art materials.

General Safety Precautions

- Read the labels on all materials used in the art room. Look carefully for the AP/CP labels. If these are not present, be suspicious. Imported art materials should be looked upon with extreme caution. Other countries have not developed the rigid safety codes adopted by the United States.

- Do not accept or use old art materials that may have been left in the school or donated by some well-meaning adult. If the materials do not bear the current safety codes, toss them out.

- Never allow food or drink in the room where art activities are being conducted. Dust and even fibers float freely in the air and can readily contaminate food or drink.

- Practice cleanliness. Have children wash their hands thoroughly with soap after using art materials.

- Use absolutely no permanent markers or solvent-based materials in the art room. If a material stains the clothes or hands and does not clean up with simple soap and water, it is not appropriate or safe for young children to use.

- Use plastic containers for washing paintbrushes; glass is dangerous in the hands of young children.

- Paper cutters should not be used by elementary-school children. The paper cutter should be kept out of the students' reach, and left in a locked position always with the blade turned to the wall.

- Do not use commercial dyes around children; use vegetable or natural dyes (flowers, teas, onion skins).

- Do not allow children in a room where a kiln is firing; both the heat and the fumes are dangerous.

Unit 1 Planning Guide

	Lesson Title	Suggested Pacing	Creative Expression Activity
Lesson 1	Expression with Lines	1:30	Create a mixed-media collage.
Lesson 2	Perception Drawing	1:15	Create a contour drawing.
Lesson 3	Geometric and Free-Form Shapes	1:15	Create a still-life drawing using a computer.
Lesson 4	Value with Hatching	1:30	Draw a model. Use hatching to show value.
Lesson 5	Value with Blending	1:15	Sketch an object. Use blended values to show form.
Lesson 6	Value Contrast	1:10	Create a scene. Use value contrast in photography.
ART SOURCE ARTSOURCE	Line, Shape, and Value in Theatre	0:45	Create a story. Feature a musical instrument.

Materials	Program Resources	Fine Art Resources	Literature Resources
9" × 12" cardboard, glue, craft sticks, paper, scissors, fabric, rope, yarn, or string	*Assessment,* pp. 9–10 *Home and After-School Connections* *The National Museum of Women in the Arts Collection* *Reading and Writing Test Preparation,* pp. 6–7	*Transparency 1* *Artist Profiles,* pp. 74, 48 *Large Prints 61, 62* *Flash Cards 1–6* *Animals Through History Time Line*	*The Wheel on the School* by Meindert DeJong
costumes with accessories, drawing paper, felt-tip pens	*Assessment,* pp. 11–12 *Home and After-School Connections* *Women in the Arts Collection* *Reading and Writing Test Preparation,* pp. 8–9	*Transparency 2* *Artist Profiles,* pp. 20, 61 *Large Prints 61, 62* *Flash Cards 1–6* *Animals Through History Time Line*	*When the Missing Piece Meets the Big O* by Shel Silverstein
computer paint program, geometric-shaped and free-form objects	*Assessment,* pp. 13–14 *Home and After-School Connections* *Women in the Arts Collection* *Reading and Writing Test Preparation,* pp. 10–11	*Transparency 3* *Artist Profiles,* pp. 11, 16 *Large Prints 61, 62* *Animals Through History Time Line*	*Going Back Home, An Artist Returns to the South* by Toyomi Igus
pencils, sketch paper, erasers, 9" × 12" white drawing paper	*Assessment,* pp. 15–16 *Home and After-School Connections* *Women in the Arts Collection* *Reading and Writing Test Preparation,* pp. 12–13	*Transparency 4* *Artist Profiles,* pp. 14, 66 *Large Print 61* *Flash Cards 1, 2, 3, 10, 11* *Animals Through History Time Line*	*Sarah, Plain and Tall* by Patricia MacLachlan
9" × 12" white drawing paper, charcoal pencils, cloth scraps	*Assessment,* pp. 17–18 *Home and After-School Connections* *Women in the Arts Collection* *Reading and Writing Test Preparation,* pp. 14–15	*Transparency 5* *Artist Profiles,* pp. 52, 49 *Large Prints 61, 62* *Flash Cards 1, 2, 3, 10, 11* *Animals Through History Time Line*	*The Big Bike Race* by Lucy Jane Bledsoe
cameras, black-and-white film	*Assessment,* pp. 19–20 *Home and After-School Connections* *Women in the Arts Collection* *Reading and Writing Test Preparation,* pp. 16–17	*Transparency 6* *Artist Profiles,* pp. 56, 3 *Large Prints 61, 62* *Flash Cards 11, 14, 17, 20* *Animals Through History Time Line*	*The First Woman Doctor* by Rachel Baker
pictures of instruments, "Voice of the Wood", pencils, notebook paper			

Unit Overview

Line, Shape, and Value

Lesson 1: Expression with lines is used to create shapes and to express ideas.

Lesson 2: Perception drawing techniques show movement, surface ridges, and edges in quick sketches.

Lesson 3: Geometric and free-form shapes are used by artists to convey ideas and to represent natural and artificial objects.

Lesson 4: Value with hatching creates light and dark areas through the use of lines.

Lesson 5: Value with blending creates gradual light and dark areas in a work of art.

Lesson 6: Value contrast is used to create emphasis in a work of art.

Introduce Unit Concepts

"Artists use the elements of line, shape, and value in their work to show movement and expression, and to mimic reality." "Los artistas usan los elementos de línea, forma y valor en sus obras para mostrar movimiento y expresión y para imitar la realidad."

Line
- Have students look around the classroom and on their clothing for examples of different types of lines (zigzag, wavy).

Shape ⭐ Language Arts
- Have students look around the room and create categories of similar shapes.
- Ask students to name the definitions that come to mind for the word *value*.

Cross-Curricular Projects
- See the *Language Arts and Reading, Mathematics, Science,* and *Social Studies Art Connections* books for activities that further develop line, shape, and value concepts.

Line, Shape, and Value

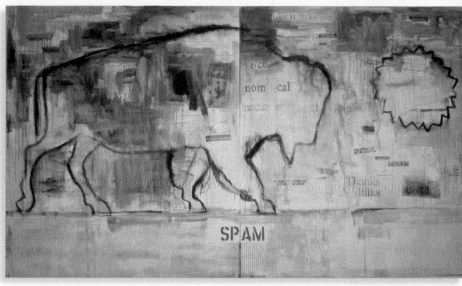

▲ **Jaune Quick-to-See Smith.** (American). *Spam.* 1995.
Acrylic and mixed-media on canvas. 60 × 100 inches (152.4 × 254 cm.). Private collection.

Line, shape, and value are used by artists to create many types of art.

Jaune Quick-to-See Smith used many kinds of lines, a variation of dark to light color, and both geometric and natural shapes to direct the viewer's eyes across *Spam*. She used contour drawing to emphasize the shape of the buffalo. This piece communicates our responsibility to our environment.

34   Unit 1

Fine Art Prints

Display **Large Prints 61** *Horses in a Field* and **62** *The Jack Pine*. Refer to the prints throughout the unit as students learn about line, shape, and value.

Large Print 61

Large Print 62

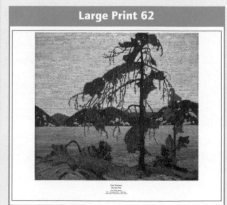

Artists use the element of **line** in works of art to create movement and shapes.

▶ What area of the picture do your eyes see first? What do you see last?

▶ What types of lines do you see? Do you see any of these lines more than once?

The element of **shape** is used by artists to create objects and people.

▶ What shapes do you see in this painting?

In This Unit you will learn about and practice how artists use line, shape, and value to create art. Here are the concepts you will study:
▶ Types of lines
▶ Shape
▶ Value

Jaune Quick-to-See Smith

(1941–)

Jaune Quick-to-See Smith grew up on a Montana reservation. Her Shoshone grandmother gave her the name "Quick-to-See" because she was quick to understand things. As a child, she often went on long trips with her father, who was a horse trainer and trader. She saw the rugged beauty of the Northwest's landscape and was inspired to draw. Smith's paintings reflect her concern for preventing the destruction of the environment and for the preservation of Native American cultures.

Unit 1   **35**

Examine the Artwork

"Let's look closely at the painting." "Vamos a observar detalladamente la pintura."

■ Have students examine *Spam* and describe what they see.

■ Have students answer the questions about line and shape on page 35.

▶ The viewer's eyes will begin with the contour drawings of the buffalo and the sun because of the contrasting value of these lines when compared to the lighter background.

▶ Curved lines, zigzag lines, vertical lines with paint, horizontal lines of text are found in *Spam*.

▶ Natural or free-form shapes are seen in this painting.

Unit Pretest

T Display ***Transparency 1*** as a pretest. Answers: 1. C, 2. B, 3. A, 4. C, 5. A

Home Connection

■ See ***Home and After-School Connections*** for family newsletters and activities for this unit.

Art History and Culture

Jaune Quick-to-See Smith

Jaune Quick-to-See Smith (zhōn kwik tōō sē smith) (1941–) was born into a large family on a Montana reservation. Her Shoshone grandmother gave her the name "Quick-to-See" because she was quick to understand things. After 22 years of supporting herself and her three children, Smith completed a master of fine arts degree. She now lives in New Mexico. Her art speaks of current issues facing Native Americans, such as the destruction of the environment and government oppression.

See pages 24–25 and 16–21 for more about art history and the subject matter.

Artist Profiles p. 53

◦ Artist Profile ◦

Jaune Quick-to-See Smith
b. 1941

Jaune Quick-to-See Smith (zhōn kwik tōō sē smith) was born into a large family on a Montana reservation. She often went hungry as a child. Her Shoshone grandmother gave her the name "Quick-to-See" because Smith was quick to understand things. When Smith was in first grade, she already knew she wanted to be an artist. Later she was told that she was not college material and that a woman could not have a career in art. Smith spent 22 years supporting herself, raising three children, finishing college, and completing a master's degree in painting. She now paints as frequently as possible in a remodeled stable

ILLUSTRATOR PROFILE
Garth Williams
(1912–1996)

Garth Williams was born in New York to parents who were both artists. His father was known for his illustrations in *Punch* magazine. Williams grew up in New Jersey and Canada until he was 10, when his family moved to England.

In England, Williams studied architecture and worked as an architect's assistant before pursuing painting and sculpture. His talents earned him a scholarship to London's Royal College of Art as well as the British Prix de Rome scholarship for his sculptures.

After serving with the ambulance unit of the Red Cross in World War II, Williams returned to the United States. He illustrated the magazine *The New Yorker* for a short time before launching his career as a children's book illustrator. His first assignment came from editors at Harper and Row, who asked him to illustrate *Stuart Little* by E. B. White. Williams would go on to illustrate White's *Charlotte's Web* as well as a multitude of classics by other children's authors, including the *Little House* books by Laura Ingalls Wilder, *The Cricket in Times Square* by George Selden, and a number of books by Margaret Wise Brown. Although Williams is most known for his work as an illustrator, he also wrote seven children's books.

Throughout Unit 1, share Garth Williams's illustrations with the class and discuss his use of line, shape, and value. Ask students these questions: What types of lines do you see? Where do you see geometric shapes? Where do you see free-form shapes? Where do you see examples of hatching, cross-hatching, stippling, blending, and contrast of value?

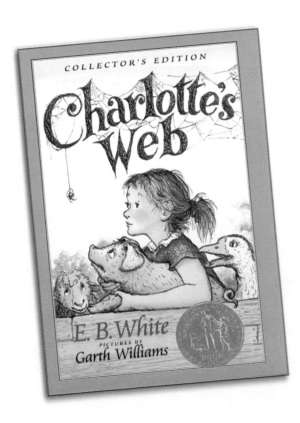

Music

Line refers to the way a melody moves higher and lower.

Shape can pertain to the melodic contour, or the way a musical phrase is "shaped" through gradual changes in volume within phrases.

Value in music relates to the ability of the performer to create subtle differences in tone.

Literature

Show the video or DVD *Jumanji*. Pause the video and have students identify various lines, shapes, and values. Ask students to explain how each of these elements contributes to what they see.

Literature and Art

Performing Arts

 Show "Voice of the Wood." Point out the use of line and shape in this video.

Artsource®

National Standards for Arts Education in Visual Arts (NSAE) 6.b

Lesson 1 Overview

Expression with Lines

Lesson 1 introduces types of lines, the emotions they represent, and how to create them. A line is a path created by a moving point or dot.

Objectives

Art History and Culture

To recognize the Mayan huipil weavings and Jackson Pollock's life and work

Creative Expression

To create a mixed-media collage using lines

Aesthetic Perception

To identify how different types of lines are used
NSAE 1.a

Art Criticism

To evaluate one's own work using the four steps of art criticism

Vocabulary Reading

Review the following vocabulary word with students before beginning the lesson.

line línea—a mark drawn by a tool such as a pencil, pen, or paintbrush as it moves across a surface

See page 59B for additional vocabulary and Spanish vocabulary resources.

Art Journal: Vocabulary

Have students add this word to the Vocabulary section of their Art Journals.

Lesson Materials

- note cards
- crayons
- 9" × 12" inch cardboard
- glue
- paper
- craft sticks
- scissors
- fabric
- rope, yarn, or string

Alternate Materials:
- scratch paper
- pencils
- drawing paper
- chenille wires
- straws

Program Resources

- *Reading and Writing Test Prep.*, pp. 6–7
- *Transparency 1*
- *Flash Cards* 1, 2, 3, 4, 5, 6
- *Artist Profiles*, pp. 74, 48
- *Animals Through History Time Line*
- *Assessment*, pp. 9–10
- *Large Prints 61* Horses in a Field and *62* The Jack Pine
- *The National Museum of Women in the Arts Collection*

Concept Trace
Expression with Lines
Introduced: Level 4, Unit 1, Lesson 1

Reinforced: Level 6, Unit 1, Lesson 1

Lesson 1 Arts Integration

Theatre

Complete Unit 1, Lesson 1, on pages 18–19 of *Theatre Arts Connections.*

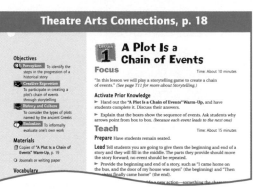

Music

Symphony No. 9 in D Minor Op. 125. Ludwig van Beethoven.

Line in music refers to the way a melody moves higher and lower (up, down, or the same). To relate the concept of line in music to line in visual art, play Beethoven's 9th Symphony, which includes a wide range of musical lines. Have students draw the vertical, horizontal, diagonal, zigzag, and curved lines that they think go with the music.

Movement & Dance

A line can travel anywhere. Stand tall and straight, using one hand and starting with a dot in space. Trace a continuous line in front, above, below, and around you. Go all the way to floor and up as high as you can. End with the dot. Explore this idea again, but this time add in a movement quality: trembling, sad, forceful, agitated and so forth.

Focus

Time: About 30 minutes

Activate Prior Knowledge

"What kinds of lines do you like to use when you create a piece of artwork? Curved lines? Straight lines?" "¿Qué tipos de líneas les gusta usar cuando hacen una obra de arte? ¿Líneas curvas? ¿Líneas rectas?"

- Discuss students' responses. Encourage them to talk about lines they have seen in other pieces of art.

Using Literature ⭐ Reading

- Share Meindert DeJong's *The Wheel on the School* with the class. Have students identify the types of lines that can be found in Maurice Sendak's illustrations, on the cover, and in the book.

Thematic Connection ⭐ Social Studies

- **Cooperation and Competition:** Discuss with students the importance of cooperation when working together and the value of competition.

Introduce the Art

Look

"Let's take a close look at the two works of art." "Vamos a observar detalladamente las dos obras de arte."

Comparing and Contrasting ⭐ Reading

- Have students compare the similarities and contrast the differences between *Huipil Weaving* and Jackson Pollock's *Convergence*. Both works of art use lines to show energy and movement. The lines used in *Huipil Weaving* are in a recognizable, planned pattern. The lines in *Convergence* appear less orderly. NSAE 5.c

Art History and Culture

Colored threads became available in the early 1950s. This huipil reflects the use of complex lines and shapes made possible by these new materials. *Convergence* is representative of Pollock's "action painting." This new approach to painting was influential in the American pop-art movement.

 Web Connection

Visit **www.anthro.fsu.edu/wovenvoices/weaving/huipil.html** or **www.mayatraditions.com/backstrap.html** for further information on Mayan huipil weaving.

 Lesson 1

Expression with Lines

Look at the artwork on these pages. The *Huipil Weaving* is part of a garment made and worn by the Cakchiquel Maya of Guatemala. In *Convergence*, Jackson Pollock created overlapping lines by dripping and sometimes splattering paint while moving in a dancelike motion around the canvas on the floor. Lines are used in both pieces of art to create mood and movement.

◀ **Artist Unknown.** (Maya/Huipil). *Huipil Weaving.* c. 1950.

Backstrap woven plain weave with supplementary-weft pattern, silk on cotton. 50 × 14½ inches (127 × 36.83 cm.). Museum of International Folk Art, Santa Fe, New Mexico.

Art History and Culture

How have these artists expressed their culture through these works of art?

Art History and Culture

Huipil Weaving

Today, in the village of Santa Catarina Palopó, Guatemala, located about two miles from the tourist hub, the main attraction is the beautiful colorful costumes worn by the people there. The *huipil* (pronounced wē´ pēl) is the Mayan women's traditional blouse, which is woven on a backstrap loom and has colorful geometric patterns, including many line types. These patterns are repeated in the design of the men's pants. *Huipil Weaving* was woven in 1950 by the indigenous women of the Cakchiquel Mayan people.

See pages 24–25 and 16–21 for more about art history and the subject matter.

Artist Profiles, p. 74

Artist Profile

Huipil Weaving

The ancient Mayan people lived in present-day Guatemala, Belize, and the western edges of Honduras and El Salvador, as well as in the Mexican states of Yucatan, Quintano Roo, Campeche, Chiapas, and Tabasco. Their civilization thrived from 700 B.C. to 900 A.D. They believed that time, space, and the physical world were connected to the supernatural world. Many Mayan gods were believed to be combinations of animals and humans. The Mayans built cities with terraced pyramids, temples, palaces, monuments, and courtyards. They also built extensive roadways that supported their trading economy.

Artist unknown (Mayan).

▲ **Jackson Pollock.** (American). *Convergence.* 1952.

Oil and enamel on canvas. $93\frac{1}{2} \times 155$ inches (237.49 × 393.7 cm.). Albright-Knox Art Gallery, Buffalo, New York.

Study both works of art to find a variety of lines.

▸ Do you see a line that zigzags?

▸ Which lines are curved?

▸ How do the lines help to create a mood?

▸ Compare the two works of art. Do you see lines that are similar?

Aesthetic Perception

Design Awareness Look around the classroom for various types of lines. What kinds of lines do you see in the furniture?

Art History and Culture

Jackson Pollock

Jackson Pollock (jak´ sən pä´ lək) (1912–1956) believed the process of creating an artwork was just as important as the finished artwork itself. During this "action painting" process, he would move in a dancelike rhythm while dripping and sometimes splattering the paint in a controlled manner onto the canvas that was placed on the floor. At a time when many artists were creating representational art, Jackson Pollock changed the rules and put the emphasis on emotion.

See pages 24–25 and 16–21 for more about art history and the subject matter.

Artist Profiles, p. 48

Artist Profile

Paul Jackson Pollock
1912–1956

Paul Jackson Pollock (pôl jak´ sən pä´ lək) was born in Cody, Wyoming, but spent his childhood in Arizona and California. He first studied painting in Los Angeles, California, at Manual Arts High School and then moved to New York City to study under Thomas Hart Benton at the Art Students League. Pollock next worked with the Mexican muralist David Alfaro Siqueiros, from whom he learned unusual painting techniques. Pollock's solo show at the Guggenheim's Art of this Century Gallery in 1943 led to a contract with the gallery that allowed him to spend all his time painting. In 1945 he married artist Lee Krasner.

Study

▸ *Huipil Weaving* uses zigzag lines within the columns as designs.

▸ Pollock: The curved lines bend and change gradually.

▸ The repeated lines in *Huipil Weaving* create a happy, or upbeat, mood. The curved and overlapped lines in *Convergence* do not break or rest, and the mood is hyper and chaotic.

▸ There are similar curved lines. NSAE 5.c

■ For more examples of abstract/nonobjective art, see *The National Museum of Women in the Arts Collection.*

Art Journal: Writing

Encourage students to imagine themselves in a place other than where they are right now. Ask them to list in their Art Journals the types of lines around them. Then have them explain how these lines create an emotion that is related to how they would feel there.

Aesthetic Perception

Design Awareness Discuss with students the lines they see first when looking at a particular piece of furniture in the classroom. Talk about what feeling these lines communicate. Find other objects in the classroom with common lines and discuss the similarities. NSAE 5.a

Developing Visual Literacy Ask students to imagine creating their own interpretation of either work of art using a different medium. Have students explain their vision of the artwork. For example, students may write a song that illustrates the mood they feel when viewing *Convergence* or a sculpture reflecting the design of *Huipil Weaving*.

Web Connection

Visit **www.nga.gov/feature/pollock** for more information about Jackson Pollock, his process, and his artwork.

each

Time: About 45 minutes

"How can you illustrate the five different kinds of lines?" "¿Cómo pueden ilustrar los cinco tipos diferentes de líneas?"

■ Discuss the definitions of the five different kinds of lines and their variations on page 38.

Practice

Materials: note cards, crayons

Alternate Materials: scratch paper, pencils, drawing paper

■ Distribute the note cards and have students follow the directions on page 38.

■ When students have finished steps 1 and 2, divide them into groups of four or five. If there is time, have the students quickly sketch the still-life poses. The note cards can be collected and used for reviewing the types of lines in this lesson.

Creative Expression

Materials: 9" × 12" cardboard, glue, craft sticks, paper, scissors, fabric, rope, yarn or string

Alternate Materials: chenille wires, yarn, or straws

■ Distribute the materials and have students follow the directions on page 39.

■ Review the Activity Tips on page 230 for visual examples of this lesson's activity.

Art Journal: Brainstorming

Have students brainstorm the types of lines they can make with their materials to express different emotions and list their ideas in their Art Journals. Then have students select one of the emotions listed and plan how they will convey this feeling in their collage.

Using Lines

A **line** is a mark drawn with a tool such as a pencil, pen, or paintbrush as it moves across a surface. Lines have different lengths, widths, and textures. Some curve and move in different directions.

 Vertical lines move up and down, creating a feeling of strength and stability.

 Horizontal lines move from side to side, creating a calm feeling.

 Diagonal lines move at a slant and express movement.

 Zigzag lines are made by joining diagonal lines.

 Curved lines bend and change gradually or turn inward to form spirals.

Lines can be long or short, thick or thin, and rough or smooth.

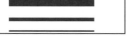  

Practice

Use lines to create a pose.

1. Choose a line type from above.

2. Draw an example of this line type on one side of a note card, and write what type of line it is on the other side.

3. Together with your assigned group, create a pose that displays the lines each of you has drawn on your note cards.

4. Pose in front of the class while the other students try to identify the lines your group has used.

38 Unit 1 • Lesson 1

Differentiated Instruction

Reteach

Have students, in the course of their school day, record two examples of each type of line reviewed in this lesson. Encourage them to record the expression these lines communicate and report their findings to the class.

Special Needs

Some collage materials may be easier than others to manipulate. Yarn may prove to be a frustrating medium for students who lack fine-motor control. Chenille wires may be a more effective material.

ELL

It might be helpful to pantomime *strength* and *stability* when describing vertical lines, *calm* for horizontal lines, and *energetic* and *slanting* for diagonal lines. Allow students to practice identifying and describing lines with a partner before they share with the entire class.

38 UNIT 1 • Line, Shape, and Value

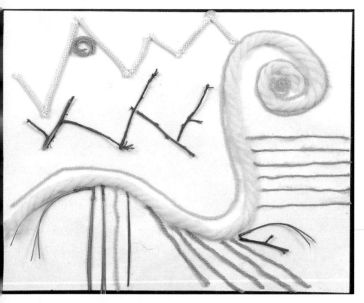

 Think about the types of lines the student artist used in this mixed-media collage.

Creative Expression

In what ways can you make lines besides drawing them? Create a mixed-media collage using lines.

1. Think about the five different types of lines. Collect linear mixed-media materials such as yarn, string, and grass.

2. Use different materials to create lines and line variations. Keep in mind the mood that certain lines suggest.

3. Arrange and glue the collage materials onto a piece of cardboard.

Art Criticism

Describe What materials did you use in your collage?

Analyze How did you use lines to express a mood in your collage?

Interpret What title would you give the collage?

Decide Were you successful in communicating the feelings that you wanted to express? If you could do this collage over again, how would you change it?

Review and Assess

"Were you able to create a mixed-media collage using lines?" "¿Pudieron hacer un collage de medios combinados usando líneas?"

Think

The student artist used vertical, horizontal, diagonal, zigzag, and curved lines.

■ Use *Large Print 62* *The Jack Pine* to have students identify and describe the use of lines in a work of art.

Informal Assessment

■ For standardized-format test practice using this lesson's art content, see pages 6–7 in *Reading and Writing Test Preparation.*

Art Journal: Critical Thinking

Have students answer the four art criticism questions—Describe, Analyze, Interpret, and Decide—in their Art Journals. In small groups, have students discuss their mixed-media collages.

Art Across the Curriculum

Use these simple ideas to reinforce art concepts across the curriculum.

★ **Narrative Writing** Have students write a short story about characters who are involved in a competition. Encourage them to incorporate the theme of cooperation in their stories.

★ **Math** When studying division, have students practice finding a fraction of the total number of lines in an artwork.

★ **Science** Look at a cross section of a tree and notice how the lines form rings that express the tree's living conditions and age.

★ **Social Studies** Review the lines of position that have been assigned on the globe.

★ **Technology** Have students practice using the tools in a paint program to draw lines with expression. Ask students to identify the mood represented in one another's work. Visit **SRAonline.com** to print out detailed instructions for this activity.
NSAE 6.b

Expression with Lines

 For the Art Specialist

Time: About 50 minutes

Focus

Study *Large Print Transparency 61 Horses in a Field* and *62 The Jack Pine*, and discuss how artists use types of lines to create mood in their artwork. NSAE 5.c

Teach

Review the three directions in which a line can move: vertical, horizontal, diagonal and the two types of lines: zigzag and curved. Discuss how artists use a variety of lines to communicate an object or emotion. Explain to students that they will be creating a nonobjective work using a variety of lines.

Reflect

Have students evaluate their works of art using the four steps of art criticism. Encourage them to locate and describe the types of lines they see in the classroom.

Alternate Activity

Materials:
- Art Journal
- 9" × 12" heavy drawing paper
- pencils, erasers
- 9" × 12" black paper
- oil pastels

1. Divide a page in your Art Journal into eight sections. Using a pencil, draw a design in the first section with only vertical lines. The lines can be broken or continuous and can vary in thickness. Experiment with horizontal, diagonal, zigzag, and curved lines in different sections. Combine the various lines in the last three sections.

2. Work directly with your oil pastel onto your drawing paper. Look at the line designs you developed in your Art Journal. Use these to create a nonobjective drawing with a variety of lines: thick, thin, rough, and smooth. Remember to use pressure when drawing with oil pastel so as to have rich colors in your drawing. You can also overlap colors.

Research in Art Education

A link exists in art education between "arts education and creative thinking, academic self-concept, and school climate" ("Learning in and Through the Arts: The Question of Transfer" in *Critical Links*, p. 66). Students in schools that have quality arts programs tend to use more creativity, take more risks, and view themselves as academically competent. As students learn about expression with lines, encourage them to express their own thoughts, feelings, and ambitions through their artwork and in journal writing.

Assessment
Use the following rubric to evaluate the artwork students make in the Creative Expression activity and to assess students' understanding of expression with lines.

Have students complete page 9 or 10 in their *Assessment* books.

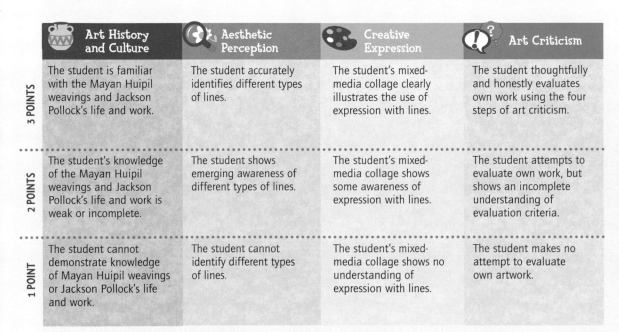

	Art History and Culture	Aesthetic Perception	Creative Expression	Art Criticism
3 POINTS	The student is familiar with the Mayan Huipil weavings and Jackson Pollock's life and work.	The student accurately identifies different types of lines.	The student's mixed-media collage clearly illustrates the use of expression with lines.	The student thoughtfully and honestly evaluates own work using the four steps of art criticism.
2 POINTS	The student's knowledge of the Mayan Huipil weavings and Jackson Pollock's life and work is weak or incomplete.	The student shows emerging awareness of different types of lines.	The student's mixed-media collage shows some awareness of expression with lines.	The student attempts to evaluate own work, but shows an incomplete understanding of evaluation criteria.
1 POINT	The student cannot demonstrate knowledge of Mayan Huipil weavings or Jackson Pollock's life and work.	The student cannot identify different types of lines.	The student's mixed-media collage shows no understanding of expression with lines.	The student makes no attempt to evaluate own artwork.

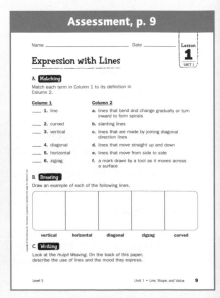

Perception Drawing

Overview

Lesson 2 introduces two types of perception drawing—gesture and contour. Gesture drawings are quick sketches that often use repeated lines and shapes to capture the motion or action of the subject. Contour drawings focus on the edges and surface ridges of a subject.

Objectives

 **Art History and Culture**

To demonstrate knowledge of the lives and works of Edgar Degas and Henri de Toulouse-Lautrec

 Creative Expression

To create a contour drawing of posed subjects

 Aesthetic Perception

To identify characteristics and uses of gesture and contour drawing techniques

Art Criticism

To evaluate one's own work using the four steps of art criticism

Vocabulary ⭐ Reading

Review the following vocabulary words with students before beginning the lesson.

contour drawing *dibujo de contorno*—drawing in which an artist keeps his or her eyes on the subject and concentrates on directions and curves

perception *percepción*—careful and deep thought about what one sees

See page 59B for additional vocabulary and Spanish vocabulary resources.

 Art Journal: Vocabulary

Have students add these words to the Vocabulary section of their Art Journals.

Lesson Materials
- drawing paper
- pencils
- costumes with accessories
- felt-tip pens

Alternate Materials:
- ballpoint pens

Program Resources
- *Reading and Writing Test Prep.,* pp. 8–9
- *Transparency 2*
- *Flash Cards* 1, 2, 3, 4, 5, 6
- *Artist Profiles,* pp. 20, 61
- *Animals Through History Time Line*
- *Assessment,* pp. 11–12
- *Large Prints 61* Horses in a Field and **62** The Jack Pine
- *The National Museum of Women in the Arts Collection*

Concept Trace
Perception Drawing
Introduced: Level 4, Unit 1, Lessons 2 and 4
Reinforced: Level 3, Unit 1, Lesson 2

Lesson 2 Arts Integration

Theatre
Complete Unit 1, Lesson 2, on pages 20–21 of *Theatre Arts Connections.*

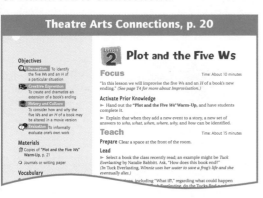

Music
SPOTLIGHT on MUSIC *Anvil Chorus* from *Il Trovatore* Giuseppe Verdi

Both works of art in this lesson are from the 19th century. Play the *Anvil Chorus* from Verdi's opera *Il Trovatore (The Troubador)* to give students a sense of 19th century European music.

Movement & Dance
Divide students into groups of four. Each person takes a turn being the model. The model turns once and takes four counts to create a pose that can be held. The members of the group position themselves around the person, viewing them from four different angles. Each traces the outline, or the contour of the model, starting at top of head or at the feet, and going clockwise. All rotate to the next angle and repeat.

Focus

Activate Prior Knowledge

"Have you ever seen light shining from behind something so brightly that you could see only the edges, or the outline, of the object?" "¿Alguna vez han visto una luz que resplandece detrás de algo y que es tan brillante que solo pueden ver los bordes, o sea, el contorno, del objeto?"

- Discuss how a silhouette can give the overall impression of an object without exposing all of the details. Explain that artists use a similar approach when making a perception drawing.

Using Literature ⭐ Reading

- Share with the class Shel Silverstein's *When the Missing Piece Meets the Big O.* Ask students to identify the use of perception drawing in the illustrations.

Thematic Connection ⭐ Social Studies

- **About Me:** Discuss with students the importance of being themselves and finding a way to express their own individuality and creativity.

Introduce the Art

Look

"Let's take a close look at the two works of art." "Vamos a observar detalladamente las dos obras de arte."

Visualizing ⭐ Reading

- Have students choose one of the two works of art in this lesson and write a paragraph about what is happening. They will have to visualize the scene that extends beyond the artwork.

 Art History and Culture

Edgar Degas painted people working in Paris's world of entertainment. His work influenced Henri de Toulouse-Lautrec who also painted similar scenes from the same time period in Paris, France. NSAE 4.a

💻 **Web Connection**

Visit **www.philamuseum.org/exhibitions/exhibits/ degas/flash/degasforkidshome.html** to learn more about Edgar Degas.

Perception Drawing

 Look at the artwork on these pages. Notice how both artists used lines to show how the people in the artwork are moving. Notice that Degas did not erase the extra lines on the ballerina's arm. Toulouse-Lautrec finished the woman's head but left the rest of her body sketched.

▲ **Edgar Degas.** (French). *Ballerinas.* 1885.
Charcoal and chalk on paper.
18 × 23½ inches (45.72 × 59.69 cm).
High Museum of Art, Atlanta, Georgia.

🏺 **Art History and Culture**

How did these European artists express their French culture through these works of art?

🏺 **Art History and Culture**

Edgar Degas

Edgar Degas (ed´ gər də gä´) (1834–1917) has been called the "master of drawing the human figure in motion." Edgar Degas is best known for his portraits of ballet dancers and racehorses. He liked to portray his subjects doing common things in common places. At that time, this was an unusual approach. Degas wanted his subjects to appear unposed even though they often were posing in a studio for hours. He often cut figures off at the edges of the canvas to make his images seem spontaneous.

See pages 24–25 and 16–21 for more about art history and the subject matter.

Artist Profiles, p. 20

Artist Profile

Edgar Degas
1834-1917

Edgar Degas (ed´ gär də gä´) was born in Paris, France, to a wealthy family. He studied law for a short time before discovering his interest in painting. Degas studied briefly at the École des Beaux-Arts in Paris around 1855. He worked at an artist's studio and traveled widely to study art. His early work showed a concern with classical painting, in subject matter as well as composition. His themes always dealt with people and city life, especially dancers at the theater. After 1909, Degas turned to sculpture due to failing eyesight. He left many wax models of dancers and horses that were cast in bronze after his death.

▲ **Henri de Toulouse-Lautrec.**
(French). *Madame Thadée
Natanson at the Theater.* 1895.
....
Gouache on cardboard. 24½ × 29½ inches
(62.23 × 74.93 cm). The Metropolitan
Museum of Art, New York, New York.

Study both works of art to find examples of
gesture and contour drawing.

▶ Where do you see gesture drawing in these works
of art?

▶ Where do you see contour drawing in these works
of art?

▶ Find a repeated gesture line that represents
movement.

▶ Can you see a beginning or an end to the
contour lines?

Aesthetic Perception

Design Awareness How would you use contour lines to draw a
classroom object? How would it appear in a gesture drawing?
Which drawing seems more fitting for representing this object?

Art History and Culture

Henri de Toulouse-Lautrec

Henri de Toulouse-Lautrec (än rē´ də too looz´ lō trek´) (1864–1901)
was influenced by the French impressionist Edgar Degas. Unlike the
impressionists' light and soft style, Toulouse-Lautrec's paintings were
often dark and mysterious. At the age of 12 he broke one of his legs,
and at 14 he broke the other. His legs never healed properly and failed
to grow. Toulouse-Lautrec's contribution to graphic arts is significant.
People clamored for his posters as soon as they were finished. He
produced over 400 lithographs in only a few years. Lautrec was
credited with helping to
reestablish the famous
Moulin Rouge, in Paris, with a
poster announcing its
reopening. The poster was
unlike anything the city of
Paris had ever seen.

See pages 24–25 and 16–21
for more about art history
and the subject matter.

Artist Profiles, p. 61

◀ Artist Profile ▶
Henri de Toulouse-Lautrec
1864–1901
Henri de Toulouse-Lautrec (än rē´ də
too looz´ lō trek´) was born in France. He
stopped growing after his legs were injured
in a childhood accident. He spent much of
his brief adult life in clubs and music halls
in Paris. Scenes from these places became
favorite subjects of his paintings. Toulouse-
Lautrec fought an addiction to alcohol
during his life, and he died at the age of 37.

Study

▶ *Ballerinas*: The repeated lines in the
ballerinas show movement. *Madame
Thadée Natanson at the Theatre*: The
wispy lines throughout the portrait
capture the motion of the scene and
show minimal detail.

▶ *Ballerinas*: the top half of the ballerina on
the left and the arm of the ballerina on the
right. *Madame Thadée Natanson at the
Theatre*: the woman's dress sleeves and her
back, neck, and head.

▶ *Ballerinas*: in the skirt of the ballerina on
the left and the back and head of the
ballerina on the right. *Madame Thadée
Natanson at the Theatre*: the skirt of the
woman, the floor beneath the person in the
back of the picture, and the person's body.

▶ There is not a definite beginning or end to
most contour lines. Contour lines show the
edges and the surface ridges of an object. In
these works of art, the contour lines
represent areas that are still and motionless.

■ For more examples of genre art, see
***The National Museum of Women in
the Arts Collection.***

Art Journal: Writing
Ask students to write something
about themselves that they are proud of.

Aesthetic Perception

Design Awareness Encourage students to look
around the classroom and identify areas of
movement. Discuss how a gesture drawing
might be a better representation of
movement than a contour drawing.

Developing Visual Literacy Have students
imagine being one of the characters in either
painting. Ask them to describe what they are
doing, feeling, hearing, and seeing from that
character's perspective.

Web Connection
Visit **www.scribbleskidsart.com/generic202.html**
to learn more about Henri de Toulouse-Lautrec and
his work.

Also visit **www.moma.org/whatisaprint/flash.html**
to learn about lithographs and other prints.

# Teach

Time: About 30 minutes

"How can you use gesture drawing to capture the feeling of motion that you see?" "¿Cómo pueden usar el dibujo de contorno para captar la sensación de movimiento que ven?"

- Discuss the definitions of perception drawing, contour, contour lines, gesture lines, and gesture sketch on page 42.

Practice

Materials: paper, pencils

- Distribute the materials and have students follow the directions on page 42.

- Have student subjects move a part of their bodies in a repeated pattern, for example, swinging one arm slowly in a designated spot. Ask students to quickly draw what they see while trying to capture the feeling of movement by using repeated gesture lines.

Creative Expression

Materials: costumes with accessories, drawing paper, felt-tip pens

Alternate Materials: ballpoint pens

- Distribute the materials and have students follow the directions on page 43.

- Select students to put on costumes and pose for the contour drawing. Remind students to pick a comfortable pose because they will need to hold this position for some time.

- Encourage students to keep their pens on their paper as much as possible without lifting them. Remind students to let their eyes follow the contours of their subjects and to move their pens at the same speed. Challenge students to look at their paper only when they feel they need to.

- Review the Activity Tips on page 230 for visual examples of this lesson's activity.
NSAE 1.b

Art Journal: Planning

Display costumes and accessories. Encourage students to plan costumes and poses and sketch their ideas in their Art Journals.

Using Perception in Drawing

Perception drawing is looking at something carefully and thinking deeply about what you see as you draw.

The **contour** of an object or figure is its edges and surface ridges. Artists often make contour drawings of objects and use them as studies before making a painting or drawing.
Contour lines are continuous, unbroken lines that show the edges and surface ridges of an object.

Gesture lines are drawn quickly to capture the movement of a person, animal, or object in a painting or drawing.

A **gesture sketch** is a drawing that tries to capture the gesture or movement of an object as quickly as possible. Unlike a contour drawing, a gesture sketch will show what the artist sees inside the object's outline.

Practice

Use a gesture sketch to capture movement.

1. Look at the subjects who are posing. Notice the lines and shapes.
2. Quickly sketch what you see. Try to capture the feeling of movement by using repeated lines.
3. Do not spend time drawing a lot of detail.
4. Share your gesture sketch with the class.
5. Identify the use of lines that show movement in the sketches.

Differentiated Instruction

Reteach
Have students create gesture drawings or contour drawings of objects from different points of view.

Special Needs
Students may have difficulty letting their eyes follow the contour lines of subjects. You may facilitate a closer look by standing near the subjects and slowly air tracing the contour lines for students to observe.

ELL
Discuss the term *gesture* with students. Review the definition and offer examples of common gestures. Suggest that students present gestures from their native cultures.

◀ **Lucas Walker.**
Age 11.

Think about how the student artist used one continuous line to draw the subject posing.

 Creative Expression

How can you improve your perception, or the way you look or think about what you see? Create a contour drawing of subjects.

1. Look carefully at the posed subjects.

2. Move your pen slowly on your paper while your eyes move around the edges or contours of the subjects.

3. Look at the subjects while you draw, and only glance occasionally at your paper.

4. Do not pick up your pen. Draw in one continuous, unbroken line.

Art Criticism

Describe Did you draw your lines using the proper procedure?

Analyze Did you use one continuous, unbroken contour line?

Interpret What mood do the lines in your drawing create?

Decide Were you successful in concentrating on the edges and surface ridges of what you saw and re-creating that on paper?

Reflect
Time: About 15 minutes

Review and Assess

"Were you able to create a contour drawing of the posing subject?" "¿Estaban a punto de crear un dibujo de contorno del tema en pose?"

Think

This student artist has created a contour drawing of the subject using only one continuous line.

- Use *Large Prints 61 Horses in a Field* and *62 The Jack Pine* to have students identify and describe the use of gesture and contour drawing in works of art. NSAE 5.c

Informal Assessment

- For standardized-format test practice using this lesson's art content, see pages 8–9 in *Reading and Writing Test Preparation.*

Art Journal: Critical Thinking

Have students answer the four art criticism questions—Describe, Analyze, Interpret, and Decide—in their Art Journals. In small groups, have students discuss their contour drawings.

Art Across the Curriculum

Use these simple ideas to reinforce art concepts across the curriculum.

★ **Poetry Writing** Have students write a poem about the value of being themselves and illustrate the poem using a contour drawing.

★ **Math** Discuss the value of estimating numbers. Like gesture and contour drawing, the details are not exact when estimating, but the ability to see the big picture is valuable and can be built upon later.

★ **Science** Have students study the shapes and contours of leaves and natural objects found outside as they practice drawing them.

★ **Social Studies** Ask students to categorize American coins according to contour. Explain that the United States Mint began putting grooves around the edges of the coins that contain gold and silver to discourage people from shaving off the edges.

★ **Technology** Have students look at a subject and use the paintbrush tool to trace the contour. Visit **SRAonline.com** to print out detailed instructions for this activity.
NSAE 6.b

Perception Drawing

 Extra! **For the Art Specialist**

Time: About 30 minutes

Focus

Study **Large Print Transparency 61** *Horses in a Field* and **62** *The Jack Pine* and discuss how artists use perception drawing in their artwork to communicate an idea. This allows viewers to make their own decisions about the subjects.

Teach

Explain to students that contour lines are the edges or ridges of an object. Demonstrate making a blind contour drawing of an object, such as a cup. Then demonstrate drawing a contour drawing of the same object. Discuss the differences. Set up a still life in an area so all students can view the objects. Include objects of varying heights.

Reflect

Have students use the four steps of art criticism to evaluate their artwork. Encourage them to locate objects in the classroom and to describe how perception drawing could be used to capture the image of each.

Alternate Activity

Materials:
- Art Journal
- newspaper
- 9" × 12" or smaller drawing paper
- pencils, erasers
- fine-line pen

1. Set up a still-life arrangement. Look closely at the objects. Notice the ridges and edges. Begin by creating several blind contours of different areas of the still life in your Art Journal. Use a full sheet of newspaper to drape over your hand as you make your blind contour drawing if you feel that you cannot keep from looking at your paper.

2. On your drawing paper create a contour drawing of a section of the still life, using pen. You may look down at your paper, but try not to pick up your pen. Try to create one continuous line.

3. Now try a second contour line drawing from a different point of view. Compare your two drawings. *Which do you feel more accurately portrayed the shapes of the objects? Why?*

Research in Art Education

Research shows that when students study art forms from minority cultures (in this case, Native American music), the instruction seems to be "effective in diminishing students' stereotypical attitudes and perceptions toward a minority culture." The arts can help teachers become "catalysts for cultural understanding and respect" ("North American Indian Music Instruction: Influences upon Attitudes, Cultural Perceptions, and Achievement" in *Schools, Communities, and the Arts: A Research Compendium*). As students work with perception drawing, discuss the perceptions, as well as the misperceptions, that people impose on unfamiliar cultures and on people who are unfamiliar to them. Discuss the dangers of these generalizations.

Assessment

Use the following rubric to evaluate the artwork students make in the Creative Expression activity and to assess students' understanding of perception drawing.

Have students complete page 11 or 12 in their *Assessment* books.

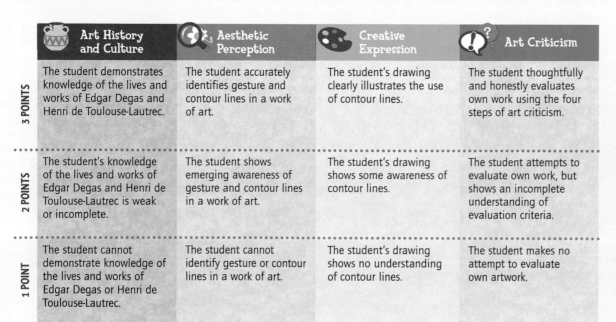

	Art History and Culture	Aesthetic Perception	Creative Expression	Art Criticism
3 POINTS	The student demonstrates knowledge of the lives and works of Edgar Degas and Henri de Toulouse-Lautrec.	The student accurately identifies gesture and contour lines in a work of art.	The student's drawing clearly illustrates the use of contour lines.	The student thoughtfully and honestly evaluates own work using the four steps of art criticism.
2 POINTS	The student's knowledge of the lives and works of Edgar Degas and Henri de Toulouse-Lautrec is weak or incomplete.	The student shows emerging awareness of gesture and contour lines in a work of art.	The student's drawing shows some awareness of contour lines.	The student attempts to evaluate own work, but shows an incomplete understanding of evaluation criteria.
1 POINT	The student cannot demonstrate knowledge of the lives and works of Edgar Degas or Henri de Toulouse-Lautrec.	The student cannot identify gesture or contour lines in a work of art.	The student's drawing shows no understanding of contour lines.	The student makes no attempt to evaluate own artwork.

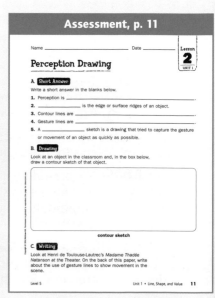

Assessment, p. 11

Geometric and Free-Form Shapes

Lesson 3 introduces the elements of geometric and free-form shapes. Geometric shapes can be described with mathematical formulas. Free-form shapes are uneven and irregular. They often are described as shapes found in nature.

Objectives

Art History and Culture

To demonstrate knowledge of the lives and works of Georges Braque and Paul Cézanne

Creative Expression

To create a still-life painting using geometric and free-form shapes in a computer paint program

Aesthetic Perception

To identify the function of geometric and free-form shapes in art

Art Criticism

To evaluate one's own work using the four steps of art criticism

Vocabulary Reading

Review the following vocabulary words with students.

shapes formas o figuras—two-dimensional forms that can be measured

geometric shapes figuras geométricas—shapes described by mathematical formulas

free-form shapes figuras abstractas—irregular shapes

See page 59B for additional vocabulary and Spanish vocabulary resources.

Art Journal: Vocabulary

Have students add these words to the Vocabulary section of their Art Journals.

Lesson Materials

- colored construction paper
- scissors
- glue
- computer paint program

Alternate Materials:
- markers or crayons

Program Resources

- *Reading and Writing Test Prep.*, pp. 10–11
- *Transparency 3*
- *Artist Profiles*, pp. 11, 16
- *Animals Through History Time Line*
- *Assessment*, pp. 13–14
- *Large Prints 61* Horses in a Field and *62* The Jack Pine
- *The National Museum of Women in the Arts Collection*

Concept Trace

Geometric and Free-Form Shapes
Introduced: Level 4, Unit 2, Lessons 1 and 2

Reinforced: Level 6, Unit 1, Lesson 2

Lesson 3 Arts Integration

Theatre

Complete Unit 1, Lesson 3, on pages 22–23 of *Theatre Arts Connections.*

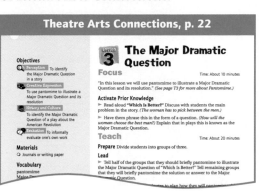

Music

 Sing, Sing, Sing Louis Prima

In music shape can pertain to the contour of the higher/lower movement of a melodic line. Play Louis Prima's *Sing, Sing, Sing* as students complete the Practice activity in which they create complex geometric shapes. Discuss the shapes students create that fit with the music.

Movement & Dance

Mark off an area on the floor, outlining it with string or tape. Six people walk in, arrange themselves in the space, and create six geometric shapes. Another six people enter, arrange themselves in and around the first group, and create free-form shapes. All twelve then take eight counts to explore moving their shapes. Switch roles.

Activate Prior Knowledge

"When you look at an object, what do you see first—the shape or the object?" "Cuando miran un objeto, ¿qué observan primero: la figura u el objeto?"

- Discuss students' responses. Ask students to name objects they would be able to identify from their shapes.

Using Literature ⭐ Reading

- Have students read and discuss the book *Going Back Home, An Artist Returns to the South* by Toyomi Igus. Encourage students to identify geometric and free-form shapes in the illustrations.

Thematic Connection ⭐ Math

- **Shapes:** Introduce students to types of polygons. Encourage students to look for examples of these shapes throughout their day, and record what they find in their Art Journals.

Introduce the Art

Look

"Let's take a close look at the two works of art." "Vamos a observar detalladamente las dos obras de arte."

Comparing and Contrasting ⭐ Reading

- Have students look at both works of fine art in this lesson. As a class, discuss the similarities and differences. NSAE 5.c

Art History and Culture

Georges Braque's *Still Life on Red Tablecloth* is an abstract painting. Paul Cézanne's *Still Life with Basket of Apples* is a realistic painting.

🖥 **Web Connection**

Visit **www.theartgallery.com.au/KidsArt/learn/ cubism/** to learn more about cubism.

Lesson 3

Geometric and Free-Form Shapes

▲ **Georges Braque.** (French). *Still Life on Red Tablecloth.* 1936.

Oil on canvas. 38¼ × 51 inches (96.52 × 129.54 cm.). The Norton Museum of Art, West Palm Beach, Florida.

Look at the artwork on these pages. In Paul Cézanne's *Still Life with Basket of Apples,* the viewer sees the table arrangement from one point of view. Georges Braque's *Still Life on Red Tablecloth* gives the viewer a chance to see the scene from many points of view. Both works of art have **geometric shapes** and **free-form shapes.**

Art History and Culture

Which of these still-life works of art is abstract?

Art History and Culture

Georges Braque

Georges Braque (zhorzh bräk) (1882–1963) studied art in Paris, where he met Pablo Picasso and was exposed to the work of Paul Cézanne. Braque believed that a piece of art should stand on its own and not be limited by reality. Together with Picasso, Braque developed *cubism.* Cubists drew what they saw and reduced the image down to a flat, geometric form that looked cubelike. The subject of a painting in cubist style was represented from many different viewpoints all at once. The viewers see all the way around the image.

See pages 24–25 and 16–21 for more about art history and the subject matter.

Artist Profiles, p. 11

◆ Artist Profile ◆

Georges Braque
1882–1963

Georges Braque (zhorzh bräk) was born in Argenteuil-sur-Seine, France. Helping his father, a house decorator, taught him much about painting. In 1900 he moved to Paris to study under a master decorator. He then spent several years painting at the Académie Humbert. Braque worked with Pablo Picasso in creating cubism, but after fighting in World War I, he ended his work with Picasso. His style constantly evolved until his death in 1963.

▲ **Paul Cézanne.** (French).
Still Life with Basket of Apples. 1895.

Oil on canvas. 23⅝ × 31½ inches (60 × 80 cm).
The Art Institute of Chicago, Chicago, Illinois.

Study both works of art to find a variety of shapes.

▶ Where do you see geometric shapes in these works of art? Describe them.

▶ Which objects have free-form shapes?

▶ Point to the solid shapes made with color and those created with outlines.

Aesthetic Perception

Seeing Like an Artist Turn a book in your hands. How many shapes can you see as you look at it from different angles?

Art History and Culture

Paul Cézanne

Paul Cézanne (pôl sā zan') (1839–1906) has been called "the father of modern art." He was a post-impressionist painter who treated the use of shape, space, and color in a unique way. Sometimes he would change the shapes that he saw to create interest and feeling in his paintings. Cézanne favored bright colors and bold brushstrokes. He was aware of how warm colors stood out and cool colors seemed to pull back; he used this to add volume and depth to his subjects. Cézanne influenced cubists, fauvists, and all modern artists of the early twentieth century.

See pages 24–25 and 16–21 for more about art history and the subject matter.

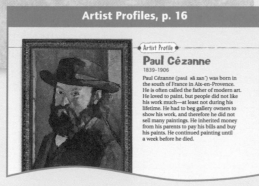

Artist Profiles, p. 16

◆ Artist Profile ◆
Paul Cézanne
1839-1906
Paul Cézanne (paul sā zan') was born in the south of France in Aix-en-Provence. He is often called the father of modern art. He loved to paint, but people did not like his work much—at least not during his lifetime. He had to beg gallery owners to show his work, and therefore he did not sell many paintings. He inherited money from his parents to pay his bills and buy his paints. He continued painting until a week before he died.

Study

▶ *Still Life on Red Tablecloth*: circles—front of the table, the pattern that moves from the center of one side of the painting to the other, objects on the table, upper center of painting; triangles—front of the table, upper-left section of the table; diamonds and rectangles—on purple section of the table, left side of the painting. *Still Life with Basket of Apples*: circles—apples, basket, plate; triangles—section of the tablecloth toward the front, block under the basket; squares and rectangles—table, napkin.

▶ *Still Life on Red Tablecloth*: the legs of the table, the shape on the lower left side of the table and the design in front of it. *Still Life with Basket of Apples*: stack of cookies, bottle.

▶ Shapes made with color and created with outlines are included in both works.

■ For more examples of still lifes, see ***The National Museum of Women in the Arts Collection.***

Art Journal: Writing

Have students look around the room and decide on a spot they would like to use for a still-life drawing. Ask students to identify the shapes they would use to re-create this scene on paper.

Aesthetic Perception

Design Awareness Discuss how shapes can be found in an object by looking at it from different angles. Have students notice the shapes created when two or more objects are placed together. Discuss the moods that are communicated by shapes. Circular shapes often create a soothing mood, whereas angular and jagged shapes represent movement and energy.

Developing Visual Literacy Ask students to describe how Georges Braque's *Still Life on Red Tablecloth* would appear if he had painted it in the style of a realist instead of in a cubist style.

Web Connection

Visit **www.artic.edu/artaccess/AA_Impressionist/pages/IMP_10.shtml** to research Paul Cézanne's *Still Life with Basket of Apples*.

Teach

Time: About 30 minutes

"How can you create complex geometric shapes?" "¿Cómo se pueden crear figuras geométricas complejas?"

- Discuss the definitions of shapes, geometric shapes, complex geometric shapes, and free-form shapes on page 46.

Practice

Materials: colored construction paper, scissors, glue

- Distribute the materials and have students follow the directions on page 46.

- Have students cut out basic geometric shapes from the construction paper. Then ask them to experiment with these cutout shapes to create complex geometric shapes.

Creative Expression

Materials: computer paint program, geometric-shaped and free-form objects

Alternate Materials: drawing paper, pencils

- Distribute the materials and have students follow the directions on page 47.

- Review procedures for working with the computer, including the use of the graphics tablet and the draw, fill, and paint tools.

- Review the Activity Tips on page 231 for visual examples of this lesson's activity.
  NSAE 1.b

Art Journal: Brainstorming

Display the free-form and geometric-shaped objects for students. Ask them to brainstorm ideas for setting up a still life using these objects and sketch their ideas in their Art Journals.

Using Geometric and Free-Form Shapes

Shapes are two dimensional and can be measured by height and width. A shape can have an outline or boundary around it, or it can be solid like a shadow. Geometric and free-form are two kinds of shapes.

Geometric shapes are shapes that can be described in mathematical formulas, and they have names. The three basic geometric shapes are the square, the circle, and the triangle. When you combine these shapes you create **complex geometric shapes** such as those below.

Parallelogram   Trapezoid   Pentagon   Hexagon   Octagon

Free-form shapes are uneven and irregular. They can be made with curved lines, straight lines, or a combination of the two. They are found most often in nature.

Practice

Create complex geometric shapes. Use paper cutouts.

1. Cut out basic shapes such as circles, squares, and triangles from paper.

2. Experiment with the cutout shapes to create complex geometric shapes.

Differentiated Instruction

Reteach
Have students create a drawing using five geometric and five free-form shapes. Students can use **Large Prints** as a guide.

Special Needs
The use of visual prompts (in the form of pre-cut geometric shapes) will help students with disabilities name and recognize the shapes found in the still-life arrangement. The use of this instructional strategy prior to the computer activity will enhance students' ability to successfully complete the task.

ELL
Students may benefit from structured practice with a fluent English speaker as they respond to the Describe, Analyze, Interpret, and Decide sections. Pair students and explain how they can ask questions, listen, and help each other with vocabulary.

◀ **Sarah Parson.**
Age 11.

Think about how the student artist created mood with shapes.

 Creative Expression

How can you create a still life by using the computer as a drawing tool?

1. Think about objects you might enjoy drawing. Select five or more different sizes and shapes.

2. Arrange the still life. Look for shape, color, and lines.

3. Using a computer, open the paint program and practice using the tools that you will use to draw your still life.

4. Using the paint program, draw the still life. Save and print your finished product.

 **Art Criticism**

Describe What objects did you draw?

Analyze How did you use lines and color to create shapes?

Interpret Is your work calm or exciting?

Decide Were you able to use a variety of shapes in the still life that you arranged?

**eflect**   **Time:** About 15 minutes

Review and Assess

"How would you explain the difference between geometric and free-form shapes?"

"¿Cómo explicarían la diferencia entre las figuras geométricas y las abstractas?"

Think

The student artist created a still life using geometric and free-form shapes.

■ Use *Large Prints 61 Horses in a Field* and *62 The Jack Pine* to have students identify and describe the use of geometric and free-form shapes. NSAE 5.c

Informal Assessment

■ For standardized-format test practice using this lesson's art content, see pages 10–11 in *Reading and Writing Test Preparation.*

Art Journal: Critical Thinking

Have students answer the four art criticism questions—Describe, Analyze, Interpret, and Decide—in their Art Journals. In small groups, have students discuss their still lifes.

Art Across the Curriculum

Use these simple ideas to reinforce art concepts across the curriculum.

★ **Descriptive Writing** Have students each write a descriptive paragraph explaining the steps used to create a still life with a computer paint program.

★ **Math** Using geometric shapes, have students create tessellations. Discuss the four types of symmetry represented in tessellations (rotation, translation, reflection, and glide reflection).

★ **Science** Discuss with students how meteorologists can predict the changes in weather by the shapes, sizes, and altitudes of clouds.

★ **Social Studies** Have students design a city park. Use a scale and graph paper to designate the space. Brainstorm the materials needed for the project, the community's needs, safety and accessibility.

★ **Technology** Use a digital camera to capture geometric and free-form shapes. Present the pictures in a presentation program while the class identifies the shapes. Visit **SRAonline.com** to print out detailed instructions for this activity.
NSAE 6.b

Geometric and Free-Form Shapes

Extra! For the Art Specialist

Time: About 30 minutes

Focus

Study **Large Print Transparency 61** *Horses in a Field* and **62** *The Jack Pine* and discuss how artists use geometric and free-form shapes in their artwork. What shapes do you see? How do these shapes affect the mood of the artwork? Where do you see two-dimensional shapes? Where do you see three-dimensional forms?

Teach

Review the various geometric and free-form shapes listed in the book. Explain to students that they will be creating a fantasy artwork. Students' work will also have geometric and free-form shapes.

Reflect

Have students evaluate their works of art using the four steps of art criticism. Encourage them to locate and describe the geometric and free-form shapes they can see in the classroom.

Alternate Activity

Materials:

- Art Journals
- 9" × 12" heavy drawing paper
- pencils, erasers, fine-point marker or pen
- tempera paint
- small detail brush
- water containers

1. In your Art Journal, draw three free-form natural objects that you like, for instance a leaf, bird, or tree. Keep the shapes simple.

2. Randomly place your three free-form shapes that you drew in your Art Journal on your paper. Outline your shapes with a fine-point marker or pen.

3. With your marker or pen, draw geometric shapes to create a fantasy drawing. Repeat your favorite geometric shape along the edges of your outlined free-form shapes.

4. Use your paints to add color to a few of your shapes. Outline your shape first with your color, and then fill it in.

Research in Art Education

Research has shown that the looking and reasoning skills learned during visual art training can be applied to scientific images ("Investigating the Educational Impact and Potential of the Museum of Modern Art's Visual Thinking Curriculum" in *Critical Links*, p. 142). Students involved in visual arts training showed less circular reasoning and more evidential reasoning when evaluating both fine art images and scientific images. As students learn about geometric and free-form shapes, encourage them to think about how objects they see change in shape over time and how this relates to their surroundings.

Assessment

Use the following rubric to evaluate the artwork students make in the Creative Expression activity and to assess students' understanding of geometric and free-form shapes.

Have students complete page 13 or 14 in their *Assessment* books.

	Art History and Culture	Aesthetic Perception	Creative Expression	Art Criticism
3 POINTS	The student can demonstrate knowledge of the lives and works of Georges Braque and Paul Cézanne.	The student accurately identifies geometric and free-form shapes in a work of art.	The student's still life clearly illustrates the use of geometric and free-form shapes.	The student thoughtfully and honestly evaluates own artwork using the four steps of art criticism.
2 POINTS	The student's knowledge of the lives and works of Georges Braque and Paul Cézanne is weak or incomplete.	The student shows emerging awareness of geometric and free-form shapes in a work of art.	The student's still life shows some awareness of geometric and free-form shapes.	The student attempts to evaluate own artwork but shows an incomplete understanding of evaluation criteria.
1 POINT	The student cannot demonstrate knowledge of the lives and works of Georges Braque or Paul Cézanne.	The student cannot identify geometric and free-form shapes in a work of art.	The student's still life shows no understanding of geometric and free-form shapes.	The student makes no attempt to evaluate own artwork.

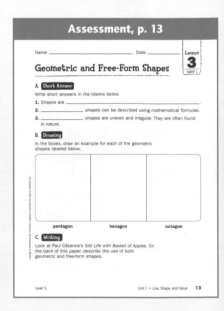

Assessment, p. 13

Name _____ Date _____ Lesson **3** UNIT 1

Geometric and Free-Form Shapes

A. Short Answer
Write short answers in the blanks below.
1. Shapes are _____
2. _____ shapes can be described using mathematical formulas.
3. _____ shapes are uneven and irregular. They are often found in nature.

B. Drawing
In the boxes, draw an example for each of the geometric shapes labeled below.

| pentagon | hexagon | octagon |

C. Writing
Look at Paul Cézanne's *Still Life with Basket of Apples*. On the back of this paper, describe the use of both geometric and free-form shapes.

Level 5 — Unit 1 • Line, Shape, and Value 13

Lesson 4 Overview

Value with Hatching

Lesson 4 introduces the element of value created by hatching. Artists create different values in their work with line patterns such as hatching, which is a series of fine parallel lines.

Objectives

Art History and Culture

To demonstrate knowledge of the works and lives of Elizabeth Catlett and James McNeill Whistler

Creative Expression

To draw a portrait using hatching to create value

Aesthetic Perception

To identify the use of lines with hatching to create values in a work of art
NSAE 3.a

Art Criticism

To evaluate one's own work using the four steps of art criticism

Vocabulary Reading

Review the following vocabulary words with students.

value *valor*—the lightness or darkness of a color or object

hatching *sombreado con rayas*—using a series of fine parallel lines

cross-hatching *sombreado con rayas entrecruzadas*—using two or more intersecting sets of parallel lines

See page 59B for additional Spanish vocabulary resources.

Art Journal: Vocabulary

Have students add these words to the Vocabulary section of their Art Journals.

Lesson Materials
- pencils, erasers
- sketch paper
- 9″ × 12″ white drawing paper

Alternate Materials:
- pens or markers

Program Resources
- *Reading and Writing Test Prep.,* pp. 12–13
- *Transparency 4*
- *Flash Cards* 1, 2, 3, 10, 11
- *Artist Profiles,* pp. 14, 66
- *Animals Through History Time Line*
- *Assessment,* pp. 15–16
- *Large Print 61 Horses in a Field*
- *The National Museum of Women in the Arts Collection*

Concept Trace
Value with Hatching
Introduced: Level 4, Unit 1, Lesson 6

Reinforced: Level 6, Unit 2, Lesson 2

Lesson 4 Arts Integration

Theatre

Complete Unit 1, Lesson 4, on pages 24–25 of *Theatre Arts Connections.*

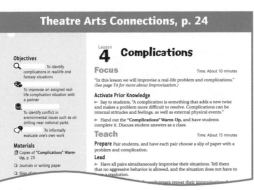

Music

 Variations on Simple Gifts from *Appalachian Spring* Aaron Copland

Value in music relates to the ability of the performer to create subtle differences in tone, sometimes referred to as *warm, cool, dark,* or *light.* In visual art, value is the darkness or lightness of an object. Play Copland's *Variations on Simple Gifts* and discuss whether students consider the music warm, cool, dark, or light.

Movement & Dance

Have a group of students demonstrate the idea of hatching. In a group of six, ask students use their bodies to create the hatching technique by creating diagonal lines that go one way and diagonal lines that cross over, going in the opposing direction. Repeat this technique in movement several times. How is light affected by this technique?

ocus

Time: About 30 minutes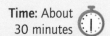

Activate Prior Knowledge

"What do you know about shading techniques?" "¿Qué saben sobre el uso de las técnicas de sombreado?"

■ Discuss students' responses. Ask students to suggest when these techniques might be used.

Using Literature ⭐ **Reading**

■ Share Patricia MacLachlan's *Sarah, Plain and Tall* with the class. Ask students to examine the front cover and identify the use of hatching to create value.

Thematic Connection ⭐ **Social Studies**

■ **Feelings:** Encourage students to brainstorm the feelings they see communicated in both works of art. Have them discuss how people from different backgrounds can experience the same feelings.

Introduce the Art

Look

"Let's take a close look at the two works of art." "Vamos a observar detalladamente las dos obras de arte."

Comparing and Contrasting ⭐ **Reading**

■ Have students look at the two works of art in this lesson and compare the similarities, then contrast the differences. Make a Venn diagram on the board to display what the class finds. NSAE 5.c

🏺 Art History and Culture

Using the context clues in *Sharecropper,* such as the title, the woman's clothes and her hat, the viewer might guess that she is looking out onto her fields. In *Weary,* the viewer might assume, because of the woman's clothes, her pose, and the title, that the woman is looking at other people in an activity, such as a dance, but is too tired to join in.

 Web Connection

Visit **www.nmaa.si.edu** for more information about Elizabeth Catlett's *Sharecropper* at the Smithsonian American Art Museum.

48 UNIT 1 • Line, Shape, and Value

 Lesson 4

Value with Hatching

▲ **Elizabeth Catlett.** (American). *Sharecropper.* 1970.
....
Color linocut. 26 × 22 inches (66.04 × 55.88 cm). Smithsonian American Art Museum, Washington, D.C.

Look at the artwork on these pages. Both Catlett's *Sharecropper* and Whistler's *Weary* are portraits. Catlett created *Sharecropper* by cutting hatching lines into linoleum. These lines appear to be white on the printed page. Whistler scratched lines into a metal plate to create value changes. Hatching was used to show changing value in both pieces.

Art History and Culture

Look at the women in these works of art. Use context clues such as their clothing and the title of the artwork to decide what they are looking at.

48 Unit 1 • Lesson 4

Art History and Culture

Elizabeth Catlett

Elizabeth Catlett (i liz´ ə bəth kat´ let) (1915–) was born in Washington, D.C. Three of her grandparents were slaves. Proud of her African American heritage, Catlett uses her art to portray the lives of those who struggled against racism, poverty, and exploitation of employees. She proudly supported the Civil Rights Movement and participated in the 1963 March on Washington, D.C. Catlett moved to Mexico in 1947, where she married artist Francisco Mora. She has played an important role in the fight for workers' rights in Mexico.

See pages 24–25 and 16–21 for more about art history and the subject matter.

Artist Profiles, p. 14

◆ Artist Profile ◆
Elizabeth Catlett
b. 1915

Elizabeth Catlett (a liz´ ə bəth kat´ lət) was born into a comfortable African American family in Washington, D.C. She went to public school there and later attended Howard University, where she graduated with honors. She also earned her master of fine arts degree from the State University of Iowa, where she studied under Grant Wood. During the 1940s, Catlett used mother-and-child themes in her realistic sculptures. During the next ten years she moved toward abstraction, generating smooth rounded forms and graceful elongated figures. During the 1960s and 1970s, she created expressionistic sculptures and prints showing African and militant themes. Catlett became a citizen of Mexico in 1962.

Study both works of art to find a variety of lines.

▶ What types of lines do you see?

▶ Where are lines close together or far apart?

▶ Which areas have dark values and which have light values?

▶ What feelings does each work express?

◀ **James McNeill Whistler.**
(American). *Weary*. 1863.
....
Drypoint. $41\frac{1}{5} \times 27\frac{3}{8}$ inches (105.4 × 69 cm.).
National Gallery of Art, Washington, D.C.

 Aesthetic Perception

Design Awareness Look at comic strips in the newspaper for examples of hatching used to show value.

Art History and Culture

James McNeill Whistler

James McNeill Whistler's (jāmz mək nēl´ hwis´ lər) (1834–1903) family moved from Massachusetts to Russia when he was nine years old. There he studied drawing at the Imperial Academy of Science. Later in life Whistler enrolled in the United States Military Academy at West Point, where he excelled in drawing classes. Whistler moved to Paris to study art. In Paris he considered himself and his work to be avant-garde and befriended other artists in the same genre. He believed that the purpose of an artwork was not to convey literary, political, or moral views. *Weary* is a portrait of a close friend who appears in a number of his most famous artworks.

See pages 24–25 and 16–21 for more about art history and the subject matter.

Artist Profiles, p. 66

⟩ Artist Profile ⟨
James McNeill Whistler
1834–1903
Although James McNeill Whistler (jāmz mək nēl´ hwis´ lər) was born in Lowell, Massachusetts, he often claimed that he was born somewhere in Europe. Whistler did spend part of his childhood in Russia—his father, an engineer, helped construct the St. Petersburg-Moscow railroad—and he studied at the Imperial Academy of Fine Arts for one year. After returning to America, Whistler attended West Point Military Academy, and then he traveled to Paris to study art. Throughout his career Whistler worked experimentally and refused to be associated with any one style of painting.

Study

▶ Catlett: short, vertical, and parallel lines. Whistler: long, horizontal, vertical, and curved lines.

▶ Lines are close together in the darkest areas. They are farther apart in the lightest areas.

▶ Dark values—Catlett: the neck, left sleeve, folds of the dress, and parts of the dress. Whistler: the woman's blouse and the background in the top of the piece. Light values—Catlett: the hair and blouse. Whistler: the face, skirt, and background in the lower half of the piece.

▶ Catlett creates a quiet, reflective, and worried mood in *Sharecropper*. Whistler's *Weary* generates a sad, bored, and tired mood.
NSAE 5.c

■ For more examples of portraits, see *The National Museum of Women in the Arts Collection.*

Art Journal: Writing

Have students write in their Art Journals about a time when they could relate to how a character in a book or a movie felt. Ask students to describe this character and the feelings they were experiencing.

Aesthetic Perception

Design Awareness Have students look at *Large Print 61* to find examples of hatching used to create value. Bring in other examples of hatching, for example, in comic strips, and ask students to find areas where hatching was used by the illustrators to create value.

Developing Visual Literacy Ask students to predict how the two works of art in this lesson might look different if the subjects were facing the viewer. Would the mood change?

Web Connection

Visit **www.artchive.com/artchive/W/whistler.html** for further information about the life and work of James McNeill Whistler.

 **each**

Time: About 45 minutes

"How are parallel lines used to create a value scale going from light to dark values?"

"¿Cómo se usan las líneas paralelas para crear una escala de valores ordenada de valores más claros a valores más oscuros?"

■ Discuss the definitions of value, hatching, and cross-hatching on page 50.

Practice

Materials: drawing paper, pencils

■ Distribute the materials and have students follow the directions on page 50.

■ Explain to students that each box of their rectangle will show a gradual value change from light to dark. In the first box, the lines will be drawn far apart; in the second box they will be slightly closer together; in the third box even closer; and so on until the last box shows the darkest value with the lines so close they are almost touching.

Creative Expression

Materials: pencils, sketch paper, erasers, 9" × 12" white drawing paper

■ Distribute the materials and have students follow the directions on page 51.

■ Review the Activity Tips on page 231 for visual examples of this lesson's activity.

■ Review the Technique Tips on page 214 for information about creating value, using pencils. NSAE 2.c

■ Encourage students to analyze each other's artwork once the class is finished drawing. Ask students to think about how hatching and cross-hatching were used to indicate value and form.

Art Journal: Brainstorming

In their Art Journals, have students create a list of many different feelings and situations or places that they associate with these feelings.

Using Hatching to Create Value

The darkness or lightness of an object refers to its **value.** Line patterns create different values. When lines are placed side by side, or parallel, value is created. The closer together parallel lines are, the darker the value. The farther apart the lines are placed, the lighter the value.

Hatching creates shading values by using a series of fine parallel lines.

Cross-hatching creates shading values by using two or more intersecting sets of parallel lines.

Practice

Using parallel lines, draw a value scale. Use a pencil.

1. Draw a rectangle and divide it into five sections.

2. Draw parallel lines far apart in the section to the left to show the lightest value. Gradually draw lines closer together until the far-right section, where the lines should be as close as you can get them without having them touch. In this way you will show the darkest value on the right side.

50 Unit 1 • Lesson 4

Differentiated Instruction

Reteach

Have students draw four shapes. Use the hatching and cross-hatching techniques learned in this lesson to show value in the four shapes that have been drawn.

Special Needs

Students may have difficulty seeing value changes in a model if there are no extreme lighting conditions. Consider having the model sit with one side to a window, or use a spotlight to illuminate only one part of the model.

ELL

Have students brainstorm a list of emotions, then dramatize short situations to illustrate a variety of feelings. Ask students to share their dramatization with the class to review and reinforce identifying emotions used in art.

◀ Lisa Kim.
Age 10.

Think about how the student artist used hatching to show value.

 Creative Expression

How can you use value to indicate form? Draw one or more models.

1. Sketch the models carefully.

2. Use hatching and cross-hatching to indicate value and form.

 **Art Criticism**

Describe How many people did you draw?

Analyze How did you use hatching and cross-hatching to create value and form?

Interpret What mood does your work express?

Decide Does the use of hatching and cross-hatching make your sketch look more realistic?

   Time: About 15 minutes

Review and Assess

"Were you able to draw a portrait using lines to create values?" "¿Pudieron dibujar un retrato usando líneas para crear valores?"

Think

The student artist used hatching to create the illusion of depth in areas of darker value when drawing this model.

■ Use *Large Print 61 Horses in a Field* to have students identify and describe the use of hatching lines to create value.

■ Present students with various photographic images and ask them to identify the moods or feelings communicated in each. Students may disagree. Allow them time to discuss and support their reasons.

Informal Assessment

■ For standardized-format test practice using this lesson's art content, see pages 12–13 in *Reading and Writing Test Preparation.*

Art Journal: Critical Thinking

Have students answer the four art criticism questions—Describe, Analyze, Interpret, and Decide—in their Art Journals. In small groups, have students discuss their drawings.

Art Across the Curriculum

Use these simple ideas to reinforce art concepts across the curriculum.

★ **Descriptive Writing** Have students each write a descriptive paragraph explaining the portrait they drew.

★ **Math** Have students use a grid to identify the darkest and lightest points on a painting. Then have students practice finding coordinates of a point on a grid.

★ **Science** Have students use the experimental method to determine how each level of darkness in the value scale is created.

★ **Social Studies** Use *Sharecropper* to discuss sharecropping before the Civil War.

★ **Technology** In a computer drawing program, have students create a picture using cross-hatching with only the rectangle tool. Notice the darker value that appears where the lines intersect at the cross-hatching. Visit **SRAonline.com** to print out detailed instructions for this activity.
NSAE 6.b

Value with Hatching

 For the Art Specialist

Time: About 30 minutes

Focus

Study **Large Print 61** *Horses in a Field* and **62** *The Jack Pine* and discuss how artists create value in a work of art using hatching. Ask students to identify areas where hatching is visible. *What effect does this have on this these areas?*

Teach

Review various techniques for creating light and dark values using lines: hatching and cross-hatching. Set up a still life using a variety of objects. Include draped fabric in the still life. Explain to the students that they will be creating a drawing of a section of the still life using both shading techniques.

Reflect

Have students evaluate their works of art using the four steps of art criticism. Encourage them to locate and describe the uses of hatching they see in illustrations found in the classroom.

Alternate Activity

Materials:
- Art Journals
- 12" × 18" black or white drawing paper
- pencils, erasers
- conte crayon (alternate material: chalk or oil pastel)

1. In your Art Journal create several quick sketches of the still life from different view points.

2. Choose either black or white paper. Select the view you like best and draw it lightly touching at least three edges of your paper.

3. Using your conte crayons complete your drawing by adding details. Use both hatching and cross-hatching to show shadows.

Research in Art Education

One large study demonstrated that students involved with the arts were "less likely to drop out of school, watched fewer hours of television, were less likely to report boredom in school, had a more positive self-concept, and were more involved in community service." These social and practical outcomes show the need to give all students a chance at arts involvement ("Involvement in the Arts and Success in Secondary School" in *Critical Links*, p. 68). As students practice working with value in this lesson, discuss the value they place on their time and their talents and how they choose to use these resources.

Assessment

Use the following rubric to evaluate the artwork students make in the Creative Expression activity and to assess students' understanding of value with hatching.

Have students complete page 15 or 16 in their *Assessment* books.

	Art History and Culture	Aesthetic Perception	Creative Expression	Art Criticism
3 POINTS	The student can demonstrate knowledge of the lives and works of Elizabeth Catlett and James McNeill Whistler.	The student accurately identifies value with hatching in a work of art.	The student's drawing clearly illustrates the use of value with hatching.	The student thoughtfully and honestly evaluates own artwork using the four steps of art criticism.
2 POINTS	The student's knowledge of the lives and works of Elizabeth Catlett and James McNeill Whistler is weak or incomplete.	The student shows emerging awareness of value with hatching in a work of art.	The student's drawing shows some awareness of value with hatching.	The student attempts to evaluate own artwork, but shows an incomplete understanding of evaluation criteria.
1 POINT	The student cannot demonstrate knowledge of the lives and works of Elizabeth Catlett or James McNeill Whistler.	The student cannot identify value with hatching in a work of art.	The student's drawing shows no understanding of value with hatching.	The student makes no attempt to evaluate own artwork.

Assessment, p. 15

Name _____ Date _____

Lesson **4** UNIT 1

Value with Hatching

A. Matching
Match each term in Column 1 to its definition in Column 2.

Column 1
___ 1. value
___ 2. hatching
___ 3. cross-hatching

Column 2
a. a shading technique used to create value by using a series of fine parallel lines
b. the darkness or lightness of an object
c. a shading technique used to create value by using two or more intersecting sets of parallel lines

B. Drawing
Draw an example of each of the following.

hatching	cross-hatching

C. Writing
Look at Elizabeth Catlett's *Sharecropper*. On the back of this paper, write about the use of hatching to change the value in the artwork.

Level 5

Unit 1 • Line, Shape, and Value 15

Value with Blending

Lesson 5 introduces the element of value achieved with blending. *Value* is the darkness or lightness of an object. Artists use value to create highlights and shadows in their artwork. Blending is the technique of gradually changing the value.

Objectives

Art History and Culture

To demonstrate knowledge of the lives and works of Charles Sheeler and Diego Rivera

Creative Expression

To create a realistic drawing showing blended value

Aesthetic Perception

To identify values created by blending to develop highlights and shadows in artwork
NSAE 2.b

Art Criticism

To evaluate one's own work using the four steps of art criticism

Lesson Materials

- cake pan
- water
- food coloring
- coffee filters
- 9" × 12" white drawing paper
- charcoal pencils
- cloth scraps

Alternate Materials:
- colored pencils
- porous white paper

Program Resources

- *Reading and Writing Test Prep.*, pp. 14–15
- *Transparency 5*
- *Flash Cards* 11, 18
- *Artist Profiles*, pp. 52, 49
- *Animals Through History Time Line*
- *Assessment*, pp. 17–18
- *Large Prints 61* Horses in a Field and *62* The Jack Pine
- *The National Museum of Women in the Arts Collection*

Concept Trace
Value with Blending
Introduced: Level 5, Unit 1, Lesson 5

Reinforced: Level 6, Unit 2, Lesson 2

Vocabulary Reading

Review the following vocabulary words with students before beginning the lesson.

value valor—the lightness or darkness of an object

blending mezclar—the gradual change from one value to another

See page 59B for additional vocabulary and Spanish vocabulary resources.

Art Journal: Vocabulary

Have students add these words to the Vocabulary section of their Art Journals.

Lesson 5 Arts Integration

Theatre
Complete Unit 1, Lesson 5, on pages 26–27 of *Theatre Arts Connections.*

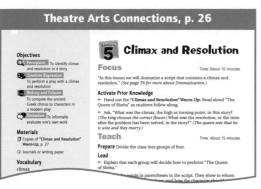

Music
Let's Run Across the Hill Heitor Villa-Lobos

Diego Rivera's *Study of a Sleeping Woman* was painted in 1921. Play *Let's Run Across the Hill* to give students a sense of Brazilian music that was composed at about the same time.

Movement & Dance
When colors are blended, they are softened at the edges. Use imagery to explore this idea in movement. Ask students to move like smooth fog, swirling, smudging, and sweeping through space. Call out each word and give students eight counts to explore, encouraging level changes and shifts of weight while maintaining a smooth quality.

Focus

Time: About 30 minutes

Activate Prior Knowledge

"In which work of art do you recall seeing the blending of values?" "¿En qué obra de arte recuerdan haber visto la mezcla de valores?"

- Discuss students' responses. Ask them to think about when an artist might use blending to create value.

Using Literature ⭐ Reading

- Use the cover of Lucy Jane Bledsoe's *The Big Bike Race* to demonstrate value with blending.

Thematic Connection ⭐ Social Studies

- **Cooperation:** Discuss the process of blending between contrasting values and how this can represent the process of meeting in the middle and cooperating with people.

Introduce the Art

Look

"Let's take a close look at the two works of art." "Vamos a observar detalladamente las dos obras de arte."

Visualize ⭐ Reading

- Have students visualize what they see in these works of art. Ask them to describe what they see, then compare and contrast students' imagined scenes.

🏺 Art History and Culture

Both Charles Sheeler's *Feline Felicity* and Diego Rivera's *Study of a Sleeping Woman* were created in the twentieth century.

💻 **Web Connection**

Visit Harvard University's oldest art museum, the Fogg Art Museum, at **www.artmuseums.harvard.edu/fogg** to find out more about both pieces of artwork in this lesson.

Lesson 5

Value with Blending

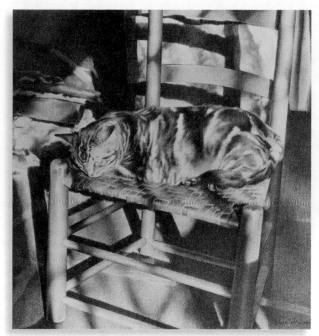

▲ **Charles Sheeler.** (American).
Feline Felicity. 1934.
....
Black crayon on paper. 22 × 18 inches (55.88 × 45.72 cm.). Harvard University Art Museums, Cambridge, Massachusetts.

Look at the artwork on these pages. *Feline Felicity* is a portrait of a lounging cat in which Sheeler re-created the image by **blending** the light and dark values. This blending emphasizes the shadows and highlights cast by the sun. In *Study of a Sleeping Woman*, Rivera also used blending to help portray a realistic image of the woman.

Art History and Culture

Both works of art were created during the same century. In which century were they created?

Art History and Culture

Charles Sheeler

Charles Sheeler (chärlz shē lər) (1883–1965) studied at the famous Pennsylvania Academy of Fine Arts in 1903. This is where he learned to paint. He later traveled in Europe and studied the works of French painters. He returned to the United States and lived in New York City, the inspiration for his popular industrial works. Sheeler practiced painting, drawing, and photography. His art focused on how these media work together to contrast and complement the subjects.

See pages 24–25 and 16–21 for more about art history and the subject matter.

Artist Profiles, p. 52

Artist Profile

Charles Sheeler
1883-1965

Charles Sheeler (chärlz shē lar), an American painter and photographer, was born in Philadelphia, Pennsylvania. He entered the Pennsylvania School of Industrial Art in 1900. He studied classical art and ornamentation. Sheeler began studying art at the famous Pennsylvania Academy of Fine Arts in 1903 and learned to paint there. Around 1906, he became friends with Morton Schamberg, a former architecture student from the University of Pennsylvania. The two shared a studio in Philadelphia where they often discussed modern French painting. These discussions were important to Sheeler. He traveled in Europe from 1908 to 1909 and studied the works of French painters. In 1919 Sheeler

▲ Diego Rivera. (Mexican). *Study of a Sleeping Woman.* 1921.
••
Black crayon on off-white laid paper. 24½ × 18½ inches (62.7 × 46.9 cm.). Harvard University Art Museums, Cambridge, Massachusetts.

Study both works of art to observe how values are created.

▶ Find the light and dark areas in both drawings.

▶ How have the artists used blending to create variations in value?

▶ Where did the artists use gradual blending?

▶ Where do you see a sudden contrast in value?

▶ What mood is suggested by the gradual blending of value in the artwork?

🔍 Aesthetic Perception

Seeing Like an Artist How would you draw a corner where the walls meet the ceiling? Would you blend the value gradually, or would the contrast between light and dark be drastic?

🏺 Art History and Culture

Diego Rivera

Diego Rivera (dē ā´ gō rē bā´ rä) (1886–1957) wanted to create art that could be enjoyed and understood by ordinary people. For this reason, he focused on simple designs and common subjects. Many of Rivera's famous works were murals. He painted more than two-and-one-half miles of murals in Mexico, San Francisco, Detroit, and New York City. While painting, he would often tell shocking and amazing stories as a crowd gathered. Rivera worked with frescoes, which are mural paintings done on fresh plaster. In 1932 he was hired by Henry Ford to paint a mural in Detroit, Michigan, which honored the American worker. This mural remains his most important painting in the United States.

See pages 24–25 and 16–21 for more about art history and the subject matter.

Artist Profiles, p. 49

◆ Artist Profile ◆

Diego Rivera
1886–1957

Diego Rivera (dē ā´ gō rē bā´ rä) was one of the most productive Mexican artists. He attended art school in Mexico but did not stay long. His first exhibition of paintings in 1907 won him a scholarship to Europe. There he studied the work of modern artists. After returning from a second trip to Europe in 1911, he became Mexico's leading mural painter. Rivera was a large man with strong opinions. His great love for his people and his country showed in his art. Crowds gathered to watch him paint his large murals on public walls. His third wife was the famous painter Frida Kahlo. They often fought and separated, but they always supported each other's artistic efforts.

Study

▶ Sheeler: Dark—along the back wall, the stripes on the cat, and the shadow cast by the chair; Light—the cat's face and stripes, the area beneath and to the left of the cat, and the curtain. Rivera: Dark—the woman's hair casts shadows on her left shoulder and her forearm. Light—the woman's dress and side of face that is tilted up.

▶ Sheeler used a gradual blend of value to create many layers of shadows being cast by different objects at different distances, throughout the cat's body, and in the objects to give them shape and dimension. Rivera: The woman's clothes create many shadows that appear gradually around her outline.

▶ Sheeler: Gradual—in parts of the cat's body, the legs and the seat of the chair, the shadows; Sudden contrast—in parts of the cat's body, shadow of the chair legs, the curtain. Rivera: Gradual—the outline of the woman's body; Sudden contrast—the woman's hair, her shoulder, the area along her left arm

▶ Gradual blending of values conveys a smooth, calm mood. NSAE 5.c

■ For more examples of genre art, see *The National Museum of Women in the Arts Collection.*

📓 Art Journal: Writing

Have students write in their Art Journals about a time when they were able to do something better because of the cooperation of others.

🔍 Aesthetic Perception

Design Awareness Find a corner in the classroom and have students discuss how they would re-create the look of the light in each area of that corner in an artwork.

Developing Visual Literacy Ask students if they have ever seen a cat sleeping in the sun. Have them describe what they saw. Ask students to compare the scene they remember to Sheeler's *Feline Felicity.*

💻 Web Connection

Visit **www.fbuch.com/diego.htm** to learn more about the life and work of Diego Rivera.

Teach

Time: About 30 minutes

"How can you use blended values to create a realistic drawing?" "¿Cómo pueden usar valores mezclados para crear un dibujo realista?"

- Discuss the definitions of blending and value on page 54.

Practice

Materials: cake pan, water, food coloring, coffee filters

Alternate Materials: colored pencils, porous white paper

- Distribute the materials and have students follow the directions on page 54.

- Fill the cake pans with colored water. Have students dip their coffee filters in the cake pans and hold them there long enough to see the color work its way up into the fibers of the coffee filters. Walk around the classroom, asking students to point out the areas where the white blends with the color.

Creative Expression

Materials: 9" × 12" white drawing paper, charcoal pencils, cloth scraps

Alternate Materials: pencils

- Distribute the materials and have students follow the directions on page 55.

- Review the Activity Tips on page 232 for visual examples of this lessons activity.

- Review the Technique Tips on page 217 for information about using charcoal.
NSAE 2.c

Art Journal: Brainstorming

Have students plan which section of the scene they will concentrate on when drawing the shadows and highlights they see in the still life. Ask them to describe the area of the scene they have chosen and, in their Art Journals, explain how they will demonstrate blending of values.

Using Blending for Value

Value describes the lightness or darkness of an object. Value depends on how much light a surface reflects.

Blending is the gradual change from one value to the next.

Practice

Experiment with value using colored liquid.

1. Dip the bottom of a coffee filter into a pan of colored water.
2. Allow enough time for the water to soak into the filter.
3. Notice where the value of the color is the darkest and how it gradually blends to a lighter color.

Differentiated Instruction

Reteach
Ask students to find pictures of the sunset in magazines or on the Internet and identify areas of value.

Special Needs
Students with disabilities may benefit from a larger surface area on drawing media. The use of ebony pencils and graphite sticks may provide more immediate blending results than a regular pencil for this lesson activity.

ELL
Frequent comprehension checks can help you monitor students' ability to follow the lesson. You can ask them for physical responses or short verbal responses to indicate their understanding.

◀ **Sarah Grainger.**
Age 10.

Think about how the student artist used blending to show realism.

Creative Expression

How can you show realism with blended values? Use blended values to sketch an object.

1. Choose one or more common classroom objects.

2. Notice how much light the surface of these objects reflects. Look for shadows and variations of value.

3. Make line drawings of the objects.

4. Use blending to add form.

Art Criticism

Describe Describe the object you included in your drawing.

Analyze In what areas have you blended the value?

Interpret How does blending affect the mood of the piece?

Decide Were you successful in creating blended values? What might you do to improve your drawing?

Unit 1 • Lesson 5   **55**

Reflect   Time: About 15 minutes

Review and Assess

"How would you explain value blending in an artwork?" "¿Cómo explicarían la mezcla de valores en una obra de arte?"

Think

The student artist has blended the value around the corners of the glue bottle to add depth and realism.

■ Use **Large Prints 61** *Horses in a Field* and **62** *The Jack Pine* to have students identify and describe the use of blending to create value.

Informal Assessment

■ For standardized-format test practice using this lesson's art content, see pages 14–15 in ***Reading and Writing Test Preparation.***

Art Journal: Critical Thinking

Have students answer the four art criticism questions—Describe, Analyze, Interpret, and Decide—in their Art Journals. In small groups, have students discuss their drawings.

Art Across the Curriculum

Use these simple ideas to reinforce art concepts across the curriculum.

★ **Poetry Writing** Have students each choose one piece of fine art from this lesson and write a poem to accompany it.

★ **Math** Discuss how shading creates the illusion of depth, and review the formula used to find the area of a cube.

★ **Science** Discuss the refraction of light in a rainbow. The blending of colors is a result of the change in energy. The light bends at slightly different degrees and causes us to see different colors.

★ **Social Studies** Look at a picture of Diego Rivera's *Pan American Unity* mural at City College of San Francisco. On a map, locate the Pan American area, including Latin America and the Caribbean Islands.

★ **Technology** Using a photo editor program, gradually change the values in a picture by adjusting the balance. Visit **SRAonline.com** to print out detailed instructions for this activity.
NSAE 6.b

Lesson 5 Wrap-Up

Value with Blending

 For the Art Specialist

Time: About 30 minutes

Focus

Study **Large Print Transparency 61** *Horses in a Field* and **62** *The Jack Pine* and discuss how artists create value in a work of art using blending. Ask students to identify areas where blending is visible.

Teach

Discuss how artists create the illusion of depth or three-dimensionality on a two-dimensional surface by using different shading techniques. Explain to the students that one technique is gradation or a gradual change of value from dark to light. Explain that they will be using blocks and spheres to arrange a group still life.

Reflect

Have students evaluate their works of art using the four steps of art criticism. Encourage them to locate and describe the use of blending they see in illustrations found in the classroom.

Alternate Activity

Materials:

- Art Journal
- 9" × 12" white drawing paper
- pencils, erasers
- wooden blocks or spherical forms such as a plastic foam ball

1. Select three or five different shapes for a group still life. Arrange them until your group is satisfied.

2. In your Art Journal, draw two quick sketches from different views of your still life. Select the one you like best.

3. Transfer your drawing onto paper. Use shading to give your objects the feeling of three-dimensionality.

Research in Art Education

Arts competencies can be beneficial when problems need to be solved in other disciplines—for example, "when a theory in science could be understood more fully through the construction of a three-dimensional mobile; or when a mathematical problem could be approached more easily through a closely observed drawing of a shell" ("Learning in and Through the Arts: Curriculum Implications" in *Champions of Change*, p. 42). As students practice using value with blending, discuss how some elements of the arts can be found in all areas of learning.

Assessment

Use the following rubric to evaluate the artwork students make in the Creative Expression activity and to assess students' understanding of value with blending.

Have students complete page 17 or 18 in their *Assessment* books.

	Art History and Culture	Aesthetic Perception	Creative Expression	Art Criticism
3 POINTS	The student can demonstrate knowledge of the lives and works of Charles Sheeler and Diego Rivera.	The student accurately identifies value with blending in a work of art.	The student's drawing clearly illustrates the use of value with blending.	The student thoughtfully and honestly evaluates own artwork using the four steps of art criticism.
2 POINTS	The student's knowledge of the lives and works of Charles Sheeler and Diego Rivera is weak or incomplete.	The student shows emerging awareness of value with blending in a work of art.	The student's drawing shows some awareness of value with blending.	The student attempts to evaluate own artwork, but shows an incomplete understanding of evaluation criteria.
1 POINT	The student cannot demonstrate knowledge of the lives and works of Charles Sheeler or Diego Rivera.	The student cannot identify value with blending in a work of art.	The student's drawing shows no understanding of value with blending.	The student makes no attempt to evaluate own artwork.

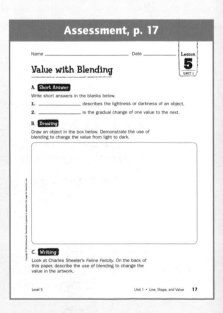

Assessment, p. 17

Name _____ Date _____

Lesson 5 UNIT 1

Value with Blending

A. Short Answer
Write short answers in the blanks below.
1. _____ describes the lightness or darkness of an object.
2. _____ is the gradual change of one value to the next.

B. Drawing
Draw an object in the box below. Demonstrate the use of blending to change the value from light to dark.

C. Writing
Look at Charles Sheeler's *Feline Felicity*. On the back of this paper, describe the use of blending to change the value in the artwork.

Level 5   Unit 1 • Line, Shape, and Value   17

Lesson 6 Overview

Value Contrast

Lesson 6 introduces the element of contrast in value. When looking at a contrast in value, the viewer will notice the degrees of difference between the lighter and darker shades present in an artwork.

Objectives

Art History and Culture
To demonstrate knowledge of the lives and works of Paul Strand and Ansel Adams

Creative Expression
To create a collage using photographs that have strong value contrast

Aesthetic Perception
To identify the use of light in photography to create contrast and to emphasize a subject NSAE 2.b

Art Criticism
To evaluate one's own work using the four steps of art criticism

Vocabulary [star] Reading

Review the following vocabulary words with students before beginning the lesson.

contrast *contraste*— the degrees of difference among color values, tones, shapes, and other elements in works of art

stippling *punteado*— shading with dots; the closer the dots are, the darker the area is

See page 59B for additional Spanish vocabulary resources.

Art Journal: Vocabulary
Have students add these words to the Vocabulary section of their Art Journals.

Lesson Materials
- drawing paper
- pencils, erasers
- cameras and black-and-white film

Alternate Materials:
- large black-and-white newspaper photographs

Program Resources
- *Reading and Writing Test Prep.,* pp. 16–17
- *Transparency 6*
- *Flash Cards* 11, 14, 17, 20
- *Artist Profiles,* pp. 56, 3
- *Animals Through History Time Line*
- *Assessment,* pp. 19–20
- *Large Prints 61 Horses in a Field* and *62 The Jack Pine*
- *Art Around the World Collection*

Concept Trace
Value Contrast
Introduced: Level 4, Unit 1, Lesson 6
Reinforced: Level 6, Unit 2, Lesson 2

Lesson 6 Arts Integration

Theatre
Complete Unit 1, Lesson 6, on pages 28–33 of *Theatre Arts Connections.*

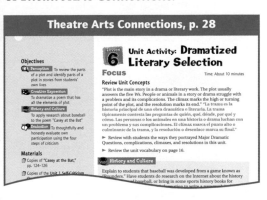

Music
The Star-Spangled Banner
Francis Scott Key

The darkness or lightness of an object is its value. Contrast is the degree of difference among the elements in a work of art. To reinforce the concept of value contrast, play or have students sing *The Star-Spangled Banner.* Discuss the contrast in the song, the high and low notes, the long and short notes, and the differences in rhythm.

Movement & Dance
Students create a nonverbal conversation with a partner that shows contrast. Number partners No. 1s and No. 2s. No. 1 has four counts to move using slashing, flinging and whipping actions. No. 1s then hold their last position. No. 2s answer them using light, dabbing, fluttering movements. Repeat this sequence three times.

Focus

Activate Prior Knowledge

"What kind of photographs do you like?"
"¿Qué tipo de fotografías les gusta?"

- Discuss students' responses. Ask them to think about the differences between color photographs and black-and-white photographs.

Using Literature 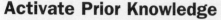 Reading

- Share Rachel Baker's book *The First Woman Doctor* with the class. This is an inspiring biography of Elizabeth Blackwell's journey to become America's first female doctor.

Thematic Connection

- **Jobs:** Ansel Adams spent many years working as a commercial photographer to fund his work in fine-art photography. Have students research a career in art that they are interested in.

Introduce the Art

Look

"Let's take a close look at the two works of art." "Vamos a observar detalladamente las dos obras de arte."

Cause and Effect Reading

- Have students experiment with light-casting shadows. If the light, or the cause, is moved, or changed, what is the effect? Ask students to record other cause-and-effect relationships they notice throughout their day.

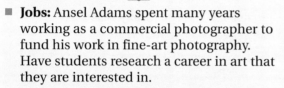

Art History and Culture

Paul Strand and Ansel Adams used photography to capture a cityscape and a natural landscape within America.
NSAE 4.a

 Web Connection

Visit **www.moma.org** for more information about Paul Strand. View Paul Strand's *Fifth Avenue, New York* (1915) and compare the value contrast with *From the Viaduct, 125th St.* (1916).

 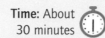

Value Contrast

▲ **Paul Strand.** (American). *From the Viaduct, 125th St.* 1916.
....
Platinum print. $9\frac{15}{16} \times 13$ inches (25 × 33.02 cm). Amon Carter Art Museum, Fort Worth, Texas.

Look at the artwork on these pages. Both photographers used strong value contrast to tell a story about an American scene. In his cityscape *From the Viaduct, New York*, Paul Strand used natural light and shadows as well as the contrast of light- and dark-valued objects. Ansel Adams reprinted *Aspens, Northern New Mexico* in 1976 to strengthen the **value contrast.** He used a deep-yellow filter to create an effect that looks more like natural sunlight.

Art History and Culture

How have these American artists expressed both similarities and differences within American settings?

Art History and Culture

Paul Strand

Paul Strand's (pôl strand) (1890–1976) father gave him his first camera when he was twelve years old. As a New Yorker, Strand had the opportunity to meet and work with many famous photographers of the time. Alfred Stieglitz would later publish Strand's *From the Viaduct, 125th St.*, in his *Camera Work* photography journal. In this journal, Stieglitz called Strand "the most important photographer developed in this country." Strand agreed with Stieglitz's theory that photography should not be altered more than through the use of light, composition, and clarity.

See pages 24–25 and 16–21 for more about art history and the subject matter.

Artist Profiles, p. 56

◆ Artist Profile ◆
Paul Strand
1890-1976
Paul Strand (pôl strand) was born in New York City to a middle-class family. He was educated at the Ethical Cultural School where practical skills, including photography, were taught. After graduating from high school, Strand learned more about photography from the New York Camera Club, a local hobby league. He traveled around America and Mexico taking pictures and developing his style. He moved to Europe in the 1950s and traveled through parts of Africa in the 1960s.

▲ **Ansel Adams.** (American). *Aspens, Northern New Mexico.* 1958. Print 1976.
....
$17\frac{7}{8} \times 22\frac{5}{8}$ inches (43.18 × 55.88 cm.). Museum of Modern Art, New York, New York.

Study both works of art to see the values that were created.

▶ Where are the darkest and lightest values in each photograph?

▶ Do you see any areas where a bright light is next to a shadow?

▶ How did each artist use value to create a mood?

Aesthetic Perception

Seeing Like an Artist Look around you. Are there areas of strong light next to dark, shadowed areas, like the ones in the photographs?

Art History and Culture

Ansel Adams

Ansel Adams (an´ səl a´ dəmz) (1902–1984) believed in the obligations that we, as humans, have to our natural world. His black-and-white photography reflects his commitment to the environment. Adams spent most of his time working in the West, especially in Yosemite National Park, a place that played a special part in his childhood. The short amount of time he spent working in New York City was in the company of Paul Strand and the Stieglitz group. Through their influence, Adams moved away from the "pictorial" style to "straight photography." Adams's photography emphasized what is felt more than what is seen in the natural environment.

See pages 24–25 and 16–21 for more about art history and the subject matter.

Artist Profiles, p. 3

Artist Profile

Ansel Adams
1902-1984

Ansel Adams (an´ səl ad´ əms) was born in San Francisco. In 1903, his family moved to a house amid the sand dunes near the ocean. Adams always believed that the sights, sounds, and smells of the ocean shaped the way he thought. Adams had a difficult time at school. With his father's approval, he quit early, intending to become a classical pianist. He became fascinated with the beauty of places such as the Yosemite valley, but was frustrated that his photography did not catch its inherent grandeur. As he pursued perfecting his photographic and development processes his talent became evident to others, and books containing his photographs began to sell. His popularity continued to increase.

Study

▶ Strand: The darkest areas are the shadow of the viaduct, along the sidewalk, and the people. The lightest areas are around the shadow on the ground. Adams: The darkest areas are around the trees. The lightest areas are the trees and ground coverings.

▶ Strand: Light areas lie all around the shadow from the viaduct. Adams: The contour of the trees appears bright next to the dark negative spaces around them.

▶ Strand blends the value contrast gradually to create a calm mood. Adams uses bold and sudden contrasts, from light to dark values, to create an exciting, energetic mood.
NSAE 5.c

■ For more examples of art from North America see the ***Art Around the World Collection.***

Art Journal: Writing

Have students write in their Art Journals about a career they are interested in learning more about.

Aesthetic Perception

Design Awareness Discuss the areas of the classroom where natural light, artificial light, and colors create areas with strong value contrast. Turn off the lights in the classroom and change the amount of natural light allowed in. Encourage students to look at the same areas and comment on the change in mood. Change the lighting again and discuss why artists might choose one mood over another in their artwork.

Developing Visual Literacy Have students imagine themselves in the settings of the artwork featured in this lesson. Ask students to write a description of the surroundings, including the air temperature, the sounds, the smells, and the sights.

Web Connection

Visit **www.zpub.com/sf/history/adams.html** to learn more about the life and work of Ansel Adams.

# each

Time: About 30 minutes

"How can you use shading techniques to create contrast in shapes?" "¿Cómo se pueden usar las técnicas de sombreado para crear contraste en las figuras?"

- Discuss the definitions of value, contrast, hatching, cross-hatching, and stippling on page 58.

Practice

Materials: drawing paper, felt-tip markers

Alternate Materials: pencils

- Distribute the materials and have students follow the directions on page 58.

- Have students each divide a sheet of paper into three sections. Ask students to draw a shape in each section of their paper and practice the shading techniques.

Creative Expression

Materials: cameras, black-and-white film

Alternate Materials: large black-and-white photographs from newspapers or magazines

- Distribute the materials and have students follow the directions on page 59.

- Review the Activity Tips on page 232 for visual examples of this lesson's activity.
NSAE 1.b
- Set up a photographic art exhibition area in the classroom. Hang students work with credit information and encourage students to analyze their peers' artwork during their free time. Encourage students to consider the use of value in the photographs.

Art Journal: Brainstorming

Have students brainstorm ideas for the subjects of photographs with strong contrasts of light and dark values. Encourage students to think of how they could tell a story or create a mood, and list their ideas in their Art Journals.

Using Value Contrast

The darkness or lightness of an object is its **value.** Value depends on how much light a surface reflects. Contrast is often created when working with values. **Contrast** is the degree of difference among color values, tones, shapes, and other elements in works of art. Using shading techniques such as stippling, cross-hatching, and hatching lines can help create value contrast in a drawing.

Contrast is the degree of difference among color values, tones, shapes, and other elements in works of art.

Cross-hatching is when two or more sets of parallel lines cross each other to create value.

Hatching is using a series of repeated parallel lines to create value.

Stippling is shading with dots. The closer the dots are, the darker the area is.

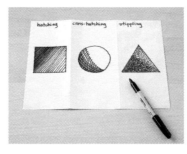

Practice

Practice creating contrast in a drawing. Use a black marker.

1. Divide a sheet of paper into three sections. Label each section a shading technique: hatching, cross-hatching, and stippling.

2. Draw a different shape in each box and practice the different shading techniques.

58 Unit 1 • Lesson 6

Differentiated Instruction

Reteach

Use the overhead projector to compare the value contrasts in transparencies of the lesson artwork with black-and-white photographs students find in magazines.

Special Needs

The use of technology such as digital cameras can help to ensure success for students with disabilities because of the immediacy of the results. The student will be able to evaluate his or her progress toward lesson objectives, and repeat the process as necessary.

ELL

You might find it helpful to restate or break down long questions at the beginning of the lesson to make them more comprehensible to students. Using pantomime and examples also can provide important clues to help students follow the lesson.

◀ **Shavonta Johnson.**
Age 11.

Think about how the student artist has shown value contrast in the photograph.

 Creative Expression

Where do you see value contrast in your environment? Take a photograph that has both bright highlights and dark shadows. Create a scene in such a way that it tells a story or expresses a mood.

1. Look around your indoor and outdoor environment. Find an interesting area, with objects or people, that tells a story or expresses a mood.

2. Use a camera. Look through the viewfinder to arrange your composition. Be sure that your photograph will have bright highlights and dark shadows. Take your photograph.

3. Have your photograph developed. Share it with the class.

 Art Criticism

Describe Describe the objects and spaces you included in your photograph.

Analyze Does your photograph have highlights and shadows? Where are they? Do your values change gradually or quickly?

Interpret Give your photograph an expressive title.

Decide Were you successful in creating a photograph that has strong value contrast and also tells a story or expresses a mood?

Unit 1 • Lesson 6   **59**

 Reflect   **Time:** About 10 minutes

Review and Assess

"Were you able to capture a photograph that has strong value contrast and expresses a mood?" "¿Pudieron capturar una fotografía con un fuerte contraste de valores y que expresa un estado de ánimo?"

Think

The artist chose a viewpoint where the dark trunk of the tree contrasts with the white boat.

■ Use *Large Prints 61 Horses in a Field* and *62 The Jack Pine* to have students identify and describe the value contrast.

Informal Assessment

■ For standardized-format test practice using this lesson's art content, see pages 16–17 in *Reading and Writing Test Preparation.*

Art Journal: Critical Thinking

Have students answer the four art criticism questions—Describe, Analyze, Interpret, and Decide—in their Art Journals. In small groups, have students discuss their photographs.

Art Across the Curriculum

Use these simple ideas to reinforce art concepts across the curriculum.

★ **Descriptive Writing** Have students each write a descriptive paragraph that explains the scene they chose to photograph.

★ **Math** Darker values can give the illusion of a solid object that has depth. Draw a three-dimensional cube and figure the volume.

★ **Science** Ansel Adams spent much of his life fighting to protect the wildlife native to the Sierra Nevada area. Have students research the plants and animals of this area and the threats they face.

★ **Social Studies** Engineers are hired to design viaducts to improve the flow of traffic in congested areas. Discuss the changes that could cause an area to need a new viaduct. How would it improve living conditions in your community?

★ **Technology** Use the tools in a paint program to create a painting that demonstrates value contrast. Visit **SRAonline.com** to print out detailed instructions for this activity.
NSAE 6.b

Value Contrast

Extra! For the Art Specialist

Time: About 30 minutes

Focus

Study *Large Print Transparency 61 Horses in a Field* and *62 The Jack Pine* and discuss how artists create value in a work of art using blending. Ask students to identify areas of value contrast.

Teach

Prior to this lesson ask students to find either a personal photograph of a person they know or of themselves. If they do not have a photograph, they can use an image from a magazine. The photograph or image they select should be a head or face shot. Black-and-white photocopies can be made of the images, and students can draw directly on these.

Reflect

Have students evaluate their works of art using the four steps of art criticism.

Alternate Activity

Materials:
- Art Journal
- 9" × 12" white drawing paper
- pencils, erasers
- collected images

1. Look closely at the image you have selected. Using a pencil, begin by lightly drawing the shape of the face onto your white drawing paper. The face shape should take up most of your paper. Add the eyes, nose, mouth and other details. Use repeated lines to create the texture of the hair.

2. Look over your practice activity. Use hatching, cross-hatching and stippling to create contrast. Use your eraser to create highlights.

3. With the side of your pencil, color in the area behind the image you drew to create a contrast between the person and the background.

Research in Art Education

Research has indicated that one important outcome of integrating arts into other curriculum areas is an increased level of classroom discussions and more time spent on problem solving. The level of teacher dedication and experience seems to influence these outcomes ("Different Ways of Knowing: 1991–94 National Longitudinal Study Final Report" in *Schools, Communities, and the Arts: A Research Compendium*). As the class studies value contrast, brainstorm successful approaches to problem solving.

Assessment

Use the following rubric to evaluate the artwork students make in the Creative Expression activity and to assess students' understanding of value contrast.

Have students complete page 19 or 20 in their *Assessment* books.

	Art History and Culture	Aesthetic Perception	Creative Expression	Art Criticism
3 POINTS	The student can demonstrate knowledge of the lives and works of Paul Strand and Ansel Adams.	The student accurately identifies value contrast in a work of art.	The student's photograph clearly illustrates value contrast.	The student thoughtfully and honestly evaluates own artwork using the four steps of art criticism.
2 POINTS	The student's knowledge of the lives and works of Paul Strand and Ansel Adams is weak or incomplete.	The student shows emerging awareness of value contrast in a work of art.	The student's photograph shows some awareness of value contrast.	The student attempts to evaluate own artwork, but shows an incomplete understanding of evaluation criteria.
1 POINT	The student cannot demonstrate knowledge of the lives and works of Paul Strand or Ansel Adams.	The student cannot identify value contrast in a work of art.	The student's photograph shows no understanding of value contrast.	The student makes no attempt to evaluate own artwork.

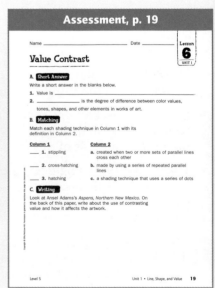

Assessment, p. 19

Name _____ Date _____

Lesson 6 UNIT 1

Value Contrast

A. Short Answer
Write a short answer in the blanks below.
1. Value is _____
2. _____ is the degree of difference between color values, tones, shapes, and other elements in works of art.

B. Matching
Match each shading technique in Column 1 with its definition in Column 2.

Column 1	Column 2
___ 1. stippling	a. created when two or more sets of parallel lines cross each other
___ 2. cross-hatching	b. made by using a series of repeated parallel lines
___ 3. hatching	c. a shading technique that uses a series of dots

C. Writing
Look at Ansel Adams's *Aspens, Northern New Mexico*. On the back of this paper, write about the use of contrasting value and how it affects the artwork.

Level 5   Unit 1 • Line, Shape, and Value   **19**

Unit 1 Vocabulary Review

blending—the gradual change from one value to the next **mezclar**—o entremezclar; el cambio gradual de un valor al próximo

complex geometric shapes—a combination of two or more basic geometric shapes **figuras geométricas complejas**—una combinación de dos o más figuras geométricas básicas

contour drawing—drawing in which artists keep their eyes on the object they are drawing and concentrate on directions and curve **dibujo de contorno**—dibujo en el cual los artistas mantienen su vista en el objeto que dibujan y se concentran en las direcciones y las curvas

contour lines—lines that show the edges and surface ridges of an object **líneas de contorno**—líneas que muestran los bordes y los surcos de la superficie de un objeto

contrast—the degree of difference among color values, tones, shapes, and other elements in works of art **contraste**—el grado de diferencia entre los valores del color, los tonos, las figuras y otros elementos de las obras de arte

cross-hatching—using two or more intersecting sets of parallel lines **sombreado con rayas entrecruzadas**—usar dos o más grupos de líneas paralelas que se intersecan

curved—lines that bend and change gradually or turn inward to form spirals **curva**—líneas que se doblan y cambian gradualmente o dan vuelta hacia adentro para formar espirales

diagonal—lines that slant and look as if they are full of energy **diagonal**—líneas inclinadas que parecen estar llenas de energía

free-form shapes—uneven and irregular shapes **figuras abstractas**—figuras irregulares

geometric shapes—shapes described by mathematical formulas **figuras geométricas**—figuras que se describen según fórmulas matemáticas

gesture lines—line drawing done quickly to capture movement **líneas gestuales**—dibujo lineal que se hace rápidamente para captar el movimiento

hatching—using a series of fine parallel lines **sombreado con rayas**—o rayado; usar una serie de líneas paralelas finas

highlights—small areas of white, or light values used to show the brightest spot **claros**—o toques de luz; pequeñas áreas de blanco o valores claros usados para mostrar el punto más brillante

horizontal—lines that move straight across from side to side **horizontal**—líneas que se mueven de lado a lado

line—a mark drawn by a tool such as a pencil, pen, or paintbrush as it moves across a surface **línea**—una marca trazada con un instrumento como un lápiz, una pluma o un pincel al desplazarlo por una superficie

perception—looking at something carefully and thinking deeply about what one sees **percepción**—mirar algo detalladamente y pensar profundamente en lo que uno ve

shadows—shaded areas in a painting or drawing **sombras**—áreas sombreadas en una pintura o un dibujo

shapes—two-dimensional forms that can be measured by length and height **figuras**—formas bidimensionales que se pueden medir según su altura y su ancho

stippling—shading with dots; the closer the dots are, the darker it is **punteado**—sombreado con puntos; mientras más cerca estén los puntos, más oscuro se verá

value—the lightness or darkness of a color or object **valor**—lo claro u oscuro de un color u objeto

vertical—lines that move straight up and down **vertical**—líneas que se mueven de arriba a abajo

zigzag—lines that join diagonal direction lines **en zigzag**—líneas que unen líneas en dirección diagonal

---

Vocabulary Practice

 Display *Transparency 37* to review unit vocabulary words.

Word Wall ⭐ Vocabulary
Designate an area in the classroom to develop a word wall. Write the words *diagonal* and *free-form shapes* on word-wall cards. Have volunteers define these words and tape them onto the wall. Add the remaining vocabulary words for this unit in this fashion. You may want to build onto the word wall using subsequent units.

Quotation Dictionary ⭐ Vocabulary
Ask students to find quotes by the artists represented in this unit in quotation dictionaries. Review how these dictionaries are used and allow students time to share the quotes they find with the class.

Spoonerisms ⭐ Vocabulary
Spoonerisms occur when the sounds in words or phrases are swapped with each other. Ask students to work in pairs, writing sentences using spoonerisms of the vocabulary words from this unit. For example, *lesture gines are line drawings done quickly to capture movement*. The *l* and the *g* were swapped in the words *gesture* and *lines*.

Art Criticism

Critical Thinking Art criticism is an organized system for looking at art and talking about art. You can criticize art without being an expert. The purpose of art criticism is to get the viewer involved in a perception process that delays judgment until all aspects of the artwork have been studied.

Describe

► The painting is called *Open Window, Nice.* Raoul Dufy created it in 1928, using oil paints on canvas. The size is $25\frac{5}{8}'' \times 21\frac{1}{8}''$. It is at the Art Institute of Chicago.

► Possible answers: This painting shows a room with open French doors and a balcony. The walls are covered with wallpaper with a design of curved leaves and flowers. There are two red chairs, with pillows, and a small table.

► The balcony overlooks a body of water. In the distance, there is land with buildings.

Analyze

► Possible answers: The French doors, balcony rail, the armoire, and the reflection all have vertical lines. The balcony rail is the only horizontal line. Diagonal lines are found in the edges of the rug. Curved lines are found in the white sofa arm.

► Possible answers: The rug is a trapezoid, as is the reflection of the balcony in the mirror. The windows in the French doors are parallelograms. The chairs, the sofa arm, and the distant hills are free-form shapes.

► The rug and the floor are the darkest values. The lightest values are in the side of the armoire, the sofa arm, and the wall.

► Cross-hatching appears in the windows.

▲ **Raoul Dufy.** (French).
Open Window, Nice. 1928.

Oil on canvas. $25\frac{5}{8} \times 21\frac{1}{8}$ inches (65.1 × 53.7 cm.).
Art Institute of Chicago, Chicago, Illinois.

Art History and Culture

Raoul Dufy

Raoul Dufy (rä ül´ dōō fē´) (1877–1953) was born in Le Havre, France, to an impoverished but happy family. He had an early interest in art and a passion for drawing. At fifteen, he enrolled at the Le Havre School of Fine Arts. There he met Georges Braque, who, with Picasso, pioneered cubism. Braque became a lifelong friend and a major artistic influence on Dufy. He was influenced by the bright colors of the fauvists but he was not a fauvist himself. Dufy had a unique style that did not fit into any category. Dufy also worked as an illustrator, fabric designer, and decorator.

See pages 24–25 and 16–21 for more about art history and the subject matter.

Artist Profiles, p. 22

Artist Profile

Raoul Dufy
1877–1953

Raoul Dufy (rä ool´ dü´ fä) was born in Le Havre, France, to an impoverished but happy family. He had an early interest in art and a passion for drawing. At the age of 15, he enrolled at the Le Havre School of Fine Arts, where he met Georges Braque, who was a pioneer of cubism, along with Picasso. Braque became a lifelong friend and major artistic influence. In 1900, Dufy received a grant to attend the École des Beaux-Arts in Paris. His interest in impressionism was directed toward fauvism under the influence of Matisse in 1905. He also worked as an illustrator, fabric designer, and decorator. *Time* magazine awarded him the moniker "Grandaddy of Modern Chic."

Art Criticism — Critical Thinking

Describe What do you see?

During this step you will collect information about the subject of the work.

- What does the credit line tell you about the painting?
- What do you see in this painting?
- What is in the background?

Analyze How is this work organized?

Think about how the artist has used the elements and principles of art.

- Where do you see vertical, horizontal, diagonal, and curved lines?
- Where do you see geometric shapes and free-form shapes?
- Where are the darkest values and lightest values in the painting?
- Where do you see cross-hatching?

Interpret What is the artist trying to say?

Use the clues you discovered during your analysis to find the message the artist is trying to show.

- Who do you think lives in this room? Describe the person, saying as much as you can deduce from this room. What does he or she read? What music does he or she like?
- What do you think this room is used for?

Decide What do you think about the work?

Use all the information you have gathered to decide whether this is a successful work of art.

- Is this painting successful because it is realistic, because it is well-organized, or because it has a strong message? Explain.

Unit 1 **61**

Interpret

- Some students might say a lady lives there because of the flowered rug and curvy table.
- Some students might say it is a living room because of the chairs and table. Others may think it is a bedroom because of the armoire.

Decide

- Some students might choose the organization, and some may choose the message.

Art Journal: Writing

Have students write answers to Aesthetic Perception in their Art Journals.

Aesthetic Perception

Critical Thinking Using all five senses, have students describe what it would be like to stand in the room seen in Raoul Dufy's painting.

Describe
- What can you see in this room and outside of this room?

Analyze
- How has Dufy used lines in this painting to express a particular mood?

Interpret
- How does this room make you feel?

- What do you think you would be doing if you were in this room?

Decide
- Why do you think Dufy added more detail to some items in the room than others?

"Artists use the elements of line, shape, and value in their work to show movement, expression, and mimic reality." "Los artistas usan los elementos de línea, forma y valor en sus obras para mostrar moviemiento, expresión e imitar la realidad."

T Review unit vocabulary with students using *Transparency 37.*

Art Journal: Writing

Have students answer the questions on page 62 in their Art Journals or on a separate sheet of paper. Answers: 1. B, 2. A, 3. C, 4. C, 5. A, 6. B

T For further assessment, have students complete the unit test on *Transparency 43.*

VISIT A MUSEUM
The Art Institute of Chicago

▶ The Art Institute of Chicago was established in 1879 as the Chicago Academy of Fine Arts. The name was changed in 1882. It is known for its architectural displays and its collection of French impressionist works. Its collections include 225,000 objects, and its membership—150,000—is the largest of any museum in the United States. Its library is the second-largest museum library in the United States.

▶ Have students describe a museum where they would want their artwork to be exhibited. The museum can be real or imaginary. They should describe the works that the museum would specialize in.

"Every child is an artist. The problem is how to remain an artist once you grow up."

—Pablo Picasso

Line, Shape, and Value, continued

Show What You Know

Answer these questions on a separate sheet of paper.

❶ A _____ is a mark drawn by a tool as it moves across a surface.
 A. dot
 B. line
 C. stippling

❷ _____ are shapes that can be described by mathematical formulas.
 A. Free-form shapes
 B. Hatching
 C. Geometric shapes

❸ _____ refers to the lightness or darkness of an object.
 A. Sketching
 B. Curved
 C. Value

❹ _____ is the gradual change of one value to the next.
 A. Blending
 B. Zigzag
 C. Value

❺ _____ is the degree of difference among color values, tones, shapes, and other elements in works of art.
 A. Stippling
 B. Contrast
 C. Cross-hatching

LET'S VISIT A MUSEUM
The Art Institute of Chicago

When it was originally established in 1879, The Art Institute of Chicago was called the Chicago Academy of Fine Arts. Today its membership reaches 150,000, the highest of any art museum in the country. Its collection has more than 225,000 works of art. There are ten different departments and galleries. The museum is known for its architectural displays and collection of French impressionist works. A large part of the museum is a school. People from all over the world attend classes in photography, painting, fashion design, and other visual arts.

▲ The Art Institute of Chicago

Unit Assessment Options

Aesthetic Perception

Practice Have students select three of the concepts in the Show What You Know section on page 62, and then find examples of each concept in the classroom.

Creative Expression

Student Portfolio Have students review all the artwork they have created during this unit and select the pieces they wish to keep in their portfolios.

Art Criticism

Activity Have students select an artwork from this unit and study it using the four steps of art criticism. (See pages 28–29 for more information about art criticism.) Have students work alone or in pairs and present their findings aloud or in writing.

Line, Shape, and Value in Theater

Voice of the Wood is a play that has been adapted from a book. The story begins with a *luthier* (a maker of musical instruments) who crafts a cello from the wood of an ancient tree. The play tells the story of his quest to discover the touch that will unlock the "voice of the wood."

What to Do Write a story that could be turned into a play.

1. Write a short story that has a musical instrument as the main character. The instrument character can have human traits and emotions, or, instead, it can be a key element in the story plot.

2. Think about the materials used in making the instrument you chose. For example, your story could begin with a reed. A reed in a clarinet, when combined with wind, produces the sounds of the music the clarinet makes.

3. Think of the characters, the setting, the problem, and how it can be solved.

4. Once your story is written, divide it into three to five scenes that can be acted.

5. Share your story with a partner.

▲ Robert Faust and Eugene Friesen. "Voice of the Wood."

 **Art Criticism**

Describe Describe the lines and shape of the instrument you are featuring.

Analyze Explain how you created a story that features an instrument.

Interpret What emotions did you give to the instrument you chose?

Decide Do you think you succeeded in writing a story that can be turned into a play?

Unit 1 **63**

 Art History and Culture

Commedia dell'Arte

The two performers in *Voice of the Wood* use half-masks derived from the Italian theatre style, Commedia dell'Arte ("professional comedy"). It originated in Venice, Italy and flourished during the 16th and 17th centuries as a form of popular comedy. There were no scripts, but rather a short outline of the plot, within which the performers improvised. There were "stock characters" where one particular trait—greed, boastfulness, etc.—was stressed. The cello, a member of the string "family," is featured in *Voice of the Wood*. Other members of this family, the violin, viola, and double bass, all evolved from ancient, plucked instruments, like the harp and the lute. The best quality string instruments are made of wood and crafted primarily by hand.

Line, Shape, and Value in Theatre

Objective: To create a story that features an instrument

Materials: Pictures of instruments, *Voice of the Wood*, perfomed by Faustwork Mask Theater. Running time: 10:00.

Focus
Time: About 10 minutes

■ Discuss the information on page 63.

 Art History and Culture

■ Have students brainstorm types of instruments and the materials from which they are made. Ask them to think of the sounds that instrument can make.

Teach
Time: About 20 minutes

 Aesthetic Perception

■ Have students list instruments and their characteristics.

■ Review criteria for writing a story.

■ Ask students to write a short story that features an instrument. Explain how they can give human traits to the instrument.

Creative Expression

■ Explain that stories can be adapted to become plays.

■ Direct students to take their story and divide it into 3–5 scenes.

■ Have students share their plays.

■ **Informal Asssessment** Comment positively on efforts to divide the elements of plot.

Reflect
Time: About 15 minutes

 **Art Criticism**

■ Have students answer the four art criticism questions on page 63 orally or in writing.

■ Did students write a story that featured an instrument character? Were they able to successfuly arrange their stories into 3–5 scenes.

Unit 2 Planning Guide

	Lesson Title	Suggested Pacing	Creative Expression Activity
Lesson 1	Positive and Negative Shapes and Space	1:15	Draw a still life emphasizing the negative space.
Lesson 2	Space in Two-Dimensional Art	1:10	Paint an outdoor scene. Include depth.
Lesson 3	Linear Perspective	1:10	Draw a city street. Use linear perspective.
Lesson 4	Shading	1:25	Draw a space station. Use shading.
Lesson 5	Form	1:05	Create a three-dimensional form. Use two-dimensional paper.
Lesson 6	Form in Architecture	1:05	Create a paper-sculpture building.
ARTSOURCE	Space, Shape, and Form in Poetry	0:35	Create a rhyming couplet.

Materials	Program Resources	Fine Art Resources	Literature Resources
12" × 18" white drawing paper, markers, large still-life objects, pencils and erasers	*Assessment*, pp. 21–22 *Home and After-School Connections* *Art Around the World Collection* *Reading and Writing Test Preparation*, pp. 18–19	*Transparency 7* *Artist Profiles*, p. 33 *Large Prints 63, 64* *Flash Card 20* *Animals Through History Time Line*	*Shadow* by Marcia Brown
chalk, tempera paint, 12" × 18" white paper	*Assessment*, pp. 23–24 *Home and After-School Connections* *The National Museum of Women in the Arts Collection* *Reading and Writing Test Preparation*, pp. 20–21	*Transparency 8* *Artist Profiles*, pp. 10, 32 *Large Print 63* *Animals Through History Time Line*	*Walk Two Moons* by Sharon Creech
12" × 18" white drawing paper, pencils and erasers, rulers, watercolor paints, paintbrushes, water dishes, masking tape, sketch paper, paper towels	*Assessment*, pp. 25–26 *Home and After-School Connections* *The National Museum of Women in the Arts Collection* *Reading and Writing Test Preparation*, pp. 22–23	*Transparency 9* *Artist Profiles*, pp. 30, 12 *Large Print 63* *Animals Through History Time Line*	*A Year Down Yonder* by Richard Peck
pencils, 12" × 18" white paper, oil pastels, recording of Gustav Holst's *The Planets*, colored pencils	*Assessment*, pp. 27–28 *Home and After-School Connections* *Art Around the World Collection* *Reading and Writing Test Preparation*, pp. 24–25	*Transparency 10* *Artist Profiles*, pp. 13, 40 *Large Prints 63, 64* *Flash Cards 1–3* *Animals Through History Time Line*	*Always Room for One More* by Nic Leodhas *Tales of the Shimmering Sky: Ten Global Folktales with Activities* by Susan Milford
paper, markers	*Assessment*, pp. 29–30 *Home and After-School Connections* *The National Museum of Women in the Arts Collection* *Reading and Writing Test Preparation*, pp. 26–27	*Transparency 11* *Artist Profiles*, pp. 54, 55 *Large Print 64* *Animals Through History Time Line*	*Call It Courage* by Armstrong Sperry
paper, thin cardboard, construction paper, towel and toilet-tissue tubes	*Assessment*, pp. 31–32 *Home and After-School Connections* *The National Museum of Women in the Arts Collection* *Reading and Writing Test Preparation*, pp. 28–29	*Transparency 12* *Artist Profiles*, pp. 37, 62 *Large Print 64* *Animals Through History Time Line*	*Rapunzel* by Paul O. Zelinsky
Our Little Blue Planet, paper, pencils			

Unit Overview

2 Space, Shape, and Form

Lesson 1: Positive and negative space are used to create mood and interest in artwork.

Lesson 2: Space in two-dimensional art is created when perspective techniques are used on a flat surface, giving the feeling of depth.

Lesson 3: Linear perspective techniques make things seem close or look far away.

Lesson 4: Shading techniques are often used to create the illusion of form and space.

Lesson 5: Form is used to create three-dimensional works of art.

Lesson 6: Form in architecture is used by architects who design buildings and structures.

Introduce Unit Concepts

"Artists use the elements of space, shape, and form to create depth in an artwork." "Los artistas usan los elementos de espacio, figura y forma para crear profundidad en una obra de arte."

Space
- Have students brainstorm the many different uses for the term *space,* such as outer space.

Shape ⭐ Math
- Have each student draw ten shapes and label them as geometric or free-form.

Form
- Discuss how form is like shape because of its height and width, but that it differs due to the third dimension of depth.

Cross-Curricular Projects
- See the *Language Arts and Reading, Mathematics, Science,* and *Social Studies Art Connections* books for activities that further develop space, shape, and form concepts.

Space, Shape, and Form

◀ **Jan Vermeer** (Dutch). *The Concert.* 1665–1667. Oil on canvas. $28\frac{1}{2} \times 25\frac{1}{2}$ inches (72.39 × 64.77 cm.). Isabella Stewart Gardner Museum, Boston, Massachusetts.

Many artists use space, shape, and form in two- and three-dimensional works of art.

Jan Vermeer relied on the use of space, shape, and form to help him create realistic paintings. He used perspective techniques in *The Concert* to create the look of depth on a flat surface. He also creates the illusion of form, using shading techniques. This makes the people and objects in *The Concert* look realistic.

64 Unit 2

Fine Art Prints

Display *Large Prints 63 The Icebergs* and *64 Eagle Man.* Refer to the prints throughout the unit as students learn about space, shape, and form.

Large Print 63

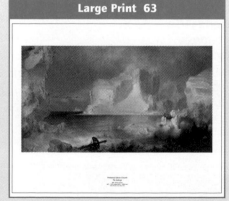

Large Print 64

Space is used by artists in paintings and drawings to give the illusion of depth on a flat surface.

▶ Notice how the tiles on the floor get smaller as they move into the painting.

Artists use several techniques to create the illusion of **form** on a two-dimensional, or flat, surface.

▶ What did Vermeer do to create form and to make the people and objects look realistic in this painting?

In This Unit you will learn about and practice techniques to create the appearance of space on a flat surface. You also will learn about three-dimensional forms. Here are the topics you will study:
▶ Space
▶ Form
▶ Perspective
▶ Shading
▶ Architectural form

Jan Vermeer.
Detail, At the Procuress'. 1656.

Jan Vermeer
(1632–1675)

Jan Vermeer was an artist who was almost unknown until about one hundred years ago. He painted fewer than forty works of art. Little was written about his life, but his paintings show that he was one of the world's greatest artists. Vermeer was interested in how scenes of everyday life might look to a person who is standing a short distance away. He used texture, value, and shape in a way that makes a scene appear to have natural light. Vermeer was only forty three years old when he died.

Unit 2   **65**

Examine the Artwork

"Let's look closely at the painting." "Vamos a observar detalladamente la pintura."

■ Have students look at Jan Vermeer's painting *The Concert*. Ask them to describe what they see.

■ Have students answer the questions about space, shape, and form on page 65.

▶ The tiles are drawn smaller in the background than in the foreground to create the illusion of depth in space using size.

▶ The people and the objects look realistic because of the details. Shading is used to create the illusion of depth and to make the people look like three-dimensional forms.

Unit Pretest

Display *Transparency 44* as a pretest. Answers: 1. A, 2. A, 3. C, 4. B, 5. C

Home Connection

■ See *Home and After-School Connections* for family newsletters and activities for this unit.

Art History and Culture

Jan Vermeer

Jan Vermeer (yän vər mer´) (1632–1675) was born in Holland. His father was an innkeeper, silk worker, and art dealer. He left the inn to Vermeer. The business kept him busy, so he painted only in his spare time. Today his artworks are some of the best known in the world. *The Concert* was stolen from the Isabella Stuart Gardner Museum in Boston in 1990, and it still has not been recovered. Vermeer painted slowly, completing only two or three works a year. Only 35 of his paintings are believed to exist today.

See pages 16–21 and 24–25 for more about art history and the subject matter.

Artist Profiles, p. 64

● Artist Profile ●

Jan Vermeer
1632–1675

Jan Vermeer (yän vər mer´) was a Dutch painter born in Delft. Little is known about his life; he married at the age of 21 and was the father of 11 children. Vermeer served a six-year apprenticeship and was admitted to the Delft painters guild in 1653. He made a modest living as an art dealer running a business that was left to him by his father. No records have been found to show that he sold any of his own works. Forgotten for almost 200 years, Vermeer is now regarded as one of the greatest painters of all time. This is remarkable because only 35 of his paintings are known to exist. This small number of works is attributed to his deliberate, methodical work habits, his short life, and the disappearance of many...

ILLUSTRATOR PROFILE
Ed Young
(1931–)

Ed Young was born in Tienstin, China, and grew up in Shanghai. Illness prevented Young from starting school at the same time as other children his age. When he finally went to school, he was preoccupied with drawing and daydreaming. At the age of 20, Young traveled to the United States, where his talent and imagination eventually led him to the Art Center College of Design in Los Angeles. He graduated in 1957 and worked for a short time in advertising, a career he readily abandoned after meeting children's book editor Ursula Nordstrom in 1962. After seeing his portfolio, Nordstrom immediately offered Young a contract.

Respect and credibility are two qualities that Young always strives to achieve in his art. After illustrating more than 70 books, he still conducts thorough research and treats each new creation with care. Young's approach to his work is also influenced by his heritage. He says, "A Chinese painting is often accompanied by words. They are complementary. There are things that words do that pictures never can, and likewise, there are images that words can never describe." Young was awarded the Caldecott Medal for his illustrations in *Lon Po Po: A Red-Riding Hood Story from China.* He also wrote and illustrated the Caldecott Honor book *Seven Blind Mice,* a retelling of an Indian tale.

Music
Color in music refers to the distinctive tone qualities, or timbre, of different instruments and voices. Have the students choose a piece of music to match the color value of their artwork in one of the lessons in this unit.

Literature
Show the video or DVD *Yonder* to introduce the concepts of space, shape, and form in landscapes. Pause the video or DVD and have students describe the use of space, shape, and form that they see.

Literature and Art

Performing Arts
ART SOURCE Show Paul Tracey's musical, *Our Little Blue Planet.* Students will write a song about a tree that interests them and consider its shape and form.

Artsource®

Positive and Negative Shapes and Space

Lesson 1 introduces positive and negative shapes and space. Artists use positive and negative shapes and space to create mood and interest in their artwork.

Objectives

 Art History and Culture

To demonstrate knowledge of the life and work of Jasper Johns

Creative Expression

To identify and emphasize the negative shapes in a still life

Aesthetic Perception

To identify the use of positive and negative spaces by artists to add interest to their work

Art Criticism

To evaluate one's own work using the four steps of art criticism

Lesson Materials
- white drawing paper
- 12" × 18" white drawing paper
- markers
- large still-life objects
- pencils and erasers

Alternate Materials:
- ink pens
- crayons

Program Resources
- *Reading and Writing Test Prep.*, pp. 18–19
- *Transparency 7*
- *Flash Card* 20
- *Artist Profiles*, p. 33
- *Animals Through History Time Line*
- *Assessment*, pp. 21–22
- *Large Prints 63* The Icebergs and *64 Eagle Man*
- *Art Around the World Collection*

Concept Trace
Positive and Negative Shapes and Space
Introduced: Level 4, Unit 4, Lesson 3

Reinforced: Level 6, Unit 1, Lesson 6

Vocabulary Vocabulary

Review the following vocabulary words with students.

space espacio—the area between, around, above, below, and within objects

positive space espacio positivo—the objects, shapes, or forms in works of art

negative space espacio negativo—the empty space that surrounds objects, shapes, and forms

See page 89B for additional vocabulary and Spanish vocabulary resources.

 Art Journal: Vocabulary

Have students add these words to the Vocabulary section of their Art Journals.

Lesson 1 Arts Integration

Theatre

Complete Unit 2, Lesson 1, on pages 36–37 of *Theatre Arts Connections.*

Theatre Arts Connections, p. 36

Objectives

1 Characters Want Something

Focus Time: About 10 minutes

"In this lesson we will use sensory recall to show a character's feelings and motivations in a story." *(See page T15 for more about Sensory Recall.)*

Activate Prior Knowledge
▶ As you read aloud "**Origin of the Pleiades**," have students imagine feelings of hunger. Discuss the positive physical sensations the children felt that led them to keep dancing. *(their bodies moving up and down, pounding hearts, and so on)* Say, "Characters in a drama act the way they do because they want something. This is called their motivation."

Teach Time: About 15 minutes

Prepare Have students stand up and spread out around the room.

Lead Tell students they are actors playing the children from the "Origin of the Pleiades."

▶ Have students begin moving rhythmically in place, imagining that their stomachs are full. Coach students, saying, "You are very, very hungry, but you still want to keep dancing. Let your actions match your hunger, but you still want to keep dancing. Let your actions match your hunger when you show great weariness and hunger

Music

SPOTLIGHT on MUSIC

Music research has found that most people associate certain instrumental sounds with the same colors. To learn to identify the sound of the orchestral families, listen to theme and variations form *The Young Person's Guide to the Orchestra*, by Benjamin Britten.

Movement & Dance

Students explore shaping negative space between the body and surfaces in the room. How can you shape negative space with the wall and your body? How can you shape negative space with the floor and your body? How can you shape negative space with another person?

Focus

Time: About 30 minutes

Activate Prior Knowledge

"Have you ever created animal shadow images on the wall using your hand and strong back lighting?" "¿Alguna vez han hecho sombras con figuras de animales en la pared usando sus manos y una luz fuerte de fondo?"

- Explain to students that shadow images on the wall are examples of optical illusions. Discuss other optical illusions.

Using Literature ⭐ Reading

- Read Marcia Brown's *Shadow*. Encourage students to identify the use of positive and negative space in the illustrations.

Thematic Connection ⭐ Science

- **Shadows:** If weather permits, take students outside to experiment with their own shadows and those cast by other objects. Discuss the rotation of Earth around the sun.

Introduce the Art

Look

"Let's take a close look at the two works of art." "Vamos a observar detalladamente las dos obras de arte."

Comparing and Contrasting ⭐ Reading

- Have students compare and contrast the use of positive and negative space in each work of art in this series by Jasper Johns.

 Art History and Culture

Students' answers might include popular musicians and entertainers, sports, fashion, or video games. NSAE 4.b

Web Connection

Visit **www.artchive.com/artchive/J/johns.html** to see more of Jasper Johns's artwork.

Lesson 1

Positive and Negative Shapes and Space

Look at Jasper Johns's lithographs, titled *Cups 4 Picasso*. They are examples of optical illusions. He has intentionally organized shapes to create a visual puzzle to interest the viewer. Johns likes to change a recognizable object to attract more attention to it. Notice the way he changed the face of the Spanish artist Pablo Picasso. Jasper Johns arranges shapes and uses color to add interest to his artwork.

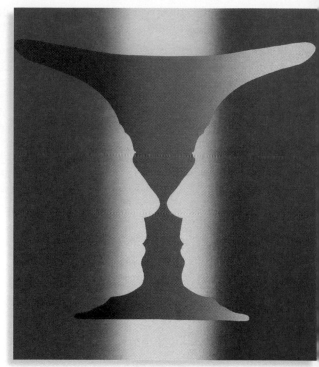

Jasper Johns. (American). ▶
Cups 4 Picasso. 1972.
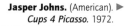
Lithograph. $14\frac{1}{2} \times 32\frac{1}{4}$ inches (35.56 × 81.28 cm.). Museum of Modern Art, New York, New York.

 Art History and Culture

Jasper Johns is a pop artist. Pop artists use objects and ideas from their popular culture in their artwork. What objects and ideas might you see in today's pop art?

 Art History and Culture

Jasper Johns

Jasper Johns (jás pər jänz) (1930–) was born in Georgia and spent his childhood in South Carolina. He served in the U.S. Army and was stationed in Japan. At age 24 he decided to throw away all the art he had made, because he wanted a fresh start. He was determined to create original art, not copies of other styles or artists. He is known for his inventive artistic styles.

See pages 16–21 and 24–25 for more about art history and the subject matter.

Artist Profiles, p. 33

▸ Artist Profile ◂

Jasper Johns
b. 1930

Jasper Johns (jas' pər jänz) was born in Augusta, Georgia. After serving in Japan with the United States Army, he moved to New York City. There he worked in a bookstore and started creating art. When he was 24, he decided to throw away all the art he had ever made. He wanted a fresh start. He was determined to create original art, not copies of the styles of other artists. Since then Johns has been known for his inventiveness.

Study both works of art to find examples of positive and negative space.

▶ What shapes do you see in each of the images in this series?

▶ How many shapes are in each view?

▶ What technique did Johns use to show which shapes are most important?

▶ What changes occur from one image to the next?

◀ **Jasper Johns.** (American).
Cups 4 Picasso. 1972.
·····························
Lithograph. 14⅛ × 32¼ inches
(35.56 × 81.28 cm.). Museum of
Modern Art, New York, New York.

Aesthetic Perception

Design Awareness Look at street signs on your way home from school today. Notice how negative and positive spaces are used to create symbols to communicate messages.

Art History and Culture

Jasper Johns

Jasper Johns is a pop artist. He takes everyday objects and transforms them into objects of art. Pop artists use mass culture, including television, billboard advertising, and cars, and bring these images into museums. Johns's work includes familiar items such as flags, targets, numerals, and maps.

See pages 16–21 and 24–25 for more about art history and the subject matter.

Artist Profiles, p. 33

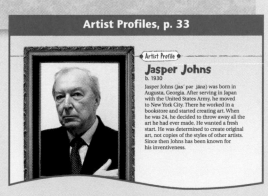

Artist Profile

Jasper Johns
b. 1930

Jasper Johns (Jas' par jänz) was born in Augusta, Georgia. After serving in Japan with the United States Army, he moved to New York City. There he worked in a bookstore and started creating art. When he was 24, he decided to throw away all the art he had ever made. He wanted a fresh start. He was determined to create original art, not copies of the styles of other artists. Since then Johns has been known for his inventiveness.

Study

▶ The shapes of Pablo Picasso's profiles stand out in the first print. They are surrounded by dark colors. The vase stands out in the second print.

▶ Each view has three shapes.

▶ Positive and negative shape reversal.

▶ The profiles become the contour of the vase.

■ For more examples of art from North America, see the *Art Around the World Collection.*

Art Journal: Writing

Have students write a diary entry from their own shadow's point of view in their Art Journal. Encourage students to share their creative writing with the class.

Aesthetic Perception

Design Awareness Ask students to identify signs or logos that use positive and negative space to identify products or to give directions. Ask students if this technique creates a two-dimensional or a three-dimensional look. Discuss how the simplicity of this style would be beneficial.

Developing Visual Literacy Ask students to share how sometimes things, as well as situations, can look different depending on what you are looking for to begin with. Encourage them to look at *Cups 4 Picasso* and explain what Jasper Johns wanted to convey with this series.

Web Connection

Visit **www.jasperjohns.com/bio.html** for more information on Jasper Johns and his artwork. Also visit **www.moma.org/whatisaprint/flash.html** to learn more about lithographs.

 **each** **Time:** About 30 minutes

"How can you draw a profile?" "¿Pueden trazar un perfil?"

- Discuss the definitions of positive space, negative space, and shape reversal on page 68.

Practice

Materials: white drawing paper, pencils

Alternate Materials: ink pens

- Distribute materials and have students follow the directions on page 68.

- Have students work in pairs. Ask them to use a pencil to make a contour drawing of a classmate's profile. Then have students turn the paper upside down and copy the profile backwards onto a second sheet of paper.

 ## Creative Expression

Materials: 12″ × 18″ white drawing paper, markers, large still-life objects, pencils and erasers

Alternate Materials: crayons

- Distribute the materials and have students follow the directions on page 69.

- Review the Activity Tips on page 233 for visual examples of this lesson's activity.

Art Journal: Brainstorming

Have students brainstorm a list of objects they might want to use for their still lifes and the angles they will be drawing from. Ask them to list the objects and sketch plans for their arrangement in their Art Journals.

Using Positive and Negative Shapes and Space

The element of art that refers to the area between, around, above, below, and within objects is **space.** Shapes and forms exist in space. It is the air around the object. There are two types of space: positive and negative.

Positive space is the objects, shapes, and forms in a work of art.

Negative space is the empty space that surrounds objects, shapes, and forms. When there is a large area of negative space in an artwork, loneliness or freedom might be expressed.

Shape reversal is when an object, shape, or form is positive space in one image and then in another image becomes negative space. Johns's lithographs show shape reversal.

Practice

Practice drawing profiles. Use a pencil.

1. Draw a profile of a classmate's head.

2. Turn your paper upside down and copy the profile backward, just as Jasper Johns did.

Differentiated Instruction

Reteach

Have students use a camera to take pictures of still-life arrangements. After the pictures are developed, ask students to compare the positive and negative spaces in the pictures with the positive and negative spaces in the negatives.

Special Needs

Students with cognitive disabilities may need guided practice in recognizing and drawing the negative spaces of an object. Prior to beginning the still-life activity, have students examine and draw just one object with negative spaces.

ELL

Some students may benefit from practice with a more English-fluent partner before they are ready to discuss their work with the group. Partners can ask each other questions to describe what they see in the artwork. Partners can offer physical and verbal clues to help with the description.

◀ **Eric Flynn.**
Age 10.

Think about where you see the negative space in the picture.

 **Creative Expression**

How can you see the shapes of negative space? Draw the negative spaces in a still life.

1. Arrange objects in a still-life pose that have large, interesting negative spaces, such as chairs or desks.

2. Look closely at the still life and find an area of it that you like. Draw what you see. Concentrate on the negative spaces around the objects.

3. Using markers, fill only the negative spaces with color. Leave the positive spaces white.

 **Art Criticism**

Describe What objects did you draw?

Analyze What shapes did you create when you colored the negative space? How do the positive and negative shapes differ?

Interpret How did reversing the positive and negative spaces affect your drawing?

Decide Were you successful in defining the negative space around your objects?

Unit 2 • Lesson 1   **69**

 **Reflect**   Time: About 15 minutes

Review and Assess

"Were you able to draw the negative shapes in a still life?" "¿Pudieron trazar las figuras negativas en una naturaleza muerta?"

Think

The student artist identified the negative space in the still life by coloring in the area around the chair with a marker.

■ Use *Large Prints 63 The Icebergs* and *64 Eagle Man* to have students identify and describe the use of positive and negative spaces and form.

Informal Assessment

■ For standardized-format test practice using this lesson's art content, see pages 18–19 in *Reading and Writing Test Preparation*.

Art Journal: Critical Thinking

Have students answer the four art criticism questions—Describe, Analyze, Interpret, and Decide—in their Art Journals. In small groups, have students discuss their still-life drawings. NSAE 2.a

Art Across the Curriculum

Use these simple ideas to reinforce art concepts across the curriculum.

★ **Narrative Writing** Have students write a story in which the main character is a person's shadow.

★ **Math** Explain how tessellations are a form of shape reversal.

★ **Science** Discuss how positive and negative space are evident during a solar eclipse.

★ **Social Studies** Have students identify the positive and negative spaces on a map of the world.

★ **Technology** Use the fill tool in a computer paint program to create a design that demonstrates positive and negative space. Visit **SRAonline.com** to print detailed instructions for this activity. NSAE 6.b

Positive and Negative Shapes and Space

Extra! For the Art Specialist

Time: About 30 minutes

Focus

Study **Large Prints 63** *The Icebergs* and **64** *Eagle Man*, and ask students to point out the positive and negative space. What shapes do you recognize in the spaces around and inside the objects? What shape is the object?

Teach

Review the concepts of positive and negative space. Explain that when the positive space becomes the negative space and the negative space becomes the positive space "shape reversal" takes place. Ask students to collect a variety of forms with interesting contours in a centralized location.

Reflect

Have students evaluate their works of art using the four steps of art criticism. Encourage them to locate and describe other areas of positive and negative space in the classroom.

Alternate Activity

Materials:
- Art Journal
- 9″ × 12″ drawing paper
- pencils, erasers
- medium-point markers
- a collection of objects with interesting contours such as vases, small sculptures, or containers

1. Select one object that interests you. In your Art Journal, create a line drawing of your object that includes all details. Use a marker to trace over the outside contours of your shape.

2. On your drawing paper, transfer only the outlined drawing. Trace with a marker.

3. Place your second sheet of paper on top of your first sheet and use your pencil to trace your image. Trace the lines with a marker.

4. Draw a repeated linear design within the contours of the positive shape of your first drawn object. In the second drawing, emphasize the same linear design in the negative space.

Research in Art Education

Research has shown that the looking and reasoning skills learned during visual-arts training can also be applied to scientific images ("Investigating the Educational Impact and Potential of the Museum of Modern Art's Visual Thinking Curriculum," in *Critical Links*, p. 142). Students involved in visual-arts training showed less circular reasoning and more evidential reasoning when evaluating fine-art images and scientific images. As students learn about positive and negative space, encourage them to think about how objects they see relate to their surroundings.

Assessment

Use the following rubric to evaluate the artwork students make in the Creative Expression activity and to assess students' understanding of positive and negative shapes and space.

Have students complete page 21 or 22 in their *Assessment* books.

	Art History and Culture	Aesthetic Perception	Creative Expression	Art Criticism
3 POINTS	The student can demonstrate knowledge of the life and work of Jasper Johns.	The student accurately identifies positive and negative shapes and space.	The student's drawing clearly illustrates the use of negative space.	The student thoughtfully and honestly evaluates own work using the four steps of art criticism.
2 POINTS	The student's knowledge of the life and work of Jasper Johns is weak or incomplete.	The student shows emerging awareness of positive and negative shapes and space.	The student's drawing shows some awareness of negative space.	The student attempts to evaluate own work, but shows an incomplete understanding of evaluation criteria.
1 POINT	The student cannot demonstrate knowledge of the life or work of Jasper Johns.	The student cannot identify positive and negative shapes and space.	The student's drawing shows no understanding of negative space.	The student makes no attempt to evaluate own artwork.

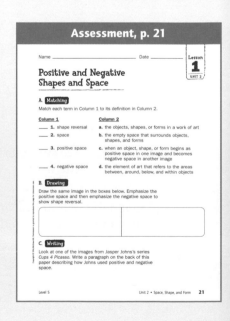

Assessment, p. 21

Name _____ Date _____

Lesson 1 UNIT 2

Positive and Negative Shapes and Space

A. Matching
Match each term in Column 1 to its definition in Column 2.

Column 1
___ 1. shape reversal
___ 2. space
___ 3. positive space
___ 4. negative space

Column 2
a. the objects, shapes, or forms in a work of art
b. the empty space that surrounds objects, shapes, and forms
c. when an object, shape, or form begins as positive space in one image and becomes negative space in another image
d. the element of art that refers to the areas between, around, below, and within objects

B. Drawing
Draw the same image in the boxes below. Emphasize the positive space and then emphasize the negative space to show shape reversal.

C. Writing
Look at one of the images from Jasper Johns's series *Cups 4 Picasso*. Write a paragraph on the back of this paper describing how Johns used positive and negative space.

Level 5 Unit 2 • Space, Shape, and Form **21**

Space in Two-Dimensional Art

Lesson 2 introduces space in two-dimensional art. Artists use perspective techniques to create the feeling of depth in a flat surface.

Objectives

 Art History and Culture

To demonstrate knowledge of the lives and work of Winslow Homer and William Adolphe Bouguereau

Creative Expression

To paint an outdoor scene using perspective techniques to create the illusion of depth

 Aesthetic Perception

To relate how artists use perspective techniques to create space in two-dimensional works of art NSAE 2.b

Art Criticism

To evaluate one's own work using the four steps of art criticism

Vocabulary  Vocabulary

Review the following vocabulary words with students.

perspective perspectiva—techniques for creating the illusion of depth on a flat surface

depth profundidad—the appearance of deep space or distance in a two-dimensional artwork

converging converger—coming together at one point or place

See page 89B for additional Spanish vocabulary resources.

 Art Journal: Vocabulary

Have students add these words to the Vocabulary section of their Art Journals.

Lesson Materials
- white drawing paper
- pencils
- 12" × 18" white paper
- chalk
- tempera paints

Alternate Materials:
- markers
- crayons

Program Resources
- *Reading and Writing Test Prep.,* pp. 20–21
- *Transparency 8*
- *Artist Profiles,* pp. 10, 32
- *Animals Through History Time Line*
- *Assessment,* pp. 23–24
- *Large Print 63* The Icebergs
- *The National Museum of Women in the Arts Collection*

Concept Trace
Space in Two-Dimensional Art
Introduced: Level 4, Unit 5, Lesson 2

Reinforced: Level 6, Unit 1, Lesson 4

Lesson 2 Arts Integration

Theatre

Complete Unit 2, Lesson 2, on pages 38–39 of *Theatre Arts Connections.*

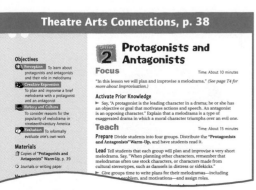

Theatre Arts Connections, p. 38

Music

 The shapes found in Western music generally contain patterns both large and small. The melodies of Native Americans are less predictable; they are more free-form. Listen to "Tekaniónton'neha." The melodic contour is generally downward, but the length of the melodies is regular, and the drum or rattle accompaniment seems to be improvisational.

Movement & Dance

Look at a picture of an Egyptian mural. Describe how the characters are depicted as two-dimensional (shoulders face forward, both feet face the same direction, face is often profile. Have the class create a wall of figures that appear to be trapped in a two-dimensional place. Students must flatten their limbs, as though they were on a two-dimensional plane. Ask students what movements would make them seem to be while showing no depth?

ocus

Time: About 10 minutes

Activate Prior Knowledge

"Have you ever noticed how things that are far away look smaller?" "¿Alguna vez han notado que las cosas que están lejos parecen más pequeñas?"

- Discuss students' responses.

Using Literature ⭐ Reading

- Use Sharon Creech's novel *Walk Two Moons* to discuss how a person's perspective can change because of the events that take place in his or her life. Use the artwork on the book's cover to find techniques used to create space in two-dimensional art.

Thematic Connection ⭐ Science

- **Enjoying the Outdoors:** Ask students to share with the class a description of a place where they enjoy being outdoors.

Introduce the Art

Look

"Let's take a close look at the two works of art." "Vamos a observar detalladamente las dos obras de arte."

Sequence ⭐ Reading

- Have students identify the order of overlapped objects in the paintings moving from back to front. Encourage students to consider how each artist planned what had to be painted first and what follows to create the correct perspective.

🏺 Art History and Culture

The children in both painting are enjoying outdoor settings. The boy in *Nooning* is relaxing in the rural farm scene of Northeast America. The girls in *The Nut Gatherers* communicate their comfort with nature. The industrial revolution had begun in both countries, but agriculture still played a major role in the economy. NSAE 4.b

💻 **Web Connection**

Have students visit **www.projectlinks.org/homer/** to research more of the life and works of Winslow Homer.

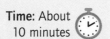 **Lesson 2**

Space in Two-Dimensional Art

▲ **Winslow Homer.** (American). *Nooning.* c. 1872.

Oil on canvas. 13 5/16 × 19 3/8 inches (33.02 × 48.26 cm.). Wadsworth Atheneum, Hartford, Connecticut.

Look at the two realistic paintings on these pages. Even though both are two-dimensional works of art, the artists successfully used techniques to make some things look farther away than others.

🏺 Art History and Culture

What can you tell about American and French culture in the late 1800s from looking at these realistic works of art? In addition to the visual clues, the titles offer clues as well.

🏺 Art History and Culture

Winslow Homer

Winslow Homer (winz´ lō hō´ mər) (1836–1910) is best known for his watercolor paintings. His art career began during the Civil War when he worked as a magazine illustrator. After spending a year in a fishing village on the coast of New England in 1881 and 1882, his focus changed. There, he concentrated on the interaction of humans and nature and developed what would become his signature watercolor technique.

See pages 16–21 and 24–25 for more about art history and the subject matter.

Artist Profiles, p. 32

◆ Artist Profile ◆

Winslow Homer
1835-1910

Winslow Homer (winz´ lō hō´ mar) was born in Boston. He had very little formal training in art, but he showed great artistic talent even in his earliest sketches. He worked as a magazine illustrator for nearly 20 years. When the Civil War began, *Harper's Weekly* sent him to the front lines to sketch both the fighting and ordinary life. Homer did not begin to paint seriously until he was 26. He taught himself the techniques he needed, and eventually settled on the Maine coast. In his later years Homer lived like a hermit, seldom seeing anyone.

Study both works of art to find how space is used.

▶ Find an object that overlaps and covers a part of another object, creating depth in each painting.

▶ Find an object that appears larger in one place and then appears smaller in another place.

▶ Where do you see strong colors? Where do the colors look weaker?

▶ Find an object near the bottom of one of the paintings and something near the top. Which of these objects seems closer to you?

▲ **William Adolphe Bouguereau.**
(French). *The Nut Gatherers.* 1882.
Oil on canvas. 34½ × 52¾ inches
(86.36 × 132.08 cm.). The Detroit
Institute of Arts, Detroit, Michigan.

🔍 Aesthetic Perception

Seeing Like an Artist When traveling home from school today, look at your surroundings. Compare the objects nearer to you to those farther away.

🏺 Art History and Culture

William Adolphe Bouguereau

William Adolphe Bouguereau (wēl´ yəm a dôlf´ bōō´ grō´) (1825–1905) was born in La Rochelle, France. As a young boy, he worked to put himself through Ecole des Bueax art school. Bouguereau is noted for his use of color and space in his paintings. Themes that emerge from his most popular works are taken from classical mythology, the Bible, and his contemporary life.

See pages 16–21 and 24–25 for more about art history and the subject matter.

Artist Profiles, p. 10

◆ Artist Profile ◆

William Adolphe Bouguereau
1825–1905

Born on the west coast of France, William Adolphe Bouguereau (wēl´ yəm a dôlf´ bōō´ grō´) grew up in a family with little money. He put himself through art school with money he earned from painting portraits, and soon was regarded as one of the best classical painters of his time. His strong work ethic was constant throughout his career, and he was known and respected for his compassion for other struggling artists. In 1883, he became president of the Society of Painters, Architects, Sculptors, Engravers, and Designers, an establishment that promoted and aided new and struggling artists. His classical style was

Study NSAE 5.c

▶ In Homer's painting *Nooning,* the overlapping trees and houses create the illusion of depth. In Bouguereau's painting *The Nut Gatherers,* the overlapping girls, nuts, and trees create the illusion of depth.

▶ In *Nooning,* the larger tree trunks seem closer. In *The Nut Gatherers,* the leaves on the ground and the trees that are larger seem to be closer than the smaller trees.

▶ In *Nooning,* the boy and the house behind him seem closer because of the bright colors used. In *The Nut Gatherers,* the viewer's eyes go first to the girls because of the clear detail used to paint them. The trees in the background have less detail.

▶ In *Nooning,* the boy is placed toward the bottom of the painting and seems closer than the house, which appears toward the top. In *The Nut Gatherers,* the leaves along the bottom of the painting seem closer than the trees along the top of the painting.

■ For more examples of genre art, see *The National Museum of Women in the Arts Collection.*

📓 Art Journal: Writing

Have students write in their Art Journals about a time when they enjoyed being outdoors or about something that they might like to do outdoors.

🔍 Aesthetic Perception

Design Awareness Take students to a window, a doorway, or outside and encourage them to notice the perspective of the surroundings. Then have them view the same spot from a different perspective and ask them to describe how the objects seem different in size, placement, detail, and color.

Developing Visual Literacy Ask students to visualize themselves in either of the paintings in this lesson. Encourage them to describe where they are, what they see, and what they are doing.

💻 Web Connection

Visit **www.hometaught.com/art_table.htm** to learn more about the life and work of William Adolphe Bouguereau.

Teach

Time: About 30 minutes

"How can you create depth in a two-dimensional piece of art?" "¿Cómo pueden crear profundidad en una obra de arte bidimensional?"

- Discuss the definitions of overlapping, size, placement, detail, color, and converging lines on page 72.

Practice

Materials: paper, pencils

- Distribute materials and have students follow the directions on page 72.

- Show students how to fold the paper into six equal parts. Have students designate each section of paper with the name of a perspective technique. Monitor as students draw an illustration for each technique.

Creative Expression

Materials: chalk, tempera paints, 12″ × 18″ white paper

Alternate Materials: markers or crayons

- Distribute the materials and have students follow the directions on page 73.

- Review the Activity Tips on page 233 for visual examples of this lesson's activity.

- See the Technique Tips on page 218 for visual information about using tempera paint.

Art Journal: Brainstorming

Have students think of places where they enjoy spending time outdoors and sketch some of these scenes from memory in their Art Journals. Encourage students to experiment with all six perspective techniques when sketching.

Space in Two-Dimensional Art

Perspective techniques are used to create the feeling of depth on a flat surface.

Overlapping When one object covers part of a second object, the first seems to be closer to the viewer.

Size Large objects seem to be closer to the viewer than the small objects. Size is often used together with placement to show depth.

Placement Objects placed in or next to the foreground seem to be closer to the viewer than objects placed in or near the background. Placement is often used together with size to show depth.

Detail Objects with clear, sharp edges and many details seem to be closer to the viewer. Objects that lack detail and have fuzzy outlines seem to be farther away.

Color Brightly colored objects seem closer to the viewer. Objects with pale, dull colors appear farther away.

Converging Lines Parallel lines seem to move toward the same point as they move farther away from the viewer.

Practice

Illustrate each of the six perspective techniques. Use a pencil.

1. Fold your paper into six equal boxes. Print the name of a perspective technique in each of the boxes.

2. Draw an illustration for each technique.

Differentiated Instruction

Reteach
Have students look at landscape photographs, drawings, and paintings. Ask them to identify the perspective techniques used.

Special Needs
Sequence instruction for students with disabilities in such a way that they add one perspective technique at a time.

ELL
As students progress through the unit, create a visual wall chart for the class to use as a reference and as a reinforcement. As a class, write concept definitions and create simple sketches or examples. Refer to the chart as you use the terminology.

◄ **Alison Thomas.**
Age 9.

Think about how the student artist used perspective techniques to paint an outdoor place.

Creative Expression

How can you use perspective techniques to create the illusion of depth? Paint a scene of a favorite outdoor place. Include depth.

1. Think of a place where you like to spend time outside.
2. Draw the scene with chalk, using at least three of the six perspective techniques.
3. Paint your scene.

Art Criticism

Describe Describe your outdoor scene.

Analyze What perspective techniques did you use to create depth in your two-dimensional painting?

Interpret Did you try to paint everything that you could remember in that outdoor area? If not, why did you choose to include some things but not others?

Decide Were you successful in creating the illusion of depth in your painting? Which perspective technique seems the most effective in creating depth?

Unit 2 • Lesson 2 **73**

Reflect
Time: About 20 minutes

Review and Assess
"How would you explain the use of space in two-dimensional art?" "¿Cómo explicarían el uso del espacio en el arte bidimensional?"

Think
The student artist used size, placement, color, and overlapping perspective techniques to paint this outdoor scene.

■ Use *Large Prints 63 The Icebergs* to have students identify and describe the use of space in two-dimensional art.

Informal Assessment
■ For standardized-format test practice using this lesson's art content, see pages 20–21 in *Reading and Writing Test Preparation.*

Art Journal: Critical Thinking
Have students answer the four art criticism questions—Describe, Analyze, Interpret, and Decide—in their Art Journals. In small groups, have students discuss their landscape paintings. NSAE 2.a

Art Across the Curriculum

Use these simple ideas to reinforce art concepts across the curriculum.

★ **Persuasive Writing** Have students write a persuasive advertisement for an outdoor recreation area.

★ **Math** When studying geometry, note which shapes have equal proportions but vary in size. Artists use the size of objects to create distance or space in two-dimensional artwork.

★ **Science** When studying the human eye, compare the use of perspective technique in artwork to create the illusion of distance with the science of corrective eyesight.

★ **Social Studies** When discussing special-interest groups in politics, incorporate the importance of perspective.

★ **Technology** Have students use a computer paint program to experiment with perspective techniques. Visit **SRAonline.com** to print detailed instructions for this activity.
NSAE 6.b

Lesson 2
Space in Two-Dimensional Art
Wrap-Up

Extra! For the Art Specialist

 Time: About 30 minutes

Focus

Study **Large Print 63** *The Icebergs,* and discuss how the feeling of depth was created in the artwork. How do the objects in the foreground differ from those in the background? What do you notice about the details on the objects? What do you notice happens to the size of the objects?

Teach

Review the six perspective techniques. Discuss how artists use the six techniques when painting and drawing outdoor scenes. Explain to the students that they will be creating an outdoor scene based on a real place using collected images from photographs or magazines. Have students begin collecting photographs and magazine images prior to this lesson.

Reflect

Have students evaluate their works of art using the four steps of art criticism. Encourage them to locate an area outside the school to draw, and describe which of the six perspective techniques they might use.

Alternate Activity

Materials:
- Art Journal
- 12" × 18" heavy white drawing paper
- pencils, erasers
- tempera paint
- paintbrushes
- cotton swabs
- water containers
- newspaper

1. As a class, make a list on the board of places you have visited, places you would like to visit, or places that are meaningful to you. Decide on one place you want to depict, and collect images of that place.

2. In your Art Journal, plan your ideas for your outdoor scene. Make sure to include the six perspective techniques.

3. Lightly draw your best ideas onto the drawing paper. Begin by painting the sky first. Your other objects will then overlap this area of your painting.

4. Paint in solid areas first and add details on top last. Use the cotton swab to paint the shape of the heads of any people that might be included in your scene. Add shadows, highlights, and textures last.

Research in Art Education

One case study showed that students who were "learning disabled and who were 'reluctant' readers" were better able to engage in reading when the creation and analysis of visual art was incorporated into their discussions of stories. This suggests that combining visual art with reading may help certain readers ("Reading *Is* Seeing: Using Visual Response to Improve the Literacy Reading of Reluctant Readers" in, *Critical Links,* p. 144). As students study the use of space in two-dimensional art, encourage them to think about the impact that illustrations have on a book.

Assessment

Use the following rubric to evaluate the artwork students make in the Creative Expression activity and to assess students' understanding of space in two-dimensional art.

	Art History and Culture	Aesthetic Perception	Creative Expression	Art Criticism
3 POINTS	The student can demonstrate knowledge of the lives and work of Winslow Homer and William Adolphe Bouguereau.	The student accurately identifies the use of space in two-dimensional art.	The student's painting clearly illustrates the use of space in two-dimensional art.	The student thoughtfully and honestly evaluates own work using the four steps of art criticism.
2 POINTS	The student's knowledge of the lives and work of Winslow Homer and William Adolphe Bouguereau is weak or incomplete.	The student shows emerging awareness of space in two-dimensional art.	The student's painting shows some awareness of space in two-dimensional art.	The student attempts to evaluate own work, but shows an incomplete understanding of evaluation criteria.
1 POINT	The student cannot demonstrate knowledge of the lives and work of Winslow Homer or William Adolphe Bouguereau.	The student cannot identify the use of space in two-dimensional art.	The student's painting shows no understanding of space in two-dimensional art.	The student makes no attempt to evaluate own artwork.

Have students complete page 23 or 24 in their **Assessment** books.

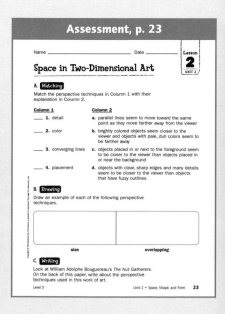

Assessment, p. 23

Name _____ Date _____

Space in Two-Dimensional Art

Lesson **2** UNIT 2

A. Matching

Match the perspective techniques in Column 1 with their explanation in Column 2.

Column 1
____ 1. detail
____ 2. color
____ 3. converging lines
____ 4. placement

Column 2
a. parallel lines seem to move toward the same point as they move farther away from the viewer
b. brightly colored objects seem closer to the viewer and objects with pale, dull colors seem to be farther away
c. objects placed in or next to the foreground seem to be closer to the viewer than objects placed in or near the background
d. objects with clear, sharp edges and many details seem to be closer to the viewer than objects that have fuzzy outlines

B. Drawing

Draw an example of each of the following perspective techniques.

size	overlapping

C. Writing

Look at William Adolphe Bouguereau's *The Nut Gatherers.* On the back of this paper, write about the perspective techniques used in this work of art.

Level 5 — Unit 2 • Space, Shape, and Form — 23

Lesson

3

Overview

Linear Perspective

Lesson 3 introduces linear perspective. Artists use linear perspective techniques to make things seem close or far away in a two-dimensional artwork.

Objectives

Art History and Culture

To demonstrate knowledge of the lives and work of Childe Hassam and Frederick Brosen

Creative Expression

To create a one-point perspective cityscape using techniques to create depth

Aesthetic Perception

To identify linear perspective techniques used in art NSAE 2.b

Art Criticism

To evaluate one's own work using the four steps of art criticism

Vocabulary Vocabulary

Review the following vocabulary words with students.

foreground frente—the part of the picture plane that seems to be closest to the viewer

background fondo—the top part of the picture plane that seems to be the farthest from the viewer

middle ground medio fondo—the area between the background and foreground

See page 89B for additional vocabulary and Spanish vocabulary resources.

Art Journal: Vocabulary

Have students add these words to the Vocabulary section of their Art Journals.

Lesson Materials

- 12" × 18" white drawing paper
- pencils and erasers
- rulers
- watercolor paints
- paintbrushes
- water dishes
- masking tape
- sketch paper
- paper towels

Alternate Materials:
- felt-tip pens
- sponges

Program Resources

- *Reading and Writing Test Prep.*, pp. 22–23
- *Transparency 9*
- *Artist Profiles*, pp. 12, 30
- *Animals Through History Time Line*
- *Assessment*, pp. 25–26
- *Large Print 63* The Icebergs
- *The National Museum of Women in the Arts Collection*

Concept Trace

Linear Perspective

Introduced: Level 4, Unit 5, Lesson 1

Reinforced: Level 6, Unit 1, Lesson 5

Lesson 3 Arts Integration

Theatre

Complete Unit 2, Lesson 3, on pages 40–41 of *Theatre Arts Connections.*

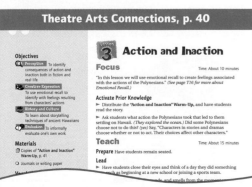

Theatre Arts Connections, p. 40

Music

 Listen to Russian "Sailors Dance" from *The Red Poppy* by Reinhold Gliere. The main melody repeats many times with variations that keep our interest. When is it the most intense? Why? Discuss the instrumentation of the variations.

Movement & Dance

Use linear perspective to show space. Demonstrate the following with a group of students. Each student finds a point in space at which to begin and travels on a straight line to a new point in space, showing the idea of moving through space in a linear way.

Time: About 10 minutes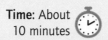

Activate Prior Knowledge

"Have you ever looked at a painting and noticed that some objects appear close and others appear to be farther away?" "¿Alguna vez han observado una pintura y han notado que algunos objetos parecen estar más cerca y otros parecen estar más lejos?"

■ Discuss the students' responses. Ask them to give specific examples, if possible.

Using Literature ⭐ Reading

■ Share Richard Peck's *A Year Down Yonder* with the class. Ask students to explain how the artwork on the cover uses the foreground, middle ground, and background to create the illusion of depth.

Thematic Connection ⭐ Social Studies

■ **Our Neighborhood at Work:** Discuss the industries important to your community.

Introduce the Art

Look

"Let's take a close look at the two works of art." "Vamos a observar detalladamente las dos obras de arte."

Point of View ⭐ Reading

■ Have students consider the artists' points of view as they painted the landscapes. An artist's point of view takes the viewer to that specific place. Some things may be hidden from view.

Cause and Effect ⭐ Reading

■ Ask students to identify objects that have been painted in the foreground, middle ground, and background. What effect does this placement have on the viewer? The viewer feels as if there is space in the two-dimensional artwork.

 Art History and Culture

Frederick Brosen's *Watts Street* appears to be a modern city scene from New York City.

🖥 **Web Connection**

Have students visit **www.spanierman.com/hassam/hassam.htm** to research more about the life and work of Childe Hassam.

 Lesson **3** Linear Perspective

◀ **Childe Hassam.** (American). *Lower Manhattan (View Down Broad Street).* 1907.
....
Oil on canvas. 30¼ × 16 inches (76.2 × 40.64 cm.). Herbert F. Johnson Museum of Art, Cornell University, Ithaca, New York.

Look at the artwork on these pages. Notice how the artists brought some objects in the paintings closer to the viewer and moved other objects farther away.

 Art History and Culture

Which of these New York City scenes appears to be modern?

🏺 **Art History and Culture**

Childe Hassam

Childe Hassam (chīld ha´səm) (1859–1935) was known for his emphasis on brilliant light, bright colors, and the shimmering quality that his paintings feature. A Massachusetts native, Hassam studied at the Boston Art School and later in Paris. He is an American impressionist. Many of his paintings and etchings are of city scenes in New York City and landscapes of New England's countryside.

See pages 16–21 and 24–25 for more about art history and the subject matter.

Artist Profiles, p. 30

◆ Artist Profile ◆
Childe Hassam
1859-1935

Childe Hassam (child has´ əm) was born in Dorchester, Massachusetts. During high school he began work as an accountant. When his father's hardware store burned down he needed to make more money, so he became a wood engraver's apprentice. His natural artistic talent helped him become a freelance illustrator while studying drawing and painting with William Rimmer and Ignaz Gaugengigl. Hassam painted in Paris, France, for a few years, and upon his return to America, he settled in New York City. In 1889 he joined a group of impressionists called the Ten American Painters, who exhibited together each year for 20 years. Hassam won many prizes and awards for his work and was elected

Study both works of art to find perspective techniques.

▶ Follow the lines of the buildings and the streets that lead to the area that looks the farthest away.

▶ What types of shapes are repeated in each painting? How did the artist make some shapes appear farther away?

▶ Identify objects in the foreground, middle ground, and background in both paintings.

▶ Describe the use of detail in both works of art.

▲ **Frederick Brosen.** (American). *Watts Street.* 1998.
....
Watercolor on paper. 30 × 47 inches (76.2 × 119.38 cm.). Forum Gallery, New York, New York.

 Aesthetic Perception

Seeing Like an Artist Look down a hallway. Compare the size of a nearby object to one that is farther away. How does the size of these objects appear to change as you walk down the hallway?

Art History and Culture

Frederick Brosen

Frederick Brosen (fre´drik brō´ sən) (1954–) has been called one of America's finest contemporary watercolor artists. Brosen is from New York City and is known for his painted cityscapes. He works primarily with watercolors. Because of his commitment to detail, people often mistake his paintings for photographs. Frederick Brosen's method consists of sketching the scene, photographing it, sketching it again, and then painting it using many layers of watercolor paint.

See pages 16–21 and 24–25 for more about art history and the subject matter.

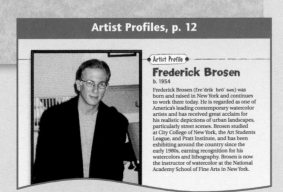

Artist Profiles, p. 12

• Artist Profile •
Frederick Brosen
b. 1954

Frederick Brosen (fre´drik brō´ sən) was born and raised in New York and continues to work there today. He is regarded as one of America's leading contemporary watercolor artists and has received great acclaim for his realistic depictions of urban landscapes, particularly street scenes. Brosen studied at City College of New York, the Art Students League, and Pratt Institute, and has been exhibiting around the country since the early 1980s, earning recognition for his watercolors and lithography. Brosen is now the instructor of watercolor at the National Academy School of Fine Arts in New York.

Study

▶ Monitor as students follow the lines of the buildings and streets with their fingers until they come to the vanishing point.

▶ Squares, rectangles, and circles are repeated in both paintings. The shapes are smaller as they move farther away.

▶ In Hassam's painting, people can be found in the foreground, buildings in the middle ground, and sky in the background. In Brosen's painting, cars can be found in the foreground; street signs, buildings, and sunlight in the middle ground; and sky in the background.

▶ In Hassam's painting, the people in the foreground appear most distinct and are painted with clearer detail than those in the middleground or background. In Brosen's painting, the street signs become blurry the farther away they appear to be.

■ For more examples of landscapes, see *The National Museum of Women in the Arts Collection.*

 Art Journal: Writing
Have students write in their Art Journals about jobs in their community that they would like to learn more about.

 **Aesthetic Perception**

Design Awareness Have students stand scattered down a hallway and rotate positions until each has stood at the end. Ask students to notice the size of their classmates when viewed from the foreground, middle ground, and background.

Developing Visual Literacy Ask students to suggest a storyline that either painting illustrates. Have students explain who the main character is in the story, where the main character is during this scene, and what is happening at this point in the story.

 Web Connection
Have students visit **www.forumgallery.com/index2 .html** to read more about the life and works of Frederick Brosen.

Teach

Time: About 30 minutes

"Were you able to see linear perspective?"
"¿Pudieron ver la perspectiva lineal?"

- Discuss the definitions of perspective, linear perspective, horizon line, and vanishing point on page 76.

Practice

Material: a hallway

- Have students follow the directions on page 76.

- Take students into the hallway of your school. Instruct them to close one eye and raise a pointed index finger to a nearby place where a wall meets the ceiling. Have students then move their fingers, without moving their feet, along this line until their eyes reach the end of the hall. Ask students to do the same with the lines where the walls meet the floor. Both times, students should end with their finger pointing at eye level.

Creative Expression

Materials: 12" × 18" white drawing paper, pencils and erasers, rulers, watercolor paints, paintbrushes, water dishes, masking tape, sketch paper, paper towels

Alternate Materials: felt-tip pens, sponges

- Distribute the materials and have students follow the directions on page 77.

- Review the Activity Tips on page 234 for visual examples of this lesson's activity.

- If time allows, ask students to paint using sponges for visual texture.

Art Journal: Sketching

Take students outside or place them at a window and ask them to sketch the landscape from at least two different vantage points in the Ideas section of their Art Journals. Encourage students to pick objects from these sketches when designing their Creative Expression activity.

Using Linear Perspective

Perspective is the method used to create the illusion of depth on a flat surface. Artists use one-point perspective to make viewers think they are looking at an object that is farther back than the rest of the image.

Linear perspective is one way of using lines to show distance and depth. In one-point perspective, all lines that move back into space meet at a single point.

The **horizon line** is the point at which the earth and the sky meet. The horizon line is always at the viewer's eye level.

The **vanishing point** is the point on the horizon line where all parallel receding lines meet.

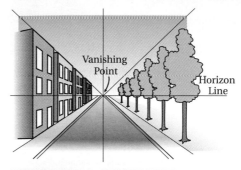

Practice

Practice seeing linear perspective.

1. Look down the length of the hallway. Point each index finger toward the lines where the ceiling meets the walls beside you.

2. While standing still, move your fingers along those lines until they are pointing to the end of the hall. Notice how your arms move together down to eye level.

3. Do this again, but this time point to the lines where the walls meet the floor. How did your arms move?

Differentiated Instruction

Reteach
Have students look through their textbooks for works of art that use foreground, middle ground, and background to create depth in a two-dimensional space.

Special Needs
Use a photograph of one-point perspective in architecture with a transparency placed over it. Have students find the vanishing point and use a marker to identify and trace the lines that converge at that point. Once the drawing is complete, the students can remove the transparency and display the two images side by side.

ELL
Have students create a three-dimensional scene with their classmates. Place some students in the foreground, some in the middle ground, and others in the background. Ask students to identify the picture planes in the posed scene.

◄ **Sally Brannen.**
Age 11.

Think about how the student artist used linear perspective.

Creative Expression

How can you use one-point perspective to create depth? Draw a city street using linear perspective.

1. Think of a place you have read about or studied. Make several sketches of objects and two or three buildings you want in your scene.

2. Lightly draw a horizon line. Mark a point where the lines will meet. Draw at least four lines coming out from the vanishing point on the horizon line. Using these guide lines, draw the buildings first, then the objects. Make the objects touch the top and bottom of the guide lines.

3. Paint your drawing.

Art Criticism

Describe Describe the cityscape you created. What objects did you include?

Analyze How did you use linear perspective in your work?

Interpret What objects communicate the kind of scene you created? Give your work a title.

Decide How could you apply the technique of linear perspective to another drawing?

Reflect

Time: About 30 minutes

Review and Assess

"Were you able to create a cityscape using one-point linear perspective?" "¿Pudieron crear un paisaje urbano usando la perspectiva líneal de un punto?"

Think

The student artist created a vanishing point in the sky. The building, windows, and street have lines that lead to the vanishing point. The student used one-point linear perspective to create the illusion of depth in this cityscape painting.

■ Use **Large Print 63** *The Icebergs* to have students identify and describe the use of depth in art.

Informal Assessment

■ For standardized-format test practice using this lesson's art content, see pages 22–23 in **Reading and Writing Test Preparation.**

Art Journal: Critical Thinking

Have students answer the four art criticism questions—Describe, Analyze, Interpret, and Decide—in their Art Journals. In small groups, have students discuss their one-point perspective cityscapes. NSAE 2.a

Art Across the Curriculum

Use these simple ideas to reinforce art concepts across the curriculum.

★ **Descriptive Writing** Have students write a descriptive paragraph about the real or imaginary city they have painted.

★ **Math** Discuss ratios after deciding how the picture plane will be divided. Compare equal proportions to those weighted differently.

★ **Science** Explain that the lines that move from the foreground to the vanishing point are called *orthogonals* and the lines that move horizontally are called *transversals*. These lines bisect and are used when studying the science of geometrical shapes.

★ **Social Studies** In Childe Hassam's painting, you can see Federal Hall in Lower Manhattan. This was the nation's first capitol, and it is where George Washington took the presidential oath. It is now the home of the New York Stock Exchange.

★ **Technology** Students can illustrate a three-dimensional form using the 3-D style in a presentation program. Visit **SRAonline.com** for further instructions. NSAE 6.b

Linear Perspective

Extra! For the Art Specialist

Time: About 30 minutes

Focus

Study **Large Print 63** *The Icebergs,* and discuss how the objects in the artwork appear to move back into space to one single point. Can you run your finger over the tops of the objects to a single point? What about the objects makes them look three-dimensional?

Teach

Discuss how artists create the illusion of depth on a flat, two-dimensional surface by using a method known as perspective. Review the six perspective techniques. Explain that linear perspective is another method used to create depth. With linear perspective, the objects appear to move back in space to a single point. This single point is called the vanishing point.

Reflect

Have students evaluate their works of art using the four steps of art criticism.

Alternate Activity

Materials:
- 9″ × 12″ white drawing paper
- rulers
- drawing boards
- pencils, erasers
- colored pencils

1. Sit in the hallway. Draw a picture of the hall using the one-point linear perspective technique. Begin by drawing the end of the hall. It will be either a rectangle or square shape. Lightly draw a dot within this shape. Line up the top and bottom sidewalls with a point. If the walls meet the corners of the end of the hall, then line up the dot with each of the four corners of your shape. If the end wall is another hall, show that by drawing a vertical line, and line up the top and bottom of that line with your dot.

2. Once the main halls are penciled in, lightly add details such as bulletin boards and doors. The top and bottom of all objects on the sidewalls will always line up with the vanishing point.

3. Add color to the completed drawing with colored pencils.

Research
in Art Education

"Children respond to art in a holistic manner; their reactions are immediate, subjective, and rarely go beyond the 'like/don't like' stage . . . It takes a sensitive teacher to help educate the vision of the child so that appreciation may occur." (Hurwitz, Al, and Stanley Madeja. *The Joyous Vision.* New Jersey: Prentice Hall, 1997.)

Assessment

Use the following rubric to evaluate the artwork students make in the Creative Expression activity and to assess students' understanding of linear perspective.

Have students complete page 25 or 26 in their *Assessment* books.

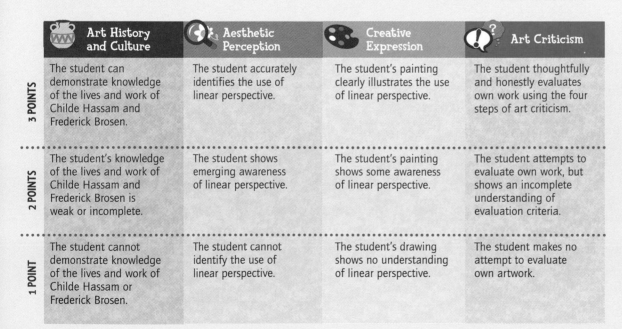

	Art History and Culture	Aesthetic Perception	Creative Expression	Art Criticism
3 POINTS	The student can demonstrate knowledge of the lives and work of Childe Hassam and Frederick Brosen.	The student accurately identifies the use of linear perspective.	The student's painting clearly illustrates the use of linear perspective.	The student thoughtfully and honestly evaluates own work using the four steps of art criticism.
2 POINTS	The student's knowledge of the lives and work of Childe Hassam and Frederick Brosen is weak or incomplete.	The student shows emerging awareness of linear perspective.	The student's painting shows some awareness of linear perspective.	The student attempts to evaluate own work, but shows an incomplete understanding of evaluation criteria.
1 POINT	The student cannot demonstrate knowledge of the lives and work of Childe Hassam or Frederick Brosen.	The student cannot identify the use of linear perspective.	The student's drawing shows no understanding of linear perspective.	The student makes no attempt to evaluate own artwork.

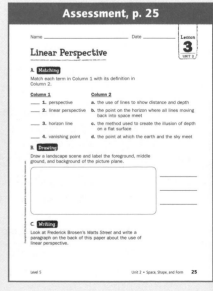

Assessment, p. 25

Name _____ Date _____

Lesson **3** UNIT 2

Linear Perspective

A. Matching
Match each term in Column 1 with its definition in Column 2.

Column 1
_____ 1. perspective
_____ 2. linear perspective
_____ 3. horizon line
_____ 4. vanishing point

Column 2
a. the use of lines to show distance and depth
b. the point on the horizon where all lines moving back into space meet
c. the method used to create the illusion of depth on a flat surface
d. the point at which the earth and the sky meet

B. Drawing
Draw a landscape scene and label the foreground, middle ground, and background of the picture plane.

C. Writing
Look at Frederick Brosen's *Watts Street* and write a paragraph on the back of this paper about the use of linear perspective.

Level 5

Unit 2 • Space, Shape, and Form 25

Shading

Lesson 4 introduces shading techniques. Artists use shading techniques to create the illusion of form and space on a two-dimensional surface.

Objectives

Art History and Culture

To demonstrate knowledge of the lives and work of Roger Brown and Robert McCall

Creative Expression

To plan and create a three-dimensional space station, using shading

Aesthetic Perception

To identify shading techniques used to create the illusion of form on a two-dimensional surface
NSAE 2.b

 Art Criticism

To evaluate one's own work using the four steps of art criticism

Lesson Materials
- 12″ × 18″ paper
- pencils
- oil pastels
- recording of Gustav Holst's *The Planets*
- colored pencils

Alternate Materials:
- markers

Program Resources
- *Reading and Writing Test Prep.,* pp. 24–25
- *Transparency 10*
- *Flash Cards* 1–3
- *Artist Profiles,* pp. 13, 40
- *Animals Through History Time Line*
- *Assessment,* pp. 27–28
- *Large Prints 63* The Icebergs and *64* Eagle Man
- *Art Around the World Collection*

Concept Trace
Shading
Introduced: Level 4, Unit 1, Lesson 6
Reinforced: Level 6, Unit 2, Lesson 2

Vocabulary Vocabulary

Review the following vocabulary word with students before beginning the lesson.

form forma—objects, either geometric or free-form, that have three dimensions

See page 89B for additional Spanish vocabulary resources.

Art Journal: Vocabulary

Have students add this word to the Vocabulary section of their Art Journals.

Lesson 4 Arts Integration

Theatre

Complete Unit 2, Lesson 4, on pages 42–43 of *Theatre Arts Connections.*

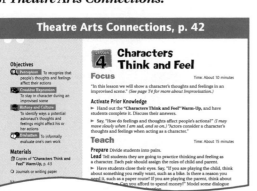

Theatre Arts Connections, p. 42

Music

As we look back in music history, one of the biggest changes is how the composers group sounds of the instruments in non-traditional ways. This gives us new tone colors. Richard Gill is a living composer from Australia. He combines the very large and the very small in "Dance for Piccolo, Oboe, Bassoon, and Side Drum." Listen to the humor created by the contrasts of sound.

Movement & Dance

Put white paper on a wall and darken the room. Give three students flashlights, which they will shine on the paper. Another group of three students moves across the pathway of the light so that shadows appear on the paper behind them. Discuss how, in art, shadows relate to shading.

Focus

Time: About 10 minutes

Activate Prior Knowledge

"Have you ever looked at a painting and noticed that things look three-dimensional?" "¿Alguna vez han visto una pintura y han notado cómo las cosas parecen ser tridimensionales?"

■ Discuss students' responses. Ask them to give specific examples, if possible.

Using Literature Reading

■ Share Sorche Nic Leodhas's book *Always Room for One More.* Ask students to identify the shading techniques that they see in this book. You may also want to use Susan Milford's book *Tales of the Shimmering Sky: Ten Global Folktales with Activities.* This book exposes children to celestial-inspired folktales from around the world.

Thematic Connection Science

■ **Space:** Have students share what they know about space exploration and travel.

Introduce the Art

Look

"Let's take a close look at the two works of art." "Vamos a observar detalladamente las dos obras de arte."

Main Idea and Details Reading

■ Have students identify the main ideas in each painting and explain how the details support the main idea.

Cause and Effect Reading

■ Have students identify the areas of shading and the effects on each painting.

 Art History and Culture

Robert McCall's *Space Station #1* was created during the Cold War and the U.S./Soviet Union race to the moon. The U.S.'s first space station, *Skylab,* was launched in 1973. At the time of Roger Brown's painting, Christa McAuliffe, a teacher, accompanied the *Challenger* crew, and the American middle class entered the age of space travel. NSAE 4.b

Web Connection

Have students visit **www.artic.edu/saic/art/brown/** to explore the life and works of Roger Brown.

78 UNIT 2 • Space, Shape, and Form

Look at the artwork on these pages. Notice the common theme and how the two artists created very different paintings by using space in their artwork. Both Robert McCall and Roger Brown used **shading** techniques to give these two-dimensional paintings the illusion of depth.

▲ **Roger Brown.** (American). *Homesick Proof Space Station.* 1987.

Oil on canvas. 48 × 72 inches (121.92 × 182.88 cm.). Phyllis Kind Gallery, Chicago, Illinois.

 Art History and Culture

How has American space travel influenced these artists and their artwork?

78 Unit 2 • Lesson 4

 Art History and Culture

Roger Brown

Roger Brown (roj´ər broun) (1941–1997) belonged to a group of artists known as the "Chicago imagists." Brown, like many of these artists, painted landscapes with few people and simple colors. His paintings were meant to express how he felt about the picture more than to portray reality. The people in his paintings are usually dark shadows in the shapes of people. From a distance, the surface of many of his paintings look patterned. Brown also used unusual scales in the same painting. For example, he sometimes made the people inside buildings look larger or smaller than life-size.

See pages 16–21 and 24–25 for more about art history and the subject matter.

Artist Profiles, p. 13

Artist Profile

Roger Brown
1941–1997

Roger Brown (roj´ər broun) was born in Hamilton, Alabama. He moved to Chicago when he was 21 and studied for several years at the Art Institute of Chicago. He received his master's degree in fine arts in 1970. His art has been shown in many museums around the United States. Even though he lived and worked in Chicago, Brown liked to paint scenes of different regions of the country. The primary focus of his art was the land and people of the United States.

▲ **Robert McCall.** (American). *Space Station #1.* c. 1968.

Mixed media on canvas. 40½ × 53 inches (102.87 × 134.62 cm.). National Museum of Air and Space, Smithsonian Institution, Washington, D.C.

Study both works of art to find forms.

▶ Find a cylinder or cube. Are there overlapping forms?

▶ Identify the shading in these works of art.

▶ What effect does it have on the subject when an object's coloring goes from light to dark?

Aesthetic Perception

Seeing Like an Artist Look around the classroom. Can you tell what objects are casting shadows? Would you know what the objects were if you could see only the shadows?

Study NSAE 5.c

▶ Overlapping forms can be seen in *Space Station #1* in the center of the space station.

▶ In *Homesick Proof Space Station,* the people are casting shadows. In *Space Station #1,* the upper part of the space station is casting a shadow in the lower part. A shadow also appears on the planet.

▶ This sharp contrast creates a feeling of floating.

■ For more examples of art from North America, see the ***Art Around the World Collection.***

Art Journal: Writing

Have students write a short paragraph in their Art Journals explaining why they would or would not like to join a team of astronauts traveling to a space station.

Aesthetic Perception

Seeing Like an Artist Have students identify an area in the classroom where they can see shadows. Determine which direction the lighting is coming from, and notice the effect it has on the objects in that area.

Developing Visual Literacy Ask students to think about the type of music they would use to further develop the mood portrayed in one of the paintings in this lesson. Encourage students to explain how it might affect the viewer's experience.
NSAE 6.a

Art History and Culture

Robert McCall

Robert McCall (rob´ ərt mə käl´) (1919–) is a graphic artist and a painter. He created paintings for such movies as *Star Trek* and *2001: A Space Odyssey.* He has painted murals at the Smithsonian Institution's National Air and Space Museum in Washington, D.C., and at the EPCOT Center in Disney World, in Florida. McCall watches spaceships take off from Cape Canaveral and then draws his impression of the events. He uses many crisp, bright colors such as blues and oranges to make the explosions look powerful and hot.

See pages 16–21 and 24–25 for more about art history and the subject matter.

Artist Profiles, p. 40

◆ Artist Profile ◆

Robert McCall
b. 1919

Robert McCall (ro´ bərt mə kōl´) was born in Columbus, Ohio. He studied art at The Columbus Art School for two years. He is interested in the wonder of the universe and the mysteries of space. Along with other artists, McCall was invited by NASA to observe the development of the space program. His drawings and paintings recorded the wonder and excitement everyone felt about exploring space. As one of the official artists of the U.S. space program, he has painted pictures of space travel for more than 30 years. He has also designed postage stamps for the U.S. government. He recently designed a large wall of stained-glass windows with his wife, Louise, who is also an artist.

Web Connection

Have students visit **www.thetech.org/2001ds/ art_mccall/01_odyssey.html** for further information on Robert McCall.

LESSON 4 • Shading **79**

each

 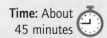

"How can you change shapes into forms?"
"¿Cómo pueden convertir las figuras en formas?"

■ Discuss the definitions of form on page 80.

Practice

Materials: white paper, pencils

Alternate Materials: markers

■ Have students follow the directions on page 80.

■ Have students draw four different shapes of their choice and label them *Hatching, Cross-Hatching, Stippling,* and *Blending.* Instruct students to change these two-dimensional shapes into forms by applying the shading technique labeled under each shape.

Creative Expression

Materials: pencils, 12" × 18" white paper, recording of Gustav Holst's *The Planets,* colored pencils

Alternate Materials: oil pastels

■ Distribute the materials and have students follow the directions on page 81.

■ Play Holst's *The Planets* while students are working.

■ Review the Activity Tips on page 234 for visual examples of this lesson's activity.

■ See the Technique Tips on page 217 for information on using oil pastels.

Art Journal: Brainstorming

Have students brainstorm ideas for designing a space station and the kinds of forms they will use. Have them list their ideas in their Art Journals.

80 UNIT 2 • Space, Shape, and Form

Using Shading

Shading is the use of dark values to create the illusion of form and texture. Shading techniques include **hatching, cross-hatching, blending,** and **stippling.**

To create the illusion of form on a two-dimensional surface, artists use shading techniques.

Hatching   Blending

Cross-hatching   Stippling

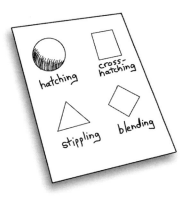

Practice

Create the illusion of forms by using different types of shading techniques. Use pencils.

1. Lightly draw four different shapes. Beneath each, write *hatching, cross-hatching, stippling,* or *blending.*

2. Make each shape appear to be a form by using the shading technique written below it.

80   Unit 2 • Lesson 4

Differentiated Instruction

Reteach
Look through *The National Museum of Women in the Arts Collection* to find examples of shading techniques used in works of art.

Special Needs
Demonstrate for students how to blend oil pastels, providing them with an opportunity to practice this skill before they begin adding color to their pictures.

ELL
Allow students to explore the multiple meanings of the word *shade* and to create visual illustrations for each.

◀ **Mike Kwon.**
Age 11.

Think about how the student artist used shading techniques to affect the appearance of the space station.

 Creative Expression

What types of forms would you use to design a space station? Draw a three-dimensional space station. Use shading techniques to create the illusion of form.

1. Use simple shapes to sketch your space station. Use the shading techniques to change these shapes into forms.

2. Draw planets. Use blending techniques to move from light to dark. Try complementary colors for shading. Add white highlights.

3. Add an atmosphere by using the side of the oil pastel to make long sweeping marks.

Art Criticism

Describe Describe your space station and the shapes you used to draw it.

Analyze What shading techniques did you use?

Interpret How did the colors affect the appearance of your space station? Would you like to live there?

Decide If you drew another space station, what would you do differently?

 **Reflect** Time: About 30 minutes

Review and Assess

"Were you able to draw a three-dimensional space station using shading techniques?"

"¿Pudieron dibujar una estación espacial tridimensional usando técnicas de sombreado?"

Think

The student artist used shading techniques to add depth to the shapes and create forms.

■ Use *Large Print 63 The Icebergs* to have students identify and describe the use of shading techniques.

Informal Assessment

■ For standardized-format test practice using this lesson's art content, see pages 24–25 in *Reading and Writing Test Preparation.*

Art Journal: Critical Thinking

Have students answer the four art criticism questions—Describe, Analyze, Interpret, and Decide—in their Art Journals. In small groups, have students discuss their space stations.
NSAE 2.b

◆ Art Across the Curriculum ◆

Use these simple ideas to reinforce art concepts across the curriculum.

★ **Personal Writing** Ask students to practice personal writing by making a list of the things they would pack for a week's vacation in a space station.

★ **Math** Students can identify geometric forms when building a three-dimensional space station.

★ **Science** Much of the information we have about our solar system was gathered by unpiloted space probes such as *Voyager 1* and *Voyager 2*. Have students research and report on the *Voyager* Project.

★ **Social Studies** Brainstorm the effect that space travel has had on our culture. Imagine vacations in space. How would this change our lives on Earth?

★ **Technology** Have students explore the use of borders and shading in a word-processing document. Visit **SRAonline.com** for further instructions.
NSAE 6.b

For the Art Specialist

Extra!

Time: About 30 minutes

Focus

Study *Large Print 63* *The Icebergs,* and ask students to point out the various shading techniques used. How do you think the artist created each of the shading techniques you see?

Teach

Review the four shading techniques: hatching, cross-hatching, blending, and stippling. Explain to students that they will be creating a nonobjective drawing using all four shading techniques to create the illusion of form. Demonstrate by using each of the shading techniques. Point out that the darkest area of an object is the area farthest from the light.

Reflect

Have students evaluate their works of art using the four steps of art criticism. Encourage them to locate and describe areas in the classroom where they would use shading to draw a scene.

Alternate Activity

Materials:
- 9" × 12" white drawing paper
- rulers
- pencils, erasers
- fine-point markers
- colored pencils

1. Randomly place a combination of five geometric shapes on drawing paper so that none touch. Use a marker to outline the shapes.

2. In one of the shapes, use a marker to draw hatching to create the illusion of form. Use cross-hatching and stippling in two other shapes.

3. In a fourth shape, use colored pencils to create blending. In the last shape, combine any two of the shading techniques.

4. Use either straight or curved lines to create a design in your background. Add color to your completed drawing using colored pencils.

Research in Art Education

There are several possible reasons for the academic achievement associated with student involvement in arts organizations. Arts organizations tend to place high expectations for achievement on participating students; they give students a chance to perform school-related tasks (such as reading, calculating, and planning), and these organizations value and encourage risk taking ("Living the Arts Through Language and Learning" in *Critical Links,* p. 78). Discuss with students the risks that are taken by artists and the risks they take in their own lives.

Assessment
Use the following rubric to evaluate the artwork students make in the Creative Expression activity and to assess students' understanding of shading.

Have students complete pages 27–28 in their *Assessment* books.

	Art History and Culture	Aesthetic Perception	Creative Expression	Art Criticism
3 POINTS	The student can demonstrate knowledge of the lives and work of Roger Brown and Robert McCall.	The student accurately identifies the use of shading.	The student's drawing clearly illustrates the use of shading.	The student thoughtfully and honestly evaluates own work using the four steps of art criticism.
2 POINTS	The student's knowledge of the lives and work of Roger Brown and Robert McCall is weak or incomplete.	The student shows emerging awareness of shading.	The student's drawing shows some awareness of shading.	The student attempts to evaluate own work, but shows an incomplete understanding of evaluation criteria.
1 POINT	The student cannot demonstrate knowledge of the lives and work of Roger Brown or Robert McCall.	The student cannot identify the use of shading.	The student's drawing shows no understanding of shading.	The student makes no attempt to evaluate own artwork.

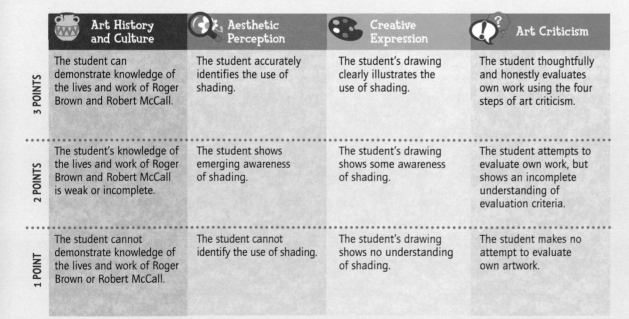

Lesson 5 Overview
Form

Lesson 5 introduces the use of form. Artists use the height, width, and depth of form to create three-dimensional works of art.

Objectives

Art History and Culture
To demonstrate knowledge of the lives and work of Frank Stella and Tony Smith

Creative Expression
To create a paper sculpture with three-dimensional forms

Aesthetic Perception
To identify the use of form in a work of art NSAE 2.b

Art Criticism
To evaluate one's own work using the four steps of art criticism

Vacabulary Vocabulary

Review the following vocabulary words with students.

form forma—a three-dimensional object that takes up space using height, width, and depth

freestanding sculpture escultura autoestable—a three-dimensional sculpture that is surrounded by space on all sides

relief sculpture escultura en relieve—a three-dimensional sculpture in which objects stick out from a flat surface

See page 89B for additional Spanish vocabulary resources.

Art Journal: Vocabulary
Have students add these words to the Vocabulary section of their Art Journals.

Lesson Materials
- papers of varied stocks, colors, and sizes
- 12" × 18" sheets of colored construction paper
- markers

Alternate Materials:
- paint and paintbrushes

Program Resources
- *Reading and Writing Test Prep.*, pp. 26–27
- *Transparency 11*
- *Artist Profiles*, pp. 54, 55
- *Animals Through History Time Line*
- *Assessment*, pp. 29–30
- *Large Print 64* Eagle Man
- *The National Museum of Women in the Arts Collection*

Concept Trace
Form
Introduced: Level 4, Unit 4, Lesson 1
Reinforced: Level 6, Unit 1, Lessons 3, 4

Lesson 5 Arts Integration

Theatre
Complete Unit 2, Lesson 5, on pages 44–45 of *Theatre Arts Connections.*

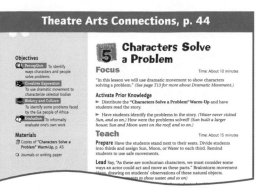

Music
Texture in music describes whether one melody is alone or with other contrasting melodies, or with harmonic accompaniment. Listen to The Moldau by Bedrich Smetana. "The Moldau" is a river in his native Czechoslovakia. The piece starts with a small flow of melody from two flutes like two streams coming out of the mountains. Listen to how the texture changes as instruments are added.

Movement & Dance
Give students Chinese jump ropes or large, circular pieces of elastic. Have students place feet or arms on the ropes to stretch them into various shapes. Working with partners, the students should find ways to put one shape inside another. Ask students to create three partner shapes and organize them into a sequence.

Focus

Time: About 20 minutes

Activate Prior Knowledge

"What do you know about how forms are used in works of art?" "¿Qué saben acerca de cómo se usan las formas en las obras de arte?"

■ Discuss students' responses. Remind students that three-dimensional sculptures and statues use forms.

Using Literature ★ Reading

■ Read Armstrong Sperry's *Call It Courage*. Discuss with students the theme of taking a stand.

Thematic Connection ★ Social Studies

■ **Taking a Stand:** Ask students to share a time when they took a stand and how that felt.

Introduce the Art

Look

"Let's take a close look at the two works of art." "Vamos a observar detalladamente las dos obras de arte."

Making Inferences ★ Reading

■ Have students discuss what the artists may have been trying to communicate through these sculptures. Ask them to explain their reasoning.

Fact and Opinion ★ Reading

■ Have students make a list of facts and opinions for each artwork. Fact: *St. Michaels Counterguard* is made from aluminum and honeycomb fiberglass. Opinion: It looks like a musical instrument.

 Art History and Culture

Artists often seek inspiration for their work in religion, literature, and other fine arts that contribute to the culture of the people around them, and in other cultures that interest them. NSAE 5.a

🖥 **Web Connection**

Have students visit **www.nga.gov/kids/stella/ stella1.htm** to practice using art interpretation skills with some of Frank Stella's sculptures.

▲ **Frank Stella.** (American). *St. Michaels Counterguard.* 1984.

156 × 135 × 108 inches (396.24 × 342.9 × 274.32 cm.). Los Angeles County Museum of Art, Los Angeles, California.

Look at the artwork on these pages. Notice how Frank Stella and Tony Smith used three-dimensional forms to create interesting sculptures. Stella's piece is a *relief* sculpture because it hangs on the wall. Smith's is a *free-standing* piece because you can walk around it.

 Art History and Culture

Smith's sculpture was inspired by a character in the book *Finnegan's Wake.* Stella's sculpture is his interpretation of Saint Michael's sword. The counterguard is the part of the sword designed to protect the inner hand and body in battle.

 Art History and Culture

Frank Stella

Frank Stella (frangk stel´ə) (1936–) belonged to a group called "hardedge" painters. This group used geometric shapes and little color in their work. He started out as a minimalist in the 1960s, painting flat black canvases with white lines on them. Stella rejected the idea of incorporating emotions into his artwork. He stripped his art down to basic shapes and occasionally incorporated bright colors. Stella later worked as an architect and used what he knew about shapes and space to create buildings with interesting geometric form and function.

See pages 16–21 and 24–25 for more about art history and the subject matter.

Artist Profiles, p. 55

◆ Artist Profile ◆

Frank Stella
b. 1936

Frank Stella (frangk ste´ la) was born in Malden, Massachusetts, in 1936. He studied painting at Phillips Academy and majored in history at Princeton University. He supported himself after college by painting houses. He moved to New York City, where he had his first successful show called *Sixteen Americans.* At the age of 23, he was the youngest artist in the show. At first people were annoyed and shocked by his style. However, his talent was noticed by a few important gallery owners and critics who felt his work was exciting and new. Later in his life he became an architect.

▲ **Tony Smith.** (American).
Gracehoper. 1971.
....
Welded steel and paint 23 feet
(7 meters). The Detroit Institute
of Arts, Detroit, Michigan.

Study both works of art.

▶ Identify the forms, both geometric and free-form, that you see in each of the sculptures.

▶ What would be different about these works of art if the artists had decided to create them out of two-dimensional shapes instead of three-dimensional forms?

▶ Which artwork is a relief sculpture? Which is a free-standing sculpture?

Aesthetic Perception

Design Awareness Look around the classroom and find at least three shapes and three forms. Remember that shapes are two-dimensional, and forms have depth.

Art History and Culture

Tony Smith

Tony Smith (tō´ nē smith) (1912–1980) was a close friend of Jackson Pollock and initially began his artistic career as a painter. As a child recovering from tuberculosis in a small house, Smith was affected by the presence of a large black stove. The influence of that stove can be seen throughout his career as a sculptor. He also often incorporated the geometric shapes of the Pueblo buildings he saw on a trip to New Mexico. Tony Smith studied art part-time while working as a toolmaker for his father. He later worked as an apprentice for the architect Frank Lloyd Wright. He used milk containers, empty boxes, and egg cartons when experimenting with forms in space.

See pages 16–21 and 24–25 for more about art history and the subject matter.

Artist Profiles, p. 54

◆ Artist Profile ◆

Tony Smith
1912–1980

Tony Smith (tō´ nē smith) was born in New Jersey, the grandson of a designer and the son of an engineer. Although he grew up among builders, his artistic talent had a traumatic beginning. When he was four, he contracted tuberculosis and was forced to live alone in a little prefabricated house in his backyard. He lived there for a few years so his family would not be exposed to his germs. It was in this tiny quarantined space that he first modeled small pueblos like those he had seen at a World's fair and took his first steps toward a career in architectural sculpture.

Study   NSAE 5.c

▶ Many geometric forms can be seen in *St. Michaels Counterguard*. One example of a free-form form is the purple section on the left of the sculpture. There are many forms in *Gracehoper*. Examples of geometric forms in this sculpture are the triangular shapes that create the legs.

▶ If designed with two-dimensional shapes, you would no longer be able to move around the pieces because they would occupy the surrounding space.

▶ Frank Stella's *St. Michael's Counterguard* is a relief sculpture. Tony Smith's *Gracehoper* is a free-standing sculpture.

■ For more examples of abstract/nonobjective art, see *The National Museum of Women in the Arts Collection.*

Art Journal: Writing

In the Writing section of their Art Journals, have students describe a time when they stood up for themselves.

Aesthetic Perception

Design Awareness Have students look around the classroom from where they are sitting and make a list of forms, categorizing geometric and free-forms.

Developing Visual Literacy Discuss what students think the artists were trying to communicate with each sculpture. Encourage students to support the reasoning behind what they propose. Ask them if the title of the sculpture influenced them. Invite students to share a time when a brand name changed what they thought about a product.

Web Connection

Have students visit **www.dia.org/collections/Modern&Contemporary/index.** to research more about the Detroit Institute of Arts and Tony Smith's *Gracehoper.*

"How can you use paper-sculpture techniques to create unique forms?" "¿Cómo pueden usar las técnicas de esculturas de papel para crear formas únicas?"

- Discuss the definitions of form, scoring a straight line, scoring a curve, pleating, curling, fringing, and tab and slot on page 84.

Practice

Materials: different types of paper, rulers, scissors

- Have students follow the directions on page 84.
- Have students use many different types of paper, rulers, and scissors to practice working with the six paper-sculpting techniques reviewed in this lesson.

Creative Expression

Materials: paper, markers

Alternate Materials: paint and paintbrushes

- Distribute the materials and have students follow the directions on page 85.
- Review the Activity Tips on page 235 for visual examples of this lesson's activity.

Art Journal: Brainstorming
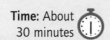
Have students plan what paper-sculpting techniques they want to use together to create a sculpture. Have them list their ideas in the their Art Journals.

Using Form

In a work of art, **form** creates space. It allows you, the viewer, to see into the artwork.

Artists use paper-sculpture techniques to create three-dimensional forms from two-dimensional paper.

Scoring a straight line

 Hold a ruler in the center of a piece of paper. Run the point of the scissors along one edge of the ruler to cut the paper in a straight line.

Curling

 Hold one end of a long strip of paper. Grip the middle of the paper strip next to the side of a pencil. With a quick motion, pull the strip firmly across the pencil.

Scoring a curve

 Gradually press a bending curve with the point of the scissors.

Fringing

 Make parallel straight cuts along the edge of a piece of paper to create a ruffled look.

Pleating

 Fold a piece of paper in from the edge. Then fold the same amount of paper in the other direction. Continue folding back and forth in this manner.

Tab and slot

 Tab and slot is a joining technique in which you cut a slot in one surface and insert a tab that has been cut out of another surface. You can glue or tape the tab for a stronger hold.

Practice

Experiment with paper-sculpture techniques.

1. Look at the paper-sculpture techniques on this page.
2. Using different kinds of paper, try each paper-sculpting technique.

Differentiated Instruction

Reteach

Have students look through the *Art Around the World Collection* to find examples of free-form sculptures and relief sculptures.

Special Needs

Students who have difficulty cutting may benefit from the use of easy-grip scissors for this lesson activity. Students could also tear the paper needed for folding and curling.

ELL

To help develop students' vocabulary skills and understanding of form, ask them to match two-dimensional shapes cut out of paper with the related three-dimensional forms.

◀ **Lauren Kaczynski.**
Age 10.

Think about how the student artist created a three-dimensional form from two-dimensional paper.

Creative Expression

How are forms created out of flat paper? Change a two-dimensional piece of paper into a three-dimensional form.

1. Use paper-sculpting techniques, especially scoring and folding to create forms. Use tab-and-slot techniques with glue to attach the pieces.

2. Cut into the paper without cutting it into two separate pieces.

3. Use markers to draw lines on the sculpture to enhance the edges of the forms.

4. Keep turning the sculpture and adding to the form so that it is interesting from many different points of view.

Art Criticism

Describe List the paper-sculpture techniques you used.

Analyze What types of forms did you create?

Interpret What mood does your artwork express?

Decide Were you successful in changing a two-dimensional piece of paper into a three-dimensional form?

Reflect

Review and Assess

"Were you able to create a paper-sculpture using the techniques you have learned?"
"¿Pudieron crear una escultura de papel usando las técnicas que aprendieron?"

Think

The student artist created a three-dimensional form using paper-sculpting techniques.

■ Use *Large Print 64 Eagle Man* to have students identify and describe the use of form in a work of art.

Informal Assessment

■ Organize an art show in which students display their portfolios. Encourage student to analyze their peers use of art elements and principles in the works of art.

■ For standardized-format test practice using this lesson's art content, see pages 26–27 in *Reading and Writing Test Preparation.*

Art Journal: Critical Thinking

Have students answer the four art criticism questions—Describe, Analyze, Interpret, and Decide—in their Art Journals. In small groups, have students discuss their three-dimensional forms. NSAE 2.b

Art Across the Curriculum

Use these simple ideas to reinforce art concepts across the curriculum.

★ **Expository Writing** Have students write the steps they used in the process of planning and building their paper sculptures.

★ **Math** Use equations to compute the area of basic geometric forms. Discuss how the element of depth adds to the space taken up by a form, as opposed to that of a two-dimensional shape.

★ **Science** Scientists asked origami expert Robert J. Lang to help design a space telescope that can fold and be stored in a rocket. Discuss with students other ways art can be a useful tool in scientific research.

★ **Social Studies** While working with paper-sculpting techniques, explore the history and craft of traditional Japanese origami.

★ **Technology** Have students create three-dimensional forms using a computer presentation program and experiment with the three-dimensional settings. See **SRAonline.com** to print detailed instructions for this activity. NSAE 6.b

Extra! For the Art Specialist

Time: About 30 minutes

Focus

Study *Large Print 64 Eagle Man,* and ask the students to explain the difference between a two-dimensional object and a three-dimensional form. Can you find the measurements in the credit line? What are they?

Teach

Look around the room for examples of form. Explain to the students that they will be creating a three-dimensional form similar to the work of Frank Stella. Demonstrate cutting posterboard or cardboard into geometric and free-form shapes no larger than your palm.

Reflect

Have students evaluate their works of art using the four steps of art criticism. Encourage them to identify shapes and forms in their work.

Alternate Activity

Materials:
- Art Journal
- 11″ × 11″ poster-board
- pencils, erasers
- scraps of poster-board and cardboard
- acrylic or tempera paints
- paintbrushes
- cotton swabs
- water containers
- newspaper

1. In your Art Journal, draw a variety of free-form shapes. Make some with only curved lines, others with only straight lines, and a few with a combination of lines.

2. Cut out 15 geometric and free-form shapes from scrap pieces of posterboard or cardboard.

3. Paint each shape and background a solid color. Use only three colors. Use a small brush and cotton swabs to add patterns.

4. Glue three to five shapes flat onto the background board. Cut and stack small squares of cardboard and glue them to the back of the remaining shapes. Glue these shapes to the background, overlapping shapes to complete the form.

Research
in Art Education

"The arts help students develop their abilities to appreciate and interpret art of other cultures and to learn about people of the past through exposure to reproductions, to art works in museums and galleries, or through discussions about contemporary artists and art works." (Andra Nyman, "Cultural Content, Identity, and Program Development: Approaches to Art Education for Elementary Educators," in *Contemporary Issues in Art Education*, edited by Y. Gaudelius and P. Speirs, 61–69. New Jersey: Prentice Hall, 2002.)

Assessment
Use the following rubric to evaluate the artwork students make in the Creative Expression activity and to assess their understanding of form.

Have students complete page 29 or 30 in their *Assessment* books.

	Art History and Culture	Aesthetic Perception	Creative Expression	Art Criticism
3 POINTS	The student can demonstrate knowledge of the lives and work of Frank Stella and Tony Smith.	The student accurately identifies the use of form in artwork.	The student's sculpture clearly illustrates the use of form.	The student thoughtfully and honestly evaluates own work using the four steps of art criticism.
2 POINTS	The student's knowledge of the lives and work of Frank Stella and Tony Smith is weak or incomplete.	The student shows emerging awareness of the use of form in artwork.	The student's sculpture shows some awareness of form.	The student attempts to evaluate own work, but shows an incomplete understanding of evaluation criteria.
1 POINT	The student cannot demonstrate knowledge of the lives and work of Frank Stella or Tony Smith.	The student cannot identify the use of form in artwork.	The student's sculpture shows no understanding of form.	The student makes no attempt to evaluate own artwork.

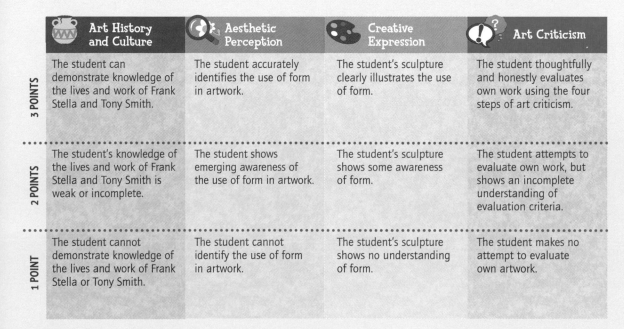

Assessment, p. 29

Form in Architecture

Lesson 6 introduces the use of form in architecture. Architects create ideas for buildings and structures for living, working, and leisure.

Objectives

 Art History and Culture

To learn more about the lives and work of Le Corbusier and Jørn Oberg Utzon

 Creative Expression

To plan and create a uniquely formed public building

 Aesthetic Perception

To identify architectural forms used by artists NSAE 2.d

 Art Criticism

To evaluate one's own work using the four steps of art criticism

Lesson Materials

- paper
- thin cardboard
- construction paper
- paper-towel and toilet-paper roll tubes

Program Resources

- *Reading and Writing Test Prep.,* pp. 28–29
- *Transparency 12*
- *Artist Profiles,* pp. 37, 62
- *Animals Through History Time Line*
- *Assessment,* pp. 31–32
- *Large Print 64 Eagle Man*
- *The National Museum of Women in the Arts Collection*

Concept Trace

Form in Architecture

Introduced: Level 4, Unit 4, Lesson 1

Reinforced: Level 6 Unit 1, Lessons 3, 4

Vocabulary Vocabulary

Review the following vocabulary words with students.

architecture arquitectura—the art of designing and planning the construction of buildings, cities, and bridges

architect arquitecto—a person who plans and designs buildings, cities, and bridges

See page 89B for additional Spanish vocabulary resources.

Art Journal: Vocabulary

Have students add these words to the Vocabulary section of their Art Journals.

Lesson 6 Arts Integration

Theatre

Complete Unit 2, Lesson 6, on pages 46–51 of *Theatre Arts Connections.*

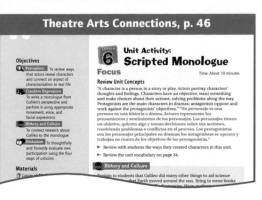

Theatre Arts Connections, p. 46

Music

SPOTLIGHT on MUSIC One innovator of sound and texture in American music was Aaron Copeland. Listen to his "Variations on Simple Gifts" from *Appalachian Spring.* He created the ballet *Appalachian Spring* for the dancer Martha Graham in 1944. His textures are open and transparent. One way he creates this openness is his sparse instrumentation; for example, he would sometimes group very high-pitched sounds with very low ones.

Movement & Dance

Study pictures of three interesting, ancient architectural structures, such as pyramids, Greek columns, or ancient temples. In small groups, students will create a design for each structure. Identify a different area of the room in which to build each structure. Each group has to find a way to travel from area to area. Use four counts to build the group design and eight counts for the group to travel.

 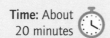
Activate Prior Knowledge

"What do you know about buildings and how they are designed? "¿Qué saben acerca de los edificios y cómo se diseñan?"

- Discuss students' responses. Ask them to think of specific buildings they are familiar with and what makes those buildings unique.

Using Literature Reading

- Share with the class Paul O. Zelinsky's *Rapunzel*. Encourage students to analyze the architectural characteristics throughout the book.

Thematic Connection Social Studies

- **Communities:** Encourage students to discuss the importance of considering the community and its needs before designing a new building for a neighborhood.

Introduce the Art

Look

"Let's take a close look at the two works of art." "Vamos a observar detalladamente las dos obras de arte."

Comparing and Contrasting Reading

- Have students list the similarities and differences between the two architectural designs in this lesson.

Point of View Reading

- Have students find other pictures of *Chapelle de Notre-Dame du Haut* and the *Opera House* in books or on the Internet.

🏺 Art History and Culture

Le Corbusier's design uses natural, free-form forms. These quiet, smooth lines blend with the hills and evoke a reverence appropriate for a church building. The 1,000-room Sydney *Opera House* looks as dramatic and innovative as the music and theatre found inside. The acoustics of the design are internationally regarded. NSAE 5.c

 Web Connection

Have students visit **www.sanford-artedventures.com/play/arch2/index.html#** to practice considering and using the elements of architectural design.

▲ **Le Corbusier.** (Swiss). *Chapelle de Notre-Dame du Haut.* 1950–1955.
....
Ronchamp, France.

Look at the artwork on these pages. Le Corbusier was an architect who designed *Chapelle de Notre-Dame du Haut* in France in 1950. The Sydney Opera House, in Sydney, Australia, was designed in 1957 by Jørn Utzon of Demark. Both architects used free-form, or organic forms found in nature, as a basis for their designs.

🏺 Art History and Culture

How have these architects designed buildings that fit the surrounding culture?

🏺 Art History and Culture

Le Corbusier

Le Corbusier (lā kôr bū zyā) (1887–1965) was the professional name of Charles Edouard Jeanneret. He was an architect, painter, and writer who had a significant effect on the development of modern architecture. *Chapelle de Notre-Dame du Haut* has been called one of the greatest buildings of modern architecture. Interestingly, the local members of the community hated it so much they denied the building water and electricity. *Chapelle de Notre-Dame du Haut* sits on a hilltop in Ronchamp, France.

See pages 16–21 and 24–25 for more about art history and the subject matter.

Artist Profiles, p. 37

▸ Artist Profile ◂
Le Corbusier
1887–1965

Le Corbusier (la kor bōō yā') is a pseudonym for Charles Edouard Jeanneret (shärl ädwär zhan nə rā). He was born in La Chaux-de-Fonds, Switzerland, and took the name *Corbusier* from a relative. A teacher encouraged him to study architecture. Le Corbusier traveled around Europe to study classical architecture on his teacher's advice. Between 1908 and 1909 he studied architecture in Paris. In 1910 he studied in Berlin, Germany. After World War I he settled in Paris. He became a French citizen in 1930. From 1921 to 1945, Le Corbusier and his cousin ran an architecture workshop. Architects from all over the world came to talk to him.

▲ **Jørn Oberg Utzon.** (Danish).
Opera House. 1957–1973
·····································
Sydney, Australia.

Study both works of art to find examples of use of form.

▶ What shapes and forms do you see in both structures?

▶ What is unique about these two buildings?

▶ Do you think both structures fit their environment? Why?

🔍 Aesthetic Perception

Design Awareness Look at the buildings in your environment. What objects in nature are similar to the forms in these buildings?

Study NSAE 5.c

▶ Free-form and rounded triangle shapes can be seen in both structures.

▶ Both buildings were designed with free-form shapes instead of geometric shapes.

▶ Both structures fit because the architects used shapes found in nature.

■ For more examples of utilitarian art, see *The National Museum of Women in the Arts Collection.*

📓 Art Journal: Writing

Have students describe how they contribute to their communities in their Art Journals.

🔍 Aesthetic Perception

Seeing Like an Artist Discuss the natural objects that students relate to the architectural structures. Ask students to compare the similarities and contrast the differences.

Developing Visual Literacy Ask students to think about the audience each architect considered when designing his structure. How is this communicated through the forms chosen by each architect? Encourage students to think about something they have written or created specifically for a particular audience. NSAE 5.a

🏺 Art History and Culture

Jørn Oberg Utzon

Jørn Oberg Utzon's (jorn ō´ bûrg ut´ zən) (1918–) *Opera House* in Sydney, Australia, is a reflection of modern expressionist art. Utzon said that his inspiration for the design came from looking at an orange. This unusual design gained him international recognition. Utzon's architectural designs are based primarily on form and function. The *Opera House* took 14 years to complete. Utzon designed the 1,000-room structure, but was unable to complete the project. The unusually shaped roof pieces are concrete sections that were delivered to the site, then assembled.

See pages 16–21 and 24–25 for more about art history and the subject matter.

Artist Profiles, p. 62

◆ Artist Profile ◆
Jorn Oberg Utzon
b. 1918
This Danish architect first learned about building from his father, a noted yacht designer. Jørn Oberg Utzon (jorn ō´ burg ut´ zon) studied at the Royal Academy of Art in Denmark. He first gained international recognition in 1957, when his design for the Opera House in Sydney, Australia, was selected from 223 entries. Utzon moved to Australia to oversee the construction. However, major delays and disagreements with local politicians forced Utzon to resign, and another architect oversaw the construction. Since then Utzon has continued to design unusual buildings. An example is a church in Copenhagen that looks like a cluster of farm buildings.

💻 Web Connection

Have students visit www.sydneyoperahouse.com/virtual_tour/vrtour2.html to further explore the *Opera House* in Sydney, Australia.

 **each**

Time: About 30 minutes

"How can you use paper to plan and create unique forms?" "¿Cómo pueden usar papel para planificar y crear formas únicas?"

- Discuss the definition of architects on page 88.

Practice

Materials: paper, pencils

Alternate Materials: charcoal pencils

- Distribute materials and have students follow the directions on page 88.

- Have students quickly sketch the shape of a building they are familiar with, including the surrounding environment. Then ask students to add architectural forms to the sketch while keeping the basic structure of the original sketch.

Creative Expression

Materials: paper, thin cardboard, construction paper, towel and toilet-paper tubes

- Distribute the materials and have students follow the directions on page 89.

- Review the Activity Tips on page 235 for visual examples of this lesson's activity.

Art Journal: Brainstorming

Have students plan what forms they want to create and how they will do this. Students should record their plan, including the materials they will use, in their Art Journals. Then have students plan how the forms will fit together to create a unique public building.

Using Form in Architecture

Architects design buildings, cities, and bridges using three-dimensional forms.

Shapes

Square   Triangle   Circle   Rectangle   Free-form

Forms

Cube   Cone   Sphere   Rectangular solid   Free-form

Practice

Practice drawing some of the architectural forms you have learned about. Use pencil.

1. Lightly sketch the overall shape of a building or house you have seen.

2. Add forms from the examples above to your sketch. Keep the basic structure of your original drawing while adding new architectural features.

88   Unit 2 • Lesson 6

Differentiated Instruction

Reteach
Have students look through travel magazines and identify forms in architecture.

Special Needs
Students with severe disabilities may not be able to create paper sculptures but are capable of making choices and expressing preferences in art making. Using pre-formed paper shapes, they can indicate to a paraprofessional or teacher where they would like each object placed.

ELL
Offer synonyms and pantomime meaning as needed for clarification of study questions for students' understanding. Students can trace shapes and forms to indicate understanding.

◀ **Cammie Valentine.**
Age 10.

Think about the purpose of the student artist's public building.

 Creative Expression

Use paper-sculpting techniques to create a uniquely formed public building.

1. Plan the building and its form. Consider what it will be used for.
2. Prepare the materials.
3. Put your building together.

Art Criticism

Describe Describe the unique building you have created.

Analyze Describe the various forms you used.

Interpret Does your building look like its function? Give it a name.

Decide Were you able to create the forms you had planned? Does the overall appearance of the building meet your expectations? What would you change?

Reflect
Time: About 15 minutes

Review and Assess
"Were you able to create a uniquely formed public building sculpture from the materials you were given?" "¿Pudieron crear una escultura de un edificio público con una forma única usando los materiales que les dieron?"

Think
The artist created these buildings for shelter and aesthetic beauty.

■ Use *Large Prints 64 Eagle Man* to have students identify the similarities and differences in the curved forms of the buildings in this lesson to living or organic forms.

Informal Assessment
■ For standardized-format test practice using this lesson's art content, see pages 28–29 in *Reading and Writing Test Preparation.*

Art Journal: Critical Thinking
Have students answer the four art criticism questions—Describe, Analyze, Interpret, and Decide—in their Art Journals. In small groups, have students discuss their unique public buildings.
NSAE 2.b

Art Across the Curriculum

Use these simple ideas to reinforce art concepts across the curriculum.

★ **Persuasive Writing** Have students write a persuasive paragraph that could be used to sell their originally designed public building.

★ **Math** Have students research advanced geometric forms, sketch them, and label them.

★ **Science** Ask students to explain how using hard, geometric shapes in place of the soft, free-form shapes would change these buildings and the effects they have on the people who use them.

★ **Social Studies** Assign cooperative groups to research the history and development of standards of measurement: length, time, weight, volume, mass.

★ **Technology** Discuss how the three-dimensional capabilities of computer-graphics programs can be useful to architects when planning their designs. See **SRAonline.com** for further instructions.
NSAE 6.b

Lesson 6 Wrap-Up

Form in Architecture

Extra! For the Art Specialist

Time: About 30 minutes

Focus

Study **Large Print 64** *Eagle Man,* and discuss form. What makes a form different from a shape? Why is this artwork considered a form? Even though the image is on a flat surface, how can you tell it is a form? What are some other clues that let us know this is a form?

Teach

Discuss how artists use a variety of materials to create architectural forms. Explain to students that they will be creating a three-dimensional architectural form using slab and coils.

Reflect

Have students evaluate their works of art using the four steps of art criticism. Encourage them to locate and describe forms they see in the classroom.

Alternate Activity

Materials:

- Art Journal
- pencils, erasers
- clay
- clay tools, rolling pins
- cotton or burlap fabric for clay mat
- kiln to fire clay

1. Create several sketches in your Art Journal of a house or building you would like to make from clay.

2. Roll out a slab of clay to the thickness of your index finger. With a pencil, lightly draw the shape of the front of your architectural design. Cut out your shape. Trace your cut out onto another slab for the back of your form.

3. Roll out another slab of clay. Draw, and cut out the sides of the building. Use your front to measure the height. Join the four slabs.

4. Make a roof using another slab of clay.

5. Using coils, small pieces of clay, and your clay tools, add the details of windows, doors, and textures.

Research in Art Education

Collaboration is an important benefit of the arts. In the visual arts, students may engage in "enterprises such as painting murals and scenery, producing books, and organizing exhibitions." They also often have the opportunity to learn to critique the work of others appropriately ("Learning in and Through the Arts: Curriculum Implications" in *Champions of Change*, p. 40). As students study form in architecture, encourage them to think of the many different situations that an architect needs to consider and the many people that he or she needs to work with when designing and building a structure.

Assessment

Use the following rubric to evaluate the artwork students make in the Creative Expression activity and to assess students' understanding of form in architecture.

Have students complete page 31 or 32 in their *Assessment* books.

	Art History and Culture	Aesthetic Perception	Creative Expression	Art Criticism
3 POINTS	The student can demonstrate knowledge of the lives and work of Le Corbusier and Jørn Oberg Utzon.	The student accurately identifies the use of form in architecture.	The student's building clearly illustrates the use of form in architecture.	The student thoughtfully and honestly evaluates own work using the four steps of art criticism.
2 POINTS	The student's knowledge of the lives and work of Le Corbusier and Jørn Oberg Utzon is weak or incomplete.	The student shows emerging awareness of the use of form in architecture.	The student's building shows some awareness of the use of form in architecture.	The student attempts to evaluate own work, but shows an incomplete understanding of evaluation criteria.
1 POINT	The student cannot demonstrate knowledge of the lives and work of Le Corbusier or Jørn Oberg Utzon.	The student cannot identify the use of form in architecture.	The student's building shows no understanding of the use of form in architecture.	The student makes no attempt to evaluate own artwork.

Assessment, p. 31

Name _____ Date _____

Form in Architecture

Lesson **6** UNIT 2

A. Short Answer

Write a short answer in the blanks below.

1. _____ is the art of designing and planning the construction of buildings and other structures in the environment.

2. An architect is a person who _____

B. Matching

Match each shape in Column 1 to its like form in Column 2.

Column 1	Column 2
___ 1. circle	a. cube
___ 2. triangle	b. sphere or cylinder
___ 3. square	c. rectangular solid
___ 4. rectangle	d. pyramid or prism

C. Writing

Look at the picture of the Opera House in Sydney, Australia, and, on the back of this paper, write about the forms that you see. Include those that make up the *Opera House* as well as the forms in the surrounding environment. Do any of these forms repeat?

Level 5   Unit 2 • Space, Shape, and Form   **31**

space—the area between, around, above, below, and within objects **espacio**—el área entre, alrededor de, arriba de, debajo de y dentro de los objetos

positive space—the objects, shapes, or forms in works of art **espacio positivo**—los objetos, las figuras o las formas de las obras de arte

negative space—the empty space that surrounds objects, shapes, and forms **espacio negativo**—el espacio vacío que rodea los objetos, las figuras y las formas

shape reversal—when a shape begins as positive space in one image and becomes negative space in another image **figura inversa**—cuando una figura empieza como un espacio positivo en una imagen y se convierte en espacio negativo en otra imagen

perspective—techniques for creating the illusion of depth on a flat surface **perspectiva**—técnicas para crear la ilusión de profundidad en una superficie plana

depth—the appearance of deep space or distance in a two-dimensional artwork **profundidad**—la apariencia de un espacio profundo o distancia en una obra de arte bidimensional

converging—coming together at one point or place **convergir**—encontrarse en un punto o lugar

picture plane—the name used to describe the surface of a drawing or painting **plano de la pintura**—el nombre usado para describir la superficie de un dibujo o una pintura

foreground—the part of the picture plane that seems to be closest to the viewer and is located at the bottom of the picture **frente**—o primer plano; la parte del plano de la pintura que parece estar más cerca del espectador y que está ubicada en la parte inferior de la pintura

background—the part of the picture plane that seems to be the farthest from the viewer **fondo**—o trasfondo; la parte del plano de la pintura que parece estar más lejos del espectador

middle ground—the area in a picture plane between the background and foreground **medio fondo**—o segundo plano; el área del plano de una pintura que está entre el fondo y el frente

form—a three-dimensional object that takes up space using height, width and depth. Forms can be geometric or free-form. **forma**—un objeto tridimensional que ocupa un espacio usando su altura, ancho y profundidad. Las formas pueden ser geométricas o abstractas.

freestanding sculpture—a three-dimensional sculpture that is surrounded by space on all sides **escultura autoestable**—una escultura tridimensional rodeada por espacio en todos sus lados

relief sculpture—a three-dimensional sculpture in which objects stick out from a flat surface **escultura de relieve**—una escultura tridimensional en la cual los objetos sobresalen de una superficie plana

architecture—the art of designing and planning the construction of buildings, cities, and bridges **arquitectura**—el arte de diseñar y planificar la construcción de edificios, ciudades y puentes

architect—the person who plans and designs buildings, cities, and bridges **arquitecto**—la persona que planifica y diseña edificios, ciudades y puentes

---

Vocabulary Practice

T Display *Transparency 38* to review unit vocabulary words.

Categorizing/Classifying ⭐ Vocabulary
Write the words *space, shape,* and *form* on the board. Have volunteers select a vocabulary word and explain under which of the three categories that it fits. Some terms may fit in more than one category.

Dictionary Entries ⭐ Vocabulary
Have students look up the definition of the word *space* in a dictionary. Discuss the multiple meanings of the word and ask which definition is the most similar to their vocabulary term.

Definitions: Demonstrate Meanings ⭐ Vocabulary
Display *Large Print 64 Eagle Man.* Ask volunteers to select a vocabulary word and demonstrate its meaning by explaining how the term is used in this work of art.

Space, Shape, and Form

Art Criticism

Critical Thinking Art Criticism is an organized system for looking at and talking about art. You can criticize art without being an expert. The purpose of art criticism is to involve the viewer in a perception process that delays judgment until all aspects of the artwork have been studied.

- See pages 28–29 for more about art criticism.

Describe

▶ This is a relief sculpture by an artist named Marisol Escobar. It is almost seven feet tall and more than five feet wide. It is made with painted wood and other materials, and it is at the Museum of Modern Art in New York City.

▶ Possible answers are: This sculpture has five people: a woman and four children. The woman is sitting, holding a baby. The woman and the baby are looking straight ahead, not smiling. The girl on the left is smiling.

Analyze

▶ The people are positive and all the white areas are negative, even though some of the white pieces are forms.

▶ The artist used shading on all of the faces and bodies to make the flat shapes look like forms.

▶ The boy is a shape because he is painted on the flat surface.

▶ Some possible answers are: The taller girl is a shape painted on the flat surface, except for the three-dimensional part of her shoes. The shorter girl's face and dress are shapes. Her legs and shoes are forms.

▶ Some possible answers are: Most of the three-dimensional part of this sculpture is geometric. The people are a combination of painted free-form shapes and carved free-form forms.

▲ **Marisol Escobar.** (Venezuelan).
The Family. 1962.
Painted wood and other found objects in three sections.
$82\frac{1}{2} \times 65\frac{1}{2} \times 15\frac{1}{2}$ inches (209.55 × 166.37 × 39.37 cm.).
Museum of Modern Art, New York, New York.

Art History and Culture

Marisol Escobar

Marisol Escobar (1930–) was born in Paris to Venezuelan parents. After her mother died, the family moved to Los Angeles, California. Escobar, with encouragement from her father, later returned to Paris to study art at the Ecole des Beaux-arts. Her sculptures are often formed from painted wood, found objects, and many times from her own clothing. Most of her sculptures are humorous portraits of people such as John Wayne, President Lyndon Johnson, and Picasso. *The Family* is based on a photograph that had been thrown away. She found it among wastepapers near her studio.

See pages 24–25 and 16–21 for more about art history and the subject matter.

Artist Profiles, p. 23

Artist Profile
Marisol Escobar
b. 1930

The Venezuelan family of Marisol Escobar (mar' ə sŏl äs kō bär') often moved and led a life of comfort despite the economic hardships of the Depression. Escobar was born in Paris, France. When her mother died in 1941, her family moved first to Venezuela and then to California, where she attended a girls' school. It was there that she began to infuse religion into her study of art. Escobar was encouraged by her father to study art, and she attended the École des Beaux-Arts in Paris before deciding to move to New York City, with its vibrant arts culture, in 1950. Her painting and drawing gave way to sculpting and creating installations. Escobar continues to create art with a wide range of materials in New York.

 **Art Criticism** Critical Thinking

Describe **What do you see?**

During this step you will collect information about the subject of the work.

- ▶ What does the credit line tell you about this work of art?
- ▶ Describe the people. What they are wearing? What they are doing?

Analyze **How is this work organized?**

Think about how the artist has used the elements and principles of art.

- ▶ Where do you see positive and negative shapes and forms in this work?
- ▶ Where did the artist use shading in this work?
- ▶ Which of the images of people are flat shapes? Which of the images of people are a combination of shapes and forms?
- ▶ Where do you see geometric and free-form shapes and forms?

Interpret **What is the artist trying to say?**

Use the clues you discovered during your analysis to find the message the artist is trying to give.

- ▶ Why are some parts two dimensional and some parts three dimensional?
- ▶ Explain the relationships of these people as you imagine they might be.
- ▶ Write a description of a day in the life of this family.

Decide **What do you think about the work?**

Use all the information you have gathered to decide whether this is a successful work of art.

- ▶ Is the work successful because it is realistic, because it is well organized, or because it has a strong message?

Interpret

- ▶ Some students will say it is meant to make us think about the importance of the people. The mother sticks out the farthest. That may make her the most important person in the family right now. Others may see this as humorous—that the artist is playing a game with us.
- ▶ Some students may say this is a happy family because they are standing close together for a family portrait. Others may say they are not happy because, except for the tall girl, they are not smiling.
- ▶ Students should look at the facial expressions for clues. Some may use the clothing as clues.

Decide

- ▶ Students' answers will vary. Some will say the strong message, while others may say the organization. Some may say realism because parts of the work look realistic.

Art Journal: Writing

Have students write answers to the Aesthetic Perception questions in their Art Journals.

 Aesthetic Perception

Critical Thinking Have students bring in a copy of a portrait of their own family or of someone else's. How does this portrait compare with Marisol Escobar's *The Family*? Discuss the similarities and differences.

Describe ▶ List and describe the shapes and forms that can be found in the family portrait.

Analyze ▶ Can any of the same shapes or forms be found in the family portrait and in *The Family*?

Interpret ▶ What moods do the faces of the people communicate in the family portrait and in *The Family*?

Decide ▶ Do family portraits always show the true picture of what is happening and how the people are feeling?

"Artists use the elements of space, shape, and form to create depth in an artwork." "Los artistas usan los elementos de espacio, figura y forma para crear profundidad en una obra de arte."

T Review the unit vocabulary with students using *Transparency 38.*

Art Journal: Writing

Have students answer the questions on page 92 in their Art Journals or on a separate sheet of paper. 1. B, 2. A, 3. C, 4. C, 5. B

T For further assessment, have students complete the unit test on *Transparency 44.*

CAREERS IN ART
Architecture

► Encourage students to evaluate the design of the school building. Brainstorm ideas to make it easier to move through, more visually appealing, and safer.

"To us art is an adventure into an unknown world, which can be explored only by those willing to take the risks."

                    -Adolph Gottlieb
                     and Mark Rothko

Wrapping Up Unit 2

Space, Shape, and Form, continued

Show What You Know

Answer these questions on a separate sheet of paper.

❶ _____ is the empty space that surrounds objects, shapes, and forms.
   A. Positive space
   B. Negative space
   C. Overlapping

❷ Parallel lines that seem to move toward the same point as they move farther away from the viewer are known as _____.
   A. converging lines
   B. horizon lines
   C. scoring a straight line

❸ One way of using lines to show distance and depth is by using _____.
   A. shape reversal
   B. curling
   C. linear perspective

❹ _____ is a technique used for darkening values by adding black or darkening an area by repeating several lines close together.
   A. Fringing
   B. Architecture
   C. Shading

❺ An _____ plans and designs building, cities, and bridges.
   A. archaeologist
   B. architect
   C. architecture

CAREERS IN ART
Architecture

Look around your neighborhood. Notice the public buildings, parks, and open areas.

Urban Design Architects design buildings, public spaces, and entire urban neighborhoods to accommodate people and their culture. Some restore buildings so that they are safe, attractive, and appear as they did when they were originally built.

Interior Design Interior designers plan the space inside homes, public buildings, businesses, or institutions. They consider color, space, shape, balance, building codes, and laws, as well as provisions for any special needs of the people that will use that space.

Marine Architects Marine architects plan, design, and oversee the building and the repairing of boats and ships.

▲ **Architect**

Unit Assessment Options

Aesthetic Perception

Practice Have students select two of the concepts in the Show What You Know section on page 92 and then find examples of each concept in the classroom.

Creative Expression

Student Portfolio Have students review all the artwork they have created during this unit and select the pieces they want to keep in their portfolios.

Art Criticism

Activity Have students select an artwork from this unit and study it using the four steps of art criticism. (See pages 28–29 for more information about art criticism.) Have students work alone or in pairs and present their findings aloud or in writing.

Space, Shape, and Form in Song Writing

Paul Tracey's musical "Our Little Blue Planet" features songs and stories that emphasize the importance of caring for Earth. Wherever we live on the planet, our actions affect people living elsewhere. One of his lyrics says "Our Little Blue Planet, our home out in space, without your environment, no human race." In his song "Save the Forest," Paul Tracey identifies a variety of trees from around the world. He researched them to point out their unique features in his lyrics. Here's an example:

► "Australia's got the *Gum* tree, koalas love to chew. In every English church yard, you'll always find a *Yew.*

► Zambia's got the *Babobab,* they say it's upside down. Its branches look like crooked roots high above the ground."

What to Do Research a specific tree and identify a feature that makes it unique.

1. Research a tree that interests you and identify its unique features. Describe its shape and form.

2. Write a rhyming couplet that includes the name of the tree and something special about it.

3. Share your line with a partner or group.

4. Combine lines and make a longer poem about trees.

▲ Paul Tracey. "Little Blue Planet."

 **Art Criticism**

Describe Did you describe the shape or form of the tree?

Analyze What did you think about as you prepared to write the couplet about this tree?

Interpret How do you feel about this tree now that you have researched it and written about it?

Decide How well did you describe this tree in poetry or lyrics?

Unit 2 **93**

 ## Art History and Culture

Paul Tracey

International troubadour Paul Tracey draws upon his cultural heritage and broad personal experience to communicate ideas about life through original songs. He proudly states that he attended "The University of the Bush" in South Africa. He learned, "If we make a mess of this planet, we can't say 'I'm leaving now.' There is nowhere else we can live. We simply have to care for our environment!"

 ## Space, Shape, and Form

Objective: to create a rhyming couplet that highlights the features of a specific tree

Materials: *Our Little Blue Planet,* featured songs are "Dead as a Dodo" and "Save the Forest," performed by Paul Tracey. Running Time: 5:00, paper and pencils or markers

Focus
Time: About 5 minutes

■ Discuss the information on page 93.

Art History and Culture

■ Have students brainstorm and list all the trees they can think of so they will have choices to research for their project.

Teach
Time: About 20 minutes

Aesthetic Perception

■ Discuss "trees" and give examples of a couplet.

Creative Expression

■ Have students select a tree to research and write about in a rhyming couplet form.

■ Have students share their couplet with a partner or small group.

■ Ask students to combine their couplets into a larger poem.

■ **Informal Assessment:** Have students share their poetry while you give positive feedback.

Reflect
Time: About 10 minutes

Art Criticism

■ Have students answer the four art criticism questions on page 93 aloud or in writing.

■ Did students select a specific tree to research and write about in a couplet form?
NSAE 6.a

	Lesson Title	Suggested Pacing	Creative Expression Activity
Lesson 1	**Monochromatic Colors**	1:10	Draw a real or imaginary animal. Use monochromatic colors.
Lesson 2	**Analogous Colors**	1:05	Create an analogous landscape. Use a computer.
Lesson 3	**Complementary Colors**	1:05	Design and create a still-life painting.
Lesson 4	**Warm and Cool Colors**	1:05	Create a collage. Use warm and cool colors.
Lesson 5	**Pattern**	1:05	Create wrapping paper. Use an original pattern.
Lesson 6	**Decorative Pattern**	1:20	Design and create a clay coil with a decorative pattern.
ART SOURCE ARTSOURCE	**Color and Pattern in Theatre**	0:45	Express scientific information using body and voice.

Materials	Program Resources	Fine Art Resources	Literature Resources
pastels, construction paper	*Assessment*, pp. 33–34 *Home and After-School Connections* *Art Around the World Collection* *Reading and Writing Test Preparation*, pp. 30–31	*Transparency 13* *Artist Profiles*, pp. 34, 33 *Large Print 65* *Flash Card 11* *Animals Through History Time Line*	*My Fellow Americans: A Family Album* by Alice Provensen
computer paint program, printer, paper	*Assessment*, pp. 35–36 *Home and After-School Connections* *Art Around the World Collection* *Reading and Writing Test Preparation*, pp. 32–33	*Transparency 14* *Artist Profiles*, pp. 46, 79 *Large Print 65* *Animals Through History Time Line*	*Streams to the River, River to the Sea* by Scott O'Dell *Black-Eyed Susan* by Jennifer Armstrong
fruit, six-inch squares of paper, watercolor paints, paper towels, scissors, colored construction paper	*Assessment*, pp. 37–38 *Home and After-School Connections* *Art Around the World Collection* *Reading and Writing Test Preparation*, pp. 34–35	*Transparency 15* *Artist Profiles*, pp. 71, 19 *Large Prints 65, 66* *Animals Through History Time Line*	*Grass Sandals: The Travel of Basho* Dawnine Spivak
construction paper in warm and cool colors, glue, scissors, 9" × 12" white paper	*Assessment*, pp. 39–40 *Home and After-School Connections* *Art Around the World Collection* *Reading and Writing Test Preparation*, pp. 36–37	*Transparency 16* *Artist Profiles*, pp. 22, 39 *Large Prints 65, 66* *Flash Card 15* *Animals Through History Time Line*	*Snowflake Bentley* by Jacqueline Briggs Martin
foam printing material, ballpoint pens, large sheets of paper, paper clips, scissors, one color of water-base ink, brayers, inking plates, oil pastels	*Assessment*, pp. 41–42 *Home and After-School Connections* *Art Around the World Collection* *Reading and Writing Test Preparation*, pp. 38–39	*Transparency 17* *Artist Profiles*, pp. 72, 69 *Large Prints 65, 66* *Animals Through History Time Line*	*A View From Saturday* by E. L. Konigsburg
earth clay, paper clips, clay tools, pencils	*Assessment*, pp. 43–44 *Home and After-School Connections* *The National Museum of Women in the Arts Collection* *Reading and Writing Test Preparation*, pp. 40–41	*Transparency 18* *Artist Profiles*, pp. 68, 57 *Large Prints 65, 66* *Animals Through History Time Line*	*Look Alikes* by Joan Steiner
resources about natural events, "On the Day You Were Born"			

3 Color and Pattern

Lesson 1: Monochromatic colors are tints and shades of one color and are used for continuity.

Lesson 2: Analogous colors are located next to each other on the color wheel.

Lesson 3: Complementary colors are located opposite each other on the color wheel.

Lesson 4: Warm and cool colors are used to create specific moods in artwork.

Lesson 5: Pattern is a repeated design that decorates the surface of fabrics and other objects.

Lesson 6: Decorative patterns are used by designers to create visual interest on the surface of an object.

Introduce Unit Concepts

"Artists use the elements of color and pattern to create mood and interest in their artwork."
"Los artistas usan los elementos del color y el patrón para crear un ánimo e interés en sus obras de arte."

Color
- Have students list the colors they can see from where they sit in the classroom. Ask students to categorize the colors they list in any way they can.

Pattern
- Ask students to look for a pattern and sketch what they see. A pattern is the repetition of a design on the surface of an object.

Cross-Curricular Projects
- See the *Language Arts and Reading, Mathematics, Science,* and *Social Studies Art Connections* books for activities that further develop color and pattern concepts.

Color and Pattern

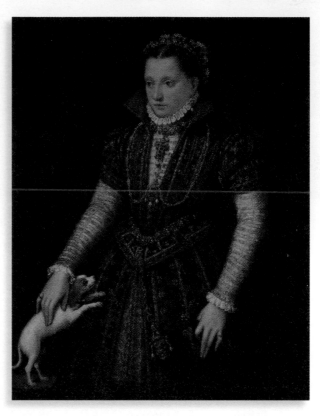

◄ **Lavinia Fontana.** (Italian).
Portrait of a Noblewoman. c. 1600
....
Oil on canvas. 45¼ × 35¼ inches
(114.3 × 88.8 cm.). National Museum
of Women in the Arts, Washington, D.C.

Many artists use color and patterns to create interest, mood, and perspective in their drawings, paintings, prints, and sculptures.

Lavinia Fontana used warm colors and detailed patterns to create a realistic portrayal of her model in *Portrait of a Noblewoman.*

94   Unit 3

Fine Art Prints

Display **Large Prints 65** *Diva* and **66** *Double Entrance.* Refer to the prints throughout the unit as students learn about color and pattern.

Large Print 65

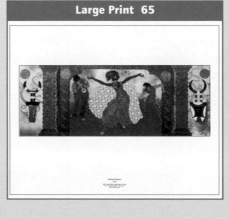

Large Print 66

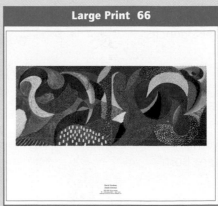

Artists use **color** to express a mood or feeling in their artwork.

- What colors do you see in this painting?
- Lavinia Fontana is noted for her attention to detail in her paintings. How does Fontana's use of color help make this portrait look realistic?

Artists use **pattern** to create designs that decorate the surfaces of fabrics and objects.

- What patterns do you see in this painting?
- Does this pattern remind you of the design you have seen on any other surface?

In This Unit you will learn and practice techniques using colors and pattern to add interest and feeling in your artwork.

Here are the topics you will study:
- Monochromatic colors
- Analogous colors
- Complementary colors
- Warm colors
- Cool colors
- Pattern

Lavinia Fontana
(1552–1614)

Lavinia Fontana was born in Bologna, Italy, in 1552. Her father, Prospero Fontana, taught her how to paint. Though it was difficult to be recognized as a female artist at that time, the city of Bologna was a great place for women to live because women's rights were recognized there more than in other places. Lavinia Fontana is considered the first female painter to have a successful career as an artist. She and her husband, Zappi, had eleven children. Zappi stayed home and took care of the family while Lavinia painted. Fontana's most notable works of art were religious and mythological paintings, in addition to her many portraits of Bolognese noblewomen. Only thirty-two of her signed and dated works exist today.

Unit 3   **95**

Examine the Artwork

"Let's look closely at the painting." *"Vamos a mirar detalladamente la pintura."*

- Have students look at Lavinia Fontana's *Portrait of a Noblewoman*. Ask them to describe what they see.
- Have students answer the questions about color and pattern on page 95.
  - ▶ Some of the many possible answers for this question are: red, white, brown.
  - ▶ A possible answer to this question is that she used brighter colors to make some things appear closer than others.
  - ▶ There are patterns in the design of the dress the noblewoman is wearing.
  - ▶ A possible answer is the comparison of the striped design on the sleeves of the dress to something else that is striped.
  NSAE 5.c

Unit Pretest

Display *Transparency 45* as a pretest. Answers: 1. B, 2. A, 3. C, 4. C, 5. A

Home Connection

- See *Home and After-School Connections* for family newsletters and activities for this unit.

Art History and Culture

Lavinia Fontana

Lavinia Fontana (Italian, 1552–1614) is one of the first female painters to have a successful career as an artist. She was born in Bologna, Italy, in 1552, and was artistically trained by her father, who was also an accomplished painter. Lavinia Fontana is noted for her attention to detail, as can be seen in *Portrait of a Noblewoman*. Some of Fontana's most notable works are religious and mythological paintings, as well as her many portraits. Only thirty-two of her signed and dated works exist today.

See pages 24–25 and 16–21 for more about art history and the subject matter.

Artist Profiles, p. 24

● Artist Profile ●
Lavinia Fontana
1552–1614

Lavinia Fontana (lə vin´ē ə fon´tä nə) was one of the first women to have a successful career as an artist. She was able to support herself and her family by painting. She received major commissions from public and private patrons for portraits and religious subjects. Fontana studied art with her father, Prospero Fontana, an artist and teacher. It was in her father's studio that she met another student, Gian Paolo Zappi, whom she married in 1577. Zappi gave up his artistic career to assist his wife in her studio. He handled the accounts of her many commissions and helped care for their 11 children. At the height of her career in 1603, Fontana and her family moved to Rome at the invitation of Pope Clement VIII

ILLUSTRATOR PROFILE
Jerry Pinkney
(1939–)

Jerry Pinkney, a native of Philadelphia, Pennsylvania, started drawing as a child because it was a hobby his older brothers enjoyed. However, Pinkney's talent and dedication soon made it apparent that art would be more than a pastime for him.

Pinkney's parents supported his interest and helped him pursue it by enrolling him in art classes. As an adolescent, Pinkney kept his sketchpad with him when he went to work at a newsstand. One day, as he sketched people passing by, Pinkney met cartoonist John Liney. Liney encouraged the young artist and helped Pinkney see that it was possible to earn a living through art.

After attending the Philadelphia Museum College of Art on full scholarship, Pinkney eventually started his own freelance business and moved to New York. In 1964 he began illustrating children's books, many of which feature multicultural themes and reflect the artist's pride in his African American heritage. Pinkney has been awarded a remarkable four Caldecott Honor Medals for his beautiful watercolor illustrations in *John Henry* by Julius Lester, *The Talking Eggs* by Robert D. San Souci, *Mirandy and Brother Wind* by Patricia McKissack, and *The Ugly Duckling* by Hans Christian Andersen.

While studying Unit 3, share Jerry Pinkney's illustrations with the class and discuss the use of color and pattern in his works of art. Ask students where they see monochromatic colors.

Music

Color in music refers to the distinctive tone qualities, or timbre, of different instruments and voices. A pattern is created when a rhythm is repeated. Quick, fast sounds in a rhythm pattern give a feeling of movement.

Literature

Show the video or DVD *Meet the Caldecott Illustrator: Jerry Pinkney.*

Literature and Art

Performing Arts

Show "On the Day You Were Born." Point out color schemes and patterns in the natural events.

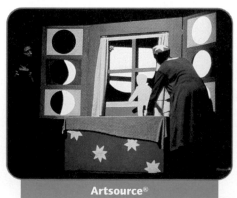

Artsource®

NSAE 6.a

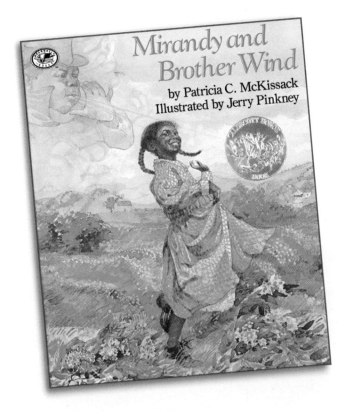

Lesson 1 Overview
Monochromatic Colors

Lesson 1 introduces monochromatic colors. Artists use monochromatic colors to bring together or unite their artwork visually.

Objectives

 Art History and Culture

To become knowledgeable about the lives and the artwork of Ben Jones and Jasper Johns

 Creative Expression

To draw a real or imaginary animal using tints and shades of one hue

 **Aesthetic Perception**

To identify monochromatic color schemes and how they are used to unite artwork

 Art Criticism

To evaluate one's own work using the four steps of art criticism

Vocabulary Vocabulary

Review the following vocabulary words with students.

monochromatic *monocromático*—a color scheme using one color plus all the tints and shades of that color

hue *matiz*—another name for *color*

tint *tinte*—a light value of a hue

shade *sombra*—a dark value of a hue

See page 119B for additional Spanish vocabulary resources.

Art Journal: Vocabulary

Have students add these words to the Vocabulary section of their Art Journals.

Lesson Materials
- rulers
- liquid tempera paints
- paintbrushes
- white paper
- newspaper
- erasers
- paper towels
- water dishes
- paper plates

Alternate Materials:
- color pencils

Program Resources
- *Reading and Writing Test Prep.*, pp. 30–31
- *Transparency 13*
- *Flash Card 11*
- *Artist Profiles*, pp. 34, 33
- *Animals Through History Time Line*
- *Assessment*, pp. 33–34
- *Large Print 65* Diva
- *Art Around the World Collection*

Concept Trace
Monochromatic Colors
Introduced: Level 4, Unit 3, Lesson 6

Reinforced: Level 6, Unit 2, Lesson 2

Lesson 1 Arts Integration

Theatre
Complete Unit 3, Lesson 1, on pages 54–55 of *Theatre Arts Connections.*

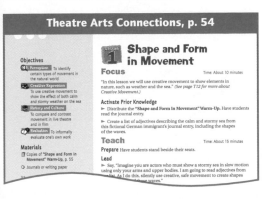

Music
 A string quartet blends the sounds of two violins, one viola, and one cello into a tone color of the string family. Listen to *String Quartet Op. 33 No. 3* "Movement 4" by Franz Joseph Haydn. There are times when the instruments are on their own, and the subtle differences among the three instruments are recognizable. Most of these differences can be attributed to the size and length of each instrument's strings. At some points the blend is so smooth they sound like one instrument.

Movement & Dance
Introduce the idea of pattern with variation. Have several students stand and create a large circle. In groups of eight, the remaining students enter the circle and move in circular patterns, creating circular movements. Each person will explore circles in their own way, and this will create variation. End in a frozen circle shape.

Focus

Time: About 20 minutes

Activate Prior Knowledge

"Would you rather dress in clothes that vary in shades but are basically monochromatic, or would you rather dress in many different colors?" "¿Preferirían vestirse con ropa que tuviera una variedad de sombras pero que básicamente fuera monocromática o preferirían vestirse con ropa de diferentes colores?"

- Discuss how monochromatic colors blend easily and are less dramatic in appearance than the use of many different hues.

Using Literature   Reading
- Use *My Fellow Americans: A Family Album,* by Alice Provensen, and *So You Want to Be President,* by Judith St. George, to incorporate this lesson's theme.

Thematic Connection   Social Studies
- **Our Country and Its People:** Discuss with students the melting pot process, in which many cultures blend to become one new culture.

Introduce the Art

Look

"Let's take a close look at the two works of art." "Vamos a observar detalladamente las dos obras de arte."

Making Inferences   Reading
- Have students make inferences about the works of art while considering the titles, the artists, and the artwork. *King Family:* Because of the title, students may be able to infer that the artwork is based on the family of Dr. Martin Luther King, Jr. The colors chosen and the facial expressions convey a somber mood. *Map:* The colors might suggest to the students a dismal mood. Students might infer that this is a statement about the United States.

 Art History and Culture

King Family honors Martin Luther King, Jr.'s fight for American's civil rights and his family's loss after his tragic death. Jasper Johns honors the U.S. map with his work of art.
NSAE 4.c

 Web Connection

Visit **www.infoplease.com/spot/mlkjrday1.html** for more information about Dr. Martin Luther King, Jr.

96 UNIT 3 • Color and Pattern

 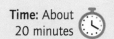

Monochromatic Colors

Look at these two works of art and notice the common hues that are repeated throughout. *King Family* is a drawing created by Ben Jones. His work shows the faces of familiar people, like the Dr. Martin Luther King, Jr., family. Jasper Johns created his collage and wax-based painting *Map,* and based it on the map of the United States. Johns's style emphasizes media rather than subject matter. Notice how both artists use color to unify their work.

◄ **Ben Jones.** (American). *King Family.* 1971.

Gouache. 40 × 30 inches (101.6 × 76.2 cm.). Collection of the Studio Museum, Harlem, New York.

Art History and Culture

How do the themes in these works of art honor American history?

Art History and Culture

Ben Jones

Ben Jones (ben jōnz) (1942–) began drawing at an early age in his hometown in New Jersey. He attended New York University and the Pratt Institute. Jones also traveled and studied in West Africa and Europe. He has exhibited widely in the United States, Africa, South America, and Paris, France. He works with mixed media and values the importance of found art. Common themes in Jones's artwork are Africa, his spirituality, political tensions, and dimensional space.

See pages 24–25 and 16–21 for more about art history and the subject matter.

Artist Profiles, p. 34

Ben Jones
b. 1942

Ben Jones (ben jōnz) was born in Paterson, New Jersey. He showed his potential as an artist as early as the age of five. His early career plan was to become an interpreter of French and Spanish. In high school he was encouraged by his art teacher, Rosalind Feinstein, to pursue a career in the arts. After college, Jones went on to participate in many group and solo exhibitions. He has traveled back and forth to Africa many times. African culture and Jones's African American heritage are strong parts of his artistic identity.

▲ **Jasper Johns.** (American).
Map. 1962.
....
Encaustic and collage on canvas.
60 × 93 inches (152.4 × 236.22 cm.).
The Museum of Contemporary Art,
Los Angeles, California.

Study the monochromatic color schemes in both pieces of artwork.

▶ What one color is used most often in each work of art?

▶ Where do you see colors that are lighter or darker than the main color?

▶ What type of lines and shapes do you see in each work of art?

▶ What feeling is expressed in each artwork? How did these artists create these feelings?

Aesthetic Perception

Seeing Like an Artist What natural objects are made up of many variations of just one color?

 Art History and Culture

Jasper Johns

Jasper Johns (jas´ pər jänz) (1930–), at age 24 decided to throw away all of the art he had ever created. He wanted a fresh start. He was determined to create original art, not copies of other styles or artists. Johns has been known for his inventive artistic styles ever since. Johns created *Map* using *encaustic,* which is pigment mixed into beeswax that is melted with a little resin. He applied heat after each layer of paint. In this way the entire artwork is set together. It is essentially a large work of wax.

See pages 24–25 and 16–21 for more about art history and the subject matter.

Artist Profiles, p. 33

◀ Artist Profile ▶

Jasper Johns
b. 1930

Jasper Johns (jas´ par jänz) was born in Augusta, Georgia. After serving in Japan with the United States Army, he moved to New York City. There he worked in a bookstore and started creating art. When he was 24, he decided to throw away all the art he had ever made. He wanted a fresh start. He was determined to create original art, not copies of the styles of other artists. Since then Johns has been known for his inventiveness.

Study

▶ Jones: The color blue is used most often. Johns: Many shades of gray are used.

▶ Jones: The darker colors are concentrated toward the bottom of the artwork; the lighter shades move from one corner to the other and up to the top of the piece. Johns: The lighter and darker shades of gray occur throughout the painting.

▶ Jones used curved lines and oval shapes. Johns used straight and zigzag lines and geometric and free-form shapes.

▶ Students will see various feelings expressed in both works.

■ For more examples of art from North America, see the **Art Around the World Collection.**
NSAE 5.c

Art Journal: Writing
Ask students to write in their Art Journals about a time when they noticed a shade of a color they really liked or did not like. Encourage students to explain the mood of this shade, where they saw it, and why they did or did not care for it.

Aesthetic Perception

Seeing Like an Artist Encourage students to point out natural objects and the common hue that can be seen in them. Talk about camouflage and how living things use monochromatic color schemes as a defense mechanism.

Developing Visual Literacy Ask students to look at Ben Jones's *King Family* and think about how they would paint their own families. What symbols would they use to identify their heritage, culture, meaningful events and hobbies? What colors and found objects would they use in this painting and why?
NSAE 4.b

Web Connection
Visit **www.jasperjohns.com/bio.html** for more information on Jasper Johns and his artwork.

each **Time:** About 30 minutes

"How can you create many different shades and tints of monochromatic colors?" "¿Cómo pueden crear muchas sombras y muchos tintes diferentes de colores monocromáticos?"

- Read and discuss the definitions of monochromatic, hue, primary hues, secondary hues, tint, and shade on page 98.

Practice

Materials: rulers, liquid tempera paints, paper plates, paintbrushes, white paper, newspaper

Alternate Materials: colored pencils

- Distribute materials and have students follow the directions on page 98.

- Have students draw three two-inch squares and label the first *hue,* the second *tint,* and the third *shade.* Ask students to choose a hue and use it to paint the first square. They will then separate the remaining paint of that hue on their paper plate and add white to half of it to create the tint and black to half to create the shade. The last two squares can then be painted and dried for a monochromatic-hue chart.

Creative Expression

Materials: pastels, construction paper

Alternate Materials: color pencils

- Distribute the materials and have students follow the directions on page 99.

- Review the Activity Tips on page 236 for visual examples of this lesson's activity.

- See the Technique Tips on page 217 for information on using pastels.

Art Journal: Brainstorming

Have students brainstorm and sketch their favorite real or imaginary animals in their Art Journals. NSAE 1.b

Using Monochromatic Colors

Monochromatic means "one color." A color scheme that is monochromatic uses only one color and the tints and shades of that color.

Hue is another name for color. Red, blue, and yellow are **primary hues.** By mixing primary hues, you create **secondary hues.** Red and blue make violet. Red and yellow make orange. Blue and yellow make green.

Tint is a light value of a hue made by adding white.

Shade is a dark value of a hue made by adding black.

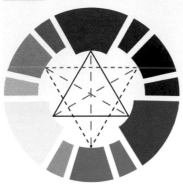

A **color wheel** is the spectrum bent into a circle.

Practice

Practice mixing monochromatic tints and shades of a hue. Use tempera paint.

1. Draw three squares. Label the first *Hue,* the second *Tint,* and the third *Shade.*
2. Choose a hue for the first square.
3. Create a tint for the second square and a shade for the third square.
4. Paint each square.
5. Experiment to create various values of the primary hue.

Differentiated Instruction

Reteach
Have students look through magazines to find examples of monochromatic color schemes. Ask them to identify the colors used.

Special Needs
This lesson contains information that for many students will be a review. For those students for whom this information is new, or for students who need help activating prior knowledge, it is important to present information about tints, shades, and color schemes in a visually understandable way.

ELL
Review with students the prefix *mono-,* meaning "one." *Chromatic* is used to describe something that relates to color. Use these word parts to explain the definition of *monochromatic.* Encourage students to make a list of other words that use the prefix *mono-.*

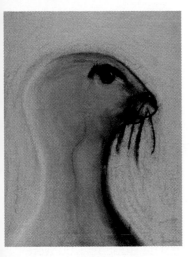

◄ **Paul Scott.**
Age 8.

Think about how the monochromatic color scheme affects the mood of the artwork.

 Creative Expression

What color dominates your favorite real or imaginary animal? Draw a real or imaginary animal. Use tints and shades of one hue. Use pastels on construction paper.

1. From your Art Journal, choose your favorite sketch of a real or imaginary animal.
2. Draw the animal large, so it fills the entire sheet of construction paper.
3. Color your animal. Use a hue, tints, and shades of that hue, and black and white pastels.

Art Criticism

Describe Describe your animal. Is it real or imaginary?

Analyze What hue did you choose? Do your tints and shades vary a lot, or are they close to the original hue?

Interpret What mood did you create with the hues that you used?

Decide Were you successful in drawing an animal, using a monochromatic color scheme?

Reflect
 Time: About 20 minutes

Review and Assess

"Were you able to draw a real or imaginary animal using tints and shades of one hue?"
"¿Pudieron pintar un animal real o imaginario usando tintes y sombras de un matiz?" NSAE 2.a

Think

The artist created a calm, cool, and maybe even sad mood by using shades of blue and gray for this seal.

■ Use *Large Print 65 Diva* to have students identify and describe the use of monochromatic color schemes used in sections of this painting.

Informal Assessment

■ For standardized-format test practice using this lesson's art content, see pages 30–31 in *Reading and Writing Test Preparation.*

Art Journal: Critical Thinking

Have students answer the four art criticism questions—Describe, Analyze, Interpret, and Decide—in their Art Journals. In small groups, have students discuss their monochromatic animal drawings.

Art Across the Curriculum

Use these simple ideas to reinforce art concepts across the curriculum.

★ **Narrative Writing** Have students use the writing process to create a story in which their real or imaginary animal is the main character.

★ **Math** When discussing degrees in math, ask students to look at the animals they have created and estimate the degrees that each tint and shade differ from the original hue.

★ **Science** Discuss the study of genealogy while viewing Ben Jones's *King Family.*

★ **Social Studies** Compare cartographers' maps of early America to those we use today.

★ **Technology** Have students create a monochromatic, nonobjective artwork using a computer paint program. Visit **SRAonline.com** to print out detailed instructions for this activity.
NSAE 6.b

Lesson 1 — Monochromatic Colors

Wrap-Up

Extra! For the Art Specialist

Time: About 30 minutes

Focus

Study the monochromatic sections of **Large Print 65** *Diva* and ask students to explain how tints and shade were used in this artwork. What areas of the work are darkest? Which areas are lightest?

Teach

If possible, take the students outside to sketch a series of tree drawings. Point out how the branches reach for the sky and how the twigs spread out like fingers. Point out that trees are not perfectly symmetrical.

Reflect

Have students evaluate their works of art using the four steps of art criticism. Encourage them to locate and describe the monochromatic colors they see around themselves.

Alternate Activity

Materials:

- Art Journals
- view finder
- pencils, erasers
- tempera paints
- paintbrushes in a variety of sizes
- water container
- mixing plates
- newspapers
- images of trees

1. Have students use the viewfinders to look at the trees. In their Art Journals, students should draw several studies of the trees they see.

2. Ask students to select their best sketches and lightly transfer them onto paper. Students should overlap the tree shapes and think about filling the page.

3. Students mix and paint the negative spaces between the trees first.

4. Using tints and shades of a selected color, students will paint their trees showing a range of values. Encourage students to paint the trees toward the front lighter, and the trees towards the back darker.

Research in Art Education

In one large study, students involved in art organizations were compared to a control group. The students who were involved in art were four times more likely to win schoolwide attention for academic achievement, four times more likely to participate in a math or science fair, three times more likely to be elected to a class office, and four times more likely to engage in community service ("Living the Arts Through Language and Learning" in *Critical Links,* p. 78). As students study the artwork in this lesson, they can see how current events, history, and politics are relevant to their own lives and can be portrayed through the arts.

Assessment

Use the following rubric to evaluate the artwork students make in the Creative Expression activity and to assess students' understanding of monochromatic colors.

Have students complete page 33 or 34 in their *Assessment* books.

	Art History and Culture	Aesthetic Perception	Creative Expression	Art Criticism
3 POINTS	The student demonstrates knowledge of the lives and work of Ben Jones and Jasper Johns.	The student accurately identifies monochromatic color schemes.	The student's painting clearly illustrates the use of monochromatic colors.	The student thoughtfully and honestly evaluates own work using the four steps of art criticism.
2 POINTS	The student's knowledge of the lives and work of Ben Jones and Jasper Johns is weak or incomplete.	The student shows emerging awareness of monochromatic color schemes.	The student's painting shows some awareness of monochromatic colors.	The student attempts to evaluate own work, but shows an incomplete understanding of evaluation criteria.
1 POINT	The student cannot demonstrate knowledge of the life and work of Ben Jones or Jasper Johns.	The student cannot identify monochromatic color schemes.	The student's painting shows no understanding of monochromatic colors.	The student makes no attempt to evaluate own artwork.

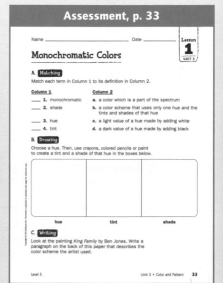

Assessment, p. 33

Name _____ Date _____ Lesson **1** UNIT 3

Monochromatic Colors

A. Matching
Match each term in Column 1 to its definition in Column 2.

Column 1
___ 1. monochromatic
___ 2. shade
___ 3. hue
___ 4. tint

Column 2
a. a color which is a part of the spectrum
b. a color scheme that uses only one hue and the tints and shades of that hue
c. a light value of a hue made by adding white
d. a dark value of a hue made by adding black

B. Drawing
Choose a hue. Then, use crayons, colored pencils or paint to create a tint and a shade of that hue in the boxes below.

hue	tint	shade

C. Writing
Look at the painting *King Family* by Ben Jones. Write a paragraph on the back of this paper that describes the color scheme the artist used.

Level 5   Unit 3 • Color and Pattern   **33**

Analogous Colors

Lesson 2 introduces analogous colors. Artists use analogous color schemes in their paintings to tie various shapes and forms together.

Objectives

Art History and Culture

To identify and compare the use of analogous colors in the artwork of Georgia O'Keeffe and in *Navajo Blanket Eye Dazzler*

Creative Expression

To use an analogous color scheme to create a nonobjective painting

Aesthetic Perception

To identify analogous colors in a work of art

Art Criticism

To evaluate one's own work using the four steps of art criticism

Vocabulary Vocabulary

Review the following vocabulary words with students.

analogous colors colores análogos—colors that sit next to each other on the color wheel and share a common color or hue

color scheme esquema de color—a plan for organizing colors

nonobjective abstracto—describes a piece of art that has no recognizable subject matter. It contains shapes, lines, and colors, not objects or people.

See page 119B for additional Spanish vocabulary resources.

 Art Journal: Vocabulary
Have students add these words to the Vocabulary section of their Art Journals.

Lesson Materials
- paper plates
- liquid tempera paints
- brushes
- pencils
- computer paint program
- printer
- paper

Alternate Materials:
- colored pencils
- paper
- markers

Program Resources
- *Reading and Writing Test Prep.*, pp. 32–33
- *Transparency 14*
- *Flash Card 17*
- *Artist Profiles*, pp. 46, 79
- *Animals Through History Time Line*
- *Assessment*, pp. 35–36
- *Large Print 65 Diva*
- *Art Around the World Collection*

Concept Trace
Analogous Colors
Introduced: Level 4, Unit 3, Lesson 6
Reinforced: Level 6, Unit 2, Lesson 4

Lesson 2 Arts Integration

Theatre

Complete Unit 3, Lesson 2, on pages 56–57 of *Theatre Arts Connections.*

Theatre Arts Connections, p. 56

Objectives
○ **Perception** To identify ways actions and movement can communicate some of the five Ws
○ **Creative Expression** To show who using dramatic movement
○ **History and Culture** To identify the five Ws of the Yupka people's movement from their ancestral lands in Venezuela
○ To informally evaluate one's own work

Materials
☐ Copies of "Movement and the Five Ws" Warm-Up, p. 57
○ Journals or writing paper

2 Movement and the Five Ws

Focus   Time: About 10 minutes
"In this lesson we will use dramatic movement to show *who* from a story."
(See page T13 for more about Dramatic Movement.)

Activate Prior Knowledge
▶ Distribute the "Movement and the Five Ws" Warm-Up, and have students read the story.
▶ Discuss the story's Five Ws and *H* in detail, including the characters, their relationships, and their surroundings. Say, "Imagine you watched actors pantomime this story. Which of the five Ws and *H* could you identify?"

Teach   Time: About 15 minutes
Prepare Have students make space. Divide them into pairs.
Lead
▶ Assign each group one paragraph from the story, excluding the opening sentence.
▶ Have pairs choose roles from their paragraphs. They should not act out together, members of each pair will use silent, dramatic movement
Say, "Think about your character..."

Music

 SPOTLIGHT ON MUSIC
In music, naming instrumental tone colors as warm, cool, or analogous is subjective. One brass instrument, the French horn, crosses over from one family sound to another family sound. For example, in a small ensemble composition, the French horn is in a woodwind quintet. Listen to "Variations on Simple Gifts" from *Appalachian Spring* by Aaron Copeland. Listen for the French horn. Why is it difficult to recognize the French horn's tone color?

Movement & Dance

Analogous colors share a common hue. Put students in groups of three. The center person is the primary color. The student begins by making a movement. To show that they have something in common with the primary color, but also that they are different, the students on either side copy the movement but change one aspect of it: level, speed, or they add on to the original movement.

# Focus

 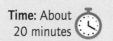

Activate Prior Knowledge

"What are some analogous colors in a box of crayons?" "¿Cuáles son algunos colores análogos en una caja de creyones?"

- Discuss students' responses. Explain how analogous colors can tie together otherwise unrelated elements in a work of art.

Using Literature ⭐ Reading

- Share Scott O'Dell's *Streams to the River, River to the Sea* with the class. This story offers an intimate look through the eyes of Sacagawea at her adventures with explorers Lewis and Clark. You may also want to share Jennifer Armstrong's *Black-Eyed Susan* with the class. This book is about an American pioneer family and their experiences.

Thematic Connection ⭐ Social Studies

- **Going West:** Discuss with students that Georgia O'Keeffe lived in the New Mexico desert and would search for objects found in nature like those in *Red and Pink Rocks and Teeth* because she found beauty in their colors, shapes, and stories. These are things that she could not find while living in New York City. The Navajo artists of New Mexico also used the warm desert colors in much of their artwork.

Introduce the Art

Look

"Let's take a close look at the two works of art." "Vamos a observar detalladamente las dos obras de arte."

 Art History and Culture

Using warm, analogous colors, the artists created a soft, warm feeling in these works of art. This mood created with color might seem ironic with O'Keeffe's chosen objects.
NSAE 4.b

 Web Connection

Visit **nmaa-ryder.si.edu/education/kids/cappy/ 9aokeeffebio.html** for more information about Georgia O'Keeffe and her artwork.

Lesson 2 — Analogous Colors

Look at these two works of art and notice how both the painting and the blanket use related colors to bring various shapes and lines together. Georgia O'Keeffe was interested in painting things that were uniquely American. She used colors found in the New Mexico desert. *Eye Dazzler* is a Navajo blanket. The Navajo of New Mexico are noted for their intricate weavings.

◀ **Georgia O'Keeffe.** (American). *Red and Pink Rocks and Teeth.* 1938.
Oil on canvas. 21 × 13 inches (53.5 × 33 cm.). The Art Institute of Chicago, Chicago, Illinois.

 Art History and Culture

What feeling from America's West have these artists reflected in their works of art?

 Art History and Culture

Georgia O'Keeffe

Georgia O'Keeffe (jôr´ jə ō kēf´) (1887–1986) was raised on a dairy farm in Wisconsin. In the eighth grade she decided to become an artist. She never veered from that path through a life of almost 100 years. She was a leader in twentieth-century art because of her strong personal vision of nature and the western deserts. She became well known for her large paintings of flowers. O'Keeffe was an early leader of the modernism movement and the wife of famous photographer Alfred Stieglitz.

See pages 24–25 and 16–21 for more about art history and subject matter.

Artist Profiles, p. 46

Artist Profile
Georgia O'Keeffe
1887–1986

Georgia O'Keeffe (jôr´ ja ō kēf´) was born in Sun Prairie, Wisconsin. At the age of ten she began taking private art lessons, but the thing she liked most was experimenting with art at home. By 13, she had decided to become an artist. She trained under experts and won many prizes for her art. For years she challenged the art world with her unique vision. She eventually became famous for her spectacular, larger-than-life paintings of natural objects, including flowers, animal skulls, and shells. She loved nature, especially the desert of New Mexico, where she spent the last half of her life. O'Keeffe was married to the famous American photographer Alfred Stieglitz and appears in many of his photographs.

▲ **Artist unknown.** (Navajo Tribe).
Navajo Blanket Eye Dazzler. 1890.
....
Wool, cotton, tapestry weave, slit tapestry, dovetailed
tapestry. 75 × 57 inches (190.5 × 144.78 cm.).
Dallas Museum of Art, Dallas, Texas.

Study both works of art
to find analogous colors.

▶ Find the red colors in
the painting and in
the blanket.

▶ What orange areas or
lines do you see in
each work?

▶ What shapes do you see
in both works of art?

▶ Find areas in both
pieces that are lighter
or darker than red.

Aesthetic Perception

Design Awareness Notice the colors used to paint your
classroom and other parts of the school. Were analogous colors
used? What mood is created with this choice of color scheme?

Art History and Culture

Navajo Blanket Eye Dazzler

The weavers of the Southwest in the 1880s liked the brilliant new
colors of the imported aniline-dyed Germantown wools. The
weavers created interactive diagonal-patterned rugs and blankets
with intensified effects. The eye-dazzler blanket was a trade
blanket. Trade blankets evolved from the original Navajo woven
blankets, after traders encouraged Navajo weavers to create rugs
and wall hangings.

See pages 24–25 and 16–21 for more about art history and the
subject matter.

Artist Profiles, p. 79

⟨Artist Profile⟩

**Navajo Blanket,
Eye Dazzler**

The Navajo people live in the Southwestern
United States. They called themselves
Dineh, "The People of the earth." In the
early 1800s, the Navajo were a powerful and
warring people. At that time, they were
called "lords of the soil." In 1863, Colonel Kit
Carson, commander of the first New Mexico
Volunteers, defeated the Navajo people and
forced them to relocate to Fort Sumner on
the Pecos River in New Mexico. The Navajos
were also forced to sign a peace treaty
promising never to fight with U.S. settlers,
Mexicans, or other Native Americans.

Artist unknown (Navajo). (United States)

Study

▶ O'Keeffe: The dark red is in the center of
the rock. *Navajo Blanket Eye Dazzler:* The
diamond shapes, the triangles at the top
and bottom, and the border at the top and
the bottom are red. There is a dark red
color in some of the zigzag lines.

▶ O'Keeffe: A section of the rock is orange.
Navajo Blanket Eye Dazzler: Some of the
zigzag lines are orange.

▶ O'Keeffe: An oval, rounded triangle, and
irregular free-form shapes are found.
Navajo Blanket Eye Dazzler: Diamonds
and triangles can be seen.

▶ O'Keeffe: The rounded triangle is darker.
Navajo Blanket Eye Dazzler: The brown
zigzag outlines are darker. The center of
the diamond is a white zigzag.
NSAE 5.c

■ For more examples of art from
North America, see the *Art Around
the World Collection.*

Art Journal: Writing

Ask students to look at a color wheel
and identify the analogous colors of a
sunset. Have students write in their Art
Journal about something else that can be
found in nature that is made up of
analogous colors.

Aesthetic Perception

Design Awareness Help students find an area
of the school that is decorated with
analogous colors. If students find none,
encourage them to suggest a new color
scheme for a room in the school using colors
located close together on the color wheel.
Discuss with the students why an area, such
as the library or a silent reading corner,
should be decorated with an analogous color
scheme. To create a calm and relaxing mood.

Developing Visual Literacy Georgia O'Keeffe
primarily used objects she found in her
surroundings of the New Mexico desert.
If you were to paint objects found in your
surroundings what would you choose
to paint?

Web Connection

Visit www.tfaoi.com/aa/2aa/2aa332.htm for more
information on the Navajo people and "eye dazzlers."

Teach

Time: About 30 minutes

"How can you mix hues to create a color wheel using primary, secondary, and intermediate colors?" "¿Cómo pueden mezclar matices para crear un círculo cromático usando colores primarios, secundarios e intermedios?"

- Read and discuss the definitions of analogous colors, color scheme, and intermediate hues on page 102.

Practice

Materials: paper plates, pencils, liquid tempera paints, paintbrushes

Alternate Materials: color pencils

- Distribute the materials and have students follow the directions on page 102.

- Model how to fold a paper plate into twelve equal sections. Ask students to identify and paint every fourth section with the primary hues of red, blue, and yellow. Then have students mix two neighboring primary hues to get the secondary hues. Students should paint these hues in the empty wedges on the left. Last, have students mix the secondary hues with the primary hues that are on either side of the remaining empty wedges to get the intermediate hues. Painting these wedges will complete the color wheel.

Creative Expression

Materials: computer paint program, printer, paper

Alternate Materials: markers

- Distribute the materials and have students follow the directions on page 103.

- Review the Activity Tips on page 236 for visual examples of this lesson's activity.

Art Journal: Brainstorming

Have students sketch ideas in their Art Journal for landscapes that they have seen in their community or imagined. Ask students to keep in mind that they will be painting these landscapes with a computer paint program and will need to use an analogous color scheme.

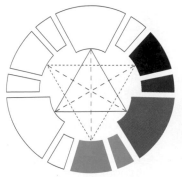

Using Analogous Colors

On the color wheel, **analogous colors** are located next to each other. They share a common color, or hue. For example, violet, blue, blue-green, and green are analogous colors. They share the color blue and are next to each other on the color wheel.

A **color scheme** is a plan for organizing colors. Analogous colors are one type of color scheme. The color scheme on the upper left shares the color blue. The color scheme on the lower left shares the color red.

Intermediate hues are made by mixing a primary hue with an adjacent secondary hue. Red and orange make the intermediate color red-orange.

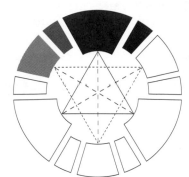

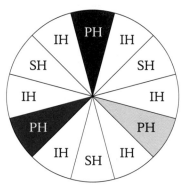

Practice

Create a color wheel. Use the primary, secondary, and intermediate colors. Use paint.

1. Fold a paper plate into twelve equal sections. Paint every fourth wedge a primary hue.

2. Combine neighboring primary hues to make secondary hues. Paint the three middle wedges with secondary hues.

3. Mix secondary hues with the primary hues to create intermediate hues. Paint the intermediate hues in the empty wedges between the secondary and primary hues to complete the color wheel.

PH–Primary hue
SH–Secondary hue
IH–Intermediate hue

Differentiated Instruction

Reteach
Have the students find examples of analogous colors in their community. Use a color wheel to have students point out the analogous colors.

Special Needs
Students may experience more success in the Practice activity if they are allowed to lightly write the name of each color onto the wedge before painting.

ELL
Discuss with students how many words, like colors, can seem to be similar but actually represent slightly different concepts. Look at the many analogous colors of blue. Then define synonymous words such as *great*, *fantastic*, and *supreme*.

◀ **Mariella Lopez.**
Age 11.

Think about how the student artist used analogous colors to create a landscape painting.

Creative Expression

How could you create a landscape painting using a computer? Use a paint program to create an analogous landscape.

1. Use the pencil tool in a paint program to create a landscape that includes a foreground, middleground, and background.
2. Check the colors in the palette for analogous color schemes.
3. Use brush, airbrush, and fill tools to paint the landscape.

Art Criticism

Describe What objects and shapes did you include in your landscape painting?

Analyze Name the analogous colors you used in your painting.

Interpret Where might you find a landscape that looks like this painting?

Decide Did you successfully use analogous colors to create a landscape painting?

eflect

 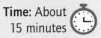

Review and Assess

"Were you able to create a landscape painting using analogous colors?" "¿Pudieron crear una pintura de un paisaje usando colores análogos?" NSAE 2.a

Think

The student artist used analogous colors to create a landscape painting using yellows and reds.

- Use *Large Print 65 Diva* to have students identify and describe the use of analogous color schemes in this work of art.

Informal Assessment

- For standardized-format test practice using this lesson's art content, see pages 32–33 in *Reading and Writing Test Preparation.*

Art Journal: Critical Thinking

Have students answer the four art criticism questions—Describe, Analyze, Interpret, and Decide—in their Art Journals. In small groups, have students discuss their analogous landscape paintings.

Art Across the Curriculum

Use these simple ideas to reinforce art concepts across the curriculum.

★ **Expository Writing** Have students write an expository paragraph explaining the steps to create a color wheel including the following key words: hue, primary hues, secondary hues, and intermediate hues.

★ **Math** Use the color wheels that students have painted when reviewing division and fraction skills in math.

★ **Science** Talk about the properties of the element on the periodic tables. Note how the properties of the elemental families vary but are analogous, or similar to each other.

★ **Social Studies** Identify the geographic area of the Navajo nation and reservation.

★ **Technology** Talk about different storage devices, like floppy disks, CDs, and zip drives. They are analogous in that they perform the same function, but vary in the way they save information. NSAE 6.b

Analogous Colors

Extra! For the Art Specialist

Time: About 45 minutes

Focus

Study **Large Print 65** *Diva* notice how analogous colors are used to tie the various shapes and lines together. What colors do you see? What common color do you see shared among the colors in the artwork?

Teach

Explain to the students that in nonobjective art the subject matter is usually about one of the art elements. Encourage the students to overlap colors and to blend their oil pastels while working on their nonobjective drawings. Demonstrate blending and overlapping the oil-pastel colors.

Reflect

Have students evaluate their works of art using the four steps of art criticism. Encourage them to locate and describe the analogous color schemes.

Alternate Activity

Materials:
- color wheel
- 9″ × 12″ black construction paper
- scrap paper
- newspaper
- oil pastels

1. Have students look at the color wheel and select a section of analogous colors. Explain that these colors should share a common hue.

2. Ask students to decide on a shape that they like. Instruct students to repeat this shape three or five times on their paper, while varying the sizes of the shapes. The shapes may overlap.

3. Students will use oil pastels to color in the shapes with the chosen analogous colors. Overlapping oil pastels will allow students to blend their colors.

4. Students should add a variety of lines and smaller shapes to complete the design.

Research in Art Education

Case studies have indicated that students perceive "that the arts facilitate their personal and social development." It also appeared that to gain the full benefit of arts education, students should be exposed to all of the arts, including fine arts, dance, theatre, and music ("Arts Education in Secondary School: Effects and Effectiveness" in *Critical Links*, p. 76). As students learn about analogous colors in fine arts, it can also be effective to incorporate how neighboring musical notes, blended movement in dance, and smooth dialogue in theatre can have the same effect on the viewer.
NSAE 6.a

Assessment

Use the following rubric to evaluate the artwork students make in the Creative Expression activity and to assess students' understanding of analogous colors.

Have students complete page 35 or 36 in their *Assessment* books.

	Art History and Culture	Aesthetic Perception	Creative Expression	Art Criticism
3 POINTS	The student demonstrates knowledge of the Navajo people and the life and work of Georgia O'Keeffe.	The student accurately identifies analogous color schemes.	The student's painting clearly illustrates the use of analogous colors.	The student evaluates own work using the four steps of art criticism.
2 POINTS	The student's knowledge of the Navajo people and the life and work of Georgia O'Keeffe is weak or incomplete.	The student shows emerging awareness of analogous color schemes.	The student's painting shows some awareness of analogous colors.	The student attempts to evaluate own work, but shows an incomplete understanding of evaluation criteria.
1 POINT	The student cannot demonstrate knowledge of the Navajo people or Georgia O'Keeffe.	The student cannot identify analogous color schemes.	The student's painting shows no understanding of analogous colors.	The student makes no attempt to evaluate own artwork.

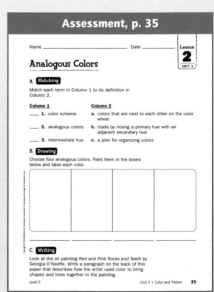

Assessment, p. 35

Analogous Colors

Complementary Colors

Lesson 3 introduces complementary colors. Artists use complementary colors to create contrast and visual excitement in their artwork.

Objectives

 Art History and Culture

To demonstrate knowledge of *Featherwork Neckpiece* from Peru and the life and artwork of Willis "Bing" Davis

 Creative Expression

To use complementary colors to create a watercolor still life

 Aesthetic Perception

To identify complementary color schemes in art and the environment

 Art Criticism

To evaluate one's own work using the four steps of art criticism

Vocabulary Vocabulary

Review the following vocabulary words with students before beginning the lesson.

complementary colors colores complementarios—colors opposite each other on the color wheel

color intensity intensidad del color—the brightness or dullness of a color

See page 119B for additional Spanish vocabulary resources.

 Art Journal: Vocabulary

Have students add these words to the Vocabulary section of their Art Journals.

Lesson Materials

- scissors
- colored paper
- posterboard
- construction paper in complementary colors
- pencils
- glue
- sketch paper

Alternate Materials:
- markers
- crayons

Program Resources

- *Reading and Writing Test Prep.,* pp. 34–35
- *Transparency 15*
- *Flash Card 12*
- *Artist Profiles,* pp. 71, 19
- *Animals Through History Time Line*
- *Assessment,* pp. 37–38
- *Large Prints 65* Diva and *66* Double Entrance
- *Art Around the World Collection*

Concept Trace
Complementary Colors
Introduced: Level 4, Unit 3, Lesson 3

Reinforced: Level 6, Unit 2, Lesson 3

Lesson 3 Arts Integration

Theatre

Complete Unit 3, Lesson 3, on pages 58–59 of *Theatre Arts Connections.*

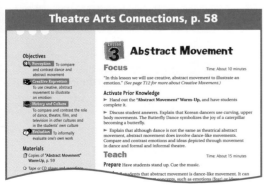

Music

 Listen to *Symphony No 9 in D Minor, Op 125 (choral)* "Fourth Movement" by Ludwig van Beethoven. Beethoven was the first composer to add voices to the blend of the orchestra in a symphony. Audiences enjoy how the orchestra, soloists, and chorus complement one another.

Movement & Dance

Organize students into a circle. Give each student a sticker or card that is either a primary or secondary color. Call out a primary color, such as red. All the students holding red move to the center of the circle and freeze in a shape. The complementary color of red is green. Students holding green move to the center of the circle and find a person holding red and connect onto their shape.

# Focus

Time: About 20 minutes

Activate Prior Knowledge

"What items can you think of that represent cultural diversity in your daily life?" "¿En qué artículos pueden pensar que representan una diversidad cultural en su vida diaria?"

- Discuss students' answers to the question. Explain how artists can use complementary colors to catch the viewer's attention.

Using Literature ⭐ Reading

- Share with the class Dawnine Spivak's book *Grass Sandals: The Travel of Basho*. It is the story of one of Japan's most noted poets and his journeys. Encourage students to notice the use of complementary colors in the illustrations.

Thematic Connection ⭐ Social Studies

- **Cultural Diversity:** Brainstorm with students a list of the many cultural influences that they come in contact with. Discuss how each of these cultures makes a difference in their lives. Encourage students to discuss the importance of understanding why and how people from many cultures live differently.

Introduce the Art

Look

"Let's take a close look at the two works of art." "Vamos a observar detalladamente las dos obras de arte."

Artist's Purpose ⭐ Reading

- Have students look at the two works of art in this lesson. As a class, brainstorm ideas for the artists' purposes when creating these works of art.

🏺 Art History and Culture

Featherwork Neckpiece honors the Incan civilization's respect for the ocean. Willis "Bing" Davis honors his African heritage by celebrating the traditional *egungun* dance in his artwork. NSAE 4.a

🖥 **Web Connection**
Visit **www.mintmuseum.org/digit/** to further explore information about the Incan civilization and pre-Columbian artifacts.

Lesson 3 # Complementary Colors

Look at the two pieces of artwork. Notice how the artists chose contrasting colors. *Featherwork Neckpiece* is an example of an adornment. An adornment decorates or adds beauty to an object or a person. Willis "Bing" Davis uses historical African patterns and forms as inspiration for his contemporary images. In Davis's work, he reflects on the images and feelings he experienced while attending a ritual dance in Nigeria.

▲ **Artist unknown.** (Peru).
Featherwork Neckpiece. c. 1350–1476.
....
Cotton, feathers, beads. Late Intermediate Period:
China style. $13\frac{1}{4} \times 11\frac{1}{2}$ inches (33.02 × 29.21 cm.).
Dallas Museum of Art, Dallas, Texas.

Art History and Culture

How have these artists honored cultural traditions through their artwork?

Art History and Culture

Featherwork Neckpiece

Neckpieces such as this one have been found by archaeologists in Incan burial graves hidden in the Andes Mountains. This neckpiece is a weaving made from llama wool, exotic bird feathers, and seashells. The importance of the ocean to the Incan civilization's survival is portrayed in the images of the pelicans and the man catching fish.

See pages 24–25 and 16–21 for more about art history and subject matter.

Artist Profiles, p. 71

> Artist Profile
> ### Featherwork Neckpiece
> The weavers of Incan society were mostly men. They traveled deep into the jungle to capture the exotic birds whose feathers they used in making ceremonial clothing.
>
> ◄ **Artist unknown (Incan).** (Peru).
> *Featherwork Neckpiece.* 1350–1476.
> Cotton, feathers, beads. Late Intermediate Period: China style.

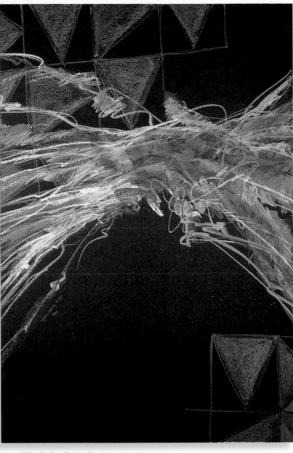

Study both works of art to find their complementary color schemes.

► What colors do you see?

► Do you see different shades or tints of these colors?

► What colors do you see repeated?

► Think about how the artist created contrast in each artwork.

▲ **Willis "Bing" Davis.** (American). *Ancestral Spirit Dance #187.*

Oil pastel. 60 × 40 inches (152.4 × 101.6 cm.). Private collection.

 Aesthetic Perception

Design Awareness Do you notice any colors on your notebooks, bags, clothes, or other objects that contrast or look bright next to each other? Which colors do you notice?

Art History and Culture

Willis "Bing" Davis

Willis "Bing" Davis (wil´ is bing dā´ ves) (1937–) became interested in art while in elementary school. Of African American heritage, Davis attended DePauw University in Indiana, Miami University in Oxford, Ohio, Indiana State University, and the Dayton Art Institute in Ohio. Davis has been an artist and teacher since 1960. His artwork includes drawings, paintings, ceramics, and jewelry.

See pages 24–25 and 16–21 for more about art history and the subject matter.

Artist Profiles, p. 19

Artist Profile

Willis "Bing" Davis
b. 1937

Bing Davis (bing dā´ vas) was born in Dayton, Ohio. He was a student with many talents and gifts, including those for athletics and the arts. Because he excelled in sports, he was awarded a scholarship to DePauw University in Indiana, where he earned a degree in art education. He continued to study and earned his master's degree from Miami University in Oxford, Ohio. Davis has pioneered such projects as the Dayton-based, now nationwide, program Artists in the Schools. Davis has had more than 50 one-man exhibitions since 1959.

Study

► *Featherwork Neckpiece:* bright orange, violet, and blue. Davis: blue, orange.

► Both works have different shades or tints of one color. Davis: tints of turquoise, blue, and violet are included.

► The repeated colors in both works are blue and orange.

► The artists created contrast in the works of art by using complementary colors.
NSAE 1.5c

■ For more examples of art from Latin America, see the *Art Around the World Collection.*

Art Journal: Writing

Ask students to think about flags they are familiar with. Have students look for the use of complementary colors in these flags and describe their findings in their Art Journals.

Aesthetic Perception

Design Awareness Look at the covers of several books, magazines, movies, and compact discs with students. Encourage students to find examples of complementary colors used by the designers in an effort to grab the attention of potential customers. Discuss with the class the reasons why designers would choose to use bold, contrasting colors when marketing products for sale.

Developing Visual Literacy Have students share with the class what they imagine hearing when looking at these works of art, and then explain what gives them this impression. Compare and contrast like and unlike sounds, and discuss the freedom that art gives the viewer to interpret the piece in his or her own way.

Web Connection

Visit www.exploris.org/learn/activities/africa/ nigeria/egungun_costume/ for more information about the egungun dance. This African festival ceremony was the inspiration for Willis "Bing" Davis's *Ancestral Spirit Dance #187.*

Teach

"How do complementary colors affect each other?" "¿Cómo se afectan entre sí los colores complementarios?"

- Read and discuss the definition of complementary colors on page 106.

Practice

Materials: scissors, colored paper

Alternate Materials: markers

- Distribute materials and have students follow the directions on page 106.

- Have students select two complementary-colored pieces of paper. Instruct students to cut a hole in just one of the pieces of paper and place this over the other piece of paper. Discuss with students how the colors appear next to each other and why an artist would choose to use complementary colors.

Creative Expression

Materials: fruit, six-inch squares of paper, watercolor paints, water, paper towels, scissors, colored construction paper

Alternate Materials: pictures of fruit

- Distribute the materials and have students follow the directions on page 107.

- Review the Activity Tips on page 237 for visual examples of this lesson's activity.

- See the Technique Tips on page 219 for more information on watercolor paints.

 Art Journal: Sketching
Have students look at the fruit or fruit pictures and make sketches of what they see in their Art Journals.

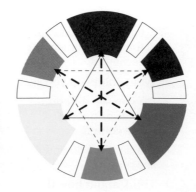

Using Complementary Colors

Colors opposite each other on the color wheel are called **complementary colors.** A complement of a color is the strongest contrast to the color. Complementary colors stand out when they are next to each other. Red and green, blue and orange, and violet and yellow are all pairs of complementary colors.

Complementary colors seem to vibrate when they are placed next to each other.

Mixing a color with its complement lowers the brightness of that color. When two complementary colors are mixed, the color becomes dull. Look at the intensity scale. The more orange that you add to the color blue, the darker it becomes.

Practice

Experiment with pieces of colored paper to see how complementary colors affect each other.

1. Choose two pieces of paper of complementary colors.

2. Cut a hole in one of the pieces of paper. Place the paper with the hole over the complementary-colored piece.

3. Notice how the complementary colors contrast.

Differentiated Instruction

Reteach
After students find an example of an artwork or advertisement that uses complementary colors, have them sketch their own version of this piece using colored pencils or crayons of analogous or monochromatic colors instead. Discuss the effects that occur by changing these color schemes.

Special Needs
To assess student understanding of complementary color schemes after the project is complete, have students use the color wheel to point out the two complementary colors they used in their artwork and one other pair of complements.

ELL
Review with students the use of a thesaurus as a reference to find synonyms. Students may have learned one English translated word but have difficulty with multiple words with similar meanings. Have students look up the word *complementary* and list the synonyms they find.

◄ **Patricia Lazzari.**
Age 10.

Think about the complementary colors that the student artist chose to use in this still life.

Creative Expression

How could you use complementary colors to make an exciting still life? Design and create a still-life painting with watercolors.

1. Select fruit of like colors.
2. Refer to the sketches in your Art Journal, and draw the fruit. Use different sizes and shapes on squares of paper.
3. Paint the fruit with shades and tints of one chosen hue.
4. Cut out the fruit shapes.
5. Arrange and glue the fruit on a complementary-colored background.

Art Criticism

Describe What objects did you include in your still life?

Analyze Which complementary colors did you use in this still life?

Interpret How do your complementary colors create contrast and visual excitement?

Decide Do the complementary colors add excitement to your still-life watercolor?

Reflect

Time: About 15 minutes

Review and Assess

"Were you able to add excitement to your still life using complementary colors?" "¿Pudieron agregar emoción a su naturaleza muerta usando colores complementarios?" NSAE 2.a

Think

The student used tints and shades of red for painting the apples and used red's complementary color, green, for the background.

■ Use **Large Prints 65** *Diva* and **66** *Double Entrance* to have students identify and describe the use of a complementary color scheme.

Informal Assessment

■ For standardized-format test practice using this lesson's art content, see pages 34–35 in **Reading and Writing Test Preparation.**

Art Journal: Critical Thinking

Have students answer the four art criticism questions—Describe, Analyze, Interpret, and Decide—in their Art Journals. In small groups, have students discuss their still-life paintings.

Art Across the Curriculum

Use these simple ideas to reinforce art concepts across the curriculum.

★ **Poetry Writing** Have students write haiku about the fruit that is featured in their watercolor paintings.

★ **Math** When studying fractions review how to count musical notes. Dancers use these beats to coordinate their moves with the music.

★ **Science** As a class, experiment with looking at green, blue, red, and yellow colors. Then switch to a plain white sheet of paper and notice how the eyes produce the complementary colors. Explain that the neurons in the retina and thalamus can only be activated by one set of these colors at a time.

★ **Social Studies** Research the African *egungun* dance in study groups. This dance is a part of the African ceremony that inspired Willis "Bing" Davis's *Ancestral Spirit Dance #187*.

★ **Technology** Have students use a paint program to make a color wheel. Visit **SRAonline.com** to print instructions for this activity.
NSAE 6.b

Lesson 3 Wrap-Up

Complementary Colors

Extra! **For the Art Specialist** Time: About 30 minutes

Focus

Study **Large Prints 65** *Diva* and **66** *Double Entrance* to have students discuss how complementary colors are often used to create contrast in an artwork. Ask students: What are the main colors used in this artwork? How are they arranged? What type of mood is created by the use of complementary colors in this work?

Teach

Explain to the students that complementary colors are across from one another on the color wheel. One is a cool color and the other is warm. Explain that they will be using a set of complementary colors to paint a papier-mâché mask. Prior to the lesson, collect milk jugs and cut them lengthwise so that they lie flat on the tabletop.

Reflect

Have students evaluate their works of art using the four steps of art criticism. Encourage them to locate and describe the complementary colors they used.

Alternate Activity

Materials:
- Art Journals
- pencils, erasers
- images of animals
- plastic milk jugs
- newspaper
- wheat paste
- containers to mix paste
- masking tape
- acrylic paints
- paintbrushes
- water containers

1. Have students create several sketches of animal faces to use for their masks in their Art Journals.

2. Students will cover the surface of the milk carton with two layers of papier-mâché. Allow this to dry.

3. Have them tape the newspaper to form the features of the animal face. When the features are securely attached, two layers of papier-mâché should be applied. Let the masks dry completely.

4. Students should paint their masks using only one set of complementary colors. Instruct students to paint the face one color and the features the complement to create a contrast.

Research in Art Education

"Just as culture shapes art, art shapes culture. Our convictions, our technology, and our imagination shape our images, and our images, in turn, shape our perception of the world." (Eisner, Elliot. *The Role of Disciplined-Based Art Education in America's Schools.* The Getty Center for Arts Education in the Arts, 1987.)

Assessment Use the following rubric to evaluate the artwork students make in the Creative Expression activity and to assess students' understanding of complementary colors.

Have students complete page 37 or 38 in their *Assessment* books.

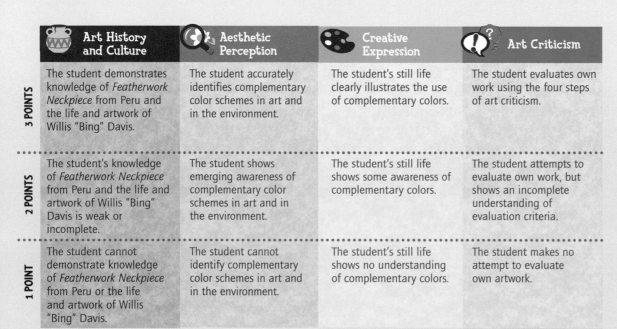

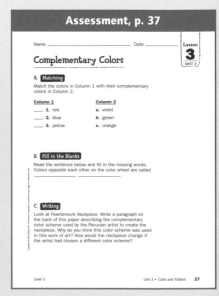

107A UNIT 3 • Color and Pattern

Lesson 4 Overview

Warm and Cool Colors

Lesson 4 introduces warm and cool colors. Artists use warm and cool color schemes to create a mood or feeling in their artwork.

Objectives

 Art History and Culture

To become knowledgeable about the lives and art of Raoul Dufy and Manabu Mabe

 Creative Expression

To create a collage using warm and cool colors

 Aesthetic Perception

To identify warm and cool colors in art and in the environment

Art Criticism

To evaluate one's own work using the four steps of art criticism

Vocabulary [★] Vocabulary

Review the following vocabulary words with students.

warm color color cálido—a color that suggests a warm mood and seems to move toward the viewer; red, orange, and yellow are warm colors.

cool color color fresco—a color that suggests a cool mood and seems to recede from the viewer; blue, green, and violet are cool colors.

See page 119B for additional vocabulary and Spanish vocabulary resources.

 Art Journal: Vocabulary

Have students add these words to the Vocabulary section of their Art Journals.

Lesson Materials

- scissors
- glue
- 9" × 12" white paper
- construction paper in warm and cool colors
- tissue paper in warm and cool colors
- water

Alternate Materials:
- markers

Program Resources

- *Reading and Writing Test Prep.*, pp. 36–37
- *Transparency 16*
- *Flash Card 15*
- *Artist Profiles*, pp. 22, 39
- *Animals Through History Time Line*
- *Assessment*, pp. 39–40
- *Large Prints 65* Diva and *66* Double Entrance
- *Art Around the World Collection*

Concept Trace
Warm and Cool Colors
Introduced: Level 4, Unit 3, Lesson 6

Reinforced: Level 6, Unit 2, Lesson 4

Lesson 4 Arts Integration

Theatre

Complete Unit 3, Lesson 4, on pages 60–61 of *Theatre Arts Connections.*

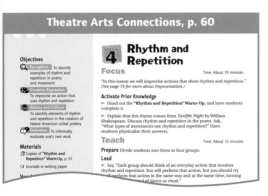

Theatre Arts Connections, p. 60

Music

 Listen to *Concerto for Two Trumpets RV 537* by Antonio Vivaldi. Trumpets are featured with a full orchestra in this composition. Describing a tone color as cool or warm is subjective. If we name the high trumpets "cool," do you hear an instrument that could be considered a "warm" color?

Movement & Dance

Brainstorm to create a list of cool-color objects and warm-color objects. For example, cool: rain, glacier, snow; warm: volcano, candle, lightning bolt. Students move for eight counts to express the warm and cool quality of each idea on the list. Then build a sequence that shows all of the ideas in the order of a cool movement followed by a warm movement.

 **Focus**

Activate Prior Knowledge

"Can the colors around you affect your mood?" "¿Pueden afectar su ánimo los colores a su alrededor?"

- Discuss how artists can use warm and cool colors to change the mood expressed by their artwork.

Using Literature ⭐ Reading

- Read *Snowflake Bentley*, by Jacqueline Briggs Martin, with the class. Encourage students to take note of the illustrator's use of cool colors and warm colors throughout the book.

Thematic Connection ⭐ Social Studies

- **Colors:** Ask students to list the colors they like. Have them identify these colors as cool or warm and explain how this might explain something about their personality.

Introduce the Art

Look

"Let's take a close look at the two works of art." "Vamos a observar detalladamente las dos obras de arte."

Comparing and Contrasting ⭐ Reading

- Have students list the similarities and the differences of these two works of art. The artists used similar warm and cool color schemes. Dufy's artwork is an abstract scene of the inside of a room with a view out onto the water. Mabe's artwork is nonobjective.

 Art History and Culture

Raoul Dufy's painting is abstract. He simplified and exaggerated the forms in this scene. Manabu Mabe's painting contains lines, shapes, and colors, but no objects or people. Therefore, this is a nonojective painting.

💻 **Web Connection**

Visit **factmonster.com/ce6/people/A0816255.html** for further information on Raoul Dufy and his artwork.

Also visit **webexhibits.org/colorart/fauve.html** to learn more about the fauvists.

Warm and Cool Colors

▲ **Raoul Dufy.** (French). *Fenetre Ouverte Devant la Mer (Window Open to the Sea)*. 1923.
Oil on canvas. 29 × 23 inches (73.66 × 58.42 cm). New Orleans Museum of Art, New Orleans, Louisiana.

Look at the artwork on these pages. Identify how the warm and cool colors affect the mood of the artwork. Dufy used the contrast of warm and cool colors in *Window Open to the Sea* to show the difference between the warm interior scene and the cool ocean scene. Mabe used contrast between light and dark as well as warm and cool to express his emotions in his nonobjective painting *Melancholy Metropolis*.

 Art History and Culture

Which work of art is abstract? Which work of art is nonobjective?

Art History and Culture

Raoul Dufy

Raoul Dufy (rä ül´ dü fē´) (1877–1953) enrolled at the Le Havre School of Fine Arts at the age of fifteen in his hometown of Le Havre, France. There he met and became lifelong friends with Georges Braque, who later became an influential cubist. Near the age of thirty, Dufy's style transitioned from impressionist to fauvist (meaning "wild beast"), due to the influence of Henri Matisse. This style lasted only four years. Dufy favored using bright, clear colors with free-moving brushstrokes. He also worked as an illustrator, fabric designer, and decorator.

See pages 24–25 and 16–21 for more about art history and the subject matter.

Artist Profiles, p. 22

◆ Artist Profile ◆
Raoul Dufy
1877–1953

Raoul Dufy (rä ool´ dü´ fä) was born in Le Havre, France, to an impoverished but happy family. He had an early interest in art and a passion for drawing. At the age of 15, he enrolled at the Le Havre School of Fine Arts, where he met Georges Braque, who was a pioneer of cubism, along with Picasso. Braque became a lifelong friend and major artistic influence. In 1900, Dufy received a grant to attend the École des Beaux-Arts in Paris. His interest in impressionism was directed toward fauvism under the influence of Matisse in 1905. He also worked as an illustrator, fabric designer, and decorator. *Time* magazine awarded him the moniker "Grandaddy of Modern Chic."

◀ **Manabu Mabe.** (Brazilian).
Melancholy Metropolis. 1961.
....
Oil on canvas. $72\frac{7}{8} \times 78\frac{7}{8} \times 1\frac{1}{4}$ inches
(185.40 × 200.5 × 2.5 cm). Walker
Art Center, Minneapolis, Minnesota.

Study both paintings to find the warm and cool colors.

- What colors do you see that remind you of water or a cool winter day?

- What colors do you see that remind you of fire?

- Imagine these works of art painted in only cool colors. How would this change the mood of these paintings?

- Imagine these works of art painted in only warm colors. How would this change the mood of these paintings?

- Why do you think these artists decided to use both warm and cool colors in these paintings?

Aesthetic Perception

Design Awareness Take time to notice how cool and warm colors are used in your school, home, and other indoor areas.

Study

▶ Dufy: blue, green, violet. Mabe: blue, violet, gray.

▶ Dufy: red, orange, yellow. Mabe: red, orange, gold.

▶ To the viewer, the artwork might seem calm, relaxed, and detached.

▶ To the viewer, the artwork might seem cozy, cramped, and energizing.

▶ Some acceptable answers for this question include: to create a realistic feel, balance, contrast, and interest.

■ For more examples of abstract/nonobjective art, see *The National Museum of Women in the Arts Collection.*

Art Journal: Writing

Ask students what colors they think of when they imagine a day in the winter, summer, fall, or spring. Have students identify these colors in their Art Journal and label them *cool* or *warm*.

Aesthetic Perception

Design Awareness Discuss with students how color choices are important when designing living spaces, work spaces, and recreational areas.

Developing Visual Literacy Ask students to describe the moods created by Dufy and Mabe in these works of art. Have students support their answers by explaining how the warm and cool colors contribute to these moods.

Art History and Culture

Manabu Mabe

Manabu Mabe (mä nä bōō mä´ be) (1924–1997) was the oldest of seven sons. He and his family moved from Shiranui, Japan, to Brazil when he was ten years old. His family owned and worked on a coffee plantation there. Manabu loved to draw as a young child. In 1945 a bad frost prevented the family from working in the field and gave Manabu an opportunity to experiment with his new oil paints. He painted many landscapes and still lifes on cardboard and on scraps of wood that he found. His family encouraged his talent. After his father's death, Manabu sold the plantation, married, and pursued a career as an artist.

See pages 24–25 and 16–21 for more about art history and the subject matter.

Artist Profiles, p. 39

● Artist Profile ●
Manabu Mabe
1924–1997
Manabu Mabe (mä nä bōō mä´ be) was born in Kumamoto, Japan. In 1934, he moved with his family to Brazil. In São Paulo, Mabe worked on a coffee plantation. He painted landscapes and still lifes in his free time. In the late 1950s, he won recognition from critics for his abstract paintings. He had many solo shows in art galleries and was featured in exhibitions worldwide.

Web Connection

Visit **www.mabe.com** for more information on Manabu Mabe and his artwork.

 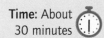

Teach

Time: About 30 minutes

"How can you use warm and cool colors in your artwork?" "¿Cómo pueden usar colores cálidos y fríos en sus obras de arte?"

- Read and discuss the definitions of warm colors and cool colors on page 110.

Practice

Materials: scissors, tissue paper in warm and cool colors

Alternate Materials: markers

- Distribute materials and have students follow the directions on page 110.

- Have students cut up squares of both warm- and cool-colored tissue paper. Then ask them to separate the warm-colored pieces from the cool-colored pieces. Encourage students to experiment with color by overlapping various combinations of colors and noting how they change.

 ## Creative Expression

Materials: construction paper in warm and cool colors, tissue paper in warm and cool colors, glue, scissors, 9" × 12" white paper

Alternate Materials: watercolor paints, paintbrushes, water container, newspaper

- Distribute the materials and have students follow the directions on page 111.

- Review the Activity Tips on page 237 for visual examples of this lesson's activity.

- See the Technique Tips on page 224 for more information on creating a collage.

Art Journal: Brainstorming

Have students brainstorm ideas in their Art Journals for creating a collage in which they will use warm and cool colors.

Using Warm and Cool Colors

Sometimes colors are divided into warm and cool colors. They make us think about warm and cool things when we see them.

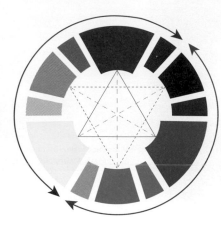

Warm colors are red, orange, and yellow. They suggest warmth and seem to move toward the viewer. They remind us of the colors of the sun or fire. Artists use warm colors to express a warm mood in their artwork.

Cool colors are blue, green, and violet. They suggest coolness and seem to move away from the viewer. Cool colors remind us of ice, water, and grass. Artists use cool colors to express a cool mood in their artwork.

Practice

Use tissue paper to experiment with warm and cool colors.

1. Cut out squares of colored tissue paper. Separate the warm colors and the cool colors.

2. Overlap warm-colored and cool-colored tissue paper. Then overlap the cool colors with each other. Do the same with the warm colors.

3. Notice how the colors change when they are placed together.

110 Unit 3 • Lesson 4

Differentiated Instruction

Reteach

Organize a schoolwide art show. Accept submissions from students and staff. Encourage students to analyze the works of art, looking for the use of warm and cool colors and other properties.

Special Needs

Students who have difficulty cutting can achieve successful results in this project by tearing paper instead.

ELL

Define the term *mood* for students as "how a person is feeling." Ask students to draw some faces representing happy, sad, mad, and calm moods. Show students some abstract artwork that relies on color, shape, and lines to convey these moods. Ask students to point to the face that matches.

◄ **Ester Stewart Dage.**
Age 11.

Think about how the warm and cool colors contribute to the mood of the artwork.

Creative Expression

How can you create a specific mood in a collage? Use warm and cool colors to create a collage.

1. Think about the warm and cool colors you like.
2. Cut free-form and geometric shapes out of colored drawing paper and tissue paper.
3. Arrange your shapes on white paper. Combine the warm and cool colors. Allow the tissue-paper shapes to overlap some of the drawing-paper shapes.
4. Use a glue-water wash to attach your shapes onto the white background.

Art Criticism

Describe What colors did you overlap? What shapes did you use?

Analyze Did you use warm and cool colors to organize your collage? Did changes occur when you overlapped colors with the tissue paper?

Interpret What mood was created with your use of colors?

Decide How would you change this collage?

Unit 3 • Lesson 4   **111**

 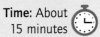 **R**eflect   **Time:** About 15 minutes

Review and Assess
"Were you able to create a collage using warm and cool colors?" "¿Pudieron crear un collage usando colores cálidos y fríos?" NSAE 2.a

Think
The artist used a mixture of warm and cool colors to create a mood that is exciting and unpredictable.

- Use *Large Prints 65 Diva* and *66 Double Entrance* to have students identify and describe the use of warm and cool colors.

Informal Assessment
- For standardized-format test practice using this lesson's art content, see pages 36–37 in *Reading and Writing Test Preparation.*

Art Journal: Critical Thinking
Have students answer the four art criticism questions—Describe, Analyze, Interpret, and Decide—in their Art Journals. In small groups, have students discuss their collages. NSAE 2.a

Art Across the Curriculum

Use these simple ideas to reinforce art concepts across the curriculum.

★ **Persuasive Writing** Have students write a persuasive advertisement for a vacation spot. Encourage students to sketch an illustration using warm or cool colors to accompany it.

★ **Math** Have students divide the number of warm colors by the number of cool colors, or visa versa, in a work of art.

★ **Science** Discuss warm and cool air-pressure systems.

★ **Social Studies** Have students locate Japan and Brazil on a world map and discuss how making this move might have affected Manabu Mabe at the age of ten.

★ **Technology** Have students create outdoor scenes with a paint program using cool and warm colors. Then ask students to reverse the cool and warm colors in an abstract outdoor scene. Visit **SRAonline.com** to print detailed instructions for this activity. NSAE 6.b

Warm and Cool Colors

For the Art Specialist

Time: About 45 minutes

Focus

Study **Large Prints 65** *Diva* and **66** *Double Entrance* to have students discuss how they can use both warm and cool colors to create a mood and to create contrast in an artwork.

Teach

Explain to the students that colors can affect the way we feel. A work of art that has predominantly warm colors can make us feel happy and secure. A work that is primarily made of cool colors is usually more calm and quiet. Ask the students to think of the emotion "blue" and how they could use color to relate that emotion.

Reflect

Have students evaluate their works of art using the four steps of art criticism.

Alternate Activity

Materials:
- Art Journal
- pencils, erasers
- 9" × 12" drawing paper
- magazines
- scissors
- tissue paper
- glue solution: two parts glue to one part water
- watercolor paints
- paintbrushes
- water containers
- oil pastels
- newspaper

1. Have students look through a magazine and for images of people or animals that communicate emotions and cut these out.

2. Students will plan out an environment in their Art Journals for these images.

3. Students will choose what colors best represent the emotion they are portraying. Tear the tissue paper and use the glue solution to cover the background. Overlap papers in some areas and allow the paper to dry.

4. Use oil pastels and watercolor paints to create the environment. Glue images on.

Research
in Art Education

"There is more to learning about art than learning to do it. Most people will not actually seek to make art in their lifetime, but all of us have daily contact with visual stimuli that deliberately (in package design, fashion, or good building) or accidentally (a pattern of leaves on snow or an unexpected bright color against a faded doorway) appeal to our aesthetic sense and offer a bit of visual order in the bustle of the everyday." (Elizabeth Vallance. "Criticism as Subject Matter in Schools and in Art Museums." *Journal of Aesthetic Education* 22. 1988. 69–81.)

Assessment
Use the following rubric to evaluate the artwork students make in the Creative Expression activity and to assess students' understanding of warm and cool colors.

Have students complete page 39 or 40 in their *Assessment* books.

	Art History and Culture	Aesthetic Perception	Creative Expression	Art Criticism
3 POINTS	The student can demonstrate knowledge of the lives and art of Raoul Dufy and Manabu Mabe.	The student accurately identifies warm and cool colors.	The student's collage clearly illustrates the use of warm and cool colors.	The student thoughtfully and honestly evaluates own work using the four steps of art criticism.
2 POINTS	The student's knowledge of the lives and art of Raoul Dufy and Manabu Mabe is weak or incomplete.	The student shows emerging awareness of warm and cool colors.	The student's collage shows some awareness of warm and cool colors.	The student attempts to evaluate own work, but shows an incomplete understanding of evaluation criteria.
1 POINT	The student cannot demonstrate knowledge of the lives and art of Raoul Dufy or Manabu Mabe.	The student cannot identify warm and cool colors.	The student's collage shows no understanding of warm and cool colors.	The student makes no attempt to evaluate own artwork.

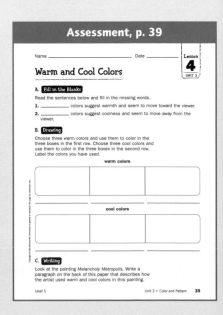

Lesson

Pattern

Overview

Lesson 5 introduces the ways patterns are used in creating surface designs by repeating lines, shapes, and colors.

Objectives

 Art History and Culture

To become familiar with the culture and the weavings of the Wari people of Peru and the Kuba group of the Congo

Creative Expression

To design wrapping paper with a random pattern using original motifs

 Aesthetic Perception

To recognize motifs and patterns in art and the environment

Art Criticism

To evaluate one's own work using the four steps of art criticism

Vocabulary ⭐ Vocabulary

Review the following vocabulary words with students before beginning the lesson.

pattern patrón—a repeated design that decorates the surface of fabrics, objects, and other things

motif motivo—the object or unit of objects that repeat in a pattern

See page 119B for additional Spanish vocabulary resources.

 Art Journal: Vocabulary

Have students add these words to the Vocabulary section of their Art Journals.

Lesson Materials

- wallpaper samples
- foam printing material
- ballpoint pens
- paper of any color
- paper clips
- scissors
- one color of water-based ink
- brayers
- inking plate
- oil pastels

Alternate Materials:
- **Large Prints**
- foam trays from grocery store with edges cut off
- foam plates
- paper plates
- pencils
- tempera paint
- stiff brushes

Program Resources

- *Reading and Writing Test Prep.,* pp. 38–39
- *Transparency 17*
- *Flash Card 14*
- *Artist Profiles,* pp. 72, 69
- *Animals Through History Time Line*
- *Assessment,* pp. 41–42
- *Large Prints 65 Diva and 66 Double Entrance*
- *Art Around the World Collection*

Concept Trace
Pattern
Introduced: Level 4, Unit 2, Lesson 3

Reinforced: Level 6, Unit 3, Lesson 1

Lesson 5 Arts Integration

Theatre

Complete Unit 3, Lesson 5, on pages 44–45 of *Theatre Arts Connections.*

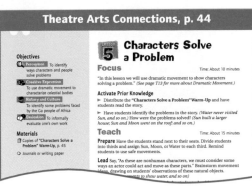

Music

 While keeping a steady beat, clap along with the words *fascinatin' rhythm* from the song *Fascinatin' Rhythm* by George Gershwin. This is the pattern Gershwin used to build the composition. Listen to the song, and find the pattern in the words and in the instruments.

Movement & Dance

Organize students into a large circle. Using a large ball of yarn or string, have students create a pattern across the circle. The first person holds onto the ball of yarn, unwinds it a little, and holding one end of the yarn, gently tosses the ball of yarn to another student. The next student holds onto the yarn in one hand, unwinds some yarn from the ball, and tosses the ball to another student. Once each person has caught and thrown, have students tilt the design at different angles to show different patterns.

Focus

Time: About 20 minutes

Activate Prior Knowledge

"Where have you seen patterns on objects in nature?" "¿Dónde han visto patrones en objetos de la naturaleza?"

- Discuss how patterns can be found in the natural world and are sometimes copied by designers to create interest on the surface of fabrics or other objects.

Using Literature ⭐ Reading

- Share with the class E. L. Konigsburg's *A View from Saturday*. After identifying the patterns that appear on the cover of this book, enjoy a story of four sixth-grade students and a special teacher working together to be the first to beat the seventh-grade Academic Bowl team.

Thematic Connection ⭐ Social Studies

- **Cooperation:** Discuss with students how a pattern can work to tie together certain motifs throughout a design, much like people working together to attain a common goal.

Introduce the Art

Look

"Let's take a close look at the two works of art." "Vamos a observar detalladamente las dos obras de arte."

Sequence ⭐ Math

- Ask students to look at the works of art in this lesson and list the order of steps the artist might have taken to create each of them.

 Art History and Culture

Both works of art use patterns in weaving to create interesting surface designs. Geometric and free-form shapes, colors, and lines are repeated in these patterns.
NSAE 5.a

 Web Connection

Visit www.metmuseum.org/collections/view1.asp?dep=20&full=0&item=29%2E146%2E23 and www.metmuseum.org/collections/view1.asp?dep=20&full=0&item=33%2E149%2E100 to learn more about Wari tunics.

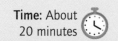 Lesson **5** Pattern

Look at the artwork on these pages and notice the patterns. Both *Half of a Tunic,* from the Wari culture of ancient Peru, and *Ceremonial Panel,* from the Kuba Group of twentieth century Congo, express aspects of each culture through the use of patterns on textiles.

◀ **Artist unknown** (Wari Culture, Peru). *Half of a Tunic.* 600–900 A.D.
....
Plain weave sections tie-dyed and recombined, alpaca. 77 × 31 inches (195.58 × 78.74 cm.). Museum of International Folk Art, Santa Fe, New Mexico.

 Art History and Culture

These works of art were created during different periods of time and in different parts of the world. What similarities do you see in these works of art?

Art History and Culture

The Wari Empire

The Wari Empire reigned from A.D. 600 to 850, at the close of Peru's classic period. During this time, Peru experienced dramatic advancements in its pottery, metalwork, and weaving arts. The complex patterns, still-vivid colors, and interesting images in the weavings suggest unrestricted creativity and show the skill of the dyers as well as the weavers. The tunic was the most common form of clothing for men in Peru during this time. The Wari tried to wipe out any trace of other cultural influences by not allowing oral traditions or ceremonial practices of any kind to be held. Because of this, only stories from the Wari culture exist from this time.

See pages 24–25 and 16–21 for more about art history and the subject matter.

Artist Profiles, p. 72

▸ Artist Profile ◂

Half of a Tunic

The Wari people, originally from the Andes Mountain region of central Peru, founded an enormous empire that extended from present-day Ecuador in the north to the border of Chile in the south. It is estimated that the Wari Empire existed during the period between 600 A.D. and 1000 A.D. In spite of the absence of any written records about its history, much has been learned about the Wari culture from the many artifacts that have been found in central Peru.

◀ **Artist unknown.** (Wari culture, Peru). *Half of a Tunic.* 600–900 A.D.

◄ **Artist unknown.** (Kuba Group, Western Kasai Province, Congo). *Ceremonial Panel.* 1950–1975.

Cut-pile and linear embroidery on plain-weave raffia palm. 22 × 23½ inches (55.88 × 59.69 cm.). Museum of International Folk Art, Santa Fe, New Mexico.

Study both weavings to find examples of patterns.

▶ Look at both works of art. Identify simple and complex geometric shapes that appear in the patterns.

▶ Find the types of lines that are used in the patterns in both textiles.

▶ What colors are used to create the patterns in these works of art?

▶ How are these two textiles similar? How are they different?

Aesthetic Perception

Seeing Like an Artist Look for interesting patterns on plants and animals. Share what you find with the class.

Study

▶ *Half of a Tunic:* Some geometric shapes in this work of art are squares and circles. *Ceremonial Panel:* Some of the geometric shapes in this work of art are triangles, squares, and hexagons. Free-form shapes exist throughout both designs.

▶ Vertical, horizontal, diagonal, and zigzag lines appear in both textile works of art.

▶ *Half a of Tunic:* Some of the repeated colors are red, black, green, gold, and white. *Ceremonial Panel:* Black and tan hues are used throughout the pattern.

▶ The two textiles are similar because of their nonobjective designs, use of geometric shapes, and the patterns within larger shapes. They differ because *Half of a Tunic* has more color and *Ceremonial Panel* has more texture.
NSAE 5.c

■ For more examples of art from Africa, see the ***Art Around the World Collection.*** Have students compare cultural themes honoring African history in these works of art.

Art Journal: Writing

Have students write in their Art Journal about a time when they were working with a group in school. Ask students to explain what they were working on, whether the people in the group cooperated or not, and how this affected the end product.

Art History and Culture

The Kuba Group

The Kuba textile has geometric shapes and mathematical patterns in its design. Almost two hundred of these motifs are known by name and can be found in other works of art in this culture. To create the ceremonial panel, the Kuba men wove a coarse cloth which the women then embroidered with softened raffia fibers. The colors in *Ceremonial Panel* are typical. The Kuba people believe that they need to be dressed in the traditional ceremonial raffia textiles in order to be recognized by their ancestors in the land of the dead.

See pages 24–25 and 16–21 for more about art history and the subject matter.

Artist Profiles, p. 69

Artist Profile

Ceremonial Panel

This ceremonial panel was made during the middle of the twentieth century by a small group of Kuba weavers of central Africa. The majority of Kuba people live in the Democratic Republic of the Congo, formerly called Zaire. The Congo is a mountainous, densely forested area. Its plentiful natural resources provide materials for Kuba works of basketry, woven textiles, sculpture, carvings, and many other types of art.

◄ **Artist unknown.** (Kuba Group, Western Kasai Province, Democratic Republic of Congo). *Ceremonial Panel.* c. 1950–1975.

Aesthetic Perception

Seeing Like an Artist Help students compile a list of things with patterns found in nature. Encourage students to identify the lines, shapes, and colors found in these patterns. Suggest that students sketch illustrations to accompany their explanations.

Developing Visual Literacy Ask students to choose a different medium, such as dance, music, or theatre, to convey the mood that one of the textiles in this lesson suggests. Encourage students to perform their interpretation or explanation of how the art would be translated in this medium. NSAE 6.a

 Web Connection
Visit www.authenticafrica.com/kubclotstrip1.html for more information on the Kuba raffia textiles.

 **Teach**

Time: About 30 minutes

"How can you use patterns in your artwork?"
"¿Cómo puedes usar patrones en tus obras de arte?"

- Read and discuss the definitions of pattern, motif, and random pattern on page 114.

Practice

Materials: wallpaper samples

Alternate Materials: Large Prints

- Distribute materials and have students follow the direction on page 114.

- Have students look through wallpaper samples to find examples of patterns with repeating lines, shapes, and colors. Encourage students to identify the motif used in each pattern they find.

Creative Expression

Materials: foam printing material, ballpoint pens, large sheets of paper, paper clips, scissors, one color of water-based ink, brayers, inking plate, oil pastels

Alternate Materials: foam trays from grocery store with edges cut off, foam plates, paper plates, pencils, colored paper, tempera paint, stiff brushes

- Distribute the materials and have students follow the directions on page 115.

- Limit students to no more than two different colors of ink.

- Demonstrate how to open a paper clip in the shape of an L. Then show students how to tape the opened clip to the back of the foam printing plate to use as a handle.

- Review the Activity Tips on page 238 for visual examples of this lesson's activity.

- See the Technique Tips on page 221 for more information on printmaking.
  NSAE 5.a

Art Journal: Brainstorming

Have students sketch in their Art Journals ideas for a motif to be used in their wrapping-paper design.

Using Pattern

A **pattern** is a repeated design that decorates the surface of fabrics and other objects.

A **motif** is the object that is repeated, or a unit of objects that is repeated, in a pattern.

In a **random pattern** the motif is repeated in no noticeable order.

Practice

Find patterns in wallpaper samples.

1. Look through the wallpaper samples provided.
2. Find patterns that use different combinations of lines, shapes, and colors.
3. Identify the motifs used in each pattern.

Differentiated Instruction

Reteach
Have students use cameras to find patterns of as many different surfaces as they can. Review the photographs with the class and encourage students to identify the motifs used in the patterns. If cameras are not available, ask students to find examples of patterns and sketch what they see.

Special Needs
Students with poor vision or motor control may benefit from using an inking tray with raised edges and having their paper taped down as they print.

ELL
Consider creating a visual wall chart for the class to use as a reference and as reinforcement. Write concept definitions, create simple sketches or examples as a class, and refer to the chart as you use the terminology.

◀ **Callie Annett.**
Age 11.

Think about how the student artist created a motif to design an original pattern.

Creative Expression

How could you create a design for wrapping paper? Create a pattern using a motif.

1. Choose your favorite motif sketch and draw it on a foam printing plate.
2. Cut out the motif and add details by etching lines with a ballpoint pen.
3. Place some ink on the inking plate. Spread out the ink using a brayer.
4. Use the brayer to roll ink onto the foam printing plate.
5. Fill the paper with a random arrangement of prints.
6. When dry, use oil pastels to add details.

Art Criticism

Describe What motif did you use to create the pattern on your wrapping paper?

Analyze Did you create a random pattern on your wrapping-paper design?

Interpret What type of gift would you wrap with this paper?

Decide How could you use this wrapping-paper to teach someone about using a motif to create a random pattern?

Unit 3 • Lesson 5   **115**

Art Across the Curriculum

Use these simple ideas to reinforce art concepts across the curriculum.

★ **Narrative Writing** Have students write a story in which cooperation is the answer to the problem the characters are facing.

★ **Math** Using the textiles artwork in this lesson, have students identify parallel, intersecting, and perpendicular lines. Students can also identify the right angles and geometric shapes that they find.

★ **Science** When studying microorganisms, explain how the parts of a cell work together to produce and sustain a living thing.

★ **Social Studies** Ask students to locate Peru and the Democratic Republic of the Congo on a world map.

★ **Technology** Have students copy and paste clip art to create a pattern in a paint program. Visit **SRAonline.com** to print detailed instructions for this activity.
NSAE 6.b

Reflect   Time: About 15 minutes

Review and Assess

"Were you able to create a design for wrapping paper using a stamp print for a motif?"
"¿Pudieron crear un diseño para un papel de envolver regalos usando un sello con un grabado para un motivo?"

Think

The students artist created a motif and used printmaking techniques to repeat the motif. This repetition was used to create an original design.

■ Use *Large Prints 65* Diva and *66 Double Entrance* to have students identify and describe the use of pattern in works of art.

■ Organize a field trip to a local museum. Prepare students with questions concerning color schemes and patterns prior to their visit. Encourage students to share their conclusions about these properties when you return to the classroom.

Informal Assessment

■ For standardized-format test practice using this lesson's art content, see pages 38–39 in *Reading and Writing Test Preparation.*

Art Journal: Critical Thinking
Have students answer the four art criticism questions—Describe, Analyze, Interpret, and Decide—in their Art Journals. In small groups, have students discuss their wrapping-paper designs.
NSAE 2.a

Lesson 5 — Pattern

Wrap-Up

Time: About 45 minutes

Focus

Study **Large Prints 65** *Diva* and **66** *Double Entrance* and ask students to discuss the use of pattern in the artwork. Describe the motif you see. How did the artist arrange the motif to create a pattern?

Teach

Explain to the students that they will be creating a stamp made from cut rubber bands and scraps of mat board. By printing and turning the rubber band stamp, an alternating pattern can be produced. They will be designing a piece of fabric.

Reflect

Have students evaluate their works of art using the four steps of art criticism.

Alternate Activity

Materials:

- Art Journals
- pencils, erasers
- 2" × 2" mat board
- rubber bands
- scissors
- glue
- paper clips
- masking tape
- printing ink
- 1" paintbrushes
- 8" × 8" or larger muslin or cotton fabric
- 9" × 9" cardboard
- newspaper

1. Draw four squares by tracing the mat-board piece in their Art Journals. Instruct them to create a different asymmetrical design in each square.

2. Choose a sketch. Then cut and glue the rubber bands onto the mat board to copy the design. Open the paperclip to form an L-shaped handle and tape it to the back of your stamp design.

3. Tape fabric to a piece of cardboard. Then apply ink to the stamp and press firmly onto the top left corner of the fabric. Ink the stamp again. Repeat this process until a pattern is created.

Research in Art Education

Schools with rich in-school art programs tend to have a more positive atmosphere—children at these schools are "more likely than children in low-arts schools to have a good rapport with their teachers. This holds true across socioeconomic lines" ("Learning in and Through the Arts: Curriculum Implications" in *Champions of Change*, p. 41). While learning about patterns and discussing cooperation in this lesson, encourage students to think about how important cooperation is in all areas of life.

Assessment

Use the following rubric to evaluate the artwork students make in the Creative Expression activity and to assess students' understanding of pattern.

Have students complete page 41 or 42 in their *Assessment* books.

	Art History and Culture	Aesthetic Perception	Creative Expression	Art Criticism
3 POINTS	The student can demonstrate knowledge of the weavings from the Wari people of Peru and the Kuba group of the Congo.	The student accurately identifies motifs and patterns in art and in the environment.	The student's wrapping paper printmaking clearly illustrates the use of patterns.	The student evaluates own work using the four steps of art criticism.
2 POINTS	The student's knowledge of the weavings from the Wari people of Peru and the Kuba group of the Congo is weak.	The student shows emerging awareness of motifs and patterns in art and in the environment.	The student's wrapping paper shows some awareness of pattern.	The student attempts to evaluate own work, but shows an incomplete understanding of evaluation criteria.
1 POINT	The student cannot demonstrate knowledge of the weavings from the Wari people of Peru or the Kuba group of the Congo.	The student cannot identify motifs and patterns in art or in the environment.	The student's wrapping paper printmaking shows no understanding of patterns.	The student makes no attempt to evaluate own artwork.

Assessment, p. 41

Name _____ Date _____

Lesson 5 UNIT 3

Pattern

A. Matching
Match the terms in Column 1 with their definitions in Column 2.

Column 1
___ 1. pattern
___ 2. motif
___ 3. random pattern

Column 2
a. the motif is repeated in no noticeable order
b. the object or unit of objects that is repeated in a pattern
c. a repeated design that decorates the surface of fabrics and other objects

B. Drawing
Create a random pattern and circle the motif once in the box below.

C. Writing
Look at *Half of a Tunic* and write a paragraph on the back of this paper describing the lines, shapes, and colors used to create a pattern in this work of art.

Level 5   Unit 3 • Color and Pattern   41

Lesson 6 Decorative Pattern

Overview

Lesson 6 introduces how artists use decorative patterns to create interest and to add personal touches in the surface designs of their artwork.

Objectives

Art History and Culture

To become familiar with the Kongo people, their artwork, and the life and art of Louis Sullivan

Creative Expression

To design and create a clay-coil bowl with a decorative pattern

Aesthetic Perception

To identify three types of patterns used by artists for surface design

Art Criticism

To evaluate one's own work using the four steps of art criticism

Vocabulary Vocabulary

Review the following vocabulary words with students.

pattern patrón—a repeated design that decorates the surface of fabrics, objects and other things

motif motivo—the object or unit of objects that repeat in a pattern

decorative decorativo—serving to make more beautiful; to adorn with ornaments

See page 119B for additional Spanish vocabulary resources.

Art Journal: Vocabulary

Have students add these words to the Vocabulary section of their Art Journals.

Lesson Materials
- paper
- pencils
- earth clay
- paper clips
- clay tools

Alternate Materials:
- air-drying clay

Program Resources
- *Reading and Writing Test Prep.*, pp. 40–41
- *Transparency 18*
- *Flash Card 18*
- *Artist Profiles,* pp. 68, 57
- *Animals Through History Time Line*
- *Assessment,* pp. 43–44
- *Large Prints 65 Diva* and *66 Double Entrance*
- *The National Museum of Women in the Arts Collection*

Concept Trace
Decorative Patterns
Introduced: Level 4, Unit 2, Lesson 3

Reinforced: Level 6, Unit 3, Lessons 1, 2, 3

Lesson 6 Arts Integration

Theatre

Complete Unit 3, Lesson 6, on pages 46–51 of *Theatre Arts Connections.*

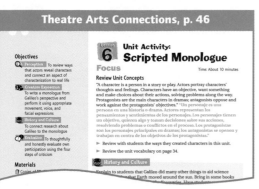

Music

 Adding a piccolo melody to a march adds a special emphasis. John Philip Sousa used a piccolo in his composition *The Stars and Stripes Forever.* Listen to *The Stars and Stripes Forever,* and identify the piccolo's piercing sound.

Movement & Dance

Organize students into a large circle. One person in the circle begins by doing a simple action or gesture, like jumping or saluting. Everyone else in the circle repeats the gesture, but has to find a way to decorate it. For example, "decorate" a jump by wiggling. Decorate a salute by turning while you salute. Repeat, so each person in the circle has a chance to create an original gesture or action.

 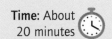

Activate Prior Knowledge

"What patterns do you particularly like on something that you own?" "¿Qué patrones les gusta en particular que se ven en algo que es de ustedes?"

■ Discuss how designers use patterns to decorate the surfaces of objects.

Using Literature ⭐ Reading

■ Use Joan Steiner's book *Look Alikes* to further demonstrate how things are not always what they appear to be.

Thematic Connection ⭐ Reading

■ **Look Again:** Brainstorm with students the many things they use throughout the day that are designed for a specific use. Look again at the shape of a pencil and discuss why some have flattened surfaces and others are round. Ask students if these pencils feel different when using them and if they have a preference.

Introduce the Art

Look

"Let's take a close look at the two works of art." "Vamos a observar detalladamente las dos obras de arte."

Visualizing ⭐ Reading

■ Have students write a news report in which one of these works of art is featured. They will have to visualize the environment in which this object is set, the people involved, and the events taking place for the report.

Art History and Culture

Both objects were designed to be used by people but were also created to have visual appeal. The artists repeated elements of art to create patterns on the surface designs of their objects NSAE 5.a

Web Connection

Visit **www.nmafa.si.edu/pubaccess/pages/ onviewfrm.htm** to learn about more art of the Kongo people featured at the Smithsonian Museum of African Art.

116 UNIT 3 • Color and Pattern

Look at the artwork on these pages. Notice how the designers used patterns to decorate the surfaces. The motif on the Kongo bowl has a random pattern created by the staining process. Louis Sullivan's *Elevator Grill* has alternating patterns throughout the design.

▲ **Artist unknown.** (Kongo peoples, Congo and Democratic Republic of the Congo). *Bowl.* Late-nineteenth to early-twentieth century.

Ceramic and resin. $5\frac{7}{8} \times 4\frac{1}{8} \times 5\frac{7}{8}$ inches (14.9 × 10.49 × 14.94 cm.). National Museum of African Art, Smithsonian Institution, Washington, D.C.

Art History and Culture

How have these artists incorporated art elements into the design of objects that will be used by their community?

116 Unit 3 • Lesson 6

Art History and Culture

The Kongo People

The Kongo people live along Africa's Zaire River. Because they believe that their royal chiefs hold the power of their ancestors' spirits, much of their art is often in the form of scepters, royal staffs, horns, bracelets, and knives. Like most of their artwork, *Bowl* resembles something found in nature. The pattern on the surface of this bowl was created by splashing it with vegetable juices while it was still hot from the kiln. The motifs that appear on the bowl remained after the mixture evaporated. The Kongo people use bowls like this for daily activities and for ceremonies.

See pages 24–25 and 16–21 for more about art history and the subject matter.

Artist Profiles, p. 68

Artist Profile

Bowl

Potters of the Kongo people were traditionally women. Ceramic bowls such as this one were made for daily use in activities such as cooking, serving food, and holding water. Despite their mundane purposes, these bowls were often decorated with beautiful designs and colorful finish glazes, making them look more like unique works of art than everyday household objects.

Study both pieces to find decorative patterns.

▶ Look at both pieces of art and identify the motifs used to create patterns.

▶ What types of lines and shapes are the motifs in the Kongo *Bowl*?

▶ What types of lines and shapes are used to create motifs on the *Elevator Grill*?

▶ Louis Sullivan created art that was functional as well as beautiful. What function would this iron design serve in an elevator door?

▶ Both designers thought about nature when creating their decorative patterns. What natural objects can you think of that look like these works of art?

◀ **Louis Sullivan.** (American). *Elevator Grill.* 1893-1894.
....
Bronze-plated cast iron. 73 × 31 inches (185.42 × 78.74 cm.). High Museum of Art, Atlanta, Georgia.

 Aesthetic Perception

Design Awareness Look at the surface designs of the objects you use today. Identify the types of patterns you see. Does the pattern help with the function of the object, or is it just decoration?

Art History and Culture

Louis Sullivan

Louis Sullivan (lōō´ əs sə´ lə vən) (1856–1924) studied architecture at the Massachusetts Institute of Technology. In 1879 he joined Dankmar Adler, an established German architect. The structures they designed together became some of the most influential of American architecture. Sullivan focused on the use of organic ornaments fashioned after what he saw in nature. *Elevator Grill* was located in Adler and Sullivan's Chicago Stock Exchange Building. The motif was inspired by seeds bursting from pods. This theme is echoed in a poem Sullivan wrote called "Inspiration." Frank Lloyd Wright worked under Louis Sullivan.

See pages 24–25 and 16–21 for more about art history and the subject matter.

Artist Profiles, p. 57

Artist Profile
Louis Sullivan
1856–1924
Louis Henri Sullivan (lōō´ əs sə´ lə vən) was born in Boston, Massachusetts, and grew up with his grandparents in South Reading, Massachusetts. When he was 16 he attended the Massachusetts Institute of Technology, where he studied architecture with some of America's leading draftsmen. His work led him to Chicago, where he designed numerous city buildings and became involved with the country's early creation of skyscrapers.

Study

▶ *Bowl:* The shape of the rings are repeated throughout the surface design of the bowl. *Elevator Grill:* The circles, perpendicular lines, dots, and *X*s are repeating motifs.

▶ The motifs in the Kongo *Bowl* are made by curved lines and free-form shapes.

▶ The motifs in *Elevator Grill* are made by the repetition of vertical lines, curved lines, and diagonal lines. The motifs also include circles, ovals, and arcs.

▶ The motifs made from wrought iron create a grate in *Elevator Grill*. This grate can protect people when riding in the elevator, yet still allow them to see through to the other side.

▶ *Bowl* resembles knotty wood found in nature. The motifs used in *Elevator Grill* were created to resemble seedpods bursting open. Some have said the design looks like splashing rain hitting the ground.

■ For more examples of utilitarian art, see ***The National Museum of Women in the Arts Collection.***

Art Journal: Writing

Have students write in their Art Journals about a time when something turned out to be different from what they thought it was. For example, students can write about a relationship with another person, a book they read, or a food they tasted.

Aesthetic Perception

Design Awareness Discuss with students how patterns can be used for function as well as aesthetics, or looks. For example, camouflage designs use stripe motifs in a random pattern for disguise in a nature environment. Braille uses a pattern of raised dots that represent letters and numbers.

Developing Visual Literacy Ask students to look at both pieces of art and suggest what their original surroundings might have looked like. For example, students can describe from their imagination the hallway in which this elevator grill appears.

Web Connection

Visit **www.geocities.com/SoHo/1469/ sullivan.html** for more information about Louis Sullivan and his architectural work.

Teach

"How can you use surface design to add interest and personality to your artwork?"
"¿Cómo pueden usar un diseño de superficie para agregar interés y personalidad a su obra de arte?"

- Read and discuss the definitions of regular pattern, alternating pattern, and random pattern on page 118.

Practice

Materials: pencils, white paper

Alternate Materials: crayons

- Distribute the materials and have students follow the directions on page 118.

Creative Expression

Materials: earth clay, paper clips, clay tools, pencils

Alternate Materials: air-drying clay

- Distribute the materials and have students follow the directions on page 119.

- Have students roll the clay in their hands in only one direction.

- The finished clay bowls will need to be fired in a kiln. The high school art department might have a kiln you could use, or you can take them to a craft shop.

- Review the Activity Tips on page 238 for visual examples of this lesson's activity.

- See the Technique Tips on page 226 for more information on clay.

Art Journal: Brainstorming

Have students brainstorm ideas in their Art Journals for a motif they would like to design out of clay and use to decorate the surface of their clay-coil bowl. Encourage students to think of an overall theme for their work.

Using a Decorative Pattern

A **regular pattern** occurs when a motif is repeated with the same amount of space between each motif.

An **alternating pattern** repeats motifs but changes positions of the motif or adds a second motif to the pattern.

A **random pattern** occurs when the motif is repeated in no apparent order.

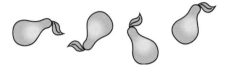

Practice

Design regular and alternating patterns using geometric shapes. Use a pencil.

1. Fold your paper in half. Label one side *regular pattern* and the other side *alternating pattern.*

2. Draw a geometric shape and repeat it to create a regular pattern.

3. To create an alternating pattern on the other side of the paper, add a second geometric shape to the shape you used in the regular pattern.

Differentiated Instruction

Reteach
Take students outside to look for patterns in natural objects. Ask students to sketch what they find and identify the type of pattern: regular, alternating, or random.

Special Needs
Have visual prompts that show examples of regular, alternating, and random pattern as students begin this project.

ELL
Give students graph paper. Ask them to fold it into thirds and label one section *Regular pattern,* another *Alternating pattern,* and the third *Random pattern.* Using a crayon of only one color, model for students each type of pattern. Then allow students to create their own surface design patterns. This sheet can be used as a reference tool.

◀ **Jamie McLachlan.**
Age 10.

Think about how the student artist used a decorative pattern to add interest to the clay bowl.

 Creative Expression

How could you design a clay coil bowl? Create a motif to decorate the surface of the bowl.

1. Make a small clay ball, and press it flat to make the base of your bowl.

2. Using a flat hand, roll pieces of clay in one direction into coils. Stack the coils on top of one another to make the walls of the bowl. Smooth out the inside coils to join them all together.

3. Make small clay shapes for the motif of your pattern.

4. Attach the motifs to the outside coils using slip and scoring techniques.

5. Scratch lines in the clay to enhance the pattern.

 Art Criticism

Describe What is the theme of your clay coil bowl?

Analyze How does this type of pattern work for the motif you used?

Interpret What does this artwork say about you?

Decide If you were to make a set of bowls, would you make them all the same or would you vary the motifs or the pattern within the same theme?

Reflect

Time: About 15 minutes

Review and Assess

"Were you able to design and create a decorative pattern for your clay coil bowl?"

"¿Pudieron diseñar y crear un patrón decorativo para su bol enrollado de arcilla?"

Think

The artist repeated a leaf motif around the outside of the clay bowl.

■ Use *Large Prints 65 Diva* and *66 Double Entrance* to have students identify and describe the uses of decorative patterns.

Informal Assessment

■ For standardized-format test practice using this lesson's art content, see pages 40–41 in *Reading and Writing Test Preparation.*

Art Journal: Critical Thinking

Have students answer the four art criticism questions—Describe, Analyze, Interpret, and Decide—in their Art Journals. In small groups, have students discuss their clay coil bowls.

● Art Across the Curriculum ●

Use these simple ideas to reinforce art concepts across the curriculum.

★ **Narrative Writing** Have students write a short story from the perspective of one of the works of art in this lesson. Encourage students to write about their travels and acquaintances they meet on their journey.

★ **Math** While students are working with multiplication tables, ask them to look for a pattern that appears in the charted numbers.

★ **Science** Ask students to find surface patterns on living things.

★ **Social Studies** Discuss the American Stock Exchange and how it plays an important role in our economy.

★ **Technology** Have students use a paint program to copy and paste pictures downloaded from a digital camera or from the Internet to create an alternating pattern. Visit **SRAonline.com** to print detailed instructions for this activity.
NSAE 6.b

Decorative Patterns

Extra! ## For the Art Specialist

Time: About 45 minutes

Focus

Study *Large Prints 65* Diva and *66 Double Entrance* and ask students to discuss the use of decorative pattern in the artwork. Do you see a shape or object that is repeated? Describe the way the artist arranged this shape of object.

Teach

Have students begin collecting objects that they would like to add to a fabric weaving. Emphasize that the objects should be related. Ask the students to collect a minimum of five objects.

Reflect

Have students evaluate their works of art using the four steps of art criticism. Encourage them to locate and describe decorative patterns.

Alternate Activity

Materials:

- 8″ × 10″ cardboard looms
- warping cord or yarn
- pre-cut fabric strips 2″ wide and 4″ longer than the loom
- scissors
- embroidery floss
- tapestry needles
- student collected objects no larger than 2″

1. Have students begin by making the loom and warping it using cord or yarn.

2. Students will need to select five fabric strips, then weave over the first string, under the second, over the third, continuing until they have reached the end of the first row.

3. Center the woven fabric strip so that equal amounts of fabric are on either side of the loom.

4. Place the collected objects on top of the weaving in a pattern and use an embroidery thread to attach these objects. Cut and tie the thread ends together to secure each object.

Research
in Art Education

"In the role of aesthetic observer, the appreciator functions in a manner which is almost the reverse of the artist's function. For example, the artist has certain emotions which are infused into the work. The appreciator looks at the artist's work and tries to extract those emotions which are inherent in the work. This is not to imply that the emotional state of the contemplative viewer would or should duplicate that of the artist at work. In appreciating artwork the viewer savors what is enjoyed." (Squires, William. *Art Experience and Criticism.* Needham Heights, MA: Ginn Press, 1991.)

Assessment
Use the following rubric to evaluate the artwork students make in the Creative Expression activity and to assess students' understanding of decorative patterns.

Have students complete page 43 or 44 in their *Assessment* books.

	Art History and Culture	Aesthetic Perception	Creative Expression	Art Criticism
3 POINTS	The student can demonstrate knowledge of the Kongo people, their artwork, and the life and art of Louis Sullivan.	The student accurately identifies decorative patterns.	The student's clay coil bowl clearly illustrates the use of patterns.	The student evaluates own work using the four steps of art criticism.
2 POINTS	The student's knowledge of the weavings from the Kongo people, their artwork, and the life and art of Louis Sullivan is weak or incomplete.	The student shows emerging awareness of decorative patterns.	The student's clay coil bowl shows some awareness of patterns.	The student attempts to evaluate own work, but shows an incomplete understanding of evaluation criteria.
1 POINT	The student cannot demonstrate knowledge of the weavings from the Kongo people, their artwork, or the life and art of Louis Sullivan.	The student cannot identify decorative patterns.	The student's clay coil bowl shows no understanding of patterns.	The student makes no attempt to evaluate own artwork.

analogous colors—colors that sit next to each other on the color wheel and share a common color or hue **colores análogos**—colores que están uno al lado del otro en el círculo cromático y comparten un color o matiz

color intensity—the brightness or dullness of a color **intensidad del color**—lo brillante u opaco de un color

color scheme—a plan for organizing color **esquema de color**—un plan para organizar el color

complementary colors—colors opposite each other on the color wheel **colores complementarios**—colores opuestos en el círculo cromático

cool color—a color that suggests a cool mood and seems to recede from the viewer; blue, green, and violet are cool colors **color frío**—o fresco; un color que sugiere un ánimo fresco y que parece alejarse del espectador. El azul, el verde y el violeta son colores fríos.

decorative—serving to make more beautiful; adorned with ornaments **decorativo**—que sirve para embellecer; adornar con ornamentos

hue—another name for *color* **matiz**—otro nombre para color

monochromatic—a color scheme using one color plus all the tints and shades of that color **monocromático**—un esquema de color que usa un color más todos los tintes y las sombras de ese color

motif—the object or unit of objects that repeat in a pattern **motivo**—el objeto o la unidad que se repite en un patrón

nonobjective—a piece of art that has no recognizable subject matter and contains shapes, lines, and colors, not objects or people. **subjetivo**—una obra de arte que no tiene un tema reconocible. Contiene figuras, líneas y colores, pero no tiene objetos ni personas.

opaque—does not let light through **opaco**—no deja que penetre la luz

pattern—a repeated design that decorates the surface of fabrics, objects and other things **patrón**—un diseño que se repite y que adorna la superficie de las telas, los objetos y otras cosas

shade—the dark value of a hue **sombra**—se refiere al valor oscuro de un matiz

tint—light value of a hue **tinte**—se refiere al valor claro de un matiz

transparent—allows light to pass through so objects on the other side can be seen **transparente**—permite que la luz penetre de modo que los objetos en el otro lado se pueden ver

warm color—a color that suggests a warm mood and seems to move toward the viewer; red, orange, and yellow are warm colors. **color cálido**—un color que sugiere un ánimo cálido y parece acercarse al espectador

Vocabulary Practice

T Display *Transparency 39* to review unit vocabulary words.

Tongue Twisters ⭐ Vocabulary

Have students work with partners to write tongue twister riddles using vocabulary words. Students can present their tongue twisters to the class when they are ready. The answers to the riddles should be a vocabulary word, for example, *This kind of color concept can concoct a calm climate in your creation. Answer: Cool Color*

Word Web ⭐ Vocabulary

Assign a vocabulary word to each group of students and ask them to create a word web using related concepts. Encourage students to share their word webs with the class.

Thesaurus ⭐ Vocabulary

Ask student pairs to look up two or three vocabulary words in a thesaurus for synonyms. Alert students that some synonyms are not perfect matches and might change the meaning of the context.

▲ **Paul Cézanne.** (French).
Pierrot and Harlequin. 1888.

Oil on canvas. 42½ × 31⅞ inches (107.95 × 80.95 cm.).
State Pushkin Museum, Moscow, Russia.

Art Criticism

Critical Thinking Art criticism is an organized system for looking at and talking about art. You can criticize art without being an expert. The purpose of art criticism is to get the viewer involved in a perception process that delays judgment until he or she has studied all aspects of the artwork.

- See page 28–29 for more about art criticism.

Describe

▶ This was painted by Paul Cézanne in 1888. It is called *Pierrot and Harlequin,* and it was painted with oil paint on canvas. It is 42½ by 31½ inches in size, and it is at the State Pushkin Museum in Moscow, Russia.

▶ Possible answers are: There are two men. They are wearing costumes. One man is dressed all in white. He is wearing a jacket with long, cuffed sleeves and a double ruffled collar. The other man is dressed in a red-orange and black diamond patterned outfit. He is wearing a black hat and black shoes. He is carrying a red and white stick tucked under his right arm. Both men seem to be facing and moving toward the right but their heads are turned to face the viewer.

▶ Possible answers are: The background has dull-yellow curtains with blue leaves and flowers on them. The floor is painted with loose brush strokes of red, brown, blue, and gray.

Analyze

▶ The orange in the man's costume and the blue wall are complementary colors.

▶ The orange in the costume and yellows in the curtains are warm colors. The blue wall and the blue flowers in the curtains are cool colors.

▶ The red-orange and black diamond pattern is a regular pattern.

Art History and Culture

Paul Cézanne

Paul Cézanne (pôl sā zan') (1839–1906) has been called "the father of modern art." As a postimpressionist painter, he was influenced by Camille Pissarro and his technique for capturing light. Cézanne constructed well-thought-out still-life arrangements with the focus on balance, form, and shape. Sometimes he would change the shapes that he saw to create interest and feeling in his paintings. His work greatly influenced French artist Henri Matisse and Spanish artist Pablo Picasso. Cézanne favored using bright colors and bold brushstrokes.

See pages 24–25 and 16–21 for more about art history and the subject matter.

Artist Profiles, p. 16

Artist Profile

Paul Cézanne
1839-1906

Paul Cézanne (paul sā zan') was born in the south of France in Aix-en-Provence. He is often called the father of modern art. He loved to paint, but people did not like his work much—at least not during his lifetime. He had to beg gallery owners to show his work, and therefore he did not sell many paintings. He inherited money from his parents to pay his bills and buy his paints. He continued painting until a week before he died.

 **Art Criticism** Critical Thinking

Describe **What do you see?**

During this step you will collect information about the subject of the work.

- ▶ What does the credit line tell you about the painting?
- ▶ Describe the people. What they are wearing? What they are doing?
- ▶ What do you see in the background?

Analyze **How is this work organized?**

Think about how the artist has used the elements and principles of art.

- ▶ What complementary colors do you see?
- ▶ Which warm colors and which cool colors do you see?
- ▶ Where do you see patterns?

Interpret **What is the artist trying to say?**

Use the clues you discovered during your analysis to find the message the artist is trying to show.

- ▶ How do the colors affect the mood of this painting?
- ▶ What kind of act do these men perform? Write a paragraph describing the act from the time the curtain opens until it closes.

Decide **What do you think about the work?**

Use all the information you have gathered to decide whether this is a successful work of art.

- ▶ Is the work successful because it is realistic, because it is well organized, or because it has a strong message?

Unit 3   **121**

Interpret

- ▶ Some students might say the mood is serious because of the dark colors and expressions on the men's faces. Others may say the feeling is happy because of the bright costumes.
- ▶ Some might say they are clowns because they recognize the harlequin costume and the baggy outfit of the other clown. Some may think they are song-and-dance men. Some may say they are serious actors about to speak lines in a drama, and others may think they are mimes.

Decide

- ▶ All three aesthetic theories apply to this work.

 Art Journal: Writing

Have students write answers to Aesthetic Perception in their Art Journals.

 Aesthetic Perception

Critical Thinking Have students think about costumes they have dressed up in or would like to someday. How do the outfits the men in *Pierrot and Harlequin* compare to the students' costumes?

Describe ▶ Describe the costumes and the accessories.

Analyze ▶ Is the costume meant to make you look like a person, an animal, or an object?

Interpret ▶ How do costumes allow performers to act in ways that they may not feel comfortable acting otherwise?

Decide ▶ How could you change this costume to change the mood that is portrayed?

▶ What element of this costume identifies it?

"Artists use the elements of color and pattern to create mood and interest in their artwork."

"Los artistas usan los elementos del color y el patrón para crear un ánimo e interés en sus obras de arte."

T Review unit vocabulary with students using *Transparency 39.*

Art Journal: Writing

Have students answer the questions on page 122 in their Art Journals or on a separate sheet of paper. 1. B, 2. C, 3. C, 4. A, 5. B

T For further assessment, have students complete the unit test on *Transparency 45.*

LEARNING ABOUT
Museums

► The Metropolitan Museum of Art was one of the first museums to be established in the United States. It is one of the world's largest and finest museums. It is visited by 4.5 million people annually. The American Wing houses the world's most comprehensive collection of American art. Prior to the museum's founding in 1870, the only public museums were in Europe.

► Have students work together in groups to design a museum that would feature the art created by students in your school.

"Our legacy is priceless. It's the gift our ancestors leave to us and what we give to future generations. It is the same way with art."

—Willis "Bing" Davis

Wrapping Up Unit 3

Color and Pattern, continued

Show What You Know

Answer these questions on a separate sheet of paper.

❶ _____ means "one color."
   A. Analogous
   B. Monochromatic
   C. Primary

❷ _____ colors are next to each other on the color wheel.
   A. Complementary
   B. Secondary
   C. Analogous

❸ _____ colors are across from each other on the color wheel.
   A. Monochromatic
   B. Warm
   C. Complementary

❹ _____ colors are blue, green, and violet. They seem to move away from the viewer.
   A. Cool
   B. Warm
   C. Motif

❺ A repeated design that decorates the surface of a fabric or other object is a _____.
   A. hue
   B. pattern
   C. shape

122   Unit 3

LEARNING ABOUT MUSEUMS
The Metropolitan Museum of Art

The Metropolitan Museum of Art in New York City is one of the world's largest museums. It has more than two million works of art, spanning 5,000 years of culture. The museum was founded in 1870 and is located in Central Park. Its Egyptian collection is second only to the one in Cairo, Egypt. Major collections in the museum, in addition to the paintings, include arms and armor, Chinese art, costumes, musical instruments, primitive art, French and American furniture, and photographs. More than 4.5 million people from around the world visit the Metropolitan Museum of Art each year.

Unit Assessment Options

 **Aesthetic Perception**

Practice Have students select one of the concepts in the Show What You Know section on page 122, and then find examples of each concept in the classroom.

Creative Expression

Student Portfolio Have students review all the artwork they have created during this unit and select the pieces they wish to keep in their portfolios.

Art Criticism

Activity Have students select an artwork from this unit and study it using the four steps of art criticism. (See pages 28–29 for more information about art criticism.) Have students work alone or in pairs and present their findings orally or in writing.

Color and Pattern in Theatre

"On the Day You Were Born" is a play based on a book by Debra Frasier. It describes events in nature on the day a child is born. The artists and actors use visual and rhythmic patterns with puppets, paintings, poems, and music to portray these natural events.

Here is a part of the text from "On the Day You Were Born."

"On the day you were born
the Earth turned, the Moon pulled,
the Sun flared, and, then, with a push,
you slipped out of the dark quiet
where suddenly you could hear…
a circle of people singing
with voices familiar and clear."

What to Do Use your body and voice to express information about science and nature.

1. List some natural events (falling tides, moving air, exploding volcanoes, and pulling gravity) to express through movement.

2. In small groups, create regular, random, or alternating patterns of movement to represent these events.

3. Think of one to three ways to interpret your natural event. Use interesting vocal sounds to accompany your movement ideas. Find a shape or design for the group to hold for the ending of the performance.

4. Perform your natural-event dance for the class.

▲ In the Heart of the Beast Theater. "On the Day You Were Born."

 **Art Criticism**

Describe Describe the way your group interpreted your natural event.

Analyze Explain why you chose specific patterns of movement or sound to express the event.

Interpret What did you learn about your natural event by interpreting it through movement and sound?

Decide Were you successful in using sound, rhythm, and movement in your dance?

Unit 3 **123**

 Art History and Culture

In the Heart of the Beast Puppet and Mask Theatre

In the Heart of the Beast Puppet and Mask Theatre, of Minneapolis, Minnesota, is known for its imaginative productions featuring puppets of all sizes and styles. Their puppets are all built by hand from recycled materials. Author/illustrator Debra Frasier and artistic director Sandy Spieler, adapted the book, "On the Day You Were Born," into a play. They storyboarded the book into sections: a prologue, an invocation, the revelation of wonders, and the birth and welcome song. Three large boxes open to reveal the text and action of the story. Both puppets and humans bring the natural wonders to life.

 Color and Pattern in Theatre

Objective: To use the body and voice to express scientific information related to natural events

Materials: Resources for information about natural events, "On the Day You Were Born" performed by In the Heart of the Beast Puppet and Mask Theatre. Running time: 8:30

Focus

Time: About 20 minutes

- Discuss the information on page 123.

- Present students with information on natural events and phenomena to prepare them to create a movement and sound study.

Art History and Culture

- Ask students to think about the natural events and phenomena that you presented. Have them add an action word to each, such as *spinning earth* and *flaming sun.*

Teach

Time: About 20 minutes

Aesthetic Perception

- Have students watch the performance and discuss the use of color and identify the patterns they see.

Creative Expression

- Divide the students into groups. Each group will select one topic to explore through sound and movement. Encourage them to take the time to brainstorm many ideas.

- Direct students to create a beginning, middle and end, incorporating sounds.

- **Informal Assessment** Comment positively on the groups working productively together.

Reflect

Time: About 10 minutes

Art Criticism

- Have students answer the four art criticism questions on page 123 orally or in writing.

- Were students successful in creating a short performance showing a natural event?

Unit 4 Planning Guide

	Lesson Title	Suggested Pacing	Creative Expression Activity
Lesson 1	Proportion	1:10	Create a sketch of a model. Use the sighting technique.
Lesson 2	Scale	1:05	Create a collage.
Lesson 3	Face Proportions	1:05	Draw a portrait.
Lesson 4	Distortion of Body Proportions	1:00	Create an original superhero.
Lesson 5	Distortion of Face Proportions	1:15	Create a papier-mâché mask.
Lesson 6	Scale and Proportion	1:20	Create a life-size soft sculpture.
ART SOURCE ARTSOURCE	Proportion and Distortion in Dance	0:45	Create distorted movement to artistically express emotions.

Materials	Program Resources	Fine Art Resources	Literature Resources
oil pastels, white paper, dustless chalk, soft erasers	*Assessment,* pp. 45–46 *Home and After-School Connections* *The National Museum of Women in the Arts Collection* *Reading and Writing Test Preparation,* pp. 42–43	*Transparency 19* *Artist Profiles,* pp. 18, 60 *Large Print 68* *Flash Cards 18, 19* *Animals Through History Time Line*	*In The Year of the Boar and Jackie Robinson* by Betti Bao Lord
white paper, glue, magazines, scissors	*Assessment,* pp. 47–48 *Home and After-School Connections* *Women in the Arts Collection* *Reading and Writing Test Preparation,* pp. 44–45	*Transparency 20* *Artist Profiles,* pp. 28, 45 *Large Prints 67, 68* *Animals Through History Time Line*	*Appalachia: The Voice of Sleeping Birds* by Cynthia Rylant
white paper, pencils, string, watercolor paints	*Assessment,* pp. 49–50 *Home and After-School Connections* *Women in the Arts Collection* *Reading and Writing Test Preparation,* pp. 46–47	*Transparency 21* *Artist Profiles,* pp. 14, 31 *Large Prints 67, 68* *Animals Through History Time Line*	*Dear Mr. Henshaw* by Beverly Cleary
pencils and erasers, white drawing paper, sketch paper, markers	*Assessment,* pp. 51–52 *Home and After-School Connections* *Women in the Arts Collection* *Reading and Writing Test Preparation,* pp. 48–49	*Transparency 22* *Artist Profiles,* pp. 9, 43 *Large Prints 67, 68* *Animals Through History Time Line*	*A Wrinkle in Time* Madeleine L'Engle *Tuesday* David Wiesner
containers for glue and water mixture, one gallon milk jugs, newspaper, liquid tempera paints, paintbrushes, paper towels, paper plates, water dishes, masking tape, scissors, yarn, found objects	*Assessment,* pp. 53–54 *Home and After-School Connections* *Women in the Arts Collection* *Reading and Writing Test Preparation,* pp. 50–51	*Transparency 23* *Artist Profiles,* pp. 81, 65, 76, 75 *Large Print 67* *Animals Through History Time Line*	*The People Could Fly: American Black Folktales* by Virginia Hamilton
clothing, shoes, gloves, stitching items, yarn, nylon stockings, scissors, newspaper, polyester filling, poster board, water dishes, sketch paper, pencils	*Assessment,* pp. 55–56 *Home and After-School Connections* *Women in the Arts Collection* *Reading and Writing Test Preparation,* pp. 52–53	*Transparency 24* *Artist Profiles,* pp. 51, 29 *Large Prints 67, 68* *Animals Through History Time Line*	*Freaky Friday* by Mary Rodgers *More Parts* by Tedd Arnold
"Lamentation" and "Satyric Festival Song"			

Unit Overview

4 Proportion and Distortion

Lesson 1: Proportion is used to show how people or things relate to one another in size.

Lesson 2: Scale is used to relate one object to another in a work of art.

Lesson 3: Face proportions are used to help artists correctly organize the features of the face.

Lesson 4: Distortion of body proportions is the changing of body features by an artist to create an expressive effect.

Lesson 5: Distortion of face proportions is the changing of facial features by an artist to express an emotion or an idea.

Lesson 6: Proportion and scale are used to create life-size sculptures.

Introduce Unit Concepts

"Artists use the elements of proportion and distortion to emphasize the realistic or unrealistic features represented in their artwork." "Los artistas usan los elementos de proporción y distorsión para enfatizar las características reales e irreales representadas en sus obras de arte."

Proportion ☆ Math

- Have students compare the sizes of their feet and their forearms. Encourage students to discuss the commonalities of the human body's proportions that they are familiar with.

Distortion ☆ Reading

- Ask students what they know about the word *distortion*. Have a volunteer read the dictionary definition aloud to the class. Brainstorm examples of distortion.

Cross-Curricular Projects

- See the *Language Arts and Reading, Mathematics, Science,* and *Social Studies Art Connections* books for activities that further develop proportion and distortion.

Proportion and Distortion

Proportion and distortion are used by artists in both sculptural forms and in pictures.

Although this statue is much larger than most human beings, the artist used normal body proportions to create it. One body part does not look unusual or out of place when compared to the other parts.

◀ **Viola Frey.** (American).
Grandmother Series: July Cone Hat. 1982.
Glazed earthenware. 86½ × 21 × 18 inches (219.71 × 53.34 × 45.72 cm.). The Nelson-Atkins Museum of Art, Kansas City, Missouri.

124 Unit 4

Fine Art Prints

Display **Large Prints 67** *Gogol* and **68** *Self-Portrait (El Coronelazo).* Refer to the prints throughout the unit as students learn about proportion and distortion.

Large Print 67

Large Print 68

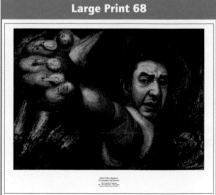

Artists use several techniques to create **proportion** in a work of art.

▶ Does Viola Frey's *July Cone Hat* look like a living person?

▶ How did Viola Frey use clothing to increase size? What effect do the shoes and hat have on the statue?

▶ How would the statue look different if there was a living person standing next to it?

Distortion is used by artists in paintings, drawings, and sculpture to express feelings and ideas.

▶ Look at the dimensions of this statue. Is the height accurate for a typical grandmother?

In This Unit you will learn about and practice techniques of proportion and distortion to add interest and feeling in your artwork. Here are the topics you will study:
▶ Body proportion
▶ Realistic scale
▶ Unrealistic scale
▶ Face and profile proportions
▶ Distortion
▶ Ratio and scale

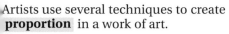

Viola Frey

(1933–)

Viola Frey grew up in the small town of Lodi, California. There was not much to do in such a small town, so she entertained herself by observing people. She studied art in high school and went on to study both painting and ceramics. Later, she taught art at the California College of Arts and Crafts. Her large statues of people are made from clay that has to be cut into many pieces, fired, and then put back together. She uses an electric lift to work on the taller parts of these sculptures. Many of her sculptures are very large and colorful, and are dressed in modern clothing. Frey describes her work as *organic* because it projects such a strong feeling of life and personality.

Unit 4 **125**

Examine the Artwork

"Let's look closely at the statue." "Vamos a mirar detalladamente a la estatua."

■ Have students look at Viola Frey's *Grandmother Series: July Cone Hat.* Ask them to describe what they see.

■ Have students answer the questions about proportion and distortion on page 125.

▶ The woman looks like a living person because her features make sense when compared to other features on her body. Her actual size is much larger than that of an average person.

▶ A possible answer to this question is that she used brighter colors to make some things appear closer to the viewer than others. The shoes and the hat make the woman seem realistic.

▶ The statue might resemble the real person but would be obviously larger than a real person.

▶ The height is not typical of a grandmother. The statue's size has been distorted by the artist.

Unit Pretest

T Display **Transparency 46** as a pretest. Answers: 1.A, 2.C, 3.C, 4.B, 5.A

Home Connection

■ See **Home and After-School Connections** for family newsletters and activities for this unit.

Art History and Culture

Viola Frey

Viola Frey (vī ō´ lə frī) (1933–) grew up in Lodi, California, a place where she says there was nothing to see other than people. Perhaps this environment influenced Viola Frey's artwork, works mostly on monumental sculptures of people. Frey studied art at Stockton Delta College, California College of Arts and Crafts, and Tulane University in New Orleans, Louisiana. Frey has said that power has been a focus of her artwork. This power is present simply in the size of her work.

See pages 24–25 and 16–21 for more about art history and the subject matter.

Artist Profiles, p. 25

◆ Artist Profile ◆
Viola Frey
b. 1933
Viola Frey (vī ō´ lə frī) was born in Lodi, California, on a farm and vineyard. She grew up with strong female role models and became a collector of found objects. She especially likes collecting little figurines from flea markets, and she inserts these objects into ceramic assemblage artwork. These sculptures represent the way the modern world has come to depend on material goods. Frey's large ceramic human figures also reference or critique the modern world and are often covered with symbols and textures that give them an appearance similar to assemblage.

Unit 4 Arts Integration

ILLUSTRATOR PROFILE

Jan Brett

(1949–)

Jan Brett was born in 1949 in Massachusetts. As a child she loved to read and draw, so she decided to become an illustrator. As a student at the Boston Museum of Fine Arts school, she spent hours admiring the artwork in the museum's collection. Brett has said that these images still come back to her in her paintings. Brett uses intricate detail in her illustrations to help readers believe that the imaginary world she is drawing really exists. She travels extensively to research the buildings and clothing that appear in her work, and often uses real people and places as inspiration for her art. Brett's illustrations often contain information that furthers the meaning or moral of the story. One example of this is Brett's retelling of *Beauty and the Beast;* the characters are shown as animals in the main illustrations, but appear in their human form in the background tapestries within those illustrations. The borders around Brett's illustrations often show information that isn't contained in the main pictures or text; Brett has said that she includes these borders to "contain the overflow of thoughts." Throughout Unit 4, share Jan Brett's illustrations with the class and discuss the use of proportion and distortion in her works of art.

Music

Proportion is not a musical term. It is always in the mind of a composer with regard to balancing various aspects of a composition. Distortion is sometimes used in music for dramatic effect. Tone colors are sometimes distorted also. In "Tubby the Tuba," the tuba's sound is distorted when Tubby accidentally "sits" on the tune.

Literature

Show the video or DVD *Masks: A World of Diversity* to introduce the concepts of proportion and distortion. Pause the video or DVD, and have students describe body and face proportions, profiles, and examples of scale, exaggeration, and distortion.

Literature and Art

Performing Arts

Show "Lamentation" and "Satyric Festival Song." Point out the use of proportion and distortion.

Artsource®

Lesson 1 · Overview · Proportion

Lesson 1 introduces proportion. Artists use proportion to show how people or things in works of art relate to one another in size.

Objectives

 Art History and Culture
To become knowledgeable about the lives and the artwork of John Steuart Curry and George Tooker

 Creative Expression
To create a drawing using the sighting technique

 **Aesthetic Perception**
To identify the use of proportion in works of art

Art Criticism
To evaluate one's own work using the four steps of art criticism

Vocabulary Vocabulary

Review the following vocabulary word with students.

proportion proporción—the principle of art concerned with the size relationship of one part to another

See page 149B for additional Spanish vocabulary resources.

Art Journal: Vocabulary

Have students add this word to the Vocabulary section of their Art Journals.

Lesson Materials
- string
- paper
- pencils
- white paper
- dustless chalk
- soft erasers

Alternate Materials:
- colored pencils
- yarn

Program Resources
- *Reading and Writing Test Prep.*, pp. 42–43
- *Transparency 19*
- *Flash Cards 18, 19*
- *Artist Profiles*, pp. 18, 60
- *Animals Through History Time Line*
- *Assessment*, pp. 45–46
- *Large Print 68* Self-Portrait (El Coronelazo)
- *The National Museum of Women in the Arts Collection*

Concept Trace
Proportion
Introduced: Level 4, Unit 5, Lessons 4, 5
Reinforced: Level 6, Unit 5, Lessons 1, 2

Lesson 1 Arts Integration

Theatre
Complete Unit 4, Lesson 1, on pages 72–73 of *Theatre Arts Connections.*

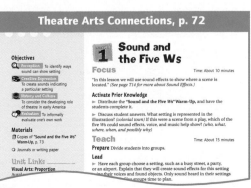
Theatre Arts Connections, p. 72

Music
 In a large form of music that has movements, acts, or stand-alone compositions, the composer takes care to balance the size of each to create unity within the whole. Listen to "Nessen Dorma" from the opera *Turandot,* by Giacomo Puccini. The form of opera is so large, that all action can stop for the singing of an aria. An aria can also stand on its own in vocal performances.

Movement & Dance
Have students stand in a neutral position. Then ask them to see if you can make themselves bigger, smaller, thinner, or wider. Encourage students to try to use their whole body first, then just one side, and then only one body part.

Focus

Activate Prior Knowledge

"Have you ever taken a photograph of something that was very little or very big and found that you could not tell what size it was because there was nothing else in the photograph to compare its size to?" "Alguna vez han tomado una fotografía de algo que era muy pequeño o muy grande y encontraron que no podían notarlo de que tamaño era porque no había mas nada con que comparar su tamaño en la fotografía?"

■ Discuss with the class how we use proportions to judge the sizes of many things.

Using Literature ★ Reading

■ Share Betti Bao Lord's *In the Year of the Boar and Jackie Robinson* with the class. Discuss how the main character survived the immigration process to the United States.

Thematic Connection ★ Science

■ **Survival:** Have students look at the two works of art in this lesson and describe the survival skills being used by the people, animals, and plants in these scenes.

Introduce the Art

Look

"Let's take a close look at the two works of art." "Vamos a observar detalladamente las dos obras de arte."

Main Idea and Details ★ Reading

■ Have students write a short news report describing what is happening in each painting as if they were reporters on the scene.

🏺 Art History and Culture

Both works of art in this lesson were painted in the setting of the artists' native environments. Why do you think this is? Some acceptable answers are: Artists tend to create variations of what they are familiar with and notice the art in their surroundings. Inspiration often comes from their surroundings.
NSAE 4.a

💻 **Web Connection**
Visit **www.tfaoi.com/newsmu/nmus5d.htm** to find more information on the life and work of John Steuart Curry.

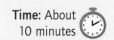
Proportion

▲ **John Steuart Curry.** (American). *Tornado Over Kansas.* 1929.
....
Oil on canvas. $46\frac{1}{4} \times 60\frac{3}{8}$ inches (117.48 × 153.34 cm.). Muskegon Museum of Art, Muskegon, Michigan.

Look at these two works of art. Notice how the two artists used accurate proportions to represent people realistically in different situations. The people in *Bird Watchers* are calm and standing vertically. The people in *Tornado Over Kansas* are active and moving diagonally.

🏺 Art History and Culture

Curry was a member of a group of artists known as American Regionalists. They painted the scenes and events of their sections of the United States.

🏺 Art History and Culture

John Steuart Curry

John Steuart Curry (jân stōō´ ərt kər´ ē) (1897–1946) grew up on a farm in Kansas. His affection for midwestern rural scenery and farm animals can be found in much of his artwork. Curry and two other artists are noted for their involvement with the regionalist movement in the art community. Most of the artists associated with this style were from the Midwest and portrayed everyday life in that environment. The house in *Tornado Over Kansas* is based on the house where he grew up.

See pages 24–25 and 16–21 for more about art history and the subject matter.

Artist Profiles, p. 18

Artist Profile

John Steuart Curry
1897–1946

John Steuart Curry (jân stōō´ art kar´ē) was born on a farm in Dunavant, Kansas, in 1897. Though he worked hard as a child, Curry was not very studious and instead liked to draw the animals and natural phenomena around him. He worked on a railroad to earn enough money to attend the Art Institute of Chicago and Geneva College. After his schooling he earned money as an illustrator for popular western magazine stories. He turned his attention to regionalism in the 1930s, capturing the everyday life and endurance of American heartlanders, especially during the Depression. Though he is best known for his regionalist paintings, Curry was also a painter of portraits and murals in both the

▲ **George Tooker.** (American). *Bird Watchers.* 1948.

Egg tempera on gesso board. 26¾ × 32¼ inches (67.95 × 81.92 cm.). New Britain Museum of Art, New Britain, Connecticut.

Study both works of art to identify the use of proportion.

▶ Look at the man's arm in *Tornado Over Kansas* and imagine it on one of the children. How would this affect the looks of the child?

▶ What does the size of the people in *Tornado Over Kansas* suggest about them?

▶ What clues do you see in each of the paintings that tell you how tall the people are?

▶ Do the people in *Bird Watchers* look shorter than average adults?

Aesthetic Perception

Design Awareness Study cartoon characters and notice how many of them are drawn with exaggerated proportions. Think about why they are drawn this way.

Art History and Culture

George Tooker

George Tooker (jorj tŏŏk´ər) (1920–) was born in Brooklyn, New York. His family moved to Long Island when George was young. He took art lessons from a friend of his mother's and attended Phillips Academy in Massachusetts. Tooker went on to study English at Harvard University. While there, he frequently visited the Fogg Art Museum and began to see art as a tool for social change. He studied at the Art Students League in New York City. There he met teachers and friends that would greatly influence his art style and direction. Tooker experimented with egg yolk with water and tempera powder. This became his favorite medium. He used it to paint *Bird Watchers.*

See pages 24–25 and 16–21 for more about art history and the subject matter.

Artist Profiles, p. 60

◆ Artist Profile ◆

George Tooker
b. 1920

George Tooker (jorj tŏŏk´ər) grew up in Brooklyn and Long Island, New York. His family was part of the upper class, and this upbringing is reflected in his paintings. He gained an understanding of a genteel lifestyle—as well the lifestyle of those who were less privileged—and he became interested in the use of art as a tool for social change. Tooker considers himself to be a reporter and he creates compositions that reflect his views of everyday life.

Study

▶ The man's arm would be too big to look realistic on any of the children.

▶ The size of the people in *Tornado Over Kansas* in comparison to each other suggests their age.

▶ The animals, trees, house, and fence all act as clues, giving the viewer references for the size of the people in these paintings.

▶ The people in George Tooker's *Bird Watchers* are shorter than the average adult. The body proportions of adults are close to seven and a half heads tall.
NSAE 5.c
■ For more examples of narrative art, see *The National Museum of Women in the Arts Collection.*

Art Journal: Writing

Have students write about a movie, play, or book that they are familiar with in which the main character has to struggle to overcome an obstacle.

Aesthetic Perception

Design Awareness With students, make a list of cartoon characters that are drawn with funny proportions. Ask students to suggest reasons why the cartoon characters are drawn that way.

Developing Visual Literacy Have students look at the characters' facial expressions in each painting. Ask them if they think the expressions accurately convey what the characters might be experiencing. Discuss with students how they could change these expressions and how this would affect the painting.

Web Connection

Visit www.rogallery.com/tooker_george/tooker-biography.htm to learn more about the life and work of George Tooker.

Teach

Time: About 45 minutes

"How can you measure human proportions or height without using a ruler or measuring tape?" "¿Cómo pueden medir proporciones o estaturas humanas sin usar una regla o una cinta de medir?"

- Read and discuss the definition of *proportion* on page 128.

Practice

Materials: string, paper, pencils

Alternate Materials: yarn

- Distribute the materials, and have students follow the directions on page 128.

- Have students find partners for this Practice activity. Ask students to take turns using the string to measure their partner's head from the top of the skull to the bottom of the chin. Then, using the measurement of the head, measure the length of their partner's arms, legs, and their overall height. The measurements should be recorded on paper and compared. Ask students how many heads tall their partner's body measurements are.

Creative Expression

Materials: oil pastels, white paper, dustless chalk, soft erasers

Alternate Materials: color pencils

- Before beginning this activity, refer to the additional notes on using the sighting method in the Activity Tips on page 239.

- Distribute the materials and have students follow the directions on page 129.

- Review the Activity Tips on page 239 for visual examples of this lesson's activity.

Art Journal: Brainstorming

Have students brainstorm and sketch both real and imaginary scenes in their Art Journals.

Using Proportion

Proportion is the principle of art related to the size relationships of one part to another, such as a hand to a wrist. Artists use several techniques to draw things in proportion.

Although people vary in size and shape, most people have the same body proportions.

Artists use the length of the head, from the chin to the top of the skull, to help them in measuring proportion. The average adult is seven and one-half heads tall. A child may be five heads tall, while an infant might be only three heads tall.

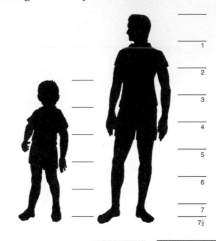

Practice

Estimate body proportions. Use string.

1. With a string, measure a partner's head from the top of the skull to the bottom of the chin. Using the length of the head as a unit of measurement, measure the rest of your partner's body. For example, the length of the arm might be two head lengths.

2. Record and compare your findings with those of your partner.

Differentiated Instruction

Reteach

Have students look though magazines and cut out pictures of people. With a ruler, students can measure the head of the person and use that measurement to determine the person's height proportion.

Special Needs

Provide visual prompts for students as they begin drawing, such as pictures of people with measuring lines dividing the body into proportionate sections. This will help students recall size relationships among body parts.

ELL

When presenting new techniques, it can be helpful to have students watch you model procedures and read the instructions aloud. This creates an oral-to-print connection with the text for students to rely on later in independent practice.

◀ **Andrew Williams.**
Age 11.

Think about the proportion this student artist used.

 Creative Expression

How can you use the sighting technique to draw a person in proportion? Sketch a model. Use the sighting technique to determine proportion.

1. Think about proportion as it relates to people. Use the sighting technique to determine the proportion of your model.

2. Use chalk and a soft eraser to lightly sketch your model.

3. Add color to your drawing by covering over all the chalk lines with oil pastels.

 **Art Criticism**

Describe Explain the steps you followed as you used the sighting technique.

Analyze How many heads tall is your figure?

Interpret What mood does your drawing convey?

Decide Were you able to successfully use the sighting technique to draw the model in proportion?

Unit 4 • Lesson 1　**129**

Reflect

Review and Assess

"Were you able to draw a model, using the sighting technique to determine the proportions of the model?" "¿Pudieron dibujar un modelo usando la técnica de reconocer por la vista para determinar las proporciones del modelo?"

Think

The student artist used correct body proportions to draw the model. Because of this, he looks realistic.

- Use *Large Print 68* Self-Portrait (El Coronelazo) to have students identify and describe the use of proportion.

Informal Assessment

- For standardized-format test practice using this lesson's art content, see pages 42–43 in *Reading and Writing Test Preparation.*

Art Journal: Critical Thinking

Have students answer the four art criticism questions—Describe, Analyze, Interpret, and Decide—in their Art Journals. In small groups, have students discuss their oil-pastel sketches.

Art Across the Curriculum

Use these simple ideas to reinforce art concepts across the curriculum.

★ **Expository Writing** Have students write instructional steps for using the sighting technique when sketching a person.

★ **Math** When studying ratios in math, look at the oil-pastel sketches students created. Have students figure the ratios of their model's proportions, using the number 1 (the measurement of the head) as the numerator.

★ **Science** Discuss the survival of endangered species and have students research what is being done to save them.

★ **Social Studies** Compare and contrast the lives of people who live in the country and in the city.

★ **Technology** Have students select a square icon and copy and paste it horizontally seven and a half times on one screen. Ask students to print and use these squares to sketch a person in proportion. Visit **SRAonline.com** to print out detailed instructions for this activity.
NSAE 6.b

Proportion

Extra! For the Art Specialist

Time: About 45 minutes

Focus
Study *Large Print 68* Self-Portrait (El Coronelazo) and ask students to closely identify the use of proportion in the artwork. Describe the person in the painting.

Teach
Explain to students that they will be selecting one of their figure studies to complete as a mixed-media painting.

Reflect
Have students evaluate their works of art using the four steps of art criticism. Encourage them to locate and describe the use of proportion.

Alternate Activity

Materials
- 12" × 18" colored paper
- color chalk
- tempera or acrylic paints
- paintbrushes
- water containers
- newspaper
- oil pastels

1. Take turns with your classmates posing for one another. Use the sighting technique to capture the pose and to determine the proportions of the model. Make at least two sketches.

2. Select your best drawing and work directly with tempera paints. Begin outlining and filling in the basic shapes. Paint the figure first. Mix the colors as needed on a mixing tray.

3. Color in the background using loose brushstrokes. Use a smaller brush to add details.

4. Once the paint has dried, use oil pastels to emphasize the important lines, shapes, shadows, and highlights.

Research in Art Education
Research suggests that when arts are integrated in schools, students tend to perform better on standardized reading and math tests. This seems to be especially true for low-socio-economic-status students at the elementary school level ("Chicago Arts Partnership in Education (CAPE): Evaluation Summary," in *Critical Links*, p. 72). As students begin to see the relevance of mathematical concepts, such as ratios used for proportion in art, the concepts will move from intangible to concrete.

Assessment
Use the following rubric to evaluate the artwork students make in the Creative Expression activity and to assess students' understanding of proportion.

Have students complete page 45 or 46 in their *Assessment* books.

	Art History and Culture	Aesthetic Perception	Creative Expression	Art Criticism
3 POINTS	The student demonstrates knowledge of the life and work of John Steuart Curry and George Tooker.	The student accurately identifies proportion used in art.	The student's sketch clearly illustrates the use of proportion.	The student thoughtfully and honestly evaluates own work using the four steps of art criticism.
2 POINTS	The student's knowledge of the life and work of John Steuart Curry and George Tooker is weak or incomplete.	The student shows emerging awareness of proportion used in art.	The student's sketch shows some awareness of proportion.	The student attempts to evaluate own work but shows an incomplete understanding of evaluation criteria.
1 POINT	The student cannot demonstrate knowledge of the life and work of John Steuart Curry or George Tooker.	The student cannot identify proportion used in art.	The student's sketch shows no understanding of proportion.	The student makes no attempt to evaluate own artwork.

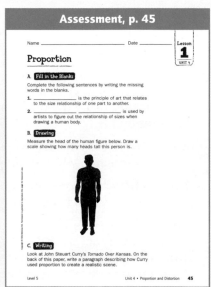

Assessment, p. 45

Name _____ Date _____

Proportion — Lesson 1, UNIT 4

A Fill in the Blanks
Complete the following sentences by writing the missing words in the blanks.

1. _____ is the principle of art that relates to the size relationship of one part to another.

2. _____ is used by artists to figure out the relationship of sizes when drawing a human body.

B Drawing
Measure the head of the human figure below. Draw a scale showing how many heads tall this person is.

C Writing
Look at John Steuart Curry's *Tornado Over Kansas*. On the back of this paper, write a paragraph describing how Curry used proportion to create a realistic scene.

Level 5 — Unit 4 • Proportion and Distortion — 45

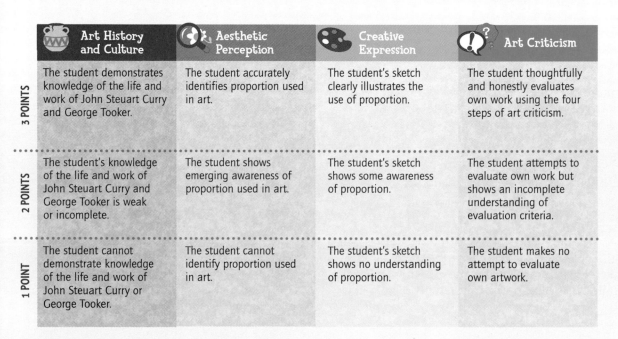

Lesson 2 Scale

Lesson 2 introduces scale. Artists use scale to relate the size of one object to the size of another in a work of art.

Objectives

 Art History and Culture

To become knowledgeable about the lives and the artwork of Domenico Ghirlandaio and Nanha

 Creative Expression

To plan and create a collage using realistic and unrealistic scale

 Aesthetic Perception

To identify the use of scale in works of art

Art Criticism

To evaluate one's own work using the four steps of art criticism

Vocabulary Vocabulary

Review the following vocabulary words with students.

scale escala—size as measured against a standard reference

realistic scale escala real—size relationships in a work of art in which everything seems to fit together and make sense

unrealistic scale escala irreal—size relationships in a work of art that do not make sense

See page 149B for additional Spanish vocabulary resources.

 Art Journal: Vocabulary

Have students add these words to the Vocabulary section of their Art Journals.

Lesson Materials

- white drawing paper
- pencils
- glue
- magazines
- scissors

Alternate Materials:
- black markers
- photographs
- newspaper

Program Resources

- *Reading and Writing Test Prep.*, pp. 44–45
- *Transparency 20*
- *Flash Cards 18, 19*
- *Artist Profiles*, pp. 28, 45
- *Animals Through History Time Line*
- *Assessment*, pp. 47–48
- *Large Prints 67* Gogol and *68* Self-Portrait (El Coronelazo)
- *The National Museum of Women in the Arts Collection*

Concept Trace

Scale

Introduced: Level 5, Unit 4, Lesson 2

Reinforced: Level 6, Unit 5, Lessons 5, 6

Lesson 2 Arts Integration

Theatre

Complete Unit 4, Lesson 2, on pages 74–75 of *Theatre Arts Connections.*

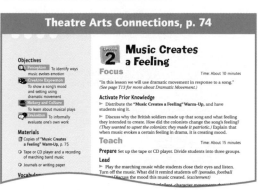

Music

 Musical compositions can be composed on any scale, from chamber music to symphonic form. Chamber music was originally written for a small group of instruments to perform in a "chamber" instead of a large concert hall. The combinations can be duos, trios, quartets, quintets, etc. Sometimes chamber music can sound like conversations between the players. Listen to *Quintet, Op. 114* "The Trout" by Franz Schubert.

Movement & Dance

Have students use their bodies to set the scale of buildings and other objects. Go outside and ask them to choose three objects to demonstrate this idea, such as a door, a tree, or a building. As one student stands next to each of the above, the class will then look at them in relationship to the object.

Focus

Time: About 20 minutes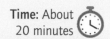

Activate Prior Knowledge

"Have you ever seen an advertisement for a product that looked really big, but when you saw the actual object, it ended up being quite small?" "¿Alguna vez han visto un anuncio publicitario para un producto que se veía muy grande pero que cuando vieron el objeto de verdad era bastante pequeño?"

- Discuss with students their answers and talk about how other nearby objects can be used to determine the actual size of something.

Using Literature ⭐ Reading

- Share Cynthia Rylant's book *Appalachia: The Voice of Sleeping Birds.* Discuss how families all over the world have things in common even though they may appear to be very different. Have students look for uses of scale in the illustrations in this book.

Thematic Connection ⭐ Social Studies

- **Families:** Encourage students to share some of their family traditions.

Introduce the Art

Look

"Let's take a close look at the two works of art." "Vamos a observar detalladamente las dos obras de arte."

Predicting ⭐ Reading

Have students predict what the fathers in the paintings are doing with their sons. Possible answers are: *Francesco Sasetti and His Son Teodoro:* The son has just asked the father a question, and the father is thinking before answering him. *Emperor Shah Jahan and His Son, Suja:* The emperor and his son are picnicking.

 Art History and Culture

Twenty thousand workers spent twenty-two years building the Taj Mahal for Shah Jahan's wife Mumtaz Mahal. Visit **www.tajmahal.net/ augEng/pano_pages.htm** for a virtual tour of the Taj Mahal.

🖥 **Web Connection**
Visit **www.ibiblio.org/wm/paint/auth/ ghirlandaio/** to learn more about the life and work of Domenico Ghirlandaio.

130 UNIT 4 • Proportion and Distortion

 **Scale**

Look at these works of art and notice how scale is used to show the differences in size between the adults and the children in the paintings.

◀ **Domenico Ghirlandaio.** (Italian). *Francesco Sasetti and His Son Teodoro.* c. 1480.
Tempera on wood. 29½ × 20½ inches (74.93 × 52.07 cm.). The Metropolitan Museum of Art, New York, New York.

 Art History and Culture

Emperor Shah Jahan had the Taj Mahal built as a tomb for his wife.

 Art History and Culture

Domenico Ghirlandaio

Domenico Ghirlandaio (dō mā´ nē kō gēr län´ dā ō) (1449–1494) was born in Florence, Italy. He was the son of a gold- and silversmith. Ghirlandaio was trained to follow in his father's footsteps, although he later left his trade and became one of Florence's most famous painters. Domenico Ghirlandaio developed his techniques in painting and mosaics while studying with Alesso Bladovinetti, a distinguished painter in Florence.

See pages 24–25 and 16–21 for more about art history and the subject matter.

Artist Profiles, p. 28

Artist Profile
Domenico Ghirlandaio
1449-1494
Domenico Ghirlandaio (dō mā´ nē kō gēr län´ dā ō) was born in Florence, Italy, in 1449. He was the son of Tommaso Bigordi, a goldsmith. *Ghirlandaio* means "garland maker." This name was given to Tommaso because of his expertise in designing silver wreaths for women to wear in their hair. Domenico inherited his father's nickname, Ghirlandaio. He developed his technique in painting and in mosaic while studying with Alesso Baldovinetti, a distinguished painter in Florence. Ghirlandaio lived in Florence most of his life, achieving great success as an artist.

▲ **Nanha.** (Indian). *Emperor Shah Jahan and His Son, Suja.* 1625–1630.
Colors on gilt on paper. 15⅝ × 10⁵⁄₁₆ inches (40.21 × 102.39 cm.).
Metropolitan Museum of Art, New York, New York.

 Aesthetic Perception

Seeing Like an Artist Compare the size of the objects in the lower-grade classrooms in your school with the size of the objects in the upper-grade classrooms.

Study both paintings to learn about scale.

► How big are the people in each work of art?

► What objects give the viewer clues to help judge the sizes of the man and his son in Nanha's painting?

► Do both children seem to be in realistic proportion and scale to the adults they appear next to?

► As a viewer, where are you in relation to each painting? How does this affect the way you see the people in these paintings?

Art History and Culture

Nanha

Nanha's (nän hä) (1582–1635) works are excellent examples of the Mogul style of painting, which was popular in India from the sixteenth to the nineteenth centuries. This art style was used mostly for book illustrations and miniature portraits. Moguls typically portrayed historical events, scenes from Persian and Indian literature and folktales, and scenes from everyday life and nature. Nanha was known for his miniature portraits of royalty and nobles. He was a designer, a painter, and a portraitist.

See pages 24–25 and 16–21 for more about art history and the subject matter.

Artist Profiles, p. 45

► Artist Profile ◄
Nanha the Mughal
c. 1582–1635
Nanha the Mughal (nän´hä the mü´gəl) was an Indian artist who was skilled enough to remain a court painter during the reigns of three emperors—Akbar, Jahangir, and Shah Jahan. Nanha's nephew, Bishan Das, also became a portrait painter.

◄ **Nanha the Mughal.** (Indian). *Emperor Shah Jahan and His Son, Suja.* 1625–30.

Study

► The boys are smaller than their fathers in both paintings.

► The bed suggests the sizes of the two; items in their hands, and their size relationship to each other.

► The child in Ghirlandaio's painting seems to be of average size. The boy in Nanha's painting appears smaller.

► Ghirlandaio: The viewer looks into the painting at eye level with the father. This gives the viewer a realistic look at the people in the painting. Nanha: The viewer is above the people in the painting. This distorts the viewer's ability to judge the sizes of the people.

■ For more examples of portraits, see *The National Museum of Women in the Arts Collection.*

Art Journal: Writing
Ask students to write in their Art Journals about a special family time they have experienced or one they are planning.

Aesthetic Perception

Seeing Like an Artist Bring in a chair from a lower-grade classroom. Ask students to compare it with one in their classroom. Discuss what features are different and why. Ask students to think of other objects that are designed in varied sizes and to explain why.

Developing Visual Literacy Would you have painted background scenery in Nanha's painting? How would the painting have a different effect if it did have background scenery?

Web Connection
Visit www.chandnichowk.com/miniatures/min_babur.htm to learn more about Mogul history and see some examples of Mogul miniatures.

Teach

"Let's draw an object to scale using one of our hands as a standard size." "Vamos a dibujar un objeto a escala usando una de nuestras manos como una medida patrón."

■ Read and discuss the definitions of *scale*, *realistic scale*, and *unrealistic scale* on page 132.

Practice

Materials: white drawing paper, pencils

Alternate Materials: black markers

■ Distribute the materials, and have students follow the directions on page 132.

■ Ask students to select an object to draw that is either smaller or larger than one of their hands. Encourage students to find a comfortable pose for the hand that they will draw. After students draw their hand in actual size, they should draw their chosen object. Discuss how the hand in the drawing offers clues to the viewer of how big the object is.

Creative Expression

Materials: white paper, glue, magazines, scissors

Alternate Materials: photographs, newspaper photographs

■ Distribute the materials, and have students follow the directions on page 133.

■ Review the Activity Tips on page 239 for visual examples of this lesson's activity.

Art Journal: Brainstorming

Have students think about a theme they would like to incorporate into their collage using unrealistic scale and list their ideas in their Art Journals. You might want to suggest that students use the lesson's theme of families for this activity.

Using Scale

Scale is similar to proportion in that it relates to size relationships. The difference is that scale refers to size as measured against a standard reference, such as the human body. A scale can be realistic or unrealistic.

Realistic Scale When an artist creates a work of art in which everything seems to fit together and make sense in size relationships, the scale is called *realistic*.

Unrealistic Scale When an artist creates size relationships that do not make sense, the scale becomes *unrealistic*.

Practice

Use a realistic scale when drawing an object. Use pencil.

1. Draw your hand to create an object of standard size.

2. Select an object that is either larger or smaller than your hand. Draw the object in realistic scale to your hand. The entire object does not have to fit on your paper.

Differentiated Instruction

Reteach

Have students look at the fine art in this program and look for examples of unrealistic scale.

Special Needs

Help students develop good composition skills by encouraging them to experiment with several different layouts of objects before gluing anything on the page.

ELL

You can provide extra exposure to art vocabulary by using both familiar and new vocabulary words. Asking students to respond using the vocabulary words will help reinforce the meanings and encourage comfort in their use. Is this scale realistic or unrealistic?

◀ **Marcia Saunders.**
Age 10.

Think about how the student artist used both realistic and unrealistic scale in this collage.

 Creative Expression

How can you use unrealistic scale to emphasize an object in your artwork? Create a collage. Use unrealistic scale.

1. Think about an indoor or outdoor background to use in your collage and the objects that you will add. Cut out pictures of objects, some that are in proper scale and one or two that are too large or too small for the other objects.

2. Arrange your collected images so that they overlap and touch the edges of your paper. Keep the arrangement organized so that it is almost realistic.

3. Glue down the background. Next, glue the remaining objects. Make sure that at least one object shows unrealistic scale.

Art Criticism

Describe Describe the objects you selected for your collage.

Analyze How are the objects arranged to create unrealistic scale?

Interpret What emotion does your collage convey?

Decide Do you feel you were able to clearly portray unrealistic scale in an organized way?

Unit 4 • Lesson 2 **133**

 **Reflect**   Time: About 15 minutes

Review and Assess
"Were you able to create a collage that reflects unrealistic scale?" "¿Pudieron hacer un collage que refleja una escala irreal?"

Think
The student artist used unrealistic scale. The children sitting on the van are too large to fit inside it.

■ Use *Large Prints 67 Gogol* and *68 Self-Portrait (El Coronelazo)* to have students identify and describe the uses of scale.

Informal Assessment

■ For standardized-format test practice using this lesson's art content, see pages 44–45 in *Reading and Writing Test Preparation.*

Art Journal: Critical Thinking
Have students answer the four art criticism questions—Describe, Analyze, Interpret, and Decide—in their Art Journals. In small groups, have students discuss their collages.

Art Across the Curriculum

Use these simple ideas to reinforce art concepts across the curriculum.

★ **Poetry Writing** Have students write a poem to accompany and reflect their collage.

★ **Math** Review the skill of estimation when solving mathematical problems. Using scale with familiar standards of measurement will improve the accuracy of estimations.

★ **Science** Review the use of scale when studying the growth stages of living things.

★ **Social Studies** Discuss how the economic concept of supply and demand works as a fluctuating scale.

★ **Technology** Have students make a bar graph with a spreadsheet program. Have students discuss how scale can represent the quantity of something. Visit **SRAonline.com** to print out detailed instructions for this activity.
NSAE 6.b

Lesson 2 — Scale
Wrap-Up

Focus

Study **Large Prints 67** *Gogol* and **68** *Self-Portrait (El Coronelazo)* to learn how artists use scale to relate one object to another object in their artwork. Have students describe the objects in the paintings and how the artists used scale in each artwork.

Teach

Have students give examples of objects that must be in scale in order to work. Cars, furniture, clothing, and architecture are some examples. Explain to students that sometimes an artist purposely creates a work in which unrealistic scale is used to communicate an idea or create a feeling.

Reflect

Have students use the four steps of art criticism to evaluate their works of art. Encourage them to identify areas of realistic or unrealistic scale.

Alternate Activity

Materials
- Art Journals
- pencils and erasers
- 12" × 18" white paper
- scissors
- magazines
- glue
- watercolor or tempera paints
- paintbrushes
- water containers
- newspaper
- fine-line markers

1. Look through a magazine and choose images that reflect your family. Because people and animals are of consistently average size, you can base your scale on your chosen images. Cut out the images.

2. In your Art Journal, work out some ideas for the environment in which to place your family images. Decide whether you will be using realistic or unrealistic scale.

3. Lightly sketch the environment onto the paper. Paint in the scene.

4. Glue the cut image into your painted environment. Use a fine-line marker to add any needed details.

Research in Art Education

"It seems without a doubt that children do, indeed, respond to and are able to talk about art in meaningful ways." Anderson, Tom. ("Talking About Art with Children: From Theory to Practice." *Art Education* 39. 1986. 5–8.)

Assessment

Use the following rubric to evaluate the artwork students make in the Creative Expression activity and to assess students' understanding of scale.

Have students complete page 47 or 48 in their *Assessment* books.

	Art History and Culture	Aesthetic Perception	Creative Expression	Art Criticism
3 POINTS	The student demonstrates knowledge of the life and work of Domenico Ghirlandaio and Nanha.	The student accurately identifies the use of scale in art.	The student's collage clearly illustrates the use of unrealistic scale.	The student thoughtfully and honestly evaluates own work using the four steps of art criticism.
2 POINTS	The student's knowledge of the life and work of Domenico Ghirlandaio and Nanha is weak or incomplete.	The student shows emerging awareness of the use of scale in art.	The student's collage shows some awareness of unrealistic scale.	The student attempts to evaluate own work, but shows an incomplete understanding of evaluation criteria.
1 POINT	The student cannot demonstrate knowledge of the life and work of Domenico Ghirlandaio or Nanha.	The student cannot identify scale used in art.	The student's collage shows no understanding of unrealistic scale.	The student makes no attempt to evaluate own artwork.

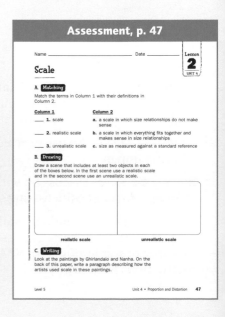

Assessment, p. 47

Face Proportions

Lesson 3 introduces proportions of the human face. Artists use standard proportions to help them correctly organize the features of the face.

Objectives

 Art History and Culture

To become knowledgeable about the lives and the artwork of Elizabeth Catlett and Robert Henri

 Creative Expression

To create a portrait incorporating correct face proportions

 Aesthetic Perception

To identify the use of face proportions in artistic portraits and on people's faces

Art Criticism

To evaluate one's own work using the four steps of art criticism

Vocabulary Vocabulary

Review the following vocabulary words with students.

face proportions proporción de la cara—used to help artists place features correctly on the human face

central axis eje central—the vertical center line used to divide a view

profile proportions proporción de contorno—the relationship of one feature of a face to another feature from the side view

See page 149B for additional Spanish vocabulary resources.

 Art Journal: Vocabulary

Have students add these words to the Vocabulary section of their Art Journals.

Lesson Materials
- white paper
- pencils
- string
- watercolor paints

Alternate Materials:
- pens
- crayons

Program Resources
- *Reading and Writing Test Prep.,* pp. 46–47
- *Transparency 21*
- *Flash Cards 18*
- *Artist Profiles,* pp. 14, 31
- *Animals Through History Time Line*
- *Assessment,* pp. 49–50
- *Large Prints 67 Gogol* and *68 Self-Portrait (El Coronelazo)*
- *The National Museum of Women in the Arts Collection*

Concept Trace
Face Proportions
Introduced: Level 4, Unit 5, Lesson 4
Reinforced: Level 6, Unit 5, Lesson 1

Lesson 3 Arts Integration

Theatre

Complete Unit 4, Lesson 3, on pages 76–77 of *Theatre Arts Connections.*

Theatre Arts Connections, p. 76

Music

In music, the form that has the formal balance of symmetry is ABA. In ABA form, the outer two sections are the same with a contrasting section in the middle. Sing or listen to "Cumbia del Sol." The form is refrain, verse, refrain.

Movement & Dance

Explore contrasting facial expressions. Have students warm up their faces by the following actions: large chewing movements, large open yawns, tightly screwing up and opening the face. Then ask them to express each of the following in a facial expression: sad, happy, curious, confused, anxious, relaxed, and silly.

Focus

Time: About 20 minutes

Activate Prior Knowledge

"Are human faces symmetrical?" "¿Las caras humanas son simétricas?"

- Discuss with students their answers to the question. Have students look closely at their own faces in a mirror and observe whether one eyebrow is slightly larger than the other, or one ear is higher than the other, and so on.

Using Literature  Reading

- Share Beverly Cleary's book *Dear Mr. Henshaw* with the class. Discuss how Leigh, the main character, uses letters to communicate his feelings and experiences. Also notice the use of face proportions on the cover art.

Thematic Connection ⭐ Social Studies

- **Communication:** Brainstorm with students the many different ways we communicate with each other. Discuss the importance of learning how to communicate what is important in an appropriate way.

Introduce the Art

Look

"Let's take a close look at the two works of art." "Vamos a observar detalladamente las dos obras de arte."

Artist's Purpose ⭐ Reading

- Ask students to infer the artists' purposes for creating the works of art that appear in this lesson. Have students support their suggestions with specific elements they see in the artwork.

🏺 Art History and Culture

"The Eight" included Arthur B. Davies, Robert Henri, George Luks, William Glackens, John Sloan, and Everett Shinn. The nickname "The Ashcan School" was given to them by a critic that did not care for their New York City subject matter.

 Web Connection

Visit **www.mojoportfolio.com/artist_search/ african_american/catlett.html#bio** to view the series *For My People* and learn more about Elizabeth Catlett's life.

Lesson 3 # Face Proportions

 Look at these works of art and notice the similar placement of the eyes in the faces.

▲ **Elizabeth Catlett.** (American). *Singing Their Songs.* 1992. From *For My People.*
Color lithograph on paper. 15¾ × 13¾ inches (40.01 × 34.93 cm).
National Museum of Women in the Arts, Washington, D.C.

🏺 Art History and Culture

Robert Henri founded a group of eight artists called "The Eight." They chose to paint everyday life as they saw it in the city. They were nicknamed the "Ashcan School."

🏺 Art History and Culture

Elizabeth Catlett

Elizabeth Catlett (ē liz' ə bəth kat' lət) (1915–) decided to become an artist while in high school. She won a scholarship to the Carnegie Institute of Technology but was not accepted because of her race. Catlett went on to receive a master of fine arts degree from the University of Iowa. There she studied under Grant Wood, who encouraged his students to "paint what you know best." Catlett followed that direction and has become famous for portraying African and African American traditions with Mexican and African American themes in her art. She often uses women as main characters in her artworks.

See pages 24–25 and 16–21 for more about art history and the subject matter.

Artist Profiles, p. 14

Artist Profile

Elizabeth Catlett
b. 1915

Elizabeth Catlett (ə liz' ə bəth kat' lət) was born into a comfortable African American family in Washington, D.C. She went to public school there and later attended Howard University. She went to graduated with honors. She also earned her master of fine arts degree from the State University of Iowa, where she studied under Grant Wood. During the 1940s, Catlett used mother-and-child themes in her realistic sculptures. During the next ten years she moved toward abstraction, generating smooth rounded forms and graceful elongated figures. During the 1960s and 1970s, she created expressionistic sculptures and prints showing African and militant themes. Catlett became a citizen of Mexico in 1962.

▲ **Robert Henri.** (American).
Tilly. 1917.
••••••••••••••••••••••••••
Oil on canvas. 24 × 20 inches
(60.96 × 50.8 cm.). Lowe Art
Museum, Coral Gables, Florida.

Study both paintings to investigate face proportions.

► What changes and what stays the same in the positions of the faces in these works of art?

► How is a mouth drawn differently in a side profile view as compared to the way it is drawn in a front view?

► Where are the ears in relation to the eyes and nose? Is this true for all faces in these works of art?

► How do the child's features compare to the adult's features?

► How are the characters in these works of art communicating?

Aesthetic Perception

Seeing Like an Artist Look at people's faces that you see throughout the day. Notice the placement of each feature and think about how you would correctly draw the features.

Study

► The positions of the faces change, but generally the proportions stay the same.

► In a profile view, the mouth is drawn with the same guide lines but is only half as large.

► The top of the ears are level with the eyes, and the end of the nose is about the height where the middle of the ear is drawn.

► The child's face is a little rounder; the features are a little smaller and closer together than those on the adult's face.

► The woman and the man in *Singing Their Songs* are singing. The girl in *Tilly* is communicating with her eyes and her body language.

■ For more examples of portraits, see *The National Museum of Women in the Arts Collection.*

Art Journal: Writing

Ask students to write about a time when they were silent but still able to communicate a message to someone. Have them explain whether the receiver was able to understand the message correctly.

Aesthetic Perception

Seeing Like an Artist Discuss with the class how each person's face has individual characteristics and can be accurately drawn using standard face-proportion guides.

Developing Visual Literacy Ask students to interpret the messages the characters in these works of art are communicating.

Art History and Culture

Robert Henri

Robert Henri (rob´ ərt hen´rē) (1865–1929) studied art at the Pennsylvania Academy and later at the Ecole des Beaux Arts in Paris. He taught art at the Women's School of Design in Philadephia, the New York School of Art, the Ferrer Center, the Arts Students League in New York, and he founded the Henri School. Robert Henri was an advocate of realism in art. He believed that artists should protect their freedom of expression through their work. Henri, and other artists that stood for this freedom, pioneered what became known as the "Ashcan" group of artists. These artists created realistic paintings that were not glamorized but portrayed people and events the way they exist in everyday life.

See pages 24–25 and 16–21 for more about art history and the subject matter.

Artist Profiles, p. 31

◆ Artist Profile ◆

Robert Henri
1865-1929
Robert Henri (rob´ art hen´ rē) was born Robert Henry Cozad in Cincinnati, Ohio. He changed his name when his father was accused of murder. Henri showed great artistic talent at a young age and was encouraged by his parents to pursue painting at the Pennsylvania Academy of Fine Arts, and later the Academie Julian and École des Beaux-Arts in Paris, France. When he returned from Paris, he became a widely known and respected teacher, emphasizing the importance of his students' creative freedom and founded The Eight, a group of American artists who joined his rebellion against the strict confines of academic art.

💻 Web Connection
Visit **monet.unk.edu/mona/pioneer/henri/henri.html** to see some of Robert Henri's artwork and learn more about his life.

Teach

Time: About 30 minutes

"Let's draw a profile." "Vamos a trazar un perfil."

■ Read and discuss the definition of *face proportions* on page 136.

Practice

Materials: paper, pencils

Alternate Materials: pens or crayons

■ Distribute the materials, and have students follow the directions on page 136.

■ Have students find a partner, and taking turns, use guide lines to draw each other's heads in profile.

Creative Expression

Materials: white paper, pencils, string for measuring, watercolor paints

Alternate Materials: crayons

■ Distribute the materials and have students follow the directions on page 137.

■ Review the Activity Tips on page 240 for visual examples of this lesson's activity

■ See the Technique Tips on page 219 for more information on how to use watercolor paints.

Art Journal: Brainstorming

Have students observe the size and shape of their partner's head, then sketch a quick contour drawing in their Art Journals for practice before measuring.

Using Face Proportions

Artists use **face proportions** to correctly draw features on human faces. Lightly drawn lines are **guide lines** used by artists to create both full-face and profile portraits more accurately.

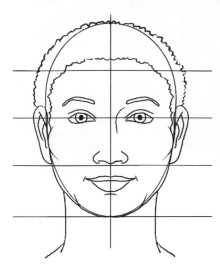
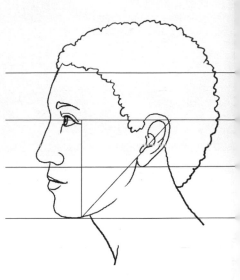

Practice

Practice drawing a profile. Use pencil.

1. Draw the shape of the head in profile. Add guide lines. Use the second drawing shown above as a reference.

2. Add the eye, nose, mouth, chin, ear, hair, and neck.

Differentiated Instruction

Reteach

Have students cut out pictures of people from magazines and draw face-proportion grids on them. Ask students to explain what they found.

Special Needs

Help students to master lesson objectives by providing visual examples of the different types of face, eye, nose, and lip shapes people have.

ELL

Long lists of detailed instructions can be overwhelming and lead to confusion. To aid students in learning the targeted vocabulary and instructions, model the procedures. Have students repeat the important vocabulary words.

◀ **Shelby Stephen.**
Age 10.

Think about how the student artist used face proportions to correctly draw a portrait.

Creative Expression

What is the best way to draw features on a portrait? Working with a partner, draw a portrait using face proportions.

1. Think about the shape and size of your partner's head.

2. Measure the size of your partner's head. Mark off the dimensions on paper. Next, lightly draw guide lines for the eyes. Keep proportion in mind.

3. Draw the hair, eyebrows, neck, shoulders and clothing.

4. Use watercolors to paint the portrait.

Art Criticism

Describe List the steps you followed to measure and draw face proportions.

Analyze What measurements did you use to place the features on the head using accurate proportions?

Interpret What does the person in your portrait seem to be thinking?

Decide Were you successful in drawing the features of your portrait in proportion? What would you do to make it better?

 Time: About 15 minutes

Review and Assess

"Were you able to draw a portrait using face proportions?" "¿Fueron capaces de hacer un retrato usando proporciones de cara?"

Think

The student artist used correct face proportions to paint a realistic portrait of the model.

■ Use *Large Prints 67* Gogol and *68 Self-Portrait (El Coronelazo)* to have students identify and describe the use of face proportions.

Informal Assessment

■ For standardized-format test practice using this lesson's art content, see pages 46–47 in *Reading and Writing Test Preparation.*

Art Journal: Critical Thinking

Have students answer the four art criticism questions—Describe, Analyze, Interpret, and Decide—in their Art Journals. In small groups, have students discuss their profile drawings.

Art Across the Curriculum

Use these simple ideas to reinforce art concepts across the curriculum.

★ **Narrative Writing** Have students write a short story about a miscommunication.

★ **Math** Use portraits when discussing balance and proportion in math.

★ **Science** Discuss the Golden Ratio with students and how it has been used in science, art, and Egyptian engineering.

★ **Social Studies** Discuss as a class who has made important contributions to the advancement of communication, for example Alexander Graham Bell and Samuel F. B. Morse.

★ **Technology** Have students use a computer paint program to redraw their portraits. Visit **SRAonline.com** to print detailed instructions for this activity.
NSAE 6.b

Face Proportions

Extra! For the Art Specialist

Time: About 45 minutes

Focus

Study **Large Prints 67** *Gogol* and **68** *Self-Portrait (El Coronelazo)* to learn how artists depict face proportions in their artwork. Describe the people you see. How old do you think they are? What clues helped you guess their age?

Teach

Have students collect photographs of a family member. Explain that they will be creating a colored chalk or oil-pastel portrait of a family member. Demonstrate dividing a face to draw the correct face proportions. Have the students interview the family members they draw. Have them write a brief biography to accompany the portrait.

Reflect

Have students evaluate their artwork using the four steps of art criticism. Encourage them to locate and describe the use of face proportions.

Alternate Activity

- Art Journals
- pencils and erasers
- 12" × 18" white or black paper
- personal photographs or magazine images
- clear plastic sandwich bags
- color chalk or oil pastels
- tissue or paper towels for blending
- newspaper

1. Collect images of a family member you would like to draw. In your Art Journal, practice drawing the face in proportion.

2. Select either white or black paper. Using a light piece of chalk, use face proportions to carefully sketch the face and features of the person.

3. Select a medium and begin to add color lightly. Once you have your basic colors down, begin overlapping and blending colors. A tissue or paper towel can be used to lightly blend and smooth colors.

4. Add details last. Then create a background.

Research in Art Education

"The elementary classroom offers an environment that can foster creativity, independence, self-awareness, self-expression, and an understanding of the visual world. Education through art can provide opportunities for exploring one's creativity, for communicating ideas, and enabling students to express themselves through the use of materials, processes, and tools." (Andra Nyman, "Cultural Content, Identity, and Program Development: Approaches to Art Education for Elementary Educators," in *Contemporary Issues in Art Education*, edited by Y. Gaudelius and P. Speirs, 61–69. New Jersey: Prentice Hall, 2002.)

Assessment

Use the following rubric to evaluate the artwork students make in the Creative Expression activity and to assess students' understanding of face proportions.

Have students complete page 49 or 50 in their *Assessment* books.

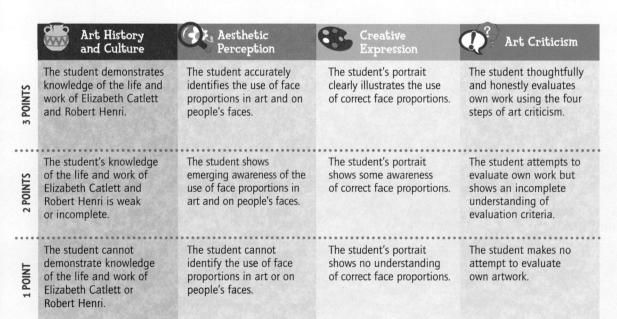

	Art History and Culture	Aesthetic Perception	Creative Expression	Art Criticism
3 POINTS	The student demonstrates knowledge of the life and work of Elizabeth Catlett and Robert Henri.	The student accurately identifies the use of face proportions in art and on people's faces.	The student's portrait clearly illustrates the use of correct face proportions.	The student thoughtfully and honestly evaluates own work using the four steps of art criticism.
2 POINTS	The student's knowledge of the life and work of Elizabeth Catlett and Robert Henri is weak or incomplete.	The student shows emerging awareness of the use of face proportions in art and on people's faces.	The student's portrait shows some awareness of correct face proportions.	The student attempts to evaluate own work but shows an incomplete understanding of evaluation criteria.
1 POINT	The student cannot demonstrate knowledge of the life and work of Elizabeth Catlett or Robert Henri.	The student cannot identify the use of face proportions in art or on people's faces.	The student's portrait shows no understanding of correct face proportions.	The student makes no attempt to evaluate own artwork.

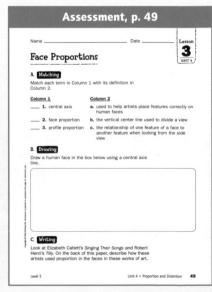

Assessment, p. 49

Name _____ Date _____ Lesson **3** UNIT 4

Face Proportions

A. Matching
Match each term in Column 1 with its definition in Column 2.

Column 1
___ 1. central axis
___ 2. face proportion
___ 3. profile proportion

Column 2
a. used to help artists place features correctly on human faces
b. the vertical center line used to divide a view
c. the relationship of one feature of a face to another feature when looking from the side view

B. Drawing
Draw a human face in the box below using a central axis line.

C. Writing
Look at Elizabeth Catlett's *Singing Their Songs* and Robert Henri's *Tilly*. On the back of this paper, describe how these artists used proportion in the faces in these works of art.

Level 5   Unit 4 • Proportion and Distortion   49

Lesson 4 Distortion of Body Proportions

Overview

Lesson 4 introduces distortion. Artists use distorted body proportions instead of real proportions to express ideas or feelings in their art.

Objectives

Art History and Culture

To become knowledgeable about the lives and the artwork of Fernando Botero and Amedeo Modigliani

Creative Expression

To plan and create an original comic-strip character using distortion of body proportions

Aesthetic Perception

To identify how artists use distortion of body proportions in works of art

Art Criticism

To evaluate one's own work using the four steps of art criticism

Vocabulary Vocabulary

Review the following vocabulary words with students.

distortion distorsión—a change from the expected or the normal

body proportions proporciones del cuerpo—ratios of one part of the body to another

See page 149B for additional Spanish vocabulary resources.

Art Journal: Vocabulary

Have students add these words to the Vocabulary section of their Art Journals.

Lesson Materials

- newspaper
- pencils and erasers
- white drawing paper
- sketch paper

Alternate Materials:

- magazines
- markers

Program Resources

- *Reading and Writing Test Prep.,* pp. 48–49
- *Transparency 22*
- *Artist Profiles,* pp. 9, 43
- *Animals Through History Time Line*
- *Assessment,* pp. 51–52
- *Large Prints 67* Gogol and *68* Self-Portrait (El Coronelazo)
- *The National Museum of Women in the Arts Collection*

Concept Trace

Distortion

Introduced: Level 4, Unit 5, Lesson 6

Reinforced: Level 6, Unit 5, Lesson 4

Lesson 4 Arts Integration

Theatre

Complete Unit 4, Lesson 4, on pages 78–79 of *Theatre Arts Connections.*

Theatre Arts Connections, p. 78

Music

Distortion is not a term used in music. However, if you lengthen a melody by making it twice as slow, it is called *augmentation.* Sing or listen to "Mongolian Sheep Herding Song." The melodic pattern is sung in quarter notes until the last phrase. What note value is used to create augmentation?

Movement & Dance

Have students stand in a neutral position. Instruct students to distort the position of their bodies and freeze when you clap your hands. After each distortion, students should return to the neutral position. Repeat this five times.

Focus

Activate Prior Knowledge

"Have you ever exaggerated or distorted a story to make one part stand out?" "¿Alguna vez han exagerado o distorsionado una historia para resaltar una parte?"

■ Discuss with students their answers to the question and how artists can make a point to the viewers by distorting proportions of a body in their work.

Using Literature ⭐ Reading

■ Share Madeleine L'Engle's book *A Wrinkle in Time* with the class. Discuss how imagination can be used to discover important truths in life. You might also want to read David Wiesner's *Tuesday* and allow students to use their imagination to create a story line for this book.

Thematic Connection ⭐ Social Studies

■ **Imagination:** Discuss with students how artists, scientists, engineers, teachers, and many other people working in professional fields use their imaginations to create pathways.

Introduce the Art

Look

"Let's take a close look at the two works of art." "Vamos a observar detalladamente las dos obras de arte."

Cause and Effect ⭐ Reading

■ Ask students to identify the areas of distortion in the two works of art in this lesson. Label this use of distortion as the cause. Then ask students to suggest the effects these distorted areas have on the artwork.

 Art History and Culture

Peter Paul Rubens was an artist and a diplomat whom Botero greatly admired. Botero painted Rubens's wife. She seems wealthy and content in this painting. Modigiani's painting of a polish woman features a female friend of his who seems weary and perhaps depressed because of World War I.

Web Connection

Visit **www.museum.oas.org/permanent/figuration/ botero/bio.html** to view some of Fernando Botero's works of art and read more about his life.

138 UNIT 4 • Proportion and Distortion

Distortion of Body Proportions

▲ **Fernando Botero.** (Colombian). *Ruben's Wife.* 1963.

Oil on canvas. 72⅛ × 70⅛ inches (183.21 × 178.13 cm.). Solomon R. Guggenheim Museum, New York, New York.

Look at these two works of art, and notice how the artists distorted body proportions in the two women. Think about how this affects the mood of the paintings.

 Art History and Culture

How have these artists communicated ideas about their culture through the use of distortion? Which subject seems wealthy and content? Which subject appears thin and weary?

138 Unit 4 • Lesson 4

 Art History and Culture

Fernando Botero

Fernando Botero (fer nän´ dō bō tā´ rō) (1932–) spent two years training to become a matador. He changed his career plans and studied art in Colombia, Spain, France, and Italy. Botero began painting in a rounded style in 1956, and this artwork sold well. Much of his work portrays his South American background, such as its food, music, religion, and architecture. Many of his sculptures and paintings have the same rounded features. He uses distortion for both humorous and serious artwork.

See pages 24–25 and 16–21 for more about art history and the subject matter.

Artist Profiles, p. 9

Artist Profile ➤ **Fernando Botero**
b. 1932

As a young man, this Colombian spent two years learning to be a matador. Fernando Botero (fer nän´ dō bōtā´ rō) changed his career plans and studied art in Colombia, Spain, France, and Italy. During this time, Botero had several exhibitions, but received little praise for his work—and fewer sales. After he began painting in a rounded style in 1956, his pictures sold well. By 1958, he was Colombia's most famous young artist. In 1960, he opened a studio in New York City. In 1973, he moved to Paris and began sculpting. He has married twice and has four children.

Study both paintings to find examples of distortion of body proportions.

▶ Where do you see a lengthened or stretched figure? A figure that is enlarged?

▶ Why do you think the artists chose to distort the figures in these ways?

▶ What emotions do these figures suggest?

▶ How would the effects of these works of art be different if they were not distorted?

◀ **Amedeo Modigliani.** (Italian).
Portrait of a Polish Woman. 1918.
Oil on canvas. $39\frac{1}{2} \times 25\frac{1}{2}$ inches
(100.33 × 64.77 cm). Philadelphia Museum
of Art, Philadelphia, Pennsylvania.

 Aesthetic Perception

Design Awareness Look at the comics section of a newspaper for examples of distortion of body proportions. What do you think was the reason for these uses of distortion?

Art History and Culture

Amedeo Modigliani

Amedeo Modigliani (ä mä dā ō mō´ dē yä´ nē) (1884–1920) was born in Italy. He studied art in France and Italy and eventually settled in Montmartre, a district in Paris where many artists lived. He began his career as a painter. Modigliani soon found that he enjoyed sculpting and focused his work on the human face. When he returned to painting, he often reproduced his sculptures as paintings. The subjects of his portraits include artists Diego Rivera and Pablo Picasso. As Amedeo Modigliani got older, his artwork became more abstract.

See pages 24–25 and 16–21 for more about art history and the subject matter.

Artist Profiles, p. 43

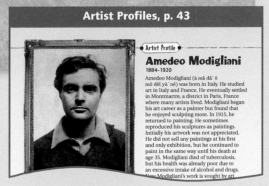

Study

▶ Botero: The woman's head and body are puffed up. Modigliani: The woman's neck and hands are stretched.

▶ Possible answers include: Botero: For humor, in keeping with his "puffed-up" style, to portray wealth. Modigliani: Use of a vertical line to create a calm mood, to accentuate the tilted head, and exaggerate the woman's long neck.

▶ Possible answers include: Botero: humor. Modigliani: sad, meditative, tired.

▶ Without the distorted body proportions, the effects that the characters have on the viewer would be more subtle. The mood would not be as obvious.

■ For more examples of portraits, see *The National Museum of Women in the Arts Collection.*

Art Journal: Writing
Have students write about a time when they imagined something to be much different than it was. Ask students to describe what they imagined and how it was distorted from reality.

Aesthetic Perception

Design Awareness If possible, bring some comic-strip pages to class for students to look at. Ask them to identify characters whose body proportions have been distorted and suggest a reason for that distortion.

Developing Visual Literacy Point out to students that neither artist included anything in the background of his painting. Why do you think they chose to do this?

Web Connection
Visit www.albrightknox.org/ArtStart/
Modigliani.html to learn more about artwork by Amedeo Modigliani.

Teach

Time: About 30 minutes

"Can you find examples of distortion featuring a famous person?" "¿Pueden hallar ejemplos de distorsión de una persona famosa?"

- Read and discuss the definition of *distortion* on page 140.

Practice

Materials: newspapers, resources for photographs of famous people

Alternate Materials: magazines

- Distribute the materials, and have students follow the directions on page 140.

- Bring editorial cartoons to class that feature recognizable public figures. Have students look for distortion of body proportions in these cartoons. Then have students find a photograph of this public figure in a magazine, on the Internet, or from another reference. Have students compare the distorted drawing of this person with their photograph and explain the similarities and differences.

Creative Expression

Materials: pencils and erasers, white drawing paper, sketch paper, markers

Alternate Materials: crayons

- Distribute the materials and have students follow the directions on page 141.

- Review the Activity Tips on page 240 for visual examples of this lesson's activity. NSAE 1.b

 Art Journal: Brainstorming

Have students brainstorm ideas for a comic-strip character and sketch ideas in their Art Journals. Ask students to think about how they will use distortion of body proportions to emphasize the superhero power of their characters.

Using Distortion of Body Proportions

Distortion is the bending or pulling of an object or figure out of its normal shape to communicate ideas or feelings.

Artists sometimes start with real body proportions and stretch, twist, shrink, or enlarge them to emphasize thoughts, feelings, and ideas.

Practice

From a newspaper, find examples of distortion in editorial cartoons.

1. Look through a newspaper for an editorial cartoon about a famous person. Next, find a photo of that same person.

2. Compare the distortion of the body proportions in the person in the cartoon with his or her features in the photo.

140 Unit 4 • Lesson 4

Differentiated Instruction

Reteach
Have students create people or animals out of clay and distort one or two features by making them larger, smaller, or stretching them out.

Special Needs
Give students the option of making this art project autobiographical by drawing themselves as a superhero. This opportunity may provide you with insight into the students' self-concepts.

ELL
Pantomime and sketch examples to help students learn the basic vocabulary needed to be successful in this lesson. You might begin with a rough sketch on a poster and have students demonstrate the meaning of words such as *lengthen, enlarge, twist,* and so on.

◄ **Kristen Patrick.**
Age 9.

 Think about how the student artist used distortion of body proportions to create an original comic-strip superhero.

Creative Expression

What kind of character would you create if you were a cartoonist? Create an original comic-strip superhero using distortion of body proportions.

1. Think about comic-strip characters you are familiar with. Then make several sketches of your own original comic-strip superhero.

2. Choose one sketch. Distort one or more body features to show the superpower of your character. Give your character a name.

Art Criticism

Describe Describe the body feature you distorted on your character.

Analyze Explain how you decided which feature to distort and how you distorted that feature.

Interpret What mood is expressed by your character? Does your character seem to be silly, serious, angry, confused, or relaxed, or does your character express a different mood?

Decide Do you like the way the distortion of body proportions changed the mood of your drawing? Explain.

Unit 4 • Lesson 4 **141**

Reflect

Time: About 15 minutes

Review and Assess

"Were you able to create an original comic-strip character using exaggeration?" "¿Fueron capaces de crear un personaje de una tira cómica original usando la exageración?"

Think

The student artist used distortion by using a frog's head and feet on a human torso.

■ Use *Large Prints 67* Gogol and *68 Self Portrait (El Coronelazo)* to have students identify and describe the use of distortion with body proportions.

Informal Assessment

■ For standardized-format test practice using this lesson's art content, see pages 48–49 in *Reading and Writing Test Preparation.*

Art Journal: Critical Thinking

Have students answer the four art criticism questions—Describe, Analyze, Interpret, and Decide—in their Art Journals. In small groups, have students discuss their comic-strip characters.
NSAE 2.b

Art Across the Curriculum

Use these simple ideas to reinforce art concepts across the curriculum.

★ **Poetry Writing** Have students write lyrics to a theme song for their comic-strip character.

★ **Math** Share with students the study of distortion in math, known as *topology.* This is the study of the properties of geometric figures or solids that are not changed by stretching or bending. Donuts and picture frames are topological examples.

★ **Science** Discuss the anatomy of the human ear and how sounds are sometimes distorted.

★ **Social Studies** Discuss the distortion of features on a flat map as opposed to features on a globe.

★ **Technology** Have students use a paint program to create a storyboard for their comic-strip character. Visit **SRAonline.com** to print out detailed instructions for this activity.
NSAE 6.b

Lesson 4
Wrap-Up

Distortion of Body Proportions

Extra! ## For the Art Specialist

Time: About 30 minutes

Focus

Study **Large Prints 67** *Gogol* and **68** *Self-Portrait (El Coronelazo)* to learn how distortion is used in a work of art. Describe the main character you see. Are any of the features larger or smaller than normal? How did the artist use distortion in each artwork? What effect does this have on the image?

Teach

Explain to students that they will be designing a political cartoon in which the main character has distorted features. Have students begin by brainstorming a list of events or concerns that affect them.

Reflect

Have students evaluate their artwork using the four steps of art criticism. Encourage them to identify and describe the use of distortion.

Alternate Activity

Materials:
- Art Journals
- pencils and erasers
- 9" × 12" white or black paper
- fine-point markers
- color pencils

1. As a class, generate a list of school concerns or current events that affect you. Look at the list for ideas to make a one-frame cartoon. Work in your Art Journals to create a character for your cartoon. While you are sketching your character, think about which feature would look best distorted.

2. Select your best sketch and carefully transfer it onto paper. Make your drawing large. Add a simple background that supports your idea.

3. Use a fine-point marker to trace over your drawing. Write dialogue and descriptive sentences.

4. Color can be added using color pencils.

Research
in Art Education

"The child's artistic responses in the early primary grades, reflecting the nuances of their world, are usually wonderfully fresh and disarmingly naive." (Kent, Robert, and Mark Luca, *Art Education: Strategies of Teaching*. New Jersey: Prentice Hall, 1968.)

Assessment

Use the following rubric to evaluate the artwork students make in the Creative Expression activity and to assess students' understanding of distortion of body proportions.

Have students complete page 51 or 52 in their *Assessment* books.

	Art History and Culture	Aesthetic Perception	Creative Expression	Art Criticism
3 POINTS	The student demonstrates knowledge of the life and work of Fernando Botero and Amedeo Modigliani.	The student accurately identifies the use of distortion of body proportions in art.	The student's comic-strip character clearly illustrates the use of distortion.	The student thoughtfully and honestly evaluates own work using the four steps of art criticism.
2 POINTS	The student's knowledge of the life and work of Fernando Botero and Amedeo Modigliani is weak or incomplete.	The student shows emerging awareness of the use of distortion of body proportions in art.	The student's comic-strip character shows some awareness of distortion.	The student attempts to evaluate own work, but shows an incomplete understanding of evaluation criteria.
1 POINT	The student cannot demonstrate knowledge of the life and work of Fernando Botero or Amedeo Modigliani.	The student cannot identify the use of distortion of body proportions in art.	The student's comic-strip character shows no understanding of distortion.	The student makes no attempt to evaluate own artwork.

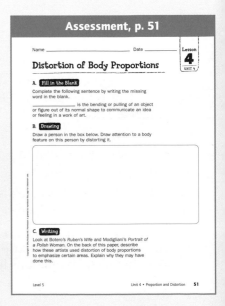

Assessment, p. 51

Name _____ Date _____ Lesson **4** UNIT 4

Distortion of Body Proportions

A. Fill in the Blank
Complete the following sentence by writing the missing word in the blank.
_____ is the bending or pulling of an object or figure out of its normal shape to communicate an idea or feeling in a work of art.

B. Drawing
Draw a person in the box below. Draw attention to a body feature on this person by distorting it.

C. Writing
Look at Botero's *Ruben's Wife* and Modigliani's *Portrait of a Polish Woman.* On the back of this paper, describe how these artists used distortion of body proportions to emphasize certain areas. Explain why they may have done this.

Level 5   Unit 4 • Proportion and Distortion   51

Lesson 5 Overview

Distortion of Face Proportions

Lesson 5 introduces distortion of face proportions. Artists distort face proportions instead of using real proportions to express ideas or feelings in their art.

Objectives

 Art History and Culture

To become knowledgeable about the people, their cultures, and their artwork in this lesson

Creative Expression

To plan and create a mask using distortion of face proportions

 Aesthetic Perception

To identify how artists use distortion of face proportions in a work of art

Art Criticism

To evaluate one's own work using the four steps of art criticism

---

Vocabulary ⭐ Vocabulary

Review the following vocabulary words with students.

face proportions proporciones de la cara—ratios of one part of the face to another

exaggeration exageración—to enlarge or increase in size

See page 149B for additional Spanish vocabulary resources.

 Art Journal: Vocabulary

Have students add these words to the Vocabulary section of their Art Journals.

Lesson Materials
- white drawing paper
- pencils
- containers for slip mixture
- one gallon milk jugs (cut in half)
- newspaper
- liquid tempera paints
- paintbrushes
- paper towels
- paper plates
- water dishes
- masking tape
- scissors
- yarn
- found objects

Alternate Materials:
- felt-tip markers
- cardboard

Program Resources
- *Reading and Writing Test Prep.*, pp. 50–51
- *Transparency 23*
- *Artist Profiles,* pp. 81, 65, 76, 75
- *Animals Through History Time Line*
- *Assessment,* pp. 53–54
- *Large Print 67* Gogol
- *The National Museum of Women in the Arts Collection*

Concept Trace
Distortion of Face Proportions
Introduced: Level 4, Unit 5, Lesson 6

Reinforced: Level 6, Unit 5, Lesson 3

Lesson 5 Arts Integration

Theatre

Complete Unit 4, Lesson 5, on pages 80–81 of *Theatre Arts Connections.*

Theatre Arts Connections, p. 80

Music

 The sound of an instrument may be distorted through change of tone production. Contemporary composers often find new ways to produce sound on traditional instruments. The singing style of another culture may sound different and "distorted." Listen to a recording of *Chinese Opera* or *Balkan Folk Songs* to hear styles very unusual to our Western ideas of vocal production.

Movement & Dance

Explore exaggerated facial expressions. Have students warm up their faces by using the following actions: large chewing movement, large open yawns, and tight squeezing and opening of the face. Ask students to make exaggerated facial expressions by tilting each expression so it is asymmetrical.

Activate Prior Knowledge

"Does it take more muscles to smile than it does to frown?" "¿Qué se usan más, músculos para arrugar la frente o para sonreir?"

■ Discuss with students their answers to the question. It does take more muscles to frown than to smile. Discuss with students that smiling and frowning are ways of distorting the face.

Using Literature Reading

■ Read *The People Could Fly: American Black Folktales* told by Virginia Hamilton. Storytelling is an important element of African American culture.

Thematic Connection Science

■ **Storytelling:** Discuss with students what they know about storytelling and oral tradition. In the Artsource® program, kindergarten level, you can find Paul Tracey's "African Folk Tale." Refer to this Web site for further information on using storytelling in your classroom: **www.turnerlearning.com/turnersouth/ storytelling/varieties.html.**

Introduce the Art

Look

"Let's take a close look at the two works of art." "Vamos a observar detalladamente las dos obras de arte."

Drawing Conclusions Reading

■ Have students look at the four masks in this lesson and identify the areas of distortion and exaggeration.
NSAE 2.b

 Art History and Culture

The *Sun Transformation Mask* was designed to convey the power of the sun. *False Face Mask* was used in healing ceremonies. This mask conveys concern. *Mask* was probably part of a sculpture to show strength. The *Kwele Face Mask* was used to announce a celebration of unity. It is peaceful and comforting.

Web Connection

Visit **www.artsmia.org/surrounded-by-beauty/ northwest/trans_home.html** to learn more about Kwakiutl transformation masks.

Distortion of Face Proportions

▲ **Charlie James.** (Southern Kwakiutl). *Sun Transformation Mask.* Early nineteenth century.
Royal British Columbia Museum, British Columbia, Canada.

▲ **Elon Webster.** (Iroquois). *False Face Mask.* 1937.
Wood. Cranbrook Institute of Science, Bloomfield Hills, Michigan.

Look at the artwork and identify the features of the faces that are distorted. Notice how different areas of the face can be stretched or changed to express an idea or emotion.

 Art History and Culture

Masks were often used to represent cultural beliefs or emotions in ceremonies. Look at these masks and identify the feelings they communicate.

 Art History and Culture

The Kwakiutl

The Kwakiutl are a group of nearly 6,000 Canadian native peoples from British Columbia. Weaving and woodworking are crafts important to their culture. The Kwakiutl people are known for their mythological stories and ceremonies involving masks.

Elon Webster

False Face Mask is typical of the Iroquois' most famous mask type. False face masks are used in healing ceremonies by the False Face Mask Society.

See pages 24–25 and 16–21 for more about art history and subject matter.

Artist Profiles, p. 65

Artist Profile

Elon Webster

Elon Webster (e´ lan web´ star) was an Onondaga carver who lived on the Tonawanda Reservation in New York during the early part of the twentieth century. *Iroquois* is a collective name for the Mohawk, Oneida, Onondaga, Cayaga, and Seneca tribes, groups that speak Iroquois-related languages and have similar cultures. Webster worked for the Works Progress Administration (WPA) on the Seneca Arts Project during the 1930s.

▲ **Artist unknown.** (Tlatilco Valley of Mexico).
Mask. c. twelfth through nineteenth century B.C.
....
Ceramic pigment. 5¼ inches tall (13.33 cm). The Metropolitan
Museum of Art, New York, New York.

▲ **Artist unknown.** (Kwele). *Kwele Face Mask.*
c. Nineteenth through twentieth century.
....
Wood and paint. 20¾ inches tall (52.71 cm). The Metropolitan
Museum of Art, New York, New York.

Study all four masks to identify the use of distortion.

▶ Which mask shows the most distortion? Which shows
the least?

▶ Use one adjective to describe the expressive quality of
each mask.

▶ What do you think was the purpose of each mask?

▶ What do all four masks have in common? How are
they different?

Aesthetic Perception

Design Awareness Look closely for distortion used in
advertisements. What are the distortions emphasizing, and why?

Art History and Culture

The Tlaticlo

The Tlaticlo region in Central Mexico was once made up primarily of
farmers and hunters. Tlaticlo ceramics were made during the pre-
classic, or the "first" period of Meso-American art. This mask is one
of the most ancient Central American ceramic artifacts that have
been found intact. It may have been part of a sculpture.

The Kwele

The Kwele people lived in the northern region of the Congo, in the
country of Gabon. The mask
in this lesson is an example
of their famous *ekuk* mask.

See pages 24–25 and 16–21
for more about art history
and subject matter.

Artist Profiles, p. 75

> *Artist Profile*
>
> **Kwele Face Mask**
>
> The Kwele tribe of Gabon is one of many
> ethnic groups living in the equatorial forest
> region of central Africa. Beginning about
> 3,000 years ago, the equatorial forest region
> was settled by farmers from various regions
> and ethnic groups. Although the equatorial
> forest region is rich in ethnic diversity, its
> people share cultural similarities and
> beliefs. One example of this is a common
> belief that the spirits of deceased family
> members are present among the living.
> Many of the people in this region believe
> that the spiritual power of ancestral relics
> can protect and benefit their communities.
>
> **unknown.** (Gabon) *Kwele Face Mask.*

Study

▶ The *Sun Transformation Mask* has the
most distortion; the Tlaticlo Valley of
Mexico's *Mask* has the least distortion.

▶ Possible answers include: stern, confused,
silly, calm.

▶ Possible answers include: ceremonies and
traditional works of art.

▶ All four masks have distortions of face
proportions. They are distorted in
different areas of the face and were
designed for different purposes.

■ For more examples of utilitarian art, see
***The National Museum of Women in the
Arts Collection.***

Art Journal: Writing

In their Art Journal, have students
write about a time they heard a story that
was exaggerated by the person speaking in
order to persuade.

Aesthetic Perception

Design Awareness Ask students to look for
and identify examples of distortion used in
advertisements. Have them analyze what the
distortions stand for and why they help to
influence the consumers who will purchase
these products or services.

Developing Visual Literacy Have students
imagine that one of the masks in this lesson
was worn by the main character in a play. Ask
them to describe that character and the play.

Web Connection
Visit **www.zyama.com/kwele/pics..htm**
to learn more about the Kwele masks.

Teach

Time: 2 50 minute sessions

"How can you illustrate distortion in a mask design?" ¿Cómo pueden ilustrar la distorsión en un diseño de una máscara?"

- Read and discuss the definitions of *distortion* and *exaggeration* on page 144.

Practice

Materials: white drawing paper

Alternate Materials: pencils

- Distribute the materials, and have students follow the directions on page 144.

- Have students brainstorm ideas for a mask that expresses something that they like or the celebration of something. Encourage students to sketch their ideas from many different angles. Tell students to distort and exaggerate features of the face to represent the main idea and the purpose of the mask.

- Set up a gallery for students to display their masks. Set aside time for the class and invite other classes to analyze the exhibit and to form conclusions about their peer's use of distortion.
NSAE 1.b

Creative Expression

Materials: containers for glue and water mixture, one-gallon milk jugs (cut in half), newspaper, liquid tempera paints, paintbrushes, paper towels, paper plates, water dishes, masking tape, scissors, yarn, found objects: paper rolls, egg cartons, and buttons

Alternate Materials: felt-tip markers and cardboard

- Distribute the materials and have students follow the directions on page 145.

- Review the Activity Tips on page 241 for visual examples of this lesson's activity.

- See the Technique Tips on page 225 for more information about papier-máché.

Art Journal: Brainstorming

Have students brainstorm what they would like their mask to look like and how they will distort the face proportions to express a certain feeling or idea and then sketch their ideas in their Art Journals.

Using Distortion of Face Proportions

Distortion can be in the form of exaggeration. **Exaggeration** is making something bigger than it normally is.

Exaggeration is used by an artist to make a feature more exciting and expressive than it would be in realistic proportions.

Practice

Design a mask. Use pencil.

1. Design a mask that expresses your enthusiasm or celebration of something. Make sketches of your mask from different angles.

2. Distort facial features of the mask by using exaggeration to emphasize what you are enthusiastic about or what you are celebrating.

Differentiated Instruction

Reteach
Find two more works of art in the program that use distortion of face proportions to create an expressive effect.

Special Needs
Students may want to use mirrors to practice some exaggerated poses in preparation for this lesson activity.

ELL
Ask students to practice sketching each other while the model poses with a distorted look on his or her face. Have students explain what features are distorted and what emotions are suggested.

◀ **Emma Sams.**
Age 10.

Think about how the student artist used distortion of face proportions in her work of art.

 Creative Expression

How does a mask express a certain emotion or idea? Create a papier-mâché mask. Use distortion in one or more of the features.

1. Tear one-inch strips of newspaper. Dip the strips into paste and squeeze off the excess liquid. Lay the strips over the outside of a plastic milk container. Overlap two layers of newspaper strips to make the base of your mask.

2. Allow the base to dry, then add the features. Distort the features. Apply two more layers of papier-mâché, and let the mask base dry overnight.

3. When it is dry, pop your mask off the container and trim the edges. Paint the mask and apply other objects.

Art Criticism

Describe List the steps you followed to create your mask.

Analyze How did you distort the features on your mask?

Interpret What emotions or ideas does your mask suggest? Which features communicate these emotions or ideas?

Decide Were you successful in creating a mask that has distorted features expressing a certain feeling or idea?

Reflect Time: About 10 minutes

Review and Assess

"Were you able to create a mask using distortion?" "¿Fueron capaces de hacer una máscara usando distorsión?"

Think

The student artist used distortion of face proportions to create larger hair and lips.

- Use **Large Print 67** *Gogol* to have students identify and describe the use of distortion.

Art Criticism

- For standardized-format test practice using this lesson's art content, see pages 50–51 in **Reading and Writing Test Preparation.**

Art Journal: Critical Thinking

Have students answer the four art criticism questions—Describe, Analyze, Interpret, and Decide—in their Art Journals. In small groups, have students discuss their masks.

Art Across the Curriculum

Use these simple ideas to reinforce art concepts across the curriculum.

★ **Descriptive Writing** Have students write a descriptive paragraph explaining the mask they designed and created.

★ **Math** Have students find the area of a square and then of a rhombus. Notice how the shape has changed and how that affects the area.

★ **Science** Define *convex* and *concave* and discuss how a flat image can be distorted with convex and concave lenses.

★ **Social Studies** Have students study folktales from different areas of the world and compare and contrast what they find.

★ **Technology** Have students create a mask in a computer paint program and then select the mask and use the stretch/skew feature to distort it. Visit **SRAonline.com** to print out detailed instructions for this activity.
NSAE 6.b

Distortion of Face Proportions

Extra! For the Art Specialist

Focus

Study **Large Print 67** *Gogol* and learn how distortion is used in a work of art. Describe the character you see. Are any of the features larger or smaller than normal?

Teach

Prior to teaching this lesson, decide whether you want the whole class to create characters based on one story or whether you want to divide the class into teams to create characters from different stories. Explain to the students that they will be using distortion to create a papier-mâché puppet based on a story.

Reflect

Have students evaluate their artwork using the four steps of art criticism. Encourage them to locate and describe the distorted face proportions.

Alternate Activity

- Art Journals
- pencils, erasers
- toilet-paper rolls cut in half
- newspaper
- wheat paste
- containers to mix paste
- masking tape
- acrylic paints
- paintbrushes
- water containers
- 12″ × 20″ fabric
- fabric, ribbon, buttons, and yarn

1. Decide which character you will create as a puppet. Create two sketches in your Art Journal of your character. Make sure that you distort at least one of the facial features to communicate your character's personality.

2. Tape a ball of newspaper to a section of cardboard roll. This will form the head and neck. Form the ears, nose, mouth, and eyes. Tape these securely in place. Apply two layers of papier-mâché to your puppet's head. Let it dry.

3. Paint your puppet's head one color. Let this dry. Use a small brush to paint the features.

Research in Art Education

The subjects on which schools typically focus reward only students with "logical-mathematical and linguistic intelligences" an opportunity to excel. One benefit of arts curricula is that they offer "many approaches to subject matter; therefore, they provide better learning opportunities for low-achieving and 'problem' students" ("The Fourth R: The Arts and Learning," in *Schools, Communities, and the Arts: A Research Compendium*). Using cross-curricular connections when studying distortion will help students find approachable pathways to understanding abstract concepts and the practicality of concepts throughout the academic areas.

Assessment
Use the following rubric to evaluate the artwork students make in the Creative Expression activity and to assess students' understanding of distortion of face proportions.

Have students complete page 53 or 54 in their *Assessment* books.

	Art History and Culture	Aesthetic Perception	Creative Expression	Art Criticism
3 POINTS	The student demonstrates knowledge of the people and the artwork in this lesson.	The student accurately identifies the use of distortion with face proportions in art.	The student's mask clearly illustrates the use of distortion.	The student thoughtfully and honestly evaluates own work using the four steps of art criticism.
2 POINTS	The student's knowledge of the people and the artwork in this lesson is weak or incomplete.	The student shows emerging awareness of the use of distortion with face proportions in art.	The student's mask shows some awareness of distortion.	The student attempts to evaluate own work, but shows an incomplete understanding of evaluation criteria.
1 POINT	The student cannot demonstrate knowledge of the people and artwork in this lesson.	The student cannot identify the use of distortion with face proportions in art.	The student's mask shows no understanding of distortion.	The student makes no attempt to evaluate own artwork.

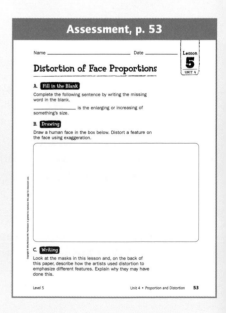

Assessment, p. 53

Name _____ Date _____

Lesson 5 UNIT 4

Distortion of Face Proportions

A. Fill in the Blank
Complete the following sentence by writing the missing word in the blank.
_____ is the enlarging or increasing of something's size.

B. Drawing
Draw a human face in the box below. Distort a feature on the face using exaggeration.

C. Writing
Look at the masks in this lesson and, on the back of this paper, describe how the artists used distortion to emphasize different features. Explain why they may have done this.

Level 5

Unit 4 • Proportion and Distortion   53

Lesson 6 Overview

Scale and Proportion

Lesson 6 introduces the use of scale and proportion together. Artists use scale and proportion to create life-size sculptures and place them in realistic settings.

Objectives

 Art History and Culture

To become knowledgeable about the life and work of George Segal and Duane Hanson

 Creative Expression

To plan and create a life-size sculpture using realistic scale and proportion

 Aesthetic Perception

To identify how artists use scale and proportion

 Art Criticism

To evaluate own work using the four steps of art criticism

Vocabulary Vocabulary

Review the following vocabulary words with students.

body proportions proporciones del cuerpo—ratios of one part of the body to another

ratio radio—a comparison of size between two things

scale escala—deals with size relationship; refers to size as measured against a standard reference, like the human body

See page 149B for additional Spanish vocabulary resources.

 Art Journal: Vocabulary

Have students add these words to the vocabulary section of their Art Journals.

Lesson Materials

- white drawing paper
- pencils
- props
- life-size clothing
- shoes and gloves
- stitching items
- yarn

- nylon stockings
- scissors
- newspaper
- polyester filling
- poster board
- sketch paper
- pencils

Alternate Materials:

- felt-tip pens
- papier-mâché

Program Resources

- *Reading and Writing Test Prep.*, pp. 52–53
- *Transparency 24*
- *Artist Profiles,* pp. 51, 29
- *Animals Through History Time Line*
- *Assessment,* pp. 55–56
- *Large Prints 67* Gogol and *68 Self-Portrait* (El Coronelazo)
- *The National Museum of Women in the Arts Collection*

Concept Trace

Scale and Proportion
Introduced: Level 4, Unit 5, Lessons 4, 5

Reinforced: Level 6, Unit 5, Lessons 1, 2, 5, 6

Lesson 6 Arts Integration

Theatre

Complete Unit 4, Lesson 6, on pages 82–87 of *Theatre Arts Connections.*

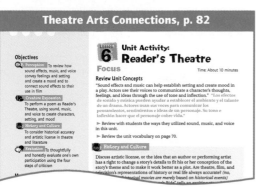

Theatre Arts Connections, p. 82

Music

Listen to *Symphony No. 9 in D Minor* by Ludwig van Beethoven to realize the scale of a symphony in the romantic period. A symphony traditionally has four parts, or movements. The first movement is lively and quick, the second is slower and smoother, the third is an energetic minuet, and the last movement is a boisterous finale. Each movement can stand on its own in performance.

Movement & Dance

Have the students sit together while five students at a time walk through a designated space. Point out how the size of their steps, their posture, and their manner of walking is different. Be aware of different body proportions and how they effect the size of the step, the tempo, the swinging of the arms, and which body part leads.

Focus

Time: About 15 minutes

Activate Prior Knowledge

"Have you ever studied mannequins in a store?" *¿Alguna vez han notado los maniquíes en las tiendas?"*

- Discuss with students their answers to the question. Ask students how real the mannequins looked and what their purposes were.

Using Literature Reading

- Read Mary Rodger's *Freaky Friday* with the class and discuss how life would be different in someone else's body. You might also want to share Tedd Arnold's *More Parts.* This book humorously explores idiom use with body parts.

Thematic Connection ★ Science

- **Body:** Discuss with students the ways that they can take care of their bodies by exercising, eating healthful and nutritious foods, and practicing safety.

Introduce the Art

Look

"Let's take a close look at the two works of art." *"Vamos a observar detalladamente las dos obras de arte."*

Sequence ★ Reading

- Have students consider the sequence the artists used when creating the sculptures in this lesson. Ask them to identify what materials would be used first and what would be added later.

Art History and Culture

Students might say that people from the eighteenth century would be confused, startled, or frightened by Duane Hanson's sculptures.

 Web Connection

Visit **www.pbs.org/georgesegal/index/index.html** to read more about the life and work of George Segal.

146 UNIT 4 • Proportion and Distortion

 Lesson 6

Scale and Proportion

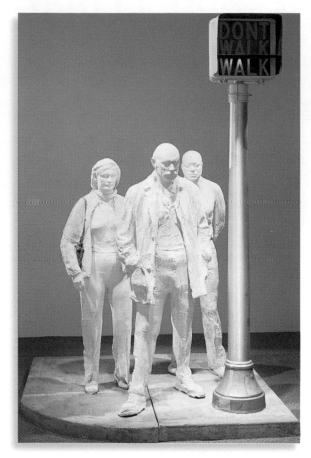

Look at the sculptures and notice how the artists have used accurate proportions. Each artist has combined objects from the real world with his sculpture. The objects and figures fit together because they have the same scale.

◄ **George Segal.** (American). *Walk Don't Walk.* 1976.

Plaster, cement, metal, painted wood, and electric light. 104 × 72 × 72 inches (264.16 × 182.88 × 182.88 cm.). Whitney Museum of American Art, New York, New York.

Art History and Culture

Duane Hanson's lifelike sculptures have been made possible because of the invention of new materials. How do you think someone from the eighteenth century would react to one of his works of art?

146 Unit 4 • Lesson 6

Art History and Culture

George Segal

George Segal (jôrj sē´ gəl) (1924–) started a chicken farm after he graduated from college and taught art in a high school to support his family. In 1958 he sold his chickens and used the buildings as his studio. He created plaster figures on wood and chicken-wire frames. At that point he started making the plaster cast. Once he removed the cast and reassembled it into a plaster human figure, he would place it in a real-life setting. With these sculptures, George Segal found himself at the center of the pop art movement. Later in his career, he had plaster sculptures cast in bronze so they could be placed in an outdoor setting, like *Walk, Don't Walk.*

See pages 24–25 and 16–21 for more about art history and the subject matter.

Artist Profiles, p. 51

Artist Profile

George Segal
1924-2000

Not long before George Segal (jorj sē´ gəl) was born, his parents emigrated from eastern Europe to the Bronx in New York. They did not consider art to be a legitimate profession, but Segal insisted on studying art in college. After graduating in 1947, he started a chicken farm in New Jersey and taught at a high school to support his wife and two children. In 1958, he sold his chickens and used the buildings the chickens were housed in as his studio. For the next two years he created plaster figures on wood and chicken wire frames. All the art teachers in that area received surplus gauze embedded with plaster from a nearby Johnson & Johnson plant to give to Segal. He used this gauze to create his sculptures.

Study both sculptures to identify realistic and lifelike objects.

▶ Which artist's work looks more realistic? Explain.

▶ What are the people doing in each sculpture?

▶ Why did the artists include real objects with their sculptures?

▶ Can you tell which objects in each work were not created by the sculptor, but were added?

▲ **Duane Hanson.** (American).
Football Player. 1981.
....
Oil on polyvinyl. 43¼ × 30 × 31½ inches
(109.86 × 76.2 × 80.01 cm.). Lowe Art Museum,
Miami, Florida.

Aesthetic Perception

Design Awareness If students in your school wanted to create sculptures to represent the school's people and activities, what would the sculptures look like?

Study

▶ Duane Hanson's sculpture looks more realistic because of the clothes, hair, color, and texture.

▶ *Walk Don't Walk:* The people are waiting at a crosswalk. *Football Player:* The athlete is resting on his helmet and drinking from a cup.

▶ The artists included real objects to increase the effect of the realistic looking sculptures.

▶ *Walk Don't Walk:* The crossing signal. *The Football Player:* The clothes, helmet, cup, pads, shoes.

■ For more examples of genre art, see ***The National Museum of Women in the Arts Collection.***

Art Journal: Writing

Have students write about their favorite ways to exercise.

Aesthetic Perception

Design Awareness Discuss with students what the sculptures would look like that would represent the people at your school and the activities there.

Developing Visual Literacy Ask students if they would have added anything to either sculpture or if they would not include something that the artists did.

Art History and Culture

Duane Hanson

Duane Hanson (dwān han sən) (1925–1996) grew up in Minnesota, where, as a boy, he carved wooden figures out of logs. His sculptures are a three-dimensional answer to works of the New Realism Movement of the 1960s and 1970s. Hanson made accurate casts of people using polyester resin compounds. Then he painted the assembled figures using oil paints. He meticulously added details, such as hair, then dressed his figures in real clothing. These sculptures are so realistic many viewers think they are real people at rest.

See pages 24–25 and 16–21 for more about art history and the subject matter.

Artist Profiles, p. 29

◆ Artist Profile ◆
Duane Hanson
1925-1996
Duane Hanson (dwān han´ sən) carved little figures out of logs using kitchen knives as a boy in his native Minnesota. Later he attended art school and taught art in Atlanta, Georgia and Miami, Florida. The same art dealer who discovered Andy Warhol arranged for Hanson's first solo exhibition. His life-size sculptures of ordinary people were an immediate success with the public. People could identify with his work. Hanson married and had five children. He continued to plan and create sculpture until the end of his life.

Web Connection

Visit **www.artmolds.com/ali/halloffame/ duane_hanson.htm** to read about Duane Hanson's life and see more of his sculptures.

Teach

Time: About 50 minutes

"Can you find examples of scale and proportion in a living sculpture?" "¿Pueden hallar ejemplos de escala y proporción para una escultura viviente?"

- Read and discuss the definitions of *body proportion, ratio,* and *scale* on page 148.

Practice

Materials: white drawing paper, pencils, props

Alternate Materials: felt-tip pens

- Distribute the materials, and have students follow the directions on page 148.

- Divide students into small groups and ask them to brainstorm scenes that George Segal or Duane Hanson might have created for a sculpture. Give students time to gather props that are either in realistic scale or unrealistic scale to their body proportions. Allow groups to take turns posing with their props for the class.

Creative Expression

Materials: life-size clothing, shoes, gloves, stitching items, yarn, nylon stockings, scissors, newspaper, polyester filling, poster board, water, dishes, sketch paper, pencils

Alternate Materials: papier-mâché

- Distribute the materials and have students follow the directions on page 149.

- Review the Activity Tips on page 241 for visual examples of this lesson's activity.

- See the Technique Tips on page 229 for more information on soft sculpture.
NSAE 2.c

Art Journal: Brainstorming

Have students brainstorm and sketch ideas in their Art Journals about the life-size sculpture they would like to create and make a list of the materials they need to make it realistic.

Using Scale and Proportion

Body proportions are defined in ratios of one part of the body to another.

A **ratio** is a comparison of size between two things. Often, artists use the measurement of the head to the length of an adult body, which is about seven times the length of the head. Therefore, the ratio is 1 (head) to 7 (heads per body length) and is written 1:7.

Scale is similar to proportion in that it relates to size relationships. The difference is that scale refers to size as measured against something that is common, such as the human body.

Practice

Find examples of scale and proportion, using props.

1. With a small group of classmates, think of a scene that George Segal or Duane Hanson might create. Collect props that are either in scale or out of scale to your body proportions.

2. Set up your living sculpture for the class to see.

Differentiated Instruction

Reteach
Ask students to think about where they have seen life-size sculptures in their community or elsewhere.

Special Needs
Use this group activity as an opportunity to showcase the strengths of students with disabilities. Assign group roles according to the strongest capabilities of each student, and model group norms of appreciation of difference.

ELL
Students will find it easier to follow instructions when working in small groups if each group has a specific list of instructions to follow. You can have students role-play their instructions as a group or tell a partner what comes next.

◄ **Fort Daniel Elementary fifth-grade class.**

Think about how the artists used scale and proportion to create a realistic-looking scene.

Creative Expression

What effect would a life-size sculpture have if you placed it somewhere in your school? Use scale and proportion to create a life-size soft sculpture. Place it in a real environment in your school.

1. Think about available items you have to make a life-size soft sculpture. Work in small groups. Plan and make sketches of your figure and of the environment.

2. Divide responsibilities. For example, some students can create a soft-sculpture head while others stuff clothes with newspaper. Others can construct the environment. Make sure your figure is in scale with the environment.

3. Make a sign that gives the title and the students' names who created the sculpture.

Art Criticism

Describe Describe the materials you used to create your sculpture and the environment.

Analyze Whom does your character represent? What is the setting of your sculpture?

Interpret What is the mood of your sculpture? What are observers likely to think your sculpture represents?

Decide Were you successful in creating a life-size sculpture that is realistic in scale and proportion? If not, what would you change?

Unit 4 • Lesson 6   **149**

Reflect

Review and Assess

"Were you able to create a sculpture using scale and proportion?" "¿Fueron capaces de hacer una escultura usando escala y proporción?"

Think

The student artists used scale and proportion to create a life-like soft sculpture that fits in the surrounding environment.

■ Use *Large Prints 67 Gogol* and *68 Self-Portrait (El Coronelazo)* to have students identify and describe the use of scale and proportion.

Art Criticism

■ Invite a cartoonist into the classroom to share their work with students. Then encourage students to share their proportion and distortion artwork chosen for their portfolios with each other and with the visiting artist. Have students analyze their peers' use of art elements and principles in the works of art.

■ For standardized-format test practice using this lesson's art content, see pages 52–53 in *Reading and Writing Test Preparation.*

Art Journal: Critical Thinking

Have students answer the four art criticism questions—Describe, Analyze, Interpret, and Decide—in their Art Journals. In small groups, have students discuss their life-size sculpture.

Art Across the Curriculum

Use these simple ideas to reinforce art concepts across the curriculum.

★ **Narrative Writing** Have students write a day-in-the-life story in which their life-size sculpture is the main character.

★ **Math** Have students practice making scale drawings using a simple ratio, for example, 1 inch equals 1 foot. This is a practical way to practice multiplication skills.

★ **Science** When studying space, have students compare the sizes of the planets in scale.

★ **Social Studies** Have students study how different cultures used dance and movement in rituals and ceremonial practices.

★ **Technology** Have students select a piece of clipart, and then draw objects, people, or a surrounding enviroment to scale. Visit **SRAonline.com** to print detailed instructions for this activity.
NSAE 6.b

Lesson 6 Wrap-Up

Scale and Proportion

Extra! For the Art Specialist

Time: About 45 minutes

Focus

Study **Large Prints 67** *Gogol* and **68** *Self-Portrait (El Coronelazo)* and ask students to study closely the use of scale and proportion in the artwork. Can you tell the approximate size of the objects and people in the work? What clues helped you determine the size of the objects?

Teach

Prior to teaching this lesson, take several photographs of daily activities around the school. Explain to students that they will be working in groups to create an installation based on an everyday scene around their school.

Reflect

Have students evaluate their artwork using the four steps of art criticism. Encourage them to identify the use of scale and proportion in their soft sculpture.

Alternate Activity

- Art Journals
- pencils, erasers
- newspaper
- wheat paste
- containers to mix paste
- masking tape
- acrylic paints
- paintbrushes
- water containers
- clothing, shoes, fabric, ribbon, buttons, yarn, and props

1. Look at the photographs and decide which scene you will recreate as a class. List all the items needed.

2. Have each group work on the papier-mâché heads with necks and hands.

3. Begin forming the head and neck by taping newspaper. Make taped newspaper forms for the hands as well. Apply papier-mâché to head and hands. Let these dry completely.

4. Paint the heads and hands one color. Use a small brush to paint the features. Use artificial hair, fur or yarn for the hair.

5. Use clothing and shoes stuffed with newspaper to form the body.

Research in Art Education

Education in the arts aids in "developing worthy citizens, people who enjoy intellectual and emotional control, people with skill and initiative, and people who are aware of their world." (Gaitskell, C. D., and Al Hurwitz. *Children and Their Art: Methods for the Elementary School*. Toronto: Harcourt, 1970.)

Assessment

Use the following rubric to evaluate the artwork students make in the Creative Expression activity and to assess students' understanding of scale and proportion.

Have students complete page 55 or 56 in their *Assessment* books.

	Art History and Culture	Aesthetic Perception	Creative Expression	Art Criticism
3 POINTS	The student demonstrates knowledge of the life and works of George Segal and Duane Hanson.	The student accurately identifies the use of scale and proportion in art.	The student's life-size sculpture clearly illustrates the use of realistic scale and proportion.	The student thoughtfully and honestly evaluates own work using the four steps of art criticism.
2 POINTS	The student's knowledge of the life and works of George Segal and Duane Hanson is weak or incomplete.	The student shows emerging awareness of the use of scale and proportion in art.	The student's life-size sculpture shows some awareness of realistic scale and proportion.	The student attempts to evaluate own work, but shows an incomplete understanding of evaluation criteria.
1 POINT	The student cannot demonstrate knowledge of the life and works of George Segal or Duane Hanson.	The student cannot identify the use of scale and proportion in art.	The student's life-size sculpture shows no understanding of realistic scale and proportion.	The student makes no attempt to evaluate own artwork.

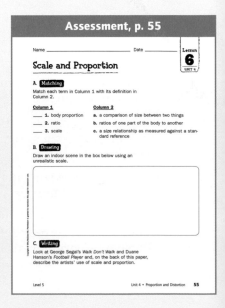

Assessment, p. 55

proportion—the principle of art concerned with the size relationship of one part to another **proporción**—el principio artistico que le interesa la relación de tamaño de una parte a la otra

scale—size as measured against a standard reference **escala**—el tamaño medido contra una referencia normal

realistic scale—size relationships in a work of art in which everything seems to fit together and make sense **escala real**—relación de tamaño en una obra de arte en que todo parece encajar y tiene sentido

unrealistic scale—size relationships that do not make sense **escala irreal**— relación de tamaño que no tiene sentido

face proportions—used to help artists place features correctly on the human face **proporción de cara**—se usa para ayudar a los artistas colocar correctamente rasgos de la cara humana

central axis—the vertical center line used to divide a view **eje central**—la línea central vertical usada para dividir una vista

profile proportions—the relationship of one feature of a face to another feature when looking from the side view **proporción de contorno**—la relación de un rasgo de la cara a otro rasgo visto por el lado

distortion—a change from the expected or the normal **distorsión**—un cambio de lo esperado o normal

body proportions—ratios of one part of the body to another **proporciones del cuerpo**—las escalas de una parte del cuerpo a otra

face proportions—ratios of one part of the face to another **proporciones de la cara**—Las escalas de una parte de la cara a otra

exaggeration—to enlarge or increase in size **exageración**—alargar o agrandar en tamaño

ratio—a comparison of size between two things **radio**—una comparación de tamaño entre dos cosas

scale—deals with size relationship; refers to size as measured against a standard reference, like the human body **escala**—se trata con relación de tamaño; se refiere a tamaño medido contra una referencia normal, como el cuerpo humano.

Vocabulary Practice

[T] Display *Transparency 40* to review unit vocabulary words.

Word Forms [★] Vocabulary

Have students identify the parts of speech for each vocabulary word using their glossary. Then assign student groups vocabulary words to use correctly in sentences. Ask groups to share their sentences on the board and discuss how that vocabulary word is used in the sentence.

Phonetic Spellings [★] Vocabulary

Assign student groups 2 or 3 vocabulary words. Ask them to look these words up in a dictionary for the phonetic spellings. Have students share what they found with the class.

Multiple Meanings [★] Vocabulary

Have student pairs look for multiple meanings of vocabulary words in a dictionary. Ask students to share the definitions that they find and identify the meaning that most closely relates to how they are using this word in unit 4.

Wrapping Up Unit 4

Proportion and Distortion

Art Criticism

Critical Thinking Art Criticism is an organized system for looking at and talking about art. You can criticize art without being an expert. The purpose of art criticism is to get the viewer involved in a perception process that delays judgment until all aspects of the artwork have been studied.

■ See page 28–29 for more about art criticism.

Describe

▶ Possible answers are: A barefoot woman who is dancing and wearing a blue-colored dress with blue trim. She has long black hair and a smiling face seen in profile. In the center of the painting is a red horse with a long curved neck. The horse's mane spirals around his curved neck.

Analyze

▶ Nothing seems in correct proportion or scale compared to the rest of the work. The woman is too short for the horse. The orange man does not relate to the woman or the horse. The black creature is too large to be a rooster and too small to be a person. The face in the bottom corner does not belong to anything.

▶ Everything seems to be distorted. The horse has an elongated, curved neck that is twisted. Its legs have no joints; they are made of curved lines. Its feet seem to be covered with human shoes. It seems to have a human smile, and its nostrils are lined up one above the other. The woman has an elongated torso and head. Her left arm has no elbow; it is made of curved lines. The man in the upper left has short arms and legs made of curved lines that bend in the opposite direction of human knees. The black creature in the center appears to be an strange combination of human and rooster.

▲ **Marc Chagall.** (Russian/French). *The Red Horse (Fiesta)*. 1942.

Gouache on paper. 26¾ × 19¾ inches (67.95 × 50.17 cm.). Norton Museum, West Palm Beach, Florida.

Art History and Culture

Marc Chagall

Marc Chagall (märk sha gäl) (1887–1985) was born in Russia but lived most of his life in France. He is known for his surreal, dream-like paintings. Chagall's work is reflective of Russian expressionism and early French cubism. Themes carried throughout his artwork include his own recollections of Russian-Jewish village scenes, his life as part of the Jewish community, and his people's treatment and theology. The use of fantasy-like paintings to tell real-life stories allows viewers of all backgrounds to feel and possibly associate with his artwork.

See pages 24–25 and 16–21 for more about art history and the subject matter.

Artist Profiles, p. 17

◄ Artist Profile ▶

Marc Chagall
1887-1985

Marc Chagall (mark sha gäl') was born in a small town in Russia, Vitebsk, which is now part of Belarus. He studied art in Saint Petersburg and then in Paris, France. After the Russian revolution he served as the director of the art academy in his hometown. From 1919 to 1922, Chagall was the art director of the Moscow Jewish State Theater. He painted murals in the theater lobby and created sets for the shows. In 1923, he moved to France. He spent most of the rest of his life there, except for a brief period of residence in the United States from 1941 to 1948.

 **Art Criticism** Critical Thinking

Describe **What do you see?**

During this step you will collect information about the subject of the work.

▶ Describe what you see in Marc Chagall's painting *The Red Horse (Fiesta)*.

Analyze **How is this work organized?**

Think about how the artist used the elements and principles of art.

▶ Where do you see realistic proportions in this painting? Where do you see unrealistic proportions?

▶ Do you see examples of distortion?

Interpret **What is the artist trying to say?**

Use the clues you discovered during your analysis to find the message the artist is trying to show.

▶ What effect does this use of distortion have on the painting?

▶ How would the painting be different if there were no distortion in it?

▶ What elements did Chagall use to create mood in this painting?

Decide **What do you think about the work?**

Use all the information you have gathered to decide whether this is a successful work of art.

▶ Do you see more things hidden in this painting the longer you look at it?

▶ Do you like how you feel when you view this painting?

Interpret

▶ The bright reds and oranges and the curving, swirling lines create this festive, happy, exciting mood. The distortion makes the scene seem dreamlike.

▶ The scene would be disconnected without the distortion.

▶ Chagall used color, shape, line, and space to create mood in this painting.

Decide

▶ Many elements in this painting will be revealed as the viewer studies this work of art.

▶ Ask students to explain their reactions to this painting.

Art Journal: Writing

Have students write answers to Aesthetic Perception in their Art Journals.

Aesthetic Perception

Critical Thinking Have students think about their favorite animals. How is this animal like other animals? What makes this animal different from other animals?

Describe ▶ Describe the features of your favorite animal.

Analyze ▶ How would you paint this animal using distortion to emphasize its most unique features?

Interpret ▶ How would distorting these proportions affect the overall appearance of this animal?

▶ Would you include other people and animals in this painting? If so, what purpose would they serve?

Decide ▶ How have you changed the effect this animal has on the viewers of the painting by distorting its features?

"Artists use the elements of proportion and distortion to express excitement and emphasis through particular areas of their artwork." "Los artistas usan los elementos de proporción y distorsión para expresar emoción y énfasis a través de áreas particulares de sus obras de arte."

T Review unit vocabulary with students using *Transparency 40.*

Art Journal: Writing

Have students answer the questions on page 152 in their Art Journals or on a separate sheet of paper. Answers: 1. B, 2. C, 3. A, 4. C, 5. B

T For further assessment, have students complete the unit test on *Transparency 46.*

CAREERS IN ART
Jewelers

► Have students identify and discuss pieces of jewelry they are wearing, own, like, or would like to own. Discuss about how jewelry is used in our culture and how it is used in other cultures. For example, you might want to talk about engagement and wedding ring practices or about Britain's Crown Jewels in the Tower of London.

"Art is something which, although produced by human hands, is not created by these hands alone, but something which wells up from a deeper source in our souls."

        -Vincent van Gogh

Proportion and Distortion, continued

Show What You Know

Answer these questions on a separate sheet of paper.

❶ _____ is the principle of art that relates to the size relationship of one part to another.
  A. Form
  B. Proportion
  C. Portions

❷ When artists create size relationships that do not make sense and look different from usual proportions, they are using _____.
  A. realistic scale
  B. ratio
  C. unrealistic scale

❸ _____ is the bending or pulling of an object or figure out of its normal shape to communicate the ideas or feelings of the artist.
  A. Distortion
  B. Dimension
  C. Scale

❹ When artists make things bigger than they normally are, they are using _____.
  A. proportion
  B. miniatures
  C. exaggeration

❺ A _____ is a comparison of size between two things.
  A. realistic scale
  B. ratio
  C. unrealistic scale

152   Unit 4

Unit Assessment Options

🔍 Aesthetic Perception

Practice Have students select three of the concepts in the Show What You Know section on page 152 and find examples of each concept in the classroom.

🎨 Creative Expression

Student Portfolio Have students review all the artwork they have created during this unit and select the pieces they wish to keep in their portfolios.

❓ Art Criticism

Activity Have students select an artwork from this unit and study it using the four steps of art criticism. (See pages 28–29 for more information about art criticism.) Have students work alone or in pairs and present their findings orally or in writing.

CAREERS IN ART
Jewelry

The art of jewelry making is the creation of ornamental objects, such as bracelets, necklaces, and rings, made with a variety of materials such as metals and gems.

Jewelry designers plan and create pieces of jewelry using materials like gold, silver, and gemstones. They combine their creative ideas with the needs and tastes of their customers to make the jewelry.

Silversmiths and goldsmiths use a metal process known as *annealing*, in which the metals are heated and slowly cooled so they can be bent and manipulated.

Jewelry appraisers decide how much a piece of jewelry is worth and how much it should cost. Because the value of one piece of jewelry can change, a jewelry appraiser must know how the rates are changing in the jewelry market.

▲ **Jeweler**

Proportion and Distortion in Dance

Martha Graham was the most important and enduring dancer and choreographer of the twentieth century. She broke with classical ballet and created her own technique. This dance, "Lamentation," is about a grieving woman. The stretchy cloth worn by the dancer exaggerates her distorted movements, creating powerful expressions of grief.

▲ Martha Graham. "Lamentation" and "Satyric Festival Song."

What to Do Perform a sequence of movements that expresses two contrasting emotions.

Think about the following ideas for expressing action and emotion:

- ▶ reaching upward; sinking downward
- ▶ a change in the tempo of music and actions from fast to slow, and vice versa
- ▶ strong, decisive, energetic motions; peaceful, fluid motions
- ▶ giving up; refusing to give up

Try walking, showing these ideas through posture and gesture.

Experiment with movements that descend and rise, showing these ideas.

Show three different shapes or body postures that capture a moment of grief or joy.

1. Walk, turn, descend, and rise for four counts each.
2. Repeat them, expressing joy. Think about the energy and direction of the movement.
3. Repeat them, expressing grief. Think about the energy and direction of the movement.
4. Do the sequence twice. Decide the order of the two emotions.

 Art Criticism

Describe Describe the ways in which you distorted movement.

Analyze What choices did you make in sequencing grief and joy?

Interpret Did you experience feelings of joy and grief when you moved?

Decide How successful were you in using distortion to express emotions through dance?

Unit 4 **153**

 Art History and Culture

Martha Graham

Modern dance pioneer Martha Graham changed the way people express themselves through dance. She choreographed great dances and trained dancers for more than seventy years. "Lamentation" is one of her most haunting pieces. "Satyric Festival Song" displays the opposite emotions from those in "Lamentation," expressing laughter, teasing wit, and self-mocking humor. Inspired by sculpture, "Lamentation" represents the essence of grief. The dancer is encased in a tube of stretch jersey, with only her hands, feet, and face visible. The movement is created through the changing forms of the costume, manipulated by the knees, legs, head, and arms underneath. In "Satyric Festival Song," Graham makes fun of her own serious works.

 Proportion and Distortion in Dance

Objective: to distort movement to artistically express emotions

Materials: "Lamentation" and "Satyric Festival Song," performed by Janet Eilber. running time: About 45 minutes.

ocus

Time: About 5 minutes

- Discuss the information on page 153.

Art History and Culture

- Have students discuss the ways in which movement can be distorted (shape, size, tempo, energy, etc.)

each

Time: About 20 minutes

Aesthetic Perception

- Have students watch "Lamentation" and "Satyric Festival Song." Talk about joy and grief.

Creative Expression

- Ask students to walk, turn, descend, and rise, using four counts for each. Then direct students to perform this sequence without emotion. Next have them perform, expressing joy and then expressing grief. Encourage them to think about energy, focus, directions, and tempo. Have students perform their improvisations in small groups.

- **Informal Assessment** Comment positively to the students that make an effort to keep time with their movements and to incorporate emotions.

eflect

Time: About 10 minutes

Art Criticism

- Have students answer the four art criticism questions on page153 orally and written.

- Were students able to successfully express joy and grief through movement?

Unit 5 Planning Guide

	Lesson Title	Suggested Pacing	Creative Expression Activity
Lesson 1	Texture	1:20	Create a memory jar.
Lesson 2	Rhythm	1:05	Create a paper weaving.
Lesson 3	Movement Through Rhythm	1:20	Create a still-life cubist drawing.
Lesson 4	Formal Balance	1:20	Create a batik-style self portrait.
Lesson 5	Informal Balance	1:05	Create a still-life mono-print.
Lesson 6	Radial Balance	1:20	Design a stained glass window.
ART SOURCE ARTSOURCE	Texture, Rhythm, and Movement in Dance	0:45	To create a mime or dance with a partner.

Materials	Program Resources	Fine Art Resources	Literature Resources
found objects, tacky glue, plastic water bottles, small slips of paper, paint	*Assessment,* pp. 57–58 *Home and After-School Connections* *The National Museum of Women in the Arts Collection* *Reading and Writing Test Preparation,* pp. 54–55	*Transparency 25* *Artist Profiles,* pp. 77, 15 *Large Print 70* *Animals Through History Time Line*	*The Great Ancestor Hunt: The Fun of Finding Out Who You Are* by Lila Perl Yerkow
pencils, scissors, 12" × 18" construction paper in warm and cool colors, 12" × ½" pre-cut strips of construction paper, white school glue	*Assessment,* pp. 59–60 *Home and After-School Connections* *Art Around the World Collection* *Reading and Writing Test Preparation,* pp. 56–57	*Transparency 26* *Artist Profiles,* pp. 27, 42 *Large Prints 69, 70* *Animals Through History Time Line*	*Bud, Not Buddy* by Christopher Paul Curtis
12" × 18" white drawing paper, pencils, erasers, rulers, colored pencils	*Assessment,* pp. 61–62 *Home and After-School Connections* *Women in the Arts Collection* *Reading and Writing Test Preparation,* pp. 58–59	*Transparency 27* *Artist Profiles,* pp. 6, 47 *Large Print 69* *Animals Through History Time Line*	*The Jazz Man* by Mary Hays Weik
black markers, 12" × 14" cardboard sheet, 10" × 12" muslin or white cotton fabric, masking tape, white school glue, toothpicks, watercolor paints, paintbrushes, water containers, newspaper	*Assessment,* pp. 63–64 *Home and After-School Connections* *Women in the Arts Collection* *Reading and Writing Test Preparation,* pp. 60–61	*Transparency 28* *Artist Profiles,* pp. 80, 49 *Large Print 69* *Animals Through History Time Line*	*The Most Beautiful Place in the World* by Ann Cameron
12" × 18" white drawing paper, pencils, paper plates, liquid tempera paints, paintbrushes, found objects, water dishes, paper towels, newspaper	*Assessment,* pp. 65–66 *Home and After-School Connections* *Women in the Arts Collection* *Reading and Writing Test Preparation,* pp. 62–63	*Transparency 29* *Artist Profiles,* pp. 5, 59 *Large Prints 69, 70* *Animals Through History Time Line*	*The Egypt Game* by Zilpha Keatley
computer, computer paint program, printer, scanner, scissors, glue	*Assessment,* pp. 67–68 *Home and After-School Connections* *Women in the Arts Collection* *Reading and Writing Test Preparation,* pp. 64–65	*Transparency 30* *Artist Profiles,* pp. 70, 4 *Large Prints 69, 70* *Animals Through History Time Line*	*Of Heros, Hooks, and Heirlooms* by Faye Silton
"Billy the Kid"			

Unit Overview

5 Texture, Rhythm, Movement, and Balance

Lesson 1: Texture is used by artists to add interest to works of art.

Lesson 2: Rhythm is the use of positive and negative space to direct the viewer's eyes.

Lesson 3: Movement through rhythm is the use of repeated colors, shapes, spaces, and forms that direct the viewer's eyes.

Lesson 4: Formal balance occurs when two halves of an artwork are identical or very similar.

Lesson 5: Informal balance occurs when unlike objects have equal visual weight.

Lesson 6: Radial balance occurs when art elements repeat from the center of an artwork outward.

Introduce Unit Concepts

"Artists use the elements of texture, rhythm, movement, and balance to organize, enhance, and control how the viewer's eyes travel though a work of art." "Los artistas usan los elementos de textura, ritmo, movimiento y equilibrio para organizar, realzar y controlar la manera en que la vista del espectador se mueve por una obra de arte."

Texture and Rhythm
- Have students brainstorm objects with the following textures: smooth, fuzzy, prickly. Ask students to work in groups to create a musical rhythm using beats and the rests.

Movement and Balance
- Ask students to try to look only at the first line of notebook paper. Brainstorm other objects with repeated elements. Display a scale with two identical items on each side. Discuss how the same principle can be applied to visual weight.

Cross Curricular Projects
- See the *Language Arts and Reading, Mathematics, Science,* and *Social Studies Art Connections* books for activities that further develop the concepts in this unit.

Texture, Rhythm, Movement, and Balance

◀ **Vincent van Gogh.** (Dutch). *Houses at Auvers.* 1890.
Oil on canvas. 29¾ × 24⅜ inches (75.56 × 61.93 cm.). Museum of Fine Arts, Boston, Massachusetts.

Artists use texture, rhythm, movement, and balance to create interesting works of art.

Vincent van Gogh applied paint so thickly to his paintings that he created ridges of paint. These raised areas are real textures that catch light and make his colors look brighter. He used the principles of rhythm, movement, and balance to organize the elements in this landscape painting.

154 Unit 5

Fine Art Prints

Display *Large Prints 69 Hmong Story Cloth* and *70 The Throne of the Third Heaven of the Nation's Millenium General Assembly.* Refer to the prints throughout the unit.

Large Print 69

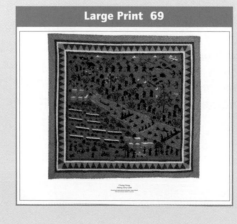

Large Print 70

Artists use both real and visual **texture** in their work.

▶ Look at the roofs of the houses in *Houses at Auvers*. How do you think they each might feel if you could touch them?

Artists use **visual rhythm** to help guide the viewer's eyes and to add visual excitement to a work of art.

▶ What lines, shapes, forms, and colors do you see repeated in *Houses at Auvers*?

Movement is used by artists to create rhythm by using positive and negative spaces, similar to musical beats and rests.

▶ What do you see in the painting that is not repeated? Notice how your eyes slow down or even stop when this happens.

Artists organize opposite sides of an artwork to create visual balance.

▶ Notice how the large house on one side is balanced by the bright-colored houses on the other side.

In This Unit you will learn about and practice using texture, rhythm, movement, and balance to create works of art. Here are the concepts you will study:
▶ Texture
▶ Rhythm
▶ Movement through rhythm
▶ Balance

Vincent van Gogh
(1853–1890)

Vincent van Gogh is considered to be one of the most important figures of modern painting. He was one of the first artists to use brightly colored canvases and thick paint to express his feelings. Van Gogh wrote almost daily to his brother Theo, who supplied him with materials. He wrote about his thoughts, feelings, and motivations. Because of these letters, historians have detailed information about the artist and his thoughts.

Unit 5   **155**

Art History and Culture

Vincent van Gogh

Vincent van Gogh (vin´ sənt van gō) (1853–1890), was the son of a Dutch Protestant pastor. At the age of 27, he began to paint. He completed more than 1,600 drawings and 750 paintings before his death at the age of 37. In 1886, van Gogh went to Paris to live with his brother Theo, who was an art dealer. There he was exposed to brightly colored impressionist paintings and Japanese prints. In 1888, van Gogh left Paris for Arles. There he painted landscapes using swirling brushstrokes and thick, bright colors to depict scenes of cypress trees, night skies, and people of the region.

See pages 24–25 and 16–21 for more about art history and the subject matter.

Artist Profiles, p. 63

◆ Artist Profile ◆
Vincent van Gogh
1853–1890
Even as a boy in the Netherlands, Vincent van Gogh (vin´ sant van gō´) cared about other people very much. He tried many jobs, including being a teacher, minister, and social worker. However, he had problems getting along with nearly everyone except his younger brother, Theo. At the age of 28, van Gogh decided that the best way he could serve others was through art. He expressed his deep feelings about people through his paintings. As he moved from place to place, he left many of his works behind. Some were burned in fireplaces for heat, and some were even used to patch holes in walls. Van Gogh was poor his entire life and often went hungry so that he could buy painting supplies. He died at age 37.

Examine the Artwork

"Let's look closely at the painting." "Vamos a mirar detalladamente la pintura."

■ Have students look at Vincent van Gogh's *House at Auvers*. Ask them to describe what they see.

■ Have students answer the questions about texture, rhythm, movement, and balance on page 155.

▶ Some roofs might feel hard and rough, like cement. Some might feel soft and uneven, as if they are made of straw. Some roofs might feel hot and slippery, like metal that has been sitting in the sun. NSAE 5.c

▶ There are curved lines repeated in the trees and the background. Short, thick lines are repeated throughout the houses, ground, and river. Free-form and rectangular shapes are repeated. Blue, green, brown, and black colors are repeated. NSAE 5.c

▶ The red color on the roof of the house is not repeated. It makes the viewer's eyes pause and take it in. NSAE 5.c

▶ The large house on the left side has a lot of visual weight, but the number of smaller houses on the right side of the painting balances, or evens out, this weight. NSAE 5.c

Unit Pretest

T Display *Transparency 47* as a pretest. Answers 1. C, 2. A, 3. C, 4. B, 5. B

Home Connection

■ See *Home and After-School Connections* for family newsletters and activities for this unit.

Unit 5 Arts Integration

ILLUSTRATOR PROFILE
Vera B. Williams
(1927–)

Free-spirited author/illustrator Vera B. Williams credits her early artistic development to the Bronx House, a community center in the New York neighborhood where she grew up. There, Williams acted, danced, told stories, and painted pictures. One of her paintings was displayed at the Museum of Modern Art when she was only nine years old.

Williams graduated from the High School of Music and Art in New York City and later earned a degree in graphic arts from the Black Mountain School in North Carolina. Along with other graduates from Black Mountain School, including poets, musicians, and potters, Williams founded an alternative community called Gate Hill Cooperative. Williams lived, worked, and raised three children there from 1953 to 1970. Several years later, when Williams was 46, single and living on a houseboat in Vancouver, Canada, she illustrated her first book.

Williams's writing consistently centers on themes of community and family, often stemming from memories of her own "fiercely scrapping, loud-talking, loving but unsettled family struggling to make a living." Her works include the Caldecott Honor Books *A Chair for My Mother* and *More, More, More Said the Baby*.

While studying Unit 5, share Vera B. Williams's illustrations with the class. Discuss the use of texture, rhythm, movement, and balance in her works of art. Ask students what kinds of texture, rhythm, movement, and balance they see in Williams's art. How did she show movement? Encourage students to identify examples of formal and informal balance in Williams's art.

Music

Balance in music is usually associated with symmetrical forms such as ABA—music having three sections with the middle section different from the two outer sections. Have students sing "Au Clair de la Lune" as an example of this. Students can also sing a round, such as "Frere Jacques," and try to balance the sound between the parts. The effect of movement in music is created primarily through the elements of beat, rhythm, and tempo.

Literature

Show the video or DVD *Rumpelstiltskin* to introduce the concepts of texture, rhythm, movement, and balance. Pause the video or DVD and have students identify these principles of art.

Literature and Art

Performing Arts

 Show "Billy the Kid." Point out how the dancer uses texture, rhythm, movement, and balance.

Artsource®

Lesson 1 Overview

Texture

Lesson 1 introduces texture. Designers combine a variety of textures to make exterior and interior spaces interesting and appealing.

Objectives

 Art History and Culture

To become knowledgeable about Victorian memory jars and the life and the artwork of George Catlin

 Creative Expression

To design and create a memory jar

 Aesthetic Perception

To identify the use of tactile and visual texture in works of art
NSAE 5.c

 Art Criticism

To evaluate one's own work using the four steps of art criticism

Vocabulary ⭐ Vocabulary

Review the following vocabulary words with students.

texture textura—the element of art that refers to how things feel or look as if they might feel if touched

tactile texture textura táctil—the way an object feels

visual texture textura visual—texture seen with the eyes

assemblage montaje—a three-dimensional work of art made of many pieces fixed together

See page 179B for additional Spanish vocabulary resources.

 Art Journal: Vocabulary

Have students add these words to the Vocabulary section of their Art Journals.

Lesson Materials

- found objects
- tacky glue
- plastic water bottles
- small slips of paper
- paint

Alternate Materials:
- plastic soft-drink bottles
- glue gun

Program Resources

- *Reading and Writing Test Prep.*, pp. 54–55
- *Transparency 29*
- *Artist Profiles*, pp. 77, 15
- *Animals Through History Time Line*
- *Assessment*, pp. 57–58
- *Large Prints 69* Hmong Story Cloth and *70* The Throne of the Third Heaven of the Nation's Millennium General Assembly
- *The National Museum of Women in the Arts Collection*

Concept Trace
Texture
Introduced: Level 4, Unit 4, Lessons 4, 5
Reinforced: Level 6, Unit 2, Lessons 5, 6

Lesson 1 Arts Integration

Theatre

Complete Unit 5, Lesson 1, on pages 90–91 of *Theatre Arts Connections.*

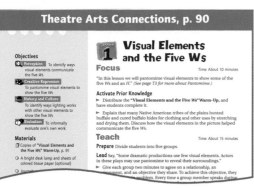

Theatre Arts Connections, p. 90

Music

 Texture in music describes whether one melody is alone or with other contrasting melodies, or with harmonic accompaniment. Listen to "The Moldau," by Bedrich Smetana. The Moldau is a river in his native Czechoslovakia. The piece starts with a small flow of melody from two flutes, depicting two streams coming out of the mountains. Listen to how the texture changes as it goes on and instruments are added.

Movement & Dance

Students work with a partner to go on a "texture walk." Ask one partner to close his or her eyes. Place various textured items on chairs and tabletops throughout the classroom. Use items with contrasting textures such as metal, fabric, wood, and plastic. Have the other partner carefully lead the person with closed eyes through the room. When they come across an object with interesting texture, they stop, and the leader helps the follower explore the object with touch (fingertips only).

Focus

Activate Prior Knowledge

"What are the textures of the outsides of the buildings in your community? What are the textures used in the furniture in the main room where you live?" "¿Cuáles son las texturas del exterior de los edificios en su vecindario? ¿Qué texturas se usaron en los muebles en el cuarto principal de donde viven?"
NSAE 5.a

- Discuss with students exterior textures that they are familiar with, such as stucco, wood, brick, and vinyl siding. Also discuss interior textures, such as the walls in a music room, and talk about their different purposes.

Using Literature ★ Reading

- Share with the class Lila Perl Yerkow's book *The Great Ancestor Hunt: The Fun of Finding Out Who You Are.*

Thematic Connection ★ Social Studies

- **Heritage:** Have students bring a symbol of their family's heritage to class and explain where it came from and what it represents.
NSAE 5.a

Introduce the Art

Look

"Let's take a close look at the two works of art." "Vamos a observar detalladamente las dos obras de arte."

Drawing Conclusions ★ Reading

- Have students look at both works of art and draw conclusions from the context clues that are given.

Art History and Culture

Students might assume that the owner or artist of *Memory Jar* was alive during the twenty-first century and valued objects used to make crafts. Students might also assume that the subject in the painting was a proud hunter because of his pose, dress, and weapon.

Web Connection

Visit http://theamesgallery.com/FolkArtPages/Memory.html to learn more about Victorian memory jars.

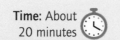
Texture

Look at the artwork on these pages. Notice the rough surface of *Memory Jar.* Your eyes tell you what it would feel like if you touched it. George Catlin's painting captures the different textures of the chief's clothing, headdress, and weapon. Can you imagine what these materials would feel like?

◀ **Artist unknown.** (North America).
Memory Jar. c. 1925.
Mixed media. 8 3/10 × 5 1/2 inches (21.07 × 14 cm.). Museum of International Folk Art, Santa Fe, New Mexico.

Art History and Culture

What can you assume about the subjects and their cultures from viewing the *Memory Jar* and painting?

Art History and Culture

Memory Jars

The origin of folk-art memory jars is unknown. Most of these jars are glass. They are covered in ordinary objects and are often painted entirely in gold or silver. Some believe that these vessels were part of an African American burial custom. Historians believe that these jars were covered with objects that were owned and used by a person who had died. Many cultures have similar rituals, which involve placing cherished or symbolic objects with the body of the deceased or at the gravesite for a comfortable transition to the afterworld. This twentieth century memory jar was made to celebrate a birthday.

See pages 24–25 and 16–21 for more about art history and the subject matter.

Artist Profiles, p. 77

Artist Profile

Memory Jar

This memory jar was made around the beginning of the twentieth century by an unknown artist. The artists who create sculptures like this come from many different ethnic groups and geographic regions, so it is difficult to determine the individual who made this particular piece.

◀ **Artist unknown.** (North America).
Memory Jar. c. 1925.

◀ **George Catlin.** (American). *Mah-To-Tóh-Pa, Four Bears, Second Chief.* 1832.

Oil on canvas. 29 × 24 inches (73.66 × 60.96 cm.). Smithsonian American Art Museum, Washington, D.C.

Study both works of art. Notice how texture is used.

▸ Where do you see a bumpy surface?

▸ Which areas look smooth or shiny?

▸ In which work of art do your eyes tell you how it would feel?

▸ In which work of art could you feel the bumpy surface with your hands?

Aesthetic Perception

Design Awareness Look around you for surfaces that are made to look like they have a rough texture but are actually smooth.

 Art History and Culture

George Catlin

George Catlin (jorj kat´ lən) (1796–1872) devoted his life to painting the lives, the cultures, and the faces of the native people of both North and South America. Catlin saw himself as a historian of the Native American people more than as an artist. He spent six years traveling throughout the Southwest. His paintings record almost fifty different American tribes, with about 300 portraits and 175 landscapes and village scenes.

See pages 24–25 and 16–21 for more about art history and the subject matter.

Artist Profiles, p. 15

◆ Artist Profile ◆
George Catlin
1796–1872

George Catlin (jorj kat´ lan) was born in Pennsylvania. He first became a lawyer, but painting lured him away from a law career. While painting miniatures in Philadelphia, he happened to meet a visiting group of Native Americans, and Catlin became fascinated by Native American culture. He made many trips into Native American territory and spent weeks studying groups that had not yet been influenced by European culture. He spent his own money to exhibit his paintings in England and France, where they were much admired. Living on a small income, Catlin traveled to South America to paint genre paintings of indigenous groups. Catlin has had more paintings displayed in the Louvre in Paris

Study NSAE 4.a

▸ The surface of *Memory Jar* looks bumpy.

▸ The areas on some of the objects of the *Memory Jar* look smooth.

▸ George Catlin's *Mah-To-Tóh-Pa, Four Bears, Second Chief* uses visual texture. The viewer cannot actually feel the texture but can imagine what it would feel like based on connecting what is seen to your previous experiences.

▸ *Memory Jar* uses tactile texture. A person could actually feel the bumps, the prickles, and the smooth areas with his or her hands.

▪ For more examples of utilitarian art, see *The National Museum of Women in the Arts Collection.*

Art Journal: Writing

Have students write about family traditions they have experienced. Encourage students to list some questions they would like to ask about their heritage and those of others.

Have students create a sketch of their family's tradition to accompany the explanation in their Art Journals.

Aesthetic Perception

Design Awareness Ask students to look for examples of imitated textures. These objects might be made to look as if they have a rough surface when the surface is actually smooth. Show students examples such as contact paper made to look like wood or brick.

Developing Visual Literacy Discuss with students how both artists in this lesson have communicated the textures of their subjects. Ask students to describe the textures of both works of art and what they might feel like if students were to touch them. Are these textures like anything else students have ever touched? Which artist in this lesson asks the viewer to imagine the texture of the subject?

Web Connection

Visit **catlinclassroom.si.edu/cl.html** to learn more about George Catlin and his artwork.

Teach

Time: About 45 minutes

"How could you use texture to make a piece of artwork interesting and meaningful?"

"¿Cómo podrían usar la textura para que una obra de arte sea interesante y significativa?"

- Read and discuss the definitions of *texture, tactile texture,* and *visual texture* on page 158.

Practice

Materials: historical family items

- Review the Practice activity directions with students on page 158.

- Allow students time to gather historical family items. Ask students to identify the texture of each of their objects on a separate sheet of paper. Give students the opportunity to share some of their favorite items with the class. If there is time, groups can work on an artifact time line using their historical family pieces. NSAE 4.b

Creative Expression

Materials: found objects, tacky glue, plastic water bottles, small slips of paper, paint

Alternate Materials: plastic soft-drink bottles, glue guns, found objects, spray paint

- Refer to the additional notes on page 242 of the Activity Tips section for steps to complete in preparation for the Creative Expression activity.

- Distribute the materials.

- Have students follow the directions on page 159.

- Review the Activity Tips on page 242 for visual examples of this lesson's activity.

Art Journal: Brainstorming

Have students brainstorm a list of possible memories they would like to save in a time capsule. One memory will be chosen to include in the Creative Expression activity. NSAE 3.b

---

Using Texture

Texture is the element of art that refers to how things feel, or how they look as if they might feel if they were touched. There are two ways in which we experience texture: by sight and by touch.

Tactile texture is how something actually feels when you touch it.

Visual texture is the way something looks like it might feel if you could touch it. It is the illusion that an artist creates to represent texture.

Tactile Texture

Visual Texture

Practice

Collect items that remind you of the past.

1. Look in different places for items that represent the history of your family.

2. Identify the texture of each item.

3. Choose some of your favorite items and share them with the class.

Differentiated Instruction

Reteach

Select random objects to display on a table in the classroom. Assign each item a number and allow students time to identify the texture of each item with corresponding numbers on separate sheets of paper.

Special Needs

Routines in art class make students feel emotionally safe. One routine that builds self-confidence is the opportunity students have to show and discuss their work. This autobiographical project is a perfect opportunity to begin or continue this routine in your class.

ELL

Students may have difficulty thinking of multiple adjectives to describe the textures of objects. Allow students to suggest objects they are familiar with that have similar textures.

◀ **Halley Stulb.**
Age 10.

Think about how the artist used texture to create an interesting memory jar.

 Creative Expression

How can you save some of your favorite items by incorporating them in a work of art?

1. Collect many small items that reflect your interests.

2. Spread tacky glue on the plastic water bottle.

3. Arrange your collected items on the bottle. Consider texture, contrast, and space.

4. Write a favorite memory on a piece of paper. Place your memory in the memory jar you have created.

5. Place the cap on the bottle. Paint the memory jar using only one color.

Art Criticism

Describe Describe the items that you chose to decorate the memory jar.

Analyze How would you describe the texture of your memory jar?

Interpret What do the items on your memory jar communicate about you?

Decide Are you satisfied with your use of texture on your memory jar?

Art Across the Curriculum

Use these simple ideas to reinforce art concepts across the curriculum.

★ **Poetry Writing** Have students each write a poem about a favorite memory to go into their memory jars.

★ **Math** Have students look at numbers in Braille and discuss how some textures serve specific purposes.

★ **Science** Ask students to compare the textures of sand, silt, and clay. Then discuss the vegetation that grows in different areas because of soil textures.

★ **Social Studies** Have students each create a family tree and include dates and birthplaces to trace their families' heritage.

★ **Technology** Have students fill shapes with visual textures in a presentation program. Visit **SRAonline.com** to print detailed instructions for this activity.
NSAE 6.b

 **Reflect** **Time:** About 15 minutes

Review and Assess

"How would you explain the difference between visual and tactile textures?" "¿Cómo explicarían la diferencia entre la textura visual y la táctil?"

Think

The artist used tactile texture to add interest and variety to this memory jar.

■ Use **Large Print 70** *The Throne of the Third Heaven of the Nation's Millennium General Assembly* to have students identify and describe the uses of tactile texture.

■ Invite a local artist into your classroom to share his or her portfolio. Ask students to research information on this artist and prepare questions about specific art elements and principles prior to the visit.

Informal Assessment

■ For standardized-format test practice using this lesson's art content, see pages 54–55 in *Reading and Writing Test Preparation.*

Art Journal: Critical Thinking

Have students answer the four art criticism questions—Describe, Analyze, Interpret, and Decide—in their Art Journals. In small groups, have students discuss their memory jars. NSAE 2.a

■ Have students look at the pieces of fine art in this lesson and compare the cultural themes honoring American traditions, such as memory jars.

Extra! For the Art Specialist

Time: About 30 minutes

Focus

Have students study **Large Print 70** *The Throne of the Third Heaven of the Nation's Millennium General Assembly* and ask students to point out the different types of textures they see.

Teach

Have students each choose two still-life objects from the classroom. The objects should have contrasting textures. Ask students to arrange the objects in a way that they would like to draw them.

Reflect

Have students evaluate their artwork using the four steps of art criticism. Encourage them to locate and describe both visual and tactile textures that they can see from where they sit in the classroom.

Alternate Activity

Materials:
- Art Journal
- 9" × 12" thick black paper
- oil pastels
- found objects
- pencils, erasers
- tacky glue

1. Arrange a still life. The objects with contrasting textures should be placed next to each other. Sketch the arrangement in your Art Journal from different points of view.

2. Choose the sketch that you like best and transfer it onto drawing paper using a pencil. Draw the objects large enough to extend from the opposite edges of the paper.

3. Add color and details using oil pastels. Be sure to add the texture of the object.

4. Glue a few of the found objects onto the drawing in the area where the objects are close. Try to find objects with textures resembling those of the chosen objects in the still-life drawing to combine visual and tactile textures.

Research in Art Education

One study showed that students on average gained eight percentile points on a standardized language arts test after one year of learning in an arts-integrated classroom and gained sixteen percentile points after two years. After three years, students "outscored non-program students on the writing and drawing assessments of social studies content learning," ("Different Ways of Knowing: 1991–1994 National Longitudinal Study Final Report" in *Schools, Communities, and the Arts: A Research Compendium*).

Assessment

Use the following rubric to evaluate the artwork students make in the Creative Expression activity and to assess students' understanding of texture.

Have students complete page 57 and 58 in their *Assessment* books.

	Art History and Culture	Aesthetic Perception	Creative Expression	Art Criticism
3 POINTS	The student can demonstrate knowledge of Victorian memory jars and the life and artwork of George Catlin.	The student accurately identifies texture used in art.	The student's memory jar clearly illustrates the use of texture.	The student thoughtfully and honestly evaluates own work using the four steps of art criticism.
2 POINTS	The student's knowledge of Victorian memory jars and the life and artwork of George Catlin is weak or incomplete.	The student shows emerging awareness of texture used in art.	The student's memory jar shows some awareness of texture.	The student attempts to evaluate own work but shows an incomplete understanding of evaluation criteria.
1 POINT	The student cannot demonstrate knowledge of Victorian memory jars or the life and artwork of George Catlin.	The student cannot identify texture used in art.	The student's memory jar shows no understanding of texture.	The student makes no attempt to evaluate own artwork.

Assessment, p. 57

Rhythm

Lesson 2 introduces rhythm. Artists use visual rhythm in much the same way that musicians use musical rhythm. The positive and negative spaces are positioned in a work of art in a way that directs the viewer's eyes in a rhythm of beats and rests.

Objectives

Art History and Culture

To become knowledgeable about the lives and the artwork of Paul Gauguin and Joan Miró

Creative Expression

To design and create a paper weaving that uses visual rhythm

Aesthetic Perception

To identify the use of visual rhythm in works of art
NSAE 5.c

Art Criticism

To evaluate one's own work using the four steps of art criticism

Vocabulary ⭐ Vocabulary

Review the following vocabulary words with students before beginning the lesson.

rhythm *ritmo*—the principle of art that shows movement by repeating elements such as lines, shapes, and colors

visual rhythm *ritmo visual*—rhythm that is perceived through the eyes, not through the hands

See page 179B for additional Spanish vocabulary resources.

Art Journal: Vocabulary

Have students add these words to the Vocabulary section of their Art Journals.

Lesson Materials

- 9" × 12" warm, and cool-colored construction paper
- magazines
- pencils
- scissors
- 12" × 18" construction paper in warm and cool colors
- 12" × ½" pre-cut strips of construction paper in warm and cool colors
- white school glue

Program Resources

- *Reading and Writing Test Prep.*, pp. 56–57
- *Transparency 26*
- *Flash Card 9*
- *Artist Profiles*, pp. 27, 42
- *Animals Through History Time Line*
- *Assessment*, pp. 59–60
- *Large Prints 69* Hmong Story Cloth and *70* The Throne of the Third Heaven of the Nation's Millennium General Assembly
- *Art Around the World Collection*

Concept Trace

Rhythm
Introduced: Level 4, Unit 2, Lessons 4, 5, 6
Reinforced: Level 6, Unit 3, Lesson 4

Lesson 2 Arts Integration

Theatre

Complete Unit 5, Lesson 2, on pages 92–93 of *Theatre Arts Connections.*

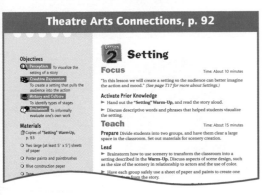
Theatre Arts Connections, p. 92

Music

Listen to "Badinerie" from *Orchestral Suite No. 2 in B Minor,* by Johann Sebastian Bach. Clap the main rhythm of the flutes. Use this rhythm to speak ordinary sentences.

Movement & Dance

Choose one student to be the class leader. The leader claps out a rhythm and the class echoes it back to the leader. Repeat, each time creating a more complicated rhythmic pattern. This can be done by adding other forms of body percussion, such as stamping, slapping body parts, and clicking. Alternate leaders.

Focus

Time: About 20 minutes

Activate Prior Knowledge

"Have you ever liked a song not because of the words or the melody but because you really liked the rhythm?" "¿Alguna vez les ha gustado una canción no por la letra o la melodía sino por el ritmo?"
NSAE 5.a

- Discuss with students how musical rhythm is created with beats and with rests that are silent between the beats.

Using Literature ⭐ Reading

- Share with the class *Bud, Not Buddy* by Christopher Paul Curtis. The story is about a ten-year-old boy who leaves an orphanage in search of his father, a jazz musician.

Thematic Connection ⭐ Social Studies

- **Beyond the Notes:** Ask students to share their experiences with music. Talk with the class about how one musical style evolves out of other styles. Students might be surprised to know that modern rhythm and blues music developed from early blues, jazz, and even country music.

Introduce the Art

Look

"Let's take a close look at the two works of art." "Vamos a observar detalladamente las dos obras de arte."

Classify and Categorize ⭐ Reading

- Joan Miró's *Hirondelle/Amour* is an abstract work of art because the viewer can see what some objects in the piece represent. A nonobjective artwork has no recognizable subject matter.

Art History and Culture

Joan Miró's *Hirondelle/Amour* is surrealistic.

Web Connection

Visit **http://www.vangoghgauguin.com/index.html** to learn more about Paul Gauguin and his work with Vincent van Gogh.

Rhythm

Look at the artwork on these pages. Notice the puppies that repeat around the bowl and the blue goblets that move your eyes from one side of the painting to the other. The spaces in between these repeated objects give your eyes a rest and help to create a rhythm. In Miró's painting the bold, warm colors are the beats in the rhythm and the cool colors are the rests.

◀ **Paul Gauguin.** (French). *Still Life with Three Puppies.* 1888.
••••••••••••••••••••••••••••••••••
Oil on wood. $36\frac{1}{8} \times 24\frac{3}{8}$ inches (91.75×62.53 cm). Museum of Modern Art, New York, New York.

 Art History and Culture

Surrealism is a twentieth-century style of art in which dreams, fantasy, and imagination are used to create artwork that moves away from realism. Which of these paintings is surreal?

 Art History and Culture

Paul Gauguin

Paul Gauguin (pôl gō gan´) (1848–1903) studied in Orléans, France, and joined a stockbrokerage firm in Paris after he graduated. He met his wife there, married, and had five children. Gauguin began to dabble in amateur painting and exhibited his work with mild success. He joined the Exhibition of Independents and spent a summer painting with Pissarro and Paul Cézanne. He left the stockbrokerage business and devoted his time to painting. Gauguin is recognized for his untraditional use of colors, lines, and shapes. Rather than copying nature, Gauguin explored combining flat, colorful shapes, broad areas of bright color, and graceful lines to create decorative patterns.

See pages 24–25 and 16–21 for more about art history and the subject matter.

Artist Profiles, p. 27

◀ Artist Profile ▶
Paul Gauguin
1848-1903
As one of France's leading postimpressionist painters, the artistic career of Paul Gauguin (pôl gō gan´) did not begin until he was a 25-year-old stockbroker. He decided to become a painter when he saw the first impressionist exhibit in Paris, France, in 1874, and throughout the next 30 years he developed his own style independent from impressionism and full of influences and experiences from his life. He was not content or fulfilled in Europe, however, and in 1891 he left his family and job to move to Tahiti and various other destinations in the South Pacific. With the exception of a two-year absence, Gauguin remained in Tahiti for the rest of his life, painting until his death in 1903.

▲ **Joan Miró.** (Spanish).
Hirondelle/Amour.
1933–1934.

Oil on canvas. 78½ × 97½ inches (199.39 × 247.65 cm.). Museum of Modern Art, New York, New York.

Study both works of art to find examples of rhythm.

▶ Which objects or elements do you see repeated in each work of art?

▶ Are there equal amounts of negative space between each repeated object or element?

▶ Imagine that the positive spaces are musical notes and the negative spaces are rests in the music. What kind of musical rhythm do the objects and elements in these paintings convey?

Aesthetic Perception

Seeing Like an Artist Look around you for examples of visual rhythm in natural and man-made designs.

Art History and Culture

Joan Miró

Joan Miró (zhô än´ mē rō´) (1893–1983) entered art school as a teenager in Spain. His teachers introduced him to modern art, but in time he developed his own style, moving from traditional painting to surreal fantasy. By the end of World War II, he was very famous. He was fascinated with symbols and encouraged many young artists, especially in the United States, to move away from realism in their paintings. He created drawings, paintings, lithographs, murals, tapestries, sculptures, and ceramics. He even designed costumes and settings for the play *Romeo and Juliet.* Miró received numerous awards for his artwork.

See pages 24–25 and 16–21 for more about art history and the subject matter.

Artist Profiles, p. 42

◆ Artist Profile ◆
Joan Miró
1893–1983

Joan Miró (hō´ än mē rō´) entered art school in his native Spain when he was a teenager. His teachers introduced him to modern art, but in time he developed his own style, moving from traditional painting to surreal fantasy. Miró lived in Spain and France and focused entirely on his art. By the end of World War II he was very famous. He painted a wall-sized mural for Harvard University, and created two ceramic walls for the UNESCO building in Paris, France. Both the cities of Houston, Texas, and Chicago, Illinois, asked him to create huge sculptures. Miró received numerous awards for his artwork. He lived a quiet life, and although his work received much attention, Miró remained in the background. Creating

▶ In Gauguin's *Still Life with Three Puppies,* the puppies, the goblets, and the fruit are repeated. In Miró's *Hirondelle/Amour* similar hands, feet, arms, legs, and faces are repeated. Colors, lines, and shapes are also repeated throughout both pieces.

▶ In *Still Life with Three Puppies* an equal amount of negative space separates the three goblets, but there is more space between the middle puppy and the one on the left than the one on the right. The negative spaces in *Hirondelle/Amour* are not equal.

▶ The rhythm of Gauguin's painting seems regular and slower than the rhythm of Miró's painting.

■ For more examples of art from Europe, see the *Art Around the World Collection.*

Art Journal: Writing

Ask students to write about the type of music they would use to accompany or express the rhythm of the two paintings in this lesson. Encourage students to use specific songs and explain how the rhythm fits each painting.

Aesthetic Perception

Seeing Like An Artist Ask students to share the examples of visual rhythm that they have found in both natural and humanmade objects and explain how the positive and negative spaces create rhythm.

Developing Visual Literacy Ask students if they have ever had a puppy or watched a litter of puppies interact with each other. Encourage students to look at Gauguin's painting and analyze how realistic the scene is. Ask students if they think some objects were arranged by the artist or if he just happened upon the scene the way it appears in the painting.

Web Connection

Visit **www.spanisharts.com/reinasofia/miro.htm** to learn more about the life and artwork of Joan Miró.

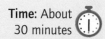

Teach

"How can you create visual rhythm in a work of art?" "¿Cómo pueden crear el ritmo visual en una obra de arte?"

- Read and discuss the definitions of *rhythm* and *visual rhythm* on page 162.

Practice

Materials: 9″ × 12″ warm- and cool-colored construction paper, magazines, pencils, scissors

- Review the Practice activity directions with students on page 162.

- Have students look through magazines to find a few images of people in action. Ask students to choose their favorite image, cut out that image, and trace it onto a piece of warm- or cool-colored construction paper three times. Students should then cut out these silhouettes of the human figure and save them to be used in the Creative Expression activity.

Creative Expression

Materials: pencils, scissors, 12″ × 18″ construction paper in warm and cool colors, 12″ × ½″ pre-cut strips of construction paper in warm and cool colors, white school glue

- Refer to the additional notes on page 242 in the Activity Tips section for steps to complete in preparation for the Creative Expression activity.

- Distribute the materials.

- Have students follow the directions on page 163.

- Review the Activity Tips on page 242 for visual examples of this lesson's activity.

Art Journal: Writing

Have students look at the images they cut out of magazines and write about the activities the people are doing.

Using Rhythm

Artists create **rhythm** by repeating elements and objects in a work of art.

In music, rhythm is created by the pauses or rests between musical sounds. A beat is followed by a rest.

Visual rhythm is the repetition of shapes, colors, or lines. Rhythm is created by repeated positive spaces that are separated with negative spaces. You can follow visual rhythm with your eyes. The shapes are the beats, and the spaces that separate them are the rests.

Practice

Create rhythm by repeating a shape three times.

1. Find an image of a person in action in a magazine. Cut out the image carefully, removing the excess paper.

2. Trace the cutout image on a piece of warm- or cool-colored construction paper three times. Cut out these shapes.

3. Arrange your shapes so you have equal amounts of space between them. Can you see the beats that are created?

4. Save your shapes to use in the Creative Expression activity.

Differentiated Instruction

Reteach	Special Needs	ELL
Have students look at the *Large Prints* and identify the uses of visual harmony.	Some students may find it helpful to begin this project by creating a musical rhythm first, then creating a piece of art to accompany it.	Students may need some focused instruction and practice to respond to questions about how successful they were. "How would your next paper weaving be different?" What would you change? Modeling first and then offering time to practice with a partner can help develop this knowledge.

◀ **Andy Valentine.**
Age 10.

Think about how this student artist used paper weaving to show rhythm.

Creative Expression

How can you show rhythm using paper weaving? Arrange paper strips on a loom and cut out images to create visual beats.

1. Use paper strips to weave over and under the warp of the prepared paper loom.

2. Glue the ends of the strips down.

3. Space your three cutout images from the Practice activity on your paper weaving to create rhythm.

4. Glue the cutout images in place.

Art Criticism

Describe What color scheme did you use? What activity is your cutout image doing?

Analyze How did you arrange the cutouts to create rhythm?

Interpret Clap out the beat to your completed piece.

Decide Do you feel your work is successful? Explain.

Unit 5 • Lesson 2   **163**

Reflect

Time: About 15 minutes

Review and Assess
"How would you explain visual harmony?"
"¿Cómo explicarían la armonía visual?"

Think

The artist used repetition of color, shape, and line to create rhythm in this weaving.

■ Use *Large Prints 69 Hmong Story Cloth* and *70 The Throne of the Third Heaven of the Nation's Millennium General Assembly* to have students identify and describe the uses of visual harmony.

Informal Assessment

■ For standardized-format test practice using this lesson's art content, see pages 56–57 in *Reading and Writing Test Preparation.*

Art Journal: Critical Thinking

Have students answer the four art criticism questions—Describe, Analyze, Interpret, and Decide—in their Art Journals. In small groups, have students discuss their paper weaving.
NSAE 2.a

Art Across the Curriculum

Use these simple ideas to reinforce art concepts across the curriculum.

★ **Persuasive Writing** Have students each write a persuasive advertisement for an event that relates to the action cut-out figure in his or her paper weaving.

★ **Math** Talk about how musical notes and rests, other than whole notes and rests, are expressed as fractions to indicate how long each is held. You may also want to discuss how beats in musical measures are designated by time signatures.

★ **Science** Color schemes based on nature are often harmonious. Discuss how Sir Isaac Newton's first color wheel, developed in 1666, changed how people use and study colors.

★ **Social Studies** Discuss as a class the many different roles music plays in cultures throughout the world.

★ **Technology** Have students copy and paste clip art into a paint program. Visit **SRAonline.com** to print detailed instructions for this activity.
NSAE 6.b

Lesson 2 — Rhythm

Wrap-Up

Extra! For the Art Specialist

Time: About 30 minutes

Focus

Have students study **Large Print 69** *Hmong Story Cloth* and **70** *The Throne of the Third Heaven of the Nation's Millennium General Assembly* and discuss how some artists create rhythm by repeating an art element within a work of art.

Teach

Discuss how artists use rhythm to arrange the art elements by having students look closely at the fine art examples. Demonstrate making a loom and using the over-under method (basket weave) prior to starting this lesson.

Reflect

Have students evaluate their artwork using the four steps of art criticism. Encourage them to locate and describe the elements repeated to create rhythm.

Alternate Activity

Materials:
- 9" × 12" cardboard
- scissors
- rulers
- pencils
- cut fabric strips or yarn in both warm and cool colors
- masking tape
- string for warping (optional)

1. Make a cardboard loom, wrap the loom, and attach a piece of string or yarn through the first slit. Pull this up to the top slit across from it, then over the back and down to the bottom.

2. Select the first piece of fabric and begin weaving. This is done by repeatedly tying the fabric at the bottom of the first string. Go over the second string, under the third, over the fourth. On the second row, weave in the opposite direction.

3. If you run out of the first piece of fabric, tie the second piece to the end. Alternate between warm and cool colors.

Research in Art Education

"If perception is basic to all learning, if selective viewing is a desirable kind of behavior, and if conceptualization comes after sensory experiences, then it becomes imperative that teachers provide paths for numerous visual and tactile explorations so as to keep all of the child's senses alive and active." (Herberholz, Barbara, and Lee Hanson. *Early Childhood Art*. New York: McGraw-Hill, 1994.)

Assessment

Use the following rubric to evaluate the artwork students make in the Creative Expression activity and to assess students' understanding of visual rhythm.

Have students complete page 59 or 60 in their *Assessment* books.

	Art History and Culture	Aesthetic Perception	Creative Expression	Art Criticism
3 POINTS	The student can demonstrate knowledge of the lives and artwork of Paul Gauguin and Joan Miró.	The student accurately identifies the visual rhythm used in art.	The student's paper weaving clearly illustrates the use of rhythm.	The student thoughtfully and honestly evaluates own work using the four steps of art criticism.
2 POINTS	The student's knowledge of the lives and works of Paul Gauguin and Joan Miró is weak or incomplete.	The student shows emerging awareness of visual rhythm used in art.	The student's paper weaving shows some awareness of rhythm.	The student attempts to evaluate own work but shows an incomplete understanding of evaluation criteria.
1 POINT	The student cannot demonstrate knowledge of the lives and artwork of Paul Gauguin or Joan Miró.	The student cannot identify visual rhythm used in art.	The student's paper weaving shows no understanding of rhythm.	The student makes no attempt to evaluate own artwork.

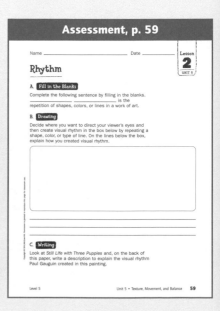

Assessment, p. 59

Name _____ Date _____

Lesson **2** UNIT 5

Rhythm

A. Fill in the Blanks
Complete the following sentence by filling in the blanks.
_____ is the repetition of shapes, colors, or lines in a work of art.

B. Drawing
Decide where you want to direct your viewer's eyes and then create visual rhythm in the box below by repeating a shape, color, or type of line. On the lines below the box, explain how you created visual rhythm.

C. Writing
Look at *Still Life with Three Puppies* and, on the back of this paper, write a description to explain the visual rhythm Paul Gauguin created in this painting.

Level 5   Unit 5 • Texture, Movement, and Balance   59

Lesson 3 Overview

Movement Through Rhythm

Lesson 3 introduces movement through rhythm. The beats and rests of visual rhythm pull the viewer's eyes through a work of art. This creates visual movement.

Objectives

Art History and Culture
To become knowledgeable about the lives and artwork of Jennifer Bartlett and Pablo Picasso

Creative Expression
To create a still-life drawing in the cubist style, repeating shapes and colors to create movement through rhythm

Aesthetic Perception
To identify the creation of visual movement through rhythm in works of art

Art Criticism
To evaluate one's own work using the four steps of art criticism.

Vocabulary Vocabulary

Review the following vocabulary word with students before beginning the lesson.

visual movement *movimiento visual*—the principle of art that leads a viewer's eyes through a work of art

See page 179B for additional vocabulary and Spanish vocabulary resources.

Art Journal: Vocabulary
 Have students add this word to the Vocabulary section of their Art Journals.

Lesson Materials
- complex and nonsymmetrical objects
- drawing paper
- 12" × 18" white drawing paper
- pencils and erasers
- rulers
- colored pencils

Alternate Materials:
- crayons

Program Resources
- *Reading and Writing Test Prep.,* pp. 58–59
- *Transparency 27*
- *Flash Cards 9, 10, 11*
- *Artist Profiles,* pp. 6, 47
- *Animals Through History Time Line*
- *Assessment,* pp. 61–62
- *Large Prints 69* Hmong Story Cloth
- *The National Museum of Women in the Arts Collection*

Concept Trace
Movement Through Rhythm
Introduced: Level 4, Unit 5, Lessons 5, 6
Reinforced: Level 6, Unit 3, Lesson 5

Lesson 3 Arts Integration

Theatre
Complete Unit 5, Lesson 3, on pages 94–95 of *Theatre Arts Connections.*

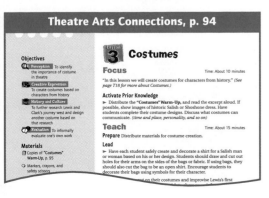

Music
Listen to "Winter," from *The Four Seasons,* by Antonio Vivaldi. This piece is a set of four concertos for violin and orchestra. In each piece, Vivaldi uses rhythms and tone colors to create the feelings of the different seasons. In "Winter," we hear music that suggests freezing cold, stamping of feet, and resting in a place that is warm. Imagine an event for the last exciting section.

Movement & Dance
Students create nonverbal, rhythmic conversations in a group. Assign each student a number from 1 through 4. The students assigned number 1 have four counts to move, using gestures, shapes, and body percussion. These students then hold their last position, and each of the other groups answers them by responding in movement for four counts.

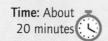

Focus

Time: About 20 minutes

Activate Prior Knowledge

"What do you associate with the word *rhythm*?" "¿Qué asocian con la palabra ritmo?"

- Explain to students that in visual art, rhythm is created by the repetition of elements such as shapes, colors, and lines, rather than sound and time as in music.

Using Literature ⭐ Reading

- Share Mary Hays Weik's Newbery Honor book *The Jazz Man* with the class. Ask students to identify the repetition of elements to create visual movement in the cover art.

Thematic Connection ⭐ Health

- **Dance and Movement:** Encourage students to share some of their experiences with dance and movement. Explain that professional football players sometimes take ballet classes to improve coordination and flexibility. Discuss other benefits dance can have. NSAE 6.a

Introduce the Art

Look

"Let's take a close look at the two works of art." "Vamos a observar detalladamente las dos obras de arte."

Visualizing ⭐ Reading

- Choose a few music selections from different genres either with the class or on your own that would appropriately accompany the artwork in this lesson. Ask students to study both works of art in the lesson while the music is playing, then close their eyes and visualize people dancing to that style of music. Encourage students to describe or share the dance movements they visualized.

🏺 Art History and Culture

Jennifer Bartlett's repetition of geometric shapes and abstract style are similar to Pablo Picasso's painting in this lesson. Bartlett's use of bold, primary colors is unlike *"Ma Jolie" (Woman with Zither or Guitar)*.

💻 Web Connection

Visit http://www.barbarakrakowgallery.com/contentmgr/showdetails.php/id/2417 to view Jennifer Barlett's House.

Movement Through Rhythm

Look at the artwork on these pages. Notice the repeated shapes, colors, and elements, and the negative spaces between them in both paintings. Pay attention to how your eyes are moved through the paintings.

▲ **Jennifer Bartlett.** (American). *Swimmer Lost at Night (for Tom Hess).* 1978.

Two silkscreen pieces on baked-enamel-on-steel units with steel plates and two oil-on-canvas panels. 6 feet 6 inches × 26 feet 5 inches (1.98 × 8.05 m.). Museum of Modern Art, New York, New York.

🏺 Art History and Culture

Art critics have said that the work of Pablo Picasso influenced Jennifer Bartlett's art. What similarities do you notice in these two works of art? What differences do you see?

🏺 Art History and Culture

Jennifer Bartlett

Jennifer Bartlett (jen´ ə fər bärt´ let) (1941–) received her master of fine arts degree from Yale University in 1965. She has developed a distinct style that combines the natural elements of water, fire, air, and earth with an organized and methodical grid that appears in most of her works of art. These repeated grids create a visual rhythm that directs the viewer's eyes in an organized way on the outer layer of Bartlett's work. Meanwhile her paintings that lie underneath often mimic nature's chaos. She cohesively blends the objects and the ideas in her art. These grid-based works that are interpretations of nature have become her signature works.

See pages 24–25 and 16–21 for more about art history and the subject matter.

Artist Profiles, p. 6

Artist Profile

Jennifer Bartlett
b. 1941

Jennifer Bartlett (jen´ ə fər bärt´ let) is an installation artist, painter, printmaker, and sculptor. She was born in Long Beach, California, and studied at Mills College and the Yale School of Art and Architecture. Yale's progressive teaching approach influenced Bartlett's early artwork in the 1960s and 1970s, and she has experimented with concepts and materials throughout her artistic career.

Study both works of art for examples of movement through rhythm.

▶ What repeated positive space directs your eyes from one side of Jennifer Bartlett's *Swimmer Lost at Night (for Tom Hess)* to the other?

▶ Where are the negative spaces in this artwork that break up the flow and create a rhythm?

▶ What elements direct your eyes through Pablo Picasso's painting?

▶ Do your eyes move smoothly through this painting, or do they jump around?

◀ **Pablo Picasso.** (Spanish). *"Ma Jolie" (Woman with a Zither or Guitar).* 1911–1912.

Oil on canvas. 39⅜ × 25¾ inches (100.03 × 65.41 cm.). Museum of Modern Art, New York, New York.

Aesthetic Perception

Seeing Like an Artist Notice how some dances have movements that are smooth, slow, and fluid, while others are rigid, quick, and choppy. How would you show these movements in a painting?

Art History and Culture

Pablo Picasso

Pablo Picasso (pä´ blō pi kä´ sō) (1881–1973) was born in Spain. His father, an art teacher, taught him to draw and paint. At the age of fourteen, Picasso had a painting accepted into an exhibition. He became the most influential artist of the 1900s. He experimented with many styles and invented what became known as cubism. Picasso's paintings changed as his life changed. When he was depressed he painted in blue. When he fell in love he painted happier scenes in shades of pink. Picasso created drawings, oil paintings, ceramic pieces, sculpture, prints, and engravings.

See pages 24–25 and 16–21 for more about art history and the subject matter.

Artist Profiles, p. 47

◆ Artist Profile ◆
Pablo Picasso
1881–1973

Pablo Picasso (pä´ blō pi kä´ sō) was born in Málaga, Spain. He did poorly in school but his father, an art teacher, taught him to draw and paint. Picasso learned quickly. When he was only 14 he had a painting accepted for an exhibition. Picasso moved to Paris, France when he was 18. At the time he was very poor. Thieves stole what little he had, yet they left his now valuable drawings. In time the outgoing Picasso made many friends. Among them were the American writers Ernest Hemingway and Gertrude Stein and the Russian composer Igor Stravinsky. Picasso painted at night and slept late most mornings. He worked hard his entire life. He completed 200 paintings the year he turned 90.

Study

▶ Each of the four panels moves the viewer's eyes from one to the other. The positive spaces separated by the grids and within each panel also direct the viewer's eyes through the two panels on the left. The repetition of the grid design that appears in the two panels on the right continues to move the viewer's eyes.

▶ The white steel grids offer the viewer's eyes rests between positive spaces and creates a rhythm.

▶ The straight lines, the repetition of similar colors, and the rectangular shapes create a rhythm and move the viewer's eye through Pablo Picasso's painting.

▶ The viewer's eyes jump unevenly through this painting.

■ For more examples of abstract/nonobjective art, see *The National Museum of Women in the Arts Collection.*

Art Journal: Writing

Have students write their own explanations of visual rhythm in their Art Journals. Ask students to describe their preferred type of visual rhythm in a work of art. Do they like random rhythms or regular rhythms?

Aesthetic Perception

Design Awareness Expose students to various genres of dance. Ask them to make connections between dance styles and movements in art.

Developing Visual Literacy Ask students to share their own explanations of the titles of the works of art in this lesson.

Web Connection

Visit **http://www.moma.org/collection/ provenance/items/176.45.html** for information about this work of art as well as many others created by Pablo Picasso.

Teach

Time: About 45 minutes

"How can you create movement by repeating shapes and color in a work of art?" "¿Cómo pueden crear movimiento repitiendo las figuras y el color en una obra de arte?"

- Read and discuss the definitions of *movement* and *visual movement* on page 166.

Practice

Materials: drawing paper, complex or nonsymmetrical objects, pencils and erasers

- Review the Practice activity directions with students on page 166.
- Ask students to select a complex or nonsymmetrical object to draw. Have students study the chosen object from different points of view and then sketch a few of these images. Ask students to overlap their drawings from each point of view and notice the changes in the object's contour.

Creative Expression

Materials: 12″ × 18″ white drawing paper, pencils, erasers, rulers, colored pencils

Alternate Materials: crayons

- Refer to the additional notes on page 243 in the Activity Tips section for steps to complete in preparation for the Creative Expression Activity.
- Distribute the materials.
- Have students follow the directions on page 167.
- Review the Activity Tips on page 243 for visual examples of this lesson's activity.

Art Journal: Brainstorming

Have students write their impression of the cubist-style paintings they have seen. Discuss how cubist works of art involve carefully calculating the position of each object to expose the viewer to viewpoints around the entire scene. Ask students to write about how their initial impression might have changed after learning about the process and purpose of cubism.
NSAE 5.b

Using Movement through Rhythm

Repeated windows on a building make your eyes move across the building. When riding in a car, have you ever noticed fence posts or telephone poles? The repeated posts and poles pull your eyes along as you are driving by. These are examples of movement. **Movement** is the principle of art that leads a viewer's eyes through a work of art.

Artists create **visual movement** in a work of art by repeating elements or objects.

Notice how the repeated lines, shapes, and colors lead your eyes through the scene below.

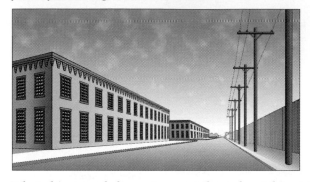

What objects and elements repeat throughout this picture?

Practice

Make sketches of one object from different points of view.

1. Choose a complex or nonsymmetrical object.
2. Sketch this object from different points of view on one sheet of paper.
3. Make the sketches overlap.
4. Notice the contour changes.

Differentiated Instruction

Reteach
Have students look through their *Art Connections* textbook for examples of visual movement. Ask students to look for a work of art that creates a slow, steady movement with large amounts of negative space, another that has a quicker rhythm with less negative space, and a third that is random.

Special Needs
Some students lacking fine-motor skills may find it difficult to create the value gradations necessary for cubism using colored pencils. Have thicker drawing media available, such as graphite or conté crayons.

ELL
Guiding students step-by-step through the text's questions can help you adjust your presentation of the lesson as needed to ensure comprehension. You can ask students to respond physically, with a partner, or chorally to questions to monitor understanding.

◀ **Seth Rujiraviriyapinyo.**
Age 11.

Think about how the artist created movement by repeating shapes and colors in his cubist-style still life.

 Creative Expression

How can you create movement by repeating an element within a work of art? Create a still-life drawing using the cubist style. Repeat shapes and colors to show movement.

1. Select your best sketch and transfer it to your drawing paper.

2. Use a ruler to draw three straight lines crossing the short span of the paper.

3. Use a ruler to draw two straight lines crossing the long span of the paper.

4. Choose cool- or warm-colored pencils, and color in your shapes.

5. Color the background using contrasting colors.

6. Do not let areas of the same color touch one another.

 Art Criticism

Describe What objects did you use? What colors did you select for your objects?

Analyze Describe how the repeated shapes and colors create rhythm.

Interpret Explain how the rhythm of the shapes and colors affect the expressive quality of your work.

Decide Do you feel your work is successful? Explain.

Unit 5 • Lesson 3 **167**

 **R** **eflect** Time: About 15 minutes

Review and Assess
"How would you explain visual movement?"
"¿Cómo explicarian el movimiento visual?"

Think
The artist repeated free-form and geometric shapes in addition to colors throughout this work of art to create visual movement.

- Use *Large Print 69* Hmong Story Cloth to have students identify and describe the use of rhythm through visual movement.

Informal Assessment
- For standardized-format test practice using this lesson's art content, see pages 58–59 in *Reading and Writing Test Preparation.*

Art Journal: Critical Thinking
Have students answer the four art criticism questions—Describe, Analyze, Interpret, and Decide—in their Art Journals. In small groups, have students discuss the use of movement in their cubist drawings.
NSAE 2.a

Art Across the Curriculum

Use these simple ideas to reinforce art concepts across the curriculum.

★ **Poetry Writing** Have students write a poem about an event from two different points of view.

★ **Math** Use creative dance movements to illustrate the use of positive and negative space to create rhythm using both physical movement and visual movements.

★ **Science** Discuss how dancers consider space, energy, and force when developing creative movement. Allow students to demonstrate scientific principles such as molecules' reaction to temperature changes with their original creative-movement arrangements.

★ **Social Studies** Trace the roots of dance styles and note how they have changed and how they have stayed the same.

★ **Technology** Have students create visual movement by copying and pasting similar shapes, colors, and clip art in original paint-program designs. Visit **SRAonline.com** to print detailed instructions for this activity. NSAE 6.b

Movement Through Rhythm

Extra! For the Art Specialist

Time: About 45 minutes

Focus

Have students study **Large Print 69** *Hmong Story Cloth* and discuss how some artists lead the viewer's eye through an artwork (movement) by repeating an art element (rhythm). Have students describe the lines, shapes, and colors they see. How was rhythm created?

Teach

Explain to students that they will be creating a mobile. By moving from lightest tint to darkest shade on cut-out shapes in ascending size, movement through rhythm will be created. Demonstrate cutting and tracing a shape.

Reflect

Have students evaluate their artwork using the four steps of art criticism. Encourage them to locate and describe the visual movement.

Alternate Activity

Materials:

- 4" × 4" mat board (5 per student)
- pencils and erasers
- scissors
- rulers (optional)
- string or thread
- hole punch
- hanger
- acrylic paints
- paintbrushes
- water containers
- mixing plates

1. Draw a shape on the first piece of board. Cut out the shape. Trace and cut three more shapes so they are different sizes.

2. Arrange shapes from smallest to largest and paint the center shape with your favorite color.

3. Mix equal amounts of this color with white and paint the next-smaller shape this tint. Then add more white to your mix and paint the smallest shape. Mix equal amounts of black and the original color and paint the next-to-largest shape this color. Add a little more black to create a darker shade for the largest shape.

4. Punch a hole in each shape. Attach a piece of thread to each shape and then to the bottom of a hanger.

Research in Art Education

Successful integration of the arts includes lesson plans based on state standards, activities with well-defined objectives and planned assessment (using rubrics or scoring guides) that match these objectives, and content and art lessons that are of equal importance ("Chicago Arts Partnership in Education," in *Champions of Change*, p. 54). Using creative movement to teach principles in academic areas such as math, science, language arts, and social studies can provide solid, meaningful, and memorable connections for students.

Assessment

Use the following rubric to evaluate the artwork students make in the Creative Expression activity and to assess students' understanding of movement through rhythm.

Have students complete page 61 or 62 in their *Assessment* books.

	Art History and Culture	Aesthetic Perception	Creative Expression	Art Criticism
3 POINTS	The student can demonstrate knowledge of the lives and artwork of Jennifer Bartlett and Pablo Picasso.	The student accurately identifies visual movement created by rhythm in art.	The student's cubist drawing clearly illustrates the use of visual movement through rhythm.	The student thoughtfully and honestly evaluates own work using the four steps of art criticism.
2 POINTS	The student's knowledge of the lives and artwork of Jennifer Bartlett and Pablo Picasso is weak.	The student shows emerging awareness of visual movement created by rhythm in art.	The student's cubist drawing shows some awareness of visual movement through rhythm.	The student attempts to evaluate own work but shows an incomplete understanding of evaluation criteria.
1 POINT	The student cannot demonstrate knowledge of the lives and artwork of Jennifer Bartlett or Pablo Picasso.	The student cannot identify visual movement created by rhythm in art.	The student's cubist drawing shows no understanding of visual movement through rhythm.	The student makes no attempt to evaluate own artwork.

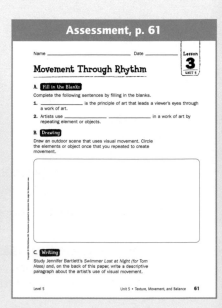

Assessment, p. 61

Name _____ Date _____ Lesson **3** UNIT 5

Movement Through Rhythm

A. Fill in the Blanks
Complete the following sentences by filling in the blanks.

1. _____ is the principle of art that leads a viewer's eyes through a work of art.

2. Artists use _____ in a work of art by repeating element or objects.

B. Drawing
Draw an outdoor scene that uses visual movement. Circle the elements or object once that you repeated to create movement.

C. Writing
Study Jennifer Bartlett's *Swimmer Lost at Night (for Tom Hess)* and, on the back of this paper, write a descriptive paragraph about the artist's use of visual movement.

Level 5   Unit 5 • Texture, Movement, and Balance   61

Lesson 4 Overview: Formal Balance

Lesson 4 introduces formal balance. Artists use formal balance to organize an artwork so that the opposite sides are equal or very similar.

Objectives

Art History and Culture
To become knowledgeable about the art of the Qing Dynasty and the life and artwork of Diego Rivera

Creative Expression
To create a modified batik self-portrait using formal balance

Aesthetic Perception
To identify the use of formal balance in art and the environment

Art Criticism
To evaluate one's own work using the four steps of art criticism

Vocabulary Vocabulary

Review the following vocabulary words with students.

balance equilibrio—the principle of design that relates to visual weight in a work of art

formal balance equilibrio formal—when equal, or very similar, elements are placed on opposite sides of a central axis

symmetry simetría—a type of formal balance that occurs when two sides are mirror images of each other

See page 179B for additional vocabulary and Spanish vocabulary resources.

Art Journal: Vocabulary
Have students add these words to the Vocabulary section of their Art Journals.

Lesson Materials
- mirrors
- sketch paper
- pencils and erasers
- black markers
- 12" × 14" cardboard sheet
- 10" × 12" muslin or white cotton fabric
- masking tape
- white school glue
- toothpicks
- watercolor paints
- paintbrushes
- water containers
- newspaper

Alternate Materials:
- light-colored bed sheets

Program Resources
- *Reading and Writing Test Prep.,* pp. 60–61
- *Transparency 28*
- *Flash Card 12*
- *Artist Profiles,* pp. 80, 49
- *Animals Through History Time Line*
- *Assessment,* pp. 63–64
- *Large Print 69* Hmong Story Cloth
- *The National Museum of Women in the Arts Collection*

Concept Trace
Formal Balance
Introduced: Level 4, Unit 6, Lesson 1
Reinforced: Level 6, Unit 4, Lessons 1, 2

Lesson 4 Arts Integration

Theatre
Complete Unit 5, Lesson 4, on pages 96–97 of *Theatre Arts Connections.*

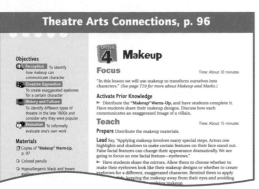

Theatre Arts Connections, p. 96

Music
 Sing or listen to "This Land is Your Land." This song is verse and refrain, but it is in AA form. What does this say about the music in the verse as compared to the refrain?

Movement & Dance
Symmetrical balance is secure and stable. Have students work with a partner to find a way to create symmetrical counterbalances together. Have partners begin with the following examples: Stand side by side with feet touching, holding hands, and lean away from each other. Lie on the floor with legs up, pressing feet together, and lift your hips off the ground. Stand back to back and walk your feet away from the center, maintaining symmetrical counterbalance by pressing your backs together.

Formal Balance

Focus

Time: About 20 minutes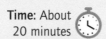

Activate Prior Knowledge

"Think about a stereo that has two speakers. What happens when you turn the balance all the way to the right? What if you put the balance in the center?" "Piensen en un equipo de sonido con dos cornetas. ¿Qué sucede cuando giran totalmente el botón de equilibrio hacia la derecha? ¿Qué pasaría si lo ponen en el medio?"

- Discuss with students their answers to the above questions. Ask students why they think balance is appealing to their eyes and their ears.

Using Literature ☆ Reading

- Share Ann Cameron's book *The Most Beautiful Place in the World* with the class. Talk about how the main character is able to balance his difficult situations by weighing what is truly important in life.

Thematic Connection ☆ Science

- **Balance:** Ask students to look around the classroom and choose two objects that they think would balance in weight, then choose two objects that seem to balance in size and compare the pairs.

Introduce the Art

Look

"Let's take a close look at the two works of art." "Vamos a observar detalladamente las dos obras de arte."

Compare and Contrast ☆ Reading

- Have students list the similarities and the differences in the two works of art. Both pieces are formally balanced. The elements seen on either side of the paintings are not identical but are very similar.

Art History and Culture

Diego Rivera studied Italian Renaissance frescos and found the medium he was searching for. When working with frescoes pigment is applied to thin layers of wet plaster then absorbed so the painting becomes part of the wall.

🖥 Web Connection

Visit **http://www.metmuseum.org/toah/hd/qing_1/hd_qing_1.htm** to learn more about the Qing Dynasty and their art culture.

Look at the artwork on these pages. Imagine a line drawn down the center from the top to the bottom of each painting and compare the opposite sides. Does one side of the painting draw your attention more than the other, or do the sides seem balanced?

◄ **Artist unknown.** (Qing Dynasty). *Portrait of Yinxiang, The First Prince of Yi. (1686–1730).* 1905.

Ink and color on silk. 73½ × 48 inches (186.69 × 121.92 cm). Arthur M. Sackler Gallery, Smithsonian Institution, Washington, D.C.

Art History and Culture

Diego Rivera is credited with reintroducing fresco painting into modern art in Mexico and the United States. Frescoes are murals painted on fresh plaster.

🏺 Art History and Culture

Qing Dynasty

In 1644 the Mongol people defeated the Ming Dynasty and introduced China to the Qing Dynasty, which reigned for almost 300 years. Because Confucian tradition states that no man can serve two dynasties, many remaining Ming loyalists left their positions of public office. This created a culture of people who now had time to pursue artistic interests. Officials removed important collections of master artists. For this reason, a large number of landscapes and portraits emerged from this time as artists looked to nature and to royalty for inspiration.

See pages 24–25 and 16–21 for more about art history and the subject matter.

Artist Profiles, p. 80

Artist Profile

Portrait of Yinxiang, the First Prince of Yi

The portrait was made by an unknown Chinese artist sometime during the Manchu Qing dynasty.

◄ **Artist unknown.** (China). *Portrait of Yinxiang, the First Prince of Yi.* 1686–1730.

Study both works of art for examples of balance.

▶ Describe how the objects, colors, and lines are arranged in each work of art. How are they similar? How are they different?

▶ Find the center of each painting. Compare and contrast what you see on the right and left sides.

▶ Are both sides of each painting identical? Where do you see differences?

▲ **Diego Rivera.** (Mexican).
Flower Day. 1925.
· ·
Oil on canvas. 58 × 47½ inches
(147.32 × 120.65 cm.). Los Angeles County
Museum of Art, Los Angeles, California.

Aesthetic Perception

Design Awareness Look around your school for examples of things that have been made to look exactly the same on both sides, for example, a basketball or a chalkboard.

Art History and Culture

Diego Rivera

Diego Rivera (dē ā´ gō rē bā´ rä) (1886–1957) wanted to create art that could be enjoyed and understood by ordinary people. For this reason, he focused on simple designs and interesting subjects. Public murals were ideal for him because people could see his art without paying. Crowds gathered to watch him paint these murals on public walls and tell stories as he worked. Rivera completed about 300 frescoes, which are paintings on fresh, moist plaster. His third wife was painter Frida Kahlo.

See pages 24–25 and 16–21 for more about art history and the subject matter.

Artist Profiles, p. 49

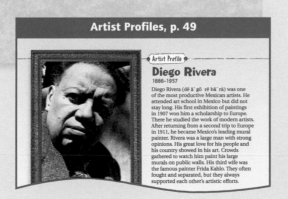

◆ Artist Profile ◆
Diego Rivera
1886–1957

Diego Rivera (dē ā´ gō rē bā´ rä) was one of the most productive Mexican artists. He attended art school in Mexico but did not stay long. His first exhibition of paintings in 1907 won him a scholarship to Europe. There he studied the work of modern artists. After returning from a second trip to Europe in 1911, he became Mexico's leading mural painter. Rivera was a large man with strong opinions. His great love for his people and his country showed in his art. Crowds gathered to watch him paint his large murals on public walls. His third wife was the famous painter Frida Kahlo. They often fought and separated, but they always supported each other's artistic efforts.

Study NSAE 4.a

▶ Similar warm colors are used in both paintings. The brighter colors are placed toward the center of both paintings. The lines in *Winxiang, Prince Yi,* are more definite and straight. The lines in Rivera's painting are rounded and softer.

▶ Very similar objects, colors, and lines are used on both sides of each work of art. The lines vary in *Winxiang, Prince Yi,* as the garment seam appears on the left side where the subject's arm is folded higher than on the right side. The people kneeling in the foreground of Rivera's painting differ. Different lines are used in the girl's braids on the left from the lines used on the right.

▶ The sides of each painting are not identical but they are similar. The differences can be seen in the subject's right arm and in his garment in the Qing Dynasty painting. There are differences in the people kneeling in Rivera's painting.

■ For more examples of portraits, see *The National Museum of Women in the Arts Collection.*

Art Journal: Writing

Ask students to look at the artwork that appears in the lesson and judge the balance of each. Ask students to explain what seems to give each side of the painting weight and how that is balanced by the opposite side.

Aesthetic Perception

Design Awareness Display examples of common school objects that are symmetrical and others that are similar but not identical on each side. Ask students to categorize each item into the two classifications.

Developing Visual Literacy Ask students if they have ever posed for a portrait and explain if it was a painting, drawing, photograph, or other form of media used to capture their image. Have students compare the mood of Prince Yi in the painting with that of their own portrait.

Web Connection

Visit **www. http://www.diegorivera.com/index.php** to learn more of Diego Rivera's life and his work. You may want to review this informational Web site before sharing it with the class.

 **each**   **Time:** About 45 minutes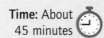

"How do you recognize formal balance in a work of art?" "¿Cómo reconocen el equilibrio formal en una obra de arte?"

- Read and discuss the definitions of *balance, formal balance, central axis,* and *symmetry* on page 170.

Practice

Materials: mirrors, sketch paper, pencils, erasers

- Review the Practice activity directions with students on page 170.

- Have students fold a piece of drawing paper in half lengthwise then unfold it leaving a crease down the length of the paper. Provide mirrors for students to use to look at themselves.
NSAE 2.b

Creative Expression

Materials: black markers, 12" × 14" cardboard sheet, 10" × 12" muslin or white cotton fabric, masking tape, white school glue, toothpicks, watercolor paints, paintbrushes, water containers, newspaper

Alternate Materials: light-colored bed sheets

- This activity is a modification of the batik process.

- Refer to the additional notes on page 243 in the Activity Tips section for steps to complete in preparation for the Creative Expression activity.

- Distribute the materials.

- Have students follow the directions on page 171.

- Review the Activity Tips on page 243 for visual examples of this lesson's activity.

Art Journal: Brainstorming

Ask students to write a list of items that are symmetrical and a list of items with approximate symmetry in their Art Journals.

Using Formal Balance

Balance is the principle of design that relates to visual weight in a work of art. One type of balance is formal balance.

Formal balance occurs when equal, or very similar, elements are placed on opposite sides of a central line called a central axis.

The **central axis** may be part of the design, or it may be an imaginary line. The central axis, or central line, divides the design in half.

Use an imaginary vertical central axis to divide this photograph. Notice that there is similar weight on both sides, but that they do not look exactly the same.

Symmetry is a special type of formal balance. The two halves of a symmetrically balanced object are the same. They are mirror images of each other.

Practice

Draw a formal self-portrait. Use pencil.

1. Fold a piece of drawing paper in half.
2. Look at yourself in a mirror.
3. Draw your self-portrait. Look at the similarities and differences on either side of the central axis.

Differentiated Instruction

Reteach

Have students look through the *Large Prints* to find examples of fine art that uses formal balance with symmetry and with approximate symmetry.

Special Needs

Consider displaying the portraits in a quilt-like format. This is a perfect opportunity to showcase the work of all students and to reinforce prior lesson concepts. Students will be able to see the ways that the repeated colors and head shapes move their eyes through the work of art.

ELL

You may want to check frequently for students' comprehension of a concept before moving to independent work. As you explain or demonstrate a concept's meaning, you might ask quick questions designed for one- or two-word responses.

Think about how the student artist used formal balance in her self-portrait.

Creative Expression

Use a batik method to create a self-portrait with formal balance.

1. Tape your self-portrait from the Practice activity to the sheet of cardboard.
2. Lay the sheet of fabric over your self-portrait and tape it in place. You should be able to see your drawing through the fabric.
3. Partially open the glue bottle, and practice drawing with the glue on a separate sheet of paper. Carefully trace your self-portrait with glue and allow it to dry.
4. Paint between the glue lines with watercolor paints.

Art Criticism

Describe What colors did you choose to paint your self-portrait? Are they realistic?

Analyze What type of formal balance did you use in your batik self-portrait?

Interpret How does the type of balance you used affect the mood of your self-portrait?

Decide Did you encounter any problems during this project? Explain.

Unit 5 • Lesson 4   **171**

Art Across the Curriculum

Use these simple ideas to reinforce art concepts across the curriculum.

★ **Descriptive Writing** Have students each write a descriptive paragraph explaining his or her self-portrait to someone who is unable to see it.

★ **Math** Have students create geometric shapes and original designs using tiles to create symmetry.

★ **Science** Ask students to collect pictures or objects that represent symmetry found in nature.

★ **Social Studies** Have students look at flags for examples of formal balance.

★ **Technology** Have students create a design with formal balance using the copy and paste options in a paint program. Visit **SRAonline.com** to print detailed instructions for this activity.
NSAE 6.b

 Reflect

Time: About 15 minutes

Review and Assess

"Were you able to create a batik-style self-portrait using formal balance?" "¿Pudieron crear un retrato estilo batik usando equilibrio formal?"

Think

The artist used formal balance to create approximate symmetry on either side of her face in this batik-style self-portrait.

■ Use *Large Prints 69* Hmong Story Cloth and *70* The Throne of the Third Heaven of the Nation's Millennium General Assembly to have students identify and describe the use of formal balance.

Informal Assessment

■ For standardized-format test practice using this lesson's art content, see pages 60–61 in *Reading and Writing Test Preparation.*

Art Journal: Critical Thinking

Have students answer the four art criticism questions—Describe, Analyze, Interpret, and Decide—in their Art Journals. In small groups, have students discuss their self-portraits.
NSAE 2.a

■ Have students look at *Large Prints 69* Hmong Story Cloth and *Winxiang, Prince, Yi* to compare cultural themes honoring Chinese history.

Lesson 4 Wrap-Up

Formal Balance

Extra! For the Art Specialist

Time: About 50 minutes

Focus

Have students study **Large Print 69** *Hmong Story Cloth* and learn how some artists use formal balance to organize an artwork so that opposite sides are the same or very similar.

Teach

Explain to students that they will be creating self-portraits using a print-making technique known as a collograph. Demonstrate cutting the shape of a face and cutting out the various eye shapes (ellipse for the eye, circle for the iris, and a smaller circle for the pupil) and layering them. Explain that a collograph is like a collage, but that a print is made with it.

Reflect

Have students evaluate their artworks using the four steps of art criticism. Encourage them to describe how formal balance was used.

Alternate Activity

Materials:
- Art Journal
- mirror
- 8" × 11" tag board
- 9" × 12" black construction paper (3 per student)
- pencils, erasers
- scissors
- white printing ink
- brayer (or brushes)
- inking tray (or paper plates)
- newspaper

1. Draw a self-portrait in your Art Journal.

2. Cut out the shape of the head and neck. Cut out the shapes needed to form the eyes, nose, mouth, ears, and eyebrows. Cut out shapes to create hair. Use glue to create a design in the background.

3. Number 1 to 3 on the back of the paper. Squirt ink into the center of the tray. Use the brayer to roll out the ink. Roll a layer of ink onto the plate making sure to create an even coating of ink. Place paper on top of the inked image. Rub the back of the paper. Gently pull off.

4. Make two more prints.

Research in Art Education

It has been proven that "at the level of neuro-function, learning experiences unequivocally impact future learning experiences." While more research is still needed on exactly how the reorganization of neural pathways and receptors impact students' transfer of skills from the arts to reading and math, it is reasonable to assume that experiences with the arts may "enhance performance in related skills" ("The Arts and the Transfer of Learning," in *Critical Links*, p. 152). When studying formal balance, students are learning to look for mathematical patterns that occur in many curricular areas.

Assessment

Use the following rubric to evaluate the artwork students make in the Creative Expressions activity and to assess students' understanding of formal balance.

Have students complete page 63 or 64 in their *Assessment* books.

	Art History and Culture	Aesthetic Perception	Aesthetic Perception	Art Criticism
3 POINTS	The student can demonstrate knowledge of the Qing Dynasty and the life and artwork of Diego Rivera.	The student accurately identifies formal balance in art and in the environment.	The student's self-portrait clearly illustrates the use of formal balance.	The student thoughtfully and honestly evaluates own work using the four steps of art criticism.
2 POINTS	The student's knowledge of the Qing Dynasty and the life and artwork of Diego Rivera is weak or incomplete.	The student shows emerging awareness of formal balance in art and in the environment.	The student's self-portrait shows some awareness of formal balance.	The student attempts to evaluate own work but shows an incomplete understanding of evaluation criteria.
1 POINT	The student cannot demonstrate knowledge of the Qing Dynasty or the life and artwork of Diego Rivera.	The student cannot identify formal balance in art or in the environment.	The student's self-portrait shows no understanding of formal balance.	The student makes no attempt to evaluate own artwork.

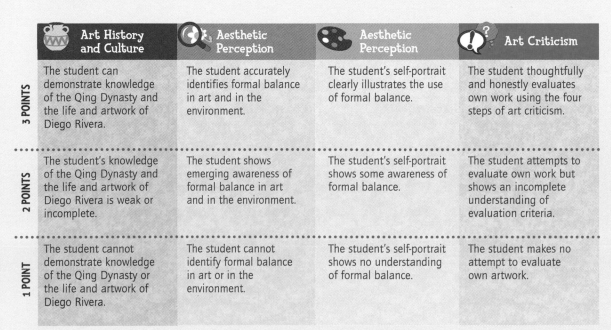

Assessment, p. 63

Name _____ Date _____

Formal Balance — Lesson 4, UNIT 5

A. Matching
Match each term in Column 1 to its definition in Column 2.

Column 1
___ 1. balance
___ 2. formal balance
___ 3. central axis
___ 4. symmetry

Column 2
a. the real or imaginary line that divides a design in half
b. the principle of design that relates to visual weight in a work of art
c. a type of formal balance in which the two halves are exactly the same
d. occurs when equal or very similar elements are placed on opposite sides of a central axis

B. Drawing
Draw a design that shows formal balance. Lightly draw the central axis.

C. Writing
Study *Flower Day* and, on the back of this paper, write a description of Diego Rivera's use of formal balance.

Level 5   Unit 5 • Texture, Movement, and Balance   63

Informal Balance

Lesson 5 introduces informal balance. Artists use informal balance when two unlike objects in an artwork have equal visual weight.

Objectives

Art History and Culture

To become knowledgeable about the lives and the artwork of Sofonisba Anguissola and James Tissot

Creative Expression

To plan and create a still-life painting using asymmetrical balance

Aesthetic Perception

To identify the use of informal balance in art and in the environment

Art Criticism

To evaluate one's own work using the four steps of art criticism

Vocabulary ⭐ Vocabulary

Review the following vocabulary words with students.

informal balance equilibrio informal—a way of organizing parts of a design so that unlike objects have equal eye attraction

asymmetry asimetría—looks balanced even if it is not the same on both sides; informal balance

negative space espacio negativo—the areas around an object or group of objects

See page 179B for additional Spanish vocabulary resources.

Art Journal: Vocabulary

Have students add these words to the Vocabulary section of their Art Journals.

Lesson Materials

- 12" × 18" white drawing paper
- pencils
- liquid tempera paint
- found objects
- paper towels and paper plates
- paintbrushes
- newspapers

Alternate Materials:
- colored pencils
- watercolor paints

Program Resources

- *Reading and Writing Test Prep.*, pp. 62–63
- *Transparency 29*
- *Flash Card 13*
- *Artist Profiles*, pp. 5, 59
- *Animals Through History Time Line*
- *Assessment*, pp. 65–66
- *Large Prints 69* Hmong Story Cloth and *70* The Throne of the Third Heaven of the Nation's Millennium General Assembly
- *The National Museum of Women in the Arts Collection*

Concept Trace

Informal Balance
Introduced: Level 4, Unit 6, Lesson 2

Reinforced: Level 6, Unit 4, Lesson 3

Lesson 5 Arts Integration

Theatre

Complete Unit 5, Lesson 5, on pages 98–99 of *Theatre Arts Connections.*

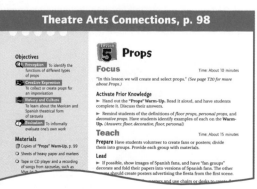

Music

Balance in music describes the manner in which different parts of a composition are performed simultaneously, to make the desired blend. Listen to "Akinla," from *African Suite,* by Fela Sowande. Discuss whether all parts are equal in dynamics at all times.

Movement & Dance

Have students work with a partner to find a way to create asymmetrical counterbalance. Have partners begin with the following examples. Extend arms forward and hold onto each other's shoulders. Lean into each other while maintaining balance. One person is a center pillar that is leaning or pulling. The other person leans away from the center pillar.

 **ocus**

Time: About 20 minutes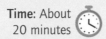

Activate Prior Knowledge

"Have you ever had to organize and arrange items in a small space?" "¿Alguna vez han tenido que organizar y ordenar artículos en un espacio pequeño?"

■ Discuss the question and then have students arrange a few items from their desks using informal balance.

Using Literature ⭐ Reading

■ Share with the class Zilpha Keatley Snyder's novel *The Egypt Game*. Have students take some time to look at the cover and find examples of informal balance, and then read an exciting tale of two girls' involvement in a fantasy game.

Thematic Connection ⭐ Social Studies

■ **Games:** Ask students to explain their favorite games and whom they play these with. Discuss games from other countries and cultures, for example, the African game *Mancala*.

Introduce the Art

Look

"Let's take a close look at the two works of art." "Vamos a observar detalladamente las dos obras de arte."

Using Literature ⭐ Reading

■ **Point of View:** Ask students to suggest where the artist was positioned while painting each of the works of art. Have students hypothesize how the painting would be different if the viewer's point of view was moved to a different area.

 Art History and Culture

King Phillip II of Spain was not only English Queen Elizabeth's enemy, but he was also her brother-in-law. He was married to Queen Elizabeth's sister, Mary. After Mary's death, King Phillip II proposed to Queen Elizabeth, but she refused. England's fleet defeated the attack of the Spanish Armada.

💻 **Web Connection**

Visit **www.italian-art.org/women/artists/ anguissola/** to see more of Sofonisba Anguissola's artwork and learn more about her life.

Informal Balance

▲ **Sofonisba Anguissola.** (Italian). *Artist's Sisters Playing Chess and their Governess.* 1555.

Oil on canvas. $28\frac{1}{3} \times 38\frac{1}{3}$ inches. (72 × 97 cm.). Poznań National Museum, Poznań, Poland.

Look at the artwork on these pages. Notice the people and objects that are arranged on each side of the paintings. Are the paintings symmetrical? The artists used different sizes, colors, textures, and positions to balance these paintings.

 Art History and Culture

Sofonisba Anguissola was one of the first women to gain an international reputation as a painter. She worked as a court portraitist from 1559 to 1573 for King Philip II of Spain.

 Art History and Culture

Sofonisba Anguissola

Sofonisba Anguissola (sō fa nēz´ bä äng gwēs´ sō lä) (1532–1625) was internationally famous in her own lifetime at a time when only men usually achieved such celebrity. She was born into an aristocratic family in Italy. As children, she and her four sisters studied with local artists. Only Sofonisba continued painting as a professional. She became a notable portraitist. Her international fame inspired many young women to pursue their dream of becoming professional artists.

See pages 24–25 and 16–21 for more about art history and the subject matter.

Artist Profiles, p. 5

Artist Profile

Sofonisba Anguissola
1532-1625

Sofonisba Anguissola (sō fō nēz´ ba ang gwō´ shō lä) was born in 1532 in the northern Italian city of Cremona. Her family encouraged her and her five sisters to take art lessons and to be creative. They were so talented that travelers would go out of their way to visit the family. Anguissola's father arranged for her to travel to Rome to study with Michelangelo, who was the best living artist in Italy. In 1559, Anguissola was invited to become the court painter of King Philip II of Spain. She remained at the court for 20 years. Her professional career as a painter ended when she married in 1560, but she continued to paint for the

▲ **James Tissot.** (French). *Women of Paris: The Circus Lover.* 1883–1885.

Oil on canvas. 58 × 40 inches (147.32 × 101.6 cm.).
Museum of Fine Arts, Boston, Massachusetts.

Study both works of art to find examples of informal balance.

▶ Identify the important figures in each painting.

▶ How are the figures arranged in these paintings?

▶ Do some of the figures in these paintings require more attention than others from the viewer?

▶ Where are the darkest and lightest areas in each painting? How does the placement of these areas affect the mood in each painting?

Study

▶ Anguissola: the sister wearing red; Tissot: the woman in the audience and the performers.

▶ Both artists have used informal balance, or asymmetry, when arranging the figures in these paintings.

▶ Possible answers: Anguissola: The game board is in the center. The trees and landscape are used to divide the sisters. Tissot: In the circus tent, the railing, the chairs, and the members of the audience divide the viewer from the perfomer.

▶ Possible answers are: Anguissola: The lightest area is the distance, or the landscape in the background. The darkest area is the trees in the middle ground. Tissot: The performing area is the lightest. The foreground and the background where the audience is sitting is the darkest. The even use of both dark and light areas balances the effects of serious and jovial moods in these paintings.

■ For more examples of narrative art, see *The National Museum of Women in the Arts Collection.*

Art Journal: Writing
Ask students to write about the rules of a game they like to play or how they would change the rules of a game.

Aesthetic Perception

Design Awareness Look for examples of informal balance on billboards and other advertisements.

Aesthetic Perception

Design Awareness Ask students to share what they found when looking for informal balance in advertisements and displays.

Developing Visual Literacy Point out the woman in each painting who is directly looking at the viewer. Have students hypothesize why the artists chose to position these women in this way.

Unit 5 • Lesson 5   **173**

Art History and Culture

James Tissot

James Tissot (jāmz tē sō) (1836–1902) recorded the modern urban life of both Paris and London scenes in a refined, polished style. His parents earned a comfortable living making clothing for wealthy customers. This led to Tissot's interest in painting stylish women in costume. He was more concerned with pleasing his customers than in developing his artistic skills. Tissot was influenced artistically by painters Edouard Manet, Edgar Degas, and James McNeill Whistler.

See pages 24–25 and 16–21 for more about art history and the subject matter.

Artist Profiles, p. 59

Artist Profile

James Tissot
1836-1902
James Tissot (jāmz tē sō') was born in France. His parents earned a profitable living making clothing for wealthy customers. This background later led Tissot to paint scenes of stylish women. As a youth, Tissot was sent away to attend religious schools, where he spent much of his time sketching his surroundings. Later he attended art school in Paris, where he became friends with Edgar Degas and other artists. His first exhibition in Paris was not a great success. Eventually, however, his artwork made him wealthy. During the Franco-Prussian War, Tissot fled from Paris to London, England, where he continued his career. Tissot never married.

Web Connection
Visit **www.ibiblio.org/wm/paint/auth/tissot/** to learn more about the life and works of James Tissot.

LESSON 5 • Informal Balance **173**

Teach

Time: About 30 minutes

"How could you demonstrate informal balance?" "¿Cómo pueden demostrar equilibrio informal?"

- Read and discuss the definitions of *informal balance, size, color, texture,* and *position* on page 174.

Practice

- Review the Practice activity directions with students on page 174.

- Divide students into groups of four or five. Instruct student groups to choose one of the ways that artists use informal-balance. Allow students time to create a pose with their group members using this informal-balance technique. Encourage groups to share their poses with the class. Ask the class to identify which technique is being used.

Creative Expression

Materials: 12" × 18" white drawing paper, pencils, paper plates, liquid tempera paints, paintbrushes, found objects, water dishes, paper towels, newspaper

Alternate Materials: colored pencils or watercolor paints

- Distribute the materials and have students follow the directions on page 175.

- Review the Activity Tips on page 244 for visual examples of this lesson's activity.

Art Journal: Brainstorming

Have students look at the display of found objects, then brainstorm and sketch ideas for still-life arrangements of these objects in their Art Journals.
NSAE 2.b

Using Informal Balance

Informal balance is a way of organizing parts of a design so that unlike objects have equal visual weight. Informal balance is also called **asymmetry.** There are several ways that artists create informal or asymmetrical balance.

 Size A large shape or form appears to be heavier than a small shape. Several small shapes can balance one large shape. To create informal balance, artists place large shapes close to the center of an artwork and place small shapes farther away.

 Color A bright color has more visual weight than a dull color.

 Texture A rough texture has an uneven pattern of highlights and shadows. For this reason, a rough surface attracts the viewer's eyes more easily than a smooth, even surface does.

 **Position** A large positive shape surrounded by a small negative space appears to be heavier than a small positive shape surrounded by a large negative space. Balance can be created by placing a large positive shape close to the center of a scene.

Practice

Demonstrate informal balance.

1. Brainstorm with your group a living scene. Include objects and people that demonstrate informal balance.

2. Model the scene for the class. Be sure to include at least two of the principles explained above.

174 Unit 5 • Lesson 5

Differentiated Instruction

Reteach
After students have completed their asymmetrical still-life paintings, have them create symmetrical still lifes using the same objects. Spend some time comparing and contrasting the two.

Special Needs
Increase interest in this project by allowing students to bring in objects from home that they would like to include in their still-life arrangements.

ELL
Students can benefit from multiple opportunities to define abstract and difficult concepts. As you describe examples of informal balance around the room, you might refer to key words and phrases written on the board. Students can also point to the corresponding illustrations in their textbooks.

◀ **Joshua Mellott.**
Age 10.

Think about how the student artist created balance in this artwork.

 Creative Expression

How can you show asymmetrical balance in a still life? Create a still life. Use a printing technique to add color.

1. Arrange the objects you have selected for an asymmetrically balanced still-life.

2. Use your thumb and index finger to form a frame around only one section of the still-life. Lightly draw this section.

3. Use a permanent marker to outline your complete drawing.

4. Paint your tabletop using watercolor paints.

5. Place your drawing right-side down on top of the painted surface. Gently rub the back of your paper and lift it to create a monoprint.

 Art Criticism

Describe What objects or sections of the still life did you select to draw? What colors did you use?

Analyze Why did you select that particular area of the still life? How did you arrange the objects on your paper?

Interpret What feeling do you get when you look at your asymmetrical still life? Give it a title.

Decide Does your painting show asymmetrical balance? How?

Unit 5 • Lesson 5   **175**

 Time: About 15 minutes

Review and Assess

"Were you able to create a still-life painting using asymmetrical balance?" "¿Fueron capaces de crear una pintura de naturaleza muerta usando equilibrio asimétrico?"

Think

The student artist created balance using size.

■ Use *Large Prints 69* Hmong Story Cloth and *70* The Throne of the Third Heaven of the Nation's Millennium General Assembly to have students identify and describe the use of informal balance.

Informal Assessment

■ For standardized-format test practice using this lesson's art content, see pages 50–51 in *Reading and Writing Test Preparation.*

Art Journal: Critical Thinking
Have students answer the four art criticism questions—Describe, Analyze, Interpret, and Decide—in their Art Journals. In small groups, have students discuss their still-life paintings.
NSAE 2.a

Art Across the Curriculum

Use these simple ideas to reinforce art concepts across the curriculum.

★ **Descriptive Writing** Have students each write a descriptive paragraph that describes the effects that informal balance has on their still-life paintings.

★ **Math** Ask students to consider a two-to-one ratio when designing their asymmetrical still lifes.

★ **Science** Remind students when they are experimenting with balance scales that informal balance is achieved when the weight of two or more objects equals the weight of one larger object.

★ **Social Studies** Relate the concept of informal balance to social studies curriculum when talking about population shifts, such as urbanization.

★ **Technology** Have students each design a game board using a paint program. The game board should be designed with informal balance in mind. Visit **SRAonline.com** to print detailed instructions for this activity. NSAE 6.b

Informal Balance

Extra! For the Art Specialist

Time: About 45 minutes

Focus

Have students study *Large Prints 69 Hmong Story Cloth* and *70 The Throne of the Third Heaven of the Nation's Millennium General Assembly* and discuss how some artists use informal balance in an artwork to give equal visual weight to both halves even though they are not the same or even similar. Have students describe how the artists arranged the objects to create informal balance.

Teach

Ask students to think of games they like to play. What type of games do they have to play sitting down? Create a list of table games on the board such as chess, cards, and board games.

Reflect

Have students evaluate their artwork using the four steps of art criticism. Encourage them to locate and describe their uses of informal balance.

Alternate Activity

Materials:

- Art Journals
- pencils and erasers
- 12" × 18" drawing paper
- fine-point ink pens
- colored pencils
- watercolor paints
- paintbrushes
- water containers

1. Draw ideas in your Art Journal of how you can show three people playing a game. For example, the subjects can be sitting at a table or huddled together on the ground. Overlap two of the people.

2. Select a sketch and transfer it to drawing paper. A fine-point ink pen can be used to trace over the lines. Hatching and cross-hatching lines should be added to show shadows.

3. Colored pencils can be used to color in the drawing. Overlap and blend the colors.

4. Complete the artwork by using watercolor paints to paint in the background.

Research in Art Education

Artistically talented students engage in more self-regulatory behavior in classes with arts integration than in classes without art integration ("Using Art Processes to Enhance Academic Self-Regulation," in *Critical Links*, p. 64). These self-regulatory behaviors included paying attention, problem solving, asking questions, taking risks, being prepared, and so on. While students are working on this lesson using informal balance, discuss how planning and organizing assignments and activities is a way of balancing or managing time.

Assessment

Use the following rubric to evaluate the artwork students make in the Creative Expression activity and to assess students' understanding of informal balance.

Have students complete page 65 or 66 in their *Assessment* books.

	Art History and Culture	Aesthetic Perception	Creative Expression	Art Criticism
3 POINTS	The student can demonstrate knowledge of the lives and work of Sofonisba Anguissola and James Tissot.	The student accurately identifies informal balance in art and in the environment.	The student's still life clearly illustrates the use of informal balance.	The student thoughtfully and honestly evaluates own work using the four steps of art criticism.
2 POINTS	The student's knowledge of the lives and work of Sofonisba Anguissola and James Tissot is weak or incomplete.	The student shows emerging awareness of informal balance in art and in the environment.	The student's still life shows some awareness of informal balance.	The student attempts to evaluate own work but shows an incomplete understanding of evaluation criteria.
1 POINT	The student cannot demonstrate knowledge of the lives and work of Sofonisba Anguissola or James Tissot.	The student cannot identify informal balance in art and in the environment.	The student's still life shows no understanding of informal balance.	The student makes no attempt to evaluate own artwork.

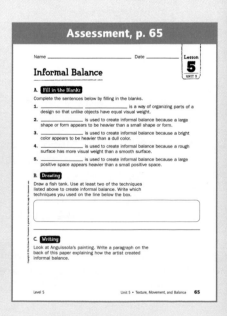

Assessment, p. 65

Name _____ Date _____ Lesson 5 UNIT 5

Informal Balance

A. Fill in the Blanks
Complete the sentences below by filling in the blanks.

1. _____ is a way of organizing parts of a design so that unlike objects have equal visual weight.
2. _____ is used to create informal balance because a large shape or form appears to be heavier than a small shape or form.
3. _____ is used to create informal balance because a bright color appears to be heavier than a dull color.
4. _____ is used to create informal balance because a rough surface has more visual weight than a smooth surface.
5. _____ is used to create informal balance because a large positive space appears heavier than a small positive space.

B. Drawing
Draw a fish tank. Use at least two of the techniques listed above to create informal balance. Write which techniques you used on the line below the box.

C. Writing
Look at Anguissola's painting. Write a paragraph on the back of this paper explaining how the artist created informal balance.

Level 5   Unit 5 • Texture, Movement, and Balance   65

Lesson 6 Overview
Radial Balance

Lesson 6 introduces radial balance. Artists use radial balance to enhance shapes and forms. Radial balance is found in natural objects and objects made by people.

Objectives

 Art History and Culture

To demonstrate knowledge of potters from Valencia, Spain, and the life and work of Noland Anderson

 Creative Expression

To create a circular stained-glass design that radiates from the center by manipulating computer-drawn segments

 Aesthetic Perception

To identify and compare the use of radial balance in art and in the environment

 Art Criticism

To evaluate one's own work using the four steps of art criticism

Vocabulary Vocabulary

Review the following vocabulary words with students.

radial balance equilibrio radial—a design based on a circle with elements radiating from the central point

mandala mandala—a radial design divided into sections or wedges, each of which contains a different image

See page 179B for additional Spanish vocabulary resources.

 Art Journal: Vocabulary

Have students add these words to the Vocabulary section of their Art Journals.

Lesson Materials
- common classroom objects
- computer
- computer paint program with mirror-image capabilities
- printer
- paper
- scanner
- scissors
- glue

Alternate Materials:
- tape

Program Resources
- *Reading and Writing Test Prep.*, pp. 64–65
- *Transparency 30*
- *Flash Card 14*
- *Artist Profiles*, pp. 70, 4
- *Animals Through History Time Line*
- *Assessment*, pp. 67–68
- *Large Prints 69* Hmong Story Cloth and *70* The Throne of the Third Heaven of the Nation's Millennium General Assembly
- *The National Museum of Women in the Arts Collection*

Concept Trace
Radial Balance
Introduced: Level 4, Unit 6, Lesson 3

Reinforced: Level 6, Unit 4, Lesson 4

Lesson 6 Arts Integration

Theatre

Complete Unit 5, Lesson 6, on pages 100–105 of *Theatre Arts Connections.*

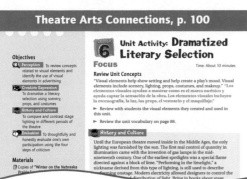
Theatre Arts Connections, p. 100

Music

 Musical forms have balance. Music in the Western tradition also has forms that create balance. Rondo form is one main musical idea played over and over again, with contrasting sections between. This form is written ABACADA. Listen to "Rondo" from *Rage Over a Lost Penny,* by Ludwig van Beethoven. How many times do you hear a section repeated?

Movement & Dance

Radial balance spreads out from the center of an object. Have students stand and create three circles, one inside the other: an outer circle, a middle circle, and an inner circle. The outside circle must have the most students to cover the circumference, the middle circle will have fewer students, and the inner circle will have the fewest students.

 **ocus**

Activate Prior Knowledge

"Imagine that you are riding a Ferris wheel. What do you notice about the wheel's movement, the arrangement of its spokes and cars, and its colors and lights?"

"Imaginense que van en una rueda mágica. ¿Qué observan acerca del movimiento de la rueda, la disposición de los rayos y los carros, y los colores y las luces?"

■ Discuss with students their responses to the question above. Explain that a Ferris wheel has radial balance because similar colors, lights, and cars radiate out from the center.

Using Literature ⭐ Reading

■ Share Faye Silton's *Of Heroes, Hooks, and Heirlooms.* This is a story of a twelve-year old Holocaust survivor's daughter.

Thematic Connection ⭐ Social Studies

■ **Things in Our Homes:** Encourage students to talk about some of their favorite things in their homes.

Introduce the Art

Look

"Let's take a close look at the two works of art." "Vamos a observar detalladamente las dos obras de arte."

Drawing Conclusions ⭐ Reading

■ Have students look at the works of art in this lesson and draw their own conclusions about each artist's original purpose for creating each piece.

🏺 Art History and Culture

Tin-glazed earthenware is essentially lead glaze made opaque by adding oxide. It was most likely developed to hide imperfections in the colors of fired-clay works of art.

 Web Connection

Visit http://www.artistica.com/about_Majolica.htm to learn more about majolica, or tin-glazed pottery.

Radial Balance

▲ **Artist unknown.** (Spain). *Deep Dish from Valencia, Spain.* 1430.

Tin-glazed earthenware painted in cobalt blue and lustre. $2\frac{6}{10} \times 19$ inches (6.7 × 48.2 cm.). Hispanic Society of America, New York, New York.

Look at the artwork on these pages. Find the central point of each one and notice how the lines, shapes, colors, and forms are repeated as they move out from the center.

🏺 Art History and Culture

Tin-glaze was used in Mesopotamia in the ninth century. Pottery dipped in a tin-glaze has a surface that colors can be applied to. This type of art reached Spain in the eleventh century under the Moors.

🏺 Art History and Culture

Valencian Pottery

A new tradition of ceramics emerged from the blending of the Spanish and Islamic cultures after the Arabs conquered Spain in the eighth century. Artists exchanged ideas and techniques using clay, glazes, and fire. This deep dish, typical of the dishes with flat centers and horizontal brims, was created around 1430. This deep dish is ceramic pottery made from clay found in this area. The fired pottery was then covered with a tin-oxide glaze, known as *majolica*. Potters of various religious and ethnic backgrounds worked together in Valencia.

See pages 24–25 and 16–21 for more about art history and the subject matter.

Artist Profiles, p. 70

Artist Profile

Deep Dish

There are no marks on this deep dish that identify the potter or workshop that created it. Although records exist that name masters of Valencian pottery, specific attribution to individual artists and their works is unknown. Potters of various religious and ethnic backgrounds worked together in Valencia.

◄ **Artist unknown.** (Spain). *Deep Dish.* 1430.

Tin-glazed earthenware painted in cobalt blue and lustre. $2\frac{6}{10}$ inches × 19 inches (6.7 × 48.2 cm.). Hispanic Society of America, New York, New York.

Study both works of art to see examples of radial balance.

▶ Where is the center of each artwork?

▶ Describe the designs that you see. How are they arranged?

▶ Can you find where these designs begin and end?

⚲ Aesthetic Perception

Seeing Like an Artist Where do you see examples of radial balance in nature?

🏺 Art History and Culture

Noland Anderson

Noland Anderson (nôl´ land an´ dər sən) (1969–) was born in Virginia in 1969. He studied art formally at the Fort Lauderdale School of Fine Arts in Florida. Anderson works as a court artist creating drawings of trials and their participants to be shown on television and in newspapers. *Blue Dome-Home Blessing* can be classified as an illumination. Historically, illuminations were the colorful illustrations alongside text in ancient manuscripts. Anderson patterned *Blue Dome-Home Blessing* after the huge, spectacular stained-glass dome in the main synagogue of Szeged, Hungary. The stained-glass dome measures ten meters in diameter.

See pages 24–25 and 16–21 for more about art history and the subject matter.

Artist Profiles, p. 4

● Artist Profile ●
Noland Anderson
b. 1969

Noland Anderson (nô´ land an´ dər sən) was born in Virginia in 1969. He studied art formally at the Fort Lauderdale School of Fine Arts in Florida. Although he works primarily in watercolors, Anderson also draws with pencil as a court artist. When a court proceeding is closed to cameras and video crews, court artists create drawings of the trial and its participants to be shown on television and in newspapers. Court artists must be able to sketch quickly and accurately in line and color. The images of people involved in court cases must be recognizable to the public. These artists often work on a freelance basis, being called in to draw courtroom proceedings when the need arises. Currently Anderson works and

Study

▶ Gold rectangles begin in the center of *Deep Dish* and repeat as they move out. In *Blue Dome-Home Blessing,* blue circles repeat from the center to the outside of the artwork. These central points meet at an axis known as the focal point.
NSAE 5.c

▶ Both designs are circular. They are arranged from the center outward.

▶ Both designs begin in the center and end at the edge.

■ For more examples of utilitarian art, see *The National Museum of Women in the Arts Collection.*

📓 Art Journal: Writing

Ask students to write about something that they have at home that has a radial design. Have students sketch this design in their Art Journals.

⚲ Aesthetic Perception

Design Awareness Bring in examples of natural radial designs found in your community for students to analyze.

Developing Visual Literacy Discuss what these artists may have been inspired by when creating these works of art.

💻 Web Connection

Visit **http://www.student.uwa.edu.au/ ~cy/szeged3.html** to see photographs of the synagogue in Szeged, Hungry. *Blue Dome-Home Blessing* was patterned after the stained-glass dome in this synagogue.

Teach

Time: About 45 minutes

"How could you create a radial design?"
¿Cómo podrían crear un diseño radial?

- Read and discuss the definition of *radial balance* on page 178.

Practice

Materials: common classroom found objects

- Review the Practice activity directions with students on page 178.

- Have students work with partners to collect objects in the classroom they will use to create a design with radial balance. Then ask students to arrange the objects they found on a desk or table using radial balance. Allow partners to travel around the room to look at their peers' work.

Creative Expression

Materials: computer, computer paint program with mirror-image capabilities, printer, paper, scanner, scissors, glue

Alternate Materials: tape

- Distribute the materials.

- Have students follow the directions on page 179.

- Review the Activity Tips on page 244 for visual examples of this lesson's activity.

Art Journal: Brainstorming

Have students think about and sketch geometric and free-form shapes they would like to use to create a radially balanced stained-glass design.

Using Radial Balance

Radial balance occurs when the elements of design (line, shape, color, and form) seem to radiate, or come out from a central point. The elements almost always are spaced evenly around the center of the design and create circular patterns.

Radial balance occurs frequently in nature. Many plants follow radial patterns of growth. Cut an orange in half and you will see the radial pattern of the segments.

People imitate nature in many objects by creating radial designs. You often see radial balance in architecture, such as in round stained-glass windows. The design always radiates out from a central point.

Practice

Create a design using radial balance.

1. With a partner, collect objects in the classroom.

2. Working together, use radial balance to arrange the objects on a desk or table.

Differentiated Instruction

Reteach

Ask student to help you collect kaleidoscopes for a class demonstration. Use a projector to display the designs created. Ask students to explain the radial balance they see.

Special Needs

Successful modifications for students with learning disabilities often include sequencing instruction into manageable steps. For this computer activity, demonstrate the steps for students and provide visual cues showing what the beginning, middle, and end of the project will look like.

ELL

Offer rehearsal time with a partner or small group. Rewrite questions as needed in more familiar language and have members of the small group extend students' language as they point out balance techniques in their own work.

◄ **Jansen Sharpe.**
Age 11.

Think about how the artist created a stained glass window design using radial balance.

Creative Expression

How can you use radial balance to create a stained glass window design? Use a computer paint program and a scanner to create radial balance with symmetry.

1. Draw a circle and divide it into eight equal triangular segments. Erase or eliminate all the segments except one.

2. Create a design in the remaining segment using the draw tool and the fill color tool.

3. Copy and paste this segment four times. Select one of the segments created, and using the option button, flip the design horizontally. Copy and paste the design three more times for a total of eight segments.

4. Print the segments. Cut them out and reassemble the segments to form a circular design. Scan the design and print.

Art Criticism

Describe List the steps you followed to make your stained glass window design.

Analyze Explain how this design shows radial balance.

Interpret Explain where and how you could use this design.

Decide Were you successful in creating a design using radial balance?

Reflect
Time: About 20 minutes

Review and Assess
"What have you learned about radial balance?" "¿Qué han aprendido acerca de un equilibrio radial?"

Think
The artist started in the center of the design and repeated elements working toward the edges.

- Use **Large Prints 69** Hmong Story Cloth and **70** The Throne of the Third Heaven of the Nation's Millennium General Assembly to have students identify examples of radial balance in each work of art.

Informal Assessment
- For standardized-format test practice using this lesson's art content, see pages 64–65 in **Reading and Writing Test Preparation.**

Art Journal: Critical Thinking
Have students answer the four art criticism questions—Describe, Analyze, Interpret, and Decide—in their Art Journals. In small groups, have students discuss their stained-glass designs.
NSAE 2.a

Art Across the Curriculum

Use these simple ideas to reinforce art concepts across the curriculum.

★ **Poetry Writing** Have students write a spiral-shaped poem and decorate it with a radially balanced design.

★ **Math** Ask students to figure the area of their stained-glass radial designs.

★ **Science** Introduce students to star maps.

★ **Social Studies** Ask students to research the development of the wheel and ask them to write a diary entry of what their day might be like if this simple machine did not exist.

★ **Technology** Have students create an original radial design experimenting with a paint program. Visit **SRAonline.com** to print detailed instructions for this activity.
NSAE 6.b

Extra! For the Art Specialist

Time: About 60 minutes

Focus

Have students study the works of art in this lesson and discuss how some artists use radial balance in an artwork to enhance a shape or form. Have students describe the lines, shapes, and colors they see. How are these elements arranged? Are they the same?

Teach

Discuss how radial designs occur in nature. Explain that artists use radial designs to decorate clothing, architecture, and religious objects. In radial design the central axis is called the focal point. The focal point is the area of the radial design that is emphasized.

Reflect

Have students evaluate their artwork using the four steps of art criticism. Encourage them to locate the focal point and describe the radial balance.

Alternate Activity

Materials:
- Art Journals
- pencils, erasers
- 9" × 9" white drawing paper
- compass or a 6" to 9" circle pattern
- fine- and medium-point felt-tip pens
- colored pencils

1. Create several sketches of combined geometric shapes. Draw some inside others in your Art Journal.

2. Lightly draw a circle on the paper using either a compass or a pattern. Fold the circle in half then in half again so that the folds cross in the center. Trace over these lines. Use a ruler to draw two diagonals to further divide the circle.

3. Draw a geometric shape in one of the pie shapes. Repeat that same shape in each wedge. Add more shapes as you move out from the center and repeat the same shape in each wedge.

4. Use a fine-tip black permanent marker to outline the radial design.

Research in Art Education

"Only through a multifaceted education program that develops divergent as well as convergent thinking—that encourages intuitive as well as rational thought processes—can today's young learner begin to be prepared to cope with the rapidly changing aspects of a technology-oriented world." (Herberholz, Barbara, and Lee Hanson. *Early Childhood Art*. New York: McGraw-Hill, 1994.)

Assessment

Use the following rubric to evaluate the artwork students make in the Creative Expression activity and to assess students' understanding of radial balance.

Have students complete page 67 or 68 in their *Assessment* books.

	Art History and Culture	Aesthetic Perception	Creative Expression	Art Criticism
3 POINTS	The student can demonstrate knowledge of potters from Valencia, Spain, and the life and work of Noland Anderson.	The student accurately identifies radial balance in art and in the environment.	The student's stained-glass design clearly illustrates the use of radial balance.	The student thoughtfully and honestly evaluates own work using the four steps of art criticism.
2 POINTS	The student's knowledge of potters from Valencia, Spain, and the life and work of Noland Anderson is weak.	The student shows emerging awareness of radial balance in art and in the environment.	The student's stained-glass design shows some awareness of radial balance.	The student attempts to evaluate own work but shows an incomplete understanding of evaluation criteria.
1 POINT	The student cannot demonstrate knowledge of potters from Valencia, Spain, or the life and work of Noland Anderson.	The student cannot identify radial balance in art or in the environment.	The student's stained-glass design shows no understanding of radial balance.	The student makes no attempt to evaluate own artwork.

Assessment, p. 67

Name _____ Date _____

Lesson **6** UNIT 5

Radial Balance

A. Short Answer
Answer the following question with a short answer. What is radial balance?

B. Drawing
Create a design that shows radial balance in the box below.

C. Writing
Look at *Deep Dish/Spain/from Valencia* and, on the back of this paper, write a description of the artist's use of radial balance.

Level 5   Unit 5 • Texture, Movement, and Balance   67

texture—the element of art that refers to how things feel or look as if they might feel if touched **textura**—el elemento del arte que se refiere cómo las cosas se sienten o lucen cómo se sienten si son tocadas

tactile texture—texture that can be felt **textura táctil**—textura que se puede sentir

visual texture—texture that is seen with the eyes **textura visual**—textura que se puede ver con sus ojos

assemblage—a three-dimensional work of art made up of many pieces fixed together **montaje**—una obra de arte tridimensional hecha de varias piezas fijadas juntas

rhythm—the principle of art that shows movement by repeating elements such as lines, shapes, and colors **ritmo**—el principio artístico que enseña movimiento por elementos repetidos como líneas, figuras o colores.

visual rhythm—rhythm perceived by the eyes, not through the ears **ritmo visual**—ritmo en que se percibe por los ojos, no por los oidos

visual movement—the principle of art that leads a viewer's eyes through a work of art **movimiento visual**—el principio artístico que lleva a los ojos del observador por una obra de arte

balance—the principle of design that relates to visual weight in a work of art **equilibrio**—el principio del diseño que se refiere al peso visual en una obra de arte

formal balance—occurs when equal, or very similar, elements are placed on opposite sides of a central axis **equilibrio formal**—ocurre cuando elementos iguales o muy parecidos están puestos en lados opuestos de un eje central

central axis—the central dividing line, which may be imaginary or part of the design **eje central**—la línea central divisoria en que puede ser imaginaria o parte del diseño

symmetry—a type of formal balance that occurs when two sides are mirror images of each other **simetría**—un tipo de equilibrio formal que ocurre cuando dos lados son imágenes idénticos

approximate symmetry—balance that is achieved when two sides are almost identical but have small differences **symetría aproximada**—se encuentra equilibrio cuando los dos lados son casi idénticos pero tienen pequeñas diferencias.

informal balance—a way of organizing parts of a design so that unlike objects have equal eye attraction **equilibrio informal**—una manera de organizar partes de un diseño para que objetos diferentes tengan la misma atracción visual

asymmetry—another name for "informal balance"; something asymmetrical looks balanced even though it is not the same on both sides **asimetría**—otro nombre para "equilibrio informal"; algo asimétrico luce equilibrado aunque no son iguales en ambos lados

negative space—the areas around an object or group of objects **espacio negativo**—el área alrededor de un objeto o grupo de objetos

radial balance—balance that occurs when elements of a design are based on a circle with features radiating outward from the central point **equilibrio radial**—equilibrio que ocurre cuando elementos de un diseño están basado en un círculo con rasgos que proyectan hacia afuera del punto central

mandala—a radial design divided into sections or wedges, each of which contains a different image **mandala**—un diseño radial dividido en secciones o cuñas, cada uno contiene una imagen diferente

Vocabulary Practice

T Display *Transparency 41* to review unit vocabulary words.

Examples ⭐ Vocabulary

Assign vocabulary words to groups of students and ask them to create or find examples of each. Attach each vocabulary word to the example and display them for reference.

Word Scrambles ⭐ Vocabulary

Have students create word scramble puzzles and trade them to solve. Students may write the definition of the words or sketch examples to be used as clues.

Syllabication ⭐ Vocabulary

Ask students to separate the vocabulary words into syllables. Teach students how to play charades with the vocabulary words. They will indicate the syllables of each word by indicating the number of fingers on their forearms.

Wrapping Up Unit 5

Texture, Rhythm, Movement, and Balance

 Art Criticism

Critical Thinking Art criticism is an organized system for looking at and talking about art. You can criticize art without being an expert. The purpose of art criticism is to get the viewer involved in a perception process that delays judgment until all aspects of the artwork have been studied.

■ See pages 28–29 for more about art criticism.

Describe

▶ The credit line indicates that Frida Kahlo painted *Self-Portrait Dedicated to Leon Trotsky* in 1937. She used oil paints on Masonite. The size is 30″ × 24.″ It is located at the National Museum of Women in the Arts in Washington, D.C.

▶ Some possible answers are: She stands in a very stiff, formal pose. She is wearing a red blouse trimmed with gold braid at the round neck. She has a ring on the middle finger of her right hand and dangling earrings. She holds a bouquet of flowers and a letter.

Analyze

▶ This is a painting, so the textures are visual. The shawl has a velvety texture. The drape of the folds tells us it is a soft fabric. The white curtains have a smooth texture. The fringes of the shawl and the pleats of the skirt ruffle look rough. The floor has the visual texture of wood.

▶ The pleats on the skirt create a visual rhythm. The curved lines on the curtains also have a visual rhythm. The planks of wood create a rhythm that moves the viewer's eyes to the back of the stage.

▶ This painting has formal balance. Equal or very similar elements such as the curtains, the arms, the two halves of the face, the skirt, and the shawl are placed on opposite sides of a central axis.

▲ **Frida Kahlo.** (Mexican). *Self-Portrait Dedicated to Leon Trotsky.* 1937.

Oil on masonite. 30 × 24 inches (76.2 × 60.96 cm.).
National Museum of Women in the Arts, Washington, D.C.

180   Unit 5

Art History and Culture

Frida Kahlo

Frida Kahlo (frē′ da kä′ lō) (1907–1954) was born in Mexico City, Mexico. As a child she had polio, which caused one leg to be smaller than the other. She had hoped to study medicine, but she was in a serious accident as a teenager that fractured her spine and crushed her pelvis. While convalescing, Kahlo taught herself to paint. She later married muralist Diego Rivera. Her life was full of pain and tragedy, and her marriage to Rivera was stormy. She used her own life as the subject matter for her art.

See pages 24–25 and 16–21 for more about art history and subject matter.

Artist Profiles, p. 35

Artist Profile
Frida Kahlo
1907–1954

Frida Kahlo (frē′ dä kä′ lō) was born in Mexico. Her life was short and painful. As a child she had polio, which caused one leg to stop growing. At 18, she was severely injured in a bus accident. Thirty-two operations did not ease her pain entirely and it often kept her in bed. Whenever possible she dressed in richly embroidered outfits, wore much jewelry, and tucked flowers in her hair. At 22, she married the famous painter Diego Rivera. He was 42 at the time and had been married twice before. Kahlo and Rivera lived in separate houses connected by a bridge. Despite their stormy relationship, she wanted to have children and was deeply disappointed that they could not. After

 **Art Criticism** Critical Thinking

Describe **What do you see?**

During this step you will collect information about the subject of the work.

▶ What does the credit line tell us about the painting?

▶ Describe the woman.

Analyze **How is this work organized?**

Think about how the artist has used the elements and principles of art.

▶ Is the texture tactile or visual?

▶ Where do you see repeated lines and shapes that create visual rhythm?

▶ What type of balance is used to organize this work?

Interpret **What is the artist trying to say?**

Use the clues you discovered during your analysis to find the artist's message.

▶ How does the use of formal balance affect the mood of this painting?

▶ Why do you think the woman is posing like this?

Decide **What do you think about the work?**

Use all the information you have gathered to decide whether this is a successful work of art.

▶ Is the work successful because it is realistic, because it is well organized, or because it has a strong message?

Interpret

▶ Some possible answers are: The formal balance makes the mood calm, stiff, dignified, and formal.

▶ Some possible answers are: The woman is posing like this because it is a very important occasion. This may be her debut. She wants everyone to pay attention to her.

Decide

▶ Some possible answers are: It is realistic. It is well organized. There is a message, but it is subtle.

Art Journal: Writing

Have students write answers to Aesthetic Perception in their Art Journals.

 Aesthetic Perception

Critical Thinking Have students bring in portraits of themselves. The portraits can be formal or casual photographs, paintings, or drawings. How do students' portraits compare with *Self-Portrait Dedicated to Leon Trotsky*?

Describe　▶ List and describe everything you see in your portrait.

Analyze　▶ What visual textures do you see in your portrait?
　　　　　▶ What type of balance do you see in your portrait?

Interpret　▶ What mood are you expressing in your portrait?
　　　　　▶ How does the light and surrounding environment contribute to this mood?

Decide　▶ What do you like about this portrait?

"Artists use the elements of texture, rhythm, movement, and balance to organize, enhance and control how the viewer's eyes will travel though a work of art." "Los artistas usan los elementos de textura, ritmo, movimiento y equilibrio para organizar, exaltar y controlar cómo los ojos del observador se mueven a través de una obra de arte."

 T Review unit vocabulary with students using *Transparency 41.*

 Art Journal: Writing

Have students answer the questions on page 182 in their Art Journals or on a separate sheet of paper. Answers: 1. B, 2. C, 3. A, 4. C, 5. B

T For further assessment, have students complete the unit test on *Transparency 47.*

VISIT A MUSEUM
The National Museum of Women in the Arts

▶ Encourage students to discuss what they have learned about this museum and what they would like to see there. Ask them to explain why this museum sounds interesting.

"Art is not a handicraft; it is the transmission of feeling the artist has experienced."

—Leo Tolstoy

Texture, Rhythm, Movement, and Balance, continued

Show What You Know

Answer these questions on a separate sheet of paper.

1 _____ is the element of art that refers to how things feel, or how they look as if they might feel if they were touched.
A. Balance
B. Texture
C. Symmetry

2 _____ is the repetition of shapes, colors, or lines.
A. Musical rhythm
B. Informal balance
C. Visual rhythm

3 _____ is the principle of art that leads a viewer's eyes through a work of art.
A. Movement
B. Texture
C. Size

4 _____ occurs when equal, or very similar, elements are placed on opposite sides of a central axis.
A. Rhythm
B. Distortion
C. Formal balance

5 _____ occurs when lines, shapes, colors, and forms seem to radiate, or come out from a central point.
A. Texture
B. Radial balance
C. Blending

182 Unit 5

VISIT A MUSEUM
The National Museum of Women in the Arts

The National Museum of Women in the Arts holds the largest and most important collection of art by women dating from the sixteenth century. In 1982 Wilhelmina and Wallace Holladay donated their art and library as the foundation of the museum. The museum opened in 1987 in a renovated building in Washington, D.C. In addition to the permanent collection at The National Museum of Women in the Arts, there are special exhibitions and exhibition series that present women artists and their artwork. The museum supports women artists and their changing roles in society. The museum has a library and an extensive research center in which 10,000 artists from all periods and countries are represented.

Unit Assessment Options

 **Aesthetic Perception**

Practice Have students choose three concepts on page 182, then find examples of each in the classroom.

 **Creative Expression**

Student Portfolio Have students review all the artwork they have created during this unit and select the pieces they wish to keep in their portfolios.

Art Criticism

Activity Have students select an artwork from this unit and study it using the four steps of art criticism. Have students work alone or in pairs and present their findings orally or in writing.

Texture, Rhythm, and Movement in Dance

This is a photo of a dancer playing a famous outlaw named "Billy the Kid." The ballet about his life and America's Westward movement was choreographed by Eugene Loring. The repeated actions of the dancers create visual rhythm in the dance. Aaron Copland composed the music with musical themes based on old cowboy songs.

What to Do Create a dance or mime using a variety of pioneer work movements.

The ballet *Billy the Kid* uses movement themes taken from pioneer life and work. It shows the Westward movement and the chores that the pioneers did to survive.

1. Select a few ideas to show in mime or movement. Experiment with exaggerating the movement. Create rhythm by repeating actions.
2. Find three ways to vary each work action. Try changing the level, the speed or direction, the movement through space, or the texture of the movements (soft and fluid or choppy and uneven).
3. Select two different actions and build a mime or movement sequence that includes both.
4. Share with a partner. Combine all four ideas and show a perspective of pioneer work life as you perform them together.

▲ Eugene Loring. "Billy the Kid."

Art Criticism

Describe Describe the way you and your partner worked together.

Analyze What things did you do to create visual rhythm in your movements?

Interpret How did it feel to perform the work of pioneers?

Decide Were you successful in creating a pioneer work dance or mime?

Unit 5   **183**

Art History and Culture

Billy the Kid

"Billy the Kid" is a ballet that has been preserved as a historical piece. It was choreographed in 1938 in the United States. It was the first ballet featuring American themes, music, and movement motifs. Eugene Loring began the choreography by organizing the events of Billy's life onto a storyboard. He placed events sequentially into scenes and then determined their dramatic impact and length. These plans were sent to Paris, to Aaron Copeland, who used them to create a musical score based on themes from cowboy songs. Loring felt there was no true movement unless there was an emotional impetus behind it. His dancers were directed to feel the emotions before doing the movements. When dancing any role, dancers explore all aspects of the characters to fully understand their motivations and perspectives.

Texture, Rhythm, and Movement in Dance

Objective: To create a pioneer work mime or dance with a partner.

Materials: "Billy the Kid" performed by The Joffrey Ballet of Chicago

Focus
Time: About 10 minutes

■ Discuss the information on page 183.

Art History and Culture

■ Have students discuss the type of work done by the pioneers in preparation for their mime or dance study on work actions.

Teach
Time: About 25 minutes

Aesthetic Perception

■ Direct students to mime a variety of different work movements from the list. Encourage them to find ways to vary their movements using levels and rhythm. Ask students to select two work actions and create movements to show them. Divide students into partners to teach and learn the two movements. They will then combine and perform them.

Creative Expression

■ **Informal Assessment** Comment positively on cooperative work and efforts to combine elements with dance movements.

Reflect
Time: About 10 minutes

Art Criticism

■ Have students answer the four art criticism questions on page 183 orally and in writing.

■ Were students able to successfully create a mime or dance?

Unit 6 Planning Guide

	Lesson Title	Suggested Pacing	Creative Expression Activity
Lesson 1	Harmony	1:25	Create a unified mural with class.
Lesson 2	Variety through Difference	1:20	Draw a school-related scene.
Lesson 3	Emphasis of an Element	1:20	Create a series of prints.
Lesson 4	Emphasis through Placement	1:20	Create an original yarn painting design.
Lesson 5	Unity through Media	1:20	Design a class quilt.
Lesson 6	Unity through Theme	1:20	Design and create a clay animal bank.
ART SOURCE ARTSOURCE	Harmony, Variety, Emphasis, and Unity in Dance	0:45	To create a "call and response" pattern.

Materials	Program Resources	Fine Art Resources	Literature Resources
12" × 18" white drawing paper, pencils, erasers, tempera paints, water containers, paintbrushes, fine-tip markers	*Assessment,* pp. 69–70 *Home and After-School Connections* *The National Museum of Women in the Arts Collection* *Reading and Writing Test Preparation,* pp. 66–67	*Transparency 31* *Artist Profiles,* pp. 7, 67 *Large Print 70* *Animals Through History Time Line*	*Play Me A Story—Nine Tales About Musical Instruments* by Naomi Adler
pencils and erasers, white drawing paper, colored pencils	*Assessment,* pp. 71–72 *Home and After-School Connections* *Women in the Arts Collection* *Reading and Writing Test Preparation,* pp. 68–69	*Transparency 32* *Artist Profiles,* pp. 58, 50 *Large Prints 71, 72* *Animals Through History Time Line*	*Antonio S. and the Mysterious Theodore Guzman* by Odo Hirsh
clay, white drawing paper, pencils, clay tools, paper clips, textured materials, tempera paints, paintbrushes, water containers, newspapers	*Assessment,* pp. 73–74 *Home and After-School Connections* *Women in the Arts Collection* *Reading and Writing Test Preparation,* pp. 70–71	*Transparency 33* *Artist Profiles,* pp. 21, 38 *Large Prints 71, 72* *Animals Through History Time Line*	*Because of Winn-Dixie* by Kate Dicamillo
pencils, 9" × 12" pieces of heavy cardboard, scissors, white glue, yarn, toothpicks, sponges	*Assessment,* pp. 75–76 *Home and After-School Connections* *Women in the Arts Collection* *Reading and Writing Test Preparation,* pp. 72–73	*Transparency 34* *Artist Profiles,* pp. 78, 73 *Large Print 72* *Animals Through History Time Line*	*El Güero* by Elizabeth Boron de Treviño
drawing paper, 6" × 6" white poster board squares, black felt-tip markers, resources for state symbols, construction paper, scissors, glue, large bulletin board	*Assessment,* pp. 77–78 *Home and After-School Connections* *Women in the Arts Collection* *Reading and Writing Test Preparation,* pp. 74–75	*Transparency 35* *Artist Profiles,* pp. 41, 26 *Large Print 71* *Animals Through History Time Line*	*One Grain of Rice* by Demi
pencils, erasers, clay, board or canvas cloth, clay tools, newspaper, slip containers, acrylic paints, paintbrushes	*Assessment,* pp. 79–80 *Home and After-School Connections* *Women in the Arts Collection* *Reading and Writing Test Preparation,* pp. 76–77	*Transparency 36* *Artist Profiles,* pp. 82, 36 *Large Print 71* *Animals Through History Time Line*	*Love That Dog* by Sharon Creech
"Dhon Dholok Cholom"			

6

Harmony, Variety, Emphasis, and Unity

Lesson 1: Harmony creates a feeling of wholeness in a work of art.

Lesson 2: Variety is the use of differences or contrasts in an artwork.

Lesson 3: Emphasis is the art principle that stresses one area of an artwork over another.

Lesson 4: Emphasis can be created through the positioning of objects in an artwork.

Lesson 5: Unity is created with the balance of harmony and variety.

Lesson 6: Unity in an artwork can be created with a theme.

Introduce
Unit Concepts

"Artists use the principles of harmony, variety, emphasis, and unity to organize works of art."
"Los artistas usan los principios de armonía, variedad, énfasis y unidad para organizar las obras de arte."

Harmony & Variety
- Have students think about harmony as it relates to music. Harmony refers to different pitches played or sung together to create a melodic sound.

- Have students look around the classroom for examples of variety. For example, they might see a variety of colors.

Emphasis & Unity
- Ask students how they have emphasized something when talking to someone and explain why.

- Have students explain what a unit is. Ask them to come up with phrases that use the word unity.

Cross-Curricular Projects
- See the *Language Arts and Reading, Mathematics, Science,* and *Social Studies Art Connections* books for activities that further develop the concepts in this unit.

184 UNIT 6 • Harmony, Variety, Emphasis, and Unity

Harmony, Variety, Emphasis, and Unity

▲ **Berthe Morisot.** (French). *The Sisters.* 1869.
....
Oil on canvas. 20½ × 32 inches (52.07 × 81.28 cm.). National Gallery of Art, Washington, D.C.

Artists use harmony, variety, emphasis, and unity to organize the elements in their work.

Morisot created harmony by posing the two sisters in the same dresses and hairdos. She introduced variety by having them sit in slightly different positions. She emphasized their faces by framing them with the dark brown hair and black necklaces. The balance between harmony and variety unify this work of art.

184 Unit 6

Fine Art Prints

Display **Large Prints 71** *El Chandelier* and **72** *Earth Is a Planet with One Peace Missing.* Refer to the prints throughout the unit as students learn about harmony, variety, emphasis, and unity.

Large Print 71

Large Print 72

Artists use **harmony** in their artwork to create a feeling of wholeness, or unity, by using separate but related elements.

▶ What elements are repeated in this work of art?

Artists use the principle of **variety** to create difference or contrast in their work.

▶ What objects introduce variety into this work of art?

Emphasis is used by artists to tell the viewer that this element or area is meant to be noticed more than those around it.

▶ How has Berthe Morisot emphasized the fan in this painting?

Artists use the principle of **unity** to tie everything together in a work of art. When a work of art has unity, everything seems to fit together well.

▶ What do you see that ties this work of art together?

In This Unit you will learn about and practice techniques to create harmony, variety, emphasis, and unity to create works of art. Here are the concepts you will study:

▶ Harmony
▶ Variety
▶ Emphasis
▶ Unity

Berthe Morisot
(1841–1895)

Berthe Morisot was born in Bourges, France, and was a member of a group of artists known as the impressionists. She was concerned with creating atmosphere and with reproducing the way light reflected off objects and people. She used a lot of white in her bright scenes of domestic life. During Morisot's painting career, the role of women in society was beginning to change. She incorporated this shift into much of her artwork.

Examine the Artwork

"Let's look closely at the painting." "Vamos a mirar detalladamente la pintura."

■ Have students look at *The Sisters*. Ask them to describe what they see.

■ Have students answer the questions about harmony, variety, emphasis, and unity on page 185. NSAE 5.c

▶ Berthe Morisot repeated the elements of line, shape, color, and visual texture to create harmony in this painting.

▶ The woman on the left is wearing a ring and the woman on the right is holding a fan. These objects introduce variety in this work of art.

▶ Morisot emphasized the fan by placing it in the center of the foreground and by painting it using a contrasting color.

▶ The patterns on the couch and in the women's dresses, the matching necklaces, hairstyles, colors, and vertical lines that move across the painting tie this work of art together and create unity.

Unit Pretest

T Display *Transparency 48* as a pretest.
Answers: 1. A ,2. C, 3. C, 4. A, 5. B

Art History and Culture

Berthe Morisot

Berthe Morisot (bârt môr ē´ sō) (1841–1895) was born in France and was the great granddaughter of painter Jean-Honoré Fragonard. She studied under French realist painter, Camille Corot. Morisot concentrated on representing light in her painting. Her works appear as if they were done quickly, with sketchy strokes that seem light and soft to the viewer. She regularly exhibited her work with the impressionists. Morisot and Mary Cassatt are considered by many to be the most important Impressionist female painters of the nineteenth century.

See pages 24–25 and 16–21 for more about art history and subject matter.

Artist Profiles, p. 44

Artist Profile
Berthe Morisot
1841–1865
Berthe Morisot (bârt môr ē´ s ō) was born in France. She was the granddaughter of the painter Fragonard. Taught by her father, she learned how to draw when she was very young. Later she took painting lessons with her sister. She began selling her paintings when she was 23, but she never felt that she was treated as an equal of male painters. When she was 33, she married Eugene Manet, the brother of Édouard Manet. They had one daughter, Julie.

Unit 6 Arts Integration

ILLUSTRATOR PROFILE

David Wiesner
(1956–)

David Wiesner was born in Bridgewater, New Jersey. He was the fifth child in a family that already had several budding young artists. Wiesner recalls spending much of his time as a child drawing and painting, lugging his sketchbook everywhere he went. Watching a cartoon introduced him to the idea of shifting realities. In the same way that the cartoon characters ran off of the filmstrip, Wiesner's imagination took flight.

As he grew older, Wiesner discovered a series of art books that further broadened and inspired his own artistic vision. He found the works of classic painters Durer, DaVinci, and Bruegel especially appealing, due in part to the fantastical landscapes in the backgrounds. However, it was the surrealists who had the greatest impact. Wiesner was "thrilled" by the works of Max Ernst, Salvador Dali, and Rene Magritte. Wiesner said, "There is a clear line of demarcation between the art I did before I discovered the surrealists and, well, everything after."

Wiesner began telling stories with his art as a teenager, and later, at the Rhode Island School of Design, he excelled in assignments that called for a series of images. Since graduating, Wiesner has published numerous award-winning children's books, including *Tuesday*, for which he received the Caldecott Medal.

While studying unit 6, share David Wiesner's illustrations with the class. Discuss his use of harmony and variety in his works of art. How did Wiesner show emphasis? How did he create unity?

Music

Harmony in music refers to different pitches, played or sung at the same time, producing chords. Have students play combinations of three pitches with one pitch in between them (C-D-E) and observe the inharmonious effect. Emphasis is a way of making a part of the music stand out. In music, it can be done with contrasts of dynamics, texture, rhythm, tone, color and speed.

Literature

Show the video or DVD *Follow the Drinking Gourd* to introduce the concepts of harmony, variety, emphasis, and unity. Pause the video or DVD and have students describe areas that use these properties.

Literature and Art

Performing Arts

 Show "Dhon Dholak Cholam." Point out how harmony, variety, emphasis, and unity are used.

Artsource®

NSAE 6.a

NSAE 6.b

Lesson 1 Overview — Harmony

Lesson 1 introduces the art principle of harmony. Harmony helps to create unity by stressing similarities of separate but related parts. In musical harmony, related tones are combined into blended sounds. In visual harmony, related art elements such as similar shapes, colors, and lines are combined.

Objectives

 Art History and Culture

To become knowledgeable about the lives and artwork of Thomas Hart Benton and Richard Yarde

Creative Expression

To use harmony to create a painting of objects for a class mural with an extracurricular activity as the theme

 Aesthetic Perception

To identify visual harmony and understand how it is used in works of art
NSAE 2.b

Art Criticism

To evaluate one's own work using the four steps of art criticism

Vocabulary Vocabulary

Review the following vocabulary words with students.

harmony armonía—the principle of art that helps to create unity by stressing the similarities of separate but related elements in an artwork

unity unidad—the quality of wholeness or oneness that is achieved by properly using the elements and principles of art

See page 209B for additional Spanish vocabulary resources.

 Art Journal: Vocabulary

Have students add these words to the Vocabulary section of their Art Journals.

Lesson Materials

- 12" × 18" white drawing paper
- pencils
- erasers
- tempera paints
- water containers
- paintbrushes
- *Art Connections* textbooks

Alternate Materials:
- markers
- colored pencils
- oil pastels

Program Resources

- *Reading and Writing Test Prep.*, pp. 66–67
- *Transparency 31*
- *Flash Cards 17, 18*
- *Artist Profiles*, pp. 7, 67
- *Animals Through History Time Line*
- *Assessment*, pp. 69–70
- *Large Prints 71* El Chandelier and *72 Earth Is a Planet with One Peace Missing*
- *The National Museum of Women in the Arts Collection*

Concept Trace

Harmony
Introduced: Level 4, Unit 6, Lesson 4
Reinforced: Level 6, Unit 6, Lessons 3, 4

Lesson 1 Arts Integration

Theatre

Complete Unit 6, Lesson 1, on pages 108–109 of *Theatre Arts Connections.*

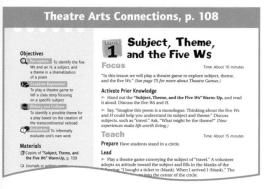

Music

 During the twentieth century, composers broke from traditional ideas of harmony. Listen to "Infernal Dance of King Kaschei" from *Firebird Suite,* by Igor Stravinsky. He wrote this piece in 1910. Three years later he deviated from the norm so drastically that a riot broke out at the premier of "The Rite of Spring."

Movement & Dance

A sense of harmony can be felt from the movement of our breathing. Breathing is continuous. When we are relaxed our breathing is even and slow, deep and flowing. Have students practice breathing in and out deeply. Ask students to inhale and create a corresponding movement. The movement should match the duration of the breath. Then have students create a movement for exhaling. Tell students to turn to face a different direction with each combined breath and corresponding movement.

Focus

 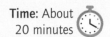

Activate Prior Knowledge

"How many different voices are there in the school choir?" "¿Cuántas voces diferentes hay en la coral escolar?"

- Discuss with students their answers to the above question. Explain that even though there are several types of voices (soprano, alto, bass, and so on), they are all combined using harmony to create one unified voice when singing in the choir.

Using Literature Reading

- Share *Play Me A Story—Nine Tales About Musical Instruments* by Naomi Adler with the class. Identify visual harmony in the illustrations and enjoy the music-related folktales from around the world.

Thematic Connection Social Studies

- **Music:** Encourage students to talk about the types of music that they enjoy and what they know about the development of those types of music.

Introduce the Art

Look

"Let's take a close look at the two works of art." "Vamos a observar detalladamente las dos obras de arte."

Fact and Opinion Reading

- Have students research and list both facts and opinions about the styles of music represented in the two works of art in this lesson. Discuss the difference between the two and note how opinions are often misrepresented as facts.

Art History and Culture

Regionalism was a very popular style of American art in the 1930s. The focus was to portray the American scene away from New York City in a clear and simple way which could be understood and enjoyed by everyone. Thomas Hart Benton, John Steuart Curry, and Grant Wood are three of the best known American Regionalists.

💻 Web Connection

Visit **www.pbs.org/kenburns/benton/** to learn more about Thomas Hart Benton and his artwork.

▲ **Thomas Hart Benton.** (American). *The Sources of Country Music.* 1975
Acrylic on canvas. 6 × 10 feet (1.82 × 3.05 m.). Country Music Hall of Fame and Museum, Nashville, Texas.

Look at the artwork on these pages. Notice the shapes, lines, and colors that are repeated throughout both paintings. Do you see repeated visual texture in each? Think about how this repetition creates unity, or oneness, in the artwork. The parts of the painting seem to fit together because of the harmony that is created.

🏺 Art History and Culture

Thomas Hart Benton was an American regionalist.

🏺 Art History and Culture

Thomas Hart Benton

Thomas Hart Benton (tom´ əs hart bent´ ən) (1889–1975) was an American regionalism painter. American Regionalist was a style that was popular with rural artists and came to prominence in the 1930s. Benton painted subjects of the American Midwest. He studied art at the Art Institute of Chicago and in Paris. Benton strongly believed that American artists should develop their own style, as opposed to copying European styles. He urged other American artists to paint scenes from their own environment. Benton began his art career as a cartoonist but is known for his narrative murals of America.

See pages 24–25 and 16–21 for more about art history and subject matter.

Artist Profiles, p. 7

Artist Profile

Thomas Hart Benton
1889-1975

Thomas Hart Benton (tom´ as hart bent´ ən) was a regional American painter known for his energetic, colorful murals. He was the son of a United States congressional representative and named after his great uncle, a famous pre-American Civil War senator. From his family, Benton developed a strong identity as an American. He studied art in Paris and at the Art Institute of Chicago. Benton believed that American artists should develop their own styles and not just copy French painting styles. Although Benton began his art career as a cartoonist, he was known for his murals depicting scenes from the rural past of the

▲ **Richard Yarde.** (American).
Savoy: Heel and Toe. 1997.
··
Watercolor. 5 × 7¼ feet (1.52 × 2.2 cm.).
Collection of Denzel and Paulette Washington.

Study both works of art. Notice how harmony is created in each painting.

▶ Look for repeated lines, shapes, colors, and textures in each painting.

▶ Is it easy to tell what the mood is in each painting?

▶ How would you describe the color schemes?

▶ Which scene would you rather be a part of?

Aesthetic Perception

Seeing Like an Artist Look for harmony in outdoor landscapes. Pay attention to repeated line, shape, color, and texture. Think about how designers imitate this natural harmony in their artwork.

Art History and Culture

Richard Yarde

Richard Yarde (ri´ ch ərd yard) (1939–) was born in Boston and now lives in Northhampton, Massachusetts. He was educated at Boston University. Yarde is an important American watercolorist. Since the 1960s, he has been using the very delicate medium of watercolor paints to create powerful images. He uses his art to express his African American culture in historical portraits of heroes and images of dance and music. His Savoy Ballroom paintings were inspired by the jazz culture of the Harlem Renaissance. Yarde created this series of paintings from 1940s *Life* magazine photographs.

See pages 24–25 and 16–21 for more about art history and subject matter.

Artist Profiles, p. 67

• Artist Profile •
Richard Yarde
b. 1939

Richard Yarde (ri´ chard yärd) was born in Boston and lives in Northampton, Massachusetts. Yarde's bright energetic watercolors have earned him national acclaim. His work can be found in more than 30 public collections. In 1991 Yarde became ill with a life-threatening kidney ailment that caused him to temporarily lose the sense of touch in his right hand. In order to fully heal he used his artwork as therapy for both his physical and emotional condition, and he created a body of work that addressed his illness and humankind's mortality. He has been a professor of art at the University of Massachusetts at Amherst since 1990.

Study NSAE 5.c

▶ Benton: There are repeated diagonal lines throughout the work in the instruments, the floorboards, the people, the train, the boat, the telephone pole, and the tree. There are repeated oranges, browns, and blues, as well as similar circle, square, and free-form shapes. Yarde: There are repeated diagonal lines expressing movement and energy. The bright yellow is repeated on both sides and in between the dancers.

▶ The mood is energetic and full of excitement in each work of art.

▶ Both artists primarily used warm colors, which bring the works close to the viewer.

▶ Students should support why they would rather be involved in one scene or the other.

■ For more examples of narrative art, see *The National Museum of Women in the Arts Collection.*

Art Journal: Writing

Have students write about a musical experience they had that made an impact on their lives. The experience might involve participating in or attending a musical, hearing a style of music or a song for the first time, learning about or meeting a musician, or studying or performing with a musical instrument.

Aesthetic Perception

Design Awareness Discuss with students how harmony is created in nature. Have students visualize different outdoor scenes and ask them to describe the sounds, lines, colors, shapes, smells, textures, and temperatures of the places. Talk about how artists mimic nature to recreate harmony in their work.

Developing Visual Literacy Encourage students to think about how the artist who created each artwork portrayed the scene. Ask students if they think the artists give the viewers a realistic look at what was happening or if they used creative license to change the scenes to appear as they wished.

Web Connection

Visit **www.savoystyle.com/yarde.html** to learn more about Richard Yarde and view the Savoy Ballroom portfolio.

Teach

Time: About 50 minutes

"How can you create harmony in a work of art?" "¿Cómo pueden crear armonía en una obra de arte?"

- Read and discuss the definition of *harmony* and how it is created with shapes, colors, and lines on page 188.

Practice

Materials: *Art Connections* textbooks

- Review the Practice activity directions on page 188 with students.

- In small groups, have students look through their *Art Connections* textbooks to find art that illustrates harmony created through the use of shapes, color schemes, and lines.

Creative Expression

Materials: 12" × 18" white drawing paper, pencils, erasers, tempera paints, water containers, paintbrushes, fine-tip markers

Alternate Materials: ink pens

- Distribute the materials and have students follow the directions on page 189.

- Review the Activity Tips on page 245 for visual examples of this lesson's activity.

- Mount students' individual paintings on a bulletin board to create a unified mural. Ask students to identify how harmony was created. NSAE 1.b

- See Technique Tips on page 218 for information on Tempera paints.

Art Journal: Brainstorming

As a class, have students brainstorm a list of their favorite extracurricular activities or interests. Together, have students decide on one activity or interest to be the theme of the class mural they will be creating. Have each student sketch three to five objects that relate to that activity in their Art Journals. For example, if dance is the theme, students might draw ballet slippers, musical notes, and people dancing.

Using Harmony

In music, harmony is created when voices blend together to create one unified sound. Artists use harmony, but instead of using combined sounds, they combine the art elements.

Harmony is the principle of art that creates unity by using separate but related elements in an artwork. Artists use harmony in two-dimensional artworks by repeating a shape, color, or texture. Harmony can also work if the space between different shapes, colors, and textures is even.

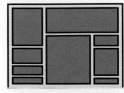

Harmony is created when related shapes of various sizes are repeated. A design using one shape is more harmonious than a design using two or more shapes.

Color creates harmony when a work is limited to only cool or warm colors.

Line creates harmony by limiting lines to either straight or curved lines.

Practice

Find examples of harmony in works of art.

1. With a small group of students, look through the textbook to find examples of harmony of shape, harmony of color, and harmony of line in works of art.

2. Share what you have found with the class.

188 Unit 6 • Lesson 1

Differentiated Instruction

Reteach

Have student groups look through the *Large Prints* to find at least four works of art that have harmony created by the use of similar shapes, colors, and lines, and four that do not. Ask students to separate these works of art into two piles and explain why each work belongs in a particular pile.

Special Needs

Provide students with visual reminders of the techniques that artists use to create harmony as they complete this activity.

ELL

By first modeling and then offering students time to practice with partners, you can help them develop the skills to critique their own work.

◄ **Natalie Tucker.**
Age 10.

Think about how the artist created harmony through repeated lines, shapes, and colors.

 Creative Expression

How can you show harmony in a mural? Create a painting of objects that are related to a favorite extracurricular activity.

1. Select your best sketch from your Art Journal and draw it large enough to fill the paper.

2. Blend your colors on a mixing tray. Paint your sketched object.

3. Use a fine-line marker to add details to your completed painting.

4. Together with your classmates, create a unified mural.

Art Criticism

Describe Describe the item you chose to paint and how it relates to the theme of the mural.

Analyze What similar art elements do you see in the mural that create harmony within the artwork?

Interpret When a work of art has harmony, what mood does it tend to create?

Decide Is there harmony throughout the mural? Is the theme communicated clearly?

Unit 6 • Lesson 1   **189**

Reflect
Time: About 15 minutes

Review and Assess

"How successful were you at creating harmony with shapes, colors, and lines? How successful was the class at creating a mural that has harmony?" "¿Pudieron crear armonía con figuras, colores y líneas? ¿Pudo la clase crear un mural que tuviera armonía?"

Think

The student artist created harmony through the use of repeated yellow stars, similar diagonal lines, and a soccer theme.

■ Use *Large Prints 71 El Chandelier* and *72 Earth Is a Planet with One Peace Missing* to have students identify and describe uses of harmony.

Informal Assessment

■ For standardized-format test practice using this lesson's art content, see pages 66–67 in *Reading and Writing Test Preparation.*

Art Journal: Critical Thinking

Have students answer the four art criticism questions—Describe, Analyze, Interpret, and Decide—in their Art Journals. In small groups, have students discuss their individual paintings and the class mural.
NSAE 2.a

■ Have students look at the works of art in this lesson and compare the cultural themes honoring traditions in American artwork.

Art Across the Curriculum

Use these simple ideas to reinforce art concepts across the curriculum.

★ **Personal Writing** Have students each write a list of extracurricular activities they would like to learn more about.

★ **Math** Discuss how writing harmonious musical notes and chords depends on mathematical ratios. Distribute blank music sheets to students and allow them to experiment with writing music. If time allows, play on a piano the notes they have written and ask them whether they hear harmony.

★ **Science** Have students look for examples of harmony created with similar lines, shapes, and colors in natural objects found on the grounds of the school.

★ **Social Studies** have students research the people and events of the Harlem Renaissance.

★ **Technology** Have students search for clip art on the computer and create a mural using a musical theme. Visit **SRAonline.com** to print detailed instructions for this activity. NSAE 6.b

Lesson 1 — Harmony

Wrap-Up

Extra! For the Art Specialist

Time: About 50 minutes

Focus

Have students study **Large Prints 71** *El Chandelier* and **72** *Earth Is a Planet with One Peace Missing* and discuss how an artist can use harmony to bring together various parts of an artwork based on their similarities. Have students describe the lines, shapes, and colors they see.

Teach

Explain to students that they will be making a group assemblage based on recycling. Ask students to begin collecting plastic bottles, containers, packaging, caps, and other objects that they normally would recycle. You can help put together the assemblage with a hot-glue gun.

Reflect

Have students evaluate their artwork using the four steps of art criticism. Encourage them to locate and describe the elements used to create harmony.

Alternate Activity

Materials:

- Art Journals
- pencils, erasers
- wire, yarn, and string
- hot-glue gun
- hot-glue sticks
- white craft glue
- collected recyclable materials

1. Divide students into groups to discuss how to create their assemblage. Will the objects be hung, stacked, displayed in boxes, or arranged with a combination of these?

2. In their Art Journals, students will sketch their ideas. If students will be hanging the objects, drawing curved lines as guide lines might be a good way to organize the assemblages.

3. Once the groups have decided how they will display their collected objects, have them begin attaching them to the prepared area using string, wire, or yarn. Encourage student to think about repeating similar shapes, colors, and lines.

Research in Art Education

An ideal arts curriculum would be "one that offers in-depth, carefully sequenced teaching in several art forms for the entire span of young people's schooling." It is also beneficial to have extended times in learning in which students may visit museums and concert halls ("Learning in and Through the Arts: Curriculum Implications:" in *Champions of Change*, p. 44). Organize a field trip to a local museum, a musical performance, or a traveling exhibition. Allow students the opportunity to analyze original exhibitions by artists and form conclusions about the artistic properties.
NSAE 5.c

Assessment

Use the following rubric to evaluate the artwork students make in the Creative Expression activity and to assess students' understanding of harmony.

Have students complete page 69 or 70 in their *Assessment* books.

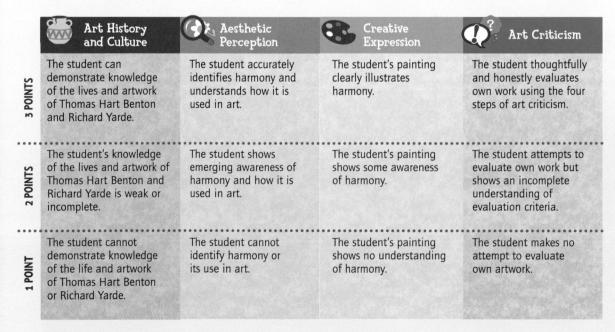

	Art History and Culture	Aesthetic Perception	Creative Expression	Art Criticism
3 POINTS	The student can demonstrate knowledge of the lives and artwork of Thomas Hart Benton and Richard Yarde.	The student accurately identifies harmony and understands how it is used in art.	The student's painting clearly illustrates harmony.	The student thoughtfully and honestly evaluates own work using the four steps of art criticism.
2 POINTS	The student's knowledge of the lives and artwork of Thomas Hart Benton and Richard Yarde is weak or incomplete.	The student shows emerging awareness of harmony and how it is used in art.	The student's painting shows some awareness of harmony.	The student attempts to evaluate own work but shows an incomplete understanding of evaluation criteria.
1 POINT	The student cannot demonstrate knowledge of the life and artwork of Thomas Hart Benton or Richard Yarde.	The student cannot identify harmony or its use in art.	The student's painting shows no understanding of harmony.	The student makes no attempt to evaluate own artwork.

Assessment, p. 69

Name _____ Date _____

Harmony — Lesson 1, UNIT 6

A. Fill in the Blank
Complete the following sentence by filling in the blank.
_____ is the principle of art which creates unity by using separate but related elements in a work of art.

B. Drawing
Create harmony using either color, shape, or line in the box below. Indicate which element you have used by writing *color, shape,* or *line* on the line provided.

C. Writing
Study Thomas Hart Benton's *The Sources of Country Music* and, on the back of this paper, write a descriptive paragraph about the elements that are repeated to create harmony.

Level 5 — Unit 6 • Harmony, Variety, Emphasis, and Unity — 69

Variety through Difference

Lesson 2 introduces variety. Variety is the principle of art created by differences or contrasts. Variety is the opposite of harmony. Artists use variety to add interest to their work.

Objectives

Art History and Culture

To become knowledgeable about the lives and artwork of Judith Surowiec and John Robinson

Creative Expression

To create variety in a drawing using a common theme

Aesthetic Perception

To identify variety and understand how it is used in works of art
NSAE 2.b

Art Criticism

To evaluate one's own work using the four steps of art criticism

Lesson Materials

- magazines
- notebook paper
- scissors
- tape
- pencils, erasers
- white drawing paper
- colored pencils

Alternate Materials:
- fine-tip pens
- markers
- white paper

Program Resources

- *Reading and Writing Test Prep.*, pp. 68–69
- *Transparency 32*
- *Flash Cards 16, 18*
- *Artist Profiles*, pp. 58, 50
- *Animals Through History Time Line*
- *Assessment*, pp. 71–72
- *Large Prints 71* El Chandelier *and 72* Earth Is a Planet with One Peace Missing
- *The National Museum of Women in the Arts Collection*

Concept Trace

Variety through Difference
Introduced: Level 4, Unit 6, Lesson 5

Reinforced: Level 6, Unit 6, Lessons 1, 2

Vocabulary Vocabulary

Review the following vocabulary words with students before beginning the lesson.

variety variedad—the principle of art created by differences or contrasts in art elements

harmony armonía—the principle of art that helps to create unity by stressing the similarities of separate but related elements in an artwork

See page 209B for additional Spanish vocabulary resources.

Art Journal: Vocabulary

Have students add these words to the Vocabulary section of their Art Journals.

Lesson 2 Arts Integration

Theatre

Complete Unit 6, Lesson 2, on pages 110–111 of *Theatre Arts Connections.*

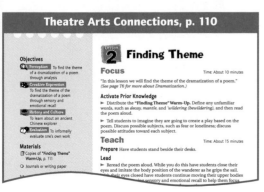

Theatre Arts Connections, p. 110

Music

SPOTLIGHT ON MUSIC Listen to the melody "change color" as it moves around the band in "East St. Louis Toddle-o," by Duke Ellington. Duke worked with superb artists—they could improvise on a melody to the point the listener might not know it is still there.

Movement & Dance

Divide students into groups of three. One student in each group is the central point. As the leader he or she will make a shape that the rest of the group imitates. Then each member of the group thinks of a slight variation for the shape. Once the students have created their variations, have them share their ideas and teach them to the leader. The leader now has his or her own shape plus two variations on the idea. The leader performs his or her shape alone.

ocus

Time: About 20 minutes

Activate Prior Knowledge

"Do all of your friends wear the same clothes and have the same personality?" "¿Todos sus amigos se ponen la misma ropa y tienen la misma personalidad?"

■ Discuss students' answers. Explain that it is the differences in the personalities and tastes of people that make them interesting.

Using Literature [★] Reading

■ Share Odo Hirsh's *Antonio S. and the Mysterious Theodore Guzman* with the class. Allow students the opportunity to identify the use of variety in the artwork and enjoy a story about imagination and creativity.

Thematic Connection [★] Science

■ **Creating from My Imagination:** Encourage students to share with the class how they use their imaginations to create original ideas and things.

Introduce the Art

Look

"Let's take a close look at the two works of art." "Vamos a observar detalladamente las dos obras de arte."

Main Idea [★] Reading

■ Have students choose one of the works of art in this lesson and outline a short story that this artwork could illustrate. Ask students to concentrate on the main ideas when first developing their outlines and note that the details will be added to the outlines later to add interest and excitement to the story.

 Art History and Culture

Student might respond by describing their personal experiences in art class or relate to a time when they created a work of art with a group of people.

Web Connection

Visit **www.theartcollective.com/theartcollective/ artistbio.asp?artistID=2** to learn more about Judith Surowiec and view some of her works of art.

190 UNIT 6 • Harmony, Variety, Emphasis, and Unity

Lesson 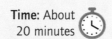 **2** # Variety through Difference

▲ **Judith Surowiec.** (American). *Art Teacher.* 1996.
....
Acrylic on canvas. 30 × 24 inches (76.2 × 60.96 cm.). Private collection.

Look at the artwork on these pages. Find the lines, shapes, colors, and textures that are different from one another. Notice the busy students at every table doing different activities in *Art Teacher*. Each person around the table in *Here Look at Mine* is also working on an individual project. Think about how this adds excitement to each painting.

 Art History and Culture

How can you relate to these works of art? Have you ever experienced a similar situation?

190 Unit 6 • Lesson 2

Art History and Culture

Judith Surowiec

Judith Surowiec (jōō´ dith sûrō´ ic) (1938–) was born in Buffalo, New York. Her family was very creative; they even made their own toys. Surowiec began to explore a more imaginative approach to painting after taking a class in Atlanta, Georgia, in 1986. She now paints more from her soul and less from her head. *Art Teacher* was created in 1996 when Surowiec visited an elementary school and shared with students how she makes her artwork. The students contributed suggestions and ideas as she painted this lively classroom scene.

See pages 24–25 and 16–21 for more about art history and subject matter.

Artist Profiles, p. 58

Artist Profile

Judith Surowiec
b. 1938

Judith Surowiec (jōō´ dith sûr ō´ ic) was born in Buffalo, New York, and grew up in a creative family. She began drawing at an early age and was encouraged by her mother to pursue creative activities. Surowiec and her family even made their own toys. She became interested in art when she encountered the watercolor paintings of her elementary art teacher, Ms. Valentine. Surowiec knew then that she wanted to study art, and she now provides a similar experience for young students by visiting classes and helping them feel excited about creativity. Surowiec lives and works in Georgia.

Study both works of art. Notice the use of variety in each painting.

▶ How many times can you find an image of the same teacher in *Art Teacher*?

▶ Is she doing the same thing or something different each time she appears in the painting?

▶ Look for different types of lines, shapes, colors, and textures that are placed next to each other in both paintings.

▶ How could you change the colors, shapes, lines, or textures to take the variety out of these paintings and add harmony?

 Aesthetic Perception

Design Awareness Look for variety used in architecture. Notice the differences in lines, shapes, colors, media, and textures used for interest in both indoor and outdoor designs.

▲ **John Robinson.** (American).
Here Look at Mine. 1980.

Acrylic on canvas. 37½ × 26½ inches (95.25 × 67.31 cm.). The Anacostia Museum and Center for African American History and Culture, Washington, D.C.

Art History and Culture

John Robinson

John Robinson (jän rä´bin sən) (1912–1995) first began painting as a child. He was forced to quit school to help support his family and had little time to practice. Robinson worked with his grandfather at a garage, where he met important members of the African American artistic community in Washington, D.C. He was able to take painting classes from some of these artists and further explore his own style and interest in art. Robinson is known for his scenes of African American communities and family life. He created many public murals of actual urban locations for churches and city streets. He would visit and study these places to capture their unique attitudes and rhythms in his paintings.

See pages 24–25 and 16–21 for more about art history and subject matter.

Artist Profiles, p. 50

• Artist Profile •
John Robinson
1912–1995

American painter John Robinson (jän rä´bin sən) is known for his scenes of African American community and family life. He first began painting when he was a child and had time to work on his art only after school. When he quit school to help support his family, Robinson continued to pursue art and painted during the little spare time he had between his many jobs. In 1929 he moved to Anacostia, in southeastern Washington, D.C., and immediately began to create paintings using the community as his subject.

▲ **John Robinson.** (American).
Here, Look at Mine. 1980.
Acrylic on canvas. 37½ × 26½ inches (95.25 × 67.31 cm.). The Anacostia Museum and Center for African American History and

Study NSAE 5.c

▶ The art teacher appears four different times in this painting.

▶ The art teacher is doing something different each time she appears in the painting. This creates variety in the painting and gives it a sense of excitement.

▶ There are many examples of lines, shapes, colors, and textures placed next to each other in each work of art.

▶ More harmony and less variety could be created by making either work of art more monochromatic, using only cool or warm colors, or using a smaller number of shapes and lines more consistently.

■ For more examples of narrative art, see *The National Museum of Women in the Arts Collection.*

Art Journal: Writing

Encourage students to write about something that they created from their imagination. Ask students to explain why they created what they did and the steps they took to take an imaginative idea and make it a reality.

Aesthetic Perception

Design Awareness Take students on a research walk in your school's neighborhood. Have each student bring a notebook and something to write with. Explain to students that they will be looking for variety in architectural designs. Students will note or sketch what they see. Allow time for students to share what they observed with the class when you return.

Developing Visual Literacy Ask students if they can relate to any of the subjects in either work of art. Have students explain how their experiences have been similar and how they have been different from those portrayed in the works of art.

Web Connection

Visit **anacostia.si.edu/Academy/artifacts/objects/object_6_frame.htm** to learn more about John Robinson and *Here, Look at Mine.*

Teach

Time: About 45 minutes

"How can you create variety in a work of art while using one common theme?" "¿Cómo pueden crear variedad en una obra de arte mientras usan un tema en común?"

- Read and discuss the definition of *variety* on page 192.

Practice

Materials: magazines, notebook paper, scissors, tape, pencils

- Review the Practice activity directions on page 192 with students.

- Have students form small groups and distribute magazines to each group. Ask students to look through the magazines and cut out photographic images they find that have a variety of shapes, lines, and colors. Ask students to tape these photographic images to notebook paper and write explanations of how variety is created in each of them.

Creative Expression

Materials: pencils and erasers, white drawing paper, colored pencils

Alternate Materials: fine-tip pens and markers on white paper

- Distribute the materials and have students follow the directions on page 193.

- Review the Activity Tips on page 245 for visual examples of this lesson's activity.

- See Technique Tips on page 215 for information on using colored pencils.

Art Journal: Brainstorming

Ask students to brainstorm a list of their favorite school activities or environments, such as physical education, science class, a hallway, the cafeteria, or the library. Have students each select one activity or place that interests them the most and create a sketch of it in their Art Journals.

Using Variety through Difference

Think about walking through a shopping center. The displays, signs, and the way the items are displayed are all varied; they look different from each other. If each store looked the same, or sold the same product, they would have a hard time staying in business. People like to have choices and are attracted to differences.

Artists use variety to add excitement to their work. **Variety** is the principle of art that is concerned with differences or contrasts. It is the opposite of harmony, which deals with similarities or common elements. Variety is created by adding something different to a design to provide a change in the artwork. Lines, shapes, and colors are used to create variety in a work of art.

Practice

Can you discover how photographers use variety in their art?

1. Work with a group to find three examples of photographic images in a magazine.

2. On a sheet of paper, list how the photographers used harmony in each image.

3. What was used to add variety to each image?

Differentiated Instruction

Reteach

Have students look through the *Art Around the World Collection* to find examples of works of art that use variety to add excitement and interest.

Special Needs

Use this lesson as an opportunity for students to show themselves performing school tasks at which they feel most successful.

ELL

Students may benefit from hearing the lesson vocabulary in a large-group brainstorming session before moving on to their individual project ideas. Consider visually recording the group brainstorming session with a simple, labeled sketch for ongoing student reference.

◀ **Nikki Gann.**
Age 10.

Think about how the artist created variety by changing her image in different places within the artwork.

 Creative Expression

How can you create variety in an artwork while using one theme?

1. Look at the sketch you have drawn in your Art Journal.

2. Place yourself three times in this sketch doing normal activities within this chosen school environment.

3. Add objects that clearly communicate who you are in the scene. Keep your clothing the same on all three of your images.

4. Lightly transfer this sketch onto your drawing paper with a pencil. Use colored pencils to complete your drawing.

Art Criticism

Describe Describe the school environment that you chose for your drawing. What objects did you include to communicate who you are in the drawing?

Analyze How did you create variety in this scene?

Interpret What are you doing during the three different times you appear in this scene? Are you communicating different moods in each of the three places?

Decide Were you successful at creating variety in this scene?

Reflect
Time: About 15 minutes

Review and Assess

"How would you explain how variety is used in a work of art?" "¿Cómo explicarían la manera en que se usó la variedad en una obra de arte?"

Think

The artist created variety by changing her image in different places in this basketball scene. Ask student to identify the artist's image within the scene, explain how they found her, and count how many times she appears.

■ Use *Large Prints 71 El Chandelier* and *72 Earth Is a Planet with One Peace Missing* to have students identify and describe the use of variety in a work of art.

Informal Assessment

■ For standardized-format test practice using this lesson's art content, see pages 78–79 in *Reading and Writing Test Preparation.*

Art Journal: Critical Thinking

Have students answer the four art criticism questions—Describe, Analyze, Interpret, and Decide—in their Art Journals. In small groups, have students discuss their drawings. NSAE 2.a

---

Art Across the Curriculum

Use these simple ideas to reinforce art concepts across the curriculum.

★ **Persuasive Writing** Have students each write a persuasive paragraph using three different points to support an opinion about a topic.

★ **Math** Discuss with students how their imaginations can be used for problem solving in mathematics.

★ **Science** Research inventors and their inventions with students. Discuss how the inventors' creativity helped in their discovery of new inventions.

★ **Social Studies** Study the demographics of different areas in the United States and discuss how the variety of people is an important part of our country's survival and success.

★ **Technology** Students can scan and alter images of themselves on the computer to create variations in what they look like. Visit **SRAonline.com** to print detailed instructions for this activity. NSAE 6.b

Variety through Difference

Extra! For the Art Specialist

Time: About 45 minutes

Focus

Have students study **Large Prints 71** *El Chandelier* and **72** *Earth Is a Planet with One Peace Missing* and discuss how some artists use variety to add interest to works of art. Have students describe the various lines, shapes, and colors they see.

Teach

Explain to students that they will each create a collage to illustrate a character in a setting from a story that they have read. They will use objects and shapes cut from newspaper and magazine photographs and combine them with wallpaper and wrapping-paper scraps.

Reflect

Have students evaluate their artwork using the four steps of art criticism. Encourage them to locate and describe the use of variety.

Alternate Activity

Materials:

- pencils, erasers
- magazines, newspapers, wallpaper and wrapping paper scraps
- 12" × 18" tag board
- scissors
- white glue, paper towels
- oil pastels
- fine-tip markers

1. Select a character from a story and make two or three sketches using flat, simple shapes.

2. Use solid blocks of colors, arrange them, and glue them in place to create a background.

3. Cut out sections of magazines, newspapers, and wallpaper and wrapping-paper scraps and assemble the character.

4. Glue the figures and objects onto the background once they are properly arranged. Use oil pastels to embellish the collage. A fine-tip marker can be used to add details.

Research in Art Education

"The making of art is an essential activity for elementary children. They need and want hands-on experiences in this 'other language.' Art lessons must include cycles of experiences with basic media and techniques, allowing students to acquire and then build upon skills fundamental to creative expression." (Kay Alexander, "Art Curricula by and for Art Educators," in *Art Education: Elementary* ed. Andra Johnson, 1992.)

Assessment

Use the following rubric to evaluate the artwork students make in the Creative Expression activity and to assess students' understanding of variety.

Have students complete page 71 or 72 in their *Assessment* books.

	Art History and Culture	Aesthetic Perception	Creative Expression	Art Criticism
3 POINTS	The student can demonstrate knowledge of the lives and artwork of Judith Surowiec and John Robinson.	The student accurately identifies variety used in art.	The student's drawing clearly illustrates the use of variety.	The student thoughtfully and honestly evaluates own work using the four steps of art criticism.
2 POINTS	The student's knowledge of the lives and artwork of Judith Surowiec and John Robinson is weak or incomplete.	The student shows emerging awareness of variety used in art.	The student's drawing shows some awareness of variety.	The student attempts to evaluate own work but shows an incomplete understanding of evaluation criteria.
1 POINT	The student cannot demonstrate knowledge of the life and artwork of Judith Surowiec or John Robinson.	The student cannot identify variety used in art.	The student's drawing shows no understanding of variety.	The student makes no attempt to evaluate own artwork.

Assessment, p. 71

Name _____ Date _____

Lesson **2** UNIT 6

Variety through Difference

A. Short Answer

Complete this sentence.
Variety is the principle of art which is concerned with _____

B. Drawing

Draw a scene from your home or your school using variety.

C. Writing

Study John Robinson's *Here Look at Mine* and, on the back of this paper, write a paragraph describing the variety in this artwork.

Level 5   Unit 6 • Harmony, Variety, Emphasis, and Unity   71

Emphasis of an Element

Lesson 3 introduces emphasis. An artist sometimes emphasizes an element of art to draw the attention of the viewer to a specific area in an artwork.

Objectives

 Art History and Culture

To become knowledgeable about the lives and the artwork of Arthur Dove and Mitch Lyons

Creative Expression

To create a series of three prints, illustrating the use of emphasis

 Aesthetic Perception

To identify emphasis of an element and understand how if affects a work of art
NSAE 2.b

Art Criticism

To evaluate one's own work using the four steps of art criticism

Vocabulary [⭐] Vocabulary

Review the following vocabulary word with students before beginning the lesson.

emphasis énfasis—the principle of art that stresses one area in an artwork over other areas

See page 209B for additional Spanish vocabulary resources.

 Art Journal: Vocabulary

Have students add this word to the Vocabulary section of their Art Journals.

Lesson Materials

- newspapers
- pencils
- clay
- paper clips
- white drawing paper
- clay tools
- textured materials (such as lace and burlap)
- tempera paints
- paintbrushes
- water containers

Alternate Materials:
- self-hardening clay

Program Resources

- *Reading and Writing Test Prep.*, pp. 70–71
- *Transparency 33*
- *Flash Card 15*
- *Artist Profiles*, pp. 21, 38
- *Animals Through History Time Line*
- *Assessment*, pp. 73–74
- *Large Prints 71* El Chandelier and *72* Earth Is a Planet with One Peace Missing
- *The National Museum of Women in the Arts Collection*

Concept Trace
Emphasis of an Element
Introduced: Level 4, Unit 6, Lesson 5

Reinforced: Level 6, Unit 4, Lesson 5

Lesson 3 Arts Integration

Theatre

Complete Unit 6, Lesson 3, on pages 112–113 of *Theatre Arts Connections.*

Theatre Arts Connections, p. 112

Music

 There are various musical devices for creating emphasis in music. A strong beat is combined with weak beats to create double or triple meter, as in boom-chick boom-chick or boom-chick-chick boom-chick-chick. The most famous dance in triple meter is the waltz. Listen to "Waltz of the Flowers," by Piotr Ilyich Tchaikovshy. Step to the beat of the music.

Movement & Dance

Have students walk, jog, skip, and slide in an open space, weaving in and around each other to the beat of a drum or other percussion instrument. Encourage students to find a way to emphasize each movement by using either weight, speed, direction, or energy changes.

Focus

Activate Prior Knowledge

"Have you ever highlighted an important word or phrase in your study notes or in a book?" "¿Alguna vez han resaltado una palabra o frase importante en sus apuntes de estudio o en un libro?"

■ Discuss with students how highlighting is a way of emphasizing text. It makes the words stand out. Ask students to think of other examples of emphasis.

Using Literature ⭐ Reading

■ Share Kate Dicamillo's *Because of Winn-Dixie* with the class. Ask students to identify how the artist used the element of color to emphasize the main character on the cover, then enjoy a story of a girl who learns the value of friendship.

Thematic Connection ⭐ Social Studies

■ **A Question of Value:** Have students each write a short paragraph about something or someone that they have come to value. Ask them to describe how they discovered the importance of this person or object.

Introduce the Art

Look

"Let's take a close look at the two works of art." "Vamos a observar detalladamente las dos obras de arte."

Making Inferences ⭐ Reading

■ Have students look at the two works of art and point to the areas they think the artists have emphasized. Students might notice that they are not all pointing to the same areas. Discuss what it means to make inferences, or educated guesses, and how there might not always be one correct answer to a question but many possible answers that all qualify as being correct.

🏺 Art History and Culture

Mitch Lyons is committed to the process of clay printing more than the final outcome. He views the prints more as a bonus than the goal.

💻 Web Connection

Visit **www.nga.gov/cgi-bin/psearch?Request=S&imageset=1&Person=8600** to learn more about Arthur Dove and his artwork.

Emphasis of an Element

▲ **Arthur Dove.** (American). *Sun.* 1943.

Wax emulsion on canvas. 24 × 32 inches (61 × 81.4 cm.). Smithsonian American Art Museum, Washington, D.C.

Look at the artwork on these pages. Notice how both artists have emphasized, or called your attention to, some parts of the artwork more than others. Sometimes artists use just one element, and other times they combine many to create emphasis in their work.

🏺 Art History and Culture

Mitch Lyons is one of the first artists to extensively explore printing with clay.

🏺 Art History and Culture

Arthur Dove

Arthur Dove (är´ thər duv) (1880–1946) is considered the first abstract American artist. His family did not support his interest in art, so he left home for New York City, where he would work as a freelance illustrator for popular magazines. During a trip to Europe, Dove was inspired by the bright colors and decorative patterns used by Henri Matisse and the fauvists. He returned to the United States a year later. Dove developed his own style of abstract painting primarily inspired by nature.

See pages 24–25 and 16–21 for more about art history and subject matter.

Artist Profiles, p. 21

Artist Profile
Arthur Dove
1880–1946

Arthur Dove (är´ thər duv) was born and raised in upstate New York and received his first painting lessons from a neighbor. His father insisted that he study law in college, but Dove chose to pursue a career in art and was forced to support himself without help from his family. He moved to New York, where he worked as a freelance illustrator for popular magazines and later was introduced to other artists influenced by European modernists. A love of nature and innovative style characterize Arthur Dove's artistic career. He is regarded as the first abstract painter in America.

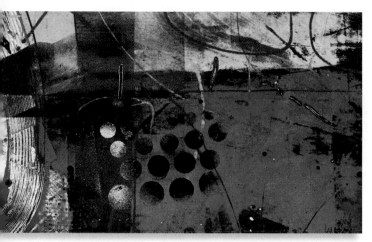

Study both works of art. Notice the areas of emphasis and how the artists have created them.

► Where do your eyes go first in each artwork?

► What draws your attention to these areas?

► What do you think the artist is trying to communicate through these works of art?

► How would the mood of these works of art be different if they were monochromatic?

▲ **Mitch Lyons.** (American). *Slip Trail.* 1997.
⋯⋯⋯⋯⋯⋯⋯⋯⋯⋯⋯
Clay monoprint. 22 × 42 inches (55.88 × 106.68 cm.). Private Collection.

 Aesthetic Perception

Design Awareness Pay attention to advertisements and how they are designed to get your attention. What has been emphasized to tell you why you should buy their product? Are you convinced?

Study NSAE 5.c

► Dove: The viewer's eyes will most likely be drawn to the bright yellow form in the upper-right corner of the artwork, then travel to the black circle within this form. Lyons: The viewer's eyes will most likely be attracted to the top of the painting first.

► The bright colors used in each painting draws the viewer's attention.

► Dove: The artist is communicating a message about the sun reflecting onto an area of flat land with mountains in the distance. Looking directly at the sun might make the form in the center appear dark because of the sun's intensity. Lyons: The artist's message is one of excitement and energy, conveyed by the many bright colors and the variety of lines.

► The mood would be more calm and fluid in monochromatic versions.

■ For more examples of abstract and nonobjective art, see *The National Museum of Women in the Arts Collection.*

Art Journal: Writing

Have students write about a time when they emphasized part of what they were saying to persuade the listener. As an example, you might ask, "Would you like to clean your room or go to the skating park?" If you emphasize the words *go to the skating park,* you can make it sound more appealing. Try saying the sentence with emphasis on *clean your room* to demonstrate the difference for the class.

Art History and Culture

Mitch Lyons

Mitch Lyons (mich lī´ ənz) earned an undergraduate degree in printmaking and a master's of fine arts in ceramics. His interest in both of these media led him to be the first known artist to expand on creating clay monoprints. In 1980 Lyons built a six-foot-by-six-foot table for his clay slab. Each print Lyons makes from this clay literally builds upon the last. This adds to the layers of color and depth of detail in each artwork. Lyons works the entire surface of the clay slab with everyday materials, simple tools, and handmade stencils. He then isolates certain areas within it from which he makes individual but related prints.

See pages 24–25 and 16–21 for more about art history and subject matter.

Artist Profiles, p. 38

◄ Artist Profile ►
Mitch Lyons
With an extensive background in ceramics, Mitch Lyons (mich lī´ ənz) established his own studio and gallery and produced handmade pots from 1971 to 1976. After experimenting with clay and printmaking in 1975, he shifted his focus to his new clay monoprint technique. As a colorist, Lyons creates prints that showcase saturated fields of layered color and builds each new composition upon the foundation of earlier prints. For the last twenty years, Lyons has been creating his innovative clay prints from his studio in Pennsylvania.

Aesthetic Perception

Design Awareness Discuss with students what elements they have noticed in advertisements. Show students some examples from magazines where color, line, shape, and placement are used for emphasis.

Developing Visual Literacy Have students study the title of each work of art in this lesson and think about how an artist might go about giving a title to a work of art. Ask students how the title of an artwork affects the viewer's perception of it.

Web Connection

Visit **www.mitchlyons.com** to learn more about Mitch Lyons and watch a slide show of his clay monoprint process.

Teach

Time: About 45 minutes

"How can you create emphasis using an element of art in a series of prints?" "¿Cómo pueden crear énfasis usando un elemento de arte en series de grabados?"

■ Read and discuss the definition of *emphasis* on page 196.

Practice

Materials: clay, newspapers, pencils, water containers, paintbrushes, paper

■ Review the Practice activity directions on page 196 with students.

■ Divide clay into a ball the size of a golf ball for each student. Direct students to press the clay into the thickness of their thumbs and use pencils to draw three lines in the clay. Two of the lines should be equal in size and width. A small amount of water should be applied to the top of the clay and then the paper can be gently rubbed on the design. Students should carefully peel off the paper and describe the prints they made.

Creative Expression

Materials: clay, white drawing paper, pencils, clay tools, paper clips, textured materials such as lace and burlap, tempera paints, paintbrushes, water containers, newspapers

Alternate Materials: self-hardening clay

■ Distribute the materials and have students follow the directions on page 197.

■ Encourage students to work quickly once the paint is applied to their clay designs. The quality of the prints will decrease once the paint begins to dry. If students are using self-hardening clay, instruct them not to leave it out very long. It will dry out and will not be reusable.

■ Review the Activity Tips on page 246 for visual examples of this lesson's activity.
NSAE 1.b

Art Journal: Brainstorming
Have student sketch ideas for their clay print designs in their Art Journals. They will need to create emphasis in each print using an element of art.

Using Emphasis of an Element

Have you ever underlined or highlighted an important word? Have you ever noticed in an advertisement how one object is made to appear more noticeable than others around it? This emphasis is meant to direct you to pay attention to an object, or idea. In art, emphasis is used in the same way.

Emphasis is the principle of design that stresses one area in an artwork over another area. Emphasis of an art element is the use of one element, such as line, color, or shape that is meant to be noticed more than the other elements around it. Sometimes the element is made so strong that it seems to take over the entire artwork. The other elements become less important to the viewer.

Practice

Create emphasis using lines.

1. Separate a piece of clay into the size of a golf ball.
2. Press the clay flat so that it is the thickness of your thumb.
3. Use a pencil to draw three lines in the clay. Make two lines the same size and width.
4. Use a small amount of water to wet the top of your clay.
5. Place a piece of paper on the top of the clay and rub gently.
6. Peel off the paper. Describe your print. Which line is emphasized?

Differentiated Instruction

Reteach
Have students look through the fine art in the *Art Around the World Collection* for examples of emphasis created with an element of art. Ask students to identify the element used to create the emphasis in each artwork and explain how effective it is in drawing their attention to that area of the work.

Special Needs
Extend learning in this project by asking students to create a landscape where one element is emphasized.

ELL
To prepare students to discuss their techniques and artwork, involve the class in a review of the entire lesson's activities. Some students might pantomime while others describe aloud. You can record key phrases on the board for later reference, if necessary.

◀ **Kord Miller.**
Age 11.

Think about how the artist created emphasis to direct the viewer to a specific area in each print.

Creative Expression

Create a series of three prints emphasizing an art element.

1. Flatten a piece of clay the size of a softball to the thickness of your thumb.

2. Use clay tools to draw repeated lines or shapes in the clay. Press textural materials into the clay and remove.

3. Paint some of your clay design. Spray a little water if the paint begins to dry out.

4. Place paper on the top of the clay plate and rub gently. Carefully peel off.

5. Add more paint. Make two more prints.

6. Label the first print $\frac{1}{3}$, the second $\frac{2}{3}$, and the third $\frac{3}{3}$.

Art Criticism

Describe Describe the lines or shapes you carved into your clay plate. Describe the designs and shapes that were created in the three prints.

Analyze How have you used an art element to create emphasis in your prints?

Interpret Is there a continuous mood throughout all three prints, or does the mood change in each?

Decide Did the prints turn out like you expected them to? How would you change the carvings in the clay plate to achieve a different look in other prints?

Reflect

 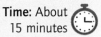

Review and Assess

"How did you create emphasis in a work of art using an art element?" "¿Cómo crearon énfasis en una obra de arte usando un elemento artístico?"

Think

The artist created emphasis by placing the main object in the center of the work of art.

- Use *Large Prints 71 El Chandelier* and *72 Earth Is a Planet with One Peace Missing* to have students identify and describe the uses of emphasis of an art element.

Informal Assessment

- For standardized-format test practice using this lesson's art content, see pages 70–71 in *Reading and Writing Test Preparation.*

Art Journal: Critical Thinking

Have students answer the four art criticism questions—Describe, Analyze, Interpret, and Decide—in their Art Journals. In small groups, have students discuss their prints. NSAE 2.a

Art Across the Curriculum

Use these simple ideas to reinforce art concepts across the curriculum.

★ **Poetry Writing** Explore how different types of poetry such as haiku, limericks, cinquains, and sonnets use emphasis. Discuss the elements of rhyme scheme and iambic pentameter within each type.

★ **Math** Explore the process of measuring to mat or frame a work of art. Convert English measurements using the metric system.

★ **Science** Have students use the experimental method to set up a questionnaire as a class that will survey how students in your school assign value and prioritize in their daily lives.

★ **Social Studies** Discuss how the field of economics includes studies of the value of things on a fluctuating basis. Talk about the principle of supply and demand using real-life examples.

★ **Technology** Have students use a computer paint program to create a nonobjective painting in which they emphasize an element of art. Visit **SRAonline.com** to print detailed instructions for this activity. NSAE 6.b

Lesson 3 Wrap-Up

Emphasis of an Element

Extra! For the Art Specialist

Time: About 50 minutes

Focus

Have students study **Large Prints 71** *El Chandelier* and **72** *Earth Is a Planet with One Peace Missing* to understand how an artist sometimes emphasizes an area in an artwork through the use of one of the art elements. Have students describe the various lines, shapes, and colors in the works of art to which their eyes are drawn first.

Teach

Discuss how a color contrast or a different shape, line, or texture can draw the viewer's attention and emphasize an area within a work of art. Explain to students that they will each be creating a painting of a cityscape and emphasizing one area using an art element of their choice. Collect city images from magazines, photographs, and postcards.

Reflect

Have students evaluate their artwork using the four steps of art criticism. Encourage them to locate and describe the emphasis of an element in their artwork.

Alternate Activity

Materials:
- Art Journals
- pencils, erasers
- city images
- 12" × 18" heavy white drawing paper
- tempera paints
- paintbrushes
- water containers
- newspapers, paper towels
- felt-tip markers

1. Brainstorm a list of daily activities that occur in the city. Then select an activity and create a sketch of this in your Art Journal. Think about which art element will be used to emphasize the main area.

2. Transfer the drawings onto paper. Center the area you want to emphasize. Carefully paint in the background shapes.

3. Paint the figures and the area to be emphasized. Once the paint has dried, use a small brush to add details.

4. Use felt-tip marker to add details.

Research in Art Education

Teachers in high-arts schools are more knowledgeable and engaged in their own learning than teachers in low-arts schools ("Learning in and Through the Arts," in *Champions of Change*, p. 45). Students in schools with high-arts integration or in "arts rich" schools scored higher on the figural creativity test, had a higher self-concept, and received higher teacher ratings on expression, risk taking, creativity, imagination, and cooperative learning.

Assessment

Use the following rubric to evaluate the artwork students make in the Creative Expression activity and to assess students' understanding of emphasis of an art element.

Have students complete page 73 or 74 in their *Assessment* books.

	Art History and Culture	Aesthetic Perception	Creative Expression	Art Criticism
3 POINTS	The student can demonstrate knowledge of the lives and artwork of Arthur Dove and Mitch Lyons.	The student accurately identifies emphasis used in art.	The student's prints clearly illustrate the use of emphasis.	The student thoughtfully and honestly evaluates own work using the four steps of art criticism.
2 POINTS	The student's knowledge of the lives and artwork of Arthur Dove and Mitch Lyons is weak or incomplete.	The student shows emerging awareness of emphasis used in art.	The student's prints show some awareness of emphasis.	The student attempts to evaluate own work but shows an incomplete understanding of evaluation criteria.
1 POINT	The student cannot demonstrate knowledge of the life and artwork of Arthur Dove or Mitch Lyons.	The student cannot identify emphasis used in art.	The student's prints show no understanding of emphasis.	The student makes no attempt to evaluate own artwork.

Assessment, p. 73

Name _____ Date _____ Lesson **3** UNIT 6

Emphasis of an Element

A. Fill in the Blank

Complete the following sentence by filling in the blank.

_____ is the principle of design that stresses one area over another area.

B. Drawing

Draw a picture of a real or imaginary animal. Emphasize an area of the picture using line, color, or shape.

C. Writing

Look at Sun and write a paragraph on the back of this paper that describes Dove's use of emphasis in this work of art.

Level 5   Unit 6 • Harmony, Variety, Emphasis, and Unity   **73**

Emphasis through Placement

Lesson 4 introduces the principle of emphasis through placement. An artist can direct the viewer's eyes by placing objects and subjects in the center or alone in a work of art.

Objectives

 Art History and Culture

To demonstrate knowledge of the Huichol people and their artwork

 Creative Expression

To create emphasis through placement in an original yarn painting

 Aesthetic Perception

To identify emphasis through placement in works of art NSAE 2.b

 Art Criticism

To evaluate one's own work using the four steps of art criticism

Lesson Materials

- picture books
- pencils
- 9" × 12" heavy cardboard
- scissors
- white glue
- various colors of yarn
- toothpicks
- small sponges or rags

Alternate Materials:
- magazines
- *Large Prints*
- oil pastels

Program Resources

- *Reading and Writing Test Prep.*, pp. 72–73
- *Transparency 34*
- *Flash Card 15*
- *Artist Profiles*, pp. 78, 73
- *Animals Through History Time Line*
- *Assessment*, pp. 75–76
- *Large Print 72* Earth Is a Planet with One Peace Missing
- *The National Museum of Women in the Arts Collection*

Concept Trace
Emphasis through Placement
Introduced: Level 4, Unit 6, Lesson 5
Reinforced: Level 6, Unit 4, Lesson 6

Vocabulary [★] Vocabulary

Review the following vocabulary words with students.

emphasis énfasis—the principle of art that stresses one area in an artwork over other areas

focal point punto focal—the area of an artwork that is emphasized

location ubicación—emphasis of an object because it has been placed in the center of an artwork

See page 209B for additional vocabulary and Spanish vocabulary resources.

 Art Journal: Vocabulary

Have students add these words to the Vocabulary section of their Art Journals.

Lesson 4 Arts Integration

Theatre

Complete Unit 6, Lesson 4, on pages 114–115 of *Theatre Arts Connections*.

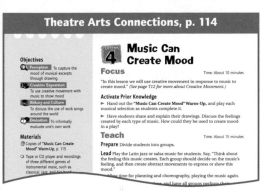

Theatre Arts Connections, p. 114

Music

 A five-eighths meter is created by a rhythm of three and two. Sing or listen to "Turn the World Around" by Robert M. Freedman and Harry Belafonte. Clap the rhythm of the refrain while you count 1-2-3-1-2. Put the emphasis on beat one.

Movement & Dance

Create an imaginary canvas outline on the floor with string or tape. Have six students walk into the space and find a way to arrange themselves on the canvas, being sure to observe the balance as they would in a painting. Ask a seventh person to enter the canvas with a prop, such as a hat or umbrella. What happens when this new person is added? How does it affect the scene and everyone's placement? Encourage students to investigate many different arrangements.

**ocus**

Time: About 20 minutes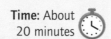

Activate Prior Knowledge

"Think about billboards you have seen. Where were your eyes attracted to first when you looked at these billboards?" "Piensen en las carteleras que hayan visto. ¿Hacia dónde se atrajo primero su vista cuando vieron estas carteleras?"

■ Discuss students' answers to the question. Billboards are designed to be seen quickly as cars travel past them.

Using Literature Reading

■ Share with the class Elizabeth Boron de Treviño's *El Güero*. Point out how the artist emphasized the character on the cover by placing his image in the center.

Thematic Connection ⭐ Social Studies

■ **Journeys:** Ask students to discuss a journey that they have taken or a trip they would like to take. Have students show on a map where they went, what they saw, and how life was different there from what they were used to.

Introduce the Art

Look

"Let's take a close look at the two works of art." "Vamos a observar detalladamente las dos obras de arte."

Comparing and Contrasting ⭐ Reading

■ Have students compare and contrast the two works of art in this lesson.

🏺 Art History and Culture

Because Huichol people depend on the sun and rain for their survival as subsistence farmers, they have developed cultural traditions that offer praise and homage to the gods that control the weather.

💻 **Web Connection**
Visit **www.mexconnect.com/mex_/huichol/ huicholart.html** to learn more about Huichol yarn paintings.

Lesson 4 Emphasis through Placement

Look at the artwork on these pages. Notice how your eyes are drawn to the center of each artwork.

▲ **Artist unknown.** (Huichol People/Mexico). *Mother of the Eagles.* 1991. Braided yarn embedded in vegetable wax on wood. $15\frac{3}{4} \times 19\frac{1}{2}$ inches (40 × 49.53 cm.). Private collection.

🏺 Art History and Culture

In their artwork, the Huichol people of Mexico often express respect for their native culture with spiritual symbols such as earth, sun, fire, water, wind, corn, deer, and rocks.

🏺 Art History and Culture

Mother of Eagles

The yarn painting *Mother of Eagles* was made by an unknown artist of the Huichol people of Santa Catarina in Jalisco, Mexico. The Huichol people, a cultural and ethnic group descended from the Aztecs, live in the mountainous central Mexican states of Jalisco and Nayarit. Huichol artists do not sign their artwork, which makes it difficult to identify the artist who created a specific piece. Within the Huichol culture, however, community members can often determine an artist's identity by observing the style, materials, and workmanship of the piece.

See pages 24–25 and 16–21 for more about art history and subject matter.

Artist Profiles, p. 78

‹ Artist Profile ›

Mother of the Eagles

The yarn painting, *Mother of the Eagles*, was made by an unknown artist of the Huichol Indians of Santa Catarina in Jalisco, Mexico. The Huichol Indians, a cultural and ethnic group descended from the Aztecs, live in the mountainous central Mexican states of Jalisco and Nayarit. Huichol artists do not sign their artwork, which makes it difficult to identify the artist who created a specific piece. Within local Huichol culture, community members can often determine an artist's identity by observing the style, materials, and workmanship of the piece.

▲ **Artist unknown.** (Huichol People, Mexico). *Mother of the Eagles.* 1991.

Study both works of art. Notice the areas in both pieces that grab your attention. Artists can emphasize an area or an object by placing it alone or toward the center of the artwork.

▶ Where do your eyes go first in each work of art?

▶ How have the artists directed your eyes to these areas?

▶ How might the works of art change if these areas were moved?

▲ **Artist unknown.** (Huichol People/Mexico).
Huichol Bead Mask. 2000.

Wood and glass beads. 5 × 3 inches. (12.7 × 7.62 cm.).
Private collection.

 Aesthetic Perception

Seeing Like an Artist Look at objects in nature. Record the items that draw your attention to the center. Do you think this area of emphasis affects the survival of this natural object?

Unit 6 • Lesson 4 **199**

Art History and Culture

Huichol Bead Mask

The bead mask was made by an unknown artist of the Huichol people of Santa Catarina in Jalisco, Mexico. The Huichol support their families by hunting and farming. The rugged landscape and dry conditions of the region make subsistence farming difficult. Because they depend on the sun and the rain for their survival, the Huichol have developed cultural traditions that offer praise and homage to the gods whom they believe control the weather. Creating masks is how the Huichol record images that come to them in dreams brought on by these ceremonies. This mask is a typical example of the pattern, style, and brilliant colors often seen in Huichol bead art.

See pages 24–25 and 16–21 for more about art history and subject matter.

Artist Profiles, p. 73

◇ Artist Profile ◇
Huichol Bead Mask
This bead mask was made by an unknown artist of the Huichol Indian peoples of Santa Catarina in Jalisco, Mexico. The Huichol Indians, a cultural and ethnic group descended from the Aztecs, live in the mountainous central Mexican states of Jalisco and Nayarit. Huichol artists do not sign their artwork, which makes it very difficult to identify the artist who created a specific piece. Within local Huichol culture, however, an artist's identity can often be determined by other members of the community by observing the style, materials, and construction of the piece.

▲ **Artist unknown.** (Huichol People/Mexico).
Huichol Bead Mask.

Study NSAE 5.c

▶ *Mother of Eagles:* The viewer's eyes travel to the center of this yarn painting first. *Huichol Bead Mask:* The viewer's eyes move to the top of the mask first and then down through the center.

▶ The artists have directed the viewer's eyes to these emphasized areas through placement.

▶ The messages of these works of art might not be as clearly stated if the areas of emphasis were moved.

■ For more examples of narrative art, see *The National Museum of Women in the Arts Collection.*

Art Journal: Writing
Have students each write a short story in their Art Journals about a character who takes an unexpected journey.

Aesthetic Perception

Design Awareness If possible, bring a Venus flytrap into the classroom. Allow students to study the plant and its unique survival skills. Discuss the fact that the seeds of many plants are stored in the center of the plants. Also discuss how insects aid in the pollination of plants by landing in the center of their blossoms.

Developing Visual Literacy Discuss with students the reasons they think the Huichol people do not sign their artwork. Ask students whether they can relate to this thinking and to explain why or why not.

Web Connection
Visit **www.mexconnect.com/mex_/huichol/art-masks1.html** to learn more about the Huichol people and their beaded masks.

LESSON 4 • Emphasis through Placement **199**

Teach

"How can you create emphasis in an artwork though the placement of objects and designs?" "¿Cómo pueden crear énfasis en una obra de arte mediante la colocación de los objetos y diseños?"

- Read and discuss the definitions of *emphasis, focal point, isolation,* and *location* on page 200.

Practice

Materials: picture books

Alternate Materials: magazines, *Large Prints*

- Review the Practice activity directions on page 200 with students.

- Have students form groups to look through picture books. Ask students to identify illustrations with strong areas of emphasis, or focal points. Allow students to share the best examples of isolation and location that they find with the class.

Creative Expression

Materials: pencils, 9" × 12" pieces of heavy cardboard, scissors, white glue, various colors of yarn, toothpicks, small sponges or rags

Alternate Materials: oil pastels

- Distribute the materials and have students follow the directions on page 201.

- If students' fingers get sticky, have them use damp sponges or cloth to clean off the glue.

- Mount or mat the finished works of art for display.

- Set up an area of the room to use as the gallery. Allow students to analyze the original artwork of their classmates during their free time in this gallery area.

- Review the Activity Tips on page 246 for visual examples of this lesson's activity.
NSAE 1.a

Art Journal: Brainstorming

Have students sketch ideas in their Art Journals for an original design in which the area of emphasis is created through isolation or location. Ask students to plan the colors, lines, shapes, value contrasts, balance, and type of emphasis they will use to make their designs.

Using Emphasis through Placement

You have learned that **emphasis** is the principle of design that stresses one area in an artwork over another area. Two types of visual emphasis can be used: emphasis of an art element and emphasis through placement. Sometimes a specific area in an artwork is emphasized. This area is called the **focal point.** There are several techniques that artists use to create emphasis.

Isolation happens when an object is placed alone and away from the other objects in an artwork. The viewer's eye is drawn to the isolated object.

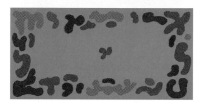

Location occurs when the viewer's eyes are naturally drawn toward the center of an artwork. Anything placed near the center of the picture will be noticed first.

Practice

Look for examples of emphasis in illustrations in literature.

1. Look though picture books with your group for illustrations that have strong focal points or areas of emphasis.

2. Share what you have found with the class.

3. Explain why you chose each illustration and how the artist created emphasis.

Differentiated Instruction

Reteach
Have students look at the Huichol yarn paintings and beaded masks that can be found on the Web sites listed in the Web Connection on pages 198 and 199. Students can print images of some of these works of art and identify the areas of emphasis.

Special Needs
Students who lack fine motor skills may benefit from using thicker yarn or applying the glue with a brush.

ELL
In small-group discussions, support students with some discussion guidelines. A speaker's turn can be indicated by holding an object and passing it to the next person. Students may also ask for assistance when it is their turn.

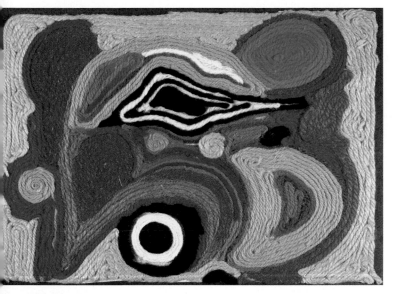

◀ **Juan Garcia.**
Age 10

Think about how the artist created emphasis through placement.

 Creative Expression

Create an area of emphasis in an original design through placement using isolation or location.

1. Pick a sketch from your Art Journal and draw it on your cardboard.

2. Place the glue on the outlines of the shapes. Fill in the shapes with strands of different colored yarn. Squeeze a line of glue for each piece of yarn as you work.

3. Use a variety of line directions, yarn, and textures. Do not leave any spaces between the yarn lines.

4. Use a toothpick to press the yarn onto the glued areas.

 Art Criticism

Describe Describe the shapes that you used in your design. Are the shapes realistic, or nonobjective?

Analyze How have you created emphasis using placement? Can you find areas of isolation or location?

Interpret Does this work of art communicate a story? What mood is communicated?

Decide Do you have an area of the artwork that turned out better than another? What is it that you like about this area?

Reflect   Time: About 15 minutes

Review and Assess

"Were you successful at creating an area of emphasis using the principle of location or isolation in your original design?" "¿Pudieron crear un área de énfasis usando el principio de ubicación o aislamiento en su diseño original?"

Think

The artist used the principle of location to emphasize the area in the center of the artwork.

■ Use *Large Print 72 Earth Is a Planet with One Peace Missing* to have students identify and describe the use of emphasis through placement.

Informal Assessment

■ For standardized-format test practice using this lesson's art content, see pages 72–73 in *Reading and Writing Test Preparation.*

Art Journal: Critical Thinking
Have students answer the four art criticism questions—Describe, Analyze, Interpret, and Decide—in their Art Journals. In small groups, have students discuss their yarn paintings. NSAE 2.a

⟡ Art Across the Curriculum ⟡

Use these simple ideas to reinforce art concepts across the curriculum.

★ **Personal Writing** Have students imagine that they have just been given passports and enough money to travel around the world in just two weeks. Ask them to make a list of what they will pack for this journey.

★ **Math** Discuss how changing the placement of a decimal point can change the value of a number.

★ **Science** Discuss how the Huichol people use little technology in their culture. Have students visualize what these people's lives might be like and how they are different from the culture students are accustomed to.

★ **Social Studies** Have students each map out five places they would like to stop on a two-week journey around the world.

★ **Technology** Have students create an artwork using a paint program in which they use emphasis through isolation or location. Visit **SRAonline.com** to print detailed instructions for this activity. NSAE 6.b

Emphasis through Placement

Extra! For the Art Specialist

Time: About 50 minutes

Focus

Have students study **Large Print 72** *Earth Is a Planet with One Peace Missing* to understand how an artist sometimes emphasizes an area in an artwork by placing it in the center of the composition.

Teach

Discuss how an object that is placed towards the center of a composition draws the viewer's attention. Tell students that simply making one object so large that it fills the paper will also create emphasis.

Reflect

Have students evaluate their works of art using the four steps of art criticism. Encourage them to locate and describe the areas of emphasis.

Alternate Activity

Materials:

- Art Journals
- pencils, erasers
- real, plastic, or silk flowers and leaves
- 12″ × 12″ white drawing paper
- color wheel
- tempera paints
- various-sized paintbrushes
- water containers
- newspapers, paper towels

1. Select a flower or leaf that you would like to draw and create several simple sketches in your Art Journal of that one object.

2. Transfer one of the sketches onto paper using pencil. Center the drawing on the paper so that it touches three edges.

3. Begin by carefully painting the flower or leaf using up to three colors. Keep one of the colors as the dominant color.

Research in Art Education

"Since the matter of aesthetic criticism is the perception of aesthetic objects, natural and artistic criticism is always determined by the quality of firsthand perception; obtuseness in perception can never be made good by any amount of learning, however extensive, nor any command of abstract theory however correct." (John Dewey, *Art As Experience*. 1934.)

Assessment

Use the following rubric to evaluate the artwork students make in the Creative Expression activity and to assess students' understanding of emphasis through placement.

Have students complete page 75 or 76 in their *Assessment* books.

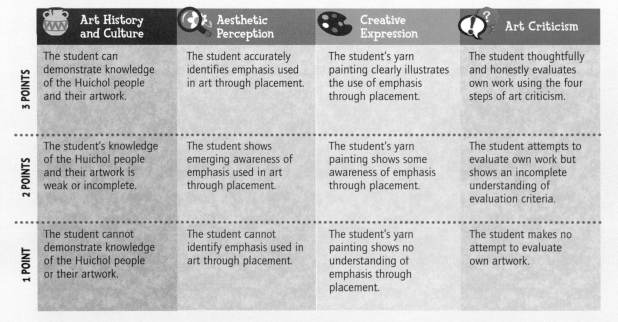

	Art History and Culture	Aesthetic Perception	Creative Expression	Art Criticism
3 POINTS	The student can demonstrate knowledge of the Huichol people and their artwork.	The student accurately identifies emphasis used in art through placement.	The student's yarn painting clearly illustrates the use of emphasis through placement.	The student thoughtfully and honestly evaluates own work using the four steps of art criticism.
2 POINTS	The student's knowledge of the Huichol people and their artwork is weak or incomplete.	The student shows emerging awareness of emphasis used in art through placement.	The student's yarn painting shows some awareness of emphasis through placement.	The student attempts to evaluate own work but shows an incomplete understanding of evaluation criteria.
1 POINT	The student cannot demonstrate knowledge of the Huichol people or their artwork.	The student cannot identify emphasis used in art through placement.	The student's yarn painting shows no understanding of emphasis through placement.	The student makes no attempt to evaluate own artwork.

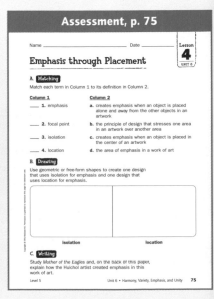

Assessment, p. 75

Name _____ Date _____ Lesson **4** UNIT 6

Emphasis through Placement

A. Matching

Match each term in Column 1 to its definition in Column 2.

Column 1	Column 2
___ 1. emphasis	a. creates emphasis when an object is placed alone and away from the other objects in an artwork
___ 2. focal point	b. the principle of design that stresses one area in an artwork over another area
___ 3. isolation	c. creates emphasis when an object is placed in the center of an artwork
___ 4. location	d. the area of emphasis in a work of art

B. Drawing

Use geometric or free-form shapes to create one design that uses isolation for emphasis and one design that uses location for emphasis.

isolation | location

C. Writing

Study *Mother of the Eagles* and, on the back of this paper, explain how the Huichol artist created emphasis in this work of art.

Level 5 | Unit 6 • Harmony, Variety, Emphasis, and Unity | 75

Lesson 5 Overview

Unity through Media

Lesson 5 introduces unity. An artist can balance the principles of harmony and variety to create unity in a work of art. Too much variety creates chaos, while too much harmony can be boring.

Objectives

 Art History and Culture

To demonstrate knowledge of the lives and work of Irene Preston Miller and Elizabeth Garrison

Creative Expression

To make a class quilt using common media to create unity

 Aesthetic Perception

To identify unity through media in a work of art NSAE 2.b

 Art Criticism

To evaluate one's own work using the four steps of art criticism

Vocabulary ⭐ Vocabulary

Review the following vocabulary words with students before beginning the lesson.

unity unidad—the quality of wholeness or oneness achieved by balancing harmony and variety in a work of art

media medio—the materials used to create something

See page 209B for additional Spanish vocabulary resources.

 Art Journal: Vocabulary

Have students add these words to the Vocabulary section of their Art Journals.

Lesson Materials

- magazines or catalogs
- notebook paper
- pencils
- drawing paper
- 6" × 6" white poster-board squares
- black felt-tip markers
- resources for state symbols
- construction paper
- scissors
- glue
- quilt-sized bulletin board large enough to fit each student's poster-board square

Alternate Materials:
- tempera paints
- paintbrushes
- newspapers

Program Resources
- *Reading and Writing Test Prep.*, pp. 74–75
- *Transparency 35*
- *Flash Cards 16, 17, 18*
- *Artist Profiles*, pp. 41, 26
- *Animals Through History Time Line*
- *Assessment*, pp. 77–78
- *Large Print 71 El Chandelier*
- *The National Museum of Women in the Arts Collection*

Concept Trace
Unity through Media
Introduced: Level 4, Unit 6, Lesson 6
Reinforced: Level 6, Unit 6, Lessons 5, 6

Lesson 5 Arts Integration

Theatre
Complete Unit 6, Lesson 5, on pages 116–117 of *Theatre Arts Connections.*

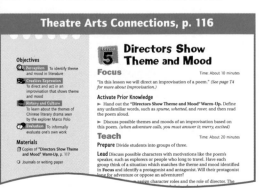

Music
Listen to "Tuileries" from *Pictures at an Exhibition.* The instrumental sounds stay high and light throughout the piece. There is a contrasting middle section, or the "B section," where the melody smooths out. Why does the total piece have a feeling of unity, even with the contrasting rhythms and phrasing of the middle section?

Movement & Dance
Divide students into equal groups. Show the students three locomotor movements that each group will perform together. Ask each group to create one original axial movement that they will incorporate into their dance. In this way there will be a sense of unity between all of the groups.

Focus

Time: About 30 minutes

Activate Prior Knowledge

"Have you ever tried to talk on the phone while someone had the television volume on too loud, someone was running the vacuum cleaner, music was playing, and noises from outside were blaring?" "¿Alguna vez han tratado de hablar por teléfono mientras otra persona tenía la televisión prendida con mucho volumen, otra persona aspiraba, se oía música y ruidos estruendosos de la calle?"

- Discuss students' answers. Talk about this and similar situations that lack unity because of too much variety.

Using Literature ★ Reading

- Share with students *One Grain of Rice* by Demi. This mathematical Indian folktale teaches the value of generosity, honesty, and charity.

Thematic Connection ★ Reading

- **Sharing Stories:** Ask students to bring to class some of their favorite stories. Create a chart to record these stories' titles, their authors, whether they are fact or fiction, and summaries. Compare and contrast the stories as the chart grows.

Introduce the Art

Look

"Let's take a close look at the two works of art." "Vamos a observar detalladamente las dos obras de arte."

Artist's Purpose ★ Reading

- Have students look at both quilts that appear in this lesson and ask them to suggest what the artist's purpose was for designing and creating each work of art.

Art History and Culture

Discuss other areas of visual arts that have developed because of technology such as screen printing, graphic design, and photography.

 Web Connection

Visit **www.womenfolk.com/historyofquilts/** to learn more about America's quilting history.

Unity through Media

▲ **Irene Preston Miller and the Hudson River Quilters.** (American). *The Hudson River Quilt.* 1969–1972.

Cotton, wool, and blends with cotton embroidery. $95\frac{1}{4} \times 80$ inches (241.95 × 203.2 cm.). American Folk Art Museum, New York, New York.

Look at the artwork on these pages. Notice how the artists have used the same materials, or media, throughout their quilts. The scenes created by the artists vary, or are different, as you look at each quilt but the cotton, wool, and embroidery stitching ties the piece together to create unity.

Art History and Culture

Prior to sewing machines, quilters commonly stitched with hidden stitches. With machines, quilters began to show stitching as a way to boast of owning a sewing machine.

Art History and Culture

Irene Preston Miller and the Hudson River Quilters

Irene Preston Miller (ī′ rēn pres′ tən mi′ lər) and thirty women created *the Hudson River Quilt* as a way of drawing attention to the beauty of the Hudson River and to gain protection for it. A plan to install a pump-storage unit near a nuclear power plant would have threatened the river's Storm King Mountain and the striped bass spawning grounds. Most of the women learned the art of quilting as they worked. *Hudson River Quilt* toured the world raising funds and environmental awareness. Each quilt block tells the story of the river's journey from the Adirondack Mountains to the New York City harbor.

See pages 24–25 and 16–21 for more about art history and subject matter.

Artist Profiles, p. 41

Artist Profile

Irene Preston Miller and the Hudson River Quilters

Irene Preston Miller (ī′ rēn pres′ tan mi′ lər), an avid quilter and seamstress, was involved with the publication of a number of sewing and quilting instruction books. One of her most substantial and well-known pieces is the *Hudson River Quilt*, which she and a group of 30 women, the Hudson River Quilters, created together.

◄ **Irene Preston Miller and the Hudson River Quilters.** (American). *The Hudson River Quilt.* 1969–1972.

◀ **Elizabeth Garrison.** (American).
Georgia. 1983.
••••••••••••••••••••••••••••••••
Cotton. 4 × 5¼ feet (1.22 × 1.6 m.)
St. Simons Island Historical Museum of
Georgia, St. Simons Island, Georgia.

Study both works of art. Notice the unity that is created from using the same media, or materials.

▶ What materials were used to make these quilts?

▶ Look at each quilt and find common colors, shapes, lines, and ideas.

▶ How does the repetition of media, materials, and ideas help to bring this artwork together as one piece?

▶ What would change if other materials were added to these quilts? What materials would you add?

🔍 Aesthetic Perception

Design Awareness Look at three-dimensional designs, such as bus-stop shelters, and notice how designers have repeated the use of media throughout the design to create unity.

Art History and Culture

Elizabeth Garrison

Elizabeth Garrison (i li´ zə beth ga´ ri sən) (1914–) designed *Georgia Quilt* for the 250th birthday of the state of Georgia quilting competition. When the quilting competition was announced, Garrison was about to leave on a trip. She made her sketches, selected her fabrics, and took all her work with her. When she returned to Georgia she sewed it together and did all the hand stitching to complete the quilt just in time for the competition. This quilt won first place in its field.

See pages 24–25 and 16–21 for more about art history and subject matter.

Artist Profiles, p. 26

◆ Artist Profile ◆
Elizabeth Garrison
b. 1914

Elizabeth Garrison (i li´ zə beth ga´ re sən) earned a teaching certificate from a two-year college in 1932, and began teaching in the small town of Benevolence, Georgia. She was paid $50 a month for eight months of work in a small country school where she taught Grades 1 through 4 in one room. Out of that $50, she paid $15 room and board, saved money to go to summer school, and helped to pay a younger brother's tuition in an Alabama prep school. After two years of teaching, she received a scholarship to go to school full time to finish her four-year degree.

◀ **Elizabeth Garrison.** (American). *Georgia.* 1983.

Study NSAE 5.c

▶ Cotton, wool, and blends with cotton embroidery were used to make these quilts.

▶ Within each quilt, the blocks share common colors, lines, shapes, and one main theme. This repetition helps to create unity in the works of art.

▶ Both quilts are made of the same materials and their blocks have a common theme, which create unified works of art. Everything in each quilt seems to fit together, which creates harmony. Because each block is different, however, variety is created in each artwork. The two concepts of harmony and variety are balanced to create unity.

▶ By adding different materials, the artists would be adding variety and excitement to the quilts. If too much variety were added, the unity will be lost.

■ For more examples of utilitarian art, see ***The National Museum of Women in the Arts Collection.***

📓 Art Journal: Writing

Ask students to each write an original story based on either quilt in this lesson.

🔍 Aesthetic Perception

Design Awareness Ask student to share the unified designs they recorded and identify what common materials created the unity. Discuss how an artist sometimes adds a quantity of variety to a design and controls whether the unity is lost or preserved.

Developing Visual Literacy Discuss the theme of each quilt in this lesson. Ask students if they have ever seen something tell a story without words or sounds and discuss the similarities and differences between this form of communication and the use of words.

💻 Web Connection

Visit **www.memory.loc.gov/ammem/qlthtml/ qlthome.html** to learn more about quilts and quiltmaking in America.

Teach

"How can you create *unity* in a work of art with your choice of media?" "¿Cómo pueden crear unidad en una obra de arte con cualquier medio que escojan?"

- Read and discuss the definition of *unity* on page 204.

Practice

Materials: magazines, notebook paper, pencils

Alternate Materials: catalogs

- Review the Practice activity directions on page 204 with students.

- Distribute magazines to student groups. Ask students to look through the magazines to find objects or sets of objects in which harmony and variety are balanced because of a common medium.

Creative Expression

Materials: drawing paper, 6" × 6" white poster-board squares, black felt-tip markers, resources for state symbols, construction paper, scissors, glue, quilt-sized bulletin board large enough to fit each student's poster-board square

Alternate Materials: tempera paints, paintbrushes, newspapers

- Prepare a large bulletin board that will hold all the students' poster-board squares in quilt fashion.

- Distribute the materials and have students follow the directions on page 205.

- Review the Activity Tips on page 247 for visual examples of this lesson's activity.

Art Journal: Brainstorming

Have students look through the state-symbol resources and select a state as a class. You might want to choose your own state, as students will be most familiar with its symbols. Each student will need to individually select the symbol he or she will be using in the quilt block and ask you to approve it to ensure variety in the finished class quilt.

Using Unity through Media

Unity is wholeness, or oneness. Artists create unity by making everything work together. When works of art have unity, all of the elements are arranged to look like they belong together. Artists create unity when they balance the art principles of *harmony,* which stresses similarities, with *variety,* which stresses differences.

Some artists use similar media, or materials, in an artwork to create unity.

Notice how the designer has used bricks in different areas to create unity here.

Quilts are often made up of many different squares, sometimes sewn by many different people, but the entire piece will work together as one artwork because it was created from similar fabric and related materials.

Practice

1. Look through a magazine with a partner. Find objects or sets of objects that have unity because they are made from one kind of media. Look for things like a wood dining room set, matching fabrics, a blanket or quilt made from just one material, a metal filing cabinet, or a set of dishes.

2. Write the characteristics of the object or set of objects that you find.

3. Explain how unity is created through media.

Differentiated Instruction

Reteach
Have students look through their textbooks to find example of works of art that balance harmony and variety to create unity. Student can then identify in these works of art the pieces that are unified through common media.

Special Needs
Use this group activity as an opportunity to model and reinforce class norms of respect and cooperation.

ELL
It can be difficult for students in the early and intermediate stages of learning a new language to talk about a subject. Use rough sketches and photographs to help with the lesson concepts and questions. Students may point out examples to help explain their answers.

◄ **Kelly Armstrong.**
Age 11.

Think about how the artist created unity through the use of common media.

 Creative Expression

How can you create unity in one artwork made by different people? Make a class quilt using state symbols.

1. Draw your chosen state symbol on a sheet of paper at least four times using different sizes. Color the drawings.

2. Cut each of the symbols out and place them on pieces of construction paper. Trace these shapes with a marker and cut them out.

3. Glue the symbols onto a posterboard square. Place the larger pieces down first. Overlap the shapes.

4. Add details with fine-tip markers.

Art Criticism

Describe Which state did your class choose? What symbol did you choose for this state?

Analyze What media was used to unify this quilt?

Interpret How many symbols can you identify while looking at this state quilt?

Decide What gives this quilt a feeling of harmony? What gives this quilt a feeling of diversity? Do these two elements seem balanced, or is one stronger than the other?

Unit 6 • Lesson 5　**205**

Reflect

 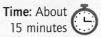

Review and Assess

"Does the class quilt balance variety and harmony to create unity?" "¿La colcha de la clase equilibra la variedad y la armonía para crear unidad?"

Think

The artist created unity through the use of paper throughout the work of art.

- Use **Large Print 71** *El Chandelier* to have students identify and describe how the artist used media to unify his work.

Informal Assessment

- For standardized-format test practice using this lesson's art content, see pages 74–75 in *Reading and Writing Test Preparation.*

Art Journal: Critical Thinking
Have students answer the four art criticism questions—Describe, Analyze, Interpret, and Decide—in their Art Journals. In small groups, have students discuss their state-symbols quilt. NSAE 2.a

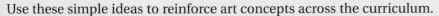

Art Across the Curriculum

Use these simple ideas to reinforce art concepts across the curriculum.

★ **Narrative Writing** Start students off with the first two sentences of a story. Time students to write as much as they can to continue the story without stopping for two minutes and then have them pass their papers to a neighbor, who will pick up the story. Continue around the room.

★ **Math** Have students use the dimensions of the quilts in this lesson to compute the size of each block.

★ **Science** Explore the environmental issues related to local bodies of water.

★ **Social Studies** Have students locate the Hudson River on a map and trace its journey from the Adirondack Mountains to the New York City harbor.

★ **Technology** Ask students to evaluate the unity in various computer designs.
NSAE 6.b

Unity through Media

Extra! For the Art Specialist

Time: About 50 minutes

Focus

Have students study **Large Print 71** *El Chandelier* to understand how an artist can use unity to bring together different objects or art elements so that everything fits together in a work of art.

Teach

Discuss how the media used often unifies the various elements in an artwork. Explain to students that they will each be creating a necklace using small metal objects, such as buttons, beads, washers, star washers, nuts, springs, and grommets. Ask students to collect a variety of small metal objects that can be strung on a piece of cording prior to beginning this lesson.

Reflect

Have students evaluate their works of art using the four steps of art criticism. Encourage them to identify the common medium that creates unity.

Alternate Activity

Materials:
- cording
- scissors
- thin jewelers' wire or thin craft wire
- variety of small metal objects
- needle-nose pliers

1. Begin by looking through the collected metal objects and select eight to ten pieces.

2. Cut a piece of cording long enough to fit over your heads once it is tied, approximately 24 inches. Loop the cording around your neck to measure the length prior to cutting it. Add an additional 2 inches for knotting.

3. Lay out your collected metal objects and decide how to arrange them on the necklace. Jewelers' wire or thin craft wire can be used to attach smaller objects to larger objects. Once you have an arrangement you like, begin assembling the necklace.

Research in Art Education

High-arts students outscore low-arts students on measures of creative thinking, elaboration, and resistance to closure. Teachers are more likely to perceive high-arts students, and students are more likely to perceive themselves, as academically competent ("Learning in and Through the Arts," in *Champions of Change*, p. 40).

Assessment
Use the following rubric to evaluate the artwork students make in the Creative Expression activity and to assess students' understanding of unity through media.

Have students complete page 77 or 78 in their *Assessment* books.

	Art History and Culture	Aesthetic Perception	Creative Expression	Art Criticism
3 POINTS	The student can demonstrate knowledge of the lives and artwork of Irene Preston Miller and Elizabeth Garrison.	The student accurately identifies unity through media used in a work of art.	The student's quilt block clearly illustrates the use of unity.	The student thoughtfully and honestly evaluates own work using the four steps of art criticism.
2 POINTS	The student's knowledge of the lives and artwork of Irene Preston Miller and Elizabeth Garrison is weak or incomplete.	The student shows emerging awareness of unity through media used in a work of art.	The student's quilt block shows some awareness of unity.	The student attempts to evaluate own work but shows an incomplete understanding of evaluation criteria.
1 POINT	The student cannot demonstrate knowledge of the life and artwork of Irene Preston Miller or Elizabeth Garrison.	The student cannot identify unity through media in a work of art.	The student's quilt block shows no understanding of unity.	The student makes no attempt to evaluate own artwork.

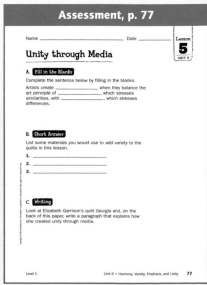

Assessment, p. 77

Name _____ Date _____

Lesson
5
UNIT 6

Unity through Media

A. Fill in the Blanks

Complete the sentence below by filling in the blanks.

Artists create _____ when they balance the art principle of _____, which stresses similarities, with _____, which stresses differences.

B. Short Answer

List some materials you would use to add variety to the quilts in this lesson.

1. _____
2. _____
3. _____

C. Writing

Look at Elizabeth Garrison's quilt *Georgia* and, on the back of this paper, write a paragraph that explains how she created unity through media.

Level 5   Unit 6 • Harmony, Variety, Emphasis, and Unity 77

Lesson 6 — Unity through Theme
Overview

Lesson 6 introduces unity achieved through a common theme in a work of art. Unity is the sense of wholeness or oneness that is communicated through the balance of harmony and variety in a work of art.

Objectives

 Art History and Culture

To demonstrate knowledge of Mexican ceramics and the life and artwork of Elizabeth Paulos-Krasle

 Creative Expression

To create a clay animal bank that has unity

 Aesthetic Perception

To identify unity through theme in works of art NSAE 2.b

 Art Criticism

To evaluate one's own work using the four steps of art criticism

Vocabulary Vocabulary

Review the following vocabulary words with students before beginning the lesson.

unity unidad—the sense of wholeness or oneness achieved by balancing harmony and variety in a work of art

theme tema—the main subject or idea of an artwork

See page 209B for additional Spanish vocabulary resources.

 Art Journal: Vocabulary

Have students add these words to the Vocabulary section of their Art Journals.

Lesson Materials
- pencils, erasers
- clay
- board or canvas cloth to work clay on
- clay tools
- newspapers
- slip containers
- acrylic paints
- paintbrushes

Alternate Materials:
- self-hardening clay

Program Resources
- *Reading and Writing Test Prep.*, pp. 76–77
- *Transparency 36*
- *Flash Cards 16, 17, 18*
- *Artist Profiles*, pp. 82, 36
- *Animals Through History Time Line*
- *Assessment*, pp. 79–80
- *Large Print 71* El Chandelier
- *The National Museum of Women in the Arts Collection*

Concept Trace
Unity through Theme
Introduced: Level 4, Unit 6, Lesson 6
Reinforced: Level 6, Unit 6, Lessons 5, 6

Lesson 6 Arts Integration

Theatre

Complete Unit 6, Lesson 6, on pages 118–123 of *Theatre Arts Connections.*

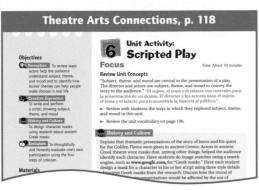

Theatre Arts Connections, p. 118

Music

 Listen to "Canon in D Major," by Johann Pachelbel. The three high voices are playing the same melodic material, but each enters at different times, which creates the "canon." The bass line, called "continuo" in Pachelbel's time, has a very simple job to create unity. What does it do?

Movement & Dance

Think of an activity such as basketball, hockey, baseball, soccer, or tennis. Ask students to demonstrate three movements from that sport. Each student will be improvising three movements of his or her own choice, but the unifying theme for everyone will be the sport that was selected. Discuss how each person made different choices in how they showed their idea.

Focus

Time: About 20 minutes

Activate Prior Knowledge

"Can you take away any part of a bike and still have it function properly?" "¿Pueden quitar una parte de una bicicleta y esperar que aún funcione adecuadamente?"

■ Discuss students' answers. Remind them that although all the parts of a bike look different and work differently, most are needed for the bike to function smoothly.

Using Literature ☆ Reading

■ Share *Love That Dog* by Sharon Creech with the class. This story is of a boy who loves his dog and also learns to love poetry.

Thematic Connection ☆ Science

■ **Animals in Art:** Ask students if they have any animals at home. Have students think about works of art that they have seen in which these animals appear.

Introduce the Art

Look

"Let's take a close look at the two works of art." "Vamos a observar detalladamente las dos obras de arte."

Sequencing ☆ Reading

■ Have students look at the two works of art in this lesson and think about the steps the artist took in planning and creating each piece.

🏺 Art History and Culture

Many cultures around the world have used natural materials to create art such as early Egyptian fabric dyes, African woodcarving masks, and Native American cave paintings.

 Web Connection

Visit **www.sa-museum.org/** to learn more about the San Antonio Museum of Art.

Unity through Theme

▲ **Artist unknown.** (Mexico). *Toy Banks.* Twentieth century.
....
Molded, single-fired, and painted earthenware. 8¼ × 13 inches (20.96 × 33.02 cm.). San Antonio Museum, San Antonio, Texas.

Look at the artwork on these pages and notice the theme. By using the same theme of animal banks, the artworks tie together and seem unified.

🏺 Art History and Culture

For thousands of years, clay found in nature has provided Mexican artists with materials for making sculptures, pottery, and many other functional, ceremonial, and decorative objects.

🏺 Art History and Culture

Toy Banks

These banks were made by an unidentified Metepec artist from Mexico. Metepec is a small town on the outskirts of the large city Toluca. Metepec is the home of many masters of ceramic art. *Toy Banks* was not signed by the artist but appears to have been made in the early twentieth century. Both ceramics and woodcarving have been important art forms throughout Mexico for thousands of years. The abundance of naturally occurring clay and numerous species of hardwood trees has provided many generations of artists with materials. *Toy Banks* was most likely made as a gift or for sale.

See pages 24–25 and 16–21 for more about art history and subject matter.

Artist Profiles, p. 82

> *Artist Profile*
>
> **Toy Banks**
>
> These banks were made by an unidentified Metepec artist from the state of México, located in central Mexico. Metepec is a small town on the outskirts of the large city Toluca. Metepec is home to many masters of ceramic art. Because the banks were not signed, it has been impossible to find the specific ceramic artist who made these pieces. It is estimated that the banks were made in the early twentieth century.

◀ **Elizabeth Paulos-Krasle.**
(American). *Puff.* 2003.
. . . .
14" inches tall (35.56 cm.). Private Collection.

Study both works of art. Notice the theme that brings the works of art together to create unity.

▶ Look at *Toy Banks* and find the common theme that carries throughout the artwork.

▶ What could you add to *Puff* to create unity by continuing a theme?

▶ If you compare *Puff* to *Toy Banks* what theme do you see?

Aesthetic Perception

Seeing Like an Artist Look at different collections and notice the common theme. For example, a collection of sports items might have a team's logo or the mascot on each item.

Study NSAE 5.c

▶ The common theme is ceramic animals in art.

▶ Dragons or other fantasy characters could be added to *Puff* to continue with the theme.

▶ Adding *Puff* to *Toy Bank* would create a theme of animal banks.

■ For more examples of genre art, see *The National Museum of Women in the Arts Collection.*

Art Journal: Writing

Ask students to write about their favorite animal and explain why it is their favorite.

Aesthetic Perception

Design Awareness Ask students to bring in their private collections. Allow students to enjoy looking at one another's collections and identify the themes.

Developing Visual Literacy Ask students to consider the dates of each work of art in this lesson. Have students discuss in small groups how artists influence one another and how they create and develop new techniques.

Art History and Culture

Elizabeth Paulos-Krasle

Elizabeth Paulos-Krasle (i li´ zə bəth kraz´ əl) (1964–) was born in British Columbia, Canada. She was raised on a fruit orchard and often passed the time making clay sculptures and bowls from the soil while ditch-irrigating vegetables. Clay was one of Paulos-Krasle's favorite media in both high school and college. Today she teaches in an elementary school and continues to develop her artwork. *Puff* is usable art. It is a toy bank made of clay, paint, and a ceramic glaze. Elizabeth Paulos-Krasle often uses textures from nature to imprint patterns into the clay as she works.

See pages 24–25 and 16–21 for more about art history and subject matter.

Artist Profiles, p. 36

◀ Artist Profile ▶
Elizabeth Paulos-Krasle
b. 1964

Elizabeth Paulos-Krasle (i li´ za bath kraz´ al) was born in 1964 in British Columbia, Canada. She was raised on a fruit orchard in Spences Bridge, British Columbia. She would often pass the time making clay sculptures and bowls from the soil. Her mother taught her how to sew, knit, and crochet in the Portuguese tradition, visually copying a pattern rather than reading it. Clay was one of Paulos-Krasle's favorite mediums in high school and college. While studying at the University of Victoria and the University of Georgia, she enjoyed hand building pieces from clay.

Web Connection

Visit **www.ilpi.com/artsource/vce/welcome.html** to explore an online exhibit of contemporary ceramics.

Teach

Time: About 45 minutes

"How can you create unity using a theme?"
"¿Cómo pueden crear unidad usando un tema?"

- Read and discuss the definition of *unity* on page 208.

Practice

Materials: clay, containers for slip, paintbrushes, scoring tools

Alternate Materials: paper clips

- Review the Practice activity directions on page 208 with students.

- Have students separate the clay into two pieces and flatten them to about the width of their thumbs. Students will need to decide which two edges they will be rejoining, score those edges, apply slip, and gently press the surfaces together. Ask students if they can hear the air pockets and slip mixture moving through the grooves they create when scoring the clay. Students will use clay tools and their fingers to smooth out the new seam and wipe away the excess slip.

Creative Expression

Materials: pencils, erasers, clay, board or canvas cloth to work clay on, clay tools, newspapers, slip containers, acrylic paints, paintbrushes

Alternate Materials: self-hardening clay

- Distribute the materials and have students follow the directions on page 209.

- Review the Activity Tips on page 247 for visual examples of this lesson's activity.

- See Technique Tips on page 226 and 228 for information on using clay.

 Art Journal: Brainstorming
Have students sketch ideas in their Art Journals for their clay animal banks. Ask students to think about how they will add texture to the clay surfaces of their animals.

Using Unity through Theme

Unity is the quality of wholeness or oneness that is achieved by balancing harmony and variety in the elements used. Unity happens when everything seems to tie together. When works of art have unity, all of the elements are arranged to look like they belong together.

Some artists use a similar or common theme in an artwork to create unity. The colors, lines, shapes, and materials might be different, but one theme pulls the artwork together.

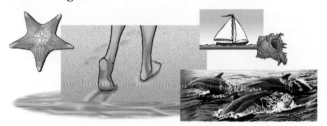

Notice how the artist used many different colors, lines, shapes, and materials, but the artwork is unified through the beach theme.

Practice

Practice slip, scoring, and smoothing clay pieces together.

1. Separate clay into two pieces and flatten. Decide which two edges you will reattach.

2. Scratch the two surfaces that will be joined with a tool.

3. Brush the slip, a creamy mixture of clay and water, onto the surface of one of the edges.

4. Gently press the two surfaces together so the slip oozes out of the seam.

5. Use clay tools or your fingers to smooth away the excess slip and smooth the new seam.

Differentiated Instruction

Reteach
Place all of the students' completed clay animal banks together and have students note the unity that is created through the theme. Ask students what different media, colors, shapes, and sizes they could add to the collection that might add variety without taking away from the theme.

Special Needs
Ensure the success of all students on this project by providing a thorough demonstration of the sculpture process and a written/illustrated list of steps.

ELL
As a way to clearly communicate the concept, give students visual examples of some collections that are connected through theme and some that are not. Ask students to organize like and unlike objects for assessment of understanding.

◀ **Camila Santos.**
Age 10.

Think about how the artist created unity through a common theme.

 Creative Expression

How can you use a common theme to create unity? Design and create a clay animal bank.

1. Create a small pinchpot base in a softball-size ball of clay. Cut a circle a little larger than the size of a quarter in this base.
2. Add clay coils onto the pinchpot for the body of the animal. Score and apply slip between each coil.
3. Make feet and a tail. Add texture and details.
4. Cut a coin slot into the back of the bank.
5. Use a flat tool to smooth the inside of the bank. Stuff newspaper inside the bank to hold the shape until the clay dries.
6. Use a ball of clay the size of a tennis ball to make a small pinch pot for the head.
7. Paint the animal bank.

Art Criticism

Describe What animal did you choose to use for your bank?

Analyze What creates unity in your animal bank?

Interpret What other pieces of art are useful?

Decide Did you change anything from the sketched design as you were working with the clay? Why was this changed? Are you satisfied with the finished product?

Reflect

Time: About 15 minutes

Review and Assess

"Was the class collection of clay animal banks clearly unified through a theme?" "¿Con el uso de un tema se unificó claramente la colección de grupos de animales de arcilla que hizo la clase?"

Think

The artist created unity through theme and media.

- Use *Large Print 71 El Chandelier* to have students identify and describe the use of unity through theme.

Informal Assessment

- For standardized-format test practice using this lesson's art content, see pages 76–77 in *Reading and Writing Test Preparation.*

Art Journal: Critical Thinking

Have students answer the four art criticism questions—Describe, Analyze, Interpret, and Decide—in their Art Journals. In small groups, have students discuss their clay animal banks. NSAE 2.a

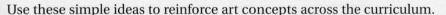

Art Across the Curriculum

Use these simple ideas to reinforce art concepts across the curriculum.

★ **Expository Writing** Have students write explanations of the planning and creative processes they used to create their animal banks.

★ **Math** Discuss how categorizing is used in math calculations.

★ **Science** Have students research seeing-eye dogs and how they are used by people who have visual impairments. Students can visit **www.seeingeye.org** to learn more.

★ **Social Studies** Discuss the concept of patriotism and how it unifies people from many different cultures within the United States as Americans.

★ **Technology** Discuss how some tasks traditionally performed by animals, such as plowing fields, are now done by machines.
NSAE 6.b

Unity through Theme

Extra! For the Art Specialist

Time: About 50 minutes

Focus

Have students study *Large Print 71 El Chandelier* to understand how artists use unity to bring together different objects or art elements so that everything fits together in a work of art. How many different objects do students see? How do the objects relate to one another?

Teach

As a class, discuss how a group of different objects can be unified if they share a common theme. Have students share themes they have used or studied in school before, such as fairy tales, a specific culture, or animals. Explain to students that they will each be creating a papier-mâché animal based on a theme selected by the class.

Reflect

Have students evaluate their works of art using the four steps of art criticism. Encourage them to identify how unity was created though a theme.

Alternate Activity

Materials:
- Art Journals
- pencils, erasers
- newspapers
- wheat paste
- containers
- masking tape
- acrylic paints
- paintbrushes
- water containers

1. Decide as a class on the animal theme you will use. Sketch ideas for animals you would like to make based on the chosen theme.

2. Keep the animal forms smaller than ten inches. Begin by taping a ball of newspaper to make the body. Then cut the length for the legs and create taped rolls to attach to the body. Form the head and neck and securely tape them to the body. Cut ears and tails from tag board and tape these in place.

3. Apply papier-mâché to the animal.

4. Let the animal dry completely, then paint a base coat using one color.

5. Use small brushes to paint features, designs, textures, and details.

Research in Art Education

"At a time when the development of thinking skills is particularly important . . . the presence of a program that fosters flexibility, promotes a tolerance for ambiguity, encourages risk taking and depends upon the exercise of judgment outside the sphere of rules is an especially valuable resource." (Eisner, Elliot W. *The Arts and the Creation of Mind.* New Haven: Yale Univ. Press, 2002.)

Assessment

Use the following rubric to evaluate the artwork students make in the Creative Expression activity and to assess students' understanding of unity through theme.

Have students complete page 79 or 80 in their *Assessment* books.

	Art History and Culture	Aesthetic Perception	Creative Expression	Art Criticism
3 POINTS	The student can demonstrate knowledge of Mexican ceramics and the life and artwork of Elizabeth Paulos-Krasle.	The student accurately identifies unity through theme in a work of art.	The student's clay animal bank clearly illustrates the use of unity.	The student thoughtfully and honestly evaluates own work using the four steps of art criticism.
2 POINTS	The student's knowledge of Mexican ceramics and the life and artwork of Elizabeth Paulos-Krasle is weak or incomplete.	The student shows emerging awareness of unity though theme used in a work of art.	The student's clay animal bank shows some awareness of unity.	The student attempts to evaluate own work but shows an incomplete understanding of evaluation criteria.
1 POINT	The student cannot demonstrate knowledge of Mexican ceramics or the life and artwork of Elizabeth Paulos-Krasle	The student cannot identify unity through theme used in a work of art.	The student's clay animal bank shows no understanding of unity.	The student makes no attempt to evaluate own artwork.

Assessment, p. 79

Name _____ Date _____

Unity through Theme

Lesson 6 UNIT 6

A. Short Answer
Answer the following questions.
1. What is unity? _____
2. How is unity created in a work of art? _____

B. Drawing
Draw three objects or designs in the boxes below that are all connected by one theme. Write what the theme is on the line provided.

C. Writing
Look at *Toy Banks* and, on the back of this paper, write a paragraph to describe how the Mexican artist created unity through theme in this work of art.

Level 5   Unit 6 • Harmony, Variety, Emphasis, and Unity   79

harmony—the principle of art that helps to create unity by stressing the similarities of separate but related elements in an artwork **armonía**—el principio artístico que ayuda a crear unidad al destacar las semenjanzas de elementos separados pero relacionados en una obra de arte

unity—the quality of wholeness or oneness that is achieved by properly using the elements and principles of art **unidad**—la calidad de la integridad que se puede obtener usando propiamente los elementos y principios artísticos

variety—the principle of art created by differences or contrasts in art elements **variedad**—el principio artístico creado por las diferencias o contrastes en los elementos artísticos.

emphasis—the principle of art that stresses one area in an artwork over other areas **énfasis**—el principio artístico que destaca un área sobre otras en una obra de arte.

focal point—the area of an artwork that is emphasized **punto focal**—el área destacada de una obra de arte.

isolation—emphasis of an object because it has been placed alone and away from other objects in an artwork **aislamiento**—énfasis de un objeto porque se ha puesto sólo y lejo de otros objetos en una obra de arte.

location—emphasis of an object because it has been placed in the center of an artwork **ubicación**—énfasis de un objeto porque se ha puesto en el centro de una obra de arte.

unity—the quality of wholeness or oneness achieved by balancing harmony and variety in a work of art **unidad**—la calidad de la integridad que se puede obtener por un equilibrio de armonía y variedad en una obra de arte.

media—the materials used to create something **medio**—los materiales usados para crear algo.

theme—the main subject or idea of an artwork **tema**—el sujeto principal o idea de una obra de arte.

Vocabulary Practice

T Display *Transparency 42* to review unit vocabulary words.

Parts of Speech ⭐ Vocabulary

Play a game of ad-libs with the class using the vocabulary words. Ask students to provide words that qualify for specific parts of speech. You may want to allow students to use their glossaries to double check their use of vocabulary words.

Similes ⭐ Vocabulary

Have student groups choose a vocabulary word to use in original similes. For example, a group might use the vocabulary word *theme* to write the simile: *The theme was as obvious as the nose on your face.*

Rebus Equations ⭐ Vocabulary

Have student groups create rebus equations for vocabulary words. For example, students might draw pictures of the following: an eye + a needle sewing + a person lying down + a lower leg with an arrow pointing to the shin = *isolation*. Collect rebuses and copy them onto one worksheet to be completed by the class.

Harmony, Variety, Emphasis, and Unity

▲ **Isabel Bishop.** (American). *Subway Scene.* 1957–1958.
Egg tempera and oil on composition board. 40 × 28 inches (101.6 × 71.12 cm.).
Whitney Museum of American Art, New York, New York.

210　Unit 6

 Art Criticism

Critical Thinking Art criticism is an organized system for looking at and talking about art. You can criticize art without being an expert. The purpose of art criticism is to get the viewer involved in a perception process that delays judgment until all aspects of the artwork have been studied.

■ See page 28–29 for more about art criticism.

Describe

▶ Possible answers: *Subway Scene* was painted by Isabel Bishop in the years 1957 and 1958. It is 40 inches tall and 28 inches wide.

▶ Some possible answers are: People are walking across the background of the painting. In the background there are vertical columns that hold up the roof.

Analyze

▶ Some possible answers are: The cool blue, violet, and gray colors and the rectangles and arches are repeated throughout the work add to the feeling of harmony.

▶ The warm color of the dispenser contrasts with all the cool colors to create variety. The vague figures that seem to be moving around the station add variety.

▶ The reflected face is emphasized because it is in the center of the artwork. It is the focal point. It is emphasized by contrast, isolation, and location.

▶ Some possible answers are: The artist used harmony of geometric shapes and harmony of cool colors to create unity. The free-form shapes of the people contrast with the geometric shapes.

 Art History and Culture

Isabel Bishop

Isabel Bishop (iz´ a bel bish´ əp) (1902–1988) was born in Cincinnati, Ohio. At age fifteen, she graduated from high school and moved to New York City to study art. For forty years she had a studio in New York. She often painted the people she saw on the streets below her in Union Square. Bishop was greatly influenced by the work of Baroque-period artist Peter Paul Rubens. She mimicked the way he used several layers of washes as an underpainting to create a sense of movement. She has been called an urban realist because she favored painting real people in the city as they went about their normal daily activities.

See pages 24–25 and 16–21 for more about art history and subject matter.

Artist Profiles, p. 8

Artist Profile
Isabel Bishop
1902-1988

Isabel Bishop (iz´ a bel bish´ əp) was born in Cincinnati, Ohio. A year later, her family moved to a run-down neighborhood in Detroit, Michigan, where her father was employed as the principal of a nearby high school. Her parents didn't think the neighborhood children made good playmates, so Bishop spent much of her time alone. She graduated from high school at age 15 and then studied art. She moved to New York City, where she continued to study art and began exhibiting her work. She loved to paint the people in Union Square.

Bishop married in 1934, moved to the suburbs, and had a son. She commuted

Art Criticism Critical Thinking

Describe What do you see?

During this step you will collect information about the subject of the work.

- ▶ What does the credit line tell us about the painting?
- ▶ Where do you see people? Where do you see objects?

Analyze How is this work organized?

Think about how the artist has used the elements and principles of art.

- ▶ What is repeated to create harmony?
- ▶ Where do you see variety?
- ▶ What is emphasized?
- ▶ How did the artist create unity?

Interpret What is the artist trying to say?

Use the clues you discovered during your analysis to find the message the artist is trying to show.

- ▶ Who is this girl and what is she doing? Write a paragraph that describes what she is thinking.

Decide What do you think about the work?

Use all the information you gathered to decided whether this is a successful work of art.

- ▶ Is the work successful because it is realistic, because it is well organized, or because it has a strong message?

Interpret

- ▶ Students will write a paragraph explaining what they think the girl in the painting is doing and thinking.
- ▶ Some possible answers are: She is checking her looks on the way to work. Others may say she is waiting to meet someone, or waiting for a train to go somewhere exciting.

Decide

- ▶ Some possible answers are: Realism but composition and message are also strong in this work.

Art Journal: Writing

Have students write answers to the Aesthetic Perception questions in their Art Journals.

Aesthetic Perception

Critical Thinking Have students share experiences in which they have used, or have imagined using forms of transportation such as subways, trains, planes, or buses.

Describe
- ▶ List and describe what you saw, who you were with, and where you were going.

Analyze
- ▶ What form of visual art media might you use to recapture the scene?

Interpret
- ▶ How did you feel while traveling?
- ▶ Do you think the people around you were feeling the same way?

Decide
- ▶ Would you choose to travel using the same form of transportation next time? Why or why not.

"Artists use the principles of harmony, variety, emphasis, and unity to organize works of art and their elements." "Los artistas usan los principios de armonía, variedad, énfasis y unidad para organizar las obras de arte y sus elementos."

T Review unit vocabulary with students using *Transparency 42.*

Art Journal: Writing

Have students answer the questions on page 212 in their Art Journals or on a separate sheet of paper. Answers: 1.C, 2. B, 3. A, 4. B, 5. A

T For further assessment, have students complete the unit test on *Transparency 48.*

CAREERS IN ART
Toy Designers

► Encourage students to discuss what they have learned about toy designers, their prior knowledge of toy designers, and what else they would like to know about them.

■ Have students complete their portfolios and prepare them for an exhibition. Set aside 30 minutes of class time for students to analyze each other's collections of artwork. Encourage students to think about the properties that were focused on with each piece.

"My work has always had the problem of where to place it. I will always be an outsider and I like that."

—Benny Andrews

Harmony, Variety, Emphasis, and Unity, continued

Show What You Know

Answer these questions on a separate sheet of paper.

❶ _____ is the principle of art that creates unity by using separate but related elements such as shape, color, or texture in an artwork.
A. Emphasis
B. Melody
C. Harmony

❷ The principle of design that stresses differences or contrasts is _____.
A. Location
B. Variety
C. Unity

❸ The principle of design that stresses one area in an artwork over another areas is _____.
A. emphasis
B. media
C. harmony

❹ Sometimes a specific area in an artwork is emphasized. This area is called the _____.
A. vanishing point
B. focal point
C. central axis

❺ _____ is wholeness or oneness. This is created when the art principles of harmony and variety are balanced.
A. Unity
B. Harmony
C. Placement

CAREERS IN ART
Toy Designers

Think about the many different toys that you have seen and played with. How are these toys different from one another, and what makes them fun?

Toy designers use computer program to create plans and to brainstorm fresh new ideas for toys. Toy designers consider what materials will be used to make the toys safe and cost effective.

These designers must think about the artistic appeal of the toy. What will make this toy more desirable than other toys? New toys are also expected to be capable of handling many technical functions.

Toy designers are problem solvers who consider cost, technology, age appropriateness, safety concerns, and enjoyment of their products for their customers.

▲ Toy designer

Unit Assessment Options

 **Aesthetic Perception**

Practice Have students choose two terms on page 212, then find examples of each in the classroom.

Creative Expression

Student Portfolio Have students review all the artwork they have created during this unit and select the pieces they wish to keep in their portfolios.

Art Criticism

Activity Have students select an artwork from this unit and study it using the four steps of art criticism. Have students work alone or in pairs and present their findings orally or in writing.

Harmony, Variety, Emphasis, and Unity in Dance

▲ Ranganiketan Manipuri Cultural Arts Troupe. "Dhon Dholak Cholam."

The drummers in the photo are from Manipur, India. They work together to play their instruments with unity, variety, emphasis, and harmony. They also dance, doing leaps and turns as they travel around in a circle. The same music has been played for thousands of years, passed on from musician to musician.

What to Do Beat out different rhythm patterns in a "call and response" form.

In India, music is learned by studying with a *guru*, or master teacher. The bond between the teacher and the student is close and respectful. The teacher plays different rhythms and also says them vocally in a "call and response" form. The student repeats the patterns and practices them until the teacher feels he or she is ready to learn more.

1. Sit at a table. Remove everything from the top so it can be used as a drum.

2. Use both hands to beat out short rhythm patterns on the edge of the table. Think of long and short sounds. Emphasize some sounds by making them stronger.

3. Beat out a short rhythmic pattern that you can repeat. Find three patterns you can play.

4. With a partner, take turns being the leader (call) and beating out one pattern at a time. Your partner will repeat each pattern after it has been played (response).

Art Criticism

Describe Describe how a pattern is different from a series of sounds.

Analyze What did you do to create variety and emphasis in your rhythm patterns?

Interpret What feeling did you have when you were the leader? How did you feel as the follower?

Decide Were you able to create rhythmic patterns using a call-and-response form?

Unit 6 **213**

Art History and Culture

Manipur

Manipur, India is called the "Jewel of India." It is a secluded state situated at India's most northeastern frontier. Located in an oval-shaped valley, it is tucked within nine ranges of Himalayan Mountains. The ancient culture of Manipur has been preserved intact for thousands of years. Dr. Singh, Director of Ranganiketan, says, "I made a choice to connect people through the language of culture rather than science." The people believe that everything is divinely inspired. As a symbol of their humility, the performers always touch the floor and then their foreheads before they begin. The dance, art, and music of Manipur is spiritual in nature. From a young age, children commit to an honored and respected relationship with a specific master teacher. The instruments include a variety of percussion, stringed and wind instruments. Many of the musicians have practiced their music since early childhood and have achieved perfection.

Harmony, Variety, Emphasis and Unity in Dance

Objective: To create rhythm patterns using a "call and response" form

Materials: "Dhom Dholok Cholom" performed by Ranganiketan. running time: 2:26

Focus

Time: About 10 minutes

■ Discuss the information on page 213.

Art History and Culture

■ Have students discuss Manipuri Indian music and also the "call and response" form to prepare them to create original rhythm patterns.

Teach

Time: About 25 minutes

Aesthetic Perception

■ Watch "Dhom Dholok Cholom" performed by Ranganiketan

Creative Expression

■ Have students sit at cleared tables to use as drums. Encourage them to "play" on the edges and beat softly with open hands. Ask them to create rhythm patterns that can be repeated. When everyone has at least three different patterns, pair them. Direct them to take turns using "call and response" to share their patterns.

■ **Informal Assessment** Comment positively on students efforts to create rhythm in patterns.

Reflect

Time: About 10 minutes

Art Criticism

■ Have students answer the four art criticism questions on page 213 orally or in writing.

■ Did students successfully create and learn a variety of rhythm patterns using a "call and response" form?

Drawing

It is important to allow the students to experiment with the drawing media. Use gentle guidance to show them how to properly hold the drawing media. Prior to use, demonstrate the techniques as they are illustrated here. Proper handling and use will increase success and establish good habits for the future. It will also make the media last longer.

Pencil

Blending is a technique of shading in which the student holds the pencil on its side between the thumb and other fingers and shades with the side of the lead.

- Primary-grade pencils with a medium-soft lead are ideal for all shading techniques.

- To create lighter values, students should press lightly and shade over the area less.

- To create darker values, students should use the side of the pencil lead, press harder, and shade over areas more than once.

- Gradations from dark to light can be created by smearing a shaded area into an area not yet shaded with a paper stump made of a tightly rolled paper towel.

Hatching is a pattern of parallel lines. How closely together the lines are drawn determines the value of that part of the drawing.

In **cross-hatching,** the parallel lines overlap each other. As with hatching, the distance of the lines from each other determines the value.

Stippling is a series of dots that create value and value changes. Careful control of the placement of all shading is important, especially stipple dots. Be sure that students are carefully drawing these dots rather than simply dotting their paper with them.

Technique Tips
Drawing
Pencil

With a pencil, you can add form to your objects with shading. With the side of your pencil lead, press and shade over areas more than once for darker values. You can also use lines or dots for shading. When lines or dots are drawn close together, darker values are created. When dots or lines are drawn farther apart, lighter values are created.

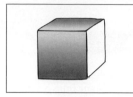
Blending

Cross-hatching

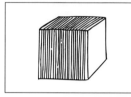
Hatching

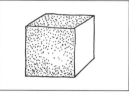
Stippling

Technique Tips

Color Pencil

You can blend colors with color pencils. Color with the lighter color first. Gently color over it with the darker color until you have the effect you want.

With color pencils, you can use the four shading techniques.

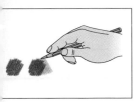

Shadows can be created by blending complementary colors.

Color Pencils

- When blending colors with color pencils, it is important to color the lighter color before the darker one. A color can be darkened easily, but it is almost impossible to lighten a color.

- To create shadows, blend complementary colors. This will create browns and darker colors.

Fine-Point Felt-Tip Pen

Felt-tip pens are a practical substitute for pen and ink. Their narrow points make them ideal for drawing details and contour line drawings.

- They can be used to draw over lightly sketched pencil drawings.

- They can be used to draw a picture which can then be painted with watercolors. (The ink is water-soluble and may run when touched by wet paint.)

- Students should avoid pressing too hard when drawing so as not to damage the tip; this is especially true when stippling.

- After use, the cap should always be replaced.

Technique Tips

Fine-Point Felt-Tip Pen

Fine-point felt-tip pens can be used to make either sketches or finished drawings. They are ideal for contour drawings.

Use the point of a fine-point felt-tip pen to make details.

Fine-point felt-tip pens can be used for hatching, cross-hatching, and stippling.

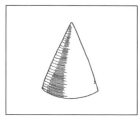 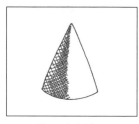 

Hatching   Cross-hatching   Stippling

Always replace the cap so the fine-point felt-tip pen does not dry out.

Technique Tips

Color Chalk

Color chalks can be used to make colorful, soft designs.

You can use the tip of the color chalk to create lines and shapes and to fill spaces. As with pencil, you can also use them for blending to create shadows.

Color chalk is soft and can break easily. Broken pieces are still usable. Colors can be mixed or blended by smearing them together with your finger or a tissue.

Oil Pastels

Oil pastels are colors that are mixed with oil and pressed into sticks. When you press down hard with them, your pictures will look painted.

Oil pastels are soft. You can use oil pastels to color over other media, such as tempera or crayon. Then you can scratch through this covering to create a design.

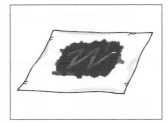

Charcoal

Charcoal is soft. It can be blended with a piece of rolled paper towel and your finger. Create dark values by coloring over an area several times. Create lighter values by erasing, or by coloring over the charcoal with white chalk.

Color Chalk

- Color chalks are used to make colorful, soft designs. The use of dustless chalk is recommended for elementary classrooms. The tip of the chalk is used much like an oil pastel to make lines. To fill a space or shape with solid color, use gentle force and color over an area more than once.

- Colors can be mixed or blended by smearing them together with a paper towel wrapped around a finger.

- Like oil pastels, color chalks break easily. Reassure the students that these pieces can still be used like new ones.

- Color chalks become dirty from use. Instruct students to mark on a paper towel until the colors are clean.

Oil Pastels

- Oil pastels are pigments that are mixed with oil and compressed into sticks. They are used like crayons. By pressing with gentle force and coloring over an area several times, students can create the effect of paint.

- Students can create lines by drawing with the tip. Large spaces can be colored with the tip or the side.

- Textures can be created by making marks such as dots and lines. Textures can also be made by layering colors and scratching through with a straightened paper clip.

- Colors can be mixed or blended by smearing them with a paper towel wrapped around a finger.

- Oil pastels break easily. Reassure the students that these pieces can still be used like new ones.

- If the oil pastels become dirty from use, instruct the students to mark on a paper towel until the colors are clean again.

Charcoal

Charcoal is a very versatile drawing medium.

- Because it is easily erased to create lighter values and blended to create shadows, it is perfect for young artists timid about drawing large or dark marks on their paper.

- Charcoal can be cleaned from hands and clothing with soap and water.

Painting

Tempera

- For best results, it is recommended that quality liquid tempera paint is used.

- To remove excess water from the brush, gently wipe the end of the brush on the inside edge of the container. This will allow the water to run back into the container. Discourage students from tapping their brushes on the rim of the container. This will prevent paint splatters.

- When mixing paints on a palette, always mix the darker color into the lighter color a little at a time until the desired color is reached. This reduces wasted paint. Paper plates work well as palettes and reduce cleanup.

- Use a thin brush for details.

- Use a wide brush for large spaces.

Painting

Tempera

1. Fill water containers halfway. Dip your brush in water. Wipe your brush on the inside edge of the container. Then blot it on a paper towel to get rid of extra water. Stir the paints. Add a little water if a color is too thick or dry. Remember to clean your brush before using a new color.

2. Always mix colors on the palette. Put some of each color that you want to mix on the palette. Then add the darker color a little at a time to the lighter color. Change your water when it gets too dark.

3. To create lighter values, add white. To darken a value, add a tiny amount of black. If you have painted something too thickly, add water and blot it with a clean paper towel.

4. Use a thin pointed brush to paint thin lines and details. For thick lines or large areas, press firmly on the tip or use a wide brush.

5. Wash your brush when you are finished. Reshape the bristles. Store brushes with bristles up.

Technique Tips

Watercolor

1. Fill water containers halfway. Dip your brush in water. Wipe your brush on the inside edge of the container. Then blot it on a paper towel to get rid of extra water. With your brush, add a drop of water to each watercolor cake and stir. Remember to clean your brush whenever you change colors.

2. Always mix colors on a palette. Put some of each color that you want to mix on the palette. Then add the darker color a little at a time to the lighter color. Change your water when it gets too dark.

3. To create lighter values, add more water. To darken a value, add a tiny amount of black. If you have painted something too quickly, add water to the paint on the paper and blot it with a clean paper towel.

4. Use a thin pointed brush to paint thin lines and details. For thick lines or large areas, press firmly on the tip or use a wide brush.

5. For a softer look, tape your paper to the table with masking tape. Use a wide brush to add water to the paper, working in rows from top to bottom. This is a wash. Let the water soak in a little. Painting on wet paper will create a soft or fuzzy look. For sharper forms or edges, paint on dry paper, using only a little water on your brush.

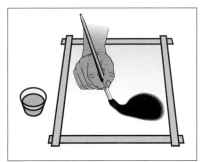

6. Wash your brushes when you are finished. Reshape the bristles. Store brushes with the bristles up.

Watercolors

- School watercolors come in semimoist cakes. Moisten each cake that is going to be used by dripping a little water from the brush onto the cake and gently stirring the water on the surface of the paint.

- Create thick lines by gently pressing down on the brush.

- Create thin lines by lightly touching the surface of the paper with the tip of the brush.

- To create textures such as stipple (dots) or lines, demonstrate these techniques:

  1. Wet a round, soft-bristled watercolor brush.
  2. Carefully squeeze excess water from the bristles.
  3. Gently divide the bristles into spikes.
  4. Carefully touch the moistened paint cake with the bristle tips so that some paint is absorbed by the bristles.
  5. Lightly touch the paper with the separated bristles. Gentle taps create irregular dots. Gentle, upward strokes create irregular lines.
  6. When finished, rinse, clean, and reshape the brush.

- To create lighter values, the hue should be thinned with water using these steps:

  1. Use a watery brush.
  2. Thin the hue on the palette with water.
  3. Brush water over an already painted area.
  4. Blot wet, painted area with a paper towel.

- To create darker values, add drops of black to the hue on the palette, *one at a time,* until the desired value is achieved.

Wash

Painting or sponging water onto the paper prior to painting will create soft lines, soft-edged shapes, and softer colors. The water should be allowed to soak into the paper before painting.

- To create sharp, clear lines and shapes, students should paint on dry paper with a damp brush.

- To create a fuzzy look, students should paint on dry paper with a dry brush and very little paint.

Technique Tips

Acrylic Paint

1. Because acrylics dry so fast, squeeze out only a little paint. If you are using a plastic palette, use a spray bottle regularly to spray a fine mist over the paint to keep it moist.

2. Keep a piece of paper towel or cloth next to your water jar, and wipe your brushes on it after you rinse them. When you are not working with your brush, keep it in the water jar.

3. If applied thickly or if mixed with a little white, all acrylic colors can be opaque. If they are diluted, they can be used like watercolors or for airbrushing.

4. Unlike a watercolor wash, when an acrylic wash dries, it is permanent and insoluble. It can be over-painted without disturbing the existing wash.

5. Because acrylics dry rapidly, you need to work fast to blend colors. If you are working on paper, dampening the paper will increase your working time.

6. Masking tape can be put onto and removed from dried acrylic paint without damaging an existing layer. This makes it easy to produce a sharp edge. Be sure the edges of the tape are firmly pressed down. Do not paint too thickly on the edges, or you will not get a clean line when you lift the tape.

7. When you are finished painting, clean your brushes. Be sure to clean inside the bristles so no paint remains.

Technique Tips

Printmaking

Making Stamps

Three methods for making stamps are listed below. You can cut either a positive or negative shape into most of these objects. Be sure to talk with your teacher or another adult about what kinds of tools you can safely use.

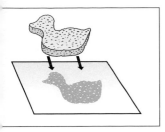

Cut sponges into shapes.

Draw or sculpt a design on a flat piece of modeling clay. Use a pencil, a clay tool, the tip of a paper clip, or another object.

Draw or sculpt a design on a flat piece of plastic foam using a pencil, the tip of a paper clip, or another object.

Printmaking

Making Stamps

- If students wish to cut a sponge into a specific shape, use thin sponges. Draw the shape on the sponge with a marker and use scissors to cut it out.

- Oil-based modeling clay can also be used to make a stamp. This is done by drawing or sculpting a design on a flat piece of modeling clay. There are a variety of tools manufactured for carving clay. Some classroom items that will work just as well include plastic eating utensils, craft sticks, and paper clips. The straightened end of a paper clip can be used to draw in the clay. The rounded end can be used as a gouge to carve clay away. To create a raised stamp, simply add pieces of clay to the bottom of the clay stamp.

Printing a Sponge Print

- Dispense colors onto individual palettes, or spread out on a surface large enough to avoid mixing. Lightly press the sponge into the paint, being careful not to get too much paint on it. Lift the sponge and lightly press it into place on the paper. The sponge should be thoroughly rinsed between colors.

Making Prints

- Below is the procedure for using a brayer, which is a soft roller, to make prints.

  1. Pour a small amount of water-based printing ink or paint onto a flat, solid surface. Roll the brayer in the ink or paint until there is an even coating on the surface and brayer.

  2. Roll the brayer over the top of the stamp. The ink should cover the stamp evenly without getting into the grooves of the design.

  3. Apply the stamp carefully to the paper, rubbing the back of the stamp with the side of the fist.

  4. Peel the paper and stamp apart.

  5. Reink the stamp as needed if you wish to make more than one print.

  6. When finished, wash the brayer, surface, and stamp.

- Another method for making prints calls for a paintbrush to apply the ink or paint. This method works better than the brayer with a raised stamp that the brayer would flatten out. Brush the ink or paint onto the stamping surface. Then follow the steps above, ending with thoroughly cleaning the brush.

Technique Tips

Printing Stamps

1. Put a small amount of water-based printing ink or some paint onto a hard, flat surface. Roll a softer roller, called a brayer, back and forth in the ink until there is an even coating of paint on both the surface and the brayer.

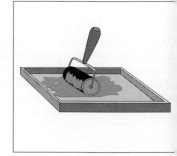

2. Roll the brayer filled with ink over the printing stamp. The ink should cover the stamp evenly without going into the grooves of your design.

3. You can also use a brush to coat the stamp evenly with paint. Whichever method you use, be careful not to use too much ink or paint.

4. Gently press your stamp onto your paper. Then peel the paper and stamp apart and check your print. If you wish to make several prints of your design, you should ink your stamp again as needed.

5. When you have finished, wash the brayer, the surface, and the stamp.

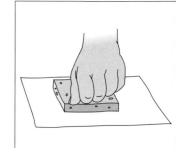

Technique Tips

Collage

In a collage, objects or pieces of paper, fabric, or other materials are pasted onto a surface to create a work of art. When planning your collage, consider such things as:

- Size of shapes and spaces
- Placement of shapes and spaces
- Color schemes
- Textures

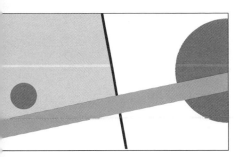

Remember that the empty (negative) spaces are also part of your design. Plan a collage as you would plan a painting or a drawing. After deciding what shapes and objects you want to use, arrange them on the paper. When you have made an arrangement you like, glue your shapes and objects to the paper.

Collage

Scissors

- It is important to teach students safety when they use scissors. They should always cut away from their bodies. Of course they should never point their scissors, at others, spin them on the table, or walk around the room with them.

- There are scissors specially made to spring open for students who are physically challenged, or who are not yet developmentally ready to use standard school scissors. Many scissors on the market today can be used with the right or left hand. If these are not available, keep a supply of left-handed scissors for students who need them.

- To cut thick yarn or fabric, encourage students to work in pairs. While one cuts, the other can stretch the yarn or fabric. This makes cutting easier and encourages cooperation.

Arranging a Design

A collage is a work of art in which pieces of paper, fabric, and other materials are glued onto a surface to create a **composition.**

- Provide a variety of textured and colored papers, yarns, fabrics, and found objects for students to use. Hard-to-cut materials should be precut for students.

- When using paper, students may choose to tear and/or cut their shapes.

- Encourage students to arrange the design first. They should pay as much attention to the negative spaces as the positive ones.

- Glue only after the final colors, shapes, and textures have been chosen and arranged. White glue will attach most porous items to the background surface.

Color Tissue Collage

- Review color mixing with students so that they do not overlap colors that do not mix. Otherwise, the colors will appear muddy.

- Wash brushes thoroughly with soap and water when finished.

Technique Tips

Color Tissue Collage

To glue color tissue, mix a solution of one part glue to one part water.

When gluing the tissue, use an old brush to put a small amount of the glue and water solution onto the drawing paper. Next, put the tissue in one place, and brush over the tissue with a small amount of the watered glue. Be careful not to get the color from the tissue on your fingers—the wet tissue is messy and fragile. You can mix colors by overlapping different colored tissues.

Be sure to rinse your brush when you change colors. When you finish, wash the brush with soapy water.

Sculpting

Papier-Mâché

The strip method of papier-mâché ("mashed paper") uses paper combined with paste. Often, papier-máché is molded over a form that helps to hold the shape until it is dry.

1. Create a supporting form, if needed. Forms can be made from clay, wadded-up newspaper, cardboard boxes and tubes, balloons, wire, or other materials. Masking tape can be used to hold the form together.

2. Tear paper into strips. Dip the strips into a thick mixture of paste, or rub paste on the strips with your fingers. Use wide strips to cover wide forms, and thin strips or small pieces to cover a small shape.

3. Apply five or six layers of strips. Lay each layer in a different direction so you can keep track of the number of strips and layers. For example, lay the first layer vertically and the second horizontally. Smooth over all rough edges with your fingers. If you are going to leave the form in place permanently, two or three layers of strips should be enough.

4. When it is dry, you can paint your sculpture.

Sculpting

Papier-Mâché

Papier-Mâché is a French term that means "mashed paper." It refers to sculpting methods that use paper and liquid paste. The wet paper and paste material is molded over supporting structures such as wadded dry paper or crumpled foil. The molded paper dries to a hard finish.

- Below are three common papier-mâché solutions:

  1. Mix one part white glue to one part water. Start by filling a sealable container halfway with white glue, and then add one quarter-container of water. Shake this mixture vigorously until mixed. Add another quarter-container of water and mix again.

  2. Make a creamy mixture of wheat paste and water. To mix wheat paste, wear a dust mask and pour dry paste into a large mixing bowl. Add water and stir until the mixture is creamy. Mash lumps with a spoon or your hands.

  3. Use liquid starch.

- Store bottles with binder in them separate from the regular glue so that students do not mistake one for the other. An alternative to the binder suggested on page 225 (one part glue to one part water), is full-strength liquid starch.

Sculpting

Working with Clay

- Always protect the work area with a cloth or newspaper. Clay dust is messy. Always wash the tables after working with clay.

- To help prevent earth clay from drying and cracking, students should not overhandle the clay. Keep damp paper towels nearby for students to keep their hands moist.

- The following steps are for modeling a person or animal from clay:

  1. Roll the piece of clay into an oval-shaped form. Describe this to the students as a "potato" shape.
  2. Pinch a head shape on one end.
  3. Pinch and pull out arms and legs.
  4. Leave some, but not too much, clay for the body.
  5. Squeeze the head, arms, legs, and body into the desired shapes.

- Clay is often sold in 25 pound bags. The bags are usually strong enough to keep the clay damp, but be sure to close the bag tightly with a twist tie or some other devise to keep it sealed. It is a good idea to place the bag inside a second bag, like a heavy-duty garbage bag, for long-term storage.

Joining Clay

- Clay is joined by using **slip,** a creamy mixture of clay and water. Slip can be made by putting a few dry pieces of clay in a container and covering them with water. When the clay dissolves, stir to achieve a creamy consistency.

- Joining clay also requires a scoring tool such as a straightened paper clip. The steps below are called the four *S*s—score, slip, smooth, and squeeze.

  1. **Score** the two pieces to be joined.
  2. Apply **slip** to one of the surfaces.
  3. **Smooth** the seam.
  4. **Squeeze** the two surfaces together.

Carving Clay

There are a variety of tools manufactured for carving clay. Some classroom items that will work just as well are plastic eating utensils, craft sticks, and paper clips. The straightened end of a paper clip can be used to draw in the clay. The rounded end can be used as a gouge to carve clay away.

Technique Tips

Clay

Pinch and pull clay into the desired shape.

Joining Two Pieces of Clay

Score, or scratch, both pieces so they will stick together.

Attach the pieces with some *slip,* which is watery clay.

Squeeze the two pieces together.
Smooth the edges.

Technique Tips

Clay Slab Construction

To roll a slab of clay, press a ball of clay into a flat shape on a cloth-covered board. Place one $\frac{1}{4}$-inch slat on each side of the clay. Use a roller to press the slab into an even thickness. With a straightened paper clip, trim the slab into the desired shape.

Wrap unfinished sculptures in plastic to keep them moist until finished.

When you are constructing a form such as a container or house with slabs of clay, it may be necessary to stuff the form with wads of newspaper to support the walls. The newspaper will burn out in the kiln.

Making a Pinch Pot

- It is important that the students gently squeeze the clay to form the pot. If they pinch the clay quickly the walls will be uneven. If they pinch the clay too hard they might make a hole in the wall of the bowl. If a student makes a hole, you might have him or her start over, or you can repair the hole by adding a small piece of clay using slip and scoring.

- The walls of the pinch pot should be the same width all around the bowl. To do this, have students hold their bowls with one thumb inside the bowl and their fingers held flat on the outside of the bowl. Then have students squeeze gently while constantly turning the bowl with their other hand. As the bowl opens up, both hands can be used to shape the walls.

- If the students are going to press designs into the walls of the bowl make sure that they have their fingers together inside the bowl to keep the bowl from collapsing.

Technique Tips

Pinch Pots

To make a clay pinch pot follow the steps below:

1. Make a ball of clay by rolling it between your palms until it is round.

2. Hold the clay ball in your hands and push a thumb into the top of the ball. Stop pushing before you reach the bottom.

3. Work your way around the clay ball while gently pinching the clay between your thumb and other fingers. Rotate the pot as you pinch.

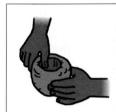

4. Continue pinching and shaping the clay until it develops into the form of a bowl.

Technique Tips

Soft Sculpture

Stuff a stocking or other stretchable material with polyester fill. Sew or glue on buttons, beads, sequins, fabric scraps, and other items to create facial features.

For hair, add yarn, string, or raffia. Try some of the stitches on this page to add details, such as eyebrows, wrinkles, or freckles.

You can use fabric paints for details.

Sew on a real hat, scarf, or head band. Use one of the stitches below.

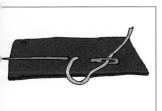
Back stitch

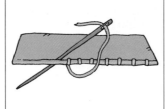
Couching stitch

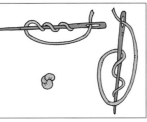
Knotted stitch

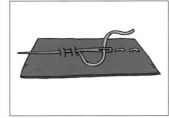
Running stitch

Soft Sculpture

- Make a variety of materials available for use in embellishing the soft sculptures. Examples include buttons, sequins, beans, seeds, yarn, raffia, fabrics, ribbons, fabric markers and paints, and articles of clothing such as scarves, ties, socks, shoes, hair bows, and hats.

- Use blunt plastic needles or blunt metal tapestry needles for the stitchery.

Activity Tips

Expression with Lines

Creative Expression

1. Think about the five different types of lines. Collect linear mixed-media materials such as yarn, string, and grass.

2. Use different materials to create lines and line variations. Keep in mind the mood that certain lines suggest.

3. Arrange and glue the collage materials onto a piece of cardboard.

Perception Drawing

Creative Expression

1. Look carefully at the posed subjects.

2. Move your pen slowly on your paper while your eyes move around the edges or contours of the subjects.

3. Look at the subjects while you draw, and only glance occasionally at your paper.

4. Do not pick up your pen. Draw in one continuous, unbroken line.

Activity Tips

Geometric and Free-Form Shapes

Creative Expression

1. Think about objects you might enjoy drawing. Select five or more different sizes and shapes.

2. Arrange the still life. Look for shape, color, and lines.

3. Using a computer, open the paint program and practice using the tools that you will use to draw your still life.

4. Using the paint program, draw the still life. Save and print your finished product.

Value with Hatching

Creative Expression

1. Sketch the models carefully.

2. Use hatching and cross-hatching to indicate value and form.

Activity Tips

Value with Blending

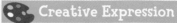 **Creative Expression**

1. Choose one or more common classroom objects.

2. Notice how much light the surface of these objects reflects. Look for shadows and variations of value.

3. Make line drawings of the objects.

4. Use blending to add form.

Unit 1 · Lesson 6 **Value Contrast**

 **Creative Expression**

1. Look around your indoor and outdoor environment. Find an interesting area, with objects or people, that tells a story or expresses a mood.

2. Use a camera. Look through the viewfinder to arrange your composition. Be sure that your photograph will have bright highlights and dark shadows. Take your photograph.

3. Have your photograph developed. Share it with the class.

Activity Tips

Positive and Negative Shapes and Space

🎨 Creative Expression

1. Arrange objects in a still-life pose that have large, interesting negative spaces, such as chairs or desks.

2. Look closely at the still life and find an area of it that you like. Draw what you see. Concentrate on the negative spaces around the objects.

3. Using marker, fill only the negative spaces with color. Leave the positive spaces white.

. . . .

Space in Two-Dimensional Art

🎨 Creative Expression

1. Think of a place where you like to spend time outside.

2. Draw the scene with chalk, using at least three of the six perspective techniques.

3. Paint your scene.

Activity Tips

Unit 2 · Lesson 3   Linear Perspective

🎨 Creative Expression

1. Think of a place you have read about or studied. Make several sketches of objects and two or three buildings you want in your scene.

2. Lightly draw a horizon line. Mark a point where the lines will meet. Draw at least four lines coming out from the vanishing point on the horizon line. Using these guide lines, draw the buildings first, then the objects. Make the objects touch the top and bottom of the guide lines.

3. Paint your drawing.

Unit 2 · Lesson 4   Shading

🎨 Creative Expression

1. Use simple shapes to sketch your space station. Use the shading techniques to change these shapes into forms.

2. Draw planets. Use blending techniques to move from light to dark. Try complementary colors for shading. Add white highlights.

3. Add an atmosphere by using the side of the oil pastel to make long sweeping marks.

234   Activity Tips

Activity Tips

Form

Creative Expression

1. Use paper-sculpting techniques, especially scoring and folding, to create forms. Use tab-and-slot techniques with glue to attach the pieces.

2. Cut into the paper without cutting it into two separate pieces.

3. Use markers to draw lines on the sculpture to enhance the edges of the forms.

4. Keep turning the sculpture and adding to the form so that it is interesting from many different points of view.

Form in Architecture

Creative Expression

1. Plan the building and its form. Consider what it will be used for.

2. Prepare the materials.

3. Put your building together.

Activity Tips

Monochromatic Colors

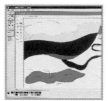

Creative Expression

1. From your Art Journal, choose your favorite sketch of a real or imaginary animal that you drew.

2. Draw the animal large, so it fills the entire sheet of construction paper.

3. Color it, using a hue, tints, and shades of that hue, and black and white pastels.

Analogous Colors

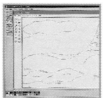

Creative Expression

1. Use the pencil tool in a paint program to create a landscape that includes a foreground, middle ground, and background.

2. Check the colors in the palette for analogous color schemes.

3. Use brush, airbrush, and fill tools to paint the landscape.

Activity Tips

Complementary Colors

 **Creative Expression**

1. Select fruit of like colors.
2. Refer to the sketches in your Art Journal and draw the fruit using different sizes and shapes on squares of paper.
3. Paint the fruit with shades and tints of one chosen hue.
4. Cut out the fruit shapes.
5. Arrange and glue the fruit on a complementary-colored background.

Warm and Cool Colors

 **Creative Expression**

1. Think about warm and cool colors you like.
2. Cut free-form and geometric shapes out of colored drawing paper and tissue paper.
3. Arrange your shapes on white paper. Combine the warm and cool colors. Allow the tissue-paper shapes to overlap some of the drawing-paper shapes.
4. Use a glue water wash to attach your shapes onto the white background.

Activity Tips

Unit 3 · Lesson 5 — Pattern

Creative Expression

1. Choose your favorite motif sketch and draw it on a foam printing plate.
2. Cut out the motif and add details by etching lines with a ballpoint pen.
3. Place some ink on the inking plate. Spread out the ink using a brayer.
4. Use the brayer to roll ink onto the foam printing plate. Repeat this until you have filled the paper with a random arrangement of prints.
5. After the print is dry, use oil pastels to add details.

Unit 3 · Lesson 6 — Decorative Pattern

Creative Expression

1. Make a small clay ball, and press it flat to make the base of your bowl.
2. Using a flat hand, roll pieces of clay in one direction into coils. Stack the coils on top of one another to make the walls of the bowl. Smooth out the inside coils to join them all together.
3. Make small clay shapes for the motif of our pattern.
4. Attach the motifs to the outside coils using slip and scoring techniques.
5. Scratch lines in the clay to enhance the pattern.

Activity Tips

Proportion

🎨 Creative Expression

1. Think about proportion as it relates to people. Use the sighting technique to determine the proportion of your model.

2. Use chalk and a soft eraser to lightly sketch your model.

3. Add color to your drawing by covering over all the chalk lines with oil pastels.

Scale

🎨 Creative Expression

1. Think about an indoor or outdoor background to use in your collage and the object that you will add. Cut out pictures of objects, some that are in proper scale and one or two that are too large or too small for the other objects.

2. Arrange your collected images so that they overlap and touch the edges of your paper. Keep the arrangement organized so that it is almost realistic.

3. Glue down the background. Next glue the remaining objects. Make sure that at least one object shows unrealistic scale.

Proportion

- Sighting is a method that will help you determine proportions. Hold a pencil vertically at an arm's length in the direction of the model. Close one eye and focus on the model's head. Hold the pencil so that the tip of the eraser is level with the top of the model's head. Slide your thumb down the pencil until it is level with the model's chin. Holding the pencil, use this measurement on the pencil to count how many heads equal the height of the model's body.

Activity Tips

Face Proportions

Creative Expression

1. Think about the shape and size of your partner's head.
2. Measure the size of your partner's head. Mark off the dimensions on paper. Next, lightly draw guide lines for the eyes. Keep proportion in mind.
3. Draw the hair, eyebrows, clothing, the neck, and shoulders.
4. Paint the portrait using watercolor paints.

Unit 4 · Lesson 4 **Distortion of Body Proportions**

Creative Expression

1. Think about comic-strip characters you are familiar with. Then make several sketches of your own original comic-strip superhero.
2. Choose one sketch. Distort one or more body features to show the superpower of your character. Give your character a name.

Activity Tips

Distortion of Face Proportions

Creative Expression

1. Tear one-inch strips of newspaper. Dip the strips into paste and squeeze off the excess liquid. Lay the strips over the outside of a plastic milk container. Overlap two layers of newspaper strips to make the base of your mask.

2. Allow the base to dry, then add the features. Distort the features. Apply two more layers of papier-mâché, and let the mask base dry overnight.

3. When it is dry, pop your mask off the container and trim the edges. Paint the mask and apply other objects.

Scale and Proportion

Creative Expression

1. Think about available items you have to make a life-size soft sculpture. Work in small groups. Plan and make sketches of your figure and of the environment.

2. Divide responsibilities. For example, some students can create a soft-sculpture head while others stuff clothes with newspaper. Others can construct the environment. Make sure your figure is in scale with the environment.

3. Make a sign that gives the title and the students' names who created the sculpture.

Rhythm

- To make the warp of the loom, look at the warm or cool color you chose for the practice activity cutouts. Select the opposite color scheme for your weaving paper.

- Fold the paper in half. Place the folded paper in front of you so that the fold is a vertical line. Draw a vertical line that is a one half-inch in from the open edge. Use a ruler and a pencil to make half-inch marks down the folded edge. Cut wavy or zigzag lines from the half-inch marks on the folded edge to the drawn line. Make sure your cut lines do not touch.

Activity Tips

Texture

Creative Expression

1. Collect many small items that reflect your interests.
2. Spread tacky glue on the plastic water bottle.
3. Arrange your collected items on the bottle. Consider texture, contrast, and space.
4. Write a favorite memory on a piece of paper. Place your memory in the memory jar you have created.
5. Place the cap on the bottle. Paint the memory jar using only one color.

Rhythm

Creative Expression

1. Use paper strips to weave over and under the warp of the prepared paper loom.
2. Glue the ends of the strips down.
3. Space your three cutout images from the Practice activity on your paper weaving to create rhythm.
4. Glue the cutout images in place.

Activity Tips

Movement through Rhythm

🎨 Creative Expression

1. Select your best sketch and transfer it to your drawing paper.

2. Use a ruler to draw three straight lines crossing the short span of the paper.

3. Use a ruler to draw two straight lines crossing the long span of the paper.

4. Choose cool- or warm-colored pencils, and color in your object.

5. Color the background using contrasting colors.

6. Do not let areas of the same color touch one another.

···

Formal Balance

🎨 Creative Expression

1. Tape your self-portrait from the Practice activity to the sheet of cardboard.

2. Lay the sheet of fabric over your self-portrait and tape it in place. You should be able to see your drawing through the fabric.

3. Partially open the glue bottle, and practice drawing with the glue on a separate sheet of paper. Carefully trace your self-portrait with glue and allow it to dry.

4. Paint between the glue lines with watercolor paints.

Activity Tips **243**

Movement through Rhythm

- As a class, set up an arrangement of objects to create a still life. Objects such as a vase, an old guitar, and plants are good. Choose two or three objects to draw. Create several sketches, keeping shapes simple and flat.

Formal Balance

- Demonstrate using a toothpick to draw through the lines of the glue so that the glue lines are consistent. To outline smaller areas, the toothpicks can be dipped in the glue and then used to trace over the lines, as if they were paintbrushes. Caution students to paint between their glue lines. The idea is to keep the glue lines white to create the effect of batik.

Activity Tips

Informal Balance

Creative Expression

1. Collect and arrange objects. Use your thumb and index finger to form a frame around the still life to help you look at only one section of it. Lightly draw your selected section of the still life.

2. Use a permanent marker to outline your complete drawing.

3. Decide on a color scheme. Paint your tabletop using watercolor paints.

4. Place your drawing right-side down on top of the painted surface. Gently rub the back of your paper and lift it to create a monoprint.

Radial Balance

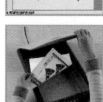

Creative Expression

1. Draw a circle and divide it into eight equal triangular segments. Erase or eliminate all the segments except one.

2. Create a design in the remaining segment using the draw tool and the fill color tool.

3. Copy and paste this segment four times. Select one of the segments created and using the option button, flip the design horizontally. Copy and paste the design three more times for a total of eight segments.

3. Print the segments. Cut them out and reassemble the segments to form a circular design. Scan the design and print.

244 Activity Tips

Activity Tips

Harmony

Creative Expression

1. Select your best sketch from your Art Journal and draw it large enough to fill the paper.

2. Blend your colors on a mixing tray. Paint your sketched object.

3. Use a fine-line marker to add details to your completed painting.

4. Together with your classmates, create a unified mural.

Variety through Difference

Creative Expression

1. Look at the sketch you have drawn in your Art Journal.

2. Place yourself three times in this sketch showing you doing normal activities within this chosen school environment.

3. Add objects that clearly communicate who you are in the scene. Keep your clothing the same in all three of your images.

4. Lightly transfer this sketch onto your drawing paper with a pencil. Use colored pencils to complete your drawing.

Activity Tips

Emphasis of an Element

Creative Expression

1. Use a piece of clay the size of a softball. Flatten it with the palms of your hands to equal the thickness of your thumb.

2. Use clay tools to draw repeated lines or shapes in the clay. Add texture by pressing textural materials into the clay and removing.

3. Paint some of your clay design. Spray a little water if the paint begins to dry out.

4. Place a piece of paper on the top of your clay plate and rub gently. Carefully peel off the paper.

5. Add more paint, making two more prints.

Emphasis through Placement

Creative Expression

1. Pick a sketch from your Art Journal and draw it on your cardboard.

2. Place the glue onto the outlines of the shapes. Fill in the shapes with strands of different-colored yarn. Squeeze a line of glue for each piece of yarn as you work.

3. Use a variety of line directions, yarn, and textures. Do not leave any spaces between the yarn lines, and be sure that no cardboard is showing.

4. Use a toothpick to press the yarn onto the glued areas.

Activity Tips

Unity through Media

🎨 Creative Expression

1. Draw your chosen state symbol on a sheet of paper at least four times in four different sizes. Color the drawings.

2. Cut out each symbol and place them on pieces of construction paper. The color of the construction paper should match the color used in your drawings. Trace these shapes with a black felt marker on the construction paper and cut them out.

3. Glue the symbols onto a posterboard square. Use fine-tipped markers to add detail to your quilt square.

Unity through Theme

🎨 Creative Expression

1. Use your thumb to create a small pinchpot base in a ball of clay the size of a softball. Cut a circle a little larger than the size of a quarter in this base.

2. Make clay coils to build onto the pinchpot for the body of the animal. Narrow the figure as you approach the neck. Cut a coin slot a little larger than the size of a quarter into the back of the bank.

3. Add a head, feet, and a tail. Add texture and details.

4. Paint the animal bank after it has been fired.

Activity Tips   **247**

Visual Index

Artist Unknown
Mask
12th–9th century
B.C. (page 143)

Artist Unknown
Half of a Tunic
A.D. 600–900.
(page 112)

Artist Unknown
Featherwork Neckpiece
c. 1350–1476.
(page 104)

Artist Unknown
*Deep Dish from
Valencia, Spain*
1430. (page 176)

Domenico Ghirlandaio
*Francesco Sasetti and His
Son Teodoro*
c. 1480. (page 130)

Sofonisba Anguissola
*Artist's Sisters Playing
Chess and their Governess*
1555. (page 172)

Lavinia Fontana
*Portrait of a
Noblewoman*
c. 1600. (page 94)

Nanha
*Emperor Shah Jahan and
His Son, Suja*
1625–1630. (page 131)

Jan Vermeer
The Concert
1665–1667. (page 64)

Charles James
Sun Transformation Mask
early 19th century.
(page 142)

Artist Unknown
Kwele Face Mask
c. 19th–20th century.
(page 143)

George Catlin
*Mah-To-Tóh-Pa, Four Bears,
Second Chief*
1832. (page 157)

James McNeill Whistler
Weary
1863. (page 49)

Berthe Morisot
The Sisters
1869. (page 184)

Winslow Homer
Nooning
c. 1872. (page 70)

William Adolphe Bouguereau
The Nut Gatherers
1882. (page 71)

James Tissot
*Women of Paris: The
Circus Lover*
1883–1885. (page 173)

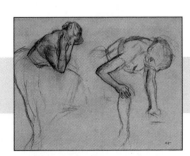

Edgar Degas
Ballerinas
1885. (page 40)

Paul Cézanne
Pierrot and Harlequin
1888. (page 120)

Paul Gauguin
Still Life with Three Puppies
1888. (page 160)

Artist Unknown
Navajo Blanket Eye Dazzler
1890. (page 101)

Vincent van Gogh
House at Auvers
1890. (page 154)

Louis Sullivan
Elevator Grill
1893–1894. (page 117)

Paul Cézanne
Still Life with Basket of Apples
1895. (page 45)

Henri de Toulouse-Lautrec
Madame Thadée Natanson at the Theater
1895. (page 41)

Artist Unknown
Bowl
Late 19th–early 20th century. (page 116)

Artist Unknown
Toy Banks
early 20th century. (page 206)

Artist Unknown
*Portrait of Yinxiang,
The First Prince of Yi*
1905. (page 168)

Childe Hassam
*Lower Manhattan
(View Down Broad
Street)*
1907. (page 74)

Pablo Picasso
*"Ma Joli" (Woman with
a Zither or Guitar)*
1911–1912. (page 165)

Paul Strand
*From the Viaduct,
125th St.*
1916. (page 56)

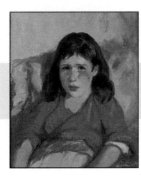

Robert Henri
Tilly
1917. (page 135)

Amedeo Modigliani
*Portrait of a Polish
Woman*
1918. (page 139)

Diego Rivera
*Study of a Sleeping
Woman*
1921. (page 53)

Raoul Dufy
*Fenetre Ouverte Devant
la Mer (Window Open to
the Sea)*
1923. (page 108)

Artist Unknown
Memory Jar
c. 1925. (page 156)

Diego Rivera
Flower Day
1925. (page 169)

Raoul Dufy
Open Window, Nice
1928. (page 60)

John Steuart Curry
Tornado Over Kansas
1929. (page 126)

Joan Miró
Hirondelle/Amour
1933–1934. (page 161)

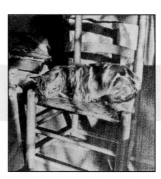

Charles Sheeler
Feline Felicity
1934. (page 52)

Georges Braque
Still Life on Red Tablecloth
1936. (page 44)

Frida Kahlo
Self-Portrait Dedicated to Leon Trotsky
1937. (page 180)

Elon Webster
False Face Mask
1937. (page 142)

Georgia O'Keeffe
Red and Pink Rocks and Teeth
1938. (page 100)

Marc Chagall
The Red Horse (Fiesta)
1942. (page 150)

Arthur Dove
Sun
1943. (page 194)

George Tooker
Bird Watchers
1948. (page 127)

Le Corbusier
Chapelle de Notre-Dame du Haut
1950–1955. (page 86)

Artist Unknown
Ceremonial Panel
1950–1975. (page 113)

Artist Unknown
Huipil Weaving
c. 1950. (page 36)

Jackson Pollock
Convergence
1952. (page 37)

Isabel Bishop
Subway Scene
1957–1958. (page 210)

Ansel Adams
Aspens, Northern New Mexico
1958 (Print 1976). (page 57)

Manabu Mabe
Melancholy Metropolis
1961. (page 109)

Marisol Escobar
The Family
1962. (page 90)

Jasper Johns
Map
1962. (page 97)

Fernando Botero
Ruben's Wife
1963. (page 138)

Robert McCall
Space Station #1
c. 1968. (page 79)

**Irene Preston Miller
and the Hudson River Quilters**
The Hudson River Quilt
1969–1972. (page 202)

Elizabeth Catlett
Sharecropper
1970. (page 48)

Tony Smith
Gracehoper
1971. (page 83)

Ben Jones
King Family
1971. (page 96)

Jasper Johns
Cups 4 Picasso
1972. (page 66)

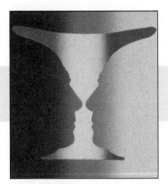

Jasper Johns
Cups 4 Picasso
1972. (page 67)

Jørn Oberg Utzon
Opera House
1973. (page 87)

Thomas Hart Benton
The Sources of Country Music
1975. (page 186)

George Segal
Walk Don't Walk
1976. (page 146)

Jennifer Bartlett
*Swimmer Lost at
Night (for Tom Hess)*
1978. (page 164)

John Robinson
Here Look at Mine
1980. (page 191)

Duane Hanson
Football Player
1981. (page 147)

Viola Frey
Grandmother Series:
July Cone Hat
1982. (page 124)

Elizabeth Garrison
Georgia
1983. (page 203)

Frank Stella
St. Michaels Counterguard
1984. (page 82)

Roger Brown
Homesick Proof Space Station
1987. (page 78)

Artist Unknown
Mother of the Eagles
1991. (page 198)

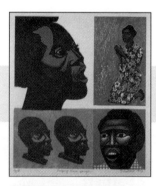

Elizabeth Catlett
Singing Their Songs
1992. (page 134)

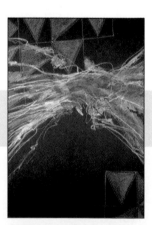

Willis "Bing" Davis
Ancestral Spirit Dance
#187
1994. (page 105)

Noland Anderson
Blue Dome-House Blessings
1995. (page 177)

Jaune Quick-to-See Smith
Spam
1995. (page 34)

Judith Surowiec
Art Teacher
1996. (page 190)

Mitch Lyons
Slip Trail
1997. (page 195)

Richard Yarde
Savoy: Heel and Toe
1997. (page 187)

Frederick Brosen
Watts Street
1998. (page 75)

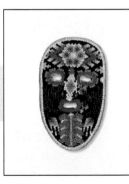

Artist Unknown
Huichol Bead Mask
2000. (page 199)

Elizabeth Paulos Krasle
Puff
2003. (page 207)

Glossary

A

alternating pattern
(ôl' tər nāt ing pat' ərn), *noun* Can repeat a motif, but change position; alter spacing between motifs or add a second motif

analogous colors
(ə nal' ə gəs kul' ərs), *noun* Colors that sit side by side on the color wheel and have a common hue. Violet, blue-violet, blue, blue-green are examples of analogous colors.

approximate symmetry
(ə 'präk sə mət sim' i trē), *noun* A type of formal balance that is almost symmetrical but small differences in the artwork make it more interesting

architects (är' kə tekts), *noun* Artists who design buildings, cities, and bridges using three-dimensional forms

architecture (är' kə tek' chər), *noun* The art of designing and planning buildings, cities, and buildings

assemblage (ä säm bläzh'), *noun* A sculpture technique in which a variety of objects is assembled to create one complete piece

asymmetry (ā sim' i trē), *noun* Another name for informal balance. Something asymmetrical looks balanced even if it is not the same on both sides.

B

background (bak' ground'), *noun* The area of the picture plane farthest from the viewer

balance (bal' ə ns), *noun* The principle of design that deals with visual weight in an artwork

blending (blen ding), *noun* A shading technique that creates a gradual change from light to dark or dark to light

body proportions
(bod' ē prə pôr shənz), *noun* The size relationship of one part of the body to another

C

central axis (sen' trəl ak' sis), *noun* A real or imaginary dividing line which can run in two directions, vertically and horizontally

collage (kō läzh), *noun*   A two-dimensional work of art made up of pieces of paper and/or fabric to create the image.

color (kul' ər), *noun*   1. The art element that is derived from reflected light; 2. In balance: a brighter color has more visual weight than a dull color; 3. In perspective: bright-colored objects seem closer, while dull or pale objects appear farther away.

color intensity (kul' ər in tem' si tē), *noun*   The brightness or dullness of a color

color scheme (kul' ər skēm'), *noun*   A plan for organizing the colors used in an artwork

color spectrum (kul' ər spek' trum), *noun*   The effect that occurs when light passes through a prism and separates into a band of colors in the order of red, orange, yellow, green, blue, and violet

color wheel (kul' ər 'wēl), *noun*   Shows the color spectrum bent into a circle

complementary colors (kom' plə men tə rē kul' ərz), *noun*   Colors that are opposite each other on the color wheel

complex geometric shapes (kom' pleks jē' ə met' rik shāps), *noun*   Combined basic geometric shapes: a pentagon or hexagon

contour (kon' tür), *noun*   The edges and surface ridges of an object or figure

contour lines (kon' tür līnz), *noun*   Continuous, unbroken lines that show the edges and surface ridges of an object or figure

contrast (kon' trast), *noun*   1. A technique for creating a focal point or area of interest in a work of art using differences in elements; 2. In emphasis: contrast occurs when one element stands out from the rest of the work.

converging (kən' vərg ing), *adj.* (verb)   Coming together at one point or place

converging lines (kən vərg ing līnz), *noun*   One of the six perspective techniques. Parallel lines seem to converge or move toward the same point as they move away from you.

cool colors (kül kul' erz), *noun*   Green, violet, and blue. They suggest coolness and move away from the viewer.

cross-hatching (krôs hach' ing), *noun*   A shading technique created when sets of parallel lines cross or intersect

curling (kərl), *verb*   Hold one end of a long strip of paper. Grip the middle of the paper strip next to the side of a pencil. With a quick motion, pull the strip firmly across the pencil.

curved (kûrvd), *adj.*   Lines that bend and change gradually or turn inward to form spirals

D

detail (dē tāl), *noun*   One of the six perspective techniques. Objects with fuzzy, blurred edges appear farther away than those with clear sharp edges.

decorative (de kē rā tiv), *adj.* Serving to make more beautiful; to adorn with ornaments

depth (depth), *noun.*   The appearance of distance in a two-dimensional artwork

diagonal (dī ag' ə nəl), *noun* (adj.) Lines that move on a slant

distortion (di stôr shən), *noun* A deviation from normal or expected proportions

E

emphasis (em' fə sis), *noun*   The principle of design that stresses one area in an art work over another area

exaggeration (eg zaj' ə rā' shən), *noun*   To increase or enlarge beyond what is expected or normal

F

face proportions (fās prə pôr shənz), *noun*   The relationship of one feature of a face to another feature

focal point (fo' kəl point'), *noun* The point which the receding lines meet. It is the first part of a composition to attract the viewer's attention

foreground (fôr' ground'), *noun* The area of the picture plane that is closest to the viewer

form (form), *noun*   A three-dimensional object that is measured by height, width, and depth

formal balance (fôr' mel bal' əns), *noun*   Occurs when equal or similar elements are placed on opposite sides of a central axis

free-form forms (frē' fôrm' fôrmz), *noun*   Three-dimensional forms with irregular edges often found in nature

free-form shapes (frē' fôrm' shāps), *noun*   Two-dimensional images made of straight or curved lines or a combination of both

freestanding sculpture (frē stan' ding skulp' chər), *noun*   A three-dimensional work of art that can be viewed on all sides because it is surrounded by space

fringing   (frinj ing), *verb*   Make parallel straight cuts along the edge of a piece of paper to create a ruffled look.

G

geometric forms (je' ə met' rik fôrmz), *noun*   Mathematically precise forms based on geometric shapes

geometric shapes (je' ə met' rik shāps), *noun* Mathematically precise shapes: circle, square, and triangle

gesture lines
(jes' chər līnz), *noun*   Lines drawn quickly to capture the movement of a person, animal or object

gesture sketch
(jes' chər skech), *noun*   Quick drawings used to capture the position or movement of the body

guide lines (gīd līnz), *noun*
Lines used by artists to create both full-face and profile portraits more accurately

H

harmony (här' mə nē), *noun*   The principle of art which creates unity by stressing similarities of separate but related parts

hatching (hach' ing), *noun*
A shading technique that looks like a series of parallel lines

highlights (hī līts), *noun*   Small areas of white or light value to show the brightest spots

horizon line (hər' ī zən līn), *noun*
The point at which the earth and sky meet. The horizon line is always at the viewer's eye level.

horizontal (hôr' ə zon təl), *noun*
Lines that move from side to side

hue (hū), *noun*   Another name for color

I

informal balance (in fôr'məl bal' əns), *noun*   A way of organizing parts of a design so that unlike objects have equal visual weight

intermediate hues
(in' tər m' de it hūz), *noun*   Yellow-green, red-orange, blue-green, made by combining a primary with either of the secondary hues that are adjacent on the color wheel

isolation (ī' sə lā' shən), *noun*   An object is emphasized by its placement apart from other objects.

L

line (līn), *noun*   The path of a moving point through space

linear perspective
(lin ē' ər pər spek' tiv), *noun*
A system used to create the illusion of depth on a flat surface

location (lō cā' shən), *noun*
Artists can emphasize an object by placing it closer to the center of the piece.

M

mandala (mən də lə), *noun*   A radial design divided into sections or wedges, each of which contains a different image

middle ground (mid' əl ground'), *noun*   The area of the picture plane that is usually towards the center

mixed-media (mikst mē dē' ə), *noun*   An art object that has been created from an assortment of media or materials

motif (mō tēf), *noun*   A unit that is made up of objects or art elements which is repeated

monochromatic
(mon' ə kro mat' ik), *adj.* A color scheme which is made up of one hue and the tints and shade of that hue

movement (müv' mənt), *noun* The principle of art that leads a viewer's eyes throughout a work of art

N

negative space (neg' ə tiv spas'), *noun* The empty space that surrounds objects, shapes, and forms

nonobjective (non' əb jek' tiv), *adj.* Art that has no recognizable subject matter

O

one-point linear perspective (wun' point lin ē' ər pər spek' tiv), *noun* A system used to create the illusion of depth on a flat surface where all receding lines meet at one point

opaque (ō pāk'), *adj.* Does not let light through

overlapping (o' vər lap ing), *noun* 1. One object covers a portion of another object. 2. In perspective: one of the perspective techniques, the object covering another will appear closer to the viewer, creating a feeling of depth.

P

paper sculpting techniques (pā pər skəlpt ing tek nēks), *noun* Six different techniques used to create paper sculptures: scoring a straight line, scoring a curve, pleating, curling, fringing, tab and slot.

parallel lines (per ə lel līnz), *noun* Lines that move in the same direction and always stay the same distance apart

pattern (pat' ərn), *noun* A repeated surface decoration

perception drawing (pər səp shən drô' ing), *verb* Looking at something carefully and thinking deeply about what you see as you draw

perspective (pər spek' tiv), *noun* The method used to create the illusion of depth in two-dimensional art: overlapping, size, placement, detail, color, converging lines

picture plane (pik' chər plān'), *noun* The surface of a drawing or painting.

placement (pləs ment), *noun* One of the six perspective techniques. Objects placed lower in the picture appear to be closer than those placed near eye level. There are three areas on a picture plane: foreground, middle ground, and background.

pleating (plēt' ing), *verb* Fold piece of paper from edge ro edge. Then fold the same amount of paper in the other direction. Continue folding back and forth in this manner.

portrait (por trət), *noun* A two- or three-dimensional artwork created in the image of a person or animal

position (pə zish' ən), *noun* In balance: a larger, positive shape and a small, negative space can be balanced by a small, positive shape and a large, negative space.

positive space (poz' i tiv spas'), *noun* Refers to any object, shape, or form in two- and three-dimensional art

primary hues (pri' mer ē hūz), *noun* Red, yellow, and blue, used to mix the other hues on the color wheel

profile (prō fīl), *noun* A side view of a person or animal

profile proportions (prō fīl prə pôr' shənz), *noun* A side view of the head that is divided by three horizontal lines

proportion (prə pôr' shən), *noun* The principle of art that is concerned with the size relationship of one part to another

R

radial balance (rā' dē əl bal' əns), *noun* A type of balance that occurs when the art elements come out, or radiate, from a central point

random pattern (ran' dəm pat' ərn), *noun* Occurs when the motif is repeated in no apparent order

ratio (rā shē ō), *noun* A comparison of size between two things

realistic scale (rē ə lis' tik skāl), *noun* When an artist creates a work of art where everything fits together and makes sense in size relation

regular pattern (reg' yə lər pat' ərn), *noun* Occurs when identical motifs are repeated with an equal amount of space between them

relief sculpture (ri ləf' skulp' chər), *noun* A sculpture in which objects stick out from a flat surface

rhythm (rith' əm), *noun* The principle of design that organizes the elements in a work of art by repeating elements and/or objects

S

scale (skāl), *noun* Size as measured against a standard reference

score (skor), *verb* The repeated scratching of the clay surface at the area that another scored piece will be attached

scoring a curve (skor' ing ā kûrv), *verb* Gradually cut bending curves in the paper with the point of the scissors

scoring a straight line (skor' ing ā strāt līn), *verb* Hold a ruler in the center of a piece of paper. Run the point of the scissors along the edge of the ruler to cut the paper in a straight line.

secondary hues (sek' ən der' ē həz), *noun* Orange, green and violet; the result of mixing two primary hues

self-portrait (self por trət), *noun* A two or three-dimensional artwork that an artist makes of him or herself

shade (shād), *noun* Any hue blended with black

shading (shād ing), *verb* Use of dark values to create the illusion of form and texture

shadows (sha dōz), *noun* Shaded areas in a painting or drawing

shape (shāp) *noun* A two-dimensional area that is measured by height and width

shape reversal (shāp rē ver səl) *noun* Occurs when an object, shape or form is positive space in one image and then in another image becomes negative space

size (sīz), *noun* 1. In perspective: objects that are closer look larger than objects that are farther away; 2. In balance: a large shape or form will appear to be heavier than a small shape, and several small shapes can balance one large shape.

slip (slip), *noun* A mixture of clay and water that is creamy to the touch and is used to attach two scored pieces of clay together

space (spās), *noun* The art element that refers to the areas above, below, between, within, and around an object

still life (stil' līf'), *noun* The arrangement of common inanimate objects from which artists draw or paint

stippling (stip' ling), *noun* A shading technique using dots to show value

symmetry (sim' i trē), *noun* A type of formal balance in which two halves of a balanced artwork are identical, mirror images of each other

T

tactile texture (tak' təl teks' chər), *noun* Actual texture, texture that can really be felt

texture (teks' chər), *noun* 1. The art element that refers to the way something feels; 2. In balance: a rough texture has an uneven pattern of highlights and shadows. For this reason, a rough surface attracts the viewer's eyes more easily than a smooth, even surface

tint (tint), *noun* Any hue blended with white

transparent (trans' per ənt), *adj.* Allows light to pass through so objects on the other side can be seen

U

unity (ū' ni tē), *noun* The feeling of wholeness or oneness that is achieved by properly using the elements and principles in art

unrealistic scale (un' rē ə lis' tik skāl), *noun* When an artist makes size relationships that do not make sense

V

value (val' ū), *noun*   The lightness or darkness of a hue

value contrast (val' ū kon' trast), *noun*   The lightness or darkness stands out from the value that surrounds it

vanishing point (vân' ish' ing point), *noun*   The point on the horizon line where all parallel receding lines meet

variety (və ri' ə tē), *noun*   The principle of art which is concerned with difference or contrast

vertical (vür' tə kəl), *noun*   Lines that move from top to bottom

visual movement (vizh' ü əl müv' mənt), *noun*   Created by repeating an art element or object in a work of art

visual rhythm (vizh' ü əl rith' əm), *noun*   The repetition of shapes, colors, or lines in a work of art

visual texture (vizh' ü əl teks' chər), *noun*   Or simulated texture, imitates real texture. It is texture if we can see how it feels.

W

warm colors (wōrm' kul' ərz), *noun*   Red, yellow, and orange. They suggest warmth and come forward toward the viewer.

Z

zigzag (zig' zag) *noun* (adj.)   Lines that are made by joining diagonal lines

Index

D

Davis, Willis Bing, 105
decorative pattern, 116–119
Deep Dish/Spain/from Valencia (Unknown), 176
Degas, Edgar, 40
detail, 72
distortion, 124–125, 138–145
Dove, Arthur, 194
Dufy, Raoul, 60, 108

E

element, 194–197
Elevator Grill (Sullivan), 117
Emperor Shah Jahan, 130
Emperor Shah Jahan and His Son, Suja (Nanha), 131
emphasis, 185, 194–201
Escobar, Marisol, 90
exaggerated features, 144
expression, 36–39

F

face proportion, 134–137, 142–145
False Face Mask (Webster), 142
The Family (Escobar), 90
Featherwork Neckpiece (Unknown), 104
Feline Felicity (Sheeler), 52
Fenetre Ouverte Devant la Mer (Dufy), 108
Flower Day (Rivera), 169
focal point, 200
Fontana, Lavinia, 94, 95
Football Player (Hanson), 147
form, 64–65, 82–89, 93
formal balance, 168–171

Francesco Sasetti and His Son Teodoro (Ghirlandaio), 130
free-form shapes, 44–47, 88
Frey, Viola, 124, 125
fringing, 84

G

Garrison, Elizabeth, 203
Gauguin, Paul, 160
geometric shapes, 44–47
Georgia (Garrison), 203
gesture art, 42
Ghirlandaio, Domenico, 130
goldsmiths, 152
Gracehoper (Smith), 83
Grandmother Series: July Cone Hat (Frey), 124
guide lines, 136

H

Hanson, Duane, 147
harmony, 185–189
Hassam, Childe, 74
hatching, 48–51, 58, 80
Henri, Robert, 135
Here Look at Mine (Robinson), 191
hexagon, 46
Hirondelle/Amour (Miro), 161
Homer, Winslow, 70
Homesick Proof Space Station (Brown), 78
Houses at Auvers (van Gogh), 154
Hudson River Quilters, 202
The Hudson River Quilt (Miller), 202
hues, 98. *See also* colors
Huichol Bead Mask (Unknown), 199
Huipil Weaving (Unknown), 36

Acknowledgments

Grateful acknowledgment is given to the following publishers and copyright owners for permissions granted to reprint selections from their publications. All possible care has been taken to trace ownership and secure permission for each selection included. In case of any errors or omissions, the Publisher will be pleased to make suitable acknowledgments in future editions.

CHARLOTTE'S WEB by E.B. WHITE. Cover Art COPYRIGHT © 1952 BY GARTH WILLIAMS RENEWED © 1980 BY GARTH WILLIAMS. Used by permission of HarperCollins Publishers.

Cover from SECTOR 7 by David Wiesner. Jacket Illustrations copyright © 1999 by David Wiesner. Reprinted by permission of Clarion Books/ Houghton Mifflin Company. All rights reserved.

Cover from FRITZ AND THE BEAUTIFUL HORSES by Jan Brett. Copyright © 1981 by Jan Brett. Reprinted by permission of Clarion Books/Houghton Mifflin Company. All rights reserved.

A CHAIR FOR MY MOTHER by VERA B. WILLIAMS. COPYRIGHT © 1982 BY VERA B. WILLIAMS. Used by permission of HarperCollins Publishers.

From MIRANDY AND BROTHER WIND by Patricia C. McKissack, copyright © 1988 by Patricia C. McKissack. Illustrations © 1988 by Jerry Pinkney. Used by permission of Alfred A. Knopf, an imprint of Random House Children's Books, a division of Random House, Inc.

LON PO PO

Photo Credits

Cover Los Angeles County Museum of Art, Los Angeles County Fund. Photo © 1999 Museum Associates, LACMA; 6 © Isabella Stewart Gardner Museum, Boston, Massachusetts, USA/Bridgeman Art Library; 7 National Museum of Women in the Arts. Washington D.C; 8 The Nelson-Atkins Museum of Art, Kansas City, Missouri (Gift of Byron and Eileen Cohen); 9 Museum of Fine Arts, Boston. Bequest of John T. Spaulding; 10 Gift of Mrs. Charles S. Carstairs, Image © 2003 Board of Trustees, National Gallery of Art, Washington; 12 (tl) Museum of Fine Arts, Boston. Bequest of John T. Spaulding, (tr) Hirshhorn Museum and Sculpture Garden, Smithsonian Institution, Gift of Joseph H. Hirshhorn, 1966, (bl) Dallas Museum of Art, Dallas, Texas, (br) © Philip Hayson/Photo Researchers Inc; 13 (tl) Honolulu Academy of Art. Honolulu, Hawaii. Gift of James A. Michener, 1955 (13,694), (tr) Purchased with funds provided by the Smithsonian Collections Acquisition Program. Photograph by Frank Khoury. National Museum of African Art, Smithsonian Institution, Washington DC, (bl) Image no.EEPA 1474. Eliot Elisofon Photographic Archives, National Museum of African Art, Smithsonian Institution, Washington, DC; (br) Royal British Columbia Museum, Catalogue No. 1908; 15 (tl) The Ogden Museum of Southern Art, University of New Orleans, Gift of the Benny Andrews Foundation, (tr) Amon Carter Museum, Fort Worth, Texas. 1999.33.E, (bl) From the Girard Foundation Collection, in the Museum of International Folk Art, a unit of the Museum of New Mexico, Santa Fe, New Mexico. Photographer: Michel Monteaux, (br) © Carl & Ann Purcell/Corbis; 16 Helen Birch Bartlett Memorial Collection, 1926.252. Photograph © 2001, The Art Institute of Chicago, All Rights Reserved; 17 © Northwest Museum of Arts & Culture. Photo by David Anderson; 18 Wadsworth Atheneum, Hartford. The Ella Gallup Summer and Mary Catlin Sumner Collection Fund; 19 (t) Dallas Museum of Art, Dallas, Texas, (b) Smithsonian American Art Museum, Washington, DC/Art Resource, NY © Elizabeth Catlett/Licensed By VAGA, New York, New York; 20 National Gallery, London/Art Resource, NY. Erich Lessing, photographer; 22 (t, tcl, tcr, br, bcr) © Photodisc/Getty Images, Inc, (bcl, bl) © Digital Vision/Getty Images, Inc; 23 (t) © Corbis, (tcl, tcr, bl, bcl, bc)© Photodisc/Getty Images, Inc, (br) © Index Stock Inc; 24, 26, 28, 30 San Francisco Museum of Modern Art. © Banco de Mexico Diego Rivera & Frida Kahlo Museum Trust. Av. Cinco de Mayo No.2, Col. Centro, Del. Cuauhtemoc 06059, Mexico, D.F; 32, 33 © Aaron Haupt; 35 © Steinbaum Krauss Gallery; 36 From the Girard Foundation Collection, in the Museum of International Folk Art, a unit of the Museum of New Mexico, Santa Fe, New Mexico. Photographer: Michel Monteaux; 37 Albright-Knox Art Gallery, Buffalo, New York. Gift of Seymour H. Knox, Jr. 1956. © 2004 The Pollock-Krasner Foundation/Artists Rights Society (ARS), New York; 38 © Eclipse Studios; 39 Frank Fortune; 40 High Museum of Art, Atlanta, Georgia, Anonymous gift, 1979.4; 42 © Eclipse Studios; 43 Randy Ellett; 44 Norton Museum of Art, Gift of R.H. Norton, 47.46. © 2004 Artists Rights Society (ARS), New York/ADAGP, Paris; 45 Helen Birch Bartlett Memorial Collection, 1926.252. Photograph © 2001, The Art Institute of Chicago, All Rights Reserved; 46 © Eclipse Studios; 47 The Metropolitan Museum of Art, Gift of Mr. and Mrs. Richard Rodgers, 1964. Photography © 1993 The Metropolitan Museum of Art; 48 Smithsonian American Art Museum, Washington, DC/Art Resource, NY. © Elizabeth Catlett/Licensed By VAGA, New York, New York; 49 National Gallery of Art, Washington, DC. Rosenwald Collection, Image © 2003 Board of Trustees, National Gallery of Art, Washington; 51 Randy Ellett; 52 Harvard University Art Museums; 53 Harvard University Art Museums. © Banco de Mexico Diego Rivera & Frida Kahlo Museum Trust. Av. Cinco de Mayo No.2, Col. Centro, Del. Cuauhtemoc 06059, Mexico, D.F; 54 Eclipse Studios; 55 Randy Ellett; 56 Amon Carter Museum, Fort Worth, Texas. P1983.17, © 1981 Aperature Foundation, Inc. Paul Strand Archive; 57 © Digital Image The Museum of Modern Art/Licensed by SCALA/Art Resource, NY. Photography by Ansel Adams. Used with permission of the Trustees of the Ansel Adams Publishing Rights Trust. All Rights Reserved; 58 © Eclipse Studios; 59 Frank Fortune; 60 The Joseph Winterbotham Collection, 1937.166. Reproduction, The Art Institute of Chicago. © Artists Rights Society (ARS), New York/ADAGP, Paris; 62 Joseph Sohm/ChromoShom/Corbis; 63 Courtesy of Faustwork Mask Theater; 64 © Isabella Stewart Gardner Museum, Boston, Massachusetts, USA/Bridgeman Art Library; 65 © Erich Lessing/Art Resource, New York; 66 The Museum of Modern Art, New York. Gift of Celeste Bartos. © Artists Rights Society (ARS), New York/ADAGP, Paris; 67 The Museum of Modern Art, New York. Gift of Celeste Bartos. © Artists Rights Society (ARS), New York/ADAGP, Paris; 68 © Eclipse Studios; 69 Randy Ellett; 70 Wadsworth Atheneum, Hartford. The Ella Gallup Summer and Mary Catlin Sumner Collection Fund; 71 Gift of Mrs. William E. Scripps. Photograph © 1996 The Detroit Institute of Arts; 73 Randy Ellett; 74 Lent by Willard Straight Hall; Gift of Leonard K. Elmhirst, Class of 1921. Courtesy of the Herbert F. Johnson Museum of Art, Cornell University; 75 © Frederick Brosen/Forum Gallery; 76 © Matt Meadows; 78 Courtesy of the Phyllis Kind Gallery; 79 National Museum of Air and Space. Smithsonian Institution, Washington, DC; 82 Los Angeles County Museum of Art, Gift of Anna Bing Arnold. © 2004 Frank Stella/Artists Rights Society (ARS), New York; 83 Founders Society Purchase with funds from W. Hawkins Ferry and Mr. Mrs. Walter Buhl Ford II Fund, Eleanor Clay Ford Fund, Marie and Alex Manoogian Fund and members of the Friends of Modern Art. Photograph © The Detroit Institute of Arts; 84 © Eclipse Studios; 85 Randy Ellett; 86 © Girandon/Art Resource, NY; 87 © Philip Hayson/Photo Researchers Inc; 88 © Eclipse Studios; 89 Randy Ellett; 90 Digital Image © The Museum of Modern Art/Licensed by SCALA/Art Resource, NY. © Marisol Escobar/Licensed by VAGA, New York, New York; 92 Photodisc/Getty Images, Inc; 93 Jody Krupin; 94 National Museum of Women in the Arts. Washington DC; 95 © Galleria degli Uffizi, Florence, Italy/The Bridgeman Art Library; 96 Collection of the Studio Museum; 97 The Museum of Contemporary Art, Los Angeles. © Jasper Johns/Licensed by VAGA, New York, New York; 98 © Eclipse Studios; 99 Randy Ellett; 100 The Art Institute of Chicago. Gift of Georgia O'Keeffe. © 2004 The Georgia O'Keeffe

Foundation/Artists Rights Society (ARS), New York; 101 Dallas Museum of Art, Dallas, Texas; 103 Randy Ellett; 104 Dallas Museum of Art, Dallas, Texas; 105 Courtesy of Willis Bing Davis; 106 © Eclipse Studios; 107 Randy Ellett; 108 The New Orleans Museum of Art; On loan from the Mrs. Frederick M. Stafford Collection. © 2004 Artists Rights Society (ARS), New York/ADAGP, Paris; 109 Collection Walker Art Center. Minneapolis, Minnesota; 110 © Eclipse Studios; 111 Frank Fortune; 112 International Folk Art Foundation Collection. Museum of International Folk Art. Santa Fe, New Mexico. Photo by: Pat Pollard; 113 International Folk Art Foundation Collection. Museum of International Folk Art. Santa Fe, New Mexico. Photo by: Pat Pollard; 114 © Eclipse Studios; 115 Randy Ellett; 116 High Museum of Art, Atlanta, Georgia, Virginia Carroll Crawford Collection, 1982.291; 117 Purchased with funds provided by the Smithsonian Collections Acquisition Program. Photograph by Frank Khoury. National Museum of African Art, Smithsonian Institution, Washington D.C; 118 © Eclipse Studios; 119 Randy Ellett; 120 © Scala/Art Resource, NY. Pushkin Museum of Fine Arts, Moscow; 122 Bob Krist/Corbis; 123 Michal Daniel; 124 The Nelson-Atkins Museum of Art, Kansas City, Missouri (Gift of Byron and Eileen Cohen); 125 Complimentary Trish Bransten; 126 Muskegon Museum of Art, Hackley Picture Fund. 35.4; 127 New Britain Museum of Art, New Britain, Connecticut; 128 © Eclipse Studios; 129 Frank Fortune; 130 The Metropolitan Museum of Art, The Jules Bache Collection, 1949. Photograph © 1978 The Metropolitan Museum of Art; 131 The Metropolitan Museum of Art, Purchase, Rogers Fund and The Kevorkian Foundation Gift, 1955. Photograph © 1980 The Metropolitan Museum of Art; 132 © Eclipse Studios; 133 Frank Fortune; 134 National Museum of Women in the Arts, Washington D.C. © Elizabeth Catlett/Licensed By VAGA, New York, New York; 135 Gift of Beaux Arts. The Lowe Art Museum, The University of Miami, Coral Gables, Florida; 136 © Eclipse Studios; 138 Guggenheim Museum, New York, New York. Photograph by David Heald © The Solomon R. Guggenheim Foundation, New York; 139 Philadelphia Museum of Art, Philadelphia, Pennsylvania; 142 (l) Royal British Columbia Museum, Catalogue No. 1908, (r) Cranbrook Institute of Science, Bloomfield Hills, Michigan; 143 (l) The Metropolitan Museum of Art, The Michael C. Rockefeller Memorial Collection, Bequest of Nelson A. Rockefeller, 1979. Photograph © 1997 The Metropolitan Museum of Art, (r) The Metropolitan Museum of Art, The Michael C. Rockefeller Memorial Collection, Bequest of Nelson A. Rockefeller, 1979. Photograph © 1997 The Metropolitan Museum of Art; 145 Randy Ellett; 146 Whitney Museum of American Art, New York. © George Segal/Licensed by VAGA, New York, New York; 147 Lowe Art Museum at the University of Miami. Coral Gables, Florida. Art © Estate of Duane Hanson/Licensed by VAGA, New York, New York; 148 © Eclipse Studios; 149 Randy Ellett; 150 Norton Museum of Art, West Palm Beach, Florida, Bequest of R.H. Norton, 53.26. © 2004 Artists Rights Society (ARS), New York/ADAGP, Paris; 152 Courtesy of Abrasha; 153 Photo Max Waldman/© Max Waldman Archives; 154 Museum of Fine Arts, Boston. Bequest of John T. Spaulding; 155 © Metropolitan Museum of Art, New York, Bequest of Miss Adelaide Milton de Groot 91876-1967), 1967 (67.187.70a); 156 International Folk Art Foundation Collection. Museum of International Folk Art. Santa Fe, New Mexico. Photo by: John Bigelow Taylor; 157 © Smithsonian American Art Museum/Art Resource, NY; 158 (tl) © Alan Abramowitz/Getty Images, Inc, (tr) © Photodisc/Getty Images, Inc, (b) © Eclipse Studios; 159 Randy Ellett; 160 © The Museum of Modern of Art, New York/Licensed by Scala/Art Resource, NY; 161 Museum of Modern Art, New York. © Art Resource, NY. © 2004 Succession Miro'/Artists Rights Society (ARS), New York/ADAGP, Paris; 162 © Eclipse Studios; 163 Randy Ellett; 164 © The Museum of Modern Art, New York/Licensed by Scala/Art Resource, NY; 165 © The Museum of Modern Art, New York/Licensed by Scala/Art Resource, NY. © Estate of Pablo Picasso/Artists Rights Society (ARS), New York; 166 © Eclipse Studios; 167 Randy Ellett; 168 Arthur M. Sackler Gallery, Smithsonian Institution, Washington, DC, Purchase Smithsonian Collections Acquisition Program and partial gift of Richard G. Prtizlaff; 169 Los Angeles County Museum of Art, Los Angeles County Fund. Photo © 1999 Museum Associates, LACMA; 170 (l) © Photodisc/Getty Images, Inc, (r) © John Parker/Getty Images, Inc; 170 © Eclipse Studios; 171 Randy Ellett; 172 Art Resource, NY; 173 Museum of Fine Arts, Boston; 174 © Eclipse Studios; 175 Randy Ellett; 176 Hispanic Society of America. New York, New York; 177 Frank Fortune; 178 (l) Steve Lupton/Corbis, (r) © Charles & Josette Lenars/Corbis, (b) © Eclipse Studios; 179 Randy Ellett; 180 National Museum of Women in the Art, Washington, DC. © Banco de Mexico Diego Rivera & Frida Kahlo Museum Trust. Av. Cinco de Mayo No.2, Col. Centro, Del. Cuauhtemoc 06059, Mexico, D.F; 181 National Museum of Women in the Arts, Washington DC; 183 Herbert Migdoll; 184 Gift of Mrs. Charles S. Carstairs, Image © 2003 Board of Trustees, National Gallery of Art, Washington; 185 © Corbis Sygma; 186 Country Music Hall of Fame and Museum. Nashville, Tennessee. © T.H. Benton and R.P. Benton Testamentary Trusts/Licensed By VAGA, New York, New York; 187 Photo by S. Petegorsky; 188 © Eclipse Studios; 189 Randy Ellett; 190 Photograph Randy Ellett; 191 Archive Center, Anacostia Museum and Center for African American History and Culture, Smithsonian Institution, Photography by Harold Dorwin; 192 © Eclipse Studios; 193 Randy Ellett; 194 Smithsonian American Art Museum/Art Resource, NY; 195 © Mitch Lyons; 196 © Eclipse Studios; 197 Randy Ellett; 199 Photograph by Randy Ellett; 200 © Eclipse Studios; 202 Collection American Folk Art Museum, New York. Gift of the J.M. Kaplan Fund. Photo by Matt Hoebermann; 204 © Corbis; 205 Randy Ellett; 207 Frank Fortune; 208 © Eclipse Studios; 209 Randy Ellett; 210 Purchase. Whitney Museum of American Art, New York; 212 © Matthew McKee; Eye Ubiquitous/Corbis; 213 Courtesy of Ranganiketan; 230 (t) © Aaron Haupt, (b) © Eclipse Studios; 231 (t) © Aaron Haupt, (b) © Eclipse Studios; 232 (t) © Eclipse Studios, (b) © Aaron Haupt; 233 (t) © Aaron Haupt, (b) © Eclipse Studios; 234, 235 © Eclipse Studios; 236 (t) Aaron Haupt, (b) © Matt Meadows; 237 (t) © Eclipse Studios, (b) © Aaron Haupt; 238 © Eclipse Studios; 239-241 © Aaron Haupt; 242,243 © Eclipse Studios; 244 (t) © Eclipse Studios, (b) © Matt Meadows; 245-247 © Eclipse Studios.

Table of Contents

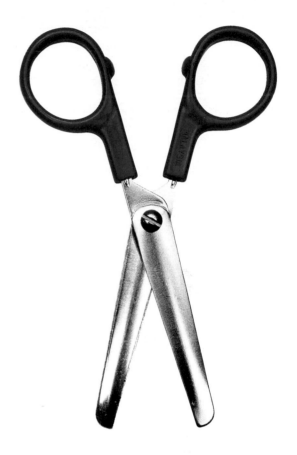

The Elementary Art Curriculum

Rosalind Ragans, Ph.D., Associate Professor Emerita, Georgia Southern University

Art education is for all students. It provides learning opportunities for the artistically talented few, as well as the many students who may never produce art outside the classroom.

A strong elementary visual arts curriculum teaches students that they can communicate a variety of ideas and emotions in many different ways. Students learn that some problems have many different solutions, and they will not be afraid to use divergent-thinking strategies. They will learn concepts and techniques that will give them control of the visual images they produce.

A strong elementary art curriculum also enables students to expand their perceptive, interpretive, and analytical abilities. They learn to find meaning in visual images, and they learn to identify aesthetic qualities in a variety of works of art and in the environment. They begin to develop the ability to make aesthetic judgments.

The visual arts have always been an integral component in the history of humanity, and through the study of art history, students will develop a better understanding of beliefs and ideas that are different from their own.

The four components of a quality art program are Aesthetic Perception, Art Criticism, Art History and Culture, and Art Production and Creative Expression.

Aesthetic Perception

Aesthetics is a branch of philosophy. In visual art, aesthetics becomes the study of the nature of beauty and art. Aesthetics is concerned with the question "What is art?" In the past, aesthetics was defined as the study of beauty because the creation of beauty was thought to be the purpose of art. Today, some aestheticians still believe that the purpose of art is to create beauty or beautifully organized arrangements of the elements of art. Some believe that art must imitate reality. Others think of art as a strong means to communicate ideas and emotions.

Aesthetic concepts are the core of the *Art Connections* curriculum. They are the framework upon which all aspects of art learning are constructed. The **About Aesthetic Perception** section in the *Student Edition* and *Teacher Edition* offers concrete methods for introducing students to aesthetics.

 Art Criticism

Works of art are the focus of every lesson. Art criticism is the sequential process used in this textbook to guide students through the procedures needed to learn from these works of art. Art criticism enables students to learn from works of art that have been created by artists from many cultures and time periods. Art criticism also provides a procedure that students can use to objectively study their own art products.

The four-step process of art criticism will help students expand their perceptive, analytical, interpretive, and aesthetic valuing abilities. The sequential steps of art criticism are similar to those used in the scientific method. During the first two steps, **Describe** and **Analyze,** students are asked to collect data objectively. During the third step, **Interpret,** students speculate about the meaning of the work based on the data collected: they make a hypothesis abut the idea, emotion, or mood expressed by the artist. During the fourth step, **Decide,** or aesthetic judgment, the students offer their conclusions about the work of art.

Art criticism helps students study a work of art before making an aesthetic judgment. Too often, beginners look at a work of art briefly and immediately make a value judgment. The sequential procedures in art criticism force the students to postpone judgment while becoming immersed in the image.

In this program art criticism is used as a higher-level method of thinking about the concepts taught in each unit. One work of art has been selected that emphasizes the elements or principles that were the focus of the lesson. Art criticism is also used to help students make a personal assessment of the artwork produced during the Creative Expression activities. The questions offered are neutral and avoid judgments involving likes and dislikes. This avoids embarrassing moments when discussing works in front of peers.

Art History and Culture

Art Connections is not an art history text, but any study of art should begin with learning something about the history of world art and the people who created it. Information about art history related to the featured work of art in each lesson is provided for the students throughout the text. The **About Art History and Culture** section provides an overview of how to include art history information in classroom instruction. Additional information is provided for the teacher in each lesson and in ancillary materials such as the *Artist Profiles* books and on the backs of the *Large Prints*. The *Art Around the World* collection and *The National Museum of Women in the Arts Collection* contain works of art from many countries and provide additional historical and cultural information.

Art Production and  Creative Expression

Each lesson includes an art production activity identified as **Practice** and **Creative Expression** in the *Student Edition*. This is the place for each student to creatively explore the lesson concept. Hands-on activities are often the most enjoyable aspect of art learning. The student integrates and internalizes the verbal and visual concepts of the lesson during the creative manipulation of art materials. While every component in the art program is equally important, every component does not need equal time. Art production requires the longest amount of time.

Do not skip the self-assessment section of the lesson. Most students would be embarrassed to offer subjective statements about their own work or the work of classmates. The four steps of art criticism offer an objective procedure for thinking about the concepts and technical procedures used during the creation of art.

Art Magazine Resources for Teachers

American Artist	*ARTnews*	*Crayola Kids*
Art Education	*Arts and Activities*	*Scholastic Art*
Art to Zoo	*Arts Education Policy Review*	*School Arts*

About Aesthetic Perception

Richard W. Burrows , Executive Director, Institute for Arts Education, San Diego, California

The Association of Institutes for Aesthetic Education promotes and fosters aesthetic education principles and practices through professional and institutional development. The Association provides policy and program leadership to the arts and education field at the national, state, and local levels.

Aesthetics has been defined as the branch of philosophy that focuses on the nature of beauty, the nature and value of art, and the inquiry processes and human responses associated with those topics.

Aesthetic perception can be most simply defined as an educational approach designed to enhance understanding of artistic expression. Aesthetic perception requires two primary elements to exist: a work of art and a viewer to perceive it. An aesthetic perception approach to viewing works of art is predicated on the belief that the arts can be studied in an active, experiential way. The focus is on developing skills of perception by using works of art as a "textbook" or a focus for study. The instruction delivered by teachers is in partnership with the work of art.

Aesthetic perception provides opportunities to heighten perception and understanding through direct encounters with a broad spectrum of works of art. Students and teachers become actively involved with the artwork—observing, listening to and discussing works of art, and exploring their perceptions of these works through participatory activities. The focus is on developing skills of perception through greater understanding of art forms, of how artists make aesthetic choices, and of how these understandings relate to other aspects of life.

Misconceptions About Aesthetic Perception

As aesthetic perception approaches have become more widely used, a number of misconceptions have developed about the purpose of aesthetic perception education in the understanding of works of art.

Multidisciplinary Versus Interdisciplinary

The purpose of aesthetic perception is not to explore the commonalities among works of art. Each work of art must be studied separately first; connections should be made after an in-depth understanding of that particular work. Every work of art has a separate intention and different meaning. If aesthetic perception is to develop a thinking- or meaning-based understanding of the work of art, then activities must reflect that point of view.

You Cannot Teach What You Do Not Like

A strong "personal" negative reaction to a work of art does not invalidate it as an object of study for students.

Arts Integration

While arts experiences must integrate with all other areas of the curriculum, it is important to understand the separate language that the arts have and acknowledge the connections with other cross-curricular areas as they arise.

The Therapeutic Value of Aesthetic Perception

Very often students and teachers will comment on the therapeutic value of aesthetic perception—it seems separate from the actual art-making processes. This is often a side effect of active engagement in artistic creation and perception. This is not the purpose of aesthetic perception, which should be seen as an alternative way of viewing the work of art and the world in which it is created.

Using Aesthetic Perception

Below are some guidelines for using an aesthetic-perception approach to education.

Deciding What to Teach

It would not be appropriate to teach the same elements over and over in connection with each work of art. Instead, knowledge of all of the elements within a given art discipline should provide the background knowledge for making a decision about what aesthetic perception experiences to design. These decisions should be based on the most predominant elements in the work of art—the responses and the backgrounds of the students.

Creating a Safe Space and Adopting a Critical Stance

It is important to create a working and learning environment with both students and teachers in which they feel comfortable taking risks and trying out new ideas. This does not mean, however, that everything that occurs in aesthetic perception has to be met with uncritical approval. Instead, experiences can be structured so that participants receive feedback on their aesthetic choices and are given an opportunity to revise and improve their solutions to problems.

Documenting the Experience

Various types of documentation serve as a way of recording the aesthetic perception events as they occur or are revisited. This documentation should include written observations, interviews, journals, and student projects. It is important in any case to record this work in order to be able to see the "habits of mind" that reveal themselves in this complex and rich way of thinking and knowing.

Aesthetic perception is a long-term undertaking and requires a patient conviction that the arts and aesthetic perception should be a part of the learning experience of young people. It requires flexibility, stamina, ingenuity, and perseverance. The rewards are astronomical in terms of student response, content understanding, and classroom relationships.

Introduction to Art History

Gene A. Mittler, Ph.D., Professor Emeritus, Texas Tech University

> "The art of the Greeks, of the Egyptians, of the great painters who lived in other times, is not an art of the past; perhaps it is more alive today than it ever was. Art does not evolve by itself; the ideas of people change and with them their mode of expression." —Pablo Picasso

One of the primary goals of education in the visual arts is to prepare students to make and support intelligent and sensitive decisions about works of art. In order to make those kinds of decisions students can employ two ways of examining and responding knowledgeably to visual art forms. One of these ways, art criticism, involves them in learning *from* works of art. Another approach is art history, which enables students to learn *about* works of art and the artists who created them.

The Art History Approach to Learning about Art and Artists

Art historians contend that no work of art can be fully understood unless it is viewed in relation to the circumstances in which it was created. Every artwork is created in a particular place at a particular time in history and to some degree is bound to reflect the prevailing conditions of that time and place. For example, an art history approach to the study of a painting by Rembrandt would include an examination of seventeenth century Holland—the time and place in which that particular artist lived and worked. Adhering to this approach would require that students focus attention on the social, religious, and economic conditions that existed in the republic at that time in history before focusing attention on the painter and his work. All these conditions would have impacted Rembrandt's choice of subject matter, medium, his way of handling materials, and the visual language he chose to use in expressing his ideas and feelings.

Art history, then, involves a study of the visual arts in relation to the times and places from which they sprang. This study will provide students with a richer, broader, and deeper understanding of the specific art objects selected for study and the world as it existed when those art objects were created. However, to determine the significance of the place of a particular work, such as a picture by Rembrandt, involves more than just an examination of the world conditions at the time that artist lived. It also requires a study of what went on in the world *before* and *after* Rembrandt painted his picture. A study of this kind will show students that Rembrandt, like all artists, took into account the works of other artists, selecting some ideas and techniques to use in his own painting while rejecting other ideas and techniques. This is a valuable lesson that students can apply to their own efforts to create art.

Consequently, a historical examination of a painting by Rembrandt would include the identification of any artists who may have influenced his style of painting. The most important of these artists was the Italian painter Caravaggio, whose paintings Rembrandt never saw, but without which his own work would not have taken on certain stylistic innovations. However, to understand Caravaggio, students would have to become acquainted with the artists *he* admired as well as the ones he rejected while arriving at his own revolutionary painting style. Thus, students adhering to an art history approach will find themselves involved in a fascinating learning process not unlike a game of dominoes, in which an entire row of game pieces is seen to collapse by upsetting the first domino in that row. The very last "domino" to fall in this comparison of art history to dominoes would be the very first visual image ever created—perhaps an image scratched on the rough wall of a cave by the very first prehistoric artist.

The Use of Historical Periods

For convenience, art historians divide the history of art into more or less artificial periods such as Medieval, Renaissance, Baroque, and Rococo. Doing so does no harm as long as students are reminded that the changes in art history identified by these labels, like changes of the seasons, are gradual. Each historical period passes into the next as smoothly as spring passes into summer.

If it can be assumed that an understanding of the present can be illuminated by a study of the past, then a chronological ordering of art history periods can be most helpful. By beginning at the beginning and observing the changes in art created from one year, decade, or century to the next, students will find it easier to understand how the art produced today has its roots in the art produced in the past. If students are to gain an understanding of art history, they should be afforded opportunities to see and learn about art examples from every corner of the world representing every historical period, not just those created by Western artists.

In every art history period students will encounter artists whose works preserve the traditional values of earlier artists, artists who chose to build upon current art trends, and still other artists who opted to explore revolutionary ways of expressing themselves through their art. Art history is filled with the stories of artists who accepted or rejected, endorsed or protested, conformed or reformed, contrasted or destroyed, dreamed of the past or conjured up visions of the future—but every one of those artists did so from the springboard of his or her own time and place, be that tenth-century China or twentieth-century America.

Art History as a Means of Understanding Each Other

Through art history students learn that a painting, a statue, or a temple is a consequence of how imaginative, sensitive members of any given society viewed and responded to the world around them. Art history also encourages students to regard works of art as more than objects that are pleasing to the eye, more than splendid and original products of human skill and inventiveness. Works of art also represent springboards for learning, revealing how differently people thought and acted at different times and in different geographical locations throughout the long history of humankind. A work of art reveals not only the customs, social habits, architecture, and technical achievements of its time and place; it also reflects the prevailing fears, beliefs, superstitions, desires, and values of people living in different ages at different geographic locations. Art history, then, is a vital part of the history of the human race.

Art History and Changing Tastes

As they study art history, students will discover that, over time, works of art do not always look the same to the people viewing them. This happens because people from different times and places look at art from different points of view. Cultures vary and change and so do tastes. Take any great artist or any great work of art from a bygone era and note how there have been periods in which that artist or work has been highly regarded, treated with indifference, or even ridiculed. For example, few today would venture a negative judgment of a painting created by Rembrandt, who is universally regarded as one of the greatest artists of all time. Yet, over the years, this Dutch master has not always been understood or appreciated. Indeed, when Italian artists first viewed a painting by Rembrandt they were puzzled and disappointed. They failed to understand why this artist was so highly regarded. His style, they concluded, was most peculiar because it made use of large areas of dark values and made no use of outlines favored by Italian artists.

Students must learn that art is a two-way process involving *both* artist and viewer. If students are to grasp more than the superficial appearance of a work of art, they must be prepared to learn its purpose, its *contemporary* meaning within the society in which it was produced, and its place in the historical process. No work of art is created in a vacuum. If students are to share in the ideas and feelings that contributed to the creation of a work of art, they must recognize the concepts, desires, and expectations of the person expressing those ideas and feelings at a particular point in time. This will result in a richer, broader, deeper understanding of both the artwork and the culture that witnessed its creation.

The Art History Operations

The study of art history is made easier for students if a plan of action is offered. One such plan makes use of four steps, or operations, that bear the same labels used to describe the four steps used in art criticism. These operations are description, analysis, interpretation, and decision. However, while these operations enable students to gain information from works of art during art criticism, they also are used to help students gather information about those works during art history. Briefly, the four art history operations are:

Description During this first operation, students seek to discover when, where, and by whom the work was created. In other words, they determine the period in which the work was created, the place where the artist lived, and, assuming it is known, the name of the artist.

Analysis This operation requires students to identify the unique features in a work of art that determine its artistic style. In the visual arts, style has come to mean the personal and unique way in which the artist uses the elements and principles of art to express ideas and feelings. For example, one artist may choose to delineate shapes in his painting by surrounding them with a heavy dark outline. Another painter might ignore the use of an outline and suggest shapes by creating areas of bright hues that contrast with the dull hues surrounding them.

> "Art historians contend that no work of art can be fully understood unless it is viewed in relation to the circumstances in which it was created."

Interpretation When interpreting a work of art, students take into account the impact of time and place upon the artist. It is during this operation that they learn that pictures of the same subject painted at the same time but in different geographic locations typically differ in appearance because they reflect different traditions and values. A landscape painted in fifteenth-century Italy will differ dramatically from a landscape painted at the same time in Japan. Moreover, a work of art created in the same country but at different times may also bear few stylistic similarities. A landscape painted by a French artist living and working in the late nineteenth century would have little in common with a landscape done by a French artist living and working at the beginning of the same century.

In an effort to express themselves in visual terms, artists make use of the materials and processes placed in their hands by the circumstances of time and place. Thus, a

nineteenth-century African artist might have carved a figure from a piece of wood to serve as a dwelling place for a departed spirit, while a seventeenth-century artist applied his brush to canvas to paint a lifelike portrait of his king. In the spotlight of history, the efforts of both artists are magnified or diminished, honored or dismissed by forces that neither could predict or control but that had little to do with the values the artists sought to express in their work. It is the desire to discover those values that motivates students when interpreting artists' works.

Decision The final art history operation requires that students make a decision about the historical importance of a work of art. They will discover that some works are more important than others because they were the first examples of a new, revolutionary style. Others are found to be significant because they are the most accomplished and successful examples of a particular style. As their knowledge and understanding of art grows, students will find themselves liking a great many more works of art than they thought possible at the start. Gradually they will gain confidence in their historical judgments and exercise skill in defending those judgments.

Art history is a fascinating, provocative learning experience affording students the opportunity to travel through time and space. It provides them with access to the inner lives of many kinds of people and offers clues to where we come from and who we are. Finally, art history reveals that artists and their art have succeeded in helping people communicate with each other in a manner we cannot express in any other way.

Art Criticism

Rosalind Ragans, Ph.D., Associate Professor Emerita, Georgia Southern University

Art criticism is organized discussion about art. The art criticism procedures used in this program were developed by Edmund B. Feldman based on his analysis of the writings of professional art critics. He organized the elaborate procedures followed by critics and summarized them into four steps. The purpose of these four steps is to delay impulse judgments of visual images and to involve the viewer in a complex interaction with the image that can result in a truly aesthetic experience.

Art criticism involves the use of high-level thinking skills. The viewer translates the visual language of the image created by an artist into everyday words. To have a truly aesthetic experience the viewer must go beyond simple identification and recognition to the types of thinking required to analyze, interpret, and judge visual clues.

Anyone can do art criticism. All that is needed are eyes to see the image and a brain to think about what is seen. Art criticism gives a viewer of any age the confidence to discuss a work of art without worrying about what other people have said about it. One does not need to know anything about the artist, the style, or the time when the work was made to get involved with the work. After the steps of art criticism have been followed in a school setting, students are usually so interested in the art that they want to know more about the who, what, where, when, and how of the work. In other words, the students are ready to learn about art history and culture.

Description

The first step of art criticism is a clue-collecting step. The purpose of this step is to get to know the work as intimately and deeply as one can. All the information from the credit line should be noted. It is important for the viewer to know whether the artwork is 20 × 30 inches or 20 × 30 feet. The medium with which the work is made is also important. Whether a piece of sculpture is modeled with clay or carved from stone affects the viewer's impression. Then the observer names everything that is seen in the image. During description the observer must remain objective. All the descriptive terms must be neutral, value-free words.

Analysis

This is an advanced form of description. It is also an objective, clue-collecting step. During this stage the viewer studies the elements of art and the principles that have been used to organize those elements. It is during this step that the viewer begins to discover how the artist has organized the formal qualities of the work to create the content or meaning. In this program you will see how the art criticism lesson at the end of each unit is used to reinforce the concepts taught during each unit. Works of art have been selected that will help the student comprehend the artist's use of the specific elements or principles that were introduced in that unit.

Interpretation

This is the most important part of art criticism. It is during this step that the viewer pulls together all the descriptive and analytical observations to make sense of the work. The viewer makes inferences about the mood, meaning, or message being conveyed by the work. This step goes beyond narration to a generalization about life. The viewer makes guesses, but these ideas must be supported by the clues collected during the first two steps. This can be the most difficult step because it requires imagination and courage. Every interpretation can be different because each is based on the feelings and life experiences of the viewer. No one individual has done or seen exactly the same things as the next person. The viewer may see ideas in a work of art that were never dreamed of by the artist. That is not wrong. It simply means that the work is so powerful that it carries special meanings for everyone.

A good interpretation goes beyond answering "What is happening?" to answering "What does it mean?"

Decision (Judgment)

This is the step where a professional critic will decide the quality of a work. Is this as good as the rest of the works by this artist? How does it measure up to the works of other artists in the same group? The students who are using this program do not have enough experience to make that level of decision, so the works of art in *Art Connections* have been selected because they have already been judged to be outstanding examples of art.

The students are asked to make personal decisions. There are two levels of judgment to be made. The first is "Do you like the work?" This opinion may be embarrassing for students to share in front of classmates, and it is best left unspoken. No one can ever tell someone else what they should like or dislike.

The second level of judgment is also subjective. We ask the student to decide why the work is successful, and we use aesthetic theories to help each individual make decisions about the work. The three aesthetic theories that we employ are the most common theories: imitationalism/realism, formalism/composition, and emotionalism/expressionism. More than one theory can be used to judge a work of art.

- Some critics think the most important thing about a work of art is the realistic presentations of the subject matter. People with this point of view think that an artwork should imitate life. This theory, called **imitationalism** or **realism,** focuses on realistic representation.
- Other critics think that composition is the most important factor in a work of art. This aesthetic theory, called **formalism** or **composition,** places emphasis on the design qualities, the arrangement of the elements of art using the principles of art.
- **Emotionalism** or **expressionism** is the theory concerned with the content or meaning of the work. This theory requires that a work of art convey a message. It must arouse a response of feelings, moods, or emotions in the viewer.

In this program we provide leading questions to help the teacher and student delve into a work of art by using the steps of art criticism. These are not all the questions that can be addressed in viewing a work, and teachers are encouraged to go beyond what is presented on the pages of these books.

Meeting National and State Standards for Art Education

Nan Yoshida

Art Connections has been carefully designed to help educators meet the standards of state and national art curriculum guidelines.

The *National Standards for Arts Education* are part of Goals 2000, the overarching plan for improving American education. Approved by the United States Congress in 1994, the standards describe what every young American student should know and be able to do in the arts.

In addition to the national standards, individual states have curriculum documents that set forth guidelines and requirements in subject areas. For example, both the *Texas Essential Knowledge and Skills for Art* and the *Visual and Performing Arts Framework for California Public Schools, Kindergarten through Grade Twelve* discuss four components of visual arts education common to most other state guidelines.

Placing the national standards side by side with the Texas and California standards, one can readily see that the documents match in their expectations of what students should know and be able to do in the visual arts.

Art Connections has been developed with these national and state expectations in mind. Every lesson in the program was designed to address the components of art education in Aesthetic Perception, Art History and Culture, Creative Expression, and Art Criticism.

Aesthetic Perception

(Artistic Perception)

Each lesson begins with Activate Prior Knowledge, which asks students to recall and visualize an image from personal experience that will help them take a purposeful look at the artwork.

Introduce the Art focuses students' attention on specific attributes of the artwork, design elements and principles, underlying structures, and functions. As students answer the questions about the work of art, they develop critical *observation* skills.

Aesthetic Perception directs students to extend their artistic perception to their environment and objects in the environment. The transition is made to use keen visual and tactile perception of formal art objects in everyday life (lifelong learning).

> "In **Art Connections** students are exposed to a variety of types and styles of art from many cultures and historical periods."

Art History and Culture

(Cultural Context)

In *Art Connections* students are exposed to a variety of types and styles of art from many cultures and historical periods. Students study art from Africa; Asia; Australia; Europe; and North, Central, and South America. They learn about the role of the artist in societies. They develop appreciation for paintings, drawings, prints, photographs, sculptures, textiles, and architecture. They relate to folk, decorative, functional, and formal arts.

While information about the works of art and the artist is necessarily brief in the *Student Edition,* teachers are encouraged to use the Art History and Culture feature of the *Teacher Edition* and the **Artist Profiles** books to provide students with enriching information about the artists, the periods of art history, and cultural perspectives.

Creative Expression

(Art Production)

Creative expression is fundamental to every art lesson. The Practice activity provides a structure for students to apply lesson concepts in meaningful practice. In the Creative Expression activity, students refine their new knowledge and skills by producing original artwork based on their personal visions. The lessons throughout the program introduce a variety of art media and techniques.

Art Criticism

(Aesthetic Valuing)

Reflection and self-assessment are inherent in the art-making process. Upon completion of the Creative Expression activity, students

evaluate their own work using the four steps of art criticism: Describe, Analyze, Interpret, and Decide. These four steps of art criticism are a method for making an informed critique of others' artwork as well.

Arts Integration

In addition to the high priority placed on teaching the visual arts as a unique discipline, both national and state standards recommend the appropriate integration or interrelation of the visual arts with the other arts disciplines of music, dance, and theatre. Toward this goal, every unit in *Art Connections* culminates with a lesson integrating one of these performing arts. In addition, connections are made to music and movement/dance in every lesson of the *Teacher Edition.*

Curriculum Integration

The *Teacher Edition* has an Art Across the Curriculum section that ties art concepts to other curriculum areas. Every lesson has a connection to Reading/Language Arts, Math, Science, Social Studies, and Technology.

National Standards for Arts Education © 1994

1. Understand and apply media, techniques, and processes.
2. Use knowledge of structures and functions.
3. Choose and evaluate a range of subject matter, symbols, and ideas.
4. Understand the visual arts in relation to history and cultures.
5. Reflect upon and assess the characteristics and merits of their work and the work of others.
6. Make connections between the visual arts and other disciplines.

The Development of Children's Art

Rosalind Ragans, Ph.D.

A child's ability to make and understand art develops along with his or her cognitive, social, emotional, and physical development. In 1947 Victor Lowenfeld was the first to identify and label the sequential stages that students move through as they create images. Since then many others have continued to study the development of children's visual images.

Understanding these stages will help you recognize what your students are doing; however, you must also understand that these stages describe untutored progression through the making of images. There are many outside influences on students, and these will show in their work. A well-meaning adult might teach a child to make stick figures, and because they are so easy to make, the child adopts this symbol.

Just as reading levels vary widely within one class, so do art abilities. Just as you teach students to appreciate differences in ability in other subject areas, you must help them understand that not everyone will have the same art abilities at the same time.

There are many different versions of the developmental stages; here we present a three-step version of art development. The stages of artistic development are useful norms that can help you, but they are **not** rules that must be followed.

The Manipulative Stage
Ages 2–5 (Grade K)

This has been called the scribble stage, and it is usually seen in children from two to five years old. During the early part of this stage, the child makes random, disordered scribbles. Making art at this stage is such a sensory experience that the child may hold crayons in both hands. Children who have opportunities to scribble produce a wide variety of lines, marks, dots, and shapes. The child who develops a variety of graphic marks during the scribble years will use them to produce complex symbolic drawings as he or she matures. Children who rarely scribble will have a more limited range of expression, and they will need a great deal of encouragement to continue drawing.

As the random scribbles become more controlled, the child starts to pull the marks into circular patterns until a mandala, or rough circle, is created. Rhoda Kellogg, who

studied thousands of children's drawings from all over the world, found that the mandala appears as the final stage between random scribbling and representation. This controlled scribble becomes a named scribble. Expressive concepts develop as children recognize the relationship between their marks and the visual outcome.

The Symbol-Making Stage
Ages 4–9 (Grades 1–4)

When a child makes the connection between images and an idea, a shape becomes a symbol. During this stage children develop a series of distinct images that stand for objects in their experiences. These symbols are eventually related to an environment within the drawing. The first representation of a person is a mandala. This can represent anyone the child wants it to be. Although this shape appears to be just a head, it represents the entire person. Soon the child adds a line and two marks, which represent a person with a mouth and two eyes. Then two lines are added to the shape to represent legs, two lines for arms, and a scribble for hair. The child is drawing what he or she knows, not what he or she sees. As children develop from the early symbolic stage into the symbol-making stage, they start to add more details and develop a symbol that includes all the body parts.

At first, space is not a consideration, and the size of symbols in a work is related to importance. Objects and people seem to float. Eventually the child wants to make people and objects stand up and will line things up on the bottom of the paper or on a baseline. Along with a baseline, the child starts to represent the sky with a strip of color across the top of the paper that includes a round symbol with radiating lines for the sun. As far as the child is concerned, the space between the sky and the baseline is air. The sky will not touch the earth until the child develops a more mature sense of perception, usually the result of sensitive art instruction.

Another spatial problem is overlap. Children realize that two objects cannot occupy the same space at the same time, and they avoid overlapping. As the environments they depict become more complex, children may use a bird's-eye view, a foldover view, or multiple views to represent space.

Children in this stage develop their own schema, or image, that resembles an actual object. Once a schema has been invented it will be used over and over. As the child continues to make art, the schema will become more detailed and sophisticated.

Giving a child this age coloring books may lead to self-doubt because of the conflict between the child's schema and the adult image. After coloring a seated dog in a coloring book, the child may become frustrated when his or her own drawing of a dog does not measure up to his or her memory of the adult image. Because children are exposed to so many adult images, many of which have low artistic quality, it is helpful for the teacher to expose children to the many high-quality works of art available in this program.

The Preadolescent Stage
Ages 8–13 (Grades 3–8)

Preadolescent children are still naturally inquisitive and creative, but they have learned to be more cautious. They have become very sensitive to peer opinion. They have reached a "crisis of confidence" regarding the images they make. If a work doesn't look exactly the way they think it should, or if it looks childlike, they reject the art product. This is the time when many children become frustrated and stop making art.

This is a critical time in students' visual development. They need to be taught to work slowly and with patience. They need to be taught drawing skills such as perspective and human proportions. They need to master the language of art and the use of design principles. They need the technical skills to master the various media such as painting, printmaking, ceramics, and sculpture.

Students need to see how different artists in the past have solved problems, and to observe what contemporary artists are doing today. Artists solve problems differently, and young people need to be exposed to many different ideas as they try to create their own solutions to visual problems.

The strong art teacher will lead students over this perilous bridge of doubt by gently stretching their minds to help them see more so that they can do more. At every stage in the child's visual development, a strong, understanding teacher can help the child move forward.

Brain-Based Learning

Jamye Ivey, K–12 Art Supervisor, Dougherty County School System, Georgia

At the end of the school day, teachers often face many unanswered questions concerning the young people whose education is their responsibility. Educators cannot help but wonder why students fail to respond to instructional strategies that were successful in their own experiences. Why is today's student so different?

Brain Research

Neuroscientists are now able to supply some of the answers that have plagued educators for years. The amazing, constantly changing world of technology has unlocked for researchers a new realm of understanding of the human brain. With the aid of advanced medical techniques and strategies using equipment such as MRI, FMRI, CAT, and PET scans, the working brain can be observed. Translating these new and often startling medical findings into the educational arena has provided the classroom teacher with practical methodologies and a better understanding of how, why, and when students learn best.

The brain is the most powerful organ in the body. Researchers have discovered that today's brains grow better in the real world than in artificial learning environments. Students must be able to connect their learning to previous experience in order for new learning to occur. For years teachers have designed and taught units with the activities culminating in field trips. When we consider these recent findings, we realize this procedure should be reversed. The field trip provides the student relevance that would facilitate learning. Without a related experience in the memory bank of past experiences, the learner finds no significance in the new material.

It is also important to note that synapses in the brain are formed, strengthened, and maintained by interaction with experience. The stronger the synapses, the faster the messaging travels and the greater the number of neural pathways that are created in the brain. This enables a person to be capable of creating more flexible thought processing and better memory.

Research confirms that environments shape brains. Teachers should create an environment that provides the best opportunities for this generation of young people to learn. Students of today need to move, talk, and touch more than previous learners did. Eric Jensen explains that the part of the brain that processes movement is the same part that processes learning. Thus, there needs to be movement in the classroom.

Today, we know that lecturing is the poorest way to present new learning. Only about fifty percent of the audience is actively listening in any given oral presentation. Students learn the most at the beginning of a presentation, the second-most at the end, and the least in the middle. Learners need breaks during teacher talk sessions. The attention span of a preadolescent is ten to twelve minutes.

This generation of children has more trouble organizing thoughts and learns on a more global scale. Expect students to want to understand the big picture before dealing with the details. One way to accomplish this is to let the class spend a few minutes looking through the whole chapter before focusing on the first page.

We know now that students cannot learn if they feel threatened or stressed. If a teacher shouts at a student, it takes fifteen minutes for the adrenaline levels to subside in all the students in the class. The glucose needed for cognitive functioning is redirected to combat stress, so all learning is governed to some extent by emotions. The constant threat of failure needs to be removed and recognition should be placed on individual performance, experience, and interest. Pressure, tension, and stress slow down or eliminate learning.

Brain-Based Learning and the Arts

Art teachers are known for using creative methods to capture the imaginations of their students. Need, novelty, meaning, and emotion are four ways to gain a student's attention, and using humor during instruction increases attention by fifty percent. A happy classroom is a more brain-compatible classroom.

The arts are an important part of effective teaching and an essential component of brain-compatible instruction. There is evidence that art-making has been around for over one million years. Brain research documents the arts as basic to the brain. Every culture in human history has one common thread: all had the arts. Stable art, music, and dance experiences not only enhance the aesthetic life of the learner, but they also provide important activity for the growing neurological system.

For both teacher and student, the most encouraging summation from recent research is that we continue to grow brain cells regardless of our age. Noted neuroscientist

Marion Diamond explains that it is best to keep the brain curious and active. In her opinion the most significant finding of her career has been that the brain can learn at any age. Be a lifelong learner and engage in physical activitities, which also helps build brain cells. Stay curious and stay active. How affirming this is for art educators because the successful teaching of art daily demands both creative curiosity and physical endurance.

References

Sousa, David A. (2002). *How the Brain Learns, Second Edition.* Corwin Press.

Sylwester, Robert (1995). *A Celebration of Neurons, an Educator's Guide to the Brain.* Alexandria, VA: Association for Supervision and Curriculum Development.

Eric Jensen (2001). *Arts With the Brain in Mind.* Alexandria, VA: Association for Supervision and Curriculum Development.

Sprenger, Marilee (1999). *Learning & Memory-The Brain in Action.* Alexandria, VA: Association for Supervision and Curriculum Development.

Armstrong, Thomas (1987). *In Their Own Way.* G.P. Putnam's Sons.

Armstrong, Thomas (1991). *Awakening Your Child's Natural Genius.* G.P. Putnam's Sons.

Classroom Management and Motivation Strategies for Teaching Elementary Art

Bunyan Morris, Art Teacher, Effingham County School System, Georgia

While motivating students to express themselves visually through creative means, the elementary art teacher is challenged with the task of maintaining proper classroom management. The purpose of this article is to provide some practical methods of motivating creative thought and action under the guidance of successful classroom management. Combine these methods with your own to give students the best learning experience possible.

Be Prepared. Begin the lesson excited and ready. Students will pick up on your mood the moment they walk into the room. If you set the tone at the beginning and grasp immediate control, it will be much easier to keep it throughout the lesson. It is important to have art prints and demonstration materials ready and in place for the initial focus. Practice an activity before demonstrating it if it is the first time that it has been taught. Something might happen that could not be foreseen; prepare for the best and the worst. Also, it might be a good idea to practice a concept or an activity that has not been taught in a long time. Even classroom veterans forget things.

Focus. For the initial focus of the lesson, gather the students into a group on the floor, in chairs, or on benches in an area of the room that is ready for discussion and demonstration. By gathering the students into a compact group, it is easier to make eye contact and to keep the attention of all learners. If there is no room for a separate demonstration and discussion spot, gather the tables or desks into a closer group so that no one is "out of reach."

Introduce the Art. Always introduce a lesson with a work of art that relates to what the students will be learning. Students get excited playing detective. Finding clues and ideas in a painting or sculpture allows them to make their own interpretations and assessments about art. They will in turn learn to apply this to their own work. The students don't have to know that this activity has a lofty term called *art criticism* to gain from its purpose. Encouraging them to ask questions and share ideas about a master work will give the students motivation and fresh ideas to take into the Creative Expression portion of the lesson.

Moving to Art Production. Always control the manner in which students move to the Creative Expression area from the Demonstration/Discussion center. Release students in a manner that will keep order but not quell their enthusiasm about the lesson. Use positive reinforcement by complimenting those who are sitting quietly, and send them first. It will not take long for the others to catch on. After time most of the students will become conditioned to this expectation. Even if they've been involved in a lively discussion, they will automatically become settled as this transitional period approaches.

Classroom Design. Not only should the students be orderly, but the classroom must also be organized and conducive to the movement of the teacher and students. The Creative Expression stations should have enough space between them for the teacher to reach every student. There should be enough space in traffic areas for student movement. Children need easy access to supply shelves and sinks, and should be able to move from one Creative Expression station to another unencumbered. The supplies should be organized on leveled shelves so that the students will return them to their proper places. If the teacher keeps the room and supplies organized, hopefully the students will too.

As well as keeping the room and supplies organized, the rest of the room should be visually pleasing. Display student art with master prints. This builds self-esteem. When possible, display every child's work. Make learning centers organized and interesting. Keep interesting objects around the room for visual reference. These objects might include plants, pottery, old bottles, discarded sports equipment, old toys, or anything that might capture the attention and interest of your students. Use these objects in still lifes and as objects of visual reference for lines, shapes, and other elements and principles of art.

When moving about the room assisting students, it is important to keep the senses alive and be aware of what is happening with the other students. See and hear what they think you can't.

Closing the Lesson. Normally one should try to close the class with a review of the lesson's objectives. This should be short and interesting. This is also the time to reward the students for good behavior. The art teacher must set the criteria for earning the award. Do not give the award if it is not earned. Of course, the students must be aware of the opportunity to earn an award ahead of time.

One method that works is to award the students with a "Super Behavior Card." This is simply a colorful card that can be given to the class to take back to their classroom teacher for having good behavior during art. This requires the cooperation of the classroom teacher to award the students in some manner for collecting a certain number of Super Behavior Cards. Awards might include a popcorn party or extra time at recess. If the classroom teacher is unwilling, you will have to provide the award in your class. Awarding of the Super Behavior Card can be coordinated with cleanup at the end of the period. Choose one student at the table who cleans up most thoroughly and quietly to carry the Super Behavior Card back to the classroom teacher. The students at each table will work together to earn the Super Behavior Card.

Hopefully these ideas and suggestions will reduce the challenge of maintaining classroom control and motivating students. The individual teacher must decide what works best for each situation. All of the motivation and management techniques suggested here have been tried and have been proven to work. Combined with each teacher's individual strategies, they will increase the probability of success in the art classroom.

A Sampling of Art Games for Home or School

Art Lotto: National Gallery of Art. Safari Limited, Miami, Florida.

ARTDECK. Aristoplay, Ann Arbor, Michigan.

The Fine Art Game. Piatnik, Wiener Spielkartenfabrik, Ferd. PIATNIK & Söhne.

Where Art Thou? WJ Fantasy, Inc., Bridgeport, Connecticut.

Art Instruction for Students with Disabilities

Mandy Yeager, Art Educator, Ph.D. Student, The University of North Texas, Denton, Texas

Art education empowers all students to look at, respond to, create, and enjoy works of art. Students who are disabled are no exception to this privilege. The arts have often been understood as an equalizing force in the education of students with disabilities; often these students experience discrimination from peers and adults because of their disability. This discrimination often manifests itself in avoidance of or lowered expectations for these students. Stereotypes of persons with disabilities cast them as helpless, unintelligent, dangerous, or contemptible. These stereotypes are maintained by a lack of knowledge or personal experiences with persons who are disabled.

The visual arts, because they use images to express ideas about the human experience, play a vital role in challenging and eliminating many of these stereotypes. The current emphasis of art education upon visual literacy allows students to examine and transform stereotypes that exist in the media regarding all types of differences (including age, race, class, gender, and ability). Artists throughout time have engaged in this process of recording and seeking to transform societal injustices through visual imagery.

The benefits of art for students with disabilities cannot be underestimated. The skills gained in visual arts often result in increased confidence and ability in other academic subjects. Arts-based learning is often effective because of the ways it engages the multiple senses and abilities of students.

The arts also give students opportunities to explore, express, and celebrate their identities. Teachers who include the work of artists with disabilities in their art curriculum help all students realize that disability is a part of the human experience and does not prevent anyone from being a creator of art.

Resources to Assist Art Educators

The first step to developing competence is to develop an understanding of the child's disability. There are a number of resources to assist the art teacher in this regard.

Resources at the School Level

Resources at the school level include special-education staff and related service providers who have contact with the child such as occupational and physical therapists. All of these staff members can provide the art teacher with insight into the child's learning strengths and needs and his or her physical and emotional development. They can also provide helpful suggestions for how a particular art medium or tool can be made accessible to a particular student.

Another valuable resource for the art teacher is the student's Individualized Education Plan (IEP). This plan exists for every student receiving special education services and provides information about learning styles, needs, and modifications. The *Individuals with Disabilities Education Act* (IDEA) requires that all regular education teachers of students with disabilities have access to the child's IEP and are provided support in implementing modifications to the general curriculum.

Art educators can design their art curricula to meet students' annual IEP goals. For instance, art criticism activities have the potential to enhance students' expressive language skills. Cooperative learning activities such as mural painting can foster social skills. Art production often produces self-efficacy in students with disabilities as they learn to trust their ability to achieve success. Art teachers who engage in this process of reviewing a child's IEP and delineating the ways that art curricula can address annual goals become more confident in their abilities to successfully instruct students with disabilities.

Art Education and Disability Organizations

VSA arts has been designated by the U.S. Congress as the National Coordinating Agency of Arts in Learning for Persons with Disabilities. The agency fulfills this role through a vast network of state affiliates. VSA arts produces art and disability awareness curricula and showcases the work of students with disabilities by regularly sponsoring national calls for art. It also provides access to the work of artists with disabilities.

The Special Needs Interest Group of the National Art Education Association (NAEA) meets annually at the NAEA convention to discuss best practices in art education and disability. This group publishes a column in the bimonthly publication *NAEA News*.

Adapting the Art Experience for Students with Disabilities

It is often necessary to adapt some aspect of the art experience for students with disabilities. Adaptations ensure that learning is accessible to every child; as such, adaptation is a principle of good instruction.

Adapting the art experience is essentially a creative activity, as many different combinations of students, media, and processes coalesce in one semester of art instruction. Accordingly, effective adaptations are individualized and begin with knowledge of a particular student's learning strengths and needs. Teachers may choose to adapt art media, instructional strategies, and/or physical space, depending upon the situation. This process of adaptation often begins by observation of students in an introductory art-making experience. If a student is having difficulty with an art task, try to determine the source of the difficulty. Consult with other school staff and use some of the resources listed below to determine what is most appropriate for the student and situation.

The adaptations accompanying every lesson in this text are provided as suggestions only, because learning needs and strengths vary with each child, medium, and project. It is hoped that art educators, upon reading this article, will feel equipped to utilize available resources to design and implement empowering learning experiences for all students.

Resources

Disability Education Organizations

National Dissemination Center for Children with Disabilities (NICHCY), www.nichy.org/index.html

The Council for Exceptional Children, www.cec.sped.org/

ERIC Clearinghouse on Disability and Gifted Education, http://ericec.org

Art and Disability Organizations and Resources

VSA arts, www.vsarts.org

Art, Disability and Expression Online Exhibit, www.vsarts.org/showcase/exhibits/disability/index.html

The National Art Education Association Special Needs Interest Group

EDGE: Education for Disability and Gender Equity, www.disabilityhistory.org/dwa/edge/curriculum/index-netscape.htm

National Arts and Disability Center (NADC), http://nadc.ucla.edu/

Safe Use of Art Materials

**Mary Ann Boykin, Director, The Art School for Children and Young Adults
University of Houston—Clear Lake, Texas**

Elementary art teachers need to be aware of safety issues that can affect the well-being of the children they teach, as well as themselves. Follow the guidelines established by the Center for Safety in the Arts to assure that neither students nor teachers are injured by the unsafe use of art materials.

Elementary teachers should do two things to prevent problems. The first is to keep all toxic and hazardous substances out of the classroom. The second is to know how to use the materials safely, because any materials can become hazardous when used inappropriately.

Toxic Substances

A toxic substance is defined by the Center for Occupational Hazards as "a poison which can damage your body's organ systems when you are overexposed to it." This harm can be immediate or can be the result of repeated exposure over time. Toxic substances can enter the body in three ways:

1. absorption through the skin
2. inhalation through the nose or mouth
3. ingestion through eating or drinking in the area where toxic materials are being used

It is up to the teacher to make sure toxic substances do not enter the classroom and that all materials are used safely to avoid problems.

Pregnant women and those who are nursing must be especially careful to prevent exposure to toxic substances. Fumes, sprays, dusts, and powders present a real hazard to the fetus, can be transferred to the infant through the mother's milk, and can be carried home to the infant or young child through dusts and residue picked up by clothing and hair. The safe path is to completely avoid exposure to any toxin by carefully reading labels and applying common sense to the situation. For example, if you plan to mix powdered tempera paint or work with chalks or clay, the safe method would include use of a respirator mask, which would prevent inhalation of these substances.

Children and Safe Art Materials

Preschool and elementary children are particularly vulnerable to unsafe art materials for a variety of reasons. Their lower body weight allows a toxic substance to become more concentrated in their bodies. Because children have a more rapid metabolism than adults, toxic substances are more quickly absorbed into their bodies. Children also tend to have more hand-to-mouth contact than adults, which allows ingestion of toxic materials. Furthermore, children are easily distracted from safety warnings regarding materials as they become involved in the art process. The tendency of children to have cuts and scratches also allows for ready entry of toxins into their bodies.

What the Labels Mean

Since 1990 our government has required the labeling of all hazardous materials. Any product labeled as hazardous is totally inappropriate for the elementary school. Safe art materials carry the statement that the material "Conforms to ASTMD-4236." A simple "nontoxic" statement on a product is not adequate.

The Arts and Crafts Materials institute developed a voluntary program to provide a safe standard for materials used by children. Products bearing the labels AP (Approved Product) or CP (Certified Product) have been tested by toxicologists in major universities and have been deemed safe for children to use. The HL (Health Label) on art products indicates that these products are appropriate to use with children 12 years old or older under the supervision of an art teacher. Products with HL labels are not safe for elementary children.

Safe Art Materials

The following are guidelines for choosing and using basic art materials in a safe manner.

Drawing Materials

- Use only water-soluble AP- or CP-designated markers. Permanent markers are extremely dangerous and can cause lung and liver damage if inhaled. Never use permanent markers in the elementary classroom.
- Do not use scented markers. This teaches children to sniff or smell materials.
- Use only dustless chalk. The amount of dust created in a classroom by twenty children wiping and blowing chalk can be irritating to those who suffer from allergies, asthma, and other respiratory problems.
- Use oil pastels; the colors are richer than crayons and the satisfaction is greater! Crayons should also bear the AP or CP label to ensure that no lead is present in these materials.

Painting Materials

- Use only liquid tempera and/or watercolor paints. If you must use powdered tempera paints, mix these outside and have the paints ready before children enter the classroom. Avoid inhaling the powders of tempera paints.
- Do not use any spray paints or fixatives. These are extremely dangerous.

Printmaking Materials

- Use only water-soluble printers' inks. Do not use any solvent-based inks.
- Use pencils to carve into unused foam trays for printing blocks. Do not use mat knives or other sharp instruments.

Collage Materials

- Sharp scissors should not be used by young children; blunt points are safe. Fourth- and fifth-graders may use rounded points with teacher supervision.
- Use only school paste or white glue for adhering papers. Do not use rubber cement unless it bears the AP or CP label. Do not use any solvent-based glues.

Sculpture and Three-Dimensional Materials

- Use premixed, moist clay for sculpture and pottery. Do not allow students to take home any unfired clay.
- Remind students to wash their hands thoroughly after using clay. The residual dust can be harmful and irritating if inhaled.
- Paint clay pieces with tempera or watercolor paints. Do not use glazes. Some have the approved labels, but they are not recommended for elementary use.
- Use pencils, craft sticks, or other blunt tools to carve clay. Soapstone should not be used for carving in a closed environment.
- Read labels carefully on pastes used for papier-mâché, because some pastes contain pesticides or preservatives that are extremely harmful.

Stitchery, Weaving, and Fiber Materials

- Use blunt plastic needles and loosely woven fabrics such as burlap for stitchery. Blunt metal tapestry needles are safe if their use is supervised.
- Young children will have trouble cutting fabric and yarn with their scissors. Precut lengths of fabric and yarn prior to introducing a task.

The Community as a Resource for Art Materials

Willis "Bing" Davis, Associate Professor Emeritus, Central State University, Ohio
President and Founder of SHANGO: The Center for the Study of African American Art & Culture

Ingenuity, resourcefulness, and creative survival have always been important to most successful art and classroom teachers when it comes to providing meaningful arts experiences for students. We are known as collectors who almost never throw anything away. Some art and classroom teachers will need to acquire the skill of always being on the lookout for resources, materials, and supplies that can supplement art materials in the classroom. It can be fun; plus, it stimulates the imagination and creative impulse. This is also a great way to build bridges and advocates for arts education.

Think of all the things you use in the art room. How many can be found locally? Safe, usable materials or supplies that can be found free or reduced in price leave more of the art budget to buy the things that have to be purchased. There are different forms of searching for inexpensive and free materials for art activities. The following are a few tried and proven ways to acquire materials, supplies, and resources that can be used for art and other educational activities.

Materials in the School Building

- Leftover wood or metal from a shop class
- Clean, empty food containers from the food-service area
- Cardboard tubes from the food-service area or copy machine
- Scrap paper from copy machines

Annual Open-House Night Resources

Open house is a great time to post a small list of hand tools needed for the art program. You would be surprised by how many extra hammers, pliers, screwdrivers, bent forks, and so on are in garages and basements. Many parents or caregivers also work at places that have by-products that could supplement the art materials in the art program.

Local Business Material Sources

- *Wood* Lumberyards are usually willing to let teachers collect boxes of scrap wood for art production. Some lumberyards will even let you leave a box with your school's name on it.
- *Wallpaper* Ask for discontinued wallpaper design sample books from paint stores.
- *Paper* Large quantities of damaged paper may be available from local paper or paper distribution companies.

> "Many local service organizations have an interest and commitment to youth and the arts."

Community Resources

- Many communities participate in the popular "Take a Child to Work" programs that allow children to see and experience where their parents or caregivers work. Almost every school also has a career day when many professional individuals visit schools to talk to students about potential careers. Both programs put schools, students, and teachers into direct contact with local businesses.
- Teachers may find that companies with national headquarters in their communities often have a strong commitment to those communities and their educational systems. Teachers can assist these companies in reaching their community commitment goals by suggesting ways to assist the school art program. Local businesses may want to sponsor the visit of a local artist or donate materials.
- Many local service organizations have an interest and commitment to youth and the arts. They often look for art and cultural events and activities to which they can

contribute. Find out how they want to contribute and help them reach their goal. These events could be funding an exhibit, hosting an art reception, donating materials and supplies, framing student artwork for display in the hallways, sponsoring a local or major art field trip, and so on.

Artist Resources

- Local and regional emerging artists live in every community and can make meaningful contributions to the school art program. Artists from the community or region offer a "realness" to the program from knowing and living in the area.
- Some artists do a good job at demonstrating, some do a good slide lecture, some are more effective in large or small groups, some do great critique sessions, and some may be better mentoring one-on-one. Each individual teacher or school district can develop an annotated artist directory listing the artists' strong points for reference.
- Most communities also have one or more local arts groups or arts organizations that can assist schools in identifying and securing the services of local artists. A local arts group may be willing to do a series of Member Art Demos over the course of the year in your school.
- Another great source of local and regional artists can be found in the colleges and universities in your area. The college or university art program can show your students some of the quality art teachers students might be working with in the future. This is a great source of judges for student competitions.

Art Agencies at Local and State Levels

While everyone is aware of the existence of the National Endowment for the Arts in Washington, D.C., many may not be aware that there are state arts agencies and many community-based arts councils that can be an important resource for your art program. Find ways to let everyone in the community help your art program to be the best it can be.

Displaying Students' Art

Jackie Ellett

"My picture is hanging in the hall!" exclaims an excited second-grader. Yes, having one's work displayed is exciting. When you display a child's artwork, you are communicating two things to that child: you value what he or she has created *and* you value the child.

Why Display Students' Art?

Students are intrigued by the work their peers produce and are eager to join in any discussion that arises from the shared experiences of the work. They often compare what they have created to the work made by their peers. A natural aesthetic experience occurs, and questions and comparisons arise. These are either verbalized or internalized, depending on the circumstance of the viewing. "Why did Erin paint that flower large and the others small?" "I like the details of the seeds that Galvin added to his painting; I'll do more details next time." These are examples of questions, comments, or thoughts that may arise when students are viewing a display. Not only do displays allow students to appreciate their completed projects, but they also allow students to aspire to better art endeavors.

A class display allows students the opportunity to stand back and critique their work. A teacher-led critique is best. Students are able to evaluate their work, gain insight into things they may not have thought about, and may learn a new solution to a problem they have encountered. Discussing their works as you would a fine-art print validates the importance of what they have created. Art is so personal that a discussion can become quite insightful.

Preschool and early elementary-aged students are eager to take their works of art home to show their parents what they have created. You should ask permission of all students to display their work. By asking permission you are showing respect for their work, and for those students as individuals.

Displays are also a good way to show administrators, parents, and the community what students are learning.

Where to Display Students' Art

Many art educators believe that the farther away from the classroom the display, the more selective the images need to be. In the classroom, every student's art may be displayed.

This area can be controlled by the teacher, students, or both. Students can be allowed to change their own work when they decide to.

Outside of the classroom there is usually an assigned area for each class to display its work. Bulletin boards made of composition board are the most desirable of all surfaces for two-dimensional art. Artwork is easily attached using staples, and the walls are protected from any damage.

Setting up a school gallery of permanent or rotating student art is wonderful for promoting the art program within a school. This should be housed in a high-traffic area where parents, administrators, and visitors can view students' art. In "Leadership and the Elementary Art Specialist: Twenty Ways to Improve Your Program's Position in the Educational System," Phillip Dunn recommends establishing a "Principal's Permanent Art Collection." Having a gallery within the school with professionally matted and framed student art communicates that students' works and the art program are valued. In an era where budget cuts are customary, promoting the work of students is very important to the survival of art programs.

Displays in local businesses, civic centers, or art centers help educate the public about the work being done within their schools. These exhibits contain a mix of student art that has gone through a selection process. Depending on the guidelines and formality of the display, the works can be mounted, matted, or framed, with three-dimensional works displayed in sculpture cases or on sculpture stands.

How to Display Students' Art

Student art can be displayed in a variety of ways. Some teachers take digital photos of their students in the process of creating a work of art and critiquing their work, and then take a photo of the finished art itself. These images can be posted on a school Web site with descriptions of the activity. Digital images are sometimes used as screen savers on the school's computer system and highlighted on closed-circuit TVs in the classrooms. The most common method of display, however, is the bulletin board. These have evolved from simple displays to elaborate descriptions of the process and documentation of student learning. Teacher-focused bulletin boards have given way to student-focused displays that often include student reflections

and interpretations. Including descriptions of the process and background information adds to better understanding of the learning that has taken place.

Two-dimensional works of art should be mounted on larger contrasting or neutral-toned paper. The top and sides are usually of equal width with the bottom larger, unless the work is square, in which case all four sides are equal in width. When matting art, a two- to three-inch mat is standard, with the bottom being an inch wider than the top and sides. The mat acts as a resting place, so when arranging mounted or matted art, the works should not overlap.

A sheet of butcher paper or bulletin-board paper can be attached to a wall to define a display area and unify the works of art. Poster board or construction paper cut wider on all sides than the largest paper used by a class can be attached to the wall as an area for mounting individual students' work. Glue a clothespin to the top of the mounted paper so students can easily change their artwork. The background papers are usually in neutral colors, although primary colors may be used in classrooms for younger children. Each background paper is individually identified by placing the child's name in large print on a label.

Three-dimensional works look best in sculpture cases or on sculpture stands. Not every school can afford these. Arranging sturdy boxes of varying heights and covering them with complementary cloths allow sculptures to be equally viewed. If sculptures are of varying sizes, the largest should always be placed toward the back and the small works in front. Arranging works in odd numbers creates interest as well.

Mobiles and kites are best displayed from the ceiling. Make certain that all materials are well attached and that the items hung from the ceiling are secure so they do not fall or set off sensor alarms. As with all displays, it is important to know your school's policies about the types of adhesives allowed. Hot glue has a tendency to peel paint, low-temperature glue guns may not work on some surfaces, and double-sided tape can leave a residue. Humidity and the wall's surface both affect what will and will not work. Reusable tacky putty sticks to most surfaces and leaves few marks.

Displays do much to enhance and rejuvenate students' spirits and allow students to communicate in a way that is neither mathematical nor verbal. The art that students make is very personal and deserves careful attention when being displayed.

Art Assessments

Assessment in art can be problematic for a variety of reasons. Many educators are reluctant to evaluate a student's creative expression as good or bad. Because there are often no right or wrong answers, students and their parents could challenge a teacher's subjective opinion of a work if it is reflected in a letter grade. Furthermore, many teachers without a strong art background do not feel qualified to grade student artwork. In addition, teachers do not want to discourage creative expression by giving a low grade or an undeserved grade. Many people also often feel that talented students have the advantage in art class and that students should not be evaluated on how talented they are, but rather on how much effort they put into their work and how much progress they make.

All of these assessment difficulties stem from the focus on art production in the art classroom, rather than a reflection of art history and culture, aesthetics, or art criticism. A broader focus in the art classroom and a variety of assessment options may help in more effective art assessment.

Assessment of Lesson Objectives

Instead of subjective opinions of whether or not one likes a student's artwork, students can be evaluated on whether or not they meet the art lesson objectives or demonstrate the knowledge and skills introduced in the lesson. In a quality art program, there are objectives for aesthetic perception, art history, and art criticism, as well as for demonstrating understanding of the elements and principles of art in art production.

In *Art Connections,* every lesson has four clear, measurable objectives. At the end of each lesson, a rubric provides evaluation criteria for each objective.

Art Production: Evaluating Student Artwork

Art teachers frequently evaluate student artwork on the basis of how well it reflects the elements and principles of art that are being stressed in the lesson and how well the student meets the criteria for the artwork. Some teachers can construct rubrics or standards for the artwork beforehand and tell students how their work will be evaluated at the time it is assigned. Other teachers use written or mental checklists of their standards as they look at student artwork. Teachers may use this form of evaluation as an opportunity to discuss the work with a student and find out whether the student thought he or she met the objectives for the artwork.

In *Art Connections,* teachers can also use the Assessment Masters in the *Assessment* book to get an idea of whether a student understands the elements or principle of art for a lesson.

Art Criticism and Aesthetic Perception: Self- and Peer-Assessment

The four-step process of art criticism (Describe, Analyze, Interpret, Decide) provides a procedure that students can use to objectively study their own art products, as well as the works of others. The sequential steps of art criticism are similar to those used in the scientific method. During the first two steps, Describe and Analyze, students are asked to collect data objectively. During the third step, Interpret, students speculate about the meaning of the work based on the data collected: they make a hypothesis about the idea, emotion, or mood expressed by the artist. During the fourth step, Decide, students offer their aesthetic judgment about the work of art. The sequential procedures in art criticism force students to postpone judgment while becoming immersed in the image. It forces them to have a fully funded visual experience before drawing conclusions about a work.

Art Connections includes art criticism questions for every Creative Expression activity. Additionally, the Aesthetic Perception feature in every lesson of the *Student Edition* provides students with an opportunity to evaluate their developing aesthetic perception.

Art History and Culture

Art is a visual record of history and diverse cultures. The goals for elementary art education are that students understand and appreciate different historical periods, cultures, and artistic styles and develop respect for the traditions and contributions of diverse societies.

In *Art Connections* every lesson introduces a work of art from a particular culture, time, and style. In the Introduce the Art strategies, teachers are encouraged to compare, contrast, and share the Art History and Culture information as well as the information provided in *Artist Profiles* to help students develop an understanding of the visual arts in relation to history and cultures. Through discussion and elements in students' own artwork, teachers can evaluate students' awareness in this area.

Portfolio Assessment

Art educators could claim to have inspired the growing use of portfolio assessment in other subject areas. Many art teachers collect the best examples of a student's work and look at the progress over time. They display it and discuss it with students and parents. Student art journals with ideas, drawings, and sketches also provide an opportunity for portfolio assessment.

In *Art Connections* students are encouraged to keep their best work in a Student Portfolio and to maintain an Art Journal. Reminders of these types of portfolio assessments appear in the *Teacher Edition.*

Performance Assessment

Unlike other subject areas, art education has a long tradition of performance assessment. In art class students make things to demonstrate what they can do. In quality art programs, teachers use performance descriptions not only for art production, but also for art criticism, art history and culture, and aesthetic perception to aid them in evaluating student demonstrations of their knowledge and skills in art.

In *Art Connections,* every work of art a student produces can be considered for performance assessment of the lesson concept. Performance assessments can also involve discussions about the works of art to introduce the lesson concept and art criticism questions.

Art not only enables teachers to evaluate student knowledge and skills in art each year, but it also provides a wonderful opportunity to assess students' growth and development over time. Students and parents are often reluctant to discard artwork and fondly review it from time to time to see how children's ideas and skills have changed. Schools often keep examples of student artwork in student portfolios from year to year.

A thoughtful and fair art assessment program enables teachers to really see how much their students are capable of accomplishing.

Art and Cross-Curricular Connections

Tina Farrell

The study and production of artwork enhances learning in all areas of the curriculum. When teachers and students connect art to other subjects, learning occurs in the natural and interrelated way that it exists in the real world. We know from experience that learning is most meaningful when it is interconnected, not isolated. Therefore, making the natural connections that exist within each discipline of study, art including, enhances total understanding and brings meaning to fragmented information.

Below are a few of the ways that art education can impact the study of other subjects.

Reading/Language Arts In the viewing and analysis of a work of art, students develop oral and written communication skills. Teachers can enhance the language process by writing art terms and concepts on the board, having students generate lists of adjectives and adverbs to describe works of art, encouraging reflective inquiry into art, having students read about art and artists, and having students use works of art as stimuli for all forms of writing.

Mathematics Mathematics concepts are enhanced through art. When math concepts are presented or expressed in a visual or manipulative manner, students can more easily grasp them. The comparison and development of shapes and forms, visual-spatial relationships, measurement, proportion, estimation, and grids and graphs, for example, all are best explained through art.

> "We know from experience that learning is most meaningful when it is interconnected–not isolated."

Science In the art-making process, children learn that multiple ways to solve problems exist. They learn to discover, imagine, try new materials and techniques, experiment, develop and test hypotheses, and observe and record visual data. These are many of the skills, objectives, and habits of mind taught in science.

Social Studies The history of the world is reflected in the functional and aesthetic works of art produced by the peoples of the world. Children can gain great insights about near and distant cultures through the study of art, artifacts, and architecture.

The Arts The arts all complement each other in the skills, elements, principles, and beliefs that are emphasized in each one. Each discipline presents a unique way to express ideas and transform emotions into song, dance, interactions, words, or images. Visual artists research, develop rough drafts (sketches), plan, develop ideas, produce completed visual ideas, and sign and title their works. These are the processes that authors, writers, dancers, composers, actors, and poets also employ.

Life Skills In art, children develop craftsmanship, self-discipline, dedication to a task, skills for working both individually and cooperatively, and pride in one's work. These skills are necessary for success in all areas of their lives.

Critical-Thinking Skills Studying the visual arts develops higher-level thinking skills as studenst analyze, compare, interpret, synthesize, and make inferences and judgments about works of art.

Art is a great integrating subject because art, first and foremost, is a form of human communication. Art is one of the first forms of communication for children. Children often express complex ideas through visual symbols that represent their beginning language systems. Art is a vehicle for children to learn about the world around them and to organize the information in a comprehensive format. As young children draw, they take textures, shapes, and colors from a complex world and form them into coherent visual images. This visual cognition, a powerful way for children to process information, is the basis for learning in and through art.

A Sampling of Art Program Resources for Schools

The California Arts Project
(http://www.ucop.edu/tcap/aeol.html)
Getty Education Institute for the Arts
(http://www.artsednet.getty.edu)
The Kennedy Center ArtsEdge
(http://artsedge.kennedy-center.org)

The Metropolitan Museum of Art
(http://www.metmuseum.org/explore/index.asp)
The Educator's Reference Desk
(http://www.eduref.org/cgi-bin/res.cgi/Subjects/Arts)

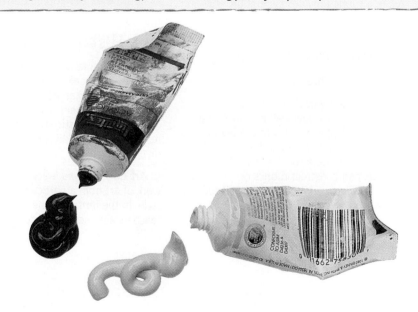

Integrating the Four Art Forms

Susan Cambigue-Tracey, Education Division, The Music Center of Los Angeles County

Albert Einstein said, "Imagination is more important than knowledge." Without exercising the imagination, knowledge is stored in the individual containers of the mind, but connections are not made. When students are taught to use the elements, skills, and content of the visual and performing arts the possibilities for synthesizing and applying what they know are multiplied. Teachers need to ensure that imagination and creativity are always nourishing the roots of learning.

The importance of artistic activity for all students goes beyond the intrinsic value of each art form in itself. Real arts investigation requires the rigor of being able to focus, make decisions, develop discipline, promote originality, and undertake research, study, and practice. Helping students to experience new ways of thinking and seeing allows them to construct personal meaning from what they experience and to build confidence and motivation.

Each art form is a discrete discipline with its own elements, vocabulary, and strategies. However, it is interesting to see connections among them where there are fundamental concepts shared across the arts and other subjects. For example, lines in art are the marks used to create images. Line in dance is the path of gestures and traveling movements, as well as body design. Line in music is a melody and also the lyrics of a song, while lines in theatre are the words that the actors speak.

A common core of knowledge is built through the arts. The principles of visual art, such as emphasis, variety, harmony, unity, and contrast, are the underlying principles used to creating anything—an architectural structure, a musical composition, a piece of literature, a dance, or a play.

It is easy to find ways to integrate one or more of the art forms and still make connections that are viable and authentic. For example, when viewing and discussing a work of art from a particular time period or culture, select music from that same time period or culture. Aztec art will have more relevance when Aztec-inspired music is played or students can view an Aztec dance and see the colors and design of the costumes. A style of music might also inspire art. Matisse did a jazz series that begs for jazz music and dance. Students can then see and hear the structural and improvisational aspects of this style in three different art forms.

When viewing or painting family scenes in art, challenge students to think of family activities that can be portrayed in a tableau, or live,

frozen picture. When viewing or creating sculpture, pair students and have one person become the "clay" and the other the "sculptor" who shapes the clay with respect and cooperation. This can extend into dance by directing the sculpted person (clay) to develop a movement idea lasting eight counts that starts and ends with the sculpted pose or form. Two people in contrasting sculptural poses can have eight counts to slowly transform from one into the other.

Three-dimensional forms in art can inspire counterbalanced (push, pull, leaning) designs made by small groups. A story, such as "The Two Skyscrapers Who Wanted to Have a Child" by Carl Sandburg, could be retold using story theatre or be portrayed in tableaux or as dramatized scenes. Students could also research musical selections to accompany their work.

> "Imagination is more important than knowledge."
> –Albert Einstein

Students will be better able to express emotions in their visual artwork if they first work with them through drama, music, and dance. Students can begin by showing a variety of emotions in the face, hands, and feet and then move toward portraying these emotions in postures such as sitting, standing, and walking. Everyday activities such as cooking or brushing teeth can be done with different emotional motivations. Students can also create short musical pieces depicting an emotion or mood or find music that expresses specific feelings or moods.

All four performing arts can become a powerful component of integrated learning. For example, during a fifth-grade project focused on the Lewis and Clark expedition, students did research in books and on the Internet to collect historical, scientific, geographical, and cultural content. This information served as the basis for group projects in music, dance, theatre, visual arts, technology, and language.

Challenged by well-designed tasks, students discussed what they knew and selected different aspects to explore through dance, music, theatre, and visual art. They learned songs of the times, listened to traditional fiddle music, and learned a rhythmic chant that was used to measure the depth of rivers. In dances, they captured the sense of traveling through "boundless space"; portrayed animals encountered during the expedition; created weather conditions such as storms; and showed the struggles in navigating rivers, waterfalls, and mountains. In theatre, students drew upon the historical characters, interpreted various scenarios, and read journal entries of Lewis and Clark. Visual art classes focused on observation drawings of plants and wild animals.

Students also created journals in which they recorded their feelings, observations, sketches, and discoveries. They were able to make connections between their own journeys and that of the Corps of Discovery. Finally, the students shared what they had learned about this epic journey in a multi-arts culmination.

The arts bring accessibility and vitality to learning, empowering students to construct meaning that has relevance for their lives. When children learn to draw, they learn to see. When children learn to act, they learn how it feels to be in different roles, cultures, and circumstances. When children learn to dance, they learn to feel comfortable in their bodies and to use movement expressively. When children learn to play an instrument, they learn perseverance and the rewards of expression through music. When children learn to sing, they release their voices and are empowered to harmonize. When children learn to write a play, they learn to observe life by thinking, reflecting, and writing. When creativity and imagination are nurtured, children learn how to use all of their resources to solve problems, to dream, and build on the ideas of others.

The Creative Process and Problem Solving

Bunyan Morris, Art Teacher, Effingham County School System, Georgia

There is great reward in watching the artistic growth of a child. Simply providing the media and the time for creating is not enough. The student's natural curiosity and desire to create must be nurtured, encouraged, and challenged. Even the brightest and most talented students need a teacher's guidance in developing the critical-thinking skills necessary for creative problem solving. The intention of this article is to provide ideas and methods for fostering creativity by developing and encouraging divergent problem solving and critical-thinking skills in elementary school art students.

Classroom Management

Fostering creativity in the art classroom is possibly an art teacher's most important skill. In order to encourage creativity, a teacher must be able to relate to students at their thinking level and then guide them to a higher level of cognitive reasoning. Classroom and behavior management are essential. There cannot be an atmosphere of creativity in a room with chaos. That is not to say that one must be a firm authoritarian. A good art teacher will learn how to walk the fine line between maintaining order and maximizing creative energy among students. Although some may not admit it, all students prefer an educational environment that is free from annoying distractions created by other students. Therefore, good behavior management is a must for maintaining a creative environment.

Visual References

Introducing a lesson with a work of art and going through the art criticism process is a tried and true method of encouraging creativity. It is important to discuss works of art that are related to the objectives of the lesson. Working strictly from imagination and memory is usually not effective. Students must have visual references from which to gather ideas.

Picture files, reference books, and the Internet are just a few sources for visual images. Photographs of people and various natural and humanmade objects provide ideas and references for drawing. Images can be collected from magazines and calendars or unwanted photographs. The image file should be organized according to subject matter or theme.

Reference books filled with images related to the lesson should be available to students. They may be checked out of the media center and kept in the room, or they may belong to the classroom. Some media specialists are willing to search for and reserve books that a teacher may need for an upcoming lesson.

An image search on the Internet is one method to help students access a visual reference that may not be available in the classroom's image file, reference books, or the school's media center.

Art Journals

Students who keep art journals maintain handy reference tools. An art journal is the best way to record ideas through sketching and writing. If art journals and writing tools are kept handy, students can jot down ideas or make sketches to save for future use. Ideas can come to mind any place or any time such as in the cafeteria, on the playground, or at the bus stop. The method or tool doesn't really matter that much. It is just important that students have a way of practicing and recording creative ideas.

Exercising the Brain

Reading should be encouraged. Students who like to read perform better in all subjects. Descriptive language stimulates the imagination. Reading a passage about the beauty of a tree or the sound of a waterfall creates a visual image in the brain. This visual image can be stored in the sketchbook and later rendered as a sculpture, painting, or drawing. Encouraging reading encourages creativity. Teachers and schools should encourage parents to limit their children's time watching television because this takes away from reading and creative play time.

Resting the Brain

Teachers should be tolerant of students taking small breaks. Sometimes students need down time to regenerate their mental energy. This down time can take the form of daydreaming or play. Both are important to the creative process. Common sense and good judgment is used to determine when a student is using time for thinking as opposed to just wasting time. Students should be reminded to get a

"Fostering creativity in the art classroom is possibly an art teacher's most important skill."

good night's sleep every night. This is not something teachers can control, but it should be encouraged. We all know that brains function better after a good night's rest.

Enriching Observation Skills

Enriched observation skills lead to more focused experimentation in art. Artists are naturally observant, but teachers know that most students are not born with natural talent. Through practice, all students can enrich their observation and critical-thinking skills. It is important to get students to slow down and see what they might not otherwise observe. One way to do this is to play an observation game. With the students' help, the teacher can set up a still life in the room. A fun game similar to "I Spy" can be played once the still life is ready. The students describe textures, lines, shapes, colors, and other elements and principles of art found within the real-life objects. The teacher writes the observations and descriptions on the board. Once the game is over and students move to the project portion of the lesson, they will be better equipped with enriched observation skills and more focused critical-thinking skills as they create.

In order to gain more focused and creative experimentation from students, an important goal of every art teacher should be to encourage creativity and divergent problem solving and critical thinking. Hopefully, teachers will find value in the ideas shared in this article and combine them with their own ideas to encourage creativity in their students.

Using Writing to Enhance Your Art Curriculum

Mary Lazzari, Ed.S., Elementary Art Teacher, Clarke County School District, Athens, Georgia

In recent decades, art teachers have expanded their area of expertise from art production to lessons that include art criticism, art history, and aesthetics. Art is being used as a vehicle not only for increasing creativity but also for developing thinking skills. One way to broaden the art experience and enhance these skills is through guided, interactive writing techniques. Writing about art is an essential component of a well-rounded art curriculum because it provides students with the opportunity to transform thoughts and feelings into words and images. It can also provide the art teacher a more personalized format for communicating with a large student population and assist art teachers in meeting the increased demand to qualify and quantify their students' learning.

> "Art is being used as a vehicle not only for increasing creativity but also for developing thinking skills."

A visual arts curriculum rich in written language activities can facilitate the development of higher-order thinking skills, such as the ability to analyze, defend, and interpret. The use of written statements can help students slow down and refine their thoughts about their own art and the art of others. Words can become the voice for a shy or inarticulate student. With writing as a means of self-expression, art educators can be more in tune with their students' inner thoughts. Some art teachers may be reluctant to incorporate writing into their curriculum because they fear a less than enthusiastic response from their students. Here are a variety of suggestions that can help motivate elementary students to write about art.

Journals

Whether it is a few sheets of paper stapled together or a spiral notebook, students enjoy having a place to write their private thoughts and feelings. Journals can be used to record the thought process from the beginning to the end of a project. It can also be a place to brainstorm ideas or vent frustrations. Art teachers can give written feedback and encouragement to each student in his or her journal.

Titles

Materials: Selected works of art, pencil and paper

At the completion of a project, students can write descriptive titles for their works of art. A title can inform, challenge, or even surprise a viewer. Younger children or students with a language deficit can dictate the title as the teacher writes. Include the student's title when displaying the artwork. Students can also think of a new title for a famous work of art. Compare it to the artist's original title and discuss the similarities and differences.

Acrostic Poems

Materials: Selected works of art, pencil and paper (for individual writings), or dry/wipe board (for group writing)

Select an artist's name or art topic and write the letters vertically. Instruct students to think of words that describe the artist or topic. Students should think of a decriptive word for each letter in the artist's name or art topic. Descriptive words can start, end, or have the letter anywhere in the selected word. Display acrostic poems with the art work that inspired them.

Venn Diagrams

Materials: Individual sheets of Venn diagrams (or draw a large diagram on the board for a whole group discussion); a set of art postcards

Place an image in each of the two outer circles of the Venn diagram. Students describe qualities they see in each of the two works of art. Qualities that are unique to each image are written in the circle that contains the image. Qualities that they have in common are written in the center of the diagram where the two circles overlap. Invite individuals or groups to share their observations. Mount and display Venn diagrams with student artwork.

Artist Statements

Materials: Pencil and paper

Direct students to write three to five sentences about their artwork. Have the students consider these questions: What did I study? What did I create? What did I learn? Display the artist statements with the completed artwork.

Writing Buddies

If you have students who are reluctant or unmotivated to write during art class, have them work in groups. Ask for a student

volunteer to be the group secretary. This student is responsible for writing down the group's thoughts and ideas. Students who are not strong in written expression will still feel success in sharing their ideas and opinions.

Brainstorming Ideas

Incorporate writing at the beginning of a lesson by having students use writing devices such as webs. The main topic is placed on the center of the page and ideas that support or expand it are written on the sides.

Vocabulary

Incorporate vocabulary into the art room. Post the "Word of the Day" on a chart or bulletin board display. Build a "Word Wall" with art vocabulary that is added throughout the year. Use word labels on art materials and equipment around the room. Create art flash cards with art words or concepts printed on them. Use the flash cards to find elements such as line, shape, and color in works of art or to review these concepts at the beginning or end of a lesson.

Try writing yourself!

Post statements about projects when displaying your students' works of art. Describe the learning objects and concepts in your statement. Use the display to inform parents, teachers and administrators about the rich and interesting learning that is taking place in your art class. Include articles about lessons, projects, and student achievements in your school or district newsletter.

Writing is an important means of creative expression. It is as valid and essential to the art curriculum as drawing or painting. Using writing to augment the art curriculum not only improves the students' ability to express ideas, it helps the art teacher communicate more effectively with every student. When art teachers integrate art instruction and writing about art, the entire curriculum is enhanced. By pairing art production, a realization of students' thoughts and ideas, with writing, a reflective way to understand and validate their opinions and feelings, art teachers can broaden the scope of the art experience. At the same time, the art teacher will develop a critical means to record and assess student learning.

The Importance of Cultural Diversity Through Art in the Elementary Classroom

Jane Rhoades Hudak, Ph.D., Professor of Art, Georgia Southern University

Culture is learned. People acquire information about the world and how to deal with it as members of a society. Individuals do not learn about their culture by themselves. Children learn about the art of their own culture and other cultures through family and friends, through the mass media, and through the Internet. The information learned this way is often valuable, but it cannot be relied upon to always give adequate and correct information. Schools are often the most effective place for giving students the opportunity to learn about the art of their culture and other cultures.

Our view of the nature of the world and our place in it is expressed and communicated culturally. Every society has institutions that teach culture—family and school are two of the best examples in our society. All societies have religions, which are bodies of cultural knowledge and practices. We also have rituals for birth and death. All cultures have objects that are used for everyday living. We express our world and views through dance, drama, music, and art. We decorate our world and our bodies. We paint our faces and the walls of our houses. We make music with instruments and our voices. All this activity is shaped by our participation in a cultural tradition.

A quality elementary art program provides a wonderful opportunity for teachers to expose students to a variety of cultures as well as their own and to help them to become culturally aware. Following are several of the areas such a program can enhance.

Art Promotes Intracultural Understanding

Through a culturally diverse art program, students begin to understand the role and function that art and artists play in society. Through learning about the art of other cultures, they have the opportunity to identify similarities and differences among their culture and others. They learn that art reflects the religion, politics, economics, and other aspects of a culture.

Through a quality art program, students can address issues of ethnocentrism, bias, stereotyping, prejudice, discrimination, and racism. Students can learn that no one racial, cultural, or national group is superior to another and that no one group's art is better than another.

Art Teaches Self-Esteem Through Diversity

Through a quality art program, students learn to recognize, acknowledge, and celebrate racial and cultural diversity through art within their own society. A good program helps promote the enhancement and affirmation of their self-esteem and encourages pride in their heritage. Personal expression is encouraged, and the result is often a statement in visual form that is both inventive and filled with personal meaning.

Art Teaches Effective Communication

When a quality art program is implemented, students are encouraged to increase their visual literacy skills. Students begin to understand that artists transmit information that cannot be disclosed through other modes of communication. Students learn visual literacy by looking, understanding, talking, writing, and making images. They learn that each society has its own way of communicating through image. Through a culturally sensitive art program, students will be able to discuss and compare art from other societies.

Art Teaches about the Past

Through a quality art program, students develop sensitivity and understanding for the history of humankind. For many periods in history, it is only through visual remains or material culture that societies' cultures can be pieced together. Experiences that students have with these art objects from the past teach them respect for others, challenge their minds, and stimulate not only their intellect but also their imagination.

Art Teaches Critical Thinking

A culturally sensitive art program encourages a variety of critical thinking skills. When students look at art from other cultures, they make critical judgments and develop their own opinions. Students are asked to identify and recall information; to organize selected facts and ideas; to use particular facts, rules, and principles; to figure out component parts or to classify; and to combine ideas and form a new whole.

Art Teaches Perceptual Sensitivity and Aesthetic Awareness

As a result of a quality art program, students develop a keen sense of awareness and an appreciation for beauty. They learn that each culture has its own criteria for beauty. Art experiences help cultivate an aesthetic sensitivity and respect for the natural and humanmade environment. Art classes are the only place in the school curriculum where students learn about what constitutes quality visual design—about harmony, order, organization, and specific design qualities such as balance, movement, and unity.

Art Teaches Creativity

When a culturally sensitive art program is implemented, creativity in all students is stimulated and nurtured. Students learn to solve problems creatively. They learn that every society has some form of creative expression. In some societies, no one special person is called an artist—everyone in the culture makes "art" objects.

Teachers can help prevent students from having a simplistic view of other cultures and help them understand the cultural context of how and why works of art are created. *Art Connections* has been carefully constructed so that students will be exposed to works of art that represent a wide variety of cultures. Questions and strategies are designed to help teachers put art in a cultural context for students. The Art History and Culture feature in the *Teacher Edition* and the *Artist Profiles* book provide additional information about the works of art and the artists.

As a teacher, you are a cultural transmitter. A quality art program taught by a culturally sensitive teacher benefits every student. When educators teach in a systematic, meaningful way, students acquire knowledge about art and cultures that will benefit them throughout their lives.

Museum Education

Marilyn J.S. Goodman, Director of Education, Solomon R. Guggenheim Museum

Museums are truly magnificent places. In recent years, these bastions of culture have taken tremendous strides toward making their collections accessible to a broader audience. Museum educators are usually eager to share new information and ideas and are delighted to assist school educators with programs and materials that can easily be incorporated into the classroom. Museums contain a wealth of treasures that offer extraordinary resources for teachers and students, and which will undoubtedly enrich the overall classroom experience.

Getting acquainted with museums in your region can be a real eye-opener. Museums collect objects that document human achievement, both in our own and in other cultures. A local historical society or farm museum might contain a variety of clothing and tools that can bring history to life. A science museum may offer interactive exhibits about phenomena in the natural or physical sciences, sensory perception, new technologies, or space exploration. A children's museum will offer hands-on displays specially designed to motivate young children to learn by doing. Art museums contain visually stunning works that reflect the diversity of human thought and experience.

Museums do not supplant classroom instruction. They enhance and reinforce what is taught by providing raw materials in the forms of objects, artifacts, and exhibits. Museums give students the chance to see and sometimes handle the real thing. It is one thing to talk about Egypt's role in the history of civilization; it is another thing entirely to see the wrappings on a cat mummy, discover hieroglyphs on a sarcophagus, or be overwhelmed by the power and grandeur of large stone sculptures of kings and queens.

When students have the chance to look at portraits, still lifes, landscapes, genre scenes, furniture, clothing, and artifacts, they learn more than by just seeing a picture of a person, place, or thing. They learn how to "read" a culture. Perhaps more importantly, they learn to develop their own process of investigation and critical inquiry. What was this person's life really like? What can one learn about the class structure of this society? What can we tell about craftspeople, available materials, or the objects this society valued? What does the clothing tell us about the climate of the region? What can we learn about the geography, topography, and vegetation? What did people eat? How did they spend leisure time? What were their religious beliefs? Is there any evidence of trade and communication with other regions? What scientific inventions were present at the time? Can one tell if they communicated through language or by writing? Because children are naturally curious, objects will motivate them to think, research, and learn.

> "A visit to a museum will make the curriculum come alive as students begin to explore objects and learn about their meanings."

A visit to a museum will make the curriculum come alive as students begin to explore objects and learn about their meanings. Museum objects give us information in a way that is very different from reading about the objects. Students must think critically to determine both the questions and answers for themselves. A first-hand, visual investigation of an object's style, material, subject matter, and physical characteristics offers preliminary clues to deciphering its meaning. When the exploration is combined with other knowledge, such as the geography and natural resources of a region; the historical context; the social, political, and economic structure of a culture; or even advances in science and technology, students can be engaged in a type of learning that is truly multidisciplinary and may lead them into other areas of study. Moreover, methods for gathering information go far beyond what people see. Exploring objects and works of art allows students to use all of their senses, combining intellect with intuition. The opportunity for experiential, emotional, and intellectual learning is always present.

Museum objects present different historical and cultural perspectives. Students can gather information about people, culture, belief systems, values, and the ways people lived in the past. Museum visits encourage students to see things from broader global and intellectual points of view, developing respect for the work, lives, and points of view of others. Students are encouraged to respond in a variety of ways and on different levels. Most importantly, students are invited to formulate and express their ideas and then discuss them with others.

To learn about museum resources, teachers can contact the education departments of museums in their region. If teachers explain the level of their students, the subjects they are studying, and the specific aspects of the curriculum they would like to supplement, the museum's education department can help to tailor the resources to the class. In addition to guided tours and workshops, the museum education department may offer materials for loan, including slides, pamphlets, posters, postcards, kits, and other printed materials. Some museums have teacher resource rooms filled with books, films, videos, CD-ROMs, and computer databases geared toward educators. Trained staff is available to answer questions or to help teachers develop a complete learning unit that can integrate museum objects with classroom studies.

Using museums is an excellent way to enrich and enliven the classroom experience. Educators can take the first step by learning all they can about the rich and diverse resources available to them and their students.

U.S. Museum Resources

Alabama

1 Birmingham Museum of Art
2000 8th Avenue North,
Birmingham
http://www.ARTSbma.org

2 Mobile Museum of Art
4850 Museum Drive, Mobile
http://www.mobilemuseum
ofart.com

3 Montgomery Museum
of Fine Arts
1 Museum Drive, Montgomery
http://www.mmfa.org

Alaska

4 Alaska State Museum
395 Whittier Street, Juneau
http://www.museums.
state.ak.us/asmhome.html

5 Anchorage Heritage Library
Museum
301 West Northern Lights
Boulevard, Anchorage
http://www.wellsfargohistory.
com/museums/alaska.ht

6 Anchorage Museum
of History and Art
121 West 7th Avenue,
Anchorage
http://www.anchorage
museum.org

Arizona

7 Heard Museum
2301 N Central Avenue, Phoenix
http://www.heard.org/

8 Phoenix Art Museum
1625 North Central Avenue,
Phoenix
http://www.phxart.org

9 Scottsdale Museum
of Contemporary Art - (SMOCA)
7380 E 2nd St, Scottsdale
http://www.scottsdalearts.org

Arkansas

10 Arkansas State
University Museum
Jonesboro, AR 72467
http://museumastate.edu

11 Historic Arkansas Museum
200 East 3rd Street,
Little Rock
http://www.arkansashistory.
com/

12 Old State House Museum
300 West Markham Street,
Little Rock
http://www.oldstatehouse.com

California

13 Asian Art Museum
of San Francisco
Golden Gate Park, San Francisco
http://www.asianart.org

14 Berkeley Art Museum
and Pacific Film Archive
2625 Durant Avenue, Berkeley
http://www.bampfa.berkeley.
edu

15 El Museo Mexicano -
Mexican Museum
Fort Mason Center,
Building D, San Francisco
http://www.mexican
museum.org

16 J Paul Getty
Center Museum
1200 Getty Center Drive,
Los Angeles, CA
http://www.getty.edu

17 Japanese American
National Museum
369 East 1st Street,
Los Angeles
http://www.janm.org

18 Korean American Museum
3780 Wilshire Boulevard
 # 220, Los Angeles
http://www.kamuseum.org

19 L A County Museum
of Art
5905 Wilshire Boulevard,
Los Angeles
http://www.lacma.org

20 San Francisco Museum
of Modern Art
151 3rd Street Building A,
San Francisco
http://www.sfmoma.org/

21 Santa Barbara
Museum of Art
1130 State Street, Santa Barbara
http://www.sbmuseart.org

22 Southwest Museum
234 Museum Drive, Los Angeles
http://www.southwest
museum.org/

Colorado

23 Aspen Art Museum
590 North Mill Street, Aspen
http://www.aspenart
museum.org

24 Boulder Museum
of Contemporary Art
1750 Thirteenth Street, Boulder
http://www.bmoca.org/

25 Denver Art Museum
100 West 14th Avenue, Denver
http://www.denverart
museum.org

Connecticut

26 New Britain Museum
of American Art
56 Lexington Street,
New Britain
http://www.nbmaa.org

27 Norwalk Museum
41 North Main Street, Norwalk
http://www.norwalkct.org/
norwalkmuseum/index.htm

28 Wadsworth Atheneum
Museum of Art
600 Main Street, Hartford
http://www.wadsworth
atheneum.org/

Delaware

29 Delaware Art Museum
800 S Madison Street
Suite B, Wilmington
http://www.delart.org

30 Sewell C Biggs Museum
of American Art
406 Federal Street, Dover
http://www.biggsmuseum.
org

31 Winterthur Museum
Route 52, Winterthur
http://www.winterthur.org/

Florida

32 Bass Museum of Art
2121 Park Ave, Miami
http://www.bassmuseum.org/

33 Key West Art and
Historical Society
281 Front Street, Key West
http://www.kwahs.com

34 Lowe Art Museum
1301 Stanford Drive, Miami
http://www.lowemuseum.
com/

35 Miami Art Museum
101 West Flagler Street, Miami
http://www.miamiart
museum.org/

36 Museum of Fine Arts,
St Petersburg
255 Beach Drive Northeast, St
Petersburg
http://www.fine-arts.org

37 Salvador Dali Museum
1000 3rd Street South,
St Petersburg
http://www.salvadordali
museum.org

Georgia

38 Albany Museum of Art
311 Meadowlark Drive, Albany
http://www.albany
museum.com/

39 High Museum of Art
1280 Peachtree Street
Northeast, Atlanta, GA
http://www.high.org

40 Morris Museum of Art
1 10th Street, Augusta
http://www.themorris.org

Hawaii

41 Contemporary Museum,
Honolulu
2411 Makiki Heights Drive,
Honolulu
http://www.tcmhi.org

42 Kauai Museum
4428 Rice Street, Lihue
http://www.kauaimuseum.org

43 University of Hawaii
at Manoa Art Gallery
University of Hawaii at Manoa,
Honolulu
http://www.hawaii.edu/
artgallery

Idaho

44 Boise Art Museum
670 Julia Davis Drive, Boise
http://www.boiseart
museum.org

45 Eagle Rock Art Museum
and Education Center, Inc.
300 S Capital Avenue,
Idaho Falls
http://www.eaglerockart
museum.org

Illinois

46 Art Institute of Chicago
111 South Michigan Avenue,
Chicago
http://www.artic.edu/aic/

47 Krannert Art Museum
500 East Peabody Drive,
Champaign
http://www.kam.uiuc.edu

48 Martin D'Arcy
Museum of Art
6525 N Sheridan Road,
Chicago
http://darcy.luc.edu

49 Mitchell Museum
of the American Indian
2600 Central Park Ave,
Evanston
http://www.mitchell
museum.org/

50 Museum of
Contemporary Art
220 East Chicago Avenue,
Chicago
http://www.mcachicago.org

51 Smart Museum of Art
5550 South Greenwood Avenue,
Chicago
http://smartmuseum.
uchicago.edu/

Indiana

52 Brauer Museum of Art
Valparaiso University Center
for the Arts, Valparaiso
http://wwwstage.valpo.edu/
artmuseum/index.html

53 Eiteljorg Museum
of American Indian
and Western Art
500 West Washington Street,
Indianapolis
http://www.eiteljorg.org

54 Indianapolis
Museum of Art
1200 West 38th Street,
Indianapolis
http://www.ima-art.org

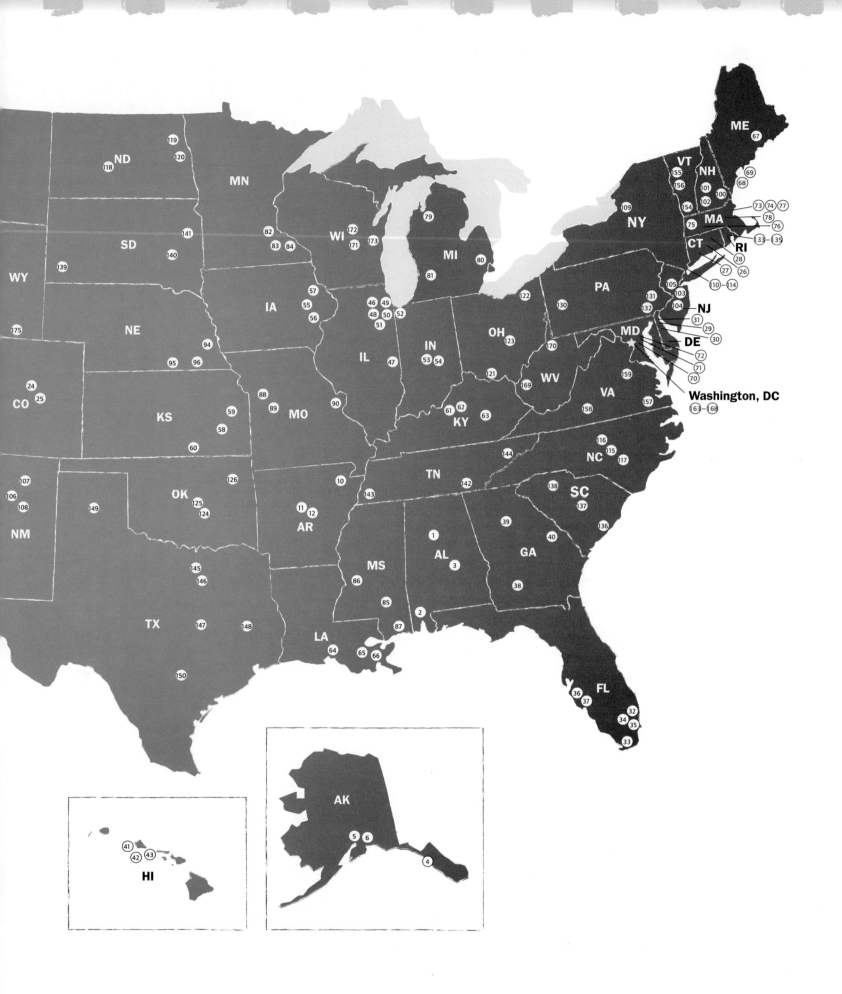

U.S. Museum Resources (continued)

Iowa

55 Cedar Rapids
Museum of Art
*410 3rd Avenue Southeast,
Cedar Rapids*
http://www.crma.org

56 Davenport Museum of Art
*1737 West 12th Street,
Davenport*
http://www.art-dma.org

57 Dubuque Museum of Art
36 East 8th Street, Dubuque
http://www.dbqart.com

Kansas

58 Coutts Memorial Museum
*110 North Main Street,
El Dorado*
http://skyways.lib.ks.us/
kansas/museums/coutts/ind

59 Spencer Museum of Art
*1301 Mississippi Street,
Lawrence*
http://www.ukans.edu/~sma/

60 Wichita Art Museum
*West Museum Boulevard,
Wichita*
http://www.wichitaart
museum.org

Kentucky

61 Kentucky Museum
of Arts + Design
609 West Main Street, Louisville
http://www.kentuckycrafts.org

62 Speed Art Museum, the
2035 South Third St., Louisville
http://www.speedmuseum.org

63 University of Kentucky
Art Museum
*Rose and Euclid Avenue,
Lexington*
http://www.uky.edu/Art
Museum/

Louisiana

64 African-American Museum
*125 New Market Street,
St Martinville*
http://stmartinparish-
la.org/tourism_africanmuseum

65 Louisiana State Museum
751 Chartres Street, New Orleans
http://lsm.crt.state.la.us/

66 New Orleans
Museum of Art
*City Park 1 Collins Diboll Circle,
New Orleans*
http://www.noma.org

Maine

67 Farnsworth Art Museum
*352 Main Street, Box 466,
Rockland*
http://farnsworthmuseum.org/

68 Ogunquit Museum
of American Art
Shore Road, Ogunquit
http://www.ogunquit
museum.org

69 Portland
Museum of Art
7 Congress Square, Portland
http://www.portlandmuseum.
org

Maryland

70 African Art
Museum of Maryland
*5430 Vantage Point Road,
Columbia*
http://www.Africanart
museum.org

71 Baltimore
Museum of Art
10 Art Museum Drive, Baltimore
http://www.artbma.org/

72 Walters Art Museum
*600 North Charles Street,
Baltimore*
http://www.thewalters.org

Massachusetts

73 Harvard University
Art Museums
32 Quincy Street, Cambridge
http://www.artmuseums.
harvard.edu/

74 Institute of Contemporary
Art
955 Boylston Street, Boston
http://www.icaboston.org

75 MASS MoCA -
Massachusetts Museum
of Contemporary Art
87 Marshall Street, North Adams
http://www.massmoca.org

76 Mead Art Museum
*Amherst College, PO Box 5000,
Amherst*
http://www.amherst.edu/
~mead/

77 Museum of Fine Arts
Boston
465 Huntington Avenue, Boston
http://www.mfa.org/

78 Worcester Art Museum
55 Salisbury Street, Worcester
http://www.worcesterart.org

Michigan

79 Cranbrook Art Museum
*39221 Woodward Avenue,
PO Box 801, Bloomfield Hills*
http://www.cranbrook.
edu/art/museum/

80 Detroit Institute of Arts
*5200 Woodward Avenue,
Detroit*
http://www.dia.org

81 Grand Rapids
Art Museum
55 Division Ave N, Grand Rapids
http://www.gramonline.org

Minnesota

82 Frederick R Weisman
Art Museum
*333 East River Road # 200,
Minneapolis*
http://hudson.acad.umn.edu/

83 Minnesota Museum
of American Art
*Landmark Center 75 West 5th
Street West, St Paul*
http://www.mmaa.org

84 Walker Art Center
*725 Vineland Place,
Minneapolis*
http://www.walkerart.org

Mississippi

85 Lauren Rogers
Museum of Art
*5th Avenue and 7th Street,
Laurel*
http://www.lrma.org/

86 Mississippi Museum
of Art
*201 E Pascagoula St
Ste 103, Jackson*
http://www.msmuseumart.
org/

87 Walter Anderson
Museum of Art
*510 Washington Avenue,
Ocean Springs*
http://www.walteranderson
museum.org/

Missouri

88 Albrecht-Kemper Art Museum
2818 Frederick Avenue, St Joseph
http://www.albrecht-
kemper.org/

89 Nelson-Atkins
Museum of Art
4525 Oak Street, Kansas City
http://www.nelson-
atkins.org/

90 St Louis Art Museum
1 Fine Arts Drive, St Louis
http://www.slam.org

Montana

91 Art Museum of Missoula
*335 North Pattee Street,
Missoula*
http://www.artmissoula.org/

92 Hockaday Museum
of Art
*2nd Avenue East at
Third Street, Kalispell*
http://www.hockadayart
museum.org/

93 Montana Museum
of Art and Culture
University of Montana, Missoula
http://www.umt.edu/partv/
famus/

Nebraska

94 Joslyn Art Museum
2200 Dodge St., Omaha
http://www.joslyn.org

95 Museum of Nebraska Art
(MONA)
2401 Central Avenue, Kearney
http://monet.unk.edu/mona/

96 Sheldon Memorial
Art Gallery and
Sculpture Garden
*University of Nebraska-Lincoln,
12th and R Streets, Lincoln*
http://sheldon.unl.edu/

Nevada

97 Las Vegas Art Museum
*9600 West Sahara Avenue,
Las Vegas*
http://www.lvam.com

98 Nevada Museum of Art
160 West Liberty Street, Reno
http://www.nevadaart.org

99 Walker African-American
Museum and Research Center
*705 W Van Buren Ave,
Las Vegas*
http://members.aol.com/
Bigbrwnsis/

New Hampshire

100 Currier Museum of Art
201 Myrtle Way, Manchester
http://www.currier.org

101 Hood Museum of Art
Wheelock Street, Hanover
http://web.dartmouth.
edu/~hood/

102 Mariposa Museum
26 Main Street, Peterborough
http://www.mariposa
museum.org

New Jersey

103 Jane Voorhees
Zimmerli Art Museum
*71 Hamilton St, Rutgers
University, New Brunswick*
http://www.zimmerlimuseum.
rutgers.edu

104 Jersey City Museum
*350 Montgomery Street,
Jersey City*
http://www.jerseycity
museum.org/

105 Princeton University
Art Museum
Princeton University, Princeton
http://www.princetonart
museum.org/

New Mexico

106 Georgia O'Keeffe Museum
217 Johnson Street, Santa Fe
http://www.okeeffe
museum.org

107 Harwood Museum of Art
*238 Ledoux Street, 4080
NDCBU, Taos*
http://www.harwood
museum.org

108 Institute of American
Indian Arts Museum
Cathedral Place, Santa Fe
http://www.iaiancad.org

New York

109 Albright-Knox
Art Gallery
1285 Elmwood Avenue, Buffalo
http://www.albrightknox.org

110 Metropolitan Museum
of Art
*6626 Metropolitan Avenue
FL 2, Flushing*
http://www.Metmuseum.org/

111 Museum of Modern Art
MoMA
11 West 53 Street , New York
http://www.moma.org/

112 New Museum
of Contemporary Art
583 Broadway, New York
http://www.newmuseum.org

113 Solomon R Guggenheim
Museum, New York
1071 5th Ave at 89th, New York
http://www.guggenheim.org
/new_york_index.html

114 Whitney Museum
of American Art
*945 Madison Avenue FL 5,
New York*
http://www.whitney.org

North Carolina

115 Ackland Art Museum
*Columbia and Franklin Street,
Chapel Hill*
http://www.ackland.org

116 Duke University
Museum of Art
*Buchanan Blvd-Trinity Avenue,
Durham*
http://www.duke.edu/web/
duma/

117 North Carolina Museum
of Art
2110 Blue Ridge Road, Raleigh
http://www.ncartmuseum.org/

North Dakota

118 North Heritage Center of
the State Historical Society of
North Dakota, Bismarck
http://www.state.nd.us/hist/
index.html

119 North Dakota
Museum of Art
Centennial Drive, Grand Forks
http://www.ndmoa.com

120 Plains Art Museum
219 7th Street South, Fargo
http://www.plainsart.org/

Ohio

121 Cincinnati Art Museum
953 Eden Park Drive, Cincinnati
http://www.cincinnatiart
museum.com/

122 Cleveland Museum of Art
11150 East Boulevard, Cleveland
http://www.clemusart.com/

123 Columbus Museum of Art
480 East Broad Street, Columbus
http://www.columbusmuseum.
org

Oklahoma

124 Fred Jones Jr
Museum of Art
*410 West Boyd Street,
University of Oklahoma, Norman*
http://www.ou.edu/fjjma/

125 Oklahoma City
Art Museum
*3113 Pershing Boulevard,
Oklahoma City*
http://www.okcartmuseum.
com/

126 Philbrook Museum of Art
*2727 South Rockford Road,
Tulsa, OK*
http://www.philbrook.org/

Oregon

127 Coos Art Museum
235 Anderson Avenue, Coos Bay
http://www.coosart.org

128 Portland Art Museum
1219 SW Park Ave., Portland
http://www.pam.org

129 University of Oregon
Museum of Art
*1223 University of Oregon,
Eugene*
http://uoma.uoregon.edu/

Pennsylvania

130 The Andy Warhol
Museum
117 Sandusky Street, Pittsburgh
http://www.clpgh.org/warhol/

131 The Palmer
Museum of Art
*Curtin Rd, The Pennsylvania
State University, University Park*
http://www.psu.edu/dept/
palmermuseum/

132 Philadelphia
Museum of Art
*26th Street and the Benjamin
Franklin Parkway, Philadelphia*
http://pma.libertynet.org/

Rhode Island

133 Museum of Art,
Rhode Island School of Design
224 Benefit Street, Providence
http://www.risd.edu/

134 Museum Of Primitive
Art & Culture
*1058 Kingstown Road,
South Kingstown*

135 National Museum
of American Illustration
*Vernon Court 492 Bellevue
Avenue , Newport*
http://www.american
illustration.org

South Carolina

136 Gibbes Museum of Art
135 Meeting Street, Charleston
http://www.gibbes.com/

137 Columbia Museum of Art
*Main and Hampton Streets,
Columbia*
http://www.colmusart.org/

138 The Spartanburg County
Museum of Art
385 S Spring St., Spartanburg
http://www.sparklenet.com/
museumofart

South Dakota

139 Journey Museum
222 New York Street, Rapid City
http://www.journeymuseum.org

140 Oscar Howe Art Center
and Middle Border Museum
*1300 E University Street P.O
Box 1071 Mitchell*
http://www.oscarhowe.com/
index.htm

141 South Dakota Art Museum
P.O Box 2250, Brookings
http://web.sdstate.edu/sites/
artmuseum/

Tennessee

142 Hunter Museum of Art
10 Bluff View, Chattanooga
http://www.huntermuseum.
org/

143 Institute of Egyptian
Art and Archaeology
*The University of Memphis,
Memphis*
http://www.memst.edu/
egypt/about.html

144 Knoxville Museum of Art
*1050 Worlds Fair Park Drive,
Knoxville*
http://www.knoxart.org

Texas

145 Dallas Museum of Art
1717 North Harwood, Dallas
http://dm-art.org/

146 Kimbell Art Museum
*3333 Camp Bowie Blvd.,
Fort Worth*
http://kimbellart.org/

147 Mexic-Arte Museum
419 Congress Avenue, Austin
http://www.mexic-arte
museum.org

148 The Museum of Fine Arts
1001 Bissonnet, Houston
http://mfah.org/

149 Panhandle-Plains
Historical Museum,
West Texas A&M University
2401 4th Ave., Canyon
http://www.wtamu.edu/
museum/

150 San Antonio Museum
of Art
*200 West Jones Avenue,
San Antonio*
http://www.sa-museum.org

Utah

151 BYU Museum of Art
*Brigham Young University,
Provo*
http://www.byu.edu/moa/

152 St George Art Museum
175 East 200 North, St George
http://www.ci.st-george.ut.us/
arts/artmuseum.php

153 Utah Museum of Fine
Arts, University of Utah
*370 South 1530 East
University of Utah , Salt Lake City*
http://www.utah.edu/umfa/

Vermont

154 The Bennington Museum
West Main St., Bennington
http://www.bennington
museum.com

155 Robert Hull
Fleming Museum
Colchester Avenue, Burlington
http://www.uvm.edu/
~fleming/home/

156 Shelburne Museum
*US Route 7, PO Box 10,
Shelburne*
http://www.shelburne
museum.org

Virginia

157 Chrysler Museum of Art
245 West Olney Rd., Norfolk
http://www.chrysler.org/

158 Maier Museum of Art
*2500 Rivermont Avenue,
Lynchburg*
http://www.rmwc.edu/
Maier/

159 Virginia Museum
of Fine Arts
2800 Grove Ave., Richmond
http://www.vmfa.state.va.us/

Washington

160 Frye Art Museum
704 Terry Ave., Seattle
http://fryeart.org/

161 Jundt Art Museum
*502 East Boone Avenue,
Spokane*
http://www.gonzaga.edu/
Campus+Resources/Museums
+an

162 Seattle Art Museum
100 University St., Seattle
http://seattleartmuseum.
org/

Washington, D.C.

163 Arthur M Sackler Gallery
and the Freer Gallery of Art
1050 Independence Avenue, SW
http://www.asia.si.edu/
default.htm

164 Corcoran Gallery of Art
500 17th Street Northwest
http://www.corcoran.org/

165 Hirshhorn Museum
and Sculpture Garden
*Independence Avenue
and 7th Street Southwest*
http://hirshhorn.si.edu/

166 National Gallery of Art
http://www.nga.gov/

167 The National Museum
of Women in the Arts
1250 New York Ave., NW
http://www.nmwa.org/

168 Smithsonian Museums
Smithsonian Institution
http://www.si.edu/

West Virginia

169 Huntington Museum
of Art
2033 McCoy Rd., Huntington
http://www.hmoa.org/

170 Oglebay Institute:
Mansion Museum and
Glass Museum
Burton Center, Wheeling
http://www.oionline.com/

Wisconsin

171 Elvehjem Museum of Art
*800 University Avenue,
Madison*
http://www.lvm.wisc.edu

172 Leigh Yawkey Woodson
Art Museum
700 North Twelfth St, Wausau
http://www.lywam.org/

173 Milwaukee Art Museum
*750 North Lincoln Memorial
Dr., Milwaukee*
http://www.mam.org/

Wyoming

174 National Museum
of Wildlife Art
2820 Rungius Road, Jackson
http://www.wildlifeart.org

175 University of Wyoming
Art Museum
2111 Willett Dr., Laramie
http://uwadmnweb.uwyo.
edu/artmuseum/

World Museum Resources

Argentina

1 Fundacion Federico Klemm
Buenos Aires, Argentina
www.fundacionfjklemm.org

Australia

2 Art Gallery of New South Wales
Sydney, Australia
www.artgallery.nsw.gov.au/

3 Australian National Art Gallery
Canberra, Australia
www.nga.gov.au/Home/index.cfm

4 Museum of Contemporary Art
Sydney, Australia
www.mca.com.au/

Austria

5 Kunsthistorisches Museum Wien
Vienna, Austria
www.khm.at/

Bahrain

6 Al Hayat Museum
Manama, Bahrain
www.beitalquran.com/

Brazil

7 Museu Historico Nacional
Rio de Janeiro, Brazil
www.museuhistoriconacional.com.br/ingles/index.htm

Canada

8 Art Gallery of Calgary
Calgary, Canada
www.artgallerycalgary.com/

9 Morris and Helen Belkin Art Gallery, University of British Columbia
Vancouver, Canada
www.belkin-gallery.ubc.ca/

10 Art Gallery of Newfoundland and Labrador
St. Johns, Canada
www.mun.ca/agnl/main.html

11 Art Gallery of Nova Scotia
Halifax, Canada
www.agns.gov.ns.ca/

12 Art Gallery of Ontario
Toronto, Canada
www.ago.net/navigation/flash/index.cfm

13 National Gallery of Canada
Ottawa, Canada
www.national.gallery.ca/

14 The Montreal Museum of Fine Arts
Quebec, Canada
www.mmfa.qc.ca/en/index.html

15 McMichael Canadian Art Collection
Toronto, Canada
www.mcmichael.com/

16 Winnipeg Art Gallery
Winnipeg, Canada
www.wag.mb.ca/

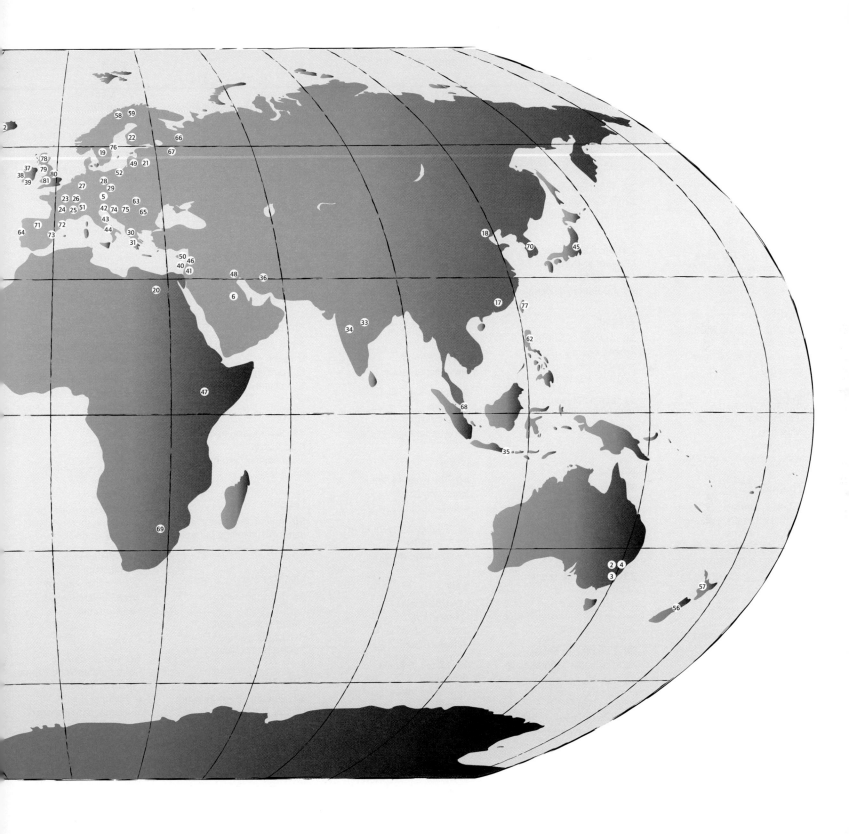

World Museum Resources

China

17 Hong Kong Museum of Art
Hong Kong, China
www.lcsd.gov.hk/CE/Museum/Arts/english/intro/eintro.html

18 Palace Museum
Beijing, China
www.dpm.org.cn/

Denmark

19 National Museum
Copenhagen, Denmark
www.natmus.dk/sw1413.asp

Egypt

20 The Egyptian Museum
Cairo, Egypt
www.egyptianmuseum.gov.eg/

Estonia

21 Estonian National Museum
Tartu, Estonia
www.erm.ee/?lang=ENG

Finland

22 The Finnish National Gallery
Helsinki, Finland
www.fng.fi/fng/rootnew/en/vtm/etusivu.htm

France

23 The Louvre
Paris, France
www.louvre.fr/louvrea.htm

24 Musee d'Orsay,
Paris, France
www.musee-orsay.fr/

25 Centre Georges Pompidou
Paris, France
www.cnac-gp.fr/Pompidou/Accueil.nsf/tunnel?OpenForm

Germany

26 Neues Museum
Nuremberg, Germany
www.nmn.de/

27 Hamburg Kunsthalle
Hamburg, Germany
www.hamburger-kunsthalle.de/

28 Alte National Galerie
Berlin, Germany
www.alte-nationalgalerie.de/

29 Bauhaus Archiv Museum of Design
Berlin, Germany
www.bauhaus.de/english/

Greece

30 Acropolis Museum
Athens, Greece
www.culture.gr/2/21/211/21101m/e211am01.html

31 Benaki Museum
Athens, Greece
www.benaki.gr/index-en.htm

Iceland

32 Living Art Museum
Reykjavik, Iceland
www.nylo.is/English/index.html

India

33 National Museum of India
New Delhi, India
www.nationalmuseumindia.org/index.html

34 Chhatrapati Shivaji Maharaj Vastu Sangrahalaya
(Formerly the Prince of Wales Museum of Western India)
Mumbai (Bombay), India
www.bombaymuseum.org/

Indonesia

35 Agung Rai Museum of Art
Ubud, Bali, Indonesia
www.nusantara.com/arma/

Iran

36 National Museum of Iran
Tehran, Iran
www.nationalmuseumofiran.com/

Ireland

37 Hunt Museum
Limerick, Ireland
www.huntmuseum.com/

38 Irish Museum of Modern Art
Dublin, Ireland
www.modernart.ie/

39 National Gallery of Ireland
Dublin, Ireland
www.nationalgallery.ie/

Israel

40 The Israel Museum
Jerusalem, Israel
www.imj.org.il/

41 Tel Aviv Museum of Art
Tel Aviv, Israel
www.tamuseum.com/

Italy

42 Uffizi Gallery
Florence, Italy
www.uffizi.firenze.it/welcomeE.html

43 Museo di Roma
Rome, Italy
www.museodiroma.comune.roma.it/PalazzoBraschi/inizio.mostra

44 Vatican Museum
Vatican City
http://mv.vatican.va/3_EN/pages/MV_Home.html

Japan

45 Kyoto National Museum
Tokyo, Japan
www.kyohaku.go.jp/indexe.htm

Jordan

46 Darat al Funun Home for the Arts
Amman, Jordan
www.daratalfunun.org/

Kenya

47 National Museum of Kenya
Nairobi, Kenya
www.museums.or.ke/

Kuwait

48 Kuwait National Museum
Kuwait City, Kuwait
www.kmia.org.kw

Latvia

49 State Museum of Art
Rīga, Latvia
www.vmm.lv/en/muzejs.html

Lebanon

50 American University of Beirut Archaeology Museum
Beirut, Lebanon

Liechtenstein

51 Kunstmuseum Liechtenstein
Vaduz, Liechtenstein
www.kunstmuseum.li/web2306e/index.html

Lithuania

52 Lithuanian Art Museum
Vilnius, Lithuania
www.ldm.lt/ldm_en.htm

Mexico

53 Museo de Arte Moderno
Mexico City, Mexico
www.arts-history.mx/museos/mam/home2.html

54 National Museum of Anthropology
Mexico City, Mexico
www.mna.inah.gob.mx/

55 Museo de Arte Contemporaneo de Oaxaca
Oaxaca, Mexico
www.arts-history.mx/museos/maco/home.html

New Zealand

56 Centre of Contemporary Art
Christchurch, New Zealand
www.coca.org.nz/

57 Auckland Art Gallery
Auckland, New Zealand
www.aucklandartgallery.govt.nz/

Norway

58 National Gallery of Norway
Oslo, Norway
www.museumsnett.no/nasjonalgalleriet/flash_versjon_engelsk/

59 Lillehammer Art Museum
Lillehammer, Norway
www.lillehammerartmuseum.com/

Panama

60 Museo de Arte Contemporaneo de Panama
Panama, Republic of Panama
www.macpanama.org/

Peru

61 Museo Arqueologico
Rafael Larco Herrera
Lima, Peru
museolarco.perucultural.
org.pe/

Philippines

62 Philippine National
Museum
Manila, Philippines
http://nmuseum.tripod.
com/

Poland

63 Polish National Museum
Warsaw, Poland
www.mnw.art.pl/

Portugal

64 Museu Calouste
Gulbenkian
Lisbon, Portugal
www.gulbenkian.pt/

Romania

65 The National Museum
of Art of Romania
Bucharest, Romania
http://art.museum.ro/
museum.html

Russia

66 The State Hermitage
Museum
St. Petersburg, Russia
www.hermitagemuseum.
org/

67 Pushkin Museum
of Fine Arts
Moscow, Russia
www.museum.ru/gmii/

Singapore

68 Singapore Art Museum
*Singapore, Republic of
Singapore*
www.nhb.gov.sg/SAM/
sam.shtml

South Africa

69 Pretoria Art Museum
Pretoria, South Africa
www.pretoriaartmuseum.
co.za/

South Korea

70 Seoul Metropolitan
Museum of Art
Seoul, South Korea
www.metro.seoul.kr/
muse/eng/

Spain

71 Guggenheim
Bilbao Museum
Bilbao, Spain
www.guggenheim-
bilbao.es/idioma.htm

72 Museu d'Art
Contemporani
Barcelona, Spain
www.macba.es/home.php

73 Valencian Institute
of Modern Art
Valencia, Spain
www.ivam.es/

Switzerland

74 Kunstmuseum Basel
Basel, Switzerland
www.kunstmuseumbasel.
ch/de/

75 Kunsthaus
Zurich, Switzerland
www.kunsthaus.ch/

Sweden

76 National Museum
Stockholm, Sweden
www.nationalmuseum.se/

Taiwan

77 National Palace Museum
T'aipei, Taiwan
www.npm.gov.tw/english/
index-e.htm

United Kingdom

78 National Gallery
of London
London, England
www.nationalgallery.
org.uk/

79 British Museum
London, England
www.thebritishmuseum.
ac.uk/

80 Tate Gallery
London, England
www.tate.org.uk/home/
default.htm

81 Victoria and
Albert Museum
London, England
www.vam.ac.uk/

Uruguay

82 Museo Nacianal
de Artes Visuales
Montevideo, Uruguay
www.mnav.gub.uy/

Elements and Principles of Art

Scope and Sequence

Elements of Art	Level K U1	U2	U3	U4	U5	U6	Level 1 U1	U2	U3	U4	U5	U6	Level 2 U1	U2	U3	U4	U5	U6	Level 3 U1	U2	U3	U4	U5	U6
Line	1-6						1-6	1					1-4							1-2				
Shape		1-6			6			1-6		1			5-6					2, 4	3-6					
Color			1-6						1-6						1-3			1, 3			1-6			
Value															4-6						1			
Space				1, 3						2, 5, 6				5-6						1-3				
Form			2-6	5						1-4		4	1-4					2, 4		4-6				
Texture				1-6						1-3							5-6					5-6		

Principles of Art	Level K U1	U2	U3	U4	U5	U6	Level 1 U1	U2	U3	U4	U5	U6	Level 2 U1	U2	U3	U4	U5	U6	Level 3 U1	U2	U3	U4	U5	U6
Pattern						1				4-5					1-2							1-3		
Rhythm						2					6				3-6							4-6		
Balance						3-4					1-2					1-2						1-4		
Proportion																								
Emphasis										3-4						3-4								3-4
Variety																		3-4						2
Harmony																		1-2						1
Unity						5-6						5-6						5-6						5-6

*Numbers indicate lesson numbers within a given unit.

Level 4						Level 5						Level 6						Level 7 Exploring Art	Level 8 Understanding Art
U1	U2	U3	U4	U5	U6	U1	U2	U3	U4	U5	U6	U1	U2	U3	U4	U5	U6		
1–6						1–2						1						Chapter 2, 6, 7, 8, 9, 10, 11	Chapter 2, 6, 8, 9, 12, 15, 16
	1–2					3	1						2					Chapter 2, 6, 8, 9, 10, 11	Chapter 2, 3, 5, 8, 9, 13, 14, 16, 17
		1–4						1–4						1–4				Chapter 2, 4, 8, 9, 11, 13	Chapter 2, 3, 4, 8, 11, 12, 14–17
		5–6					4–6							2–3				Chapter 14	Chapter 13, 14, 15
			1–3				1–3								5–6			Chapter 2, 4, 10, 12	Chapter 6, 7, 13, 15
		1–3					4–6								3–4			Chapter 2, 6, 11, 12, 13	Chapter 6, 14, 15
			4–5							1					5–6			Chapter 2, 14	Chapter 3, 5, 6, 11–16

Level 4						Level 5						Level 6						Level 7 Exploring Art	Level 8 Understanding Art
U1	U2	U3	U4	U5	U6	U1	U2	U3	U4	U5	U6	U1	U2	U3	U4	U5	U6		
	3						5–6						1–3					Chapter 3, 6	Chapter 7, 8, 10, 15, 17
	4–6							2–3					4–6					Chapter 3, 4, 7	
		1–3						4–6							1–4			Chapter 3, 11, 12	Chapter 5, 7, 9, 10, 11, 13
			4–6					1–6								1–6		Chapter 3, 11, 14	Chapter 5, 11, 12
			6		5				3–4						5–6			Chapter 3, 11	Chapter 5, 10, 11, 12, 16
					5				2								1–2	Chapter 3, 6, 13	Chapter 3, 4, 5, 10, 15
					4				1								3–4	Chapter 3, 6, 7	Chapter 4, 5, 7, 12, 16
					6				5–6								5–6	Chapter 3	Chapter 7

Media

Scope and Sequence

Media	Level K						Level 1						Level 2						Level 3					
	U1	U2	U3	U4	U5	U6	U1	U2	U3	U4	U5	U6	U1	U2	U3	U4	U5	U6	U1	U2	U3	U4	U5	U6
Collage	6	2	2, 3		1	3	3		5			3, 4	5	5					4					
Drawing	2, 4, 5	4, 5	1, 4, 5	1	2	1, 2	1	1–3, 5	1, 4		2, 6	1, 5				2, 3	2–4, 6	4	1, 2, 5, 6	3	1	1	3, 5	6
Fiber Arts				4, 6							5						5						6	2
Mixed Media		6		3, 4	3			5		5	1	2	2, 6	2	2, 3	6				6	4, 6			4
Painting	1		6				1, 2, 4	4	3, 6	6			3, 4	6	1, 4–6		1, 3		3	2	2, 3, 5	4		
Photography																								
Printmaking		3									4					1				1			1	
Three-Dimensional Forms				2, 5, 6	5	4, 6				1–4	3	6	1	1, 3, 4		4	1	5		4, 5		2, 3	4, 6	1, 5
Technology	3	1				5	6	6	2							5		2, 6				5	2	3

*Numbers indicate lesson numbers within a given unit.

| Level 4 | | | | | | Level 5 | | | | | | Level 6 | | | | | |
U1	U2	U3	U4	U5	U6	U1	U2	U3	U4	U5	U6	U1	U2	U3	U4	U5	U6
	6	3				1		4	2		5	6					1
1–6	3, 4	2		1, 2, 4, 5		2, 4, 5	1, 4	1, 5	1, 4	3	2	1	3	1, 2, 4	3–5	1, 2, 5	
			3, 6								2	4	2				3, 5
	1, 5		4, 5			1, 4				1			6			6	4
		4–6				2, 5	2, 3	3	3	4, 5	1	5		1, 2, 4	5	1	
		3				6											2
																	3
			1–3				5, 6	6	5, 6		6		3, 4	3, 6	6	3	6
	2	1	6	6		3		2			6		5		2	4	

Level 7 Exploring Art	Level 8 Understanding Art
Chapter 1, 6, 10	Chapter 10
Chapter 2, 7, 11, 14	Chapter 3, 15, 16
Chapter 1, 2, 3, 13	Chapter 7, 8, 10, 12
Chapter 5, 13	Chapter 2, 3
Chapter 2, 3, 4, 5, 6, 9, 11, 14	Chapter 1–8, 10, 11, 13–17
Chapter 10	Chapter 1, 17
Chapter 3, 4, 8	Chapter 1, 3, 6, 8, 14–17
Chapter 2, 3, 4, 5, 7, 12, 13	Chapter 1, 2, 3, 5–13, 15–17
Chapter 4, 11, 15	Chapter 3, 17

Program Glossary

A

active lines *noun* Lines that show action and add energy and movement to a work of art. Diagonal, zigzag, and curved lines are examples of active lines.

additive sculpture *noun* When something is added to either relief or freestanding sculpture

alternating pattern *noun* Can repeat a motif, but change position; alter spacing between motifs or add a second motif

analogous color scheme *noun* Uses colors that are side by side on the color wheel and have a common color

analogous colors *noun* Colors that sit side by side on the color wheel and have a common hue. Violet, blue-violet, blue, blue-green are examples of analogous colors.

angle *noun* A shape formed when two lines extend in different directions from the same point

animal forms *noun* A three-dimensional representation of an animal

ant's view *noun* Viewers feel they are looking up, toward an object or figure.

appliqué *noun* An art form in which cutout fabrics are attached to a larger surface

approximate symmetry *noun* A special kind of formal balance where both sides of a design are almost exactly the same. One example is the human face: each side is almost the same as the other.

arc *noun* Any portion of a curved line from a circle

architects *noun* Artists who design buildings, cities, and bridges using three-dimensional forms

architecture *noun* The art of designing and planning buildings, cities, and bridges

armature *noun* A framework for supporting material used in sculpting

art form *noun* A type of art

assemblage *noun* A sculpture technique in which a variety of objects is assembled to create one complete piece

asymmetrical balance *noun* Another name for informal balance

asymmetry *noun* Another name for informal balance. Something asymmetrical looks balanced even if it is not the same on both sides.

atmospheric perspective *noun* The effects air and light have on how we perceive an object

axis *noun* A real or imaginary line across the center of a work of art

B

background *noun* The area of the picture plane farthest from the viewer

balance *noun* The principle of design that deals with visual weight in an artwork

bird's-eye view *noun* Or aerial view; viewers feel they are looking down on a scene.

black ▮▮▮▮

blending *noun* A shading technique that creates a gradual change from light to dark or dark to light

blind contour drawing *noun* A drawing that is made by looking at the object being drawn, not at the paper.

blob *noun* A type of free-form shape

body forms *noun* Three-dimensional representations of a person

body proportions *noun* The size relationship of one part of the body to another

brass *noun* A metal made by combining copper and zinc

bright colors *noun* colors that appear to reflect light

broken (line) *noun* A line that is made of a series of dashes, not solid

building *noun* a structure where we live, work, meet, or play

C

calm lines *noun* Lines that give a work of art a quiet and peaceful mood. Horizontal and vertical lines are calm lines.

carving *noun* Art made by cutting into the surface of the medium.

central axis *noun* A real or imaginary dividing line that can run in two directions, vertically and horizontally

circle *noun* A round, geometric shape made when all points are placed the same distance from a center point.

close-up view *noun* Viewers feel they are right next to an object, or are a part of the action in a picture.

coil *noun* A long roll of clay joined into a circle or spiral. Clay coils are used to make pottery.

collage *noun* A two-dimensional work of art made up of pieces of paper and/or fabric to create the image.

collograph *noun* A printmaking technique where cut papers or thin boards are arranged to create an image on a stiff printing plate.

color *noun* 1. The art element that is created from reflected light; 2. In balance: a brighter color has more visual weight than a dull color; 3. In perspective: bright-colored objects seem closer, while dull or pale objects appear farther away.

color intensity *noun* The brightness or dullness of a color

color scheme *noun* A plan for organizing the colors used in an artwork

color spectrum *noun* The effect that occurs when light passes through a prism and separates into a band of colors in the order of red, orange, yellow, green, blue, and violet.

color wheel *noun* Shows the color spectrum bent into a circle

column *noun* A supporting pillar on a building

complementary color scheme *noun* Uses one set of complementary colors; for example, red and green, blue and orange, and yellow and violet

complementary colors *noun* Colors that are opposite each other on the color wheel

complex geometric shapes *noun* Shapes made by combining simple geometric shapes such as triangles, squares, and rectangles. Some examples of complex geometric shapes are diamonds, pentagons, trapezoids, hexagons, parallelograms, and octagons.

contour *noun* The edges and surface ridges of an object

contour hatching *noun* A shading technique that follows the form of an object

contour lines *noun* Continuous, unbroken lines that show the edges and surface ridges of an object or figure

contrast *noun* 1. A technique for creating a focal point or area of interest in a work of art using differences in elements; 2. In emphasis: contrast occurs when one element stands out from the rest of the work; 3. showing differences between things

converging *adj.* (*verb*) Coming together at one point or place

converging lines *noun* One of the six perspective techniques. Parallel lines seem to converge or move toward the same point as they move away from you.

cool colors *noun* Green, violet, and blue. They suggest coolness and move away from the viewer.

cool hues *noun* Blue, green, and violet. Cool hues are associated with cool things like snow, water, and grass.

cross-hatching *noun* A shading technique created when sets of parallel lines cross or intersect

culture *noun* Another word for custom

curling *verb* Hold one end of a long strip of paper. Grip the middle of the paper strip next to the side of a pencil. With a quick motion, pull the strip firmly across the pencil.

curved *adj.* Lines that bend and change gradually or turn inward to form spirals

curved (line) *noun* A line that changes directions slowly and bends in arcs

curving movement *verb* Using curved lines to move the viewer's eyes through a work of art and make the viewer feel that objects in the work of art are moving along curves

D

dark lines *noun* Created by using less water for watercolor paints

dark value *noun* A value that has more black added to it

decorative *adj.* Serving to make more beautiful; to adorn with ornaments

depth *noun* 1. The appearance of distance; 2. How far something extends toward or away from the viewer.

detail *noun* One of the six perspective techniques. Objects with fuzzy, blurred edges appear farther away than those with clear sharp edges.

diagonal *noun* (*adj.*) Lines that are slanted. They look as if they are falling or rising. They make things look active.

diagonal movement *verb* Using diagonal lines to move the viewer's eyes through a work of art and make the viewer feel that objects in the work of art are moving along diagonals

dimension *noun* A measurement of the amount of space an object takes up in one direction

diorama *noun* A display of a scene using sculpted, miniature figurines

directional lines *noun* How a line moves: diagonally, vertically, or horizontally

distortion *noun* A deviation from normal or expected proportions

dominant *noun* (*adj.*) The part of the work of art that seems more important to the viewer. Dominant elements have been emphasized.

dominant element *noun* The element in a work of art that is noticed first.

dull colors Colors that are not bright

E

earthenware *noun* Ceramics made out of clay and fired at a low heat

elongate *verb* To stretch out or make long

embroidery *noun* The art of decorating designs with needle and thread

emphasis *noun* The principle of design that stresses one area in an art work over another area

even balance *adj.* Both halves are equal. Left side and right side are the same.

exaggerate *verb* To make much larger than actual size

exaggeration *noun* To increase or enlarge beyond what is expected or normal

F

facial proportions *noun* The relationship of one feature of a face to another feature

faraway view *noun* Or eye-level view; viewers feel they are standing far away from the scene.

fiber *noun* A material used to make baskets and cloth. Grass, yarn, and straw are kinds of fibers.

flowing lines *noun* Create a feeling of calm and gracefulness. Flowing lines are fluid; they change direction and size.

flowing rhythm *noun* Created when curved lines or shapes are repeated

focal point *noun* The point where the receding lines meet. It is the first part of a composition to attract the viewer's attention.

foreground *noun* The area of the picture plane that is closest to the viewer

form *noun* A three-dimensional object that is measured by height, width, and depth

formal balance *noun* Occurs when equal or similar elements are placed on opposite sides of a central axis

Program Glossary (continued)

free-form forms *noun* Three-dimensional forms with irregular edges often found in nature

free-form shapes *noun* Two-dimensional images made of straight or curved lines or a combination of both

freestanding *noun* Forms that can be seen from all around

freestanding sculpture *noun* A three-dimensional work of art that can be viewed on all sides because it is surrounded by space

fringing *verb* Make parallel straight cuts along the edge of a piece of paper to create a ruffled look.

frontal proportions *noun* A front view of the head that is divided by three horizontal lines across the central axis

futurists *noun* A group of Italian artists during the early twentieth-century who repeated and overlapped shapes and lines to create the illusion of movement

G

geometric forms *noun* Mathematically precise forms based on geometric shapes

geometric shapes *noun* Mathematically precise shapes: circle, square, and triangle

gesture *noun* An expressive movement

gesture drawings *noun* Quick drawings used to capture the position or pose of the body

gesture lines *noun* Lines drawn to capture the movement of a person, an animal, or an object in a painting or drawing

gesture sketch *noun* Quick drawings used to capture the position or movement of the body

guide lines *noun* Lines used by artists to create both full-face and profile portraits more accurately

H

hand tools *noun* Simple instruments for carving or sculpting

harmony *noun* The principle of art that creates unity by stressing similarities of separate but related parts

hatching *noun* A shading technique that looks like a series of parallel lines

height *noun* A vertical measurement, or how tall something is

high-intensity color *noun* A pure hue such as red

highlights *noun* Small areas of white or light value to show the brightest spots

horizon line *noun* The point at which the earth and sky meet. The horizon line is always at the viewer's eye level.

horizontal *noun* (*adj.*) A line that moves from side to side

hues *noun* The spectral colors, or colors of the rainbow. Hues do not include black or white. Hues are red, orange, yellow, green, blue, and violet.

I

informal balance *noun* A way of organizing parts of a design so that unlike objects have equal visual weight

installation *noun* An artwork that was created for a specific place, such as a gallery or outdoor location

intensity *noun* The brightness or dullness of a color

interior designers *noun* Artists who decorate the inside of a building

intermediate colors *noun* Colors made by mixing a primary color and a secondary color. There are six intermediate colors—red-orange, yellow-orange, yellow-green, blue-green, blue-violet, and red-violet.

intermediate hues *noun* Yellow-green, red-orange, blue-green, made by combining a primary hue with either of the secondary hues that are adjacent on the color wheel

invented texture *noun* Created when an artist uses lines or other elements to make a textural look without any specific texture in mind

irregular *adj.* Does not follow a rule or pattern

isolation *noun* An object is emphasized by its placement apart from other objects.

J

jeweler *noun* An artist who designs and makes jewelry

jewelry *noun* Three-dimensional artwork that is made for people to wear

K

kinetic movement *noun* Actual or real movement

kinetic sculpture *noun* A three-dimensional form that actually moves in space

L

landscape *noun* a picture of the outdoors

light lines *noun* Created by adding more water to watercolor paints

light value *noun* A value that has more white added to it

line *noun* A mark drawn by a tool such as a pencil, pen, or paintbrush as it moves across a surface

line variety *noun* The different possibilities in the character of lines. For example, lines can be long or short, thick or thin, rough or smooth, and broken or solid.

linear perspective *noun* A system used to create the illusion of depth on a flat surface

lines *noun* One of the six perspective techniques. Parallel lines seem to converge or move toward the same point as they move away from the viewer.

location *noun* Artists can emphasize an object by placing it closer to the center of the piece.

low-intensity color *noun* A dull hue made by mixing a color with its complement

M

mandala *noun* A radial design divided into sections or wedges, each of which contains a different image

maquette *noun* A small model for a larger sculpture

mask *noun* A three-dimensional art form of sculpted faces

matte *noun* A dull, sometimes rough finish

medium *noun* The supply an artist uses to create art. Some media are clay, paint, or wood.

middle ground *noun* The area of the picture plane that is usually toward the center

minimal details *noun* Used in gesture sketches to complete the drawing

mix a neutral color *verb* Mix a neutral color with another color to change its value

mixed-media *noun* An art object that has been created from an assortment of media or materials

mobile *noun* A moving sculpture in which shapes are balanced and arranged on wire arms and suspended from the ceiling to move freely in the air currents

monochromatic *adj.* A color scheme that is made up of one color and the tints and shade of that color

monochromatic color scheme *noun* Uses only one color and the values of that color

monotonous *adj.* Lack of variety; boring

monumental sculptures *noun* Sculptures that are larger than human forms

motif *noun* A unit that is made up of objects or art elements that can be repeated

movement *noun* The principle of art that leads a viewer's eyes throughout a work of art

mural *noun* A painting done on a wall

N

negative space *noun* The empty space that surrounds objects, shapes, and forms

neon *noun* A special kind of light that can be made to be many bright colors

neutral color scheme *noun* Uses black, white, and a variety of grays

neutral colors *noun* Black, white, and gray; give hues a range of values

nonobjective *adj.* Art that has no recognizable subject matter

O

one-point linear perspective *noun* A system used to create the illusion of depth on a flat surface where all receding lines meet at one point

opaque *adj.* Does not let light through

outline *noun* a line drawn around the edge of an object

overlap *verb* To place one object on top of another object and partially cover the first object up

overlapping *noun* 1. One object covers a portion of another object. 2. In perspective: one of the six perspective techniques; the object covering another will appear closer to the viewer, creating a feeling of depth.

P

painting *noun* An art form using paint on a flat surface

paper sculpting techniques *noun* Six different techniques used to create paper sculptures: scoring a straight line, scoring a curve, pleating, curling, fringing, tab and slot.

parallel lines *noun* Lines that move in the same direction and always stay the same distance apart

pattern *noun* A repeated surface decoration

perception drawing *verb* Looking at something carefully and thinking deeply about what you see as you draw

perspective *noun* The method used to create the illusion of depth in two-dimensional art: overlapping, size, placement, detail, color, converging lines

perspective techniques *noun* The six techniques an artist uses to create the illusion of depth in two-dimensional art: overlapping, size, placement, detail, color, converging lines

photograph *noun* A picture taken using light-sensitive film and a camera

picture plane *noun* The surface of a drawing or painting

placement *noun* One of the six perspective techniques. Objects placed lower in the picture appear to be closer than those placed near eye level. There are three areas on a picture plane: foreground, middle ground, and background.

pleating *verb* Fold piece of paper from edge to edge. Then fold the same amount of paper in the other direction. Continue folding the paper back and forth in this manner.

point of view *noun* The angle at which the viewer sees an object

portrait *noun* A two- or three-dimensional artwork created in the image of a person or animal

posed *verb* Arranged in a special way

position *noun* In balance: a larger, positive shape and a small, negative space can be balanced by a small, positive shape and a large, negative space.

positive space *noun* Refers to any object, shape, or form in two- and three-dimensional art

primary colors *noun* Red, yellow, and blue. They cannot be made by mixing colors.

primary hues *noun* Red, yellow, and blue, used to mix the other hues on the color wheel

print *noun* An image created by using a stamp or printing plate. When artists make prints, they can make many identical images.

printing *verb* Pressing a shape from one thing to another many times

printing plate *noun* A plate that holds the image that will be used to create a print

prism *noun* A wedge-shaped piece of glass that bends light as it passes through

profile *noun* A side view of a person or animal

profile proportions *noun* A side view of the head that is divided by three horizontal lines

proportion *noun* The principle of art that is concerned with the size relationship of one part to another

Program Glossary (continued)

R

radial balance *noun* A type of balance that occurs when the art elements come out, or radiate, from a central point

rainbow *noun* An arc of spectral colors, usually identified as red, orange, yellow, green, blue, indigo, and violet, that appears in the sky opposite the sun

random pattern *noun* Occurs when the motif is repeated in no apparent order

ratio *noun* A comparison of size between two things

real texture *noun* Texture you can feel

realistic scale *noun* When an artist creates a work of art where everything fits together and makes sense in size relation

rectangle *noun* A four-sided geometric shape made of all right angles and whose opposite sides are equal in length.

regular pattern *noun* Occurs when identical motifs are repeated with an equal amount of space between them

relief *noun* A type of sculpture where forms project from a flat background

relief sculpture *noun* A sculpture in which objects stick out from a flat surface

repeated lines *noun* Used to give the feeling of movement or motion in a gesture drawing

repetition *noun* Lines, shapes, colors, or textures that are repeated throughout an artwork

rest *noun* The negative space between repetitions of the motif

rhythm *noun* The principle of design that organizes the elements in a work of art by repeating elements and/or objects

rough *noun* (*adj.*) A surface that has ridges; not smooth

rough (line) *noun* A line that has jagged, uneven edges

S

sail *noun* A type of free-form shape

scale *noun* Size as measured against a standard reference

score *verb* The repeated scratching of the clay surface at the area that another scored piece will be attached

scoring a curve *verb* Gradually cut bending curves in the paper with the point of the scissors

scoring a straight line *verb* Hold a ruler in the center of a piece of paper. Run the point of the scissors along the edge of the ruler to cut the paper in a straight line.

sculpture *noun* Three-dimensional art

sculpture model *noun* The study or detailed example of what the sculpture will look like when completed

secondary colors *noun* Orange, green, and violet. These colors are made by mixing two primary colors.

secondary hues *noun* Orange, green, and violet; the result of mixing two primary hues

self-portrait *noun* A two- or three-dimensional artwork that an artist makes of him or herself

sets of complementary colors *noun* There are three sets on the color wheel: red and green, blue and orange, and yellow and violet.

shade *noun* Any hue blended with black

shading *noun* A technique for creating dark values or darkening an area by repeating marks such as lines or dots

shadows *noun* Shaded areas in a painting or drawing

shape *noun* A two-dimensional area that is measured by height and width

shape reversal *noun* Occurs when an object, shape, or form is positive space in one image and then in another image becomes negative space

shiny *noun* Bright from reflected light

silhouette *noun* The shape of a shadow

simulated texture *noun* Imitates real texture, see also visual texture

size *noun* 1. in perspective: objects that are closer look larger than objects that are farther away; 2. In balance: a large shape or form will appear to be heavier than a small shape, and several small shapes can balance one large shape.

slip *noun* A mixture of clay and water that is creamy to the touch and is used to attach two scored pieces of clay together

smooth *noun* A surface free from roughness; even

smooth (line) *noun* A line that has even edges

solid (line) *noun* A line that has no breaks, gaps, or holes

space *noun* The art element that refers to the areas above, below, between, within, and around an object

spectral color scheme *noun* Uses all the colors of the rainbow: red, orange, yellow, green, blue, and violet

spectral colors *noun* The colors of the light spectrum: red, orange, yellow, green, blue, and violet

spectrum *noun* The range of colors that it is possible to see; the rainbow

splash *noun* A type of free-form shape

square *noun* A four-sided geometric shape where all sides are the same length and all angles are right angles

statue *noun* Three-dimensional art that is a body form

still life *noun* The arrangement of common inanimate objects from which artists draw or paint

stippling *noun* A shading technique using dots to show value

stitchery *noun* Art made with yarn on cloth

storyteller doll *noun* A Native American sculpture that shows one person relating the history of the culture to many children

style *noun* A unique quality of an object

subordinate *noun* The parts of the artwork that seem less important. Subordinate objects are not emphasized.

subtractive sculpture *noun* When an artist carves pieces away from a form

surrealism *noun* An art movement that emphasized art in which dreams, fantasy, and the subconscious served as inspiration for artists

symmetrical When two sides of a work of art are mirror images of each other

symmetry *noun* A type of formal balance in which two halves of a balanced artwork are identical, mirror images of each other

T

tactile texture *noun* The texture that can be felt

texture *noun* 1. The art element that refers to the way something feels; 2. In balance: a rough texture has an uneven pattern of highlights and shadows. For this reason, a rough surface attracts the viewer's eyes more easily than a smooth, even surface.

thick (line) *adj.* Wide

thick line *noun* Created by beginning with a thin line and gradually pressing the brush down

thin (line) *adj.* Narrow

thin line *noun* Created when a brush is held vertically to paper and touched lightly with the tip of the brush

three-dimensional *adj.* Has measurements in three directions: height, width, and depth

three-dimensional patterns *noun* Patterns that have depth and are formed on the surface of a sculptural form

three-dimensional rhythm *noun* A principle of design that indicates movement by the repetition of elements in a form

tint *noun* Any hue blended with white

transparent *adj.* Allows light to pass through so objects on the other side can be seen

triangle *noun* A three-sided geometric shape

two-dimensional *adj.* Shapes that are flat and can be measured by length and width

two-dimensional decoration *noun* Flat decoration produced on the surface of a work of art

U

unity *noun* The feeling of wholeness in a work of art. Artists use repetition and grouping to show that different parts of a work belong together.

unrealistic scale *noun* When an artist makes size relationships that do not make sense

V

value *noun* The lightness or darkness of a hue

value contrast *noun* The lightness or darkness stands out from the value that surrounds it

vanishing point *noun* The point on the horizon line where all parallel receding lines meet

variety *noun* The principle of art which is concerned with difference or contrast

vertical *noun* (*adj.*) Lines that move straight up and down. They make things look tall, steady, and calm.

visual movement *noun* Occurs when the eye is pulled through a work of art by a rhythm of beats and rests

visual rhythm *noun* The feeling of movement created when artists repeat colors, shapes, lines, and textures to lead the viewer's eyes through a work of art

visual texture *noun* Or simulated texture, imitates real texture. It is the illusion of a three-dimensional surface.

visual weight *noun* cannot be measured on a scale; it is measured by which objects the viewer's eyes see first.

W

warm colors *noun* Red, yellow, and orange. They suggest warmth and come toward the viewer.

warm hues *noun* Red, orange, and yellow. Warm hues are associated with warm things such as fire or sunshine.

weave *verb* To interlace or interweave strips or strands of material

width *noun* A horizontal measurement, or how long across something is

Z

zigzag *noun* (*adj.*) A line that is made by joining diagonal lines

Program Index

Program Index (continued)

Program Index (continued)

Program Index (continued)